THE ART OF THE OLD SOUTH

THE ART OF THE OLD SOUTH

Painting, Sculpture, Architecture & the Products of Craftsmen

1560-1860

JESSIE POESCH

HARRISON HOUSE
NEW YORK

This 1989 edition is published by Harrison House,
distributed by Crown Publishers, Inc.,
225 Park Avenue South, New York, New York 10003,
by arrangement with Alfred A. Knopf, Inc.

Printed and Bound in the United States of America

Library of Congress Cataloging-in-Publication Data

Poesch, Jessie J.
The art of the old South : painting, sculpture, architecture & the
products of craftsmen, 1560–1860 / Jessie Poesch.
p.   cm.
Reprint. Originally published: New York : Knopf, 1983.
Bibliography: p.
Includes index.
ISBN 0-517-68053-X
1. Art, American—Southern States.   2. Art, Colonial—Southern
States.   3. Art, Modern—17–18th centuries—Southern States.
4. Art, Modern—19th century—Southern States.   I. Title.
[N6520.P63   1989]   88-38491
709'.75—dc19   CIP
ISBN 0-517-68053-X
h   g   f   e   d   c   b   a

CONTENTS

Acknowledgments

*I*N GATHERING INFORMATION for this book, I tried to see as much as possible of the wide range of arts and crafts produced in the South before the Civil War. I had become familiar with some of the work during my almost twenty years of living in the Deep South, but made a concerted effort to expand my awareness as part of the research for this study. It involved travel by train, plane, bus, and automobile through wind, rain, and bright sunshine, and contact with a wide variety of people who helped me.

Curators and staff members of various art, educational, and historical institutions were key people, and universally helpful during my research, showing me the collections in their charge, often providing me with basic catalogue information from their records, and making helpful suggestions. I remember each contact with pleasure and wish to thank each and every one; because there are so many, I must needs list them in alphabetical sequence:

Gail Andrews of the Birmingham Museum of Art; Rita Adrosko of the National Museum of American History; H. Parrott Bacot of the Anglo-American Museum of Louisiana State University; Edward Barnwell of the Columbia Museum of Art and Science; Patti Carr Black of the Mississippi State Historical Museum; Robin Bolton-Smith of the National Museum of American Art; Mary Rose Boswell of the Association for the Preservation of Virginia Antiquities; Doris Bowman of the National Museum of American Art; Dr. J. Turner Bryson of Callaway Plantation in Washington, Georgia; Amelia K. Buckley of Keeneland Race Track; Cary Carson of Colonial Williamsburg; Mary E. Carver of the J. B. Speed Museum; Dr. Robert A. Cason of the Alabama Department of Archives and History; Elizabeth Childs of the Valentine Museum; Stiles T. Colwill of the Maryland Historical Society; William Cullison III of Tulane University; John Davis of Colonial Williamsburg; Anthony Dees of the Georgia Historical Society; Caldwell Delaney of the City of Mobile Museum; Anne W. Dibble, a field researcher in Charleston for the Museum of Early Southern Decorative Arts; Sallie

Doscher of the South Carolina Historical Association; William Voss Elder III of the Baltimore Museum of Art; Jean Federico of the DAR Museum; William Barrow Floyd with Historic Properties of Kentucky; Gregg Free of the Mississippi Department of Archives and History; Dianne Gamaway of the Tennessee Fine Arts Center at Cheekwood; Alexander V. J. Gaudieri of the Telfair Academy of Arts and Sciences; Anne C. Golovin of the National Museum of American History; Wallace Gusler of Colonial Williamsburg; Virginius Hall of the Virginia Historical Society; Carroll Hart of the Georgia Department of Archives and History; John Burton Harter of the Louisiana State Museum; Morrison H. Heckscher of the Metropolitan Museum of Art; Graham Hood of Colonial Williamsburg; the late Dr. Milo Howard of the Alabama Department of Archives and History; Sona Johnston of the Baltimore Museum of Art; Louise Lambert Kale of the College of William and Mary; Patricia Kane of the Yale University Art Gallery; Mildred Lanier of Colonial Williamsburg; Dennis Lawson of Drayton Hall; Sarah Lytle of Middleton Place; Roseanne McCaffrey of the Historic New Orleans Collection; Millie McGehee of The Hermitage; John Mahe of the Historic New Orleans Collection; Ethel Moore of the Georgia Museum of Art; Susan Myers of the National Museum of American History; Edward Nygren of the Corcoran Gallery; William D. Paul, Jr., of the Georgia Museum of Art; Linda Peters of the Augusta-Richmond County Museum; Lisa Reynolds of the Atlanta Historical Society; Beatrix Rumford of the Abby Aldrich Rockefeller Folk Art Center; Nadine Russell of Gallier House; Martha Severens of the Gibbes Art Gallery; Feay Shellman of the Telfair Academy of Arts and Sciences; Romaine Somerville of the Maryland Historical Society; Rodger Stroup of the Historic Columbia Foundation; Mrs. J. Allen Tison of the Owens-Thomas House; Dell Upton of the Virginia Historic Landmarks Commission; Mary O'Neill Victor of the Fine Arts Museum of the South at Mobile; Martha B. Vogelsang of the Filson Club; Gene Waddell of the South Carolina Historical Association; Paula Welshimer of Old Salem; Susan Williams of the Corcoran

Gallery; Richard B. Woodward of the Virginia Museum of Fine Arts; and Kitty Zainiecki of the Mississippi State Historical Museum.

Private collectors have been equally generous in allowing me to study their collections and sharing their knowledge and enthusiasms. These are William N. Banks, Dr. and Mrs. Benjamin Caldwell, Dr. Robert Coggins, John Geiser III, Augustus T. Graydon, Mr. and Mrs. Henry D. Green, Dr. Georgeanna Greer, Dr. and Mrs. Jack Holden, Dr. and Mrs. Robert Judice, Mr. and Mrs. Earl Long III, James Ricau, Hugh Smith, Roy A. Swayze, Will Theus, and William E. Wiltshire III.

In the course of my research, Frank Horton, John Bivins, Jr., Bradford Rauschenberg, and other staff members of the Museum of Early Southern Decorative Arts were particularly helpful in making available their superb photographic and research files. So, too, Graham Hood and the expert curatorial staff of Colonial Williamsburg who are identified individually above. Martha Shipman Andrews and her staff at the Bicentennial Inventory of American Painting, the staff of the Archives of American Art, and those at the library of the National Museum of American Art, all in Washington, were equally helpful. Mr. Leonard Mee gave permission to quote from the John Wood Dodge Papers. At the Library of Congress, Ford Peatross and Mary Ivon, who work with the records of the Historic American Building Survey, helped in the search for appropriate photographs. Richard Harwell, Special Collections, University of Georgia Libraries, allowed me to see items in their collection. E. L. Inabinett and Eleanor Richardson of the South Caroliniana Library at the University of South Carolina introduced me to the treasures in their care. Mills Lane of the Beehive Press kindly allowed me to read the text of Kristian Huidt's *Von Reck's Voyage* while still in page proof. The majority of the bibliographical research and writing was done at the Howard-Tilton Library of Tulane University, and I wish to thank Philip Leinbach and his staff for their help and encouragement throughout, particularly those in the Louisiana Collection and the Special Collections divisions.

A number of individuals took time to provide specific detailed information or helpful leads, and to them, too, I am grateful. Among these are Captain Richard Anderson; W. H. Britton; Charles E. Brownell; John Burrison; Richard Doud; Prof. Joseph Ewan; Roy Eugene Graham; Paul P. Hoffman; Nancy H. Holmes; Leonard Huber; Margaret Rose Ingate; Harvie Jones;

Louis C. Jones; Peggy Jo Kirby; Henry Krotzer; Charles L. Mackie; Philip A. Mason; Ann and Frank Masson; Caroline Mesrobian; Roderick Moore; Mary Lane Morrison; David Pettigrew; Mrs. Silas Read; Martin Schmidt; David M. Sherman; Michael O. Smith; Harrison Symmes; Curt Thomas; Mary Louise Tucker; David Warren; Gregory Weidman; James A. Williams; Samuel Wilson, Jr.; and Lyn Allison Yeager.

Personal friends and acquaintances were among those who guided me in their local area, provided hospitality, or shared a portion of my travels. These include Shannon DuBose of Camden and Columbia; Dr. and Mrs. Clyde Huggins of Mobile; Annibel Jenkins of Atlanta; Mrs. Sarah McGehee and Mr. and Mrs. Ronald Miller in Natchez; Mrs. Woody S. Moore in Marion, Alabama; Penny Morrill in Alexandria, Virginia; Joseph Newell and Terry McGough during a trip in Alabama; Belle Pendleton in Fredericksburg; Rodris Roth of Washington; Sidney Adair Smith in Mobile; James Whitnell in Columbus, Georgia; and Mrs. Wesley Wright, Jr., in Richmond. They smoothed the way and increased the pleasure of research.

Throughout the preparation of this study, Ann Close, as editor, has provided ever-wise advice and help, coordinated and shared in the gathering of the photographs, and has been a pleasure to work with. Ivor Noël Hume, John Bivins, Jr., and Letitia Galbraith read short portions of the text, while Carolyn Weekley, Jean Farnsworth, Donald and Joan Caldwell, Richard Lattner, and Carroll Mace each read one or more sections. I am particularly grateful for their helpful and constructive comments and questions. It goes without saying that I am responsible for any and all errors. This study was first initiated by Carter Smith of Media Projects, Inc., and my thanks go to him and to his staff, who handled many of the complex details of securing the photographs. The institutions, individuals, and photographers who provided these are acknowledged elsewhere; I am grateful to them. The pictures are absolutely essential to the text. Doris Antin transformed my scratchy handwriting into beautiful typed copy; Jody Blake prepared bibliography cards. The administrators of Newcomb College and Tulane University allowed me to take time off from my teaching duties in order to research and write this study. To them, and to my many colleagues and friends—some of whom I may inadvertently have omitted—who shared in one way or another in the preparation of this book, I am grateful.

JESSIE POESCH
New Orleans

Introduction

A SEEMING MULTITUDE of books has been written about the history, literature, and "mind" of the South, as if it were a special and identifiable entity, as in many ways it is or has been.* Though a variety of specialized studies now exist, few books have been written that provide a general view of the arts in the South. Until relatively recent times, many aspects of the history of art in the South were poorly researched; paintings, buildings, and furniture were in poor condition, and access to materials was difficult. The diffuse nature of the culture, distances between major cities, and unfamiliarity with the region are also possible reasons for this lack.

Those who have made special studies of distinctive aspects of the South have wrestled with geographical, political, and cultural definitions. Many of these have been written in the twentieth century and thus from a post–Civil War perspective. A rough geographical definition is the area below the Mason-Dixon line and its extension westward, a line originally determining the border between Pennsylvania and Maryland; the extension became the border between the slave states and the free states. Within the geographical area defined as the South there is infinite variety in the terrain: low-lying swamps and fields, lands bordering tidewater bays, rivers and creeks, gently rolling countryside, mountain ranges where fog catches in the valleys and the peaks are hidden in blue mist. There are large sections of hill country and tracts of piney woods where the soil is ungenerous. In parts of Alabama, Mississippi, and Louisiana the soil along the ancient riverbeds is rich and black, in the upland country of the Carolinas and Georgia it ranges from ashen gray to copper red, while near Vicksburg one sees unusual loess deposits which can be cut like a cake. Relative common denominators are that the summers are hotter for longer periods, sometimes brutally hot and humid, and the winters shorter, sometimes wonderfully mellow and mild. The growing seasons are long.

Politically the South has been variously defined, most consistently as the slaveholding states before the Civil War—and these included Maryland, Kentucky, and the District of Columbia—or the area included in the Confederate states. The existence of a biracial society underlies these definitions.

The cultural delineation of the South is the most complex; it is a culture notably diffuse. Here the attempt has been to show a consciousness among Southerners themselves of having mind sets, value systems, and ways of life distinct from the rest of America. Most would agree that, however complex, there has been an ebb and flow in this sense of distinctiveness through the years. Historically, until around 1770 the South was not a self-conscious social and cultural entity, though already signs of differences in cultural and economic patterns were there, influenced by the growth of the plantation system and the large size of the black slave population. With the birth of the new nation, sectional awareness gradually evolved, first coming to a peak in 1819–1820 with the Missouri Controversy and Compromise, and again in 1833 with the Nullification Crisis, a conflict that hinged on issues of tariff rates and states rights. Political separation, of course, occurred at the time of the Civil War, the war for Southern independence. During that war and in the immediate aftermath of defeat the political differences and the geographical area were clearly defined, although the number of individuals who struggled with divided loyalties suggests that even then the sense of political, social, and cultural distinctiveness was less clearly delineated than is generally thought. Until relatively recent times, all views of the South, both by Southerners and those not native to the region, were influenced by the experience and perception of the Civil War. The circumstances of the long post–Civil War period have also been factors in our knowledge, understanding, and interpretation of the arts in the South.

"The South" was, in some senses, frozen geographically and politically from the end of the Civil War until after World War I, and was most isolated, most separate culturally, from the rest of the United States in this period. It was during the first half of the twentieth century that a great flowering of Southern literature took place, a flowering nourished by factors that seem to have resulted from the relative isolation and distinctive qualities of Southern life—a greater sense of continuity with the past, the

*Quotations, research, and factual information are referenced in the notes section beginning on p. 337.

experiences of defeat and poverty, a sense of evil and of guilt, a mingled sense of pride and shame in one's heritage, lack of mobility, strength of family ties, a biracial society, emphasis on setting, sense of place, and a romanticized view of the past. With the memories of the Civil War now fading and with changed economic and political situations, the traditions that formed this literature and the perception of the South as a distinctive sectional and cultural society are gradually eroding. The South is growing more and more like the rest of America, and many things thought to be peculiarly Southern—intricate race relations, jazz and country music, even Coca-Cola—have, for better or for worse, been assimilated into the broader culture of America. Historians, sociologists, and literary critics have studied and sifted through the complex forces that created the sense of separateness, and those that now seem to be breaking down these differences. At the same time they have acknowledged that, given all the differences, the South has always been a part of the United States. Paradoxically, the very definition of the South as separate has depended upon its being a part of the whole.

In this study of the visual arts in the South before the War of 1861–1865, the arts are seen as a part of the larger setting of colonial America and the growing United States. No major brief is made for their being peculiarly or especially Southern, though they often cast an illuminating light on life as lived in the American South in this broad period. The appearance of the Anglican colonial churches in Virginia and Maryland reflects the particular form of Protestant Christianity practiced; it was a mixture, Anglican in form but strongly influenced by Calvinistic austerity. Certain persistent characteristics in vernacular architecture show a response to the climate. Mourning portraits are a reminder of the high incidence of disease experienced in the South, sporting paintings of the racing and horse-breeding that were associated with the region. A number of the important early depictions of America's natural history were done in the South. Ceremonial chairs created for Masonic lodges are an index to the value systems held by many of the founding fathers of this country. Special tables designed for making beaten biscuits are tangible evidence of a favorite food; sugar chests and huntboards reflect local custom. The family seat in the country, the pillared plantation house, has become a part of a mythological image of the pre–Civil War South, and this has influenced twentieth-century perceptions of the area.

One reason for a study such as this is that there has been previous neglect: comparatively few examples from the South are shown in the various surveys of visual arts in America. A more important reason is that much new material has come to light in recent years. So much, in fact, that this volume is in itself a broad survey. The study of American architecture, painting, and other arts and crafts is still relatively new, and each discovery reveals more facets of a rich and diverse heritage.

For much of the time from the earliest European settlements in those parts of North America that have become the United States, the population in the American South has been less than in the North. For example, in 1790 the slave states from Maryland southward contained virtually half (49.9 percent) of the nation's total population and 40.1 percent of the whites. By 1830

the relative percentages were down to 45.3 and 34.6 percent, and by 1860 the percentages were still lower, to 39.1 and 29.9 percent, respectively. That is, the population growth in the areas to the north and east was more rapid than that in the South. There is not necessarily a direct relation between size of population and creation of works of art as defined within the traditions of Western European culture but, as the Marquis de Chastellux observed in 1783, the arts often flourish best where a greater number of men are assembled. As a friend of the new nation, he hoped that America would eventually give rise to cities where the arts would flourish, but he recognized that this was a hope for the future rather than a present reality. Given the smaller population and the rural character of much of the American South until recent times, it is probably true that, relatively speaking, fewer buildings, paintings, sculpture, and finely crafted objects were actually produced in the South. The region also seems to have had more than its share of natural and man-made disasters. A succession of hurricanes and fires, which swept through Southern shores and Southern cities, are among natural calamities that have destroyed part of the architectural and artistic heritage. Hot and humid weather is unkind to things, particularly painted canvases and textiles. During the Revolutionary War the British systematically looted parts of the South: in South Carolina they are known to have packed and sent off quantities of silver and other valuables in rice barrels. The Civil War also ravaged certain sections of the South, and at times looting was rampant, some of it officially fostered. All these things help to account for the relative dearth of surviving objects of various kinds. Therefore, in any broad survey of the arts in America, the proportion of examples shown from the South will be appropriately fewer.

In the study of architecture, distinguished mansions and public buildings in the South have received their proportionate due. Recent and specialized studies, some taking advantage of new archaeological methods, as well as surveys of state and city architecture, have revealed a variety of important vernacular traditions. The study of painting in the South has been considerably overlooked, partly because of a seeming paucity of evidence, diffuseness of available material, and unfamiliarity with the region. However, in recent years many museums, historical societies, and private individuals have rescued paintings from storage and deterioration. Thanks to such conservation we can now see paintings long hidden from view.

The study of the objects created by skilled craftsmen in the South was likewise largely neglected. Those interested in the subject were made sharply aware of this in 1949 when, at an Antiques Forum held in Williamsburg, two speakers reported that they could point to no group of Southern furniture comparable in quality or quantity to that of any *one* of the Northern centers. Another stated that he knew of only three examples of silver made in colonial Virginia. Though a few studies of crafts in the South existed, the general lack of knowledge was disturbing. Earlier assumptions had been that most fine household furnishings were imported from England and that only a few crude things were made on the plantations—a kind of romanticized Cavalier interpretation of the South. (Other possible and unrecorded reasons for such a lack of knowledge of the history of fine craftsmanship are the general lack of awareness, even indifference, to Southern history and life among those in the Northeast at that time, and, on the part of Southerners, a neglect, partly excusable by poverty, of disciplined study of this aspect of the past.) It was immediately recognized that these were probably not valid assumptions and that research was needed. A committee was organized and a major exhibition of Southern furniture from 1640 to 1820 was shown at the Virginia Museum of Fine Arts in January 1952. Since that exhibition there have been many studies involving the various "decorative arts," and a wealth of material is still being discovered, only a portion of which can be reported on here.

In examining the arts in the South I have tried to suggest the historical context and the social and cultural milieus that prompted their creation. When possible I have tried to identify patrons, architects, artists, and craftsmen because awareness of their purposes and circumstances often lends a dimension of meaning to the purpose and use of the object, insight into the nature of the society, and a feeling for the texture of life of the period. The ways of life in the South were as diverse as the soil. Especially in the earliest period, almost all works of art or craft served utilitarian purposes, therefore both art, in the more traditional sense, and artifact are included here. In addition to functional purposes such as providing shelter, most arts serve other human and societal functions—to instruct, to record, to define status, to delight and distract the eye and the mind, to satisfy a sense of order and measure. The borderline between art and artifact can sometimes be extremely narrow and, arguably, in the eye of the beholder. Both illuminate our understanding of the societies that produced them, and both are part of the larger heritage of our material culture. Throughout this study, I have tried to select those examples in which there is revealed that extra care or flair that gives satisfaction to the eye and spirit and thus makes it appropriate to identify as art. This decision is dictated both by choice and limitations of space. Even so, it has not been possible to include examples of certain traditional craft products, such as baskets, wood carvings, weaving, some forms of needlework, ironwork, and pottery. In virtually all cases the objects created before 1860 in these arts have worn out and disappeared. Fortunately, some craftsmen today still practice these time-honored crafts in traditional ways, ways passed on from parent to child or from craftsman to apprentice. In the South these traditions have persisted, for example, among the highlanders of the upland South and the Afro-Americans of the coastal regions of South Carolina and Georgia. Excellent exhibitions and rewarding studies have been and are being made of such craftsmen and their heritage. By the same token, it has not been possible to include the fine artifacts and paintings that were imported by some Southerners from Europe and which formed a part of their domestic settings.

This book is divided into four major chronological periods, starting with the first European settlements and ending with the immediate antebellum period. The period from about 1560 to 1735 represents a time of beginnings; during the years between 1735 and 1788 a sense of an established society evolved, at the end of which self-confident colonists declared, fought, and won their independence. Southerners were prominent in leading and shaping the new nation in the period from 1789 to 1824, and

during the years beginning around 1825, or a little earlier, until the outbreak of the Civil War, there was a growing sense of separation between North and South. There are not necessarily sharp changes in style or taste between each of these periods—history and the history of art are essentially seamless—yet in order to relate changes in taste or mood to the historical and cultural context, divisions into periods acording to major changes are useful.

In the earliest period conditions were sometimes startlingly primitive, and remained so for some settlers. Others managed to adapt to the new circumstances, create new forms, borrow and adapt ideas from the Indians, and also create an immediate ambience similar to what they had known before.

After the struggles and precarious nature of life during the first years, the settlements along the Eastern Seaboard finally achieved a relative stability, and this continued until the political upheaval of the Revolutionary War. Dominated by those of English descent, the society, value systems, and way of life seemed in many ways similar to that in the homeland—eighteenth-century England. For example, the idea that high status was achieved by having an estate and home in the country—that is, that the life of the English country gentleman was a condition to be sought—prevailed among some, and given the abundance of land and circumstances of the new country, many seized the opportunity for upward mobility.

The strong imprint of English values and English taste in the arts upon the way of life in the South has remained powerful. The fact that during the long post–Civil War period fewer immigrants chose to settle in the Southern parts of the United States also meant that in certain places there has been a stronger retention of English traditions among both rich and poor, and a vague allegiance to England. This may be more obvious in speech and song than in the visual arts, but it is an important facet of the history of the South and has shaped Southerners' perception of their history and of their art. At the same time, it was on the Southern fringes of this country that the political struggle among the English, French, and Spanish for control of various territories took place. Among these were the skirmishes over settlements in Florida and the Carolinas, the back and forth ascent and exchange of power along the Gulf Coast and the Mississippi Valley, and the Texas struggle for independence from Mexico. Thus it is in some of the arts in the South that the influence of the French and Spanish can still best be seen and felt. The Germans, Swiss, Scotch-Irish, and Africans practiced their crafts and have also left their mark on building and artistic practices in the South.

When the new nation was formed, Southern leaders, as well as architects, builders, painters, and craftsmen, helped in shaping its environment. Their ideals and ideas of the role of the arts in giving a sense of place and of history influenced the direction and character of some of those arts. The area west of the Appalachians was opened for settlement, and the citizens of the infant country pushed westward.

From the late 1820s to the beginning of the Civil War, much of the population was on the move, uprooting themselves from older communities and reestablishing themselves frequently in areas that had been wilderness or tracts of canebrake. Patrician values and patterns of living often gave way to a society more essentially bourgeois. Great prosperity, a depression, and a growing sense of separation characterized the years immediately before the Civil War, affecting the arts indirectly and sometimes directly.

For each period, examples of architecture, painting, sculpture, and the products of craftsmen have been included. Each art or craft tradition has its own constants of problems and technique, and there are good reasons for studying each tradition separately. Architects and builders must provide shelter and symbols of purpose and status; practitioners must know about plumb lines, materials for building walls, and contours of moldings. Painters of pictures learn about sizing of canvases, qualities of pigments and oils, brush sizes and, for the period under discussion, how to create illusions of form on flat surfaces. Cabinetmakers know about joining of parts, the use of turning lathes and of a variety of chisels, gouges, planes, and grooving planes. They must know the relative qualities of different woods when being carved and must be familiar with human proportions and social customs. Needleworkers must know the difference between plain sewing and varied embroidery stitches, and between the straight and bias of a piece of fabric, in order to fashion useful and attractive objects.

Artists and craftsmen also respond to and influence other attitudes of mind and spirit, and share in enthusiasms for certain ideas and tastes, such as a feeling for the crisp and classical, or for the moody and picturesque. As artists and craftsmen participate in, and interact with, their society, they produce quite different products, yet there are relationships and interactions among them. In this way they help to stamp certain special qualities, even a general ambience, upon the period in which they live. These relationships are not always easy to define, but can be sensed more easily if a variety of products of the same period are seen together.

In surveying the art of the South before 1860 within a chronological framework, I found that, since in each successive period the population grew and the area of settlement also became larger, the number of noteworthy examples for each period increased. The selections shown here will reveal something of the complexity and diversity of the multifaceted culture of the early South as well as certain strong continuities within it.

PART ONE

Beginnings

1560-1735

A SINGLE WATERCOLOR survives from the forty-two or more Jacques Le Moyne de Morgues made on the basis of his work while with the French settlement in Florida in 1564–1565. His duties with the second French expedition to Florida in the spring of 1564 were to map the seacoast and harbors, the towns and courses of the rivers, to depict the dwellings of the natives and to record whatever else he considered worthy of observing. His commander, René de Laudonnière, had been a member of an earlier French expedition. Two years before, Jean Ribaut had claimed the area near St. John's River for France, left a small group to maintain a fort, and returned home to write a glowing report. Difficulties occurred and the survivors returned to France within a year.

During the fourteen months or so that Le Moyne was part of the small French outpost at Fort Caroline, which probably was at what is now Mayport on St. John's River, he must at first have devoted much of his time to visiting among the Timucua Indians in the region, watching them as they hunted and fished, planted crops, prepared and stored their food. He observed them caring for the sick, and saw their ceremonials for the dead. He witnessed one of the battles between Indian tribes in which the French unwisely involved themselves, and attended a victory ceremony. We surmise this because forty-three engravings based on Le Moyne's paintings were published in Frankfurt many years later, in 1591, by Theodore De Bry. The latter also published Le Moyne's narrative account of his adventures, an account written after he had returned to the Old World. Le Moyne probably wanted to publish these himself, but he died in 1588.

This second French expedition was meant to establish a colony for Huguenots on the shores of the New World, thus helping to solve an uncomfortable minority problem at home. The beginnings of life at Fort Caroline among the 300 Frenchmen and four women who accompanied René de Laudonnière were peaceful enough, but disarray soon set in, and Le Moyne would have had less and less time to attend to his duties. His account records dissension within the company, an attempted mutiny, and the departure of some members. In their eagerness to ally themselves with Indians who could lead them to gold, the French broke faith with the Indians who had first befriended them. Thinking the land naturally abundant, they did not bother to plant for food and grain, and when supplies ran out, the Indians, upon whom they depended for sustenance, were no longer friendly. Some of the French died of starvation during the winter, and the surviving half-starved men could secure food only by foraging many miles from the fort. When they were very near the end, the English naval officer and slave-trader Sir John Hawkins unexpectedly put in at the fort on August 4, 1565, apparently to secure a supply of fresh water, but also to reconnoiter the condition of the French for Queen Elizabeth. The English, French, and Spanish were keeping a wary eye on each other in the far-flung reaches of the New World, and were to continue to do so for the next two centuries or more. Though Hawkins may have intended to destroy the fort, he was apparently impressed by the miserable state of the French and, moved by mercy, gave them enough provisions, dried beans, and peas to enable them to return to France, which they decided to do. Preparations were made, and they burned the fort and waited for a change in the winds so they could set sail. To their surprise and joy, on August 13 a fleet of seven French ships under Jean Ribaut arrived with supplies and men. Immediately they began to rebuild the fort.

No sooner was this underway than on September 3 they sighted another six ships. These were under the command of the Spaniard Pedro Menendez de Avilés, who had been sent out by Philip II shortly after the Spanish learned of Ribaut's departure from France. After a series of contacts and feints, and after a frightful hurricane of the kind still familiar to residents of the Southern coasts of the United States, the Spanish captured the fort. When Le Moyne later wrote his version of what had happened he told how Menendez had rounded up a sizable number of French survivors and offered to make terms. After each group had given up its arms the men's hands were tied and they were marched toward him in groups of ten. He ordered that as each group disappeared from view they were to be massacred, not as Frenchmen but as Lutherans, killing all but a few who ultimately returned to Europe to tell the story. Menendez did this on two successive occasions, September 29 and October 12.

LAVDONNIERVS ET REX ATHORE ANTE COLVMNAM A PRÆFECTO PRIMA NAVIGATIONE LOCATAM QVAMQVE VENERANTVR FLORIDENSES
Jacobus Le Moyne dictus de Morgues ad vivum pinxit

Jacques Le Moyne de Morgues. "Réné de Laudonnière and the Indian Chief Athore Visit Ribaut's Column." After 1564. Watercolor on vellum. New York Public Library, New York.

When word finally reached Europe of these events there was a tremendous outcry against the Spanish, giving rise to the famous "Black Legend," though in truth their behavior may have been no more or less cruel than other current European acts of war.

Jacques Le Moyne was with those who managed to escape the fort, hide in the woods, walk waist-deep in the swamps, and find their way to one of the two ships that eventually reached Europe. He spent the last years of his life, from 1572 on, in London, where he had lodgings at Blackfriars, provided by his patron, Sir Walter Raleigh. The latter, always a friend to the Huguenots, had his own interests in the New World. There is no record of any drawings of Florida made directly from life by Le Moyne, but there is a slim chance that he managed to save some rough field sketches during the harrowing end of his sojourn there. (Nowhere does he mention the loss of his drawings.) It is conceivable that he made additional sketches from memory during the return voyage or soon thereafter. According to Hakluyt, it was Raleigh who charged the artist to make "liuely drawen in coulours" of things he recalled from his voyage, and these were the basis of De Bry's 1591 engravings. They would seem to represent a remarkable feat of visual memory, and if they included a hermaphrodite or two, perhaps he (or De Bry) can be forgiven for wanting to make a good tale better. Le Moyne died in London and his widow subsequently sold the watercolors to De Bry.

The single watercolor that survives from the group of forty-two or more is shown above. We see the Indian chief Athore as he greeted the returning French officer, Laudonnière, and several of his harquebusiers on June 2, 1564, shortly after their arrival. Together they visited the stone column, one of two that had been erected by the French two years earlier when Ribaut first visited the Florida-Carolina shores and Laudonnière had been his lieutenant. The columns, erected in what is now Beaufort County, South Carolina, had been brought from France. The one shown is carved with the arms of France surmounted by a crown and encircled by the collar of the Order of St. Michael, a symbol of French sovereignty. Le Moyne's narrative says that by this time the column was worshiped as an idol, and he shows the adoring Indians on the left.

This heartening ceremonial event no doubt looked something like this when it happened, but as the artist enriched the details, the memory image seems to have become a picture of what he hoped would or could still be: Europeans and North American Indians side by side in peaceful harmony, the bountiful produce of the New and Old Worlds a still further testimony of this peace. (The image was quite contrary to his own experience.) Three of the garlands that encircle the column are of ivy, oak, and laurel, a clearly European choice of plants associated since antiquity with noble virtues—friendship and fidelity, strength, glory and steadfastness, victory and peace. In the left foreground are two bottle gourds being used as jars for perfumed oils. A bundle of white and red ears of corn is conspicuously placed on the right. Le Moyne, who was knowledgeable about plants, must have been impressed with the high degree of cultivation to which the Indians had brought this crop, a crop that was to provide foods basic to the diet (cornbread, spoonbread, hominy grits, hush puppies) of later inhabitants of the American South. Most of the fruits and vegetables identifiable in the other baskets appear to be European—a pear, plums, turnips, possibly beets, as well as squashes, which could be either. He may have included these by intent, to show what he felt could be grown, or because he had forgotten exactly which fruits and vegetables he had seen. For Le Moyne the event he depicted was a memory to be cherished, and for Europeans, and adventurers such as Raleigh, a relationship to be hoped for.

Technically the watercolor is rendered with the precision of a skilled limner or miniaturist of the sixteenth century. The colors are clear and sharp and partly applied with a stipple technique; gradations of tone are used, but there are few real shadows. Ethnographically it is less valuable, giving a somewhat inaccurate rendering of the appearance of the Timucuans. Their upswept hairdress, their use of delicate patterned tattoos, and the long fingernails fancied by the men may be correct, but the proportions and their complexions are based on European artistic concepts. It is however a rare document and the earliest authentic surviving European painting of a scene in North America.

Le Moyne's other drawings are known only through the engravings based on them as published by De Bry. One of these, De Bry's Illustration 10, shows Fort Caroline with its related buildings. The text accompanying the pictures says that the commander's house had a porch all around it. This porch does not show in the engraving but, if the statement is correct, the commander's house must have been the first building of any kind in North America with an encircling porch or covered passage, and an interesting portent of the vernacular architectural forms that later developed in the South. The other engravings showing the various activities of the Indians are valuable ethnographical documents, even if not wholly accurate. They were copied and modified by other publishers and thus helped to shape the European vision of the New World during the ensuing decades.

Each of the earliest settlements in North America was part of the larger complex of political jousting among the European powers, especially the three-cornered diplomatic and real battles between Spain, France, and England. The French had already laid claim to Quebec and the more Northern parts of the newly discovered continent. When they made their attempt to establish the Florida-Carolina colonies, they were careful to see that the sites they chose would have given them—had they succeeded—a chance to challenge the Spanish, plunder their ships, and expand the boundaries of their own territory. The French also hoped to find other sources of the fabled gold that was making the Spanish rich.

As a direct result of the bold French attempt to found a colony at Fort Caroline, the Spanish, having captured and destroyed it, then built several forts of their own along the Florida coast and established themselves at St. Augustine, the oldest surviving settlement in what is now the United States. The massive Castillo San Marcos there, a fairly pure example of a European fortress with star-shaped bastions, was built much later (from 1672 to 1756), in response to the expanding English colonies. Now restored, it stands as a symbol of the longtime, though never truly strong, Spanish presence in Florida.

The Spanish initially laid claim to the whole Southeastern coast of North America, and Spanish ship captains were familiar with some of the contours of Florida and the Chesapeake area in the early sixteenth century. Small portions of the interior were explored, and the Spanish made several attempts to plant colonies, such as one in 1526 near the Pee Dee River and another in 1528 near Pensacola. In both cases bad weather, inadequate food, poor relations with the tribes of the region, illness, and internal dissension contributed to their collapse.

In the spring of 1539 Hernando de Soto, who had gained a fortune in gold in Peru, commenced an exploratory expedition into the interior that was to last almost four years, during which he traversed a large portion of the American South. He started out with a troop of 600 to 900 men, horses, pigs, ammunition, and other supplies. By persuasion or force de Soto and his men secured Indian guides along the way. Starting from the west coast of Florida they apparently first went north into Georgia, across parts of the Carolinas, and then into the rising hills of northeastern Georgia. The gold they sought turned out to be copper reserves in the mountainous southeastern corner of what is now Tennessee. They seem to have passed near present Chattanooga and then southward into Talladega County, Alabama. Their entire journey was marked by frequent cruel treatment of the Indians, which earned them nothing but hatred. With their numbers already thinned by starvation, by fighting, and by hardships of the trek, they lost men (the Indians lost more) and horses in a bitter and brutal encounter with the Mavilians, between the Alabama and Tombigbee rivers. Their second winter was spent in the northern part of the present state of Mississippi, and in April 1541 they came upon the great Mississippi somewhere below Memphis. They managed to cross it and wintered in Arkansas. By April of the next spring the tattered remnants turned back. De Soto died in May 1542, shortly after they again reached the great river, where his body was ignominiously given to its waters. Unable to recross, the straggling force headed toward the Gulf and New Spain. Ultimately a diminished band of hardy survivors reached Mexico City. The Spanish thus had the opportunity to gain an extraordinary familiarity with the interior geography and resources of the South, but they failed to exploit this knowledge in any way.

From these and hosts of later forays the Europeans slowly gained acquaintance with the land from the Indians, and the importance of that heritage in the American Southeast can best be underlined (as it could in other parts of the United States) by recalling a few of the many place-names that derive from the language of the earliest inhabitants: Wateree, Santee, Congaree, Combahee, Tombigbee, Potomac, Accomack, Chesapeake, Pamunkey, Chickahominy, Appalachia, Appomattox, Tuscaloosa, Tallapoosa, Tuscumbia, Natchez, Mobile (from the Mobilias Indians), Atchafalaya, Paducah, Pascagoula, Dahlonega, Alabama and Mississippi, Chattanooga and Tennessee. De Soto's men would not recognize many of these places today, but they probably heard most of these names; and many miles of modern roads and highways follow the trails made by red-skinned men.

John White. "Sabatia or Marsh Pink." c. 1585–1590. Watercolor on paper. British Museum, London.

the first reconnaissance voyage, which lasted from April to September of 1584. The English sailed as far as Chesapeake Bay and made an all-important contact with the friendly Algonkian tribes on Roanoke Island, taking two of the Indians back with them.

It was on the second expedition to Roanoke, when the English made their initial attempt to plant a colony, that John White did the fieldwork for his watercolors. This collection, now housed in the British Museum, provides a wonderfully fresh, richly factual, and rare record of the life of the Indians they encountered and of the flora and fauna they observed. White must have made sketches on the spot, and then prepared more carefully finished versions. Perhaps the latter were done while still in Virginia, as the area was broadly called, or on board ship, or more probably in England after he and all other members of this colony returned. Fortunately, White's original finished drawings have survived and, thanks to recent publications, are becoming increasingly well known.

This first colony lasted from the landing on June 26, 1585, to June 18, 1586; Sir Ralph Lane was the governor and the youthful, distinguished mathematician, Thomas Hariot, was the surveyor. It would appear that Hariot and White worked as a team, exploring the countryside, examining and collecting examples of plant and animal life in order to see if a larger colony could be established. They observed the ways of the Indians and learned as much as possible from them about the lands they were unable to explore. The colonists planted crops, and in general planned carefully and behaved wisely during their sojourn. However, there was some dissension among them, and in the end trouble and misunderstandings with the Indians. A final, fatal storm prompted them all to return to England with Sir Francis Drake (who had just devastated St. Augustine, requiring the Spanish to start anew there), when he appeared with fresh supplies. Very shortly after their return Hariot published his *A briefe and true report of the new found land of Virginia*, a remarkably lucid if occasionally too optimistic account of the prospects for development of this land whose climate was "like Persia." He carefully listed possible marketable commodities, then crops for sustenance. He, too, noticed the usefulness of Indian corn as well as tobacco, and also noted a variety of fruits, vegetables, trees, and animals. He then described the nature and manners of the native peoples whom he thought "shall haue cause both to feare and loue us." Among his too optimistic reports was the expectation that pearls would be an important exportable commodity and that silk culture could be easily developed (a hope of colonial planners and dreamers in England that was to recur often), and the idea that with twenty-four hours' labor a year's crop could be sown that would require no more work until harvested.

Of marketable commodities he identified the cedar or cypress as a wood from which "sweet & fine bedsteads, tables, deskes, lutes, virginalles & many fine things else" could be made, adding "of which there hath beene proofe made already," suggesting that the colonists had tried their hand at joinery. Indeed a document exists recording that a bed of "cypress or cedar" was later given by Sir Walter Raleigh to the Earl of Northumberland, a bed that does not seem to have survived.

John White's watercolors bring Hariot's descriptions to life. We see the Indian village Secoton, right, which was probably in

From their encounters with Europeans, the Indians, not without guile themselves, also capable of exquisite cruelties and willing to use the Europeans in their warfare with each other, slowly learned the unpredictable and bewildering value systems, different concepts of property, and often cruel powers of the Europeans. Le Moyne's watercolor depicts one of the moments of friendship between the two peoples. In the next two centuries the Europeans gradually encroached on the territories of the Indians and they were frequently in conflict.

Since the Huguenot Le Moyne was associated with Sir Walter Raleigh in his later years, it is no surprise that the English artist John White must have had some contact with him or his drawings. White copied two of Le Moyne's drawings and also used details from the Frenchman's Florida map in his own more general one of southeastern North America, which he made following his own voyages to America in conjunction with the first English efforts to colonize the new continent.

The English yearned to have a share in the riches of the New World, and as early as 1510 John and Sebastian Cabot had explored parts of the Northern coast of North America, but no effective attempts were made to plant colonies until those carried out under Sir Walter Raleigh's patent, obtained from Queen Elizabeth on March 25, 1584. John White seems to have been on

what is now North Carolina, in which the artist shows the three different plantings of corn, one "newly sprong," another green, and a third ripe. Here, as in a view of another village, he shows "the true forms of their howses, couered and enclosed some wth matts, and some wth barcks of trees." When De Bry later published the engraving based on this scene, his craftsmen made it even more prosperous-looking, for they added a patch of tobacco, some sunflowers, and a row of pumpkins. Hariot had described the tobacco plant as among those useful for sustenance, and noted its healthful effects: "it purgeth superfluous fleame." Moreover, "We owr selues during the time we were there vsed to suck it after their maner, as also since our returne." (Hariot was to die of cancer of the nose.)

The uptilted view of the town is what one might call a cartographer's perspective, clearly showing the divisions of the land. The lighting is very even. All of the watercolors were unfortunately soaked with water in an accident in 1865, probably making the contours and colors softer than they had been originally. Other watercolors show the Indians fishing, their methods of cooking soups in earthenware pots (strong enough to withstand the heat of an open fire), preparing what is probably hominy, and other simple scenes of domestic life. One of the loveliest of the natural history renderings is that of the *Sabatia*, left, which is known as the sea pink or marsh pink in North Carolina, and which still grows in the salt marshes of the East Coast from Florida to Massachusetts. Here, too, the rendition is direct, correctly proportioned, unshaded.

White was to return to Roanoke yet a third time, as governor of the next colony the English tried to establish. He stayed for a while with the new settlers, then they asked him to return for more supplies, which he did; his daughter and her newborn child, Virginia Dare, were among those left behind. White was delayed for almost three years in England and when he returned the colony had disappeared—the famous lost colony. He went home finally, a broken-hearted man.

It was probably while White was on this last voyage in 1590 that his drawings were published as engravings by the enterprising De Bry. The book in which they were issued came out in four languages (Latin, English, French, and German), and went through at least seventeen printings. Thus the two books issued by De Bry, the Virginia volume with engravings after White and with a text prepared by Hariot, and the Florida book with Le Moyne's text and pictures, shaped the European vision of the New World for the next half-century and more. Pictures from both were copied and recopied in books and on maps. The illustrations on the title page of John Smith's 1624 *Generall Historie of Virginia,* for example, are borrowed from White's work, the Indians made less attractive, and copies are even found on eighteenth-century Spanish pottery. The stories of the hardships were gradually forgotten, but the dream of the New World as a land of fertile soil, abundant crops, a source of exportable goods (a good investment), and of friendly and handsome natives who might be taught to obey, fear, love, and honor the white man, persisted.

Though several sixteenth-century expeditions to South and Central America were accompanied by artists or draftsmen, the presence of men like Le Moyne and White was the exception rather than the rule, and there were no comparable visual chronicles of North America for the next hundred years. The intense curiosity of the first discoverers had, in fact, given way to the more mundane work of establishing permanent settlements.

After the failure at Roanoke, the English waited twenty years before attempting to establish another settlement on the North American coast, which they did at Jamestown in 1607. The Spanish maintained their hegemony in Mexico and on some of the islands as well as a precarious foothold in Florida. The

John White. "Indian Village of Secoton." c. 1585–1590. Watercolor on paper. British Museum, London.

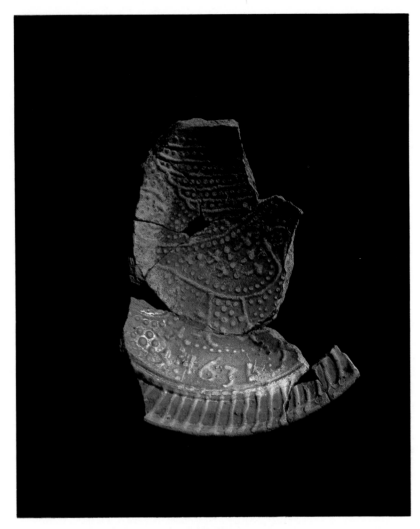

*Fragment of slip-ware pottery, dated 1631. From the English
settlement in Martin's Hundred, Virginia. The earliest dated
British-American pottery known. Colonial Williamsburg.*

French founded a trading station at Québec in 1608, but did not
penetrate into the South until La Salle's journey down the Mississippi in 1682, while Mobile, New Orleans, and Natchez were
not established until the early years of the eighteenth century.

Like all previous ventures in the New World, the first years
of the Jamestown and nearby settlements of the Chesapeake
were ones of continual struggle and near-fiasco, with the colonists ill-prepared to build a new society in a wilderness to which
they had come with often false and unrealistic expectations. In
London, the shareholders had planned that such industries as
iron mining, smelting, glassmaking, silk and wine production
would provide profitable exports. They failed to realize the need
for a supportive agricultural and food system, and there were few
yeomen and husbandmen among the first groups sent over.
"Starving times" were the unfortunate result. In addition some
of the colonists envisaged only a short stay in the New World;
they hoped to make a quick fortune and were not interested in
establishing roots or a permanent abode. This continued to be so
even after a better-growing tobacco plant was introduced from
the West Indies around 1617 and the crop began to bring in a
good income after 1619. The same problems that had plagued
each of the earlier settlements beset Jamestown: poor management, poor relations with the Indians, inadequate supplies, and
an appallingly high death rate as disease and famine struck.

Even so, there were craftsmen who practiced their trades in
these beginning years; documentary and some archaeological
evidence confirms their presence. Among these were boat builders, carpenters, woodcutters and sawyers, a mason, and a blacksmith. There was a short-lived ironworks at Falling Creek, upriver from Jamestown, which was in operation for a year or so
from about 1620 to 1622, when Indians massacred the workers
and the furnace was destroyed. Once tobacco became a major
commodity, coopers, who made barrels, casks, and the like,
were steadily employed. As early as 1610 mention is found of
church furniture being built. The most exotic workers were a
group of eight Dutchmen and Poles brought over in 1608 to start
a glass industry, in accord with London's plans. A glass furnace
of sorts was erected but the enterprise soon failed. Again in 1621
six Italian glassworkers were sent, and for three years spasmodic
attempts were made to manufacture glass. The gap between
what the London merchants and planners thought possible and
the actual conditions in the isolated wilderness was often unbridgeable.

Very temporary, improvised shelters, as well as some sturdier
structures based on familiar methods from the homeland, appear
to have been erected during the first phase of settlement. In
these, some of the English learned and borrowed Indian methods. William Strachey, writing in 1610, noted: "A delicate
wrought fine kind of mat the Indians make with which (as they
can be trucked for or snatched up) our people do dress their
chambers and inward rooms, which make their houses so much
the more handsome. The houses have wide and large country
chimneys, in the which is to be supposed (in such plenty of
wood) what fires are maintained; and they have found the way to
cover their houses now (as the Indians) with barks of trees, as
durable and as good proof against storms and winter weather as
the best tile, defending likewise the piercing sunbeams of summer and keeping their inner lodgings cool enough, which before
in sultry weather would be like stoves, whilst they were, as at
first, pargeted and plastered with bitumen or tough clay. And
thus armed for the injury of changing times and seasons of the
year we hold ourselves well apaid, though wanting arras hangings, tapestry, and gilded Venetian cordovan, or more spruce
household garniture and wanton city ornaments."

Strachey was obviously familiar with well-appointed English
interiors hung with Arras tapestries or with walls covered with
fine leather. In the New World he, and other settlers of his class,
satisfied their urge for decoration beyond bare utilitarian form by
using Indian mats. He seems to have enjoyed the challenge.

Recently the archaeologist Ivor Noël Hume and his staff discovered several early seventeenth-century sites in an area once
called "Martin's Hundred" on the James River. Since archaeolo-
gists have yet to find any of the original fortified settlement
at Jamestown (part of which may have washed away), these
pre–1650 sites represent the earliest material evidence found
thus far of life, and death, in the Virginia colony. The finds
provide vivid evidence of the settlers as they tried to transplant
their known society to an unknown wilderness setting. Two remarkable metal close helmets, bits of chain mail, and an elbow
section from a suit of armor show the sort of military equipment
they brought to protect themselves, equipment ill-suited for war-

fare in woodlands and swamps, be it with Indians or Spaniards. An inch-long piece of woven gold of the type which would have been used to adorn a gentleman's garment has been found. It may have belonged to the "governor," William Harwood, of the Martin's Hundred area, founded in 1619 and destroyed by Indians in 1622.

There is firm evidence of the practice of the potter's craft. The date 1631 is clear on the fragment of a dish decorated with yellow slip ornament on the left; it is the oldest dated piece of British-American pottery yet found. Other pieces of pottery made locally include parts of different-shaped bowls and pots and a colander, below. Though undated themselves, they can be placed between 1620 and 1645. These utilitarian earthenware pieces are representative of the earliest known group of colonial Virginia pottery.

The excavations suggest that life at these early settlements must often have been full of sharp contrasts—between the familiar and the unfamiliar, between the sick and the well, between the fortunate and those less so. People brought with them familiar objects, and tried to fashion an environment that had some resemblance to the settings they had known. A few individuals and a few households must have enjoyed many of the amenities they had known before. For most, life was extremely harsh and primitive. The marks of postholes found in excavations on these sites show what one settlement in Martin's Hundred, Wolstenholme Towne, was like. There was a fort with a palisade of post-and-plank construction and a watchtower, where the community members could retreat in time of danger. The leader may have had his house within this enclosure. Outside were other buildings, including what was probably a storehouse and a longhouse adjoined by a stable.

The vision of the Virginia Company, and later of the Crown, was for a group of agricultural villages like Wolstenholme Towne, each with a church, storehouse, market square, and houses evenly laid out, with provision for military protection, surrounded by outlying farms. Each was to be the commercial and social center of an area. It was a concept with which the English had had some experience, rooted in the plans used for English-controlled medieval towns, or *bastides*, in southwestern France, and practiced as well by the English after their conquest of Wales and in their Irish colonies. Jamestown was to be the first of these, and there was in fact a semblance of a town there until the Revolution, long after it was abandoned as the capital in 1698. A continuous record of renewed official attempts to improve the town, such as the 1662 "Act for Building a Towne," suggests how slowly the small community grew (it also suffered several fires). Most settlers chose to live on their farms or plantations scattered along the rivers rather than in a town. The chief function of Jamestown was thus as a court and political center. It apparently never became important as a commercial center for the surrounding farms or as a place where trades and crafts genuinely flourished. Indeed, as late as 1705 Robert Beverley was prompted to write that the Virginians "have not any one Place of Cohabitation among them, that may reasonably bear the Name of a Town."

Whether in town or on outlying lands, it appears that during the first sixty or so years, settlers in Virginia lived in a variety of vernacular structures, many of which were relatively short-lived (ten to twenty years). Although more permanent than the first improvised shelters, they were less permanent than the buildings erected after 1680 or 1690. From a report of 1623: "But the plantations are farr asunder and their houses stand scattered one from another, and are onlie made of wood, few or none of them beeing framed houses but punches (posts) sett into the Ground and couered wth boards so as a firebrand is sufficient to consume them all." The buildings of posthole construction, based on English vernacular architectural practice and subject to a number of variations, had vertical elements or posts that were set directly three or four feet into the ground. There were often no sills, or sills were laid between the posts, and they were "earth fast." A number of these buildings seem to have been as small as 8 by 8 feet or 10 by 10 feet.

A 1647 act passed by the Assembly concerning the problem of escaping prisoners indirectly provides additional evidence about the unsubstantial housing "wee frequently inhabitt" and also suggests that a sturdier "Virginia house" had evolved by that date. The latter must have been sufficiently different from English models to justify the characterization: "Whereas divers escapes have been made by prisoners, and more likely to be, for want of sufficient prisons in severall countyes, to which the poverty of the countrey and want of necessaries here will not admitt a possibillitie to erect other than such houses as wee frequently inhabitt. . . . *Be it therefore enacted*, That such houses provided for that purpose shall be accompted sufficient prisons as are built according to the forme of Virginia houses, from which noe escape can be made without breaking or forcing some part of the prison house. . . ."

A clue to what the "Virginia houses" might have been is found in a tract written in 1656 to attract settlers, in which the writer, John Hammond, says the colonists, most of whom are settled along the rivers, are "Pleasant in their building, which

Pieces of utilitarian pottery made in Virginia between 1620 and 1645. Colonial Williamsburg.

Cary Carson. Conjectural drawing of St. Mary's City, Maryland, c. 1634. Conjectural drawings need periodic revision. This drawing should not have included sheep, horses, nor so many dwellings. In 1982, however, archaeological excavations confirmed the approximate location and outline of the fort. St. Mary's City Commission.

although for the most part they are but one story besides the loft, and built of wood." The unpretentious interiors were described as "contrived so delightfull, that your ordinary houses in England are not so handsome, for usually the rooms are large, daubed and whitelimed, glazed and flowered, and if not glazed windows, shutters which are made pritty and convenient." Thus by the middle of the century some of the structures being built, though still modest and not necessarily long-lived, had an air of substance.

No pure examples of these "Virginia houses" have survived, but careful examination of interior portions of several surviving buildings of seventeenth-century origin, which have been modified and added to in subsequent years, suggests that the "Virginia house" of the seventeenth century was similar to the type just described, and was probably a one- or one-and-one-half-story frame dwelling, one or two rooms long, covered with unpainted riven clapboards and with gable and chimneys.

One of the variations from the simplest posthole construction was to use a regular joined timber frame but to place this on piers or blocks (rather than on a foundation) which, in archaeological excavation, look much the same as postholes. This somewhat sturdier method of building, which was different from traditional English practice, apparently became the norm by the end of the century. Whereas earlier the Virginians thought of their methods as less substantial than English ones, by the end of the century they saw them as better, and by 1692 one finds a reference to "good Substantial Virginia Built." Seventeenth-century ways of building were modified in the eighteenth century, but many of

the essential methods continued in use and were basic to the construction of most colonial Virginia frame structures.

The extensive archaeological and documentary investigation still underway continues to shed new light on the probable appearance of the earliest settlement in Maryland. George Calvert, first Lord Baltimore, was granted a charter by Charles I for the proprietary colony of Maryland in 1632. In March 1634, 200 colonists under Leonard Calvert arrived on the banks of the Chesapeake. A conjectural drawing, above, prepared in 1972 for St. Mary's City Commission, shows how that little community may have looked in 1634. All of the first buildings were probably within the "pallizado" which Calvert reported as built, the eight "pieces of Ordnance" brought with them placed at the four corner bastions. A blockhouse may have been at the point where the two cross streets intersected. The "gentlemen adventurers," little more than twenty, probably had timber-framed cottages of posthole construction, while their indentured servants (who could not afford to pay their own passage) probably lived in very simple earth-built or sod huts. The timber-framed cottages were, relatively speaking, of more durable construction. The fort was adjacent to a Yaocimico Indian village and one of their lodges served for a time as chapel for the colonists.

It was the Indian crop, tobacco, exported for cash, that gradually helped the settlers in both Maryland and Virginia to establish a more stable and cohesive society. To some of the settlers the New World became home, a place of permanent residence for themselves and their children rather than a place to make quick money from a few years of good crops. The other Indian crop, corn, and then wheat, gradually gained in importance. They were used both for food and partly as market crops. Enough cattle were raised so that some could be exported to Barbados. Prosperity attracted new colonists with capital to the colony, and additional groups of indentured servants were added to the population. With this stability came more permanent buildings.

The finest surviving house in Virginia of the second half of the century, and very probably the oldest surviving brick house in English North America, is the Arthur Allen house in Surry County, Virginia, to the right. It is frequently called Bacon's Castle because it was here in 1676 that the forces of the headstrong Nathaniel Bacon, revolting against the colonial government, were quartered for a time.

The house is a tall, two-story brick structure with steeply pitched roof. The entry was in the central vertical projection or tower, while a staircase to the second floor was in a similar tower at the rear. A large room or hall was on either side. The watercolor rendering, done around 1820, shows both a front view and a side elevation of the then already venerable building. The doorway was ornamented with a triangular pediment of molded brick, and there are raised and plastered brick frames around both the first- and second-story windows, which provided decorative accents to the exterior. (These first-floor frames were removed in the 1850s.) The original windows were leaded casements with

R. H. Cocke. "Arthur Allen House." c. 1800–1820. Watercolor on paper. Built c. 1665, Surry County, Virginia. Association for the Preservation of Virginia Antiquities, Richmond.

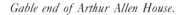

Gable end of Arthur Allen House.

mullions and transoms—the shuttered sash windows in the watercolor reflect a modernization that had already taken place by 1820. The curved and stepped gables end with tall diagonally set chimney stacks, left, and are the outstanding feature of the house. They indicate that the owner and builder were conversant with stylistic modes familiar in England, whence Arthur Allen had only recently come. The pronounced verticality of the whole building reflects the lingering medieval taste in England, but the symmetrical plan, the nicely balanced decorative elements, and the Flemish curved gables all demonstrate that both builder and owner were aware of the architectural styles that had slowly spread across Europe and reached England through the Netherlands and Flanders. The house is also modern for its time in having the service facilities, such as the kitchen and storage areas, in the basement. This elegantly conceived house, with a certain architectural self-consciousness, is a portent of the great eighteenth-century plantation houses of Tidewater Virginia and

Maryland. It has long been believed that the Arthur Allen house was built around 1655, but new dendrochronological analysis of cores taken from timbers in the house indicate the building probably was not under construction until a decade later.

As the two colonies continued to grow and prosper, settlers moved ever farther along the rivers and bays near the seaboard. The Roanoke lost colony had been in what is now North Carolina. As early as 1660 a permanent English settlement was established by colonists from Virginia at Albemarle on the Chowan River, which also became part of North Carolina. The boundary between the two colonies was set in 1633 when Charles II granted a charter to the Lords Proprietors of Carolina for a large tract extending south from the Virginia border to Spanish Florida. Almost from the beginning the new Carolina territory was

Maurice Matthew, surveyor. "Plat of Joseph West." 1680.
Watercolor on parchment. South Carolina Historical Society,
Charleston.

thought of in terms of a northern and southern section—in the northern area the early years were marked by poverty and political turbulence, including several uprisings, in the southern one life was more ordered. By 1712 the divergence was such that North Carolina was given its own governor.

The initiative for the Carolina colony had come from the English at Barbados because their island was already crowded. Once again, the first efforts at new settlement were sporadic and unsuccessful. However, by 1680 Charles Town (Charleston) had been laid out between the Ashley and Cooper rivers. It was a simple grid plan with an open square in the middle, all surrounded by a stockade. The process of allocating land grants depended upon the careful measuring and mapping by surveyors, whose fundamental role in the establishment of new territories we are apt to forget.

A rare illuminated vellum from this early period, left, is the work of the surveyor Maurice Matthew and represents the boundaries of the grant of land "scittuate upon ye westermost side of ye westermost branch of the Cooper River and belonging to the honourable Colonel Joseph West Governor and Landgrave of the Province of Carolina" in 1680. The surveyor or one of his men was not content simply to show the geographical limits of the grant, for he decorated it with tiny vignettes showing trees, a stream, and even a tiny windmill. He further lavished it with a patterned border, almost three inches wide, of fruits and flowers. There is a nicety of observation, and a desire to particularize and make a local identification in the yellow flowers that appear to be a native wild jessamine; strawberries and pomegranates are also shown. The arms of Governor West are detailed in carefully rendered calligraphy. The whole has the finished and decorative quality one would expect from a disciplined and trained European craftsman of the seventeenth century performing a task for an important client. This was a new venture in a new world, but it was to have the order, decorum, and measure of the old. West had provided just such orderly leadership as governor during 1671, a year of great hardship for the colony, and again between 1674 and 1682 and in 1684.

Charleston traders were soon penetrating deep into Indian country, especially into Cherokee territory. This trade began to transform the latter's society from a subsistence-planting-hunting economy into one based on deerskins, and although the herds were gradually depleted, much of the first wealth of the colony came from this trade. This early, friendly relationship with the Cherokees also helped the troops from South Carolina sent to North Carolina to fight in the short-lived Tuscarora War of 1711–1713, because the Indians joined the whites in attacking their ancient enemies. According to tradition, the South Carolinians paid their Indian colleagues for each scalp taken.

Sketches of schematic rows of trees, brightly colored compass and calipers, and decorated cartouches to enframe texts enhance the military map, right, of a battle that took place in March 1713 near the end of the Tuscarora War. The decoration by an anonymous cartographer again goes considerably beyond the military necessity of recording and reporting. In two of the three encampments the unknown artist has indicated the mixed nature of the force by showing two European-style tents alongside rows of Indian-style curved shelters. The South Carolinians captured

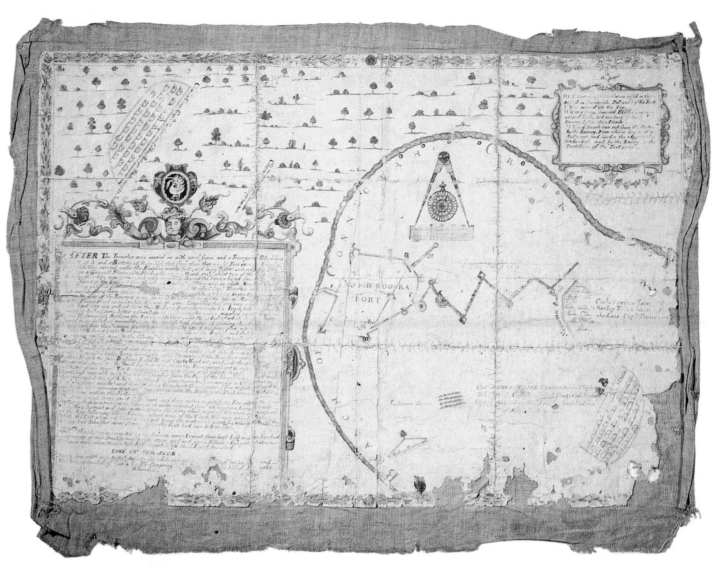

Artist unknown. "Map of Tuscarora Expedition." 1713. South Carolina Historical Society, Charleston.

the Tuscarora "fort" of Noo-he-roo-ka. After this victory a small contingent of the Tuscarora remained in the Carolinas, while the greater part of the tribe found refuge with the Oneida Nation to the north. During their trek they stayed two years in Pennsylvania, but then removed to New York, where they joined the Iroquois confederacy as the sixth nation. Theirs was one of many treks to unfamiliar territories American Indians were to make in the face of the inexorable outward thrust of the white settlements. For the land-hungry whites, with their concept of measured individual property, such battles were necessary to make themselves secure; for the Indians they meant the end of their known way of life.

One of the means of creating a cohesive society was the establishment of churches. This was seen as important to most of the founder-investors of the colonies, who wished for stability and were fearful of the chaos which could be created by religious upheaval and dissension.

The English in Virginia took care to divide their counties into parishes as early as 1612 and to establish churches. The Virginia Company resolved from the beginning that the official religion was to be Church of England; this policy was reinforced when Virginia became a Crown colony in 1624, and continued to be official policy until the American Revolution. In Maryland, even though the proprietor, Lord Baltimore, was a Roman Catholic, the original charter required that the province be governed by the laws of England, and hence the official religion was Church of England. From its settlement in 1634 until 1692 there was a great deal of religious freedom in Maryland, and during the English Commonwealth the Puritans actually took control. In 1692 when Baltimore's proprietorship ended, the Church of England was again named the established church in Maryland. The code of laws for the Carolina colony drawn up by the famous English philosopher John Locke, in 1669, granted freedom of worship to "every church and profession," and from an early date people of a variety of religious faiths settled there—French Huguenots, Scotch and English Presbyterians, New England Congregationalists, Lutherans, Quakers, Baptists, Roman Catholics, and Sephardic Jews. Non-Anglicans actually outnumbered the Anglicans in Carolina, though the latter represented the largest single group of one faith. The inevitable jockeying for power among rival groups came to a head in 1705–1706; religious and political issues intermingled. There was a Church Party and a Dissenters Party, and in 1706 the Church Act was passed, making the Church of England the established church. Thus in the three major seaboard colonies of the South founded in the seventeenth century, the Church of England was the official church by 1706, if not before. However, despite insistence on its jurisdiction, the Church of England never appointed a bishop to oversee and supervise its American churches, and as a result a number of native institutions, and patterns of discipline and governance, grew up

Merchant's Hope Church, Prince George's County, Virginia, c. 1657.

traditional cruciform plan and a steeple or bell tower in front. Newport Parish Church, now called St. Luke's, has a square tower, buttressed walls, and is in the late Gothic vernacular style. It looks like a small English parish church, and is frequently used as a textbook example of an early Virginia or Southern church. It may have represented the ideal form, transplanted from the mother country, but it is not typical of what was built. For instance, only three of the 250 or so churches or chapels in colonial Virginia are known to have buttressed walls, and only a few more had bell towers or steeples. Though these two are frequently illustrated, they appear somewhat exceptional.

In essence, the typical early Virginia Church of England house of worship was a simple rectangular building, plain, almost austere on the exterior, and therefore with something of a domestic air. Most were without steeples or bell towers of any kind. They were thus considerably more modest in appearance than their English counterparts. They are neat and well built, but minimal. Most were designed to conform to certain traditional English ecclesiastical precepts, such as having the long axis of the church set east and west, with the altar in the east end. But the services themselves often differed in degree from those in England and hence the pulpit or reading desk sometimes had, relatively speaking, more prominence than the altar.

The precedents for these structures were set in the seventeenth century. A Swiss traveler, Francis Louis Michel, writing in 1702, probably gave an accurate, if brief, description of the Virginia churches then surviving when he wrote that most were "of timber, without towers or bells." He also noted, without further elaboration, that they were "not all built alike." Thus the steepleless church was characteristic by the end of the seventeenth century, and there was some variety in the plans and elevations.

None of these seventeenth-century timber churches, which must have been quite simple, plain structures, has survived, although records suggest that as many as fifty small parish churches were erected. Most were replaced with brick buildings. The majority of the latter, to judge by the fifty-two that now remain, reflect or express the restrained choices of the colonists.

An early example of these modest and austere structures is Merchant's Hope Church, Prince George County, to the left. It is located on the south side of the James River, ten miles east of the present city of Hopewell, and is one of the relatively few brick churches built in Virginia during the seventeenth century. The name probably derives from the name of a plantation in the area. The date of 1657 is inscribed on a roof rafter, and though it cannot be firmly proved, this may be the date of completion. In 1655 an Act of Assembly urged the founding of parishes and building of churches, and in the same year a merchant in this area willed a fund of tobacco for repairing the existing church or for building a new one.

The church is a simple shedlike structure, with brick laid in English bond below the beveled water table, and in Flemish bond above it. The walls are extremely well built and though the building underwent many vicissitudes in the late eighteenth and nineteenth centuries, very few repairs were made to the basic fabric. The brick headers were glazed, giving subtle color variation and texture to the wall surface. The surround of the arch of

to meet the needs of the colonial parishes. Local vestries, committees set up to help govern the church, were responsible for performing the various duties of the church for the parish, such as upkeep of buildings, care of the poor and aged, and were to a large degree self-governing.

Religious life in the early South was more varied than is sometimes implied. Moreover, Southern colonial houses of worship were more diverse in appearance than is probably generally known. Given the dominance of the Church of England and the desire of many of the colonists to pursue a way of life based on English models, one would expect the majority of church buildings of the colonial period to be fairly close copies of English parish churches. Some few are, but considerably more are so much simpler as to appear different in kind.

Notable high-style examples that fit the official ideal are the Newport Parish Church, Isle of Wight County, Virginia, and the Bruton Parish Church in Williamsburg. The latter, begun in 1711, was essentially the state church for the capital city; it has a the doorway on the west end is of smooth rubbed brick slightly different in color, as are those of the windows. The eaves of the gable are canted outward. The dentiled cornice and some of the interior woodwork and plaster are apparently part of an 1870 restoration. The round-arched windows are the most overt statement of the religious or institutional character of the building. The pulpit is believed to have been in the middle of the south wall. Thus if there was a service when holy communion was not given, the pulpit or reader's desk would have been the architectural focus, and the attention away from the altar of the east end. Other original interior arrangements are not known.

The reasons for the plainness of the early timber churches (which sometimes must have looked similar to early New England meetinghouses) and of churches such as Merchant's Hope are difficult to identify precisely but seem to result from circumstances in rural Virginia. The early colonists persisted in a pattern of scattered settlements along the rivers, where there were virtually no village or town centers. Thus the churches came to be situated deep in the country, often easily accessible by river, at a site where drinking water was available, and more or less between plantations. The absence of steeples, bell towers, and bells may be accounted for in part by the fact that bells could not be heard from a great distance and, given the economic hardships of the first century of Virginia settlements, such niceties were expensive. By the time the colonists could afford them it appears to have become more or less traditional to do without.

Whether or not the modesty and austerity of these churches had to do with questions of liturgy, faith, and the number of available ministers is at best a moot question.

During the sixteenth, seventeenth, and eighteenth centuries in Europe, with the rise of the Reformation, there was much controversy and much experiment concerning forms of worship, which in turn affected the shape and form of buildings for worship. Reformers stressed the need for the service to center on Scripture and to be in the language of the people. They wished the services to be easily heard by all members of the congregation, and all acts of the service to be visible. Some old churches were stripped of ornamentation; elaborate "popish" decoration was frowned upon. Pulpits were given a new dominance and a more central position. Communion tables replaced altars. Sometimes (in both Scotland and the Netherlands, for example) these tables were put in the aisles and the congregation received communion sitting at them, or communion was served to the seated parishioners rather than their coming forward to kneel—thus giving greater emphasis to the communal nature of the Last Supper than to the sacramental aspect. Galleries were introduced so more people could hear easily. In England there were movements for reform both within and without the established church. Some reforming groups eschewed institutional buildings altogether and met in private houses, hence the term meetinghouses. The changes that took place in the architectural settings for worship during the sixteenth century largely resulted from modifications to existing buildings; a few "auditory" churches with open, central spaces were erected in England in the early seventeenth century.

In America during the seventeenth century, Puritans in New England evolved and created in their meetinghouses a distinct architectural type. These served both as places of worship and as centers of village government, and were located in the towns. No single form was consistently used, though most were simple rectangular or square buildings, frequently with galleries, usually well lighted; the exteriors were derived in part from English village market halls. In the examples built in the late seventeenth century the entrance was generally on the south side (rather than on the west end) and the pulpit opposite, with the seats or pews facing the pulpit. The communicants received the Lord's Supper seated in their pews.

Though the early colonists of Virginia adhered to the Church of England, there were those among them who favored reforms. The distinguished scholar Perry Miller has pointed out that during the earliest period of settlement, when the Virginia Company professed allegiance to the Church of England, the "ecclesiastical complexion always shows itself more 'low' than 'high,'" and that at this time the Virginians' "sense of their relation to God, was so thoroughly Protestant as to be virtually indistinguishable from the Puritan." The religious impulse that underlay the founding of the Virginia Company, however, collapsed with the company's failure in 1624. From that time on religious dedication and values played a lesser role; emphasis turned to creating a financially successful colony. Church building and religious affairs took second place to other activities. Later, in the turbulent seventeenth century, when the Virginia colonists officially remained loyal to the church despite Cromwell, a tolerant latitudinarianism prevailed so long as individuals were not openly disloyal to king or colonial government.

A major feature of Anglican church services is supposed to be the regular celebration of communion. However, in rural colonial Virginia there was often a dire shortage of ministers, and therefore most parishes celebrated the sacrament of holy communion only three times a year, and seldom more than four. Thus the regular communion so essential to Anglican service was usually omitted in the Virginia religious devotions. Services were sometimes conducted by lay readers, by ministers who had not been officially ordained, or "ordained" by local vestries. Some ministers who served were dissenters of the Genevan or Presbyterian faith. Due to circumstances, in some parishes the conduct of special religious services, such as funerals and marriages, was slipshod and casual by English standards. Some services seemed, to outsiders, closer to those of the dissenting or reform churches than to the Church of England. Michel, the Swiss traveler of 1702, who noted the absence of steeples and towers on the early Virginia churches, also recorded, without elaborating or giving specifics, "Regarding religious services it may be said that they are held according to the principles of the reformation, as in our Swiss churches, although with some customs in the English language not current among us." Hints as to the diversity among services in Virginia parishes are to be found in the report published by the Reverend Hugh Jones in 1724. He had taught at William and Mary College, served as chaplain to the General Assembly, then returned to England in 1722. He noted that in some parishes, "In several respects the Clergy are obliged to omit or alter some minute Parts of the *Liturgy*, and deviate from the strict *Discipline and Ceremonies* of the *Church* . . . and in some Parishes where the People have been used to receive Commun-

Christ Church, Lancaster County, Virginia, built 1722–1728.

ion in their Seats (a Custom introduced for Opportunity for such as are inclined to *Presbytery* to receive *Sacrament* sitting) it is not an easy matter to bring them to the *Lord's Table* decently upon their knees." Kneeling or not kneeling was an issue symptomatic of broader theological arguments, and this passage suggests that in some parishes the religious concepts of the reforming Presbyterians had been accepted and assimilated. In the same context Jones also remarked, "Every Minister is a kind of *Independent* in his own parish." Thus economics, geography, and the willingness of some congregations to accept certain concepts of the reformers—such as not kneeling at communion or eschewing elaborate ornamentation—help to explain the austere and domestic character of many Virginia churches.

The Great Fire of London in 1666 destroyed many of the old churches of that city, and as is well known, Sir Christopher Wren was responsible for the design and rebuilding of more than fifty churches in the City of London from 1670 to 1722. He deliberately created variety; no two were alike. Most were graced with steeples or campaniles that towered above neighboring buildings. The Wren churches had an important influence on subsequent church building in both England and America.

Wren was well aware of the concepts enunciated by reformers and dissenters, and of the modifications in religious services which they introduced. In planning his new churches he sought to adapt the interior spaces so as to accord with the principles of those who sought reform from within the church. In a letter to a friend, written in 1708, he noted, "The Churches therefore must be large; but still in our reformed Religion, it should seem vain to make a *Parish-church* larger than that all who are present can both hear and see. The *Romanists,* indeed, may build larger Churches, it is enough if they hear the Murmer of the Mass, and see the Elevation of the Host, but ours are to be fitted for Auditories." Thus Wren further developed and made popular in England the "auditory" church, where ministers could be clearly seen and heard. The pulpit was given prominence; sometimes it was combined with the reading desk. Both were placed near the congregation, sometimes to the right and left of the center aisle. The well-lighted, open quality and the use of decorative architectural embellishments of classical vocabulary are the chief characteristics of the varied parish churches he designed. Many of the floor plans were simple, open rectangles. Wren's variations or experiments represent the modification of medieval forms as handled or "reformed" within the tradition of the Church of England (which in itself was and is Protestant vis-à-vis the Roman Catholic church), and typify the English art of compromise. Official "high" church practices and reform concepts were combined.

The interior "auditory" plans of Wren were congenial to the

next generation of Virginians since their own church buildings appear to have evolved in the same direction. Although with the growing prosperity and stability of the colony during the early eighteenth century, many of the wooden churches were replaced with brick ones, the exteriors of most of the surviving Virginia churches of this period are still austere, minimal, and almost domestic in appearance.

Christ Church in Lancaster County, Virginia, left, tall and of imposing scale, served not only as a parish church but also as a family church. It is one of the finest colonial buildings in America, yet even here, where money was no problem, there remains an air of restraint. Though the brickwork and detailing are superb, the elegant ornament is extraordinarily discreet, so that the net impression is of great, albeit elegant, plainness. The design is within the still-new Wren fashion, but is also well within the tradition of austere Virginia church design. Most of the original fabric is intact, though some repairs have been made. It was built at the expense and munificence of Robert "King" Carter somewhere between 1726 and 1733. Carter had acquired great wealth, including an estate of 300,000 acres of land and about 1,000 slaves, and comported himself in such a way as to earn the nickname King. His manner of living epitomizes what later generations thought of as Virginia Cavalier.

The plan of Christ Church is that of a Latin cross, though the nave is proportionately short and the impression is almost of the equidistant Greek cross—indeed, the total length of the cross-arms or transepts is the same as that of the nave and chancel. The brickwork, in Flemish bond with scattered glazed headers, is superb. The west doorway, which is 21 feet high, is framed in molded and rubbed brick pilasters topped by an entablature and a segmental arched pediment. The side doorways on the east and west are 12½ feet high and have triangular pediments. There are small oval windows over each of the doorways: these are framed in rubbed brick, as are the semicircular arches over the tall windows. The capitals and bases of the pilasters of all three doorways are of Portland stone, as are other decorative details. The eaves of the tall hipped roof are beautifully canted out, thus giving a sharper definition to the elegant form and proportions of the roof. The walls are three feet thick.

The designer or architect is unknown, but clearly he and the craftsmen who worked on the church were men of skill who knew their trades. As was typical at this time, bricks were made at the building site, for in Carter's will, drawn up in 1726, he directed, "the bricks that are made & burnt shall be appropriated to the building of the said Brick church or as many thereof as will perfect the building." Among his white servants were a carpenter, a ship's carpenter, a glazier, a blacksmith, and a bricklayer, and among his Negroes were four carpenters. They may have been among those who built the church, but it seems probable that still other craftsmen were called upon in the course of the enterprise. Carter must have felt confident that there were enough skilled workers to carry out his plans, and that the design was fully understood, for in his lengthy will and codicils he allots only one paragraph to his wish that "the Vestry of Christ Church Parish shall undertake to build a brick church where the present Church stands." In a world of face-to-face business dealings, it was obviously not considered necessary to elaborate further on

Interior, Christ Church.

things that must have been discussed. Some of the craftsmen may have worked on Carter's own house, Corotoman, or on Rosewell, which was built for his son-in-law, Mann Page, around 1726–1730, a handsome building, now in ruins.

The tradition is that by 1726 the earlier parish church, built by Carter's father in 1669, had become too small, and the congregation wished to erect a new one at a more convenient location. However, the vestry agreed to have the new one built at the same site when Robert Carter agreed to pay for it. The church was on the family property, and another of the stipulations in Carter's will was that money be given for the new church, "provided alwaies the Chancel be preserved as a burial

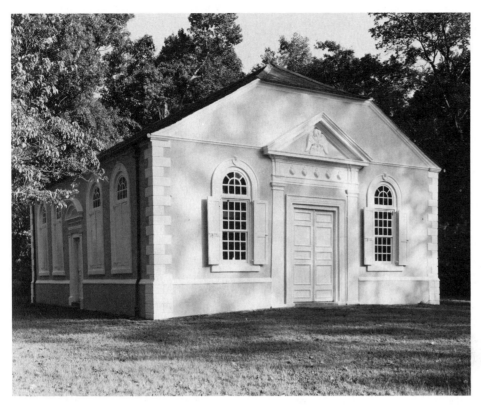

St. James's Church, Goose Creek, South Carolina, 1706–1719.

place for my family as the present chancel is, and that there be preserved to my family a commodious pew in the new chancel." He also willed that his own body was "to be laid in the yard of Christ Church near and upon the right hand of my Wives." These conditions were followed. Thus Christ Church was built and designed as a traditional parish church, but with the additional character of a family, and memorial church. Carter further accentuated this link by building a road, bordered by two tall hedges to cover the three miles between his house and the church. Perhaps most revealing was the fact reported in 1838 by Bishop William Meade, who saw an old vestry book, now disappeared, that the congregation did not enter the church on Sunday until after Carter's coach had arrived.

In keeping with Carter's proprietary relationship to the church, all the seating space in the north transept was reserved for his tenants and servants. The desire to have space allotted to his own plantation community may have been one reason for the choice of the cruciform plan. The Bruton Parish Church in Williamsburg begun in 1711 was built in the form of a Latin cross, and is the most immediate and only known precedent for a cruciform church in Virginia. Since Bruton Parish Church was essentially the state church for the capital city, the transept pews were reserved for the House of Burgesses when that body was in session. Carter and/or his designer may have known of a number of cruciform churches in Great Britain, most especially in Scotland, but it has not been possible to prove any single immediate precedent or model. The cruciform plan, particularly with the appearance of a Greek cross, was an unusual choice for a Virginian to make at that time, but it was a reasonably well-known form. The sister parish church (the two congregations shared a minister for years) of St. Mary's White Chapel was built around 1740, also in

Lancaster County, and also in the form of a cross, possibly in emulation of Christ Church. After 1732 a number of other Virginia churches followed this plan.

The interior of Christ Church, previous page, has the same mixture of elegance of details, fine proportions, yet overall sense of restraint, which characterizes the outside. The walls are white, and light pours in from the great windows. A fine walnut molding is at the spring line of the ceiling. Above this rises the plastered and vaulted ceiling which is 33 feet at its highest point. The wood of the liturgical furniture, the three-decker pulpit, the altar-piece on the east wall, and the paneling on three sides of the chancel are of polished black walnut, shaped with great skill. The high box pews are of pine. The altar table and the font are at the east end, while the pulpit with reading desk is situated at the southeast angle of the crossing. Thus the two "liturgical centers" were and are both completely visible to the congregation. Bishop Meade held services there in 1838, and reported his pleasure in preaching "from the high and lofty pulpit, which seemed, as it were, to be hung in the air. Perfectly delightful it was to raise the voice . . . in a house whose sacred form and beautiful arches seemed to give force and music to the feeblest tongue beyond any other building in which I ever performed." It is the auditory church par excellence.

The majority of the surviving colonial churches in Maryland and North Carolina are also Anglican and, as in Virginia, most also are of brick. In both states, but especially in Maryland, where forty-nine colonial churches remain, modest, well-built, rectangular churches without steeples or bell towers—comparable to Merchant's Hope in Virginia—are found. Among these are Old Wye Church in Wye Mills, Maryland, c. 1717, and St. Thomas's Church at Bath, North Carolina, 1734.

There is a greater variety in style and scale among the surviving colonial churches of South Carolina. One of the earliest is the exquisite, small St. James's of Goose Creek, above. It was planned sometime after 1706 when the General Assembly of the colony passed an act making the Church of England the established church in Carolina. Nine parishes were laid out: St. James's was one. The vestry journal records that it was finished in 1719. It, too, is in a rural setting, and is without bell tower or steeple, though it is less austere than some of its Virginia counterparts. It is a single-storied rectangular church with a single tier of arched windows on either side, three bays wide, five bays long. There are doors on the front and west end, in the center, and on both sides.

Here one senses the tie with Barbados. The brick walls were stuccoed and tinted in a brick red that has now faded, while the architectural accents are white, a practice still followed in the British West Indies. The use of quoins, the round-arched windows, the pilastered and pedimented door frame, all reflect an awareness of "correct" architecture of the time. We do not know the designer-builder, but Arthur Middleton, son of a planter who had come from Barbados, was apparently a prime mover. He gave four acres for the parsonage and was awarded a pew in the church immediately upon its completion. Nine other pews were so awarded; the rest, as was the tradition, were sold. The majority of the first parishioners, "Goose Creek Men," were English settlers from Barbados. The basic shape of this one-story rectan-

Interior, St. James's Church.

gular church, including the jerkinheaded gable, was followed in several later South Carolina rural churches.

The pelican placed over the doorway, succoring its young, a traditional symbol of Christ's sacrifice, was the official emblem of the Society for the Propagation of the Gospel in Foreign Parts. (The present sculpture is cast from an earlier one, and may be the fourth one in this place.) This was the newly formed mission society of the Church of England. Between 1702 and 1772 they sent fifty-four missionaries or preachers to Carolina. The first missionary-minister to Goose Creek was an English-speaking native of France, sent perhaps because the society was thinking of the French Huguenots in the region. Other architectural details include the frieze over the door, flaming hearts in the metopes alternating with classical triglyphs. The keystones of

the window arches are carved with cherub heads. The religious intent of the building is explicit.

In the interior, above, the tall pulpit beneath its sounding board dominates the end wall. It stands over and above the communion table and the reading desk. The three liturgical activities are thus concentrated together. There was some precedent for such an arrangement in a few English country churches. The pulpit is directly in front of a large arched window, and is flanked by tablets on which the Decalogue, the Lord's Prayer, and the Creed are inscribed. These tablets are each placed against two fluted pilasters, painted to look like marble, with capitals of the composite order. These, in turn, support an entablature and an elaborate broken-scroll pediment which unites the two sides. All of this is of painted plaster. The pilasters and pediment visually

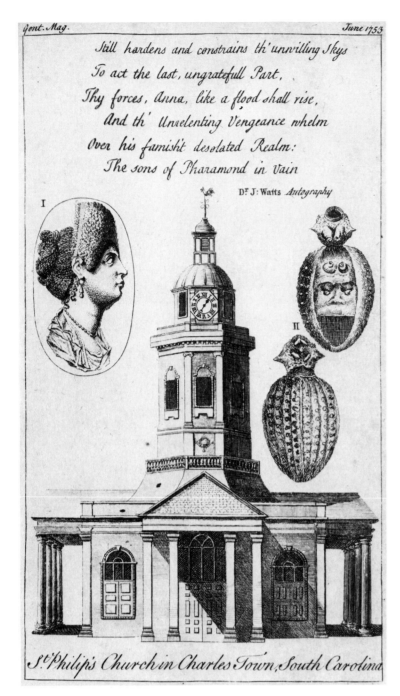

Still hardens and constrains th'unwilling Skys
To act the last, ungratefull Part,
Thy forces, Anna, like a flood shall rise,
And th' Unrelenting Vengeance whelm
Over his famisht desolated Realm:
The sons of Pharamond in vain

Dr. J. Watts Autography

I

II

St. Philip's Church in Charles Town, South Carolina

"*St. Philip's Church in Charles Town, South Carolina.*"
Engraving from GENTLEMAN'S MAGAZINE, *London,*
June 1753. Avery Library, Columbia University,
New York, N.Y.

frame the pulpit. A Bible supported by two cherubim forms the keystone of the arched window. Directly above this are the royal arms in high relief and full color. The whole unit makes a statement on the close relation between church and state. At the same time, the central and dominant placement of the pulpit seems to proclaim the missionary role of the church where the Word was given great emphasis. The Goose Creek men were among the staunchest supporters of the Church of England in the early colony, and as such were strong in the Church Party. In South Carolina religious and political control went hand in hand, as they did in the symbolism used here.

The grandest, and the most English of colonial churches in the American South, was no doubt St. Philip's in Charleston,

built around 1710–1723. Because it was destroyed by fire in 1838 it receives little or no mention in most standard studies of American architecture, yet it was identified more than once during the eighteenth century as one of the finest edifices in the new country. Its imposing appearance can be guessed at from an engraving, left, published in the London *Gentleman's Magazine* of June 1753. There it was described as "one of the most regular and complete structures of its kind in America." In a chauvinistic text that accompanied an engraving of a view of Charleston published in 1739, based on a drawing by Bishop Roberts, we are told "ye Church of St. Philip, may Justly be reckoned ye finest structure in America."

Edmund Burke, in his *Account of the European Settlements in America*, published in 1761, echoes these words: "The church is spacious, and executed in a very handsome taste, exceeding everything of that kind which we have in America."

St. Philip's was the second Anglican church built for the young city of Charleston. There is no evidence that a church was built at the original settlement at Albemarle Point ("Old Town") in 1670, but when the site of the new town was laid out in 1680 a "convenient place" was reserved for "a church, town house and other public structures." Sometime thereafter a wooden building of cypress was erected. It must have been inadequate or in poor condition, for in 1710 an act was passed "for the erecting of a new brick church . . . to be the Parish Church of St. Philip's, Charlestown." Again, we do not know who the builder, architect-designer, and craftsmen were, although they must have been very knowledgeable, because the engraving shows a commanding and impressive structure, with not one but three giant porticoes of the Tuscan order, one on the west, and one each facing the north and south. This was probably the first use of giant-order porticoes in the present United States. Dr. Frederick Dalcho wrote an extensive description of the church in 1820. The nave was about 74 feet long, the vestibule or belfry 37 feet. The church was 62 feet wide and 40 feet high. The steeple totaled about 80 feet; two bells were within one course, dial plates of a clock on another. The interior roof was arched (a barrel vault), and two rows of Tuscan pillars supported five arches on each side. The galleries, which were added somewhat later, were attached to these pillars. "Over the centre arch on the south side, are some figures in heraldic form, representing the infant colony imploring protection of the King." Here again was a mixture of imagery of church and state. There was no chancel, and the communion table stood "within the body of the Church." The pulpit and the reading desk were at the east end, at the northeast corner of the middle aisle. The east end was "pannelled Wainscot, ornamented with Corinthian Pilasters, supporting the Cornice of a Fan-light." Though the pulpit was slightly off center, it had the prominence found in an auditory church of the period. The treatment of the east wall (reredos was a term seldom used at that time) seems to have been reminiscent of that seen at St. James's, Goose Creek.

In South Carolina, as in Virginia, the Anglican services were apparently "low" rather than "high," though the reasons for this may have been somewhat different: in the 1705–1706 struggle for power between the Church Party and the Dissenters Party, political, religious, and legal issues were intermingled, for part of the struggle had to do with complete or limited rights for holding, purchasing, and transferring land under English law. Though a group of French Huguenots in old Craven County were essentially Calvinist and dissenters in faith, only months before the passage of the 1706 Church Act they succeeded in having their settlement made an Anglican parish—their minister therefore given an allowance from taxes. Thus in the complex politics of the moment, the Huguenots came into opposition with the Dissenters Party, and it was their vote that helped to bring about the passage of the 1706 Church Act. This act included the provision that rites and services could be conducted in the French language provided a translation of the Book of Common Prayer was used. In essence, some Huguenots, and in time more, assimilated themselves, or were assimilated, into the established church—and into the ruling group in South Carolina. Thus their clergy were supported by taxes, and in other ways they were allowed full participation in the political life and control of the colony. The Anglican church in South Carolina may have been "low" without the addition of the Huguenots with their Calvinist beliefs, but the participation of a fair number of them in the established church helped to keep it so.

St. Philip's, then, was built to accommodate the largest congregation of the established church in South Carolina at the time. It was a visible symbol of that church and, indeed, of the triumph of the Church Party (which kept a firm control over the clergy). Elections for the parish were in fact held there during the colonial period. In having the church built, the vestry must have sought out someone who knew well the newest and most fashionable ideas in church architecture. The three giant porticoes projected out from the walls and were baroque in their boldness. A 1776 traveler recorded that it was "modeled after the Jesuit's church in Antwerp," which seems farfetched, though both have barrel-vaulted interiors. It is remotely possible that someone of European origin assisted in the design. St. Philip's, long simply called "the Church," was so beloved that the new building of 1838, which replaced the 1710–1723 structure, was modeled on it in large part though, significantly, a chancel was added.

One of the original purposes of the Society for the Propagation of the Gospel in Foreign Parts, which provided the Anglican clergy to the province of South Carolina, was to convert "the Heathens and Infidels"; that is, the Indians and the Negroes and other likely lost souls. Several of the clergy conscientiously tried to do this; others found the task daunting. One of the early missionaries indicated that he had "too many profane to awaken, some few pious to build up, and many Negroes [and] Indians to begin withall." Moreover, the ministers soon learned that not all owners of slaves were eager to have their subjects taught lest they take off from work or get ideas about earthly freedom. Nonetheless, in some congregations slaves were instructed in religion and attended services, and in a number of cases the galleries were especially built to accommodate the slave population. Since galleries were common features of auditory churches in both England and America the presence of a gallery in a Southern church does not necessarily mean it was for Negroes.

Despite the political control of the Church Party a number of denominations flourished in South Carolina. The diversity in religious beliefs was reflected in the appearance of their houses of worship. One associates meetinghouses primarily with New England Puritans or Pennsylvania Quakers. However, according to the artist Charles Fraser, who published a memoir of his life in Charleston in 1854, only the two Anglican houses of worship in that city were called churches, all the others were called "meeting houses." The congregations were made up of various dissenting groups. One of the meetinghouses he knew would have been a forty-foot-square building, probably built in the 1680s, long known as the Presbyterian Meeting or the White Meeting House. The official name was the Independent Church of Charleston, and its congregation was made up of French Huguenots, Presbyterians from Scotland and Ireland, and Congregationalists from both England and New England. A separate Huguenot congregation as well as the Baptists and the Quakers each had houses of worship—meeetinghouses—in Charleston in the early eighteenth century.

Trade in deerskins with the Indians, the exportation of naval stores—wood products, staves, turpentine, and tar—and the raising of cattle and hogs for Barbados were among the ways the enterprising Carolinians first began to develop their economy. As in Virginia, some planted and experimented with a variety of seeds in an effort to find crops suitable to the low-lying land. There were those who succumbed to the eternal will-o'-the-wisp that mulberry trees might be the basis for a silk industry and make the new colony another Levant. Others planted grapes, and the proprietors hoped that indigo, cotton, ginger, and olives might also prove congenial to the climate and soil and provide income for them. Indigo and cotton were to become important crops later in the eighteenth and nineteenth centuries, but it was the development of rice culture that brought the first great economic boom to the lowland country of South Carolina at the beginning of the eighteenth century, and with it the burgeoning of a plantation society. The scholar Peter H. Wood has convincingly suggested that the development of rice culture might in fact owe a great deal to the Negro slaves from the west coast of

Thomas Coram. "Residence and Slave Quarters of Mulberry Plantation." c. 1800. Oil on paper. Built 1714 for Thomas Broughton. Carolina Art Association/Gibbes Art Gallery, Charleston.

Africa who brought with them knowledge and skill in growing that crop. Rice became important in the two decades after 1685, and it was in this period that the number of Africans brought to the colony increased so much as to equal and then surpass the number of whites. As early as 1619 a Dutch ship had brought twenty Negroes to Virginia, but the slave system did not take hold immediately there, probably because it was easier and cheaper for those who were gaining control of the land to use white indentured servants as laborers: they were treated virtually as chattel or short-term slaves. By 1650 there were still no more than 500 Negroes in Virginia, but as the number of available indentured whites declined or became too expensive, Virginians did turn to slaves as a source of labor, and during the first half of the eighteenth century the number of Negroes increased substantially. The planters who came to Carolina from Barbados were familiar with the slave system long in use there, and some brought slaves with them. Men and women of black skin were an integral part of the Carolina economy from the beginning.

A small oil painting, on the part title and previous page, done around 1800 by the English-born Thomas Coram, shows what was probably a typical early eighteenth-century complex of mansion house and "street" or row of small houses where servants and field hands lived. The plantation depicted, called Mulberry, still stands on the Cooper River. The mansion house was built around 1714 and is one of the earliest surviving Carolina country houses. It is a relatively low brick building with projecting rectangular appendages at all four corners, each of which is capped

with a double-canted bell-shaped roof topped with a finial. It was built for Thomas Broughton, who had come from England and was both planter and politician. As is so often the case, we do not know as much as we would like about the mental equipment and technical abilities brought to the wilderness world by successive newcomers, white and black. The central block, laid in English bond brickwork, is symmetrically ordered and in keeping with English building taste of the time. Some parallels in plan with certain English houses—Wollaton Hall, for example—can be identified. However, the source of the unusually shaped roofs and flared eaves of the four corner pavilions are a puzzle and seem to recall buildings in Holland and France. Protestant Huguenots and Dutch traders were among the national and racial mix of people who mingled on the streets of the growing town of Charleston, and one of them may have worked with Broughton in drafting the plan. The "street" houses for the slaves appear to have been neatly built one-room structures with sharply pitched hipped roofs. It is possible that their character owed something to African building traditions.

A sprig of mulberry within a horseshoe frame is carved on the pediment of Broughton's house. It is another wistful reminder of the hope that silk culture could be developed, and an example of the use of a plant as an emblem of the new land. In fact, rice seems to have been Broughton's most important crop.

"A Ground Plat of the City and Port of Annapolis." Manuscript copy made in 1748 of a manuscript plan of Annapolis, Maryland, drawn by James Stoddert in 1718. Maryland Hall of Records, Annapolis.

In 1695 the little community of Arundel Towne, located in the center of colonial Maryland where the Severn River enters Chesapeake Bay, was designated the capital, replacing straggling St. Mary's, and renamed Annapolis in honor of Queen Anne. Four years later the village of Middle Plantation in Virginia, where the new College of William and Mary had already been established, was chosen as the capital of Virginia, and renamed Williamsburg, honoring the former English sovereign. In both cases a more central—and healthier—site was selected for the growing colony, and in both cases a new plan for the town was drawn up. The one for Annapolis, left, involved an imaginative, if occasionally slightly awkward, combination of two central circles—a "public" circle and a "church" circle where the statehouse and church were to be—over a grid underlay, with an adjacent, residential "Bloomsbury Square." At Williamsburg the Capitol building was placed as the terminal of one of the major streets, the Governor's Palace as the terminal of another. Though the act for establishing Williamsburg was passed in 1699, the town developed slowly and not exactly according to the first plan. Surveying was not done until 1712.

Both of these plans for small communities with important strategically placed institutional, symbolic, and focal buildings show that the designer had assimilated many of the concepts of town and landscape planning then current in Europe. These would have included knowledge of the layouts of great palaces and country houses such as Versailles, as well as of the plans presented by Sir Christopher Wren and John Evelyn for rebuilding London after the Great Fire, and recent real estate developments in London, where residential squares were being laid out.

The two plans are among the most successful by far in colonial America. Williamsburg, designed as a community for only

2,000 or so, but to be "a commodious place, suitable for the reception of a considerable number and concourse of people," served the state as capital until 1779, while Annapolis remains the attractive seat of government for Maryland, and retains the basic configuration of its baroque town plan. In restored Colonial Williamsburg one can experience the town much as it was originally laid out, with several long vistas, the spaces between in a grid pattern. In Annapolis the Capitol building, the third on the site of the State or Public Circle, still dominates the community, and a church still stands on Church Circle. The man responsible for initiating these two pleasing and effective schemes was probably Sir Francis Nicholson. He served as a British colonial official first in New York and Virginia, then as governor in Maryland and subsequently Virginia. He was a talented and capable man whose Cambridge education and travels in Europe would have given him a gentleman's knowledge of architecture, landscape, and town planning, and he obviously had a genuine enthusiasm for these subjects. In each place he served he left behind solid accomplishments, some of which can still be seen, although some of his contemporaries described him as difficult, stubborn, strong-willed, and arrogant.

Robert Beverley was one who was not too fond of the mercurial governor. In his *History & Present State of Virginia*, written in 1705, he expressed skepticism about the new community Nicholson was creating. "There he flatter'd himself with the fond Imagination, of being the Founder of a new City. . . . There he procur'd a stately Fabrick to be erected, which he placed opposite to the College, and graced it with the magnificent Name of the *Capitol*." To Beverley it was audacious that a building designed for the conduct of affairs of state, virtually always called a statehouse at the time, should be identified with the ancient Roman Capitolium, the temple of Jupiter overlooking the Forum. It was the first use of the term in the English colonies, and was seldom if ever used elsewhere in America until after the Revolution. It presages the identification with classical forms and ideas that shaped the thinking of such later Virginians as Washington and Jefferson in their creation of a new Republic. That the Capitol or governmental and ceremonial center was the raison d'être of the new town was in no doubt, for the building was given precedence in the 1699 *Act directing the building the Capitoll and the City of Williamsburgh*. Thanks to the skillful reconstruction of the Capitol (the original burned in 1747) by the Colonial Williamsburg Foundation, we know what it must have looked like. It was focally placed at the end of the major street, Duke of Gloucester, with the already established College of William and Mary at the other end. Though he thought the name audacious, Beverley nonetheless conceded that the "two fine Publick Buildings are the most magnificent of any in *America*." About two generations later, in 1761, Edmund Burke recorded a similar judgment. Williamsburg was "yet but a small town. However, in this town are the best public buildings in British America." To his reporter's eye the college resembled Chelsea Hospital in London—as it does to others who believe the design for the building may have come from the office of Sir Christopher Wren. The reporter admired the church "in the form of a cross," and liked the placement of the Capitol "at the other end of the design of a noble street." (The Capitol his reporter saw would

Brush-Everard House on Palace Green, Williamsburg, Virginia, c. 1720.

have been the second one on the site.) Nicholson's vision was justified.

The public buildings, though placed and designed as focal points, did not and do not overwhelm by their size. As we see them in the Colonial Williamsburg restoration, the private and public buildings are unified in scale. (It should be remembered that eighty-one of the buildings seen in the restoration were not reconstructed; and that the latter task has been done only after the most meticulous research.) This unity is not a result of accident, but partly of law. The assembly set certain controls and restrictions on placement and height of houses on the Duke of Gloucester Street. All were to be six feet from the street line and were to "front a like." They were also to be not "less than tenn Foot Pitch." In 1705 these were modified slightly, but it was also decreed that all lots on that street were to be enclosed with "a Wall Pales or Post and Rails." There thus seems to have been enough regulation to ensure a unified scale and regularity, but not so much as to be restrictive or preclude variety.

There are in Williamsburg a number of examples of typical early eighteenth-century Virginia buildings. We may not know exactly what a "Virginia house" of the seventeenth century was, but the Brush-Everard house on the Palace Green, above, built around 1720, well represents one of several variable types of frame dwelling found in the colony in the eighteenth century. Though brick was used for some public edifices and large country houses, wood was commonly used for most buildings. The first owner, John Brush, was a blacksmith, gunsmith, and armorer. His house, as was typical of most frame houses, was not large. Most timber did not exceed a 20-foot span, so this length

Brafferton Hall, College of William and Mary, Williamsburg, Virginia, 1723.

became a sort of construction module or limit that probably influenced the proportions attainable. One can partially read the internal plan of the Brush-Everard house from the exterior. There is a central passage with staircase on the ground floor, and a room on either side. Two low bedrooms upstairs completed the original one-and-a-half-story house. Additions were apparently intended from the beginning, for the two chimneys were placed at what was originally the back, so they could eventually serve two more rooms. The back additions were made at different times, providing in the end four rooms on the ground floor, with another small chamber and storage space built onto the exterior. The builders followed the canons of taste and used the simple but well-defined classical molding shapes found in handbooks or remembered from their experience in England. Subtle finishing touches that are characteristic of early eighteenth-century building practices are the use of rake boards directly under the roof at the gable ends and of corner boards—the vertical boards nailed

on the exterior at the corners. Both give definition to the form, like a heavier line that defines major features in a drawing.

Builders of eighteenth-century houses in Tidewater Virginia adapted seventeenth-century building techniques, as well as plans and elevations, to changing needs and tastes. Plans varied somewhat, but fairly consistent elements on the ground floor included a hall or parlor—that is, a formal room for visitors—a passageway, the somewhat more private dining room, and the still more private chamber. In the case of farm or plantation houses, outbuildings served to separate the servants' living quarters from the main house, while others—kitchen, dairy, stables, barns—fulfilled specialized functions. The accumulated group suggested a small village. Detailing and many of the building techniques were similar to those known in England, but the consistent choice of structures of modest scale, often one-and-a-half-story, low-lying rectangular buildings, shaped a vernacular tradition. It is my impression also that in American towns the wider aspect of such colonial houses more often than not faced the front or street. Therefore the impression of the street vista of, say, colonial Williamsburg was rather different in appearance from a village in England of the same period when more gable ends faced front; this seems an American nuance. These modest-sized houses were built for and by many farmers, craftsmen, and some plantation owners. Mount Vernon started as such a vernacular structure. They are as typical, if not more so, as some of the grander mansions. Many have a balanced façade in front, with a door in the middle and double-hung sash windows with small panes, flanked by shutters, on the ground floor. The windows and doors were usually trimmed in moldings. The houses were raised slightly, and one went up three to five steps to enter. There may have been a small porch with balustrades, but this was not roofed. Some houses had cellars. Chimneys were of brick, some placed at the exterior ends, some in the interiors.

One of the surviving Williamsburg buildings that needed little restoration is the Brafferton, or Brafferton Hall, a 1723 brick

structure, left, built for the College of William and Mary to house the Indian school. One solution to the presence of the Indians was to convert and assimilate them. In retrospect we may be skeptical of the motives involved in such an effort, but on the part of some of the colonists there was a genuine belief that they would do the Indians a great good by "propagating the Christian religion among the infidels." Much earlier, in the 1620s, there had been a scheme for a college at Henrico that would have included Indians, a scheme never carried out because the Indians saw it as an encroachment on their territory and attacked the settlers. The monies for the Brafferton came from the will of no less a distinguished Englishman than the great philosopher, chemist, and inventor of the air pump, Robert Boyle. (His charities included the printing of the Scriptures in Irish, Welsh, Turkish, and Malayan.) The Brafferton was used as an Indian school until the Revolution, though the enrollment was never high.

The building is a well-proportioned two-story one of brick laid in Flemish bond with glazed headers; this variation in tone

Benjamin Henry Latrobe. "Green Spring Mansion." Drawn 1796. Watercolor on paper. Begun 1646–1652, remodeled several times. Maryland Historical Society, Baltimore.

Court cupboard, Tidewater Virginia, c. 1660–1680. Oak frame; yellow pine top and panels; walnut applied ornaments. Museum of Early Southern Decorative Arts, Winston-Salem, N.C.

pacious enough to serve as Berkeley's headquarters, and the Assembly met there. What we see in the picture is the house as it probably had been further extended and modified by members of the Ludwell family after Berkeley's death. The latest of these additions was probably made during the first half of the eighteenth century. The tall chimneys and the shape of the dormers as well as the hipped roof with cornice appear to be from that time, while the tall entrance way with round-arched roofline is probably a little older. When Latrobe saw Green Spring it was already partially in ruins, and is now gone. Archaeological excavations have helped to give an idea of some of the outlying structures. These included a pottery kiln, which was probably in operation as early as 1660–1680, and in which simple unglazed and undecorated red wares were made. During the time Berkeley lived in the original manor house he planted an orchard and a vineyard, made attempts at silk and rice culture, and grew hemp and tobacco.

Builders, carpenters, and masons were among the craftsmen who were able to practice their trades, at least part-time, in the seventeenth and early eighteenth centuries in the Chesapeake, tidewater, and lowland areas of Maryland, Virginia, and the Carolinas. This can be amply demonstrated by surviving buildings, though more of these, as we have seen, were built in the early eighteenth century than in the seventeenth; by then a fairly stable society had developed in these areas. In addition to farms and plantations, a network of small towns or trading centers had

between glazed and unglazed bricks enhances the wall by giving it textural variety, an effect favored in the late seventeenth and early eighteenth centuries. The general proportions and the steep angle of the hipped roof are similar to those of the Governor's Palace, although Brafferton Hall has less ornamentation and is simpler in mien. The water table, a string course, and the cornice give definition to the horizontals. The façade of five bays is symmetrical. There is a transom over the central doorway, and a brick modillioned pediment. It very possibly was built by Henry Cary, Jr., who took over the completion of the Governor's Palace from his father three years earlier, and who is known to have built the very similar William and Mary president's house as well as the college chapel. In the eighteenth century the Brafferton might have been characterized as "neat"—elegant, yet simple, free of unnecessary embellishments, well proportioned, with a sense of measure and decorum.

While many buildings were new-built to meet the needs of the expanding population, some evolved by accretion. Green Spring Mansion was of this genre; it was originally built by the durable Governor Berkeley and later lived in by his widow and subsequent generations of the Ludwell family into which she married after Berkeley's death. We can see it as it looked in 1796, previous page, when the young Englishman Benjamin Henry Latrobe saw it and painted a watercolor view. A fairly large house was there by around 1646–1652, but it burned. A new house was built adjacent to it around 1670 when Sir William remarried. During Bacon's Rebellion in 1676 the house was ca-

Clothespress, Tidewater Virginia, c. 1680. Walnut primary; yellow pine secondary. Museum of Early Southern Decorative Arts, Winston-Salem, N.C.

slowly evolved. These included Annapolis, Williamsburg, Norfolk, Edenton, New Bern, Yorktown, and Charleston, which were becoming small cultural centers and represented the first beginnings of urban life. Here a variety of tradesmen and some craftsmen could also gain a livelihood.

Relatively little work of joiners, turners, cabinetmakers, and metalworkers is known from the period before about 1675 in the colonial South. Probably not many men trained or skilled in these crafts could have sustained a livelihood by practicing full time in the marginal agricultural economy and difficult living conditions that prevailed. There is evidence to suggest that some individuals and families had only the most fundamental equipment for cooking and sleeping. Simple chests, boxes, and trunks served as furniture. Also, as judged by the standards of later centuries, the everyday physical surroundings found in the homes of many seventeenth-century men and women, whether rich or poor, whether in America or Europe, were in fact often lacking in comfort, though dress, fabrics, and individual objects were sometimes elaborate and extravagant.

Throughout the first hundred years or so of settlement, the officials and the more prosperous kept up close social and cultural ties with England and Europe, and imported some fine objects of craftsmanship. It is a truism to say that in both the North and the South, until well past the Revolution, men and women of taste and education saw themselves as part and parcel, inheritors and transmitters of English and European cultures, even as they forged new patterns of political, social, and economic life on new shores and were proud of, or daunted by, their ability, or inability, to cope in a frequently harsh environment. Those of humbler station basically shared the same concepts. And from the time Jean Ribaut first described the new lands as "the fairest, fruitfullest and pleasantest of all the world," the new country beckoned to men and women in all stations of life willing to venture or driven by desperation. Among this steady infusion of "newly arrived" were craftsmen who brought their special skills.

The solidly built cupboard, upper left, is a rare survival from the period 1660 to 1680. Such cupboards provided some storage space, here enclosed in the lower portion, with open surfaces for display in the upper area. The four posts that support the top, with their thick and decisively rounded turnings, and the split spindles and round bosses at the lower portions, are characteristic of the kind of heavy, vigorous ornament that was used in England under Charles II and James II. The frame is of oak, the applied ornament of walnut. The yellow pine of the tops and panels suggests that it comes from the South, as does the fact that it was found in Tidewater Virginia in the Yorktown area. We can guess that this piece, with its several types of decoration, was found in a home whose owner had status in the upper side of the colonial community. The simpler and more completely utilitarian pieces were probably worn out and discarded by their owners. As with many surviving pieces of furniture, there are few or no records. Craftsmen rarely signed their products, and it is only by adding up a variety of kinds of evidence that the origins of an article can be arrived at, although perhaps never with absolute certainty.

On a storage piece of different form, a press, lower left, prob-

Blanket chest, Tidewater Virginia, probably late seventeenth century. Yellow pine with maple feet. Descended in Rowell family of Surry County. Private collection.

ably used for storing clothing and linens, split spindles are again used as applied decoration. Three successive molded lozenges decorate the panel which, unevenly, divides the two sections of the interior—shelves are located on the narrow side, while pegs for hanging things are found on the other. The piece is fashioned of walnut, with yellow pine in the obscure or "secondary" areas. The use of walnut, the fine grain of which lends itself to fine carving, was only just becoming common in England in the Jacobean period, and the choice here reminds us that the wood was more readily available to joiners working in America.

The much simpler chest of yellow pine, above, also believed to have been made in Virginia, was perhaps more typical of those to be found in humbler dwellings. The bun feet are characteristic of the rounded forms, turned on lathes, which were favored shapes at this time.

Gateleg tables, complex structures whose side leaves could be raised or dropped upon need, were popular from the last quarter of the seventeenth century. The Virginia example, following page, is primarily of walnut, with an oak center support. For good reason, those who cherish furniture of this period delight in seeing the robustness of the turnings, the flow of pressure from in to out, the liveliness of the profile created thereby. All this is quite unnecessary from a structural point of view. We do not know how the seventeenth-century cabinetmaker or joiner or his customer spoke of these qualities—no doubt with less self-conscious esthetic language than that of some twentieth-century connoisseurs—but they must have enjoyed the forms or they would not have lavished the time and care required to create them.

A table of a similar genre, but with more restrained vase-shaped turnings, following page, is believed to have been made in the Charleston area. It descended in the Manigault family of Silk Hope plantation, and is of cypress, one of those woods which Hariot thought could be used for joinery and that as "fraite with other principal commodities will yeeld profite." Cypress subsequently became an important building material throughout the low-lying Deep South and was used as a secondary wood in furniture until the supply began to give out in the twentieth century.

Gateleg table, possibly Virginia, probably late seventeenth century. Walnut; oak in center drawer support. Private collection.

A smaller table, with stretchers connecting the legs, upper right, is also of cypress and from the Charleston area. The turnings here are elongated vase shapes, with ringed moldings at the base, neck, and top. Some fragments of red paint suggest that this piece may have once lent a colorful note to a room at Limerick plantation, whence it probably came. The use of connecting stretchers and the more restrained form places it around 1700–1720, and it represents a simple version of a type that became popular during the reign of William and Mary.

Chairs were not common pieces of furniture in either Europe or America in the early seventeenth century. Benches and

Gateleg table, Charleston, traditionally believed to have come from the Manigault family of Silk Hope Plantation, c. 1700. Cypress with red cedar gate frame. Charleston Museum.

stools—or tops of chests—frequently sufficed for seating purposes. Since so few examples from this period survive, it is difficult to say if any given example is typical. In one extant armchair of the period, far right, the back consists of two rows of turned spindles joined to the turned cross-pieces. The supporting front and back posts are ringed with light turnings. The arm supports extend out over the front posts. Though there is no known reason, this handling appears on a number of Southern armchairs while a counterpart example in New England would have the arm support fitted or mortised into the front post, with this post then ending in a turned knob. This chair is of cherry, an unusual wood for this time. It may have originated in the Carolinas.

In another armchair, lower right, of the same type and from the same region, the craftsman used maple and white oak. The turning on the spindles is much simpler, but the turnings and terminals on the supporting posts are by contrast more shapely and far more interesting.

The inventories of estates, which were often done with meticulous care during the period, give evidence of a wider variety of furniture than is shown here or than is to be found among the still small amount of known seventeenth-century pieces believed to have been crafted in the South. A "table and forme," "18 leather chairs," a "couch (trussell)," a top supported by a frame, a "trundle bed," and "old cradle," a looking glass, and several old chests and trunks are found in the 1690 estate inventory of one Mr. Robert Ruffin of Lawnes Creeke of Surry County, Virginia. However, as one follows the assessors around in one's mind's eye, it is the bolsters, pillows, bedstead curtains, and valances that seem to have dominated three of the four living chambers and a shed in Ruffin's home, and which in fact were most valued. For example, the table and form and the eighteen leather chairs in the hall, or major living room, were valued as equivalent to 700 pounds of tobacco, while one feather bed, bolster, two pillows with bedstead curtains and valance, a bed rug or cover, and a blanket were exactly double in value. Four heifers were less in value than the bed and its equipment, being worth only 1,200 pounds of tobacco. The high valuation on these accessories was because fabrics were rare and expensive; they served a utilitarian function but were probably colorful and decorative as well. In a 1693 estate inventory of a shopkeeper in Norfolk County, Virginia, one can compare the value of three pounds of woolen fringe for valances, given as eleven shillings, to the ten-shilling value of "one cane with silver head & a gold ring" to get an idea of the importance and value put upon fabric used as ornament.

The earliest of the Virginia settlers were content to use Indian mats rather than Arras tapestries for decorating their primitive shelters. One or two generations later some of the inhabitants of Virginia, Maryland, and the Carolinas could afford and had the occasion to commission portraits to embellish their walls. Some officials and some planters and merchants in the latter part of the seventeenth century may have brought paintings with them or had portraits made when they visited England or Europe, as a few surviving pieces of art attest. It is not until the early years of the eighteenth century that we can definitely identify the work

Byrd II of Westover, helped with Byrd's gardens, and learned what he could from that amateur but knowledgeable naturalist. He traveled into the country, into the lower piedmont, and followed the James River to its sources in the Appalachians. Though during this period Catesby did not contemplate publication, his work so impressed his scientifically minded colleagues that after he returned to England members of the Royal Society pledged funds so that he could go back to America. Among these was the intellectually alert Sir Francis Nicholson, then first royal governor to South Carolina, after his earlier tenures in Maryland and Virginia. Catesby returned, going first to Charleston in February 1722. This time he collected specimens and seeds as before but also used paints and paper to record what he saw. In 1724 he was again in the mountainous Cherokee country, and he spent time at Fort Moore on the Savannah River opposite present Augusta. He subsequently traveled to Bermuda and returned to London in 1726.

While in America on his second sojourn, Catesby apparently made watercolor studies in the field. Of his problems and skills as a painter he was to write, in the introduction to his book, *The Natural History of Carolina, Florida and the Bahama Islands:* "As I was not bred a Painter I hope some faults in Perspective, and other niceties, may be more readily excused: for I humbly con-

Mark Catesby. "Summer Redbird." c. 1724. Watercolor on paper. Royal Library, Windsor Castle, England.

Catesby's work is generally known through the lively engravings in his book, which he himself etched under the tutelage of a French-born watercolorist, Joseph Goupy. However, the original watercolors are in three bound volumes at the Royal Library at Windsor, and it is only within the last decade or so that they have been identified by specialists and their significance appreciated. They are believed to be Catesby's own, though Goupy may have had a share in their execution. Catesby wrote that he always drew his plants while "fresh and just gathered" and the birds "while alive." A sense of vitality radiates from the beautifully rendered watercolor of the summer redbird, left. The colors and contours of the bright redbird, lifting its head as if to burst into song, and the shaded green leaves are strong and well defined. Catesby was a pioneer in introducing habitat settings in natural history illustrations. Though the bird is shown in profile and the leaves mostly frontally—that is, in the flat—Catesby had enough knowledge of shading, if not of perspective, to create an illusion of layered space if not of great depth. Fresh as this composition is, one would nevertheless guess that it is not one of his sketches, made directly from the live bird and plants, but is what artists of this period would have called a finished watercolor, based upon the preliminary sketches.

The pattern and color of the trumpet vine which attracts the tiny hummingbird dominate the composition at far right. The leaves, flowers, and the bird are each essentially flat, but the whole is full of life. The making of the engravings and the publication of his fieldwork extended over a twenty-year period, the labor of a lifetime. Catesby's was the first attempt to delineate the natural history of the Carolinas and Florida since John White's tentative beginnings more than a century earlier. He knew of his predecessor's work, for he included in his publication seven plates and part of an eighth that were copied from plates based on White's Roanoke drawings. Catesby's work, in which birds predominate, formed the basis for Southern ornithological studies, and his method of depicting birds and other creatures in a natural setting influenced natural history illustration in both Europe and America.

By the 1730s, the Charleston that Catesby knew was flourishing as a community; it was a port, the commercial, legal, social, and cultural center for the surrounding country. It was to be the most important town, and only genuine urban center, in the South for the next decades. In 1731 Jean Pierre Purry, who was writing about South Carolina in order to attract fellow Swiss Protestants, said, "The people of *Carolina*, except those who give themselves up to Debauchery, are all rich, either in Slaves, Furniture, Cloaths, Plate, Jewels, or other Merchandizes, but especially in Cattle." The good Swiss would have been as attracted to the prospect of owning cattle as of owning fine plate, and indeed a Swiss settlement, Purrysburgh, was established the following year in South Carolina on the northern shore of the Savannah River. Some of the plate and furniture and jewels the prospering citizens owned was imported from England and Europe. At the same time a growing artisan class was beginning to supply the desires for luxury products. Probably the two earliest silversmiths to practice in Carolina were the Huguenots Solomon Legare and Nicholas De Longuemare, Jr. Both seem to have left France as a result of the Revocation of the Edict of Nantes.

ceive that Plants and other Things done in a Flat, tho' exact manner, may serve the Purpose of Natural History, better in some Measure, than in a bold and Painter-like way."

Catesby was very conscious that he chose to do his paintings "in a Flat . . . manner" for reasons of accuracy. His rationale, however, is one that may well have prevailed with other and later artists who, somewhat unsure of their talents, also seem to have recognized that they could get more "exact" renderings by working in a flat manner and not trying for the subtle shading needed to create the illusion of roundness and depth. This rationale would appear to underlie the style of painters who are variously identified as naïve, folk, or self-trained or partially trained artists.

Legare was in Charleston by 1696, De Longuemare by 1699. Legare lived to a ripe old age, dying in 1740, De Longuemare in 1711. In 1700 Legare was among petitioners who asked the Lords Commissioners for Trade and Plantations to be permitted to send an expedition to explore for the silver mines they still believed were to be found in the mountainous areas of the province: the silver and gold that De Soto and others had failed to discover. A rare early account book of De Longuemare survives. It reveals that he shaped a variety of silver forms, some of which he also engraved, and that his business also included much mending of clocks and watches.

Among the earliest surviving pieces of silver made in Charleston is a flat-topped silver tankard, below. It bears the mark of Luke or Lucas Stoutenburgh, a man of Dutch ancestry who was born in New York and by 1718 was living in Charleston. The tankard, with corkscrew thumbpiece and scroll handle, reveals his skill and would have served as an ample sign of the wealth and well-being of its original owner. In style it is parallel in form and decoration to work done in England and New York of the same period. Work of this quality is a good indication that the British colonies were prospering.

While the British established themselves firmly in scattered settlements along the Atlantic coast from the Carolinas to Maine, the French gained a foothold in the West Indies, with small colonies at Santo Domingo and elsewhere, and made settlements at Quebec, Montreal, and along the St. Lawrence in the north. From the latter they gradually pushed westward, the fur traders following the river and lake systems, learning the terrain from the Indians, the Jesuits often following with missions, and collecting and recording knowledge of the geography of the land. As if to draw a vast circle around the territories claimed by the Brit-

Mark Catesby. "Hummingbird." c. 1724. Watercolor on paper. Royal Library, Windsor Castle, England.

Luke (Lucas) Stoutenburgh. Silver tankard, Charleston, c. 1720–1730. Marked: "LSB" in trefoil, at lip, each side of handle. Mabel Brady Garvan Collection, Yale University Art Gallery, New Haven, Connecticut.

ish, the French began to search for the great river that flowed to the south which the Indians called Mesippi. Louis Joliet, fur trader and explorer, and Jacques Marquette, a Jesuit, and a group of *voyageurs* journeyed in 1673 from the mission station in Mackinac, across the Fox-Wisconsin portage, to the upper reaches of the Mississippi. They continued down the river, past the point where the Missouri poured in, and probably got as far south as the Arkansas. No gold and no route to the Pacific were found, but they surmised that the river emptied into the Gulf of Mexico, and they recognized the agricultural potential of the fertile lands. No immediate effort was made to follow up their discoveries until 1681–1682 when the far more ambitious René

35

Jean Baptiste Michel Le Bouteux. "The Camp at New Biloxi, Dec. 1720." Pen and wash drawing on paper. Inscribed in French: "View of the Camp of the Concession of Monseigneur Law at New Biloxi, coast of Louisiana, by Jean Baptiste Michel Le Bouteux, 10 December, 1720." Newberry Library, Chicago, Illinois.

Robert Cavalier Sieur de La Salle set out to find the mouth of the river as part of a grand scheme to develop a series of forts and commercial trading posts along the inland waterways. If achieved, this would serve to hem in the English to the east and the Spanish to the south. Though he hoped to go down the Mississippi with a flotilla of armed vessels, in the end he carried out the first part of his plan by traveling by canoe with a company of Frenchmen and Indians. They did in fact reach the Gulf, having passed through the lands of the Choctaw and Natchez along the southern reaches of the river. On April 9, 1682, with a show of ceremony, the singing of hymns, a volley of muskets, La Salle erected a cross and a column with the arms of France, and "took possession of that river, of all rivers that enter it and of all the country watered by them." It was a ceremony very like that in which Jean Ribaut had claimed the Florida territory for France more than a century earlier. The country was named Louisiana, honoring their king, Louis XIV.

In 1684 the French government sponsored La Salle, then in France, to attempt a settlement near the mouth of the Mississippi. He sailed too far west and thus failed to find the mouth of the great river; the expedition was rendered a complete failure when he was assassinated by one of his own men in 1687. An indirect effect of La Salle's presence in the Gulf was to spur the

Spanish to greater vigilance, and in 1698 they established a small fort at Pensacola. (It was captured by the French in 1719 and restored to the Spanish in 1723.)

It was not until 1698 that the French, who had been preoccupied with affairs in Europe, essayed another attempt at settlement in the South, this time under Pierre le Moyne de Iberville, a French-Canadian soldier-sailor. They found the Spanish already established at Pensacola, so went on to Mobile Bay, arriving on January 31, 1699. During the next months they located the mouth of the Mississippi, and went upriver at least as far as the tall red stick (present Baton Rouge) that the Indians used to demarcate the hunting grounds between the Houmas and Bayagoulas. They then established a fort, Maurepas, near present Ocean Springs, Mississippi. Iberville left the small garrison of seventy-six men in May under the command of his brother, Jean-Baptiste le Moyne de Bienville, and returned in January of the next year and built another small fort. In 1701 the tiny settlement was moved to Mobile Bay and Fort Louis established there. The little colony struggled on during these first years. Iberville died in 1706. After a flood in 1710 Bienville, who was now governor, moved the settlement to the mouth of Mobile River and a plan for a town was drawn up. By 1714 the French had also established a fort in what is now western Louisiana, near

Natchitoches, to protect their claims against the Spanish. Fort Rosalie was established in 1716 farther north, on the bluffs of the Mississippi, the site of present-day Natchez. Wealthy Antoine Crozat was granted trading rights to the new territory in 1712, and hoped that mining and trade with the Spaniards would yield an income, but these efforts were largely illusory. A new and grandiose scheme was launched under John Law, a Scottish financial speculator whose persuasive powers were such that his Company of the West was granted a twenty-five-year monopoly on trade in Louisiana, and thousands of investors gave him funds. Part of the plan was to establish a city on the Mississippi, and the site selected, that of present New Orleans, was the Indian portage between the river and Lake Pontchartrain. Bienville brought a small force from Canada to clear the land in 1718. By 1720 Law's shaky financial scheme fell apart and the "Mississippi Bubble" burst. Bienville seems to have taken matters in hand, persuading some of the settlers, including a disenchanted group of Germans who had been landed upriver in Arkansas, to stay. Thus by 1720 there were a thousand or so settlers in the Louisiana territory and tiny settlements at Mobile, Biloxi, and New Orleans.

A rare watercolor, left, shows the camp of Law's concession near Biloxi. A busy and orderly place is depicted, with one large warehouse and a series of tents and temporary structures, such as the triangular huts covered with palmetto in the foreground. The warehouse, with its very French-looking steeply pitched hipped roof, appears to be of timber-frame construction, filled in by vertical wooden planks. The sills are laid directly on the ground. Unfortunately, little or nothing is known concerning the artist, Jean Baptiste Michel Le Bouteux. He was obviously more than a well-trained draftsman, for he handles perspective and tone with skill.

In 1721, the engineer Adrien de Pauger arrived at New Orleans and helped to survey the lands and lay out the new town or trading post. He took as a model a plan developed—but never used—by the military engineer La Blond de la Tour, for a fortified town near Biloxi. The finished plan provided by De Pauger was a grid scheme with a central square facing the water; the square was to be dominated by a church. This plan remains the core of the present city of New Orleans and is the most substantial legacy of the fragile early settlement. The square continues to be one of the most attractive urban spaces in America.

A detail from another rare watercolor, below, by Jean Pierre Lassus, done in 1726, shows the central portion of the new settlement, with the church in the foreground and a scattering of small houses. The cypress swamps that surrounded the clearing loom up in the background. Lassus and his younger brother had come as surveyors for the colony, and he gives a general picture of how the little village probably looked.

The first parish church of St. Louis was also designed by De Pauger. It had brick foundations, made at a newly established brickyard, a timber frame with brick fill, and walls that were

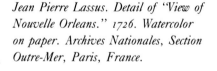

Jean Pierre Lassus. Detail of "View of Nouvelle Orleans." 1726. Watercolor on paper. Archives Nationales, Section Outre-Mer, Paris, France.

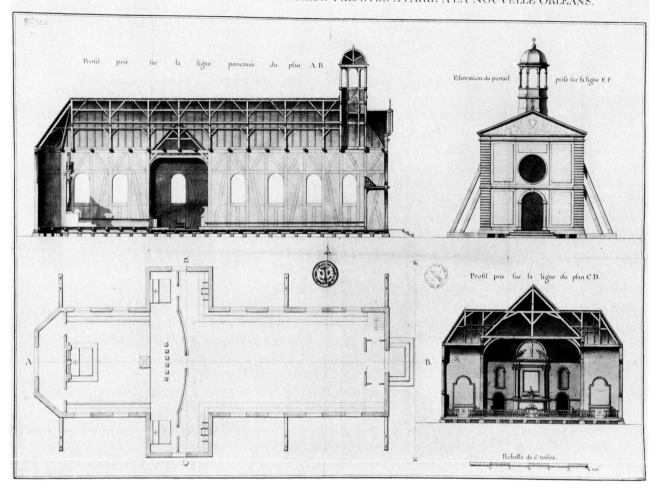

Profil pris sur la ligne ponctuée du plan A.B.

Elevation du portail. prise sur la ligne E.F.

Profil pris sur la ligne du plan C.D.

Echelle de 6 toises.

Adrien de Pauger. "Plan, sections, and elevation of the church proposed to be built at New Orleans." Ink and watercolor. Signed: "de Pauger." Dated: "May 29, 1724." Archives Nationales, Section Outre-Mer, Paris, France.

covered with chamfered planks. By 1763 it was in such disrepair that it was abandoned for a while, then repaired, but finally destroyed in the great fire of 1788. De Pauger's elevations and plans for this cruciform structure, above, survive in the French National Archives. Once the frame was filled with brick, the timber buttresses, which De Pauger originally thought necessary to help the building withstand hurricanes (a disastrous one had struck in 1722), were not considered necessary and never placed. De Pauger died before the building was finished and asked to be buried within it, as he was. The present St. Louis Cathedral stands on this site.

The first small houses had timber frames with sills laid directly on the ground, were usually covered with wide boards, and often were roofed with strips of bark; as in the other colonies, these early structures were short-lived. Within a few years several other somewhat more substantial structures were built. One of these was the first Ursuline Convent, put up from 1727 to 1734. It was of exposed timber frame with brick fill (the brick between posts, *briqueté entre poteaux*, characteristically found in French specifications), which did not last in the humid climate. It had to be replaced by 1745. However inept or negligent the French were in developing their scattered colonies and forts spread out along the Gulf and the lower Mississippi, they kept

remarkable records, and carefully finished architectural drawings showing plans and elevations for a number of buildings erected between 1699 and 1749 still survive. Except for the second Ursuline Convent building, none of the actual buildings survive.

In 1729 Indians destroyed Fort Rosalie at Natchez, and in the years between 1729 and 1740 the French were engaged in a series of wars with Indians. These were not continuous, and Indians in a peaceful state were drawn by Alexandre De Batz, yet another of the French military architect-engineers who served in the New World. A group of six pen-and-ink drawings show glimpses of the Indians of the lower Mississippi Valley. In one of these, right, De Batz showed an Acolapissa temple and a chief's cabin. At the top of the temple were three reedwork pyramids from which protruded canes sharpened to points, and atop these were three colored and sculptured figures, the tail of which resembled that of a turkey, the head that of an eagle. This must have been a fairly impressive structure, to judge by the small scale of the Indian figures alongside. It served as the sepulcher for the chiefs of the nation. He then describes the cabin as built of posts in the ground, plastered with clay or earth mortar and covered with mats. According to De Batz, all of the cabins of the savages were of similar construction and round. (The technique of using a mixture of mud and moss as a kind of earth mortar was apparently adapted by the French, who used such a mixture, *bousillage*, as fill instead of bricks in many of their buildings; a practice that continued in Louisiana well into the nineteenth century.) The artist noted that the picture was "Surveyed and sketched at the Village of the Acolapissa the fifteenth of April of the present year. Redrawn at New Orleans the twenty-second of June 1732," thus spelling out the procedure probably also used by Jacques Le Moyne, John White, and Mark Catesby. De Batz might have known of the published works of Le Moyne and White, and perhaps he hoped that he, a member of a later generation of soldier-explorers, could produce a new series. However, he seems to have completed only a few drawings, which had less complete information and none of the freshness that characterized the earlier men's work.

Despite their careful plans and layouts of forts, towns, and buildings, the French attracted only a small number of settlers to their far-flung settlements or trading posts. Their most important Southern plantation at New Orleans grew only very slowly in the first decades after its establishment.

Georgia was the last of the English colonies in the present American South to be established. After South Carolina became a Crown colony in 1729, George II in 1732 granted the southern portion, of which the borders with Spain were ill-defined, to the Trustees for Establishing the Colony of Georgia in America. The early French and English settlements, or attempts at settlements, had been based on a complex web of dream and reality. They hoped to find gold, or pearls, or land that would support the mulberry and the olive. They made plans to plunder the ships or otherwise gain access to the riches the Spanish had truly found in Peru and Central America. Their efforts were related to military and political strategies, and the desire to solve population problems, be they asylum for Huguenots or more land for the English at Barbados. The mind of the remarkable man, James Edward Oglethorpe, who led the first settlers to Georgia, was filled with some of these same visions and realistic concerns. He, too, hoped that silk culture could be developed—initially the Georgia Trustees specified that each settler plant a certain number of mulberry trees per acre—and he recognized the importance of establishing a colony to the south of the Carolinas as a buffer against the Spanish in Florida and the French on the Gulf and the Mississippi. By this time the British had much experience with colonies in America, and Oglethorpe had studied some of the results with passionate interest. His, and that of his fellow Trustees, was a broad vision; they hoped that Georgia would not only be commercially successful and militarily useful, but that through it some of the social evils in England could be ameliorated. This new colony was to be for "unfortunate People in the Kingdom of reputable Families, and of liberal, or at least easy Education," people who had been "undone" by various misfortunes. It was to be a society of yeomen freeholders, each of whom would have his own plot of land. Thus by their own labor each would not only be able to sustain himself but would "at the same Time enrich their Mother Country."

Oglethorpe himself accompanied the first group of 114 people to the new colony. They arrived first at Charleston, then Oglethorpe lodged the settlers in barracks at Beaufort while he and a smaller party selected a site on the Savannah River several miles inland. He was delighted with his choice, and in February 1732 wrote of it: "The river here forms a half-moon, along the south side of which the banks are about forty foot high, and on the top flat, which they call a bluff. The plain high ground extends into the country five or six miles, and along the river side about a mile. Ships that draw twelve foot water can ride within ten yards of the bank. Upon the river-side in the centre of this plain I have laid out the town."

Thus almost casually did Oglethorpe refer to the first unit of a town plan that is rightly considered one of the most agreeable in the United States, a plan about which much has been written and conjectured. In the same letter he goes on to say: "The whole people arrived here on the first of February. At night their tents were got up. Till the seventh we were taken up in unloading, and making a crane, which I then could not get finished, so took off the hands, and set some to fortification, and began to fell the woods. I marked out the town and common, half of the

Alexandre De Batz. "Temple and Cabin of the Chief, Acolapissa." 1732. Colored pen and ink on paper. Peabody Museum of Archaeology and Ethnology, Cambridge, Massachusetts.

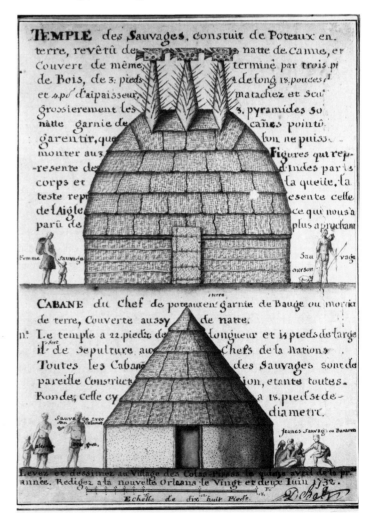

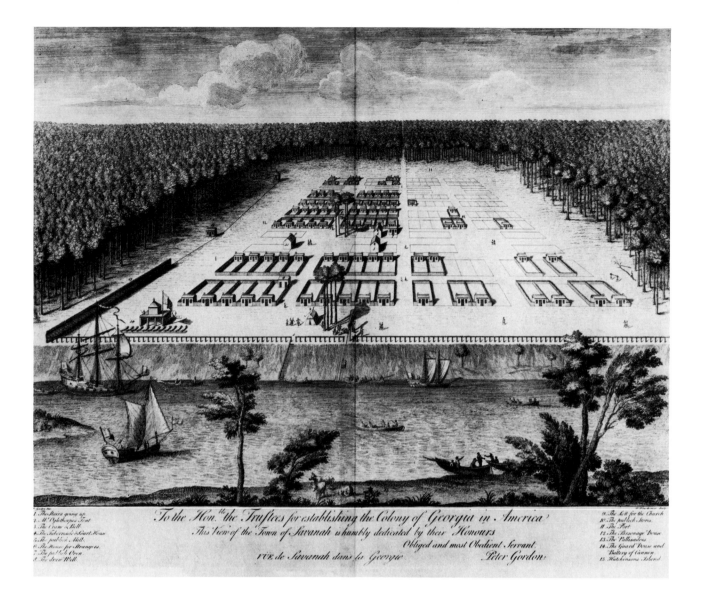

To the Hon.ble the Truftees for establiſhing the Colony of Georgia in America

This View of the Town of Savanah is humbly dedicated by their Honours

Obliged and moſt Obedient Servant,

VUE de Savannah dans la Georgie Peter Gordon

Peter Gordon. "View of Savannah, March 29, 1734." Engraving. University of Georgia Libraries, Athens.

former is already cleared, and the first house was begun yesterday in the afternoon."

An engraving after a drawing by Peter Gordon, above, shows the layout of the town as it appeared in 1734. The bluff that served, and still serves, to separate the river life of the port from the town is in the foreground. This same bluff was militarily useful since from it could easily be spotted all who approached from the river side. The artist indicated the steps Oglethorpe's men cut into the bluff for the first settlers to climb up as well as the crane they erected. On the left is the beginning of a palisade and guardhouse, and near the center the tent in which Oglethorpe chose to stay while houses were being erected can be seen.

The first unit of the town plan consisted of four blocks parallel to the river, separated by three major streets. The town extended back for six shorter blocks. In the second and fifth of these, open squares for use as parks, markets, and parade grounds were laid out on the axes of the first and third cross streets. Thus in the original plan four squares, or four neighborhood units or wards, were provided for. The genius of the plan is that it provides for a pattern of successive neighborhood units, each around a square. By great good luck subsequent surveyors

and builders in the city recognized this and continued it, as can be seen in the plan, far right, as it had been extended by 1749. By this date Oglethorpe's good friend, the Indian chief Tomochichi, had been buried in the central square. The idea of units of blocks, with squares in the center, was kept up until the middle of the nineteenth century, so that in the central part of present-day Savannah one still moves through an attractive succession of tree-lined streets and quiet, green squares.

Visitors often find that the squares remind them of those in English cities, especially London. The comparison is not far-fetched; it is highly probable that they were derived from these. In London the pleasant and profitable idea of urban real estate developments, with a core of one or more residential squares surrounded by buildings of uniform scale, sometimes with a church or other public building as a central accent, had evolved in the seventeenth century. By the time Oglethorpe and/or his colleagues drew up their plans this was a familiar concept. These urban schemes were usually carved out of the family estates or landholdings that surrounded the City and Westminster and were often skillfully fitted into odd-shaped pieces of land; in Savannah there was an open and uncluttered expanse of land so that the scheme could grow in linear sequences. By the 1730s long-established London squares included Bloomsbury and St. James's. (In the Annapolis plan one of the squares was even named Bloomsbury.) Newer ones were Soho and Red Lion. In Oglethorpe's own time Hanover Square and the complex of streets around Grosvenor Square were being built.

Oglethorpe's writings and those of the Trustees indicate that he and they had thought about the nature and experiences of colonies, including those of the Romans, the Dutch, the English in Ireland and in America, before drawing up plans for the new settlement. A treatise by William Penn was included in a series of tracts probably published by the Trustees as part of their propaganda for the Georgia colony, and special mention is made of the way Philadelphia had been laid out, with "proper Spaces" for markets and public buildings. Thus the Philadelphia grid plan with regularly spaced squares was familiar to them, as were the plans laid out by the British for Londonderry in Ireland. Still another plan that Oglethorpe and the Trustees knew of and were probably influenced by was Sir Robert Montgomery's remarkably elaborate scheme for the Margravate of Azilia, a 1717 proposal for a separate province to be established between the Savannah and Altamaha rivers, a scheme that never came to fruition but which included an urban center plus open parks, and a series of square acreages for individual farms. (The Savannah plan, in addition to the town where the houses were to be built, included outlying plots for individual gardens and still others for larger farm plots.) It seems fair to conclude, as has the scholar John Reps, that it was Oglethorpe and his colleagues who conceived the particular pattern of Savannah. Oglethorpe at the time of his leadership of the Georgia colony was a vigorous man in his middle thirties with European military experience on the Danube and elsewhere, service in Parliament, and a man whose friends included the scholarly but indigent ("undone") Robert Castell, who wrote a treatise on architecture called *Villas of the Ancients.* It is reasonable to suppose that the plan may have been designed by him in consultation with the other Trustees; thus in Oglethorpe's letter to them discussing the plan, he did not feel compelled to elaborate upon it in any detail.

The small houses shown in Peter Gordon's engraving are probably those belonging to the common freeholders that Francis Moore saw in 1735 and described as made of "a Frame of sawed Timber, 24 by 16 Foot, floored with rough Deals, the Sides with feather-edged Boards unplained, and the Roof shingled." These tiny structures may have been similar to the simplest of the early Virginia houses. Moore reported that dwellings of the first forty freeholders were all alike, but even by 1735 there were other houses, "100 or 150, many of these much larger, some of 2 or 3 Stories high, the Boards plained and painted." In yet another report, written by the young German aristocrat Baron von Reck, who accompanied a party of settlers from Salzburg in 1734, we learn that "all of the houses here are built of wood, for building stones are not to be found in Georgia and there has not been time to make bricks. Because of the great hurricanes that blow with great force the houses are built no higher than one story and an attic." Here, too, there is a parallel with the houses that were being built by farmers and planters in Virginia, which also had one and a half stories.

Oglethorpe, when in Savannah, occupied one of the small freeholders' structures, but ten years later it was described as "a ruinous Heap." The fragility of the early houses, plus the effects of several devastating fires, was such that the old section of Savannah as we know it today is largely made up of nineteenth-century buildings (just as are some of the London squares that were laid out much earlier), but it is the felicitous plan, the underlying skeletal structure of the city, that contributes so much to its special character—an urban place of human scale punctuated by green and open spaces.

Recently a group of watercolor drawings, based on a visit to Georgia in 1736, has been found among the possessions of the Royal Library in Copenhagen. There is no record of how they came to the library, but they were probably given, around 1790–1791, by the then elderly German aristocrat Philip Georg Friedrich von Reck, who lived the last decades of his life in a Danish provincial town.

"Savannah in 1757," as printed in William de Brahm, HISTORY OF THE PROVINCE OF GEORGIA, 1849. *University of Georgia Libraries, Athens.*

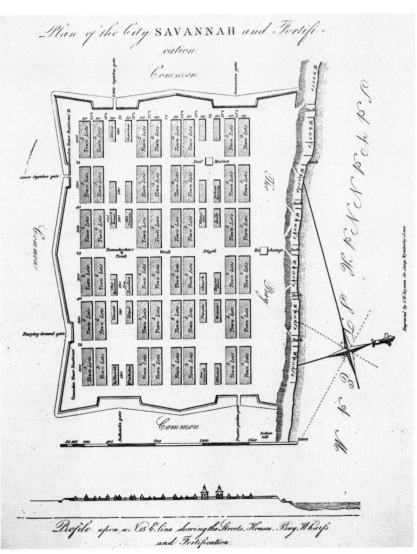

Philip Georg Friedrich von Reck. "Indian Festival." 1736.
Watercolor on paper. Royal Library, Copenhagen, Denmark.

Protestants who had been summarily expelled from Salzburg in 1732 by a zealous archbishop attracted the sympathy of the Georgia Trustees, several of whom were members of the Society for Promoting Christian Knowledge. They arranged to transport some of these refugees to their new colony, and in 1734 a small group sailed for Savannah. Oglethorpe helped to establish them in a community slightly further inland, which they named Ebenezer—Rock of Help. They were accompanied by the bright but temperamental young von Reck, who, having seen them safely established, returned in August of the same year to London and to Europe. A second group went out in the fall, reaching Georgia in December.

Von Reck was eager to return. Writing to the secretary for the Society for Promoting Christian Knowledge, he said he wanted to transport "Good Laborius and Industrious Men," and wanted to forward husbandry, vineyards, and trade. In order to effect

this he would make an exact description of the country, and on his return they could "Expect from me an ocular proof." This suggests that he had in mind the express idea of making visual records.

He was granted his wish and in late 1735 he accompanied the "third transport" of Salzburgers and others whom he had recruited. They arrived in February 1736 to find the infant community of Ebenezer in disarray. Seeds had spoiled, the soil was barren, the water unhealthy. They had suffered through a hot summer with inadequate supplies and a cold winter in shelters without fireplaces. After some misunderstandings and after persuading Oglethorpe of the necessity—though it meant violating a treaty he had made with the Indians—it was agreed to move the settlement to a new site. This was named New Ebenezer, lest it be thought the project had completely failed.

Von Reck was too impetuous to be an effective administrator.

Moreover, there were already on hand, from the first and second transports, a minister and a keeper of stores who were in contention with each other. By July the hot-tempered young man decided to leave, in August he was racked with fever, and finally in October he left the shores of America, weak and defeated. A short report he wrote was printed, rather obscurely, in Augsburg in 1740. During this period he also apparently succeeded in making some of the "ocular proof" he had promised. Although the watercolors are not signed and were not published with the 1740 report, there is every reason to believe Von Reck is the artist.

The fifty or so watercolor and pencil sketches show a few scenes of the settlers as they were building their first shelters at New Ebenezer, several depictions of members of the nearby Yuchi Indians, and flora and fauna of the region. They are of uneven quality. Several, such as his rendering of a squash, below, are painted with broad, free-flowing, soft-edged strokes; the transition from green to orange tones on the squash is skillfully rendered. Another of the drawings, on the left, shows an Indian festival and one of their shelters. Hanging from the rafters are what appear to be European guns, an indication of the trade between the two peoples.

The drawings are an invaluable record. They especially shed new light on the life and language of the Yuchi and the Creeks. While working on the sketches, the artist must have become familiar with the Indians' languages, since many are not only captioned in German, French, and English but also in Yuchi and Creek. Some of the plants depicted were not formally described by botanists until the nineteenth century, so these drawings now provide earlier references. There are plants illustrated which do not normally grow in Georgia, such as the pineapple and the ginger tree; these would appear to represent specimens grown in the Trustees' experimental garden at Savannah. Most have small figure number notations, indicating that the artist probably intended them to be used in a publication.

Though the Georgian settlements started out with high hopes and with logical (perhaps too logical) and carefully thought-out plans, they, too, had a precarious existence in the early years. In an effort to avoid what he saw as evils and problems in the other colonies, Oglethorpe and the Trustees in 1734 passed measures prohibiting slavery and the sale of rum, and set up a licensing system to facilitate peaceful trade with the Indians. The prohibition against slavery seems to have been motivated by at least the seeds of moral revulsion against the institution as well as by the desire to limit the size of the slave population, which had just become a majority in Carolina, and by the fear that slaves escaping into Spanish territory would participate in wars or uprisings against the English. (In 1738, in fact, the Spanish announced that all slaves fleeing the English colonies would be granted land and protection in Florida.) Though some of the settlers were well pleased with this prohibition, more found it hard to compete with the slave economy immediately to the north and there was steady pressure to change. The strict limitations on size of landholdings and inheritance, which were part of the original plan, created resistance, and after these broke down so did the slave prohibition. Oglethorpe established good relations with the Indians, but this aroused the ire of the Carolinians because the Georgians were cutting in on the lucrative trade enjoyed by the

former. Oglethorpe began to devote more and more of his time, and incurred large debts for the Trustees, in developing the military fort at Frederica as a southern outpost against the Spanish. In fact, military affairs dominated the last of his years in Georgia. War with the Spanish broke out in 1739. Oglethorpe led an abortive attack on St. Augustine in 1740, and in 1742 the Spanish launched a counterattack on Fort Frederica. Thanks to a series of confusing events, the English under Oglethorpe managed to repulse the Spanish and the uneasy truce was maintained. Oglethorpe returned to England in 1743 and in 1753 Georgia became a Crown colony. Georgia successfully served as a buffer state, but its internal economy was weak until a new fusion of immigrants came in the 1750s.

All of the first settlements in the Southern parts of what was to become the United States were very slow in getting established. The mild and balmy winters and springs that evoked visions of Persia and the Levant were succeeded by cruelly hot summers, which the Europeans learned to endure only after "seasoning." The unreal expectations of both proprietors and colonists gradually gave way to more practical exploitation of the resources of the new land through the two cash crops, tobacco and rice, as well as corn and wheat, and the development of fur trade, stock raising, and trade in naval stores. In this paradoxical land that seemed to offer such abundance there was famine, illness, sheer confusion, exploitation of first a servant class and then permanent servitude for black Africans. The European powers were

Philip Georg Friedrich von Reck. "Squash." 1736. Watercolor on paper. Royal Library, Copenhagen, Denmark.

vying with each other for the resources of the new lands and for positions of influence in Europe. The Indians were seen as a source of help, an avenue of trade, and a barrier to expansion.

It could be argued that the arts that played a role in the lives of the colonists who first settled in the American South—as with their counterparts farther north—were the useful arts. But one of the many "uses" of art is the emotional satisfaction it provides both in its creation and viewing, a difficult value to describe or weigh. We know that in every human society, whether very "primitive" or highly "civilized" there are things—objects— which seem to have been created, consciously or unconsciously, with this kind of "use" as a component.

From the very beginning of the efforts to establish settlements in the Southern part of this country, there was an effort to record and depict the inhabitants and the products of the new land. The modest, essentially didactic natural history renderings are nonetheless among the freshest and freest of this genre. The work of Mark Catesby, who saw the close relationship between creatures and their environment, and drew them in habitat settings, had an important influence on the subsequent history of natural history illustration.

Somewhat impermanent buildings served as adequate shelters for the first decades of settlement. The whitewashed interiors of some of these, with shutters "pritty and convenient," were nonetheless attractive. There is pleasure, too, in looking at the well-formed shapes of the utilitarian pottery made at Martin's Hundred. The fragment of decorated pottery tells us that a craftsman spent time and effort to decorate one or more pieces with different colors and designs.

Gradually a sense of identification with place developed, and more permanent buildings came into being, buildings of carefully calculated proportions, finished with skillfully crafted panelings, moldings, door and window frames, and other embellishments. Luxury items such as paintings, fine plate, and fabrics were acquired and displayed by some.

The dreams and unreal expectations included the laying out of new towns: some of these never developed as communities and their dirt streets now lie under plowed fields. But among those that survived are Charleston, Annapolis, Williamsburg, New Orleans, and Savannah, communities whose distinctive characters today still owe much to the planners, surveyors, and builders of the first generations of settlers.

PART TWO

An Established Society

1735-1788

A MEASURE OF PEACE and stability characterized the colonial settlements on the Eastern Seaboard by the third decade of the eighteenth century. The youthful Eliza Lucas, newly arrived in Charleston in 1739, found that "the people live very Gentile and very much in the English taste." This was an astute observation. In this colony far from the shores of England a way of life closely based on the English model had been established. Merchants and planters practiced the "gentle" manners, or decorum, of upper-class English gentry, and identified with them. Whether one looks at architecture, painting, furniture, or silver, English taste is dominant. This dominance held despite the fact that in some areas, such as lowland South Carolina, the setting and circumstances were in some ways most un-English: the summers were steaming hot, the winters often milder than an English summer, half the population was black, and rice, then indigo, unfamiliar in Albion, were planted in the fields. (The latter crop was first cultivated by young Eliza Lucas, who ran her father's plantation while he was away in the West Indies.) Adapting to these circumstances after the early years of struggle, those of English descent now dominated politically and economically in Virginia, Maryland, the Carolinas, and in the sparse settlements in Georgia.

Beneath this surface dominance there was diversity. Differences show up in the buildings and artifacts created in areas where French, German-Swiss, and Spanish peoples still prevailed, and on the frontier. In architecture, the hot climate often influenced builders to make particular choices or to modify traditional designs.

The French were gaining a foothold in the lower Mississippi Valley. The French Huguenots in South Carolina, who had first entered into the ruling clique by joining the Anglican church, were fairly well assimilated culturally and linguistically within two decades. The peoples of Germanic descent who helped to settle the back- and up-country during the middle years of the eighteenth century retained a large measure of cultural identity, and this is manifest in the things they built and created. Pioneer conditions prevailed on the frontier, which began to extend beyond the Appalachians, where many new arrivals were of Scot-

tish ancestry. The Spanish retained a foothold in St. Augustine, Florida, and that town continued to be Spanish in appearance even after the English took control in 1764. The few British Floridians did not join the revolt against the motherland in 1776.

Under the aegis of the English, especially after 1700, a large population of blacks of African descent were brought to the English colonies in the South, and between 1710 and 1740 they formed the majority of South Carolina's population. In Virginia the black population grew from about 10,000 to 100,000 between 1700 and 1750. The growth and prosperity of the burgeoning plantation economies of tobacco, rice, and the newly introduced indigo depended upon the labor of these enslaved people. From this time on, the society of the American South was biracial—the nuances, complexities, and richness of which we are still learning to understand. By the 1740s, after the Stono rebellion in South Carolina, the slave population was held in fairly firm submission throughout the South, and although blacks contributed immeasurably to the growing strength and wealth of Southern society, they shared only marginally in it.

The shrewd English traders maintained ties with the Indians even as they steadily laid claim to the lands the relatively sparse Indian population had once used for hunting and cultivation. The military helped to establish security, and after the Tuscarora and Yamasee wars of 1711–1713 and 1715, the Europeans along the seaboard felt little danger of attack from the Indians. Inconclusive wars with the Spanish in the 1740s made relationships between the English and Spanish relatively quiescent, aided by the fact that as Spain's power in Europe and on the international scene waned, that of England grew.

The French and Indian War of 1754–1763 further confirmed Britain's power on the North American continent. Most of the territory the French had laid claim to east of the Mississippi and part of Spanish Florida came under English control. The area west of the Alleghenies was thus opened for exploration and development by British colonists. In the Deep South, however, the Cherokee and the Creek remained a barrier to the white man's expansion until after the American Revolution.

In England itself there was also a period of prosperity. This

Drayton Hall, on the Ashley River, South Carolina, c. 1735–1742. Land side.

created additional wealth for the landed aristocracy and for a rising merchant and manufacturing class. The latter eagerly identified with the values of the aristocracy; it was difficult to join the ranks of nobility, but it was possible through money, marriage, and manners to become one of the gentry. Elegant country houses and the related life-style of the landed gentry became symbols of social prestige. Within the ever-subtle boundaries of class, there was great social mobility in England at this time.

The possibility of rising socially and economically was even greater in the provincial social centers of the colonies. There was surely truth as well as irony in the comments of a correspondent of the *South Carolina Gazette and Country Journal*, who wrote in 1773: "If we observe the Behavior of the polite Part of this Coun-

try, we shall see, that their whole Lives are one continued Race; in which everyone is endeavouring to distance all behind him, and to overtake or pass by, all before him; everyone is flying from his Inferiors in Pursuit of his Superiors, who fly from him with equal Alacrity. . . .

"Every Tradesman is a Merchant, every Merchant is a Gentleman, and every Gentleman one of the Noblesse. We are a Country of Gentry, *Populous generosorum:* We have no such Thing as common People among us: Between Vanity and Fashion, the Species is utterly destroyed."

As in England, one of the ways to show one's status was to erect fine houses and to furnish them generously. The delight in material things, fortunately often combined with a sobriety of

from the plan there appear to be five openings to the outdoors at either end, whether doors or windows is not quite clear. Whitefield named his house Bethesda, or House of Mercy, after the Scriptural passage in the Gospel of St. John, chapter 5, where Jesus miraculously healed the sick. Whether or not the five openings were meant to repeat the "five porticoes" of the Biblical text can only be conjecture; if so the given Biblical name had a physical and tangible expression as well as a symbolic connotation.

Whitefield, who went back and forth to England a number of times during his career, did not spend long periods at the orphanage. He made it virtually an intercolonial charity and preached about it from Maine to Georgia. Benjamin Franklin contributed after he heard the eloquent Whitefield. When the naturalist William Bartram was in Savannah in 1765 he took time to see "this celebrated building" and described it in some detail as "a neat brick building, well finished and painted both within and without; its dimensions 60 feet by 40, with cellaring all the way through; two stories high, with good garrets, and a turret and bell on top. Piazzas, ten feet wide, project on every side, and form a pleasant walk, both winter and summer, round the house. The inside apartments are well divided. On the ground floor a passage runs from end to end, at the extremities of which a stair case of red bay, not unlike mahogany, leads to the upper story. On one side of this passage are three rooms, a parlour, chappel, and library; on the other side, a long dining room and parlour. The upper story corresponds with the lower, and the garrets are also conveniently divided."

On the basis of this description, it would appear that only one of the two staircases shown in the plan was built and that a chapel was placed in the other available space. Also of interest is the reference to red bay wood being used instead of mahogany. Though most of the red bay that grows in the Southern United States is now relatively small there were early trees of considerable girth, and references to or examples of the use of red bay as a cabinet wood occur from time to time. When Bartram saw the institution there was a handsomely laid-out garden and an orchard, and a functioning plantation worked by Negroes.

A drawing in the French archives for a building that was to house the *corps de garde* and a prison cell at the harbor post at Balize near the mouth of the Mississippi, following page, shows that a *galerie* or porch was to extend around two sides of the small hip-roofed building. It is dated February 1734 and signed by Bernard Deverges, an engineer who served with the French in the New World. Louisiana buildings with a porch or sheltered walkway across the front have their roots in French farmhouse buildings. Such simple country buildings with projecting roofs supported by posts are seen in the early seventeenth-century prints of Jacques Callot; even earlier examples are found in the sixteenth-century designs for small farmhouses originated or recorded by Sebastiano Serlio.

The Deverges plan not only shows a gallery on two sides but indicates that the building is to be raised on low piers, thus preventing the rotting of sills that took place when structures were placed directly on the ground. Raising the building off the ground also provided for some circulation underneath, making it a little cooler and drier in damp, humid conditions or in minor

floods. Though the *corps de garde* building that was erected at Balize did not follow this plan exactly, the design indicates the direction of French thinking at the time.

The 1749 designs for the residence of the Commissary, Commissaire Ordonnateur, or Intendant—that is, the chief offi-

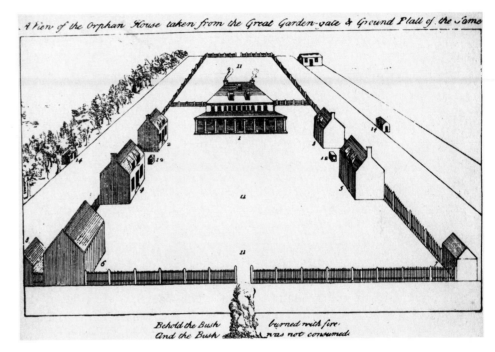

View of the Orphan House, Bethesda, near Savannah, Georgia. 1740. University of Georgia Libraries, Athens.

Plan of the Orphan House, Bethesda.

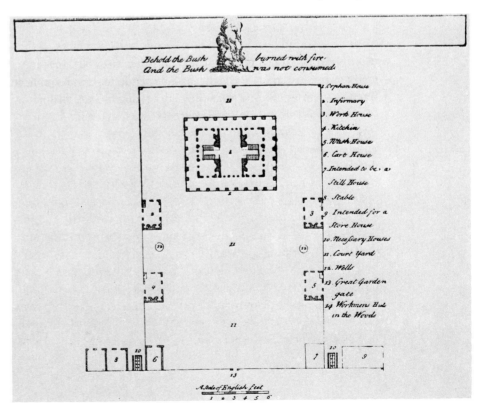

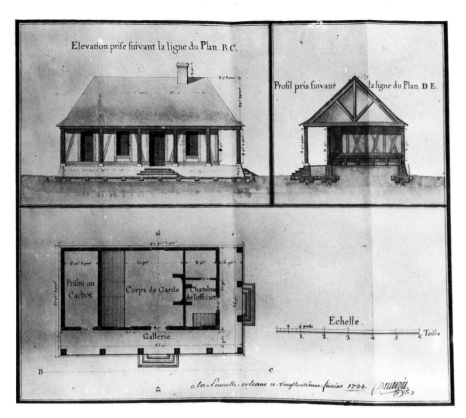

Bernard Deverges. "Plan, section, and elevation of a corps de garde and prison cell projected for the port of Balize." Signed: "A la Nouvelle orléans ce vingthuitième fevrier 1734 DEVERGES." Archives Nationales, Section Outre-Mer, Paris, France.

cial dealing with civil affairs in French-colonial Louisiana—show a two-story *galerie* on the front and rear of the building. As can be seen on the section drawing, far right, columns on the ground floor were to be of brick and the slimmer colonnettes on the upper level of wood. The roof was to be canted out in order to extend at a more agreeable angle over the galleries. The structure was to be of brick and, as in the design for the Balize *corps de garde*, was raised somewhat off the ground. The plan of the ground floor, right, shows a capacious interior with a variety of rooms, including one for archives. There is no real central hall or corridor, rather the rooms are arranged in the French *enfilade* manner, with one room leading into another, an economical arrangement that does not waste space, though it does not always guarantee privacy. The design was the work of a French engineer, Ignace François Broutin. By this time Louisiana had become a colony of the king; Honoré Michel de la Rouxillière was intendant, Pierre de Rigaud, Marquis de Vaudreuil, was governor. The nine years of the latter's administration, 1745–1753, were ones of peace and prosperity, during which a social and cultural life developed. It was during this time, too, that the Jesuits experimented with the planting of sugar cane on a more extensive scale and laid the foundations for the cane industry that was to be so central to Louisiana's economy in the nineteenth and twentieth centuries.

For several reasons this building was never erected. The drawing is, however, very important since it represents what in many ways is the prototype, or reflects a vernacular solution already begun, of the plan for what was to be the typical Louisiana plantation house of the second half of the eighteenth and early

nineteenth centuries, with its double galleries on two or more sides, brick piers below and wooden colonnettes above, and double-canted roof. These houses, too, were early identified by some as being "in the West-India style." Though these forms may have first developed in the West Indies, it is difficult to pinpoint direct influences or exact prototypes, while evidence for their gradual development in French Louisiana can be traced, as we have seen, with some ease. One common source may be in the sixteenth- and seventeenth-century farm buildings of France, mentioned above. African and American Indian building traditions may also have played a role.

Thus, the practice of attaching or building sheltered porches, piazzas, or galleries, as they were variously called, had become fairly common by about 1750 in the most Southern and low-lying regions of the American South. A detail, bottom of page 56, from a drawing of New Orleans as seen from the opposite side of the river, done by an unknown Englishman in 1765, shows a variety

Ignace François Broutin. "Plans of the Ground Floor and First Story of the Intendance Building Projected to be Constructed in Brick Masonry at New Orleans." Ink and watercolor. Signed: "Broutin." Dated: "August 23, 1749." Archives Nationales, Section Outre-Mer, Paris, France.

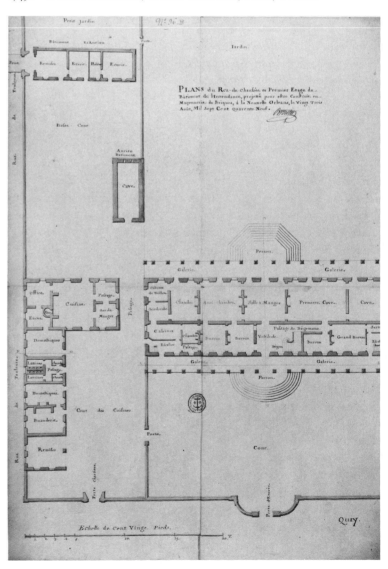

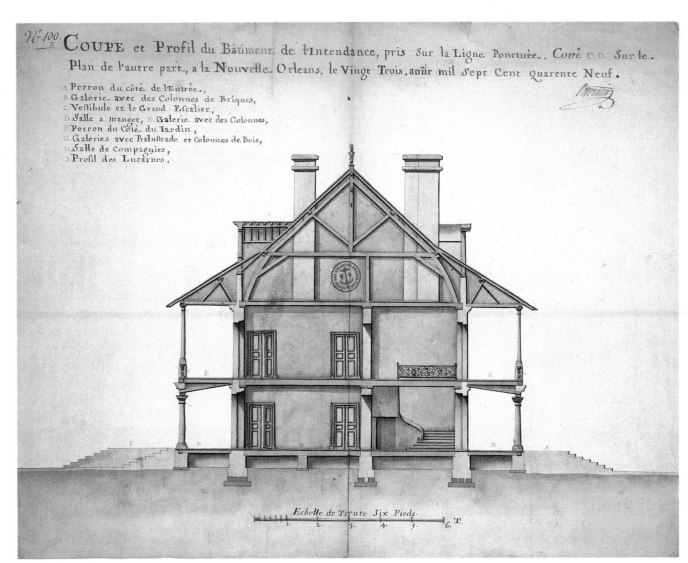

COUPE et Profil du Bâtiment de l'Intendance, pris sur la Ligne Ponctuée. Coté C.D. Sur le
Plan de l'autre part, a la Nouvelle Orleans, le Vingt Trois, aout mil sept Cent Quarante Neuf.

A. Perron du côté de l'Entrée,
B. Galerie avec des Colonnes de Briques,
C. Vestibule et le Grand Escalier,
D. Salle a manger, E. Galerie avec des Colonnes,
F. Perron du Côté du Jardin,
G. Galeries avec Balustrade et Colonnes de Bois,
H. Salle de Compagnies,
I. Profil des Lucarnes.

Echelle de Trente Six Pieds.

Ignace François Broutin. "Section and Profile of the Intendance Building at New Orleans." Ink and watercolor. Signed: "Broutin." Dated: "August 23, 1749." Archives Nationales, Section Outre-Mer, Paris, France.

of vernacular structures, many with galleries. There are one- and two-story structures with galleries across the front. Some are raised off the ground. Others have galleries on two or more sides. All indicate that builders had introduced a number of different building types, most with at least one porch or gallery, suitable to the climate.

The drawing may well have been done by a British intelligence officer. Following the end of the Seven Years' War (the French and Indian War) in 1762–1763, France ceded all its Canadian claims, as well as Louisiana east of the Mississippi, except for the "island" of New Orleans, to England. Spain gave up Florida for the return of Cuba and the Philippines. Thus the English were now in control of the whole Gulf Coast. At the same time the French secretly ceded New Orleans and the rest of Louisiana to Spain, though the citizens of New Orleans were not apprised of this until 1764. Spain did not really attempt to take possession of New Orleans until 1766 and did not gain full and official control until 1769.

Despite the presence of the Spanish, New Orleans and Louisiana west of the Mississippi remained predominantly French in character and in many cases French officials continued to serve. The design for the Spanish commandant's house in Baton Rouge, dated 1788, top of page 56, in the Archives at

Seville, is similar to the vernacular structures already evolved by the French. In this case the widespreading double-angled roof shelters an open walkway on four sides.

Several types of vernacular Carolina buildings appear to have evolved by the third quarter of the eighteenth century. One example is Richmond, a low country plantation house that was situated on a hill above the Cooper River, part title and bottom of page 57. It belonged to Colonel John Harleston, was probably built sometime in the second half of the eighteenth century, and was accidentally burned at the end of the nineteenth century. The watercolor shown here was done in 1803 by the miniaturist Charles Fraser. From this we can see that it was a four-square structure raised on a high foundation, with a hipped roof. The porches or piazzas were sheltered by simple shed-roofs. This arrangement is typical of many low country plantation houses that are less well known than those with more elaborate and bookishly "correct" classical porticoes.

A similar but narrower vernacular structure is the Philip Alston house, top of page 57, situated in Carthage in the rolling hill country of Piedmont, North Carolina, and built before 1781. The tall, thin frame structure has shed-roofs over porches on the ground floor on either side, supported by simple wooden columns. There are massive chimneys at either end. It is a form,

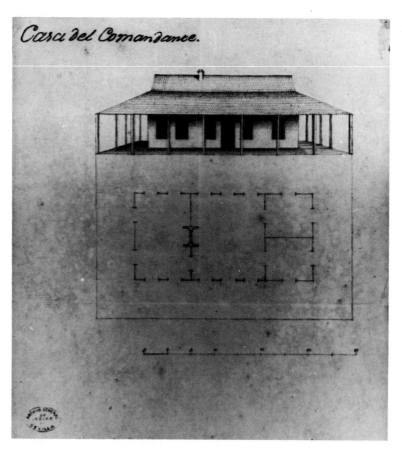

Unknown artist. "Commandant's house, Baton Rouge."
1788. Drawing. Archivo General de Indias, Seville, Spain.

plain or square building, which looks more like a schoolhouse than a church, may have been built when the congregation was founded in St. Bartholomew's Parish in 1728, or may have been built a few years later. The round-arch windows seem to have been the one concession to churchlike detail the builders allowed themselves. The sketch also reveals that the shutters and doors were paneled. Old Colleton County was an area settled largely by English dissenters and here they established their congregations. Fraser also drew at least one other of their Presbyterian meetinghouses, Stony Creek Meeting in Prince William's Parish. It, too, was a plain, unostentatious building with a high hipped roof. The interiors were very probably austere, with tall pulpits. These eighteenth-century South Carolina meetinghouses may have been as architecturally distinctive in their way as the seventeenth-century meetinghouses of New England.

A traveler visiting New Bern, North Carolina, in 1787 recorded, "There are to many of the houses Balconies or Piazzas in front or sometimes back of the house. This Method of Building is found convenient on account of the great Summer Heats here—These Balconies are often two Stories high, sometimes one or both ends of it are boarded up and made into a Room." The same might have been said of other towns or villages. Vernacular traditions were born. Forms varied from region to region, but wherever the heat was extremely intense, builders and architects made adaptations.

with variations, also frequently found in up-country South Carolina, in communities such as Winnsboro and Spartanburg, or near Camden. During this period the back-country of the Carolinas and Virginia was filling up. Some of the settlers moved inland from the coastal areas. Others poured down through the Valley of Virginia from Pennsylvania and western Maryland.

A simple shed-roof supported by posts was also found across the front of a meetinghouse of the Bethel Congregation of Pon-Pon, which was located in old Colleton County, southwest of Charleston, top of page 58. This 1799 watercolor by Charles Fraser is one of the rare visual records of the meetinghouses used by various dissenter congregations (in this case Presbyterian) once found in some numbers in parts of South Carolina. This

The influence of national country of origin or bookish designs was sometimes muted as the builders moved toward regional adaptations, though in details of decoration, such as door frames, moldings and fireplace and overmantel treatment, they usually followed the current taste. The specific influence of the national origins of a still diverse people can be seen, however, in several mid-eighteenth-century public buildings.

The major structure surviving in Louisiana or the Gulf Coast from the period of French domination is the Ursuline Convent in New Orleans, bottom of page 58, completed in 1753. An earlier building, erected from 1727–1734, of exposed timber-frame construction, with bricks used as fill, and with no outside sheathing, deteriorated within a decade of completion. It served as convent, school, and orphanage. New plans were drawn up in 1745 under the supervision of Broutin, and the present convent was built

Unknown artist, probably English. Detail of a "View of New Orleans from the Opposite Side of the River." 1765. Ink drawing. Louisiana State Museum, New Orleans.

Philip Alston House in the Horseshoe,
Carthage, North Carolina,
before 1781.

under the direction of Claude Joseph Villars DuBréuil. The latter, one of the wealthiest of the French inhabitants, was a building contractor and canal engineer. This time they had determined to put up a more substantial structure, for as Governor Vaudreuil wrote to France, they wanted to create "durable buildings, to prevent the repairs which are often repeated, as we have had the experience in the colony, far exceeding what it would have cost to build something solid at first." It is a two-and-a-half-story brick masonry structure, covered with stucco. There is a pedimented central bay, edged by bold quoins, and the corners are finished with quoins. The edges of the great hipped roof are slightly canted at the bottom in a traditional French manner. The windows are topped with segmented arcs, giving a soft, slightly rococo feeling. The economical French reused the handsome cypress staircase from the earlier convent. The building

has withstood the vicissitudes of time, weather, and some neglect, and has recently been repaired and restored. Originally the front of the building faced toward the river, but with the growth of the city the area between it and the river has been filled in. It is now approached from what was originally the rear, or land, side. The convent became the residence of the bishops and archbishops of New Orleans after 1824, and has served other functions through the years. The Ursulines still maintain an academy in another part of the city.

Two rare watercolors made by an anonymous British artist in 1764, perhaps a soldier or engineer, give us an idea of the appearance of the Governor's house, page 59, and the main guardhouse, page 60, at St. Augustine at the time the British took over. The watercolors themselves represent the artistic talent occasionally found among the military who served in America. The artist used pale color washes to enliven the topographical rendering and to produce an ephemeral effect. The Governor's house was situated on the far side of the plaza, facing the sea, and the building shown in the watercolor was originally built in 1706 and remodeled in 1759. The guardhouse was on the plaza itself, closer to the sea. It, like the Governor's house, was built after a devastating 1702 fire ignited by British-Carolinians who had besieged the community and its forts.

Charles Fraser. "Richmond. Home of Colonel John Harleston, built second
half of eighteenth century." 1803. Watercolor. Carolina Art Association/
Gibbes Art Gallery, Charleston.

Charles Fraser. "Meeting-House near Jacksonborough—
Bethel Congregation of Pon-Pon." 1799. Watercolor.
Carolina Art Association/Gibbes Art Gallery, Charleston.

St. Augustine was essentially a garrison town near a fort, and had been such since its founding in 1565. Sir Francis Drake burned the settlement with its wooden houses in 1586, but the tiny community was rebuilt. The majority of the houses were again simple wooden structures, mostly roofed by palm thatch. In 1598 a central plaza facing the sea was laid out under the direction of Governor Gonzalo Mende de Canzo, and the first

Governor's house on that site, presumably a wooden structure, was erected. Though this governor was optimistic about the possibilities of the community as a base for exploration, as a center for converting the Indians, and as a home for shipwrecked people, the Spanish did little other than provide some minimum support to the fort and the small settlement. It was only after the English colony in Virginia began to show greater strength and

Ursuline Convent, New Orleans, Louisiana,
designed 1745, completed 1749–1753.

Unknown artist, English. "View of the Governor's House, St. Augustine, in E. Florida, Nov. 1764." Watercolor. British Museum, London.

perseverance and repeated pirate attacks that plans were begun for a strong masonry fort. In 1671 work started on the impressive fort, the Castillo San Marcos, now restored. It took twenty-five years to build. Skilled workers were brought from Cuba and the stone quarried from nearby Anastasia Island. And it was only after the fort was virtually completed that permission was given to build a masonry structure for the governor. However, the siege and fire of 1702 intervened, and the building shown in the watercolor was begun around 1706.

Though most structures in St. Augustine were of wood, the Governor's house had masonry walls 22 inches thick, made of the local "coquina" or shellrock, a conglomerate consisting of fragments of various shells. The projecting roof balcony on the street side (a *balcon de la calle*) was there from at least 1713, when it was reported that the governor and his lady flung silver coins to the populace below. Nineteenth-century photographs and descriptions of other buildings in St. Augustine suggest that such balconies on two-story houses were fairly common. So, too, were walls extending from the house along the street side, though probably

none had an entrance gate as elaborate as that in the watercolor. It is flanked by pairs of engaged columns. Most had simple stone lintels over the entrance way. Atypical also was the watchtower in the rear. Though the sketch shows an entrance on the street floor, the major entrance to the living quarters, which were on the second floor, was reached from the interior courtyard, via a masonry staircase leading to a porch or gallery. There were also several outbuildings, a garden, and an orchard in the rear.

Though the Governor's house was probably grander than others, evidence, written and archaeological, indicates that many of the Spanish-built houses of the 1702–1763 period had the main entrance on an inner courtyard. In this inner yard there usually was a loggia or porch alongside the house, sometimes a one-story, sometimes a two-story—a sheltered area to catch the breezes.

The governor, and the British artist who did the watercolor, could look from the balcony or window across the plaza to the waterfront and see the guardhouse. It, too, was a masonry structure that had gable parapets on the center section, and what

*Unknown artist, English. "Military guardhouse, the Plaza. View
from Governor's House, looking east toward bay and ocean."
c. 1764. Watercolor. British Museum, London.*

appears to be a flat-roofed arched loggia on the north side. This
was topped by small castellations, giving it a faintly medieval
look.

In neither of the watercolors do we see the projecting structures, or *rejas*, often built in front of the windows on the street
side of the ground floor. Travelers' descriptions and old photographs indicate that these were characteristic of some of the
houses that crowded the narrow streets of old St. Augustine.
They made this Florida community look very Spanish or Mediterranean. *Rejas* were made of close gratings of wood that extended a foot or more into the street, creating a kind of open, but
screened and private, bay window. John Bartram described some
of these when he visited St. Augustine in the 1750s: "They had
no glass windows, but the best houses had large windows next
the street, all bannistered and projecting a foot or more from the
house wall. . . . All these windows had strong shutters within
side, many of which had a little one in each, and many windows
had a lattice with holes one inch square, reaching half way or
more up the window." Even though the British came in 1764
and stayed for twenty years, the old part of the city retained

much of its Spanish and Mediterranean air well into the nineteenth century, through the second Spanish period, and into the
American era.

Politics and power were very much in the minds of the
French and Spanish as they established their outposts in the
New World (even as they neglected them for other political
power plays in Europe). None of the German states were directly
involved in the establishment of settlements in America, though
people from Germany and Switzerland formed an important sub-
group among those who came to live on the American shores.
Some came because of the religious freedom offered to those
who belonged to pietistic faiths. These included the Mennon-
ites, who settled in Pennsylvania as early as the 1680s, and some
of the German and Swiss refugees who came into North Carolina
(New Bern) in the first decade of the eighteenth century.

The special character of the German contribution can best be
seen in the beautifully restored community of Old Salem in
North Carolina. Fortunately most of the buildings remained
through the years, and have now been returned as much as possible to their original appearance. The work of restoration was

facilitated because the German Moravians who established Salem kept careful and copious records, in some cases even writing down the colors and mixtures of pigments to be used for painting woodwork.

The Moravian Brethren originated among followers of the fifteenth-century religious leader John Huss of Bohemia, survived through the turbulent years of the Reformation, and founded what is possibly the oldest of the Protestant churches. In Europe they pioneered public education, were the first Protestants to translate the Bible from Latin into their native tongue, and were the first to publish a hymnal for congregational use. Their members were persecuted during the Counter-Reformation, and it was not until the early eighteenth century, when Count Zinzindorf of Saxony, a Lutheran sympathetic to their views, gave them shelter on his estates that their religious community once again began to prosper. They were zealous in their dedication to the belief that their faith must find expression in the acts of daily life and that they must shape their lives in the pattern of the original apostles. They established a communal village, called Herrnhut, on Zinzindorf's estates, in which each member was to contribute according to his ability and to share according to his need, a way of life at once simple and fulfilling, yet highly regulated, rigid, and demanding, tempered fortunately by a belief in education, hard work, and great joy in music. Their vigor and success at this time increased their missionary zeal.

Zinzindorf helped to find shelter for them in the New World by purchasing the tract of land for them in Georgia, where, as we have seen, a group went in 1735. They conscientiously objected to bearing arms in the war between the Spanish and English in Florida and so removed from Georgia in 1740, going to Pennsylvania. There they built several towns, including Bethlehem, on the pattern of Herrnhut, and carried on their missionary work among the Indians and, more successfully, among their white neighbors.

Their discipline and diligence helped them to prosper as settlers, and they were encouraged by the Land Proprietors of North Carolina to come there. After an initial visit, they bought nearly 100,000 acres in the central Carolina Piedmont. Here they established several settlements between 1753 and 1759, and in 1766 laid out what was to be their major community, a place of peace, Salem.

One of the oldest surviving buildings, a structure of generous proportions, is the Single Brothers' house, right, where the unmarried men of the community lived and ate their meals. Many of the workshops for the crafts practiced by the Moravians were located here. These included a gunsmith's, shoemaker's, and joiner's shop. The older portion of the building, shown in the foreground, is timber-frame construction on a stone foundation. The raising of the already carefully cut and measured half-timber framing took just two days in May 1769, after which, so it is recorded, "the musicians blew their trumpets from the top of the house." The brick used for filling was then added, the interior fittings completed, and the walls plastered and whitewashed on the inside. Seeing it as it faces the central square of Old Salem, or as one descends the main street of the original village in which it is located, one feels as if a piece of late medieval Germanic Europe has been transplanted, as in a sense it was. The overall proportions, the timbers patterned in squares, rectangles, and with diagonal bracing, and the use of exposed brick remind one of the buildings shown in some of Dürer's paintings. As with many continental buildings, the eave of the roof has a characteristic spring or kick outward at the bottom. A shingled pent roof girdles the building just above the first floor.

By 1786 the community had become an important regional center for marketing and for purchasing the products of the skilled craftsmen. The Single Brothers' house was expanded, hence the all-brick addition to be seen on the downhill side of the building. Its arched window heads are characteristic of Salem structures of this slightly later date. The new addition housed a large *Saal*, equipped with an organ, for services and meetings, a new dining hall and kitchen, as well as vaulted cellars for food storage.

Most of the public architecture in eastern or coastal Maryland, Virginia, and the Carolinas in this period reflects, of course, the dominant English or Georgian taste. Like the domestic ones, public buildings are characterized by a feeling for proportion and decorum, and by the consistent use of a given artistic vocabulary. By this token, public structures in the Southern colonies were seldom overly large in scale and were frequently endowed with an almost domestic character. In both, a fine sense of dignity and elegance was achieved.

This is true of several Virginia churches of the third quarter of the eighteenth century, such as Pohick Church in Fairfax County, following page, built 1769–1774. It is one of three closely similar in design. Plans for the other two, Christ Church

Single Brothers' House, Old Salem, North Carolina, 1769 and addition of 1786.

Pohick Church, Fairfax County, Virginia, 1769–1774.

in Alexandria, 1767–1773, and Falls Church, 1767–1769, were made by a Colonel James Wren, and it is probable that he was also the designer of Pohick. Some records for Pohick are remarkably complete. The first builder or contractor was Daniel French, who died in 1771. George Mason (the Revolutionary statesman) then took over and supervised the completion of the work. Both George Mason and George Washington were on the building committee, and the church was conveniently near their plantations, Gunston Hall and Mount Vernon. Each of these three brick churches is rectangular in shape, two stories in height, and with two tiers of windows. (Considerable alterations have been made to Christ Church, Alexandria, and the Falls Church building.) At Pohick the central doorway of "good white freestone" is on the south side, the long side of the rectangle. There are two doors, one for men and one for women, on the west end. The carving of these three doors, though weathered, is particularly fine. Each is framed by Ionic pilasters and topped by a triangular pediment. Stone quoins are on each of the four corners. The roof is hipped and there is a modillioned cornice under the eaves. The windows are completely domestic in scale. Those on the first floor have flat arches; those on the second floor are semicircular. There is no steeple.

On the inside (which has been somewhat altered and restored

since the destruction of the interior during the Civil War) the "Alter-piece" was to be "done with wainscot after the Ionic order." The floor of "the Communion Place"—the word chancel was not used in the specifications—was to be raised twelve inches higher than the floor of "the House." There was to be a Communion Table of black walnut "of a proper size." As was requisite in Anglican churches, the Apostles' Creed, the Lord's Prayer, and the Ten Commandments were to be "neatly painted on the Alter-piece in black letters." These were and are on the east end.

The pulpit, canopy, and reading desks were "to be of pine, wainscoted with proper cornice, and executed in the Ionic Order." It was placed, then as now, in the center of the north wall, so that as one enters the main south door the eye focuses directly on the pulpit. If one enters one of the west doors, the focus is on the "Alter-piece" and communion table. There are two aisles, one north-south, one east-west, which cross approximately in the center. The font presently stands at this crossing. Thus, architecturally the two major liturgical centers are given equal emphasis. The pews, with seats on several sides, made it possible for the parishioners to shift position, if they wished, when one or the other of these centers was the focus of attention. Since communion was given only three or four times a year, as mentioned earlier, the focus was more frequently on the pulpit. All aspects of the service could be easily seen and heard.

Though the specifications recorded in the vestry book are in some cases quite detailed, in others they are general or vague. It was understood that a good craftsman would know how to do a "Modillion cornice" or what kind of paneling would be needed for the pews if they were to be "wainscoted." In addition to Daniel French and George Mason as builders or contractors, William Bernard Sears did some of the "carved work." William Copein, another craftsman involved, was responsible for the design of a font. We know that craftsmen sometimes used various English pattern books to guide them, but in this case the source was recorded: "William Copein having undertaken to make a stone Font for the Church according to a Draught in the 150th plate in Langley's Designs being the upermost on the left hand for the price of six pounds. . . .—the Vestry agree to pay him that sum for finishing the same."

This would have been Plate 150 from Batty Langley's *The City and Country Builders and Workman's Treasury of Design*, first published in 1740. Either Copein, one of the other craftsmen, or one of the members of the building committee owned this volume. (The doorways are based on Plate 35.)

As the work approached completion the vestry ordered that the church be "furnished with a Cushion for the Pulpit and Cloths for the Desks & Communion Table of Crimson Velvett with Gold Fring, and that Colo. George Washington be requested to import same." Another entry indicates that Washington provided gold leaf for ornamenting the tabernacle frames and "also the Eggs on the Cornice of the small Frames if the Gold will hold out."

The church was Anglican, with the "Alter-piece" highlighted by gold leaf and the communion table covered with gold-fringed crimson velvet at the east end. The restrained elegance and austerity of the interior are characteristic of the balance achieved by the Anglicans between their desire, which they shared with dissenters, not to be "popish," and their wish to retain a sense of the importance of the sacraments. Yet one cannot but be struck by the simplicity and domestic air of the exterior. As was customary in Virginia, there was no steeple. For this reason, perhaps, there is an uncannily close relation between the exterior of Pohick (also of Falls Church and Christ Church, Alexandria, as they originally appeared) and several Nonconformist chapels built in England after the Act of Toleration of 1687 had allowed the licensing of such structures. Three English chapels—Old Meeting (Norwich, 1693), Friars Street Chapel (Ipswich, 1700), and Underbank Chapel (Stannington, near Sheffield, 1742)—are also two-storied, hipped-roof buildings with most windows on a domestic scale, and with the pulpit on the long side. In this period of experimentation in the designs for buildings of worship, there was no set formula for the style of English meetinghouses, just as there were none for the form of a New England meetinghouse or for Anglican churches. Therefore, the close parallel between the outside of Pohick and English Nonconformist chapels may be sheer accident; still, the relationship is so close as to suggest that similar underlying attitudes led to the selection of similar designs.

It may be relevant that in the three decades preceding the building of these churches reformers and dissenters had gained adherents in Virginia. The preachers of the Great Awakening had aroused religious excitement and engendered discontent with the established church; some clergy and vestry, in turn, were disquieted by the presence of "itinerant" preachers and their appeal to emotions, although some allowed these men to preach in their churches. Quite a few people defected from the established church to the New Light Presbyterianism. These were often considered not only religious dissenters but also in revolt against traditional authority. At the same time, several settled communities of foreign Protestants in Virginia (Huguenots and the Germans) were quietly allowed by the authorities to go their way. Ultimately the General Assembly of Virginia in 1759 promulgated a law that largely ended official attempts to restrict the New Light Presbyterians. After this, Presbyterianism gained acceptance, respectability, and a large measure of religious freedom. By the 1760s the Anglicans and Presbyterians were even sometimes united against the disaffection being created by the Separate Baptists.

Whether Pohick and its sister churches represent a continuation of religious architectural traditions already established in Virginia or whether their designs somehow represent a modification in the direction of Presbyterian or Nonconformist tastes remains a matter of conjecture. In appearance they were far less "churchly" than Bruton Parish in Williamsburg or St. Philip's in Charleston, and were by choice or accident somewhat similar in appearance to meetinghouses built by dissenting Presbyterian congregations in London. In a curious way, the designs of this group of three Virginia churches seem to reflect the democratic leanings, religious tolerance, and freedom in the Virginia of the 1770s.

It is unusual to have records as complete as the vestry minutes of Pohick Church, which tell us the names of its builders and some of its craftsmen. Few or no facts are known about the men who applied their talents to the wall, following page, of the ornate drawing room found originally in Marmion, from the outside a modest wooden house situated in the Rappahannock Valley in King George County, Virginia, dating from the middle years of the eighteenth century. The interior of this room is unusually well preserved and reveals a lavish decorating scheme. The walls are sheathed in paneling. Fluted and stop-fluted Ionic pilasters provide measure and frame the door, windows, fireplace, and corner cupboards. A fully decorated cornice completes this elaborate architectural interior. The skills of painters were called upon to further enrich the room, perhaps at the time it was built, or (according to one tradition) a few years later. The pilasters, cornice, and dado are painted to look like richly grained marble, and are now a muted purplish brown. The panels, in contrast, are fairly light, while the rococo ornamentation is done in yellow and gold. There are reds, greens, and blues in the landscape scenes. It is one of the finest surviving decorated rooms of colonial America, and it is appropriate, though a little sad since the house still stands, that this carved and painted interior has been installed in the Metropolitan Museum of Art in New York.

The technique of painting pine or other inexpensive woods

to look like the finest grained woods or marble (false graining and false marbleizing) was an old one known to skilled craftsmen. It may have been used in America more than is realized. Certainly it is easy to find nineteenth-century examples of fine and imaginative woodwork painting of this genre in houses in Kentucky, Tennessee, Mississippi, Louisiana, Alabama, and Texas. The 1705 specification for the Capitol in Williamsburg read, "That the Wainscot and other wooden work on the first and second floor in that part of the Building where the Genll Court is, be painted like marble, and the wainscot and other wooden work on the two first floors in the other part of the Building shall be painted like Wainscot." This technique was carried out by skilled craftsmen during Colonial Williamsburg's reconstruction of the Capitol.

Advertisements confirm the presence of such craftsmen working in the South at this time. One Richard Marten's ad, placed in the July 17, 1736, issue of the *South Carolina Gazette and Country Journal,* was quite specific about his talents: "Work done after the best manner, imitation of Marble, Walnut, Oak, Cedar, etc. at five Shillings a yard."

Craftsmen skilled in the arts of ornamental stucco and plasterwork also found patrons from time to time. A craftsman of sure talent and familiarity with the rococo taste popular in Ireland and England did the decoration in the dining room of the Colonel William Rhett house in Charleston, on the right. The shape of the flowing and delicate curling tendrils, the molded

branches and flowers as if newly plucked, the baskets of flowers and garlands, are reminiscent of the elaborate, skillfully wrought, and joyous ornament found in mid-eighteenth-century country houses in Ireland. It is just possible that this anonymous craftsman was "newly arrived" from Ireland. The work is unusual among surviving examples from Charleston and colonial America. The house was built about 1712, but this particular room was probably redecorated sometime around 1750.

Having conquered the land and made it productive, some of the colonists lavished time, money, and affection domesticating and beautifying that land with gardens. This was particularly true of those who built their mansions along the Ashley, the Cooper, the James, and the Potomac rivers. The Middleton gardens, on the Ashley near Charleston, page 66, represent a rare survival and rejuvenation of the most ephemeral of arts, landscape gardening. They were laid out beginning in 1741, shortly after Henry Middleton married Mary Williams. Mary's dowry was the Williams family house and plantation where they lived. They named their estate Middleton Place. The house stood on high ground, set back a quarter of a mile from the river that flowed around a bluff.

Tradition has it that it took ten years and the labor of a hundred slaves to lay out the gardens and achieve the terracing and planting. It is a formal plan, with a strong central axis from the riverfront side of the house to the succession of terraces that slope down to two symmetrically shaped "butterfly" lakes. The view extends across the lakes to the forest-bordered river beyond. On the north side of the property a flat reflecting pool and an azalea pond form the outer boundaries of a succession of smaller gardens; the groupings fit alongside the angle of the river and the adjacent rice fields. The diagram reveals the geometric precision with which this scheme was worked out, fitting it into the contours of the land. To move through the succession of smaller gardens is as if to move consciously through a series of rooms and spaces, some open but bordered, others more closed and intimate, a sundial here, a mound there, with different plants, textures, colors, lights, and shadows.

There is also a tradition that an English architect or gardener helped and planned the creation of this garden. Henry Middleton, grandson of the first Middleton who had come to South Carolina from Barbados, was born in South Carolina and educated in England. At the time of his marriage he had already inherited large landholdings from his father and was one of the wealthiest men in the colonies. He would have been familiar with English gardening practices and together with his gardener-architect must have spent many hours shaping this grand setting for his home and family. Later members of the family introduced new plants and more statuary, extended the boundaries, and introduced an informal wood walk. After the Civil War and the 1886 earthquake, the gardens were neglected and became overgrown. Since 1916, they have gradually been rejuvenated to their former grandeur.

The garden of Crowfield in Goose Creek, owned by Middleton's brother, must have rivaled that of Middleton Place. Ac-

Interior of Colonel William Rhett House, Charleston, South Carolina. The house was built c. 1715, the plasterwork added c. 1750.

Aerial view of Henry Middleton's gardens on the Ashley River, South Carolina. The central axis extended from the chief residence (no longer standing) to two "butterfly lakes" along-side the river. Laid out c. 1741–1751.

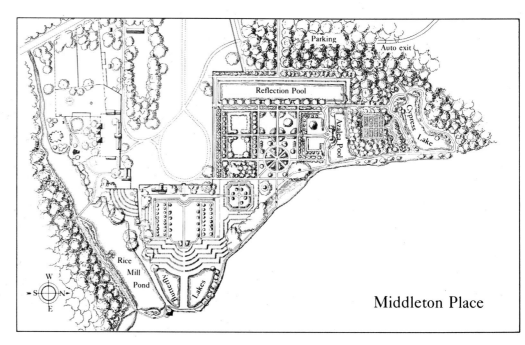

Middleton Place

Plan of the gardens, Middleton Place. The formal gardens on the right, bordered by the Reflection Pool and Azalea Pool, were laid out in the eighteenth century.

cording to a description by Eliza Lucas, it was replete with a serpentine walk, a thicket of young live oaks, a sunken bowling green, a double row of flowering laurels, several "Mounts," a Roman temple, and two large fish pools. The Ashley, the Cooper, and Goose Creek came to be called the "seated rivers" because of the impressive rows of plantation houses in landscaped settings that lined their banks. In Virginia and Maryland, in Georgia and Florida, where rare ornamental trees and flowers were planted in the governor's garden, and in far-off New Orleans, where old maps show patterns of formal gardens, the colonists shaped and carefully cultivated parts of their land. In Colonial Williamsburg's historic district replicas of the well-kept gardens of the tradesmen and town dwellers can be seen today. Even the smallest usually had a formal, linear, and patterned quality. The informal "English" gardens were to come later.

Elegant and sophisticated townhouses fronting the street often had their gardens in back. This is true of the Miles Brewton house, right, in Charleston, finished in 1769. The residence is one of the finest in Charleston and must always have been deemed so. An exemplar of the kind to which others aspired, it twice received the indirect accolade of being selected as the headquarters of occupying military officials. During the Revolutionary War it served as British Army headquarters and both Sir Henry Clinton and Lord Cornwallis used the premises. In the Civil War it became headquarters for Generals Meade and Hatch in 1864 and 1865.

These military officers found an elegantly appointed brick mansion, the design of which was based on Palladian concepts. It stands behind a high wall that separates the grounds from the street. The projecting two-story double-portico has Doric columns of Portland stone on the first level and Ionic wooden columns on the second. The entablature above the Ionic order extends around three sides of the house and is ornamented with an angular Chinese fret pattern. Thanks to a controversy among some of the workmen, and therefore a rather lengthy notice in the *South Carolina Gazette and Country Journal* of April 22, 1769, by Ezra Waite, we learn that he "calculated, adjusted, and draw'd at large for to work by, the Ionick entablature, and carved the same in the front and round the eaves, of Miles Brewton, Esquire's House on White Point for Mr. Moncrieff." In this same notice Waite identified himself as "Civil Architect, House-builder in general, and Carver from London," and called attention to the fact that he had "twenty-seven years experience both in theory and practice, in noblemen and gentlemen's seats." This newspaper notice provides insight into the blended roles and skills of craftsmen-architects who practiced in the eighteenth century. Moncrieff (or Moncrief) appears to have been the contractor. The carpenter, who seems to have maligned Waite, was Mr. Kinsey Burden, and a rivalry seems to have developed between Burden and Waite. Waite died two months after he placed his ad; Burden lived until 1791 and may have helped to design and build some other of Charleston's distinguished houses; he was, in fact, a partner with Moncrieff, while Ezra Waite was apparently employed by Moncrieff for this job. A number of other joiners, along with Waite himself, carried out much of the carving in the Brewton house, the designs having been drawn by Waite. We do not know the exact role of the

Miles Brewton House, Charleston, South Carolina, c. 1769.

owner, Miles Brewton, or of his wife, Mary Izard Brewton, in determining the scale and character of the house. She was the sister of Elizabeth Izard Blake who, with her husband, Daniel Blake, lived in the well-proportioned house at 34 Meeting Street known as the Daniel Huger house, built in 1760. It is very possible that Brewton and his wife made it clear to the workmen involved that they wanted a home similar to or finer than the Blakes'.

The interior of the Brewton house is equally if not more impressive than the exterior. The intricate carving over the doorway and the cornices of the first-floor drawing room, following page, further attest to the skill of Ezra Waite, who claimed responsibility for the carving in the four principal rooms. Leaf and floral ornamental plasterwork on the ceiling add to the room's richness.

The large second-floor drawing room, which extends across

Interior, first-floor drawing room, Miles Brewton House.

most of the front of the house, far right, is testimony to the taste for elegant living that characterized Charleston in the period before the Revolution. This seventeen-foot-high room has a coved ceiling, the central portion of which is painted blue. The original glass chandelier designed for the house is still in place. The woodwork decorations are in the Corinthian order; the door frames and their pediments, the fireplace surround and overmantel are beautifully carved.

For a few brief years the Brewtons enjoyed the house. Josiah Quincy, Jr., of Boston visited Charleston in 1773, and kept a journal of his impressions, not all favorable. He was a dinner

guest of the Brewtons and recorded: "Dined with considerable company at Miles Brewton, Esqur's, a gentleman of very large fortune: a most superb house said to have cost him 8000 sterling. The grandest hall I ever beheld, azure blue satin window curtains, rich blue paper with gilt, mashee borders, most elegant pictures, excessive grand and costly looking glasses, etc. . . . At Mr. Brewton's side board was very magnificent plate; a very large exquisitely wrought Goblet, most excellent workmanship and singularly beautiful." Quincy was not disturbed by what must have been a favorite pet of either Mr. or Mrs. Brewton. "A very fine bird kept familiarly playing over the room, under our chairs and the table, picking up the crumbs, etc., and perching on the window, side board and chairs: vastly pretty!" (The birds sometimes seen in colonial paintings may have been genuine pets, not necessarily the symbols or emblems they are sometimes interpreted to be.)

In August 1774, Brewton, who was a member of the South Carolina Provincial Congress and who had been among those expressing the grievances of the colonists to the royal governors, but who sensed the political strain which was to come and who was therefore hesitant to endorse a total break with Great Britain, wrote to Quincy: "I have quitted trade and am now winding up my labours for twenty-one years past. I long for shelter; when once I get under the shade it is not a little will bring me out again." In August 1775, as tension was mounting between the British and the colonists, Brewton, his wife, and family set sail for Philadelphia, where he had relatives. The newspapers reported heavy gales off the coasts of North Carolina and Virginia; the family was never heard from again. The estate, including much valuable furniture, silver, and china, was divided between his two sisters. Rebecca, Mrs. Jacob Motte, inherited the townhouse and until very recently members of the family continued to live there among some of the possessions of the original owners.

In 1769, the year in which the Miles Brewton house was completed, one of several impressive Georgian houses in Annapolis, the Chase-Lloyd house, was begun. It shows the excellent proportions and fine detailing found in a number of town and country houses built in the seaboard colonies in the 1760s. It is especially notable because a number of features, including the plasterwork in the upper stair hall, following page, mark this as one of the earliest buildings in America in which the influence of the "Adam" or neoclassic taste being made fashionable in England at the time appears. The majority of buildings in America showing such features were built after the Revolution and are often identified as "Federal." The use of this new style in the Chase-Lloyd house at such an early date indicates that some of the Southern colonists on the Eastern Seaboard kept themselves au courant with changing modes, and introduced new fashions surprisingly soon.

The house was begun for Samuel Chase, a young lawyer and enthusiast for the cause of the colonies, who soon found the costs beyond his means. He sold the unfinished brick shell to Edward Lloyd, a member of a wealthy Maryland family whose prosperity came from tobacco lands. According to tradition, Chase brought a craftsman named Scott from England to oversee the building of the new house, and he may have been responsible for the elaborate "Venetian" doorway flanked by two windows, a form more usually associated with post-Revolutionary houses in America.

Interior, second-floor drawing room, Miles Brewton House.

Upper stair hall in the Chase-Lloyd House, Annapolis, Maryland, 1769–1774.

Scott seems to have disappeared from view, and in 1770 Lloyd called upon William Buckland to supervise and carry out the interior structure and decoration. Buckland at that time had been in America for fifteen years and had a well-established reputation as master-builder, designer, and architect, having started out as an indentured servant and carpenter-joiner for George Mason of Gunston Hall in Virginia. In 1770 Buckland was one of the most sought-after architect-builders in Annapolis. In 1772, probably because Buckland was busy with several other commissions, a Mr. William Noke, who had recently come to Maryland, took

over supervision of the building for Lloyd. Among the surviving bills, during the period November 1772–October 1774 when Noke was in charge, are those from Rawlings and Barnes for decorative plasterwork. Those two men were probably responsible for the decoration in the upper stair hall. The craftsmen divided the ceiling into several geometric shapes, rectangles, a circle, and small triangles, and the spare and delicate ornamental work is confined to those areas. The tendril forms within the circle represent a survival of the rococo, while the other abstract shapes are characteristic of the new decorative work found in buildings designed and built by the architect Robert Adam and his brother in England. The former had visited Italy and Dalmatia in 1757 and upon his return introduced a subtle variety of different kinds of ornament in their buildings. Some of this was specifically based on motifs he had seen in ancient classical monuments while on the Continent. Others were vaguely or freely derived from such designs. Adam's work acquired intellectual cachet after the publication of his *Ruins of the Palace of the Emperor Diocletian at Spoleto* in 1764. Rawlings and Barnes advertised in the *Maryland Gazette* of Annapolis on February 14, 1771, that they were "Plasterers and Stucco-Workers, late from London," and that "Gentlemen may be waited on with designs for ceilings and cornices on the shortest notice." The frequent mention in the advertisements of craftsmen in the colonies that they were "late from London" or "from Bristol" or "from Edinburgh" implied that they were acquainted with the newest fashions. By employing such craftsmen a colonial patron reinforced his identification with the taste and life-style of the mother country. It can be presumed that Rawlings (or Rawlins) and Barnes were familiar with the work of Robert Adam and were emulating the new taste for the Chase-Lloyd house.

The two classical niches for statuary on either side of the central bedroom door, as well as the arched doorways on either side, contribute to the austere neoclassic ambience of this interior; such niches had been used by the Adam brothers in England. We do not know whether it was Noke, or Lloyd, or Rawlings and Barnes, who suggested these features, but together they created a noble stair hall of grace and style that represented the latest mode.

While well-to-do planters, landowners, and merchants were building town and country houses that would have looked natural in English settings, other colonists were building homes for themselves, particularly those in the inland frontier settlements, of a quite different character and with little or no concern for the niceties of fashion. Among these were some of log or hewn-log construction and some of stone.

Houses built of joined logs or log cabins appear to have been introduced into North America by the Swedes and Finns who settled in Delaware; and the Germans who came to Pennsylvania either adopted the form or used similar techniques familiar to them. The Scotch-Irish who migrated to western Pennsylvania, and then to Maryland, Virginia, North Carolina, and Kentucky, were quick to adopt this method of building for their houses.

As early as 1728 William Byrd II, owner of Westover, made two references to the use of log structures by North Carolina colonists in his manuscript, *History of the Dividing Line Betwixt Virginia and North Carolina Run in the Year of Our Lord 1728*. In the first of these he is commenting about Norfolk, Virginia: "The method of building wharves here is after the following manner. They lay down long pine logs that reach from the shore to the edge of the channel. These are bound fast together by cross pieces notched into them, according to the architecture of the log houses in North Carolina."

In the second he is writing of a neighborhood somewhere between the Dismal Swamp and Edenton on the Albemarle Sound: "Most of the houses in this part of the country are log houses, covered with pine or cypress shingles, three feet long and one broad. They are hung upon lathes with pegs, and their doors, too, turn upon wooden hinges and have wooden locks to secure them, so that the building is finished without nails at all, and, indeed, more securely than those that are nailed."

A surviving log house located in the back-country of Piedmont North Carolina, but of a later date, is the John Allen house, below. It was erected around 1782 in the town of Snow Camp and in recent years has been moved to another site in Alamance County. It is a single-unit structure with sheathing on the gable and a shed-roof extending out over front and back, a simple variation on the sheltering porches or verandas so often found in the South. Three simple posts support the roof; the single front door is placed to one side. The interstices between the logs on houses such as this were usually chinked or filled with thin stones or wedges of wood or shingle, and then daubed with some kind of mortar.

Because few logs exceeded twenty-four feet in length, most single-unit log houses were less than this in length. Typical examples were often around 18 feet long by 16 feet deep. These units were called "pens," and were sometimes divided into two rooms. If two units were combined they were called double houses or "double-pens." Sometimes the two units were linked together by an open central passage. Such structures, which seem to have originated in the northern part of the Shenandoah Valley, acquired colorful appellations in the nineteenth century, such as dog-trot, dog-run, possum-trot, or breezeway houses. Varying examples of these vernacular houses can still be found in Virginia, North Carolina, Tennessee, Kentucky, Mississippi,

John Allen House, originally in Snow Camp, now at Alamance Battleground, Alamance County, North Carolina, c. 1782.

Cyrus McCrackin cabin, Woodford County, Kentucky, built after 1755.

Kentuckians today are rightly proud of the number of "rock houses" or houses of stone laid without mortar which have survived in their state, some now bearing such evocative names as Stony Lonesome or Cave Spring. Quite a few of these are of gray limestone; the walls are often two feet thick. After the masonry courses were laid, outside joints were sealed with mortar, and the spaces between the rocks on the inside filled with mud.

There are 300 or more surviving rock houses which were built between the late 1780s and 1820. One of the earliest of these is the stone cabin of Cyrus McCrackin in Woodford County, right, built after 1755, in the famed bluegrass region. With a sure instinct for the best land the earliest settlers had found their way either down the Ohio River or through and over the mountains of southeastern Kentucky, through the Cumberland Gap, and into the beautiful rolling land of north central Kentucky. Though some white men had penetrated into Kentucky much earlier, the first recorded expedition into what was then still a part of Virginia was that led by Thomas Walker in 1750. Daniel Boone and the small band of hunters and explorers who came from their frontier homes on the Yadkin River in North Carolina (the Boones lived in a log cabin there) traversed the mountains, and first came upon the rolling plains of central Kentucky in the spring of 1769. The first permanent white settlement in the area was at Harrodsburg, begun in 1774 and firmly established in 1775. The first buildings were all of logs. It was after a battle with the Shawnee, at Point Pleasant, in present West Virginia, when the British defeated the Indians, that the way was opened for settlement by white men. Boonesborough, near present Richmond, was established in 1775.

Cyrus McCrackin was an early pioneer who came from Pennsylvania into Kentucky. His neat stone cabin is reminiscent of the Pennsylvania fieldstone houses that were built there by both the English and Germans. The McCrackin cabin has virtually no architectural embellishments. It is a two-room dwelling located on a hillside, and is in effect two structures linked together. Some other of the larger Kentucky stone houses have carved door frames and paneled interior woodwork, but even these are quite simply and conservatively handled.

McCrackin's name suggests that he was of Scotch-Irish descent. A careful study of the sixty-three first owners of surviving rock houses that can be identified reveals that 57 percent had Scotch or Irish names, as opposed to 35 percent with English names. Thus, these characteristically Kentucky stone houses seem to have been built largely by the Scotch-Irish, as were many of the log structures, for they were the frontiersmen of this era.

Painting

A number of artists found patrons in communities along the Southeastern seaboard during the middle years of the eighteenth century. Some settled in one place for the rest of their lives, others were somewhat itinerant, remaining for a season, or for several years, and then moving on. Their numbers were relatively few, but their very presence is yet another indication of a more stable and maturing society. Among them were a man of

Alabama, Louisiana, and as far west as Texas—and elsewhere. Many were built in the nineteenth century, some are sheathed in clapboard and others are forthrightly rustic, the round or hewn logs fully exposed. Still other variants on the double cabin or two-pen structure had two rooms joined together by a common chimney. This variation has been called a "saddle-bag."

Logs were used for buildings other than homes. The Waxham Presbyterian Church in South Carolina, later called "Old Waxham," in the up-country on the border between North and South Carolina, was a log structure, built around 1755–1756. Its remains were still extant in 1870. Mount Zion College at Winnsboro, another Presbyterian institution in the hills of Piedmont South Carolina, consisted initially of two log cabins, between which a frame building was placed. This institution, patterned after the College of New Jersey (Princeton), was incorporated in March 1785. The Waxham congregation sought a preacher from Scotland. The first instructor at Mount Zion was a Mr. McCaule. Colonists either from Scotland, or who were descendants of Scots who had colonized Northern Ireland and then come to America, were among those who helped to establish these two up-country institutions, and it was they who were familiar with the methods of building log structures.

sixty-five who accompanied his daughters and a son to Virginia in 1735 and spent six to eight years in the colony before returning home to die; a dancing master; a Swiss-born artist who painted the likeness of many a Charlestonian in the more than thirty years he practiced his skill in that city; an artist who may have received his training from a London drapery painter and who found ready patrons among the families of the planters of Virginia and Maryland; an American-born son of a Swedish painter in Philadelphia who settled in Maryland and was a responsible churchman and landowner as well as an artist. Portraits by these artists have survived and are identifiable. From records and from other surviving paintings we know there were a number of other artists who also worked in the South during this period. Some of these offered their skills as painters of landscapes, altar-pieces, and sea-pieces, but virtually nothing has survived to show the success of their enterprise. Fortunately, a group of watercolors and drawings by John Bartram has survived. He was a talented native-born artist-naturalist whose wanderings took him deep into the South, where he recorded what he saw for his scientific colleagues.

The portraits of Mann Page II and his wife, below, are now believed to be the work of Charles Bridges (c. 1670–1747), the artist who arrived in the fullness of years in Williamsburg in 1735. On the back of Mrs. Page's portrait is an inscription that is copied directly from what had been the eighteenth-century signature, "Charles Bridges fecit." This is one of several interrelated clues that have led to the identification of a group of paintings as the probable work of this artist.

In the pair, the warm and brilliant colors in the male portrait of Mann Page II contrast with the muted and cooler tones in the portrait of Mrs. Page and child. There is a sense of openness and spaciousness in both compositions because in each case a substantial area of the canvas is given to background. In both, the backgrounds are umber with an admixture of reds. The face of Mann Page is well modeled; the flesh tones are warm and ruddy, the shadow of the nose and the line of the brows, as well as the flesh of a double chin, firmly delineated. The white of the lace stock and shirt, and of the gloves, contrasts with the scarlet waistcoat. The edges and the highlights of the coat are done in a brighter tone, and put in with long, broad brush strokes. It is a strong and forceful portrait.

The portrait of Mrs. Mann Page II is more austere and somewhat awkward. The composition is based on a mezzotint by Smith after a painting by Kneller of the Duchess of Ormonde.

Charles Bridges. "Mann Page II." c. 1743. Oil on canvas. College of William and Mary, Williamsburg, Virginia.

Charles Bridges. "Mrs. Mann Page II and Child." c. 1743. Oil on canvas. College of William and Mary, Williamsburg, Virginia.

Charles Bridges. "John Bolling, Jr." 1735–1743. Oil on canvas. College of William and Mary, Williamsburg, Virginia.

The hand is turned at a characteristic angle, and the transition from cheekline to background fairly sharp. Her gown is cut in the simple loose and flowing lines that were characteristic of the period. The modeling is done in broad, toned areas with several sharply delineated folds of drapery to further define major shapes. The overall proportions of the body do not quite work; the torso is too long and the transition to the lap marked by the use of a dark blue drape. The upper part of her right hand is too long, and the hand hangs awkwardly. The child's head does not rest convincingly on the neck, and a cloak of dull red conveniently eliminates the problem of rendering the contours of the child's clothing and body. In both portraits there is a somber dignity.

When Bridges arrived in Williamsburg with his children he had introductions to both the lieutenant governor and the president of the College of William and Mary, for they wrote back to colleagues in London that they had met him and would encourage him. Soon Colonel William Byrd II of Westover reported that Bridges had "drawn" his own children and several others in the neighborhood, and commended his services to former Lieutenant Governor Spotswood, comparing Bridges with the English court painters, Sir Peter Lely and Sir Godfrey Kneller. "And tho' he have not the Masterly hand of a Lelly, or a Kneller, yet had he lived so long ago when places were given to the most Deserving, he might have pretended to be the Ser-

Attributed to William Dering. "Mrs. Mordecai Booth." c. 1745–1749. Oil on canvas. Private collection.

74

and women in the mid-eighteenth century. His virtuosity as a drapery painter can best be seen in some of his three-quarter-length portraits of women.

Among Wollaston's most charming paintings are those of children. In a portrait of the young Virginia girl, Mary Lightfoot, left, the figure is set off against a dark brown-black background and placed within an oval. The edges are soft, and some melt into the background. She gazes directly at the viewer. Her features are well defined. She had the large eyes that are characteristic of the artist. She is serious but not solemn. The tones in the rose-pink gown are highlighted by an almost chalky white. The lace is rendered with soft grace. The gown of the girl is similar in cut to those worn by women; she holds herself in the erect posture that stiff stays enforced upon adult females—either she had been taught to so hold herself or there were a few stays in her dress. She lightly fondles a well-dressed doll, an adult doll clothed in a golden yellow gown or shift. This elegantly clad doll appears in a number of Wollaston's paintings of children and must have been a prop he used to help the child pose. Anyone familiar with a number of Wollaston's portraits finds it easy to recognize his characteristic manner and certain idiosyncrasies. Among the latter is a lack of understanding of the bone structure of the hand, as can be seen here in the flaccid left hand of the girl. Oftentimes the large eyes are slightly down-tilted giving the sitter a slightly exotic and sensuous mien, and there is a certain sameness in characterization. At his best Wollaston shows his subjects as both warm in feeling and elegant in appearance. His work, too, is rococo in its grace and finesse. In fact, he helped to introduce and popularize this style in America.

Mary Lightfoot was the daughter of the king's counselor, William Lightfoot. She later married Colonel William Allen, of Surry County, Virginia, a descendant of Arthur Allen, and they lived in Bacon's Castle, the family's house.

From 1760 to his death in 1778 the painter John Hesselius made his permanent residence in Anne Arundel County in Maryland, not far from Annapolis. He was the son of Gustavus Hesselius, a Swedish-trained painter who came to America in 1711 and settled in Philadelphia. The father was one of the first well-trained Europeans to establish himself in the American colonies, though his surviving oeuvre is small. The son, John, born in 1728, would have gained familiarity with the basic techniques and materials of painting from his father. He then seems to have set off on his own; his first signed painting, in 1750, is of a Virginia subject, and soon he had other patrons in Virginia, Maryland, and Delaware. He very probably saw and was influenced by Wollaston's work. He was established in Anne Arundel County by 1760, and in 1763 married a Maryland woman. He lived there the rest of his life, and he continued to paint acquaintances in Maryland and in Virginia.

One of the legal documents that helps to trace the course of Hesselius's career is the sale to Governor Horatio Sharpe in 1763 of some land adjacent to that on which Sharpe built his fine country house, Whitehall, in 1764–1765. Around this same time Hesselius painted Sharpe, a military man who was Colonial Governor of Maryland from 1753 to 1769, right. He is shown in uniform against a dark background. The pose, with one hand resting on the hip and the other on a table, is a typical masculine pose of the period, at once controlled and at ease. It can be seen in the work of Robert Feke, the New York–born artist who worked in Boston and Philadelphia, and who may have influenced Hesselius early in his career. John Singleton Copley painted at least one subject with a similar stance. It was also used by Joseph Blackburn, an English artist who worked in Boston from 1755 to 1760, and is similar to poses recorded in English mezzotints. There is a mezzotint probably published between 1755 and 1767 by McArdell after a painting of Lord Townshend in which the uniformed subject has a stance only slightly different from that of Sharpe. Theus quite clearly used the same mezzotint as the basis for his portrait of Colonel Barnard Elliott, and interestingly enough, the pose which Peter Manigault took for the English artist Allan Ramsay is somewhat similar. In this case Hesselius and Sharpe may have selected the pose because they consciously or unconsciously knew how right and fashionable it was, having seen its like a number of times, or the mezzotint may have been the direct model. The painting is highly finished, which is typical of Hesselius's work.

John Hesselius. "Horatio Sharpe, Colonial Governor of Maryland." c. 1760. Oil on canvas. Private collection.

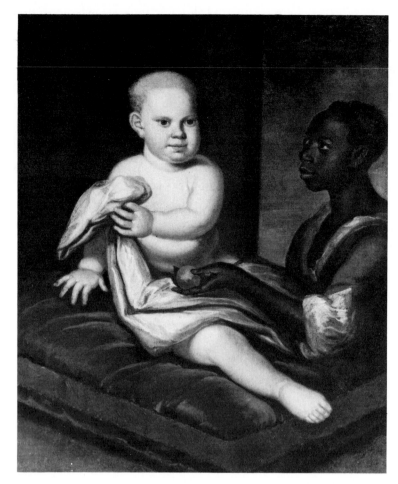

John Hesselius. "Gustavus Hesselius, Jr., and Servant Girl." c. 1767. Oil on canvas. Baltimore Museum of Art.

and forms, and here all Hesselius might have learned from looking at the paintings of Feke and Wollaston is displayed. There is a sense of dignity and gravity that may partly have been engendered by the character of the subject, for Quakers eschewed pretension, yet respected solid material things, such as well-made clothing of fine fabrics. Whatever the conscious intent, the artist has created a somber and sympathetic portrait. The pose could once again be said to be typical of the period and to have its prototype in an English mezzotint. But this is virtually irrelevant, for by this time Hesselius had assimilated these formulas and made them his own, eliminating all that was fussy and busy in them.

Among other portraitists who worked in Virginia were John Durand and Matthew Pratt. William Dunlap, the first historian of American art, reported in 1834 that Durand "painted an immense number of portraits in Virginia; his works are hard and dry, but appear to have been strong likenesses, with less vulgarity of style than artists of his *calibre* generally possess." Matthew Pratt was a Philadelphian who spent several years in England, returning in 1768. He was in Virginia in 1773.

John Hesselius's father, Gustavus, is believed to have executed the first religious painting to be commissioned in colonial America, a *Last Supper*, now probably lost, for St. Barnabas's

John Hesselius. "Elizabeth Sprigg" (née Galloway). 1764. Oil on canvas. Inscription on back of original canvas: "Elizabeth/Sprigg/Aetat 43/J. Hesselius/1764." Art Institute of Chicago.

A touching family portrait, above, by Hesselius shows his infant son, Gustavus Hesselius, Jr., who lived only from 1765 to 1767, with a young servant girl. The painting of the child is probably posthumous, so it is no surprise that the pose of the baby on its cushion comes directly from an English mezzotint, that of Lord Brey by Smith, after a painting by Kneller. The rather mature face given to the infant has the full cheeks, slightly receding high forehead, and forward-jutting jaw that occurs in a number of Hesselius's paintings. The portrait of the young servant girl is sensitively rendered from life, and he has conveyed a sense of dignity and sorrow in the sober presentation of this young black woman.

In his mature works Hesselius produced some memorable portraits, one of which is the three-quarter-length portrait of the forty-three-year-old Elizabeth Sprigg, painted in 1764, right. Mrs. Sprigg was a wealthy Quaker who, as a widow herself, lived for many years with her widowed mother at Cedar Park, a family estate in Anne Arundel County. A suggestion of open park and sky breaks up the dark background. The face of the plain and rosy-cheeked matron is framed with a white cap of thin material, her full figure garbed in a dress of fine gray satin. There are no fetching laces at the sleeve or neck, merely a scarf of sheer fabric that covers the subject's throat and bosom. The bright blue drapery enlivens the composition. The artist has captured a variety of textural and tonal qualities in his rendering of the clothing. Drapery painting is something of an exercise in abstract shapes

Bishop Roberts. "Prospect of Charles Town." c. 1735–1739. Watercolor and India ink. Colonial Williamsburg.

Church in Queen Anne's Parish, Prince George's County, Maryland, in 1720. There are scattered references to other religious paintings or to paintings other than portraits. In 1764 Mrs. Elizabeth Stith of Surry County, Virginia, bequeathed money to her Parish of Southwark: "I would have Moses and Aaron drawn at full length holding up between them the Ten Commandments . . ." She did not say by whom this was to be executed. In 1857 Bishop Meade recorded a letter in which a woman described her own and her mother's recollection of a painting of the Last Judgment that once hung in the Old Poplar Spring Church in Gloucester, Virginia, near Rosewell: "I remember seeing part of what seemed a very large cord and tassel. Mamma said there used to be an angel just where the curtain was drawn on one side, with a trumpet in his hand, and rolling on toward him were vast bodies of clouds with angels in them, and that she used to fancy one of the faces was like her dear little brother John, who was drowned when only ten years old. . . . I feel sure that then I first understood about the Last Judgment." Unfortunately, no other record of this work, so evocative to the child, remains.

We have the names of literally dozens of other painters, limners, miniaturists, and drawing teachers who may have practiced their craft, sometimes briefly, in the colonial South of the Eastern Seaboard. So far it appears that little of their work has survived, though there is always the hope that new discoveries will be made. How many commissions did Warwell, "PAINTER from London," get after he placed elaborate advertisements in the *South Carolina Gazette and Country Journal* of January 21, 1766, and how genuinely versatile was he? He said he could paint history-pieces, heraldry, altar-pieces, coaches, landscapes, window blinds, sea-pieces, chimney blinds, flowers, screens, and fruit. Moreover, he offered to paint rooms in oil or water in "a new taste." He could also do "Deceptive Temples, Triumphal Arches, Obelisks, Statues, etc. for Groves and Gardens."

His career was cut short by death in June of the following year. Equally tantalizing are the short careers in Charleston of John and Hamilton Stevenson. On September 12, 1773, John placed an advertisement in which he described himself as a limner who could paint history, portrait, landscapes, and miniatures, family and conversation-pieces (small-scale group portraits), as well as perspective views, from nature, of towns, streets, villas, or plantations. By 1774 he was joined by a relative, possibly his brother, Hamilton, and they announced the opening of a Drawing and Painting Academy in which they offered to teach these subjects "after the Manner they are taught in the Roman Schools." The war probably cut short their plans, and by 1780 both were in Jamaica. In 1782, when the British were occupying the city, Hamilton reappeared in Charleston. Since no more is heard of him, it is possible he left in December of the same year when the British evacuated.

A watercolor and India ink drawing of Charleston, above, done by Bishop Roberts between 1735 and 1739, has survived. In the background are the red brick or stucco buildings along the Battery as seen from the opposite shore. Red and green tiles are on the roofs. On the far left the British flag flies from what was Granville's bastion, and on the far right the tower of St. Philip's can be seen. The foreground is filled with all manner of ships— skiffs and rowboats, sailing ships and sloops—a record of the marine craft of an increasingly important harbor. Bishop Roberts and his wife are first recorded in Charleston in 1735. He died in 1739 and she lived until 1761. He advertised that he could do portrait painting, engraving, heraldry, landscapes for chimney-pieces, and "draughts" or views of houses. The limited range of colors in this watercolor can be explained because it was apparently done as a basis for a print. The engraving, done by W. H. Toms, was printed in London in 1739. A lengthy text accompanied the print, extolling the prosperity and products of the port

William Bartram. "American Lotus or Water Chinquapin." 1761–1762. Pencil on paper. Fothergill Album, British Museum, London.

which he made as a young man of twenty-two, to the home of his uncle on the Cape Fear River in Bladen County, North Carolina.

Bartram (1739–1823) was the son of the Philadelphia naturalist John Bartram. He had begun to draw birds and plants by the age of fourteen; when he was sixteen his father wrote Collinson that botany and drawing were his son's "darling delight." William Bartram spent the years 1773–1777 exploring the Southeast for Fothergill, gathering seeds and specimens. The Seminole Indians affectionately called him Pucpuggy—the flower-hunter. He returned to Philadelphia during the Revolution, and in 1791 his well-known *Travels*, a rambling narrative of his observations and experiences, was first published. A joy to read, the book was a great success and the basis for his fame. Between 1791 and 1799 it was republished in London, published in Philadelphia and Dublin, and translated into German, Dutch, and French. It was and is important for its accurate information about the flora and fauna of the Southeast—Florida, the Carolinas, and Georgia—but also for what it tells about the Indians. More than that,

William Bartram. "Marsh Pink." Watercolor on paper. Fothergill Album, British Museum, London.

of Charleston, and thus serving as a propaganda piece for the royal province. By the time Mrs. Roberts had it for sale in Charleston in 1740 the artist was in his grave. The watercolor suggests he was essentially a draftsman and perhaps had had experience as a marine painter. His wife tried to pursue a career as an engraver/painter but had great difficulty. A miniature has recently been identified as by her hand.

The watercolors and drawings of William Bartram were intended for the eyes of Peter Collinson, Dr. John Fothergill, and others in Britain who were deeply interested in gathering all the information they could about American natural history. A small album of them ultimately found its way to the security of the great natural history collection of the British Museum and has recently been published. In a bold and exuberant rendering of the American lotus, or water chinquapin, above, Bartram combines an upright and flat depiction of the leaf with what might be called a heron's-eye view of the flowers and leaves as they rise out of the water. As a naturalist Bartram succeeded completely in showing the exact appearance of the leaves and blossoms in various views and stages, but he does so with a poetic and artistic imagination, untutored in the traditional sense, which makes for a strong and pleasing composition. On the left the Venus's-flytrap is rendered in smaller scale. This is in fact the first historic sketch of this plant, which the Indians called Tipiti-wicket, and which is noted for its sensitive leaves that close when touched. Bartram probably did the drawing during a visit in 1761–1762,

Travels has a lyrical, poetical quality that has attracted and influenced poets and writers from Coleridge and Wordsworth to Emerson, Thoreau, and Lafcadio Hearn. The visual and esthetic component of his imagination is all-important. It has been said that in his writing, he, as much as anyone, embodied or expressed the eighteenth-century movement of *sentiment de la nature*.

Bartram's watercolor of the marsh pink *(Sabatia grandiflora)*, lower left, is a more conventional botanical drawing. This is the same marsh flower depicted many years earlier by John White (page 6). The specimen plucked by White may have just happened to have a straight stem, and that by Bartram a curvilinear form, but each blossom, stem, and leaf in the Bartram rendering seems to have a light, lyrical, or vigorous thrust of its own not seen in the sixteenth-century example.

The career of Henry Benbridge (1743–1812) covers a span from the colonial into the period of the early Republic. Born in Philadelphia, his first awareness of painter's techniques may have come from seeing Wollaston's work. Young Benbridge was helped by his wealthy stepfather to study in Italy and England from 1765 to 1770. He was one of the many young Americans who were encouraged by Benjamin West in London. While in Italy, Benbridge was commissioned by the famed journalist Boswell to paint the Corsican hero Pascal Paoli, a portrait which established his reputation in Florence and in London. By 1772 he was in Charleston, where he succeeded Theus as the most popular painter in that city. There is a subtle idealizing and classicizing quality about his portraits which may be the result of his European training at the time the neoclassic taste was coming to the fore.

Benbridge's professionalism in handling paint can be seen in his portrait of Charles Cotesworth Pinckney, right, done while the latter was in his late twenties, and already launched on his long career in public service as soldier, diplomat, and legislator. Benbridge placed his subject in a relaxed pose against a dark-toned background, opening up to light on the right and a little on the left. The bright red turnings of the uniform and sash add color and dash. Careful analysis of this painting by staff members of the National Portrait Gallery has indicated that when it was first painted Pinckney was shown wearing the red coat of a British officer, that is, when he was a member of the pre-Revolutionary Charles Town Militia, around 1773. The present, visible uniform is that of the Second South Carolina Regiment, which was organized to be responsible for local defense. Thus parts of the portrait were probably repainted in 1775.

Pinckney was the son of Charles and Eliza Lucas Pinckney (who as a young girl had introduced indigo as a crop). He went with his family to England as a youth, was educated at Oxford and Middle Temple, and studied botany, chemistry, and military science in France. When he returned to America he was immediately involved in public service, maintaining at the same time his law practice and an interest in agriculture. He was, among many things, a supporter of the movement which led to the founding of South Carolina College. During his career, his portrait was taken by a number of artists. Although perhaps in this case the painting was done at his own or his family's request on the eve of his departure for a military campaign, later portraits may have

Henry Benbridge. "Charles Cotesworth Pinckney." c. 1773–1774. Oil on canvas. National Portrait Gallery, Washington, D.C.

been at the request of others. He was one of a series of "Heroes" painted by J. Paul and engraved by C. Tiebout in the early 1800s.

Benbridge took the side of the patriots and was one of those held prisoner in Charleston harbor during the war. He was back in the city by 1784 and in 1788 he represented limners in a parade celebrating the adoption of the Federal Constitution. Around 1800 he settled in Norfolk. His wife was apparently an accomplished miniaturist. Little is known of her work, though a small group of miniatures has been attributed to her.

American artists and patrons generally showed little interest at this time in what academic painters and connoisseurs identified as "history" painting. These were complex subject paintings, based on classical or religious themes, expressing an idea or telling a heroic story with intent to elevate or uplift the mind. Neither were a large proportion of artists in England interested in such paintings, though they gave lip service to the idea, and patrons were more liable to purchase them abroad. Interestingly, two transplanted Americans, West and Copley, were among the more successful history painters in the second half of the eighteenth century. Their success was partly due to the fact that they selected for their subjects well-known and relatively recent events, thus creating a type of painting that was heroic reportage and not quite "history" painting in the sense that, say, a French

academician of the seventeenth century would have understood it. The painting of *Washington and His Generals at Yorktown*, above, probably by Charles Willson Peale, is close to this concept of reportage and is no more than that. It is a serene work, capturing the character of the landscape along the river, and showing ships at sail, military aides leading horses, windmill and buildings in the distance. It is only after looking twice that the tops of sunken ships, dead horses on the shore, and the details of the fort, "Fuselliers' Redoubt" are noticed. On the far right a group of military officers is clustered. There is a sense that the landscape was largely finished before the military group was put in—in essence it is a landscape painting, but the hints of the strife of war and the presence of the officers make it something more, a document memorializing the victory over Cornwallis in October 1781.

Robert Gilmor, Jr., a noted collector of his generation, writing in 1845, described this piece as "a curious relic of our Revolutionary history, being a view of Yorke-Town in Virginia . . . painted by the venerable Charles W. Peale." Though unsigned, it is generally believed to be by that artist. (Two other versions exist; one, less developed in detail, has an old inscription that says it was painted by James Peale, who was the brother of C. W. Peale.) Charles Willson Peale's forte was portraits, but he sometimes included landscape vistas in the backgrounds. He had painted each of the officers shown during the war years so he could have composed this group using his own paintings as sources. The group represents the meeting of the generals of the American and French armies at Yorktown. All wear the black-and-white cockade of the Franco-American alliance. General Washington is shown in the center. As he points toward the river with his riding crop his arm crosses the figure of the Marquis de Lafayette, painted in an American uniform. Between them is the head of General Benjamin Lincoln, who in 1778 was given command of the Southern Department. Comte de Rochambeau and his chief of staff, General de Chastellux, are shown in their blue-and-scarlet French uniforms. Washington's aide-de-camp and military secretary, Lieutenant Colonel Tench Tilghman, is on the far right. He was a close friend of Peale's. There is no attempt to be dramatic or to emphasize the heroic aspects of the battle and siege, but rather the quiet aftermath is depicted, history as record, and here record of place as much as people.

Peale was born in Annapolis in 1741 and started out as an apprentice to a saddler. He set up his own business in 1762 but was soon attracted to painting. He received his first lesson from John Hesselius. Subsequently he made a trip to New England and was able to see the work of Smibert and spend a day with Copley. Between 1767 and 1769 he was in London, studying with Benjamin West. He returned to Annapolis and there began his career as a painter. He traveled widely in Virginia and Maryland, and also had commissions in Philadelphia. He then served three years in the Continental Army. In 1778 he settled permanently in Philadelphia, where he enjoyed a long career as painter, museum keeper, scientist, and inventor, in what was the foremost city in the country. Throughout his life he kept close ties with his Southern connections. His sons, especially Rembrandt, spent parts of their careers there.

Peale probably wouldn't have felt himself capable of the kind of large-scale and complex composition that a heroic history painting would have required, nor would he have had the time. In 1786 Peale opened his museum in the State House (Independence Hall) in Philadelphia and made a concerted effort to paint important Americans—again, he was concerned to make a record for the future. His subjects included Revolutionary officers, men who had been signers of the Declaration of Independence, members of the Continental Congress, and other political leaders, and then gradually a roster of distinguished men of science, explorers, architects, and others. Many Southerners were among his sitters.

One of Peale's most engaging portraits of his Maryland acquaintances is that of *William Smith and Grandson*, below, done in 1788. The sitter is shown in a relaxed pose, resting one arm on a marble table; he rests his other hand affectionately on the head of his grandson. A pair of columns and a grandiose building are no doubt figments of Peale's imagination, designed to serve as background in the European tradition. More interesting is the landscape scene to the left, showing Eutaw, Smith's estate outside Baltimore, named for the Battle of Eutaw Springs where the Americans, under the command of Smith's son-in-law, had a decisive victory. Smith's house is a vernacular building with a gambrel roof and porch across the entire front; a mill is also shown. Peale noted the progress of the painting in his journal, from the stretching of the canvas, the individual sittings of Smith and his grandson—first the faces and then the drapery—through the finished composition. This included a journey with the son-in-law to the "county seat 4 miles distant, where I made 3 drawings with the machine and returned in the Evening." Peale apparently had a camera obscura or similar instrument to help him in drawing a perspective view.

Peale also recorded the time spent in painting the books on the table. The one in the foreground is opened at a page headed GARDENING, and alongside there is a pruning knife. The child holds a peach, and a cut branch rests on the table. A visual pun is suggested; the child is a branch from the Smith tree. Peale, who loved natural science, sometimes created excellent vignettes of still life and landscape in his paintings, often to shed light on the character of his subject. However, he seldom produced an entire canvas in these genres.

In this case it was the son-in-law, General Otho Holland Williams, who commissioned the painting rather than the subject. Williams had already been painted by Peale. A combination of affection for his father-in-law and pride in his own son, a desire to have family continuity recorded, friendship with Peale and a respect for the latter's talents, might have prompted the commission. William Smith, the subject, was an important Baltimore merchant and active in public affairs.

There is a certain amount of overlap and continuity among the lives of the painters who worked in the South before and during the Revolutionary years. Dering appears in Williamsburg at the time Bridges departs. Benbridge follows Theus in Charleston. Wollaston paints in Maryland and Virginia for a number of years, succeeding Dering and surpassing him in quality and quantity.

The young Hesselius learned from his father and assimilates a sense of style from men such as Feke and Wollaston. Peale gets his first painting lessons from Hesselius. Benbridge may have had contact with Wollaston. Though each worked to a degree in isolation there were connections and the beginnings of a sense of community among these artists. Patronage is from individuals and families, and only occasionally from a church or institution. Some families established a tradition of patronage and saw to it that members of each generation were painted, making for impressive records and collections. Some of these families remained rooted in the same house, so that one can still see and appreciate the cumulative effect of their continued patronage.

Sculpture

The talents of the artisan carvers and stonecutters who worked in the South in the pre-Revolutionary years were largely employed

Charles Willson Peale. "William Smith and Grandson." 1788. Oil on canvas. Virginia Museum of Art, Richmond.

Tombstone of George Hesket. George Hesket was born in Boston, Massachusetts, in 1690, died August 31, 1747. Slate. Churchyard of the Circular Congregational Church, Charleston, S.C.

two in New York. The Southern statues were commissioned from England by the citizens of South Carolina and Virginia in the third quarter of the eighteenth century, in both cases to commemorate a distinguished person and to enhance their capital city. The commissions were given only after due consideration and with full support of a legislative body. The decision to erect such public monuments suggests the sense of permanence, the sense of a well-established society which the colonial peoples now felt.

The Commons House of Assembly of South Carolina ordered a statue of William Pitt "to be done in the most finished and elegant manner" in 1766. They chose to honor Pitt because he had defended "freedom . . . by promoting a repeal of the Stamp Act." The erection of a major piece of sculpture was no everyday event. When it was put in place on July 5, 1770, "almost the whole of the inhabitants" turned out, twenty-six cannons were discharged, and three huzzas shouted. The figure was of marble, "the habit Roman," that is, garbed in a toga as a Roman orator. Thus the artist, responding to the increased admiration for the antique and a theory of current taste, sought to endow a contemporary hero with a timeless, classical image. Carved by Joseph Wilton, the statue was a replica of one he had made for a similar commission for New York. It has suffered vicissitudes but still stands, now in Washington Park behind City Hall, in Charleston.

The Virginians chose to honor their governor, Norborne Berkeley, Baron de Botetourt, who died in Williamsburg on October 15, 1770. He had been admired for his good will, and in 1771 the Virginia legislature voted "with one united voice" monies for an appropriate statue. It was assumed that an English artist would be needed, and in due time Richard Hayward was selected. Hayward not only did figures but had been employed to do decorative architectural sculpture in major English country houses such as Blenheim. The sculpture, right, arrived in June 1773 and was erected in the plaza in front of the Capitol. The head was based on a wax medallion. The figure is fully clothed in contemporary dress, including a large cloak that gives mass; the structure of the figure itself is poorly executed, and the whole seems to lack dignity.

Though the sculptor did not depict Botetourt in the antique manner, he did, on the pedestal, upper right, introduce the neoclassical. Most noticeable is the use of the Greek anthemion or palmette motif across the top. This statue and other smaller objects helped to introduce the new taste to Williamsburg in the years immediately before the war.

After the Revolution, the Assembly of Virginia was quick in wanting to memorialize the leaders responsible for bringing the new nation to fruition. In 1781 they commissioned the French sculptor Jean Antoine Houdon to make a portrait bust of Lafayette. Houdon had done a bust of Benjamin Franklin and knew a number of Americans in Paris. In 1784 the Virginia Assembly resolved that "a statue of George Washington, to be of the finest marble and best workmanship" be commissioned. By that time, the Assembly was already sitting in Richmond. As early as 1776 Jefferson drew up the act calling for the transfer of the capital to a location closer to the center of population, which was expanding steadily westward. The act passed in 1779 and the transfer took place in 1780. Six blocks were allocated for the construction

in the building or furniture trades, in tomb-cutting, or other commemorative work. The high level of carving on some of the furniture that has been identified as having been done in the South attests to their skill. So does work found in Drayton Hall or the Miles Brewton house, or in churches such as St. Michael's in Charleston. However, formal or monumental sculpture was still a luxury beyond the aspiration of most individual colonists or communities.

Some tombstones in Charleston and Georgetown, South Carolina, were imported from New England, where slate was plentiful, but others may have been carved locally since several craftsmen advertised their skills in Charleston newspapers. An example may be the tombstone of George Hesket, above, in the churchyard of the Circular Congregational Church (originally the Presbyterian Church). A portrait bust in low relief is carved within a circle; this is framed in the pediment with leafy foliage similar to that which might grace furniture or a mantelpiece. The formula of a portrait in a circle, within a pediment with foliated border, is found on several Charleston tombstones.

Two of the four monumental sculptures that were erected in the colonies before the Revolution were in the South, the other

Detail of pedestal of the Botetourt statue.

of public buildings, and Jefferson no doubt already had visions of classically republican buildings for the new Commonwealth.

When the Assembly commissioned the statue of Washington, Jefferson was in Paris, and wrote back recommending that Houdon, whose reputation was "unrivaled in Europe" be chosen. Moreover, he suggested that Houdon be sent to America in order to take Washington's features from life. Houdon was caught up in the French admiration for the budding nation and immediately offered to come, "to leave the statues of kings unfinished, & to go to America to take the true figure by actual inspiration & measurement."

Houdon arrived in September 1785 and by October 2 was at Mount Vernon. He took a life mask, modeled a bust in terra cotta, and took careful measurements of the tall war hero. It was decided that the statue was to be life-sized. Houdon spent October 2–19 at Mount Vernon, then departed on Washington's barge to Alexandria and thence by stage to Philadelphia. The sculptor was back in Paris by January 1786 and worked on the statue in his studio during the next two years. Houdon had apparently planned to show the hero-patriot in "the garb of antiquity." However, Washington, learning of this, tactfully suggested that a taste for modern dress had been introduced by Mr. West (he was referring to West's heroic interpretation of the *Death of General Wolfe*) and that there might be "some little deviation in favor of the modern costume." This was agreed upon. The clay statue was finished in 1788. It was put into marble, which was brought from Italy to Paris, between 1788 and 1791, but it was not put into place in the new Virginia Capitol building until 1796. The statue, right, is a noble and impressive work, timeless yet immediate. It has the dignity and presence that was apparently one of Washington's special qualities. He is shown wearing the uniform of the Revolution, but this has been simplified so that details are unobtrusive. He rests his arm on a bundle of thirteen rods or fasces, symbolic of the thirteen colonies. His sword is hung on this, the battle is over. Behind him is a plow, representing the farmer-statesman. He is represented as a modern Cincinnatus, a citizen-soldier who has retired to his fields. This imagery was fully understood. A group of officers, with Washington as their first president, organized themselves into the Society of the Cincinnati, dedicated to perpetuating the ideals of the Revolution, maintaining the friendships, and aiding those officers and families who might be in need. They chose their name for the Roman general who had first proclaimed the ideal of citizen-soldier. The favorable reception of Virginia's venture in commissioning a monumental sculpture encouraged other states to follow suit.

Products of Craftsmen

In the eighteenth century in Europe, for reasons that are not fully understood, furniture attained a more important place in everyday life of the middle classes than heretofore. This was probably in part because there was an expansion in the size of the population and a related rise in the size of the middle class. A variety of furniture for special uses was introduced, and astonishing levels of artistry were achieved. A testimony to the vitality and suitability of the forms created in this period is the fact that many of them have been revived, copied, and modified in the nineteenth and twentieth centuries. To look at "traditional" furniture in the present day is to see types, shapes, and forms created in large part in the eighteenth century.

American craftsmen and their patrons shared in this seeming upsurge of interest and concern with furniture. Among surviving pieces there are not only handsome examples created for domestic use but also some very interesting ceremonial or institutional ones.

Research extending over the last fifty years or more, intensified during the last decade, has made possible the identification of a remarkable amount of furniture made in what is now the American South during the middle years of the eighteenth century, remarkable because earlier it was thought that little fine furniture was made in this region. The number of surviving Southern pieces seems to be fewer than that in areas to the north, perhaps because the South had fewer and smaller urban centers where craftsmen could flourish, or there may have been more losses due to fires, hurricanes, wars, and earthquakes. Hot, humid weather is hard on objects, and thus more pieces may have deteriorated and decayed. Several periods of great prosper-

J. A. Houdon, Paris. "George Washington." 1788. Marble. State House, Richmond, Virginia.

ity, when old furniture was discarded for new, also account for losses.

Although this new research is increasingly broadening into the study of the lives of the craftsmen who made the furniture and of the business and working relationships among them, our knowledge of eighteenth-century furniture and furniture-making in the South is still incomplete and uneven. A good deal is now known about Williamsburg. Charleston was probably the most important center for craftsmanship on the Southeastern seaboard. There is ample documentation in newspaper advertisements and elsewhere to indicate that from around 1730 onward a sizable number of cabinetmakers worked there. However, few of the known individual pieces of furniture from Charleston can be directly documented to the maker's workshop, so it is not yet possible to define as many interrelationships among surviving examples as has been done for the Williamsburg area. Annapolis, in Maryland, was yet another center for cabinetmaking and some fine pieces can be attributed to that city with some certainty. The diverse products of North Carolina craftsmen are gradually coming to light. Less is known of early work in Georgia. Documented evidence about craftsmen who worked in the growing city of New Orleans is scanty.

The table shown in the upper right is believed to have been made in 1740 in New Ebenezer, Georgia, by one of the group of Protestant Salzburgers whom Oglethorpe had invited to settle in the newly established colony. The bulbous turnings of the splayed legs suggest a lingering taste for the familiar forms of the slightly earlier style which the craftsman probably knew in his homeland. The stretchers and the base are of hard yellow or "southern yellow" pine native to the South and frequently used, especially as a secondary wood, in furniture. The presence of this pine supports the traditional Southern history of the piece. The legs are of sweet gum and the apron of yellow poplar.

The communion table, lower right, is also of yellow pine, with legs of poplar. The vase-shape turnings reflect the more restrained taste of the style called William and Mary. In both this and the preceding piece the four stretchers at the base give added strength to the form and visually assure the viewer of its solidity. The ball feet of the communion table represent a continuity of form between the styles of the late seventeenth and early eighteenth centuries.

This table was "always," so far as is known, in the Fork Church (St. Martin's) in Doswell, Virginia, Hanover County, which was built in 1736–1740, and whose rector for many years was Patrick Henry, the uncle of the patriot. St. Martin's is an Anglican church and the table is typical of the form and dimensions of communion tables that came into usage in England in the late seventeenth and early eighteenth centuries. They were relatively small and movable and were usually placed at the east end in front of the altar-piece. A similar table, with heavier proportions, which was used in Yeocomico Church in Westmoreland County, Virginia, has survived.

The architectural chair for the Speaker of the House of Burgesses, following page, made for the Capitol in Williamsburg, is, like the communion table, a ceremonial or public piece of furniture. It is of American black walnut with yellow pine, poplar, and oak as secondary woods, and was most likely fashioned in Williamsburg itself sometime around 1730. There is a very similar chair in the Chowan County Courthouse in North Carolina, which seems to have been based on this Virginia chair. Both are close in form to the Speaker's chair used in the British House of Commons. The extraordinary paneled and pedimented back of the Williamsburg example bespeaks status. The chair was unusual enough to prompt a visitor in 1777 to record it in his notebook with a sketch emphasizing the splayed and curling arm terminals, which are the kind found in furniture in the William

Stretcher table, Georgia, c. 1740. Yellow pine, yellow poplar, sweet gum, top restored. Museum of Early Southern Decorative Arts, Winston-Salem, N.C.

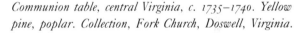

Communion table, central Virginia, c. 1735–1740. Yellow pine, poplar. Collection, Fork Church, Doswell, Virginia.

and Mary style. The columnar vase supports are classically detailed, more so than those of the communion table. The cabriole legs and pad feet show a response to the new taste for curved forms associated with the Queen Anne style. (This is the usual term, although, in fact, the style with its characteristic smooth curving lines evolved during the reigns of George I and George II, and many of the forms derive from Dutch, Chinese, and Indian furniture.)

The subdued but curved flowing line of the cabriole legs dominates the silhouette of the tea table, right, which has descended in the Galt family of Williamsburg. The curved or contoured skirt serves as a perfect transition to the top. There is a spare but elegant feeling. The tea table is linked by style to the Speaker's chair, and also displays a number of features of construction, such as the way that pieces forming the skirt pass across the top edge of the cabriole legs and are mitered at the corners, which have been found in still other pieces associated with Williamsburg.

These are the first links in a series of interrelationships which, thanks to the careful collecting and documentation that have gone on at the Colonial Williamsburg Foundation since 1930, help to provide a fairly comprehensive picture of cabinetmaking in and around Williamsburg from 1710 to 1790. Because it was the political center in Virginia in the eighteenth century, the cabinetmakers there may well have been among the most important providers of fine furniture of the region. Comparable research on other possible centers of craftsmanship, such as Norfolk, Winchester, Fredericksburg, Alexandria, and Richmond, Virginia, remains incomplete, and it may never be possible to assemble as much data about them. (A devastating fire, for example, burned Norfolk on January 1, 1776.)

A number of chairs, believed to have been made in Virginia for household purposes, have also been identified. From these we can imagine something of the range, from fairly elaborate to quite simple, that characterized the workmanship there. All are very English.

A chair, upper right, having a pierced and carved splat with an interlacing lozenge design, is believed to have descended in the family of Alexander Spotswood, Lieutenant Governor of Virginia from 1710 to 1722. His descendants owned land at Germanna near Fredericksburg. The center of the crest is scrolled backward, and the ears likewise scroll back. The stiles flare outward and give a firm sense of support. Shells with bellflower pendants are carved on the knees of the cabriole legs which terminate in claw and ball feet in front and in shaped feet in the back. There are parallels with London-made furniture, and it is possible to hypothesize a craftsman familiar with London techniques and styles. Several armchairs and side chairs having very similar back splats and showing similar methods of construction are known. A pair of these are at Shirley plantation in Charles City County, Virginia, not far from Williamsburg. Another pair of side chairs, now at the Virginia Historical Society, may belong to the same set. A single armchair has descended in the Ferneyhough family of Fredericksburg. Still another may have been owned by Thomas Jefferson. The fact that several of these, and a few other related pieces, have come down in families with Fredericksburg connections has led to the idea that

they originated in the Fredericksburg-Falmouth area. It has been argued convincingly, however, that they originated in Williamsburg, and were probably made in the shop of Peter Scott. There were close familial ties between the two communities, and it is also possible that a cabinetmaker trained in Williamsburg might have moved to Fredericksburg. From a broader perspective, what is important is that the chairs share a number of

Speaker's chair, Virginia House of Burgesses, Williamsburg, c. 1730. Walnut, poplar, yellow pine, oak. Commonwealth of Virginia, on loan to Colonial Williamsburg.

Tea table, Williamsburg, c. 1735. Mahogany, yellow pine, oak. Colonial Williamsburg.

Side chair, attributed to the shop of Peter Scott, Williamsburg, c. 1740. Mahogany, beech slip seat. Colonial Williamsburg.

Side chair, descended in the Stansbury family of "Snowden" in Fredericksburg, Virginia, third quarter, eighteenth century. Cherry. Private collection.

common features, despite small differences. From noting these characteristics—such as a typical one-piece shoe at the base of the splat—we can begin to see relationships which suggest the work of one shop, one craftsman, or several interrelated shops, and hence get some insight into the way craft practices were shared or passed from one man to another.

A less complicated version of the same general form is seen in the chair shown in the lower right. This descended in the Stansbury family of "Snowden" in Fredericksburg. The supposition is that a less expensive chair was desired and so the craftsman, familiar with the more elaborate model, created a simpler, but pleasingly satisfactory version.

A side chair, following page, of even simpler design, and not directly related to the examples just mentioned, descended in the Galt family of Williamsburg, and probably came from a shop there. It is typical of a group of quite plain chairs made around 1770. Here the splat is unpierced, almost as if waiting for the carver's pattern. There is no shaped yoke, and there are no "ears." Indeed, its simple outline shows an almost direct relationship to Plate IX of the first edition of Thomas Chippendale's *The Gentleman and Cabinet-Maker's Director*, published in London in 1754, page 93. In this plate a very similar chair is shown in outline to demonstrate how to draw a chair in perspective. It may not have been intended as an actual model for a chair at all.

Side chair (one of four), Williamsburg, c. 1770. Walnut primary; yellow pine secondary. Galt Family Collection, Colonial Williamsburg.

to chairs in the "Queen Anne" or George II style of the late 1730s, but the back splat is pierced and carved rather than solid. The major motif within the splat is one of an interlocking diamond and figure eight. There is at least one English example of "pre-Chippendale design" with a similar silhouette and motif. Therefore, the craftsmen who made this pair undoubtedly had close ties with England and may have been trained there. The diamond and figure-eight motif, interestingly enough, turns up in American chairs from other regions, though differently framed. The design may have been circulated among a number of craftsmen, or pieces with this design may have been copied by various craftsmen.

Along with the Virginia Speaker's chair, there are several other remarkable ceremonial chairs that have recently been identified as having been made in Virginia; four are Masonic chairs. While most of the surviving Virginia chairs made for household usage are quite plain, though well constructed, the Masonic chairs served a different function and are very elaborately carved and decorated.

Of the four chairs carved with Masonic emblems, one of the most impressive is that now owned by the Unanimity Lodge No. 7, in Edenton, North Carolina, page 94. We do not know which lodge it was originally made for. The name of Benjamin Bucktrout is stamped in the back of the chair's central capital, a

In common parlance "Chippendale" is used to indicate English, Irish, and American mid-eighteenth-century designs similar to those found in the book of patterns published by the London cabinetmaker and entrepreneur of that name in 1754, and then again in 1759 and 1762. These books were very important to provincial craftsmen in England and in the colonies; by using them they could fashion furniture similar to that being made in London. In the desire to identify visual sources found in this and other popular pattern books, the importance of the oral and manual transmission of ideas shared by working craftsmen may be underestimated. In chair design the chairs shown on page 91, for example, have been identified as in the "Chippendale style," because they have pierced splats and well-defined ears. In point of fact, in none of the group of chairs directly related to these do the chair backs have a direct one-to-one relationship to a plate in Chippendale's book. The designs seem to be the kind which one craftsman might have copied or learned from another, modifying them in small ways.

Yet another skillfully carved armchair of easy, broad proportions and of varied curved parts is that shown to the right. It is one of a pair. They have a history associated with Hertford, North Carolina, on the Perquimans River, near both Albemarle Sound and the Virginia border. Several related pieces have been recently discovered, and it seems probable that they were all made in Edenton, North Carolina. The basic silhouette is similar

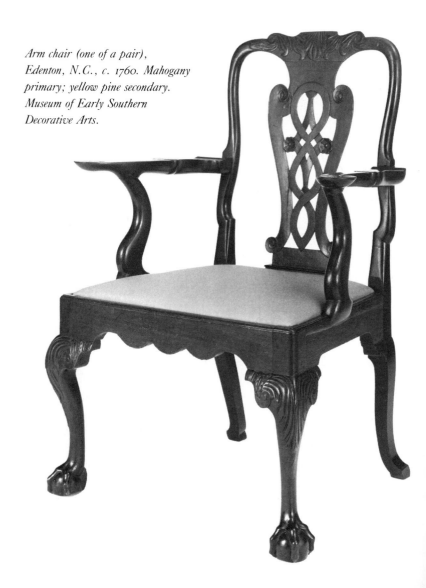

Arm chair (one of a pair), Edenton, N.C., c. 1760. Mahogany primary; yellow pine secondary. Museum of Early Southern Decorative Arts.

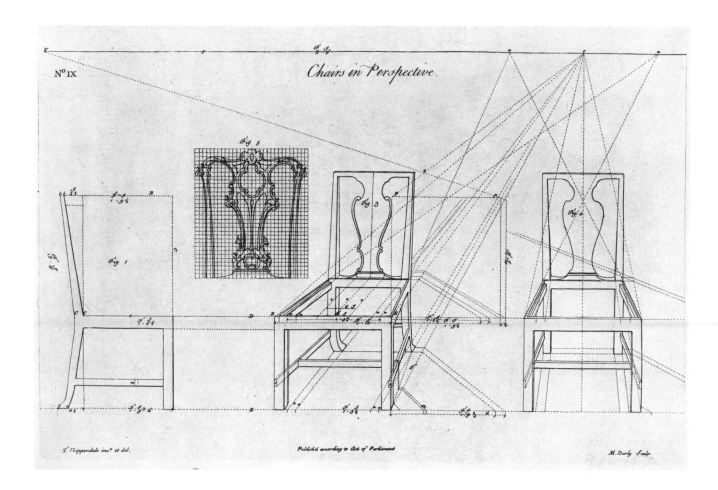

Thomas Chippendale's DIRECTOR,
1st edition (London, 1754).
Plate IX. Library of Congress,
Washington, D.C.

rare example of signed Virginia furniture, and was probably made between 1767 and 1770 when he was working as a cabinetmaker. Bucktrout was one of several men who worked in, or ran, a cabinet shop on Nicholson Street in Williamsburg for a period of more than twenty years. A variety of newspaper advertisements and legal papers help to document its activity. In recent times the site has been excavated, yielding a rich harvest of artifacts, even including an unfinished table leg and a carved leg of an easy chair. An important group of furniture has been attributed to the occupants of this shop, whose careers were intertwined. The first master of the shop was Anthony Hay, who had it from 1751 to 1776. His employees included his two sons and a slave named Wiltshire. Even though other masters took over the shop, it was still often referred to as "the Shop formerly kept by Mr. Hay." In 1776 Hay "removed" himself in order to take over the Raleigh Tavern. He enjoyed the upward mobility that a number of craftsmen and tradesmen did, becoming land and property owners after a successful career in their craft. For a time another skilled craftsman, "James Wilson, Carver, from LONDON," worked in Hay's shop; then in 1767 Benjamin Bucktrout, who advertised as a cabinetmaker from London, bought it. He was briefly a partner with one William Kennedy and had at least one apprentice (who ran away). In 1771, after Hay's death, Bucktrout apparently moved his business to another location, for Edward Dickinson took over the Hay premises. Somewhat like Hay, Bucktrout became involved in other enterprises. Until around 1779 he ran a retail shop and sold upholstery and other articles while he continued his cabinetmaking; in later years he served as

town surveyor. He died in Williamsburg in 1813. (One of his enterprises still survives as the Bucktrout Funeral Service.)

Bucktrout's successor at the Hay premises, Edmund Dickinson, apparently enjoyed success, for he had to advertise for journeymen-cabinetmakers to help him. In 1774 he was joined in his shop by George Hamilton, "carver and gilder, just from Britain." The ad indicated that he could do a variety of objects and ornaments "after the new Palmyrian taste." This is another indication that awareness of the new neoclassical style reached the colony before the Revolution.

Thus for a period of twenty-five years the shop of Anthony Hay was a center of cabinetmaking in Williamsburg and at least six highly skilled craftsmen worked there. This is an unusually complete record of a continuing business enterprise, and the attribution of a number of pieces to this shop seems valid.

In the Masonic chair shown here, which is impressed with Bucktrout's name, the arm supports, skirt, and carved legs are related to English examples. Several craftsmen under Bucktrout's supervision were probably involved. The carved dolphin legs are among the most elaborate, if not *the* most elaborate, found in eighteenth-century American furniture. It has been shown that these are copied directly from Plate XXI of Chippendale's *Director*. Likewise the configuration of the three capitals on the back: the two of the Corinthian order and the central one of the Composite order seem to derive directly from plates in the same book. A copy of "Chippendale's Designs" was listed among the property of Edmund Dickinson after his death in 1778. Since he can be documented at the Hay shop before and after Bucktrout

Masonic chair, stamped signature of Benjamin Bucktrout, Williamsburg, c. 1767–1770. Mahogany primary; walnut secondary; original black leather upholstery. Unanimity Lodge No. 7, Edenton, N.C.

posed to the working craft of masonry, apparently had its modern beginnings as a society in England with the founding of the Grand Lodge in 1717. Not long after that, in 1733, the first "regular" lodge was established in Boston. Savannah, Charleston, and other local lodges soon followed. The tools of the mason's trade became symbols of fraternal behavior. Though once there was secrecy concerning the symbolism, since the 1830s much of this has come into the public domain and, in fact, has been made available by the Masons themselves.

Thus even a novice can "read" this chair in part, and to read it is to be partially instructed in the principles of behavior and ideas espoused by the Masons. Freemasonry was seen by its members as a "handmaiden to religion," a system of morality, and as a "science which is engaged in search after Divine Truth, and which employs symbolism as its method of instruction." Obviously Masonry had a tremendous appeal to men of the Enlightenment who were seeking out rational principles of behavior as well as rational explanations of the workings of the universe.

A basic idea of Freemasonry is to express symbolically the idea of a man passing through the pilgrimages of life. Therefore there are various degrees by which a candidate ascends from a lower to a higher condition of knowledge. The names of the three primitive degrees are Entered Apprentice, Fellow Craft, and Master Mason. A still more advanced degree is that of Royal Arch. One or more mason's tools were adopted as the "working tools" or emblems of each degree. Thus on this chair the twenty-four-inch gauge, the straight bar near the top, is one of the working tools of the Entered Apprentice, the square is a working tool of a Fellow Craft, and the trowel the special tool of the Master Mason. The gauge represents "time well spent" (the divisions on the gauge represent twenty-four hours); truthfulness and honesty are embodied by the square, and the trowel was understood as a symbol of spreading affection, kindness, and brotherly love. The square and compass together remind members to square their actions and to keep them within bounds.

The sun and moon are shown on the left and right. The sun was an all-important symbol to the Mason, as a source of natural light and a reminder of "that intellectual light of which he is in constant search." The sun, which governs the day, and the moon, which governs the night, together exemplified that the Worshipful Master should "rule and govern his lodge with equal regularity and precision."

In the center, directly below the gauge, is the Bible, opened to I Kings 7, the text that describes the building of Solomon's Temple. The Temple of Solomon is a prominent and pervading symbol of Freemasonry, and in their symbolic language the "interior and spiritual man" is represented by a material temple, a symbol of this life. To Masons of the Royal Arch the temple symbolism was carried further; to them the temple erected on the ruins of the first, the Temple of Zerubbabel, is a symbol of life eternal where the lost truth shall be found, the future life. The small pickaxe, on the right, is one of the Royal Arch working tools, teaching him "to loosen from his heart the hold of evil habits."

On the left tip of the square on this chair, the diagrammatic proof of Euclid's 47th proposition, the Pythagorean theorem, is inscribed. This proof was used by practicing masons in trying

took over, it appears he also worked there during the time Bucktrout occupied the property, and may have been responsible for some of this work.

The chair back is literally too weighted with Masonic symbols to be pleasing esthetically, but as a tour de force of cabinetmaking, it is extraordinary. Also, the elaborate care lavished on this and other Masonic chairs attests to the important role Freemasonry must have played in the lives of some colonists, a role that is extremely hard to evaluate since it was, and is, a secret society. Within it, important bonds of friendship, and even concepts of government, were no doubt forged. A chair as elaborate as this must have been time-consuming and expensive to make, but deemed worthy of the effort to those who commissioned it in order to have their beliefs symbolized in tangible form.

Freemasonry, speculative or philosophic Masonry, as op-

their squares, and is a recurring symbol of Freemasonry. It is also a symbol of the Master Mason's degree. Therefore, to Masons, the devotion to learning which this proof represents is a memento "instructing them to be lovers of the arts and sciences."

A level is shown near the bottom, between the two columns. It is a symbol of equality, although the definition of equality is an eighteenth-century definition. It is "not of that social equality which would destroy all distinctions of rank and position, and beget confusion, insubordination and anarchy; but of that fraternal equality which, recognizing the fatherhood of God, admits as a necessary corollary the brotherhood of man. . . . In this vein, the level teaches us that all men are equal, subject to the same infirmities, hastening to the same goal, and preparing to be judged by the same immutable law." It is an equality of fate, of common humanity, and not of rank or distinction. It seems to respect the basic human dignity of all, and to foster a respect for individuals of all classes, even as rank and position are retained. This is very probably how a man like Washington, a Mason, understood the meaning of equality and this interpretation may also have influenced Jefferson, a Mason as well. The level is a "working tool" of a Fellow Craft and the official ensign of the Senior Warden.

The whole complex is topped by an arch with a keystone. This may possibly refer to the Royal Arch, which at one time or another may have formed part of the Master Mason's degree. The keystone also had an important place "in the legend of the Royal Arch Degree." It is, of course, the stone which secures the others in an arch and establishes stability. It is at least possible that this chair was made for men who attained the Royal Arch. Three brothers were raised to that degree at Fredericksburg Lodge 4 on December 22, 1753, the first in America to do so.

Under the keystone, and atop the composite capital, is a beautifully carved bust, right. It has been identified as based on, or indirectly copied from, a stone sculpture of Matthew Prior (1664–1721), the poet, in Westminster Abbey. Why this should be is a mystery. There were in circulation ceramic busts based on the Abbey sculpture, which might simply have been identified as "Prior," and one of these might have seemed an appropriate model for the craftsman because that is also an appellation for a superior of the Order.

As the earliest example of signed Virginia furniture this exceptional chair is the keystone in the study of cabinetmakers and their craft. It is also a remarkable monument in wood, proclaiming the moral system and hierarchy of Masons in eighteenth-century Virginia—a system governed by ideas of enlightened reason, moderation, discipline, and the brotherhood of man.

It is difficult to judge how this world of secret brotherhood influenced or complemented the development of democratic and republican ideas of virtue and government that are embodied in the Constitution, but many of the men who were patriots during the Revolution and leaders in the new Republic were Masons. George Washington, perhaps the most famous Mason of all, was initiated into the Fredericksburg Lodge on November 4, 1752, and remained active until his death. Benjamin Franklin, Thomas Jefferson, and General Lafayette were all members. Southerners among this number included William Blount of Edenton, North Carolina, later territorial governor of Tennessee; David Carroll of

Detail of Masonic chair.
Carved head.

Baltimore; James Madison; Charles Pinckney of Charleston; and Edmund Randolph of Williamsburg.

The importance of the Masons in some colonial communities can also be sensed by the placement of the Masonic Hall. In Fredericksburg, Virginia, for example, it was and is close to both the Anglican church and the town hall. In more than one Southern town it is found on the main street.

A more frivolous object, a tea or "china" table, following page, may also have been made in Anthony Hay's shop when Benjamin Bucktrout was there. In it, too, there is a touch of symbolism. Once thought to be English, it is now believed to have been made in America. Furniture in the Chinese taste was popular at this time, and Chippendale and other compilers of craftsmen's handbooks, such as William Halfpenny, included a variety of models. An effect of great lightness and delicacy is achieved by the open pierced fretwork within a straight outline, a frequently found element of the book designs. The table is of solid mahogany. The fact that each leg is cut from a single piece of wood, rather than being of three or so laminated layers as in English examples, supports the hypothesis of American origin—fine woods were cheaper in the New World. (There may originally have been block feet and a column inside each leg such as are found in a related example.) A bird is shown in profile in

China table, Williamsburg, c. 1770. Mahogany. Colonial Williamsburg.

conspires to make this town the politest, as it is one of the richest in America." It was the market, political, and legal center for the whole of South Carolina. All the produce from the area was brought there, and it was the chief port from which goods were shipped. The reporter noted that Charleston traders dealt "near 1000 miles into the continent." Rice, indigo, deerskins, pitch, turpentine, furs, tanned leather, seeds, oranges, pease and corn, candles, butter, beeswax, stones, shingles, lumber, pork, beef, tallow, oil of turpentine, rosin, and bacon were among the exports. It was also the seat of the government, the place where the General Assembly met, the place where the courts were held (until 1773 the only place in the state), records kept, and indeed

Desk and bookcase, Williamsburg, c. 1770. Walnut primary; yellow pine and walnut secondary. Colonial Williamsburg.

the center of the skirt. Oral tradition has it that the table descended in the Lewis family of Gloucester County, Virginia. One of the Lewises, Susan, married William Powell Byrd, son of William Byrd III of Westover. The bird therefore may be a family emblem.

A Chinese fret pattern decorates a desk and bookcase, right, which has come down in the Galt family of Williamsburg. The fret is less complex and more angular than usually found, and may have come out of a handbook of the London Society of Upholsterers called *Genteel Household Furniture*. It is used along the top of the slant-top desk, the frieze of the pediment, and, in larger scale, on the tympanum of the pediment, lending a muted decorative note to an otherwise sober but well-constructed piece. A rather surprising refinement is that the molding of the pediment is carved in perspective. There was originally a fret pattern on the plinth of the finial, and the finial was topped with a pointed tip. This is one of the finest storage or case pieces to survive from colonial Williamsburg. Other examples include several very simple but well-made chests of drawers, and a bookcase on a stand.

Virtually every traveler who recorded his impressions of Charleston in the middle years of the eighteenth century noted the luxurious quality of life enjoyed by the well-to-do. The *London Magazine* reported in 1762, "Here the rich people have handsome equipages; the merchants are opulent and well-bred; the people are thriving and extensive, in dress and life; so that everything

"the business of the province transacted." Charleston drew its wealth from the commerce and services it provided for the region; it was the largest city south of Philadelphia.

The thoughtful farmer who lived for a time in Pennsylvania, J. Hector St. John Crèvecoeur, writing sometime shortly before the Revolution, identified Charleston lawyers as well as planters and merchants as among those who had wealth, power, and influence. For him the only comparable city in the New World was Lima, Peru. He found the scale of luxury "far superior to what are to be seen in our northern Towns. . . . An European at his first arrival must be greatly surprised when he sees the elegance of their houses, their sumptuous furniture, as well as the magnificence of their tables—can he imagine himself in a country the establishment of which is so recent?" Though he was impressed by the business and commerce, he was disturbed by the conditions among the slaves who helped to produce the city's wealth.

Among the variety of tradesmen who lived and worked in Charleston between 1735 and 1780 there were at least sixty cabinetmakers or furniture craftsmen who plied their trade for shorter or longer periods. Information about them has been gleaned from legal records, and the occasional advertisement, though some were so busy they had little need to advertise. From these, from a rare surviving account book, and from some estate inventories, it is clear that every kind of fashionable furniture was made: "sophas," "Mahogany Couches," "Desk and Book Cases with Arch'd Pediment and O.G. Heads," "Chest of Drawers of all fashion fluted or plain," breakfast tables with "fluted legs & Chinese brackets," beds, and a wide variety of chairs. John Lord, a furniture carver from London, knew his Chippendale, for on May 12, 1767, he placed an ad in the *South Carolina Gazette and Country Journal* indicating he did carving "in the Chinese, French and Gothic tastes."

The account book for an eight-year period, 1768–1775, of the cabinetmaker Thomas Elfe has survived. During this period his shop produced 1,302 fairly large pieces of furniture—bedsteads, chests of drawers, clothes presses, side chairs, easy chairs, tea tables, etc.—and 200 additional smaller items such as fire screens and picture frames. The many coffins he built are not included in this listing. This is only eight years of a working career of twenty-eight years, and he was only one craftsman among many.

Elfe had the services of five handicraft slaves who were joiners and cabinetmakers as well as of four sawyers in his shop at various times. The accounts show that occasionally he also had work, such as carving, done for him by other craftsmen. Twice he was in a business association with another craftsman, for a brief time with John Forbes and for a long time, off and on, with Thomas Hutchinson. His customers included many well-known Charleston citizens; for example, Charles Cotesworth Pinckney and John Drayton. He not only made completely new pieces of furniture but performed a variety of repair jobs such as mending clockcases and "japann'd" tea tables. Several times he sold mahogany picture frames to the painter Jeremiah Theus.

Unfortunately, there are few signed or labeled pieces of Charleston furniture, and so far no signed pieces by Thomas Elfe have been found; although those attributed to him show similarities to architectural decorative work known to have been done by

Tea table, Charleston, second quarter, eighteenth century. Mahogany primary; cypress secondary; top and brasses restored. Private collection.

his shop. In fact, of the prodigious amount of furniture that the records suggest was made in Charleston, the number of surviving pieces is small. Charleston suffered more than the usual number of disasters, among which were major fires in 1740, 1778, and 1796, and a notable hurricane in 1752. Most of the surviving furniture shows close affinities with English styles and with English methods of construction, not surprising given the close commercial ties between Charleston and Britain.

Fine craftsmanship and appreciation of good proportions went into the making of a mahogany tea table in the Queen Anne style, above. The curves of the legs are imbued with vitality. The swelling and tapering at the knees are defined by slim C-scrolls, and the pad feet express the idea of solid footing. (The top and the brasses are restored.) Mahogany was used frequently and generously by Charleston cabinetmakers. Given the closeness to the West Indies, it was apparently easy and cheap to import the logs and board from there. There must have been a large trade, for in 1740 the Assembly repealed duty on mahogany plank, making it even cheaper. Cypress is used as the secondary wood.

A bed from Charleston, following page, whose classically fluted and stop-fluted bedposts surmount organically shaped cabriole legs with claw-and-ball feet is made of solid mahogany. The headboard is set in grooves for easy removability. According to tradition, during the hot summer months in South Carolina, beds were placed in the middle of the rooms with headboards removed, allowing for a maximum amount of air circulation. This bed is finely detailed and was possibly fairly expensive. However, estate inventories reveal that people of middle income

*Bed, Charleston, c. 1750. Mahogany. Museum of Early
Southern Decorative Arts, Winston-Salem, N.C.*

The combination of desk and bookcase, now frequently called a secretary, was apparently popular in Charleston. From the 1750s mahogany desks and bookcases with glass (mirror) doors were often listed in estate inventories. Fluted and stop-fluted Ionic pilasters frame the sides of the tall mahogany bookcase, page 100. The fret adds a touch of chinoiserie. The shell which serves as a finial is rendered very naturalistically.

It has been suggested that the cabinetmaker for this very architectural piece was William Axson, Jr., because the fret, as well as the treatment of the carved edges of the mirrors, are very similar to the details of the woodwork at Pompion Hill Chapel and St. Stephen's Church, in Berkeley County, built in 1763 and 1767. At Pompion Hill Chapel, Axson, who was active in the Wambaw Lodge of Freemasons, put his name and small, precisely inscribed Masonic emblems on the wall; at St. Stephen's he made similar inscriptions on two bricks above the Palladian window. A practicing craftsman, he was proud to be a member of philosophic Masonry as well.

As in Williamsburg, there were overlapping relationships among the craftsmen in Charleston. Axson, for example, was a partner with another cabinetmaker, Stephen Townsend, between 1763 and 1768. (Their shop burned to the ground in 1765.) During this time Axson also worked with the builder Zachariah Villepontoux and his nephew in the building of the two churches.

In 1767 John Fisher, a cabinetmaker from London, announced his intention to engage in "the Cabinet Business in all its branches." In 1769 Ezra Waite, who had done the frieze and other work on the Miles Brewton house, left a sum of money in his will for the same John Fisher; probably Fisher helped Waite in some of the interior woodwork. For an unknown period before May 27, 1771, John Fisher was in partnership with Thomas Elfe. On June 3 of the same year Fisher announced that he had bought out Townsend's business, including the "Negroes brought up" in the trade. Though Fisher and Elfe were no longer partners,

owned mahogany furniture. Elfe's records also indicate that he frequently made cheaper bedsteads of poplar, though there are not yet any known surviving poplar pieces from Charleston or South Carolina.

A number of craftsmen who worked in Charleston indicated in their advertisements that they came from London or had someone in their employ who did. Those who did not could use Chippendale's or similar publications as a source of inspiration. In the case of a mahogany breakfast table, right, one can readily imagine how the craftsman took the two tables shown in Plate 53 of the third edition of the *Director*, upper right, and combined them to create his own individual version. The basic configuration is based on the diagram to the right, including the shaping of the leaves and saltire, or cross stretchers. Rather than a drawer the craftsman has substituted a fret, simplified and different from that in the diagram to the left, but like it in concept. The straight legs, which the craftsman subtly shaped, are closer to those shown on the left.

Breakfast table, Charleston, third quarter, eighteenth century. Mahogany primary; ash secondary. Charleston Museum.

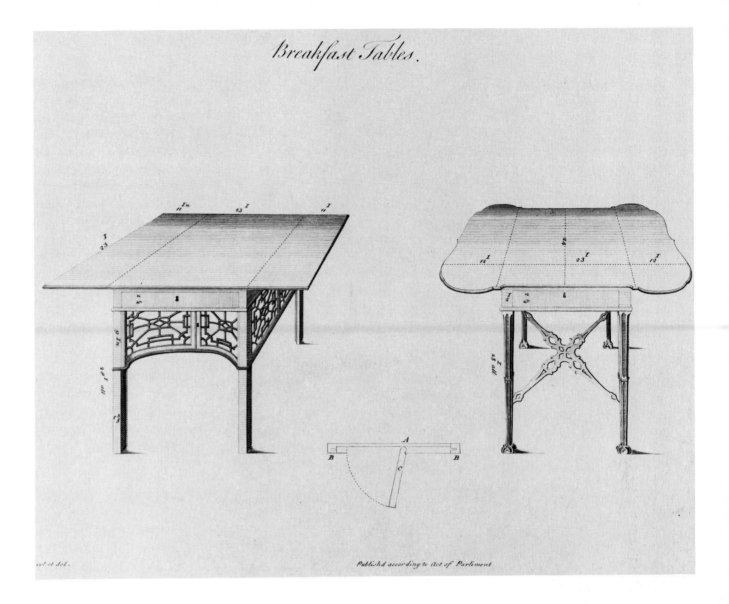

Thomas Chippendale's DIRECTOR, *3rd edition (London, 1754), Plate* LIII. *Henry Francis duPont Winterthur Museum, Winterthur, Delaware.*

Elfe's accounts show that on occasion he paid Fisher to do certain jobs. For example, in May 1773 Elfe paid Fisher 40 shillings for cutting a "frett" and 30 shillings for cutting a pediment board. Elfe also had had several business transactions with Townsend; and occasionally he employed a number of fellow craftsmen to do carving for him. These included John Crips and Abraham Pearce.

During the period recorded by his account book, Thomas Elfe made twenty-eight double chests of drawers, also called chests-on-chest. The example shown on the following page descended in the family of John Deas of Charleston (1735–1790). It is one of a number having similar proportions and construction details. The fret across the top, a kind of figure eight with a loop-ended diamond inside it, is associated with Thomas Elfe, and he or craftsmen in his shop may have made this. Carved rosettes terminate the two ends of the broken-arch pediment, and the pediment itself is filled in with an open-loop fret pattern. Chamfered fluted and stop-fluted pilasters are at the sides of the upper section. These finish in carved lambs' tongues. The tops of the flutes end in inverted crescents with a large dot superimposed. The chest itself is of mahogany. The sides and bottoms of the drawers are of cypress.

The double chest of drawers was made in other American colonies, but it appears to have been made more frequently in Charleston. The high chest of drawers, popularly called a highboy, seems not to have been made or used in Charleston. Nor was it a form popular in Virginia. As is well known, it was popular in the middle colonies and in New England.

Upholstered or stuffed easy chairs are listed in Charleston estate inventories and must have looked similar to the example shown on page 101. According to tradition, it descended directly in the family of Deputy-Governor Robert Daniel, though it would probably have been made after his term of service. The knees are embellished with carved leaf fronds and the front legs terminate in claw-and-ball feet. The tapered back legs have simpler, shaped feet. Stretchers are used to join the legs and provide added support. In the period of his account book Thomas Elfe made only nine easy chairs, most with "eagle claws." He also repaired easy chairs by putting on new stretchers—perhaps similar to those shown here.

The type of furniture most frequently made in Thomas Elfe's workshop during the years 1768–1775 was the side chair. He lists 643. Inventories reveal that it was not uncommon to have thirty or forty chairs in a single home. Other craftsmen may

Desk and bookcase, attributed to William Axson, Jr., Charleston, c. 1765–1780. Mahogany primary; cypress secondary. Museum of Early Southern Decorative Arts, Winston-Salem, N.C.

by the British attempts to capture it in 1776, which were successfully repulsed, then by a blockade of the harbor, and finally by attacks again in 1779. In May of 1780 the Americans surrendered and Charleston was under military rule from 1780 to December 1782. On October 28, 1777, Martin Pfeniger placed an advertisement in the *South Carolina Gazette and Country Journal* telling his customers that he was sorry "to leave off his business of Cabinet-making" for lack of mahogany. The British blockade apparently cut off supplies, and during the war there was a hiatus in the production of furniture. Citizens were torn in their loyalties, as can be seen by the fate of a few individual craftsmen. Abraham Pearce, a cabinetmaker and carver from London who did

Chest-on-chest, Charleston, c. 1778. Mahogany primary; cypress and yellow poplar secondary. Colonial Williamsburg.

have made equal quantities. A surviving example is shown on the far right. The silhouette is a typical Chippendale configuration. The figure-eight and diamond motif in the center of the open carved splat is quite similar to that seen in the Edenton chair on page 92, though the framing is different. The motif is close to that seen, in smaller scale, on "Elfe" frets. The wings and handhold of this chair are gilded. Other side chairs believed to have been made in Charleston range from ones with quite uncomplicated splats to those which are considerably more intricate and close to elaborate English models.

During the Revolutionary War Charleston was first affected

*Easy chair, Charleston, c. 1750–1790. Mahogany primary;
cypress and yellow pine secondary. Descended in family of
Deputy-Governor Robert Daniel. Colonial Williamsburg.*

group of handsome townhouses was being erected, one of the
finest groups of domestic buildings of the period. When the
English civil servant William Eddis first came to Annapolis in
1769 he noted that "At present, this city has more the appearance of an agreeable village than the metropolis of an opulent
province . . ." Despite the smallness of the community, he
was soon surprised to observe: "The quick importation of
fashions from the mother country is really astonishing. I am almost inclined to believe that a new fashion is adopted earlier by
the polished and affluent American than by many opulent persons in the great metropolis. . . . In short, very little difference
is, in reality, observable in the manners of the wealthy colonist
and the wealthy Briton."

There were several cabinetmakers who worked in Annapolis
between 1760 and 1780 for as long as a decade, though so far no
corpus of clearly identifiable work by these men has been established. There are one or two elegant and exceptional pieces with
a long history of ownership in Maryland families that may have
been made there, possibly by some of the obviously skilled
craftsmen in woodwork who were also engaged in the building
trades. Some unpretentious utilitarian furniture has also survived.

The craftsman who seems to have dominated the local cabinetmaking trade in Annapolis from 1772 until at least 1816 (he
died in 1829) was John Shaw. Born in Glasgow in 1745, the son
of a Scots carpenter, he was in Annapolis by 1763, a young man

work for Elfe from time to time, petitioned to be admitted to the
status of British citizen. After the war he was ordered banished
and his estate confiscated, and there is no further record of him.
Jacob Sass, a native of Germany who came to Charleston only in
1773, wholeheartedly supported the colonial cause, reestab-
lished his business in Charleston after the war, and had a long and
productive career until his death in 1828. Stephen Townsend,
erstwhile partner of Elfe, also signed a petition to be reinstated
as a British citizen. Though initially his estate was ordered confiscated, he appears to have gotten off with a 12 percent
amercement, which was the lot of many Loyalists. William
Axson, Jr., enrolled in the militia, was captured by the British,
and held in one of the grim prison ships anchored in the harbor.
His wife and two children were banished to Philadelphia, apparently for not taking an oath of allegiance to the Crown. He returned and took part in the Federal Procession of 1788 as a cabinetmaker.

*Side chair, probably Charleston,
mid-eighteenth century. Mahogany
primary; long leaf pine secondary;
wings and handhold are gilded.
Heyward-Washington House,
Charleston Museum.*

Annapolis was a small community, with a population still under
1,400 in 1769. In the 1760s and the 1770s, as we have seen, a

Slant-top desk, labeled on the back of the central interior compartment by John Shaw, Annapolis, c. 1776–1786. Talbot County Historical Society.

Baltimore was one of the towns that showed a marked growth in population during the 1760s and 1770s. The number of white settlers living in the inland back-country or up-country areas of the South also grew steadily in these years. Peter Manigault who, in the 1770s, was managing the plantation of a South Carolinian who lived in London, wrote, in order to explain the rise in the price of Negroes, "You must know that since you left Carolina, the back parts of the Province have settled extremely fast, inasmuch, that it is computed that there have been at least 10,000 White Inhabitants come in from the Northern Colonies in one Year only. They all traveled by land, so that We upon the Sea Coast did not perceive with what Rapidity o[u]r Colony was increasing." The vast majority of the people filling up the back settlements came via what was known as the Great Wagon Road. It started outside Philadelphia, to Lancaster and York in Pennsylvania, then across the Potomac and into the Shenandoah Valley in Virginia, through Winchester, Staunton, and south to Roanoke. There it veered east close to the Blue Ridge and into North Carolina to Wachovia, the first Moravian settlement. Beginning in 1760 it then went on down through Piedmont North Carolina to Salisbury, through the Catawba Valley into South Carolina to Pine Tree (Camden). It continued west and south, crossing the Congaree and forking for the towns of Ninety-Six and Augusta. During the last decade or so of the colonial period apparently tens of thousands traversed this path, and these settlers became an important force in the new Republic.

One walnut dressing table, below, has a long history of ownership in Camden, South Carolina, one of the trading centers of the developing back-country. It carries with it a story that is a footnote to the history of that settlement during the Revolution. In general, it is Queen Anne in style, with cabriole legs and flat pad feet, typical of furniture made around 1735. It is unusual in

Dressing table, South Carolina, c. 1735–1780. Walnut primary; yellow pine secondary. Private collection.

of eighteen years. He must already have been trained, since by 1771 there is a record indicating that he had made two mahogany dining tables, a full dozen mahogany chairs, and two card tables for the well-to-do planter James Brice. Most of the documented furniture by Shaw, who was twice in partnership with a fellow Scotsman, Archibald Chisholm, dates to the post-Revolutionary period and will be discussed in the next section. The slant-top desk, above, bears his label, and was probably made between 1776 and 1786. It bears out Eddis's conclusion that new fashions were quickly transmitted to the colonies, for though the form is essentially Chippendale, the presence of the arch of parallel string-inlay, with keystone and impost blocks, is a portent of the taste for linear and inlay decoration so popular in the Federal styles of late eighteenth and early nineteenth centuries. An almost identical desk bears the label of Joseph Middleton, a fellow Annapolis craftsman, showing once again how closely various cabinetmakers sometimes worked with each other.

This desk was made for the merchant John Stevenson of Falls Point, Baltimore. According to Eddis, Stevenson was an Irishman, who had "first conceived this important project of rendering [the port of Baltimore] the grand emporium of Maryland commerce" by commencing to have wheat shipped from there. The first section of what is now Baltimore was laid out in 1729. By 1745 there were twenty-five houses and 200 inhabitants. The shipment of wheat from the port began around 1754 and from that time onward the village grew in prominence until it became one of the most important cities of post-Revolutionary America.

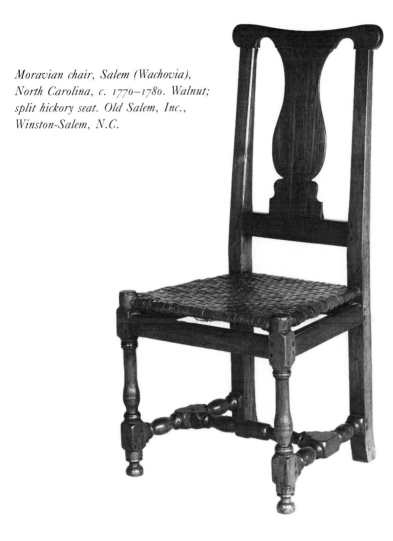

Moravian chair, Salem (Wachovia), North Carolina, c. 1770–1780. Walnut; split hickory seat. Old Salem, Inc., Winston-Salem, N.C.

another reason for thinking it might have been made away from a center of high fashion. It may also be of a later date than the style suggests, or a craftsman from France may have been responsible for it.

Despite the early style, there is a family tradition that it was new (newly acquired?) around 1780. It has descended in the family of Joseph Kershaw who came to Charleston from the West Riding of Yorkshire in England sometime in the third quarter of the eighteenth century. He worked first for James Laurens in Charleston and then for the factors Ancram, Lance, and Laocock in Pine Tree (Camden), building a house there around 1775–1780. General Cornwallis chose this house to live in when he occupied Camden. Kershaw was captured and sent to Honduras. Mrs. Kershaw first lived with her daughters in the attic. She was then allowed to move into a small house in the country which they owned, and permitted to take a few pieces of furniture. This piece was one that she took because it was new. (Cornwallis departed Camden in 1781, leading his troops northward to Virginia where he hoped to join with Clinton's Army. It was a difficult campaign; the British suffered losses at Cowpens and Guilford; Clinton failed to arrive on time and Cornwallis surrendered at Yorktown in Virginia.)

Just as the architecture in the Moravian settlements of Wachovia and Salem, in Piedmont North Carolina, was built on the basis of old-fashioned and Germanic traditions, so, too, the furniture. This conservatism can be seen in a Moravian side chair, left, believed to have been made around 1770–1780. The turned stretchers and front legs hark back to the fashion at the beginning of the century, while the shape of the back splat, straight and upright, is in the Queen Anne style.

The walnut sawbuck table, with X-shaped supports, below, was found near Winston-Salem and is believed to have been made during the early years of the settlement at Wachovia. It shows close parallels with tables made by the Moravians in Pennsylvania. The basic design is an old and utilitarian one; such

the exceedingly sprightly curve of the legs, and in the back feet, which are hoof-shaped and close to those found on French furniture. The secondary wood is yellow pine. This suggests that it might have been made in an outlying district such as Camden, which is located in the sandhill section of South Carolina, where yellow pine grows. Unless other closely related pieces are found, it stands as a slightly eccentric but still sophisticated example—

Moravian sawbuck table. Salem (Wachovia), North Carolina. Walnut. Old Salem, Inc. Winston-Salem, N.C.

Blanket chest, Eastern Shore of Virginia, c. 1770. Yellow pine with original green and white paint. Colonial Williamsburg.

tables are sometimes depicted in medieval manuscripts. It is also as new as the latest outdoor picnic table—one of those forms that has an extraordinary history of continuity.

The simple low chest is another form with a long history; many more must have existed than have survived. A painted yellow pine chest, above, is believed to have been made on the Eastern Shore of Virginia. It is like a number of other examples found there. The design on the panels is similar to that found in local architecture. The combinations of four triangles, and of a diamond and four quarter-circles, would seem to be available to anyone handy with a compass and square; yet in fact these two designs appear to be based on Plates XXIII and XXVI in William Salmon's *Palladio Londinensis*. This was a popular handbook first

Blanket chest, Southern (Maryland, Virginia, or North Carolina), c. 1760–1790. Tulip poplar. Colonial Williamsburg.

published in London in 1734, which went through nine editions before 1774. It seems to have been widely used by joiners in eighteenth-century Virginia.

The Eastern Shore, which is separated from the Virginia mainland by the Chesapeake Bay, is neither up-country nor back-country. The communities there, however, lived somewhat in isolation and the designs of the furniture of the area do not conform closely to the mode prevalent on the mainland.

Some painted furniture was decorated to simulate woodgraining. The tulipwood blanket chest, lower left, has bands of different patterns of simulated graining. It is believed to be Southern, possibly from Maryland, Virginia, or North Carolina. Some forms of painted furniture were also made in South Carolina, although a large proportion of the furniture was made of mahogany. For example, there are three references to poplar bedsteads that were listed as "coloured" or painted in Thomas Elfe's account book.

The few surviving pieces of eighteenth-century furniture from the French settlements in the lower Mississippi Valley and New Orleans are decidedly French in form and type. Those that probably date to the eighteenth century are Louis XV in style. An example is the elegantly simple rectangular table of solid walnut, upper right. There is a lively spring to the curve of the legs, which terminate in delicately carved, cloven-hoofed doe's feet, opposite. (In the French version of the cabriole leg there seems to be less emphasis on the "knee." The gradation of the curve is more even and sinuous.) The curve and scallops of the apron continue the line of the curve of the leg. The top of the table has a curved edge, with beading. The pegs which secure the joined construction are exposed. This table belonged to the Ursuline Convent. The first group of nuns arrived in 1727 in order to teach girls, including orphans, and to help in the military hospital. The convent, which has moved its quarters several times, has had a continuous existence in New Orleans since that time. Unfortunately, some of the account books of the convent have been lost and others are lacking in specifics. The records indicate that from time to time payments were made to *menusiers* for work done or for tools, but there is no description beyond that. Most of the few surviving pieces from the early days at the convent are of native woods, walnut and cypress, and some of mahogany.

The study of early furniture of Louisiana is of much more recent date than that of other areas in the South, and the resource materials are limited. Fires, hurricanes, and the great prosperity of the early years of the nineteenth century all probably contributed to the destruction of furniture. There were no newspapers until 1794. A beginning has been made in gleaning data on the presence of craftsmen from a variety of sources. The early censuses of 1726 and 1732 reveal the presence of a number of turners, carpenters, and cabinetmakers. Unfortunately, inhabitants were not listed by trades in the censuses of 1741, 1770, and 1805. From the characteristics of surviving pieces of furniture, which are different from Canadian and French counterparts, it seems clear that craftsmen worked in the city. Some of these were probably trained in Europe and apprentices might have

Table, New Orleans or Louisiana, c. 1760–1780. Walnut. From Ursuline Convent. Private collection.

Detail of walnut table. Doe's foot or pied de biche.

building contractor and engineer responsible for the Ursuline Convent, sale lots included "nine cabinet-maker's tools," "thirty-two cabinet-maker's tools," "a whole outfit of cabinet-maker's tools," "five cabinet-maker's work-benches," "four other cabinet-maker's work-benches" as well as other quantities of building materials, bricks and tiles and brick molds, black-smithing and carpentry tools, and other goods and chattel. Some of the farmers and plantation owners made their own furniture. During the Spanish administration, an official, Don Francisco Bouligny, reported about the Creoles: "There are few houses of which the furniture has not been made by the owners them-selves, and men of means do not disdain to pass entire days handling a plane, in the carpenter shop, or the blacksmith shop."

Estate inventories also indicate that a wide variety of furni-ture was used by the inhabitants of lower Louisiana in the second half of the eighteenth century. There are armchairs; easy chairs, or *bergères* with cushions and upholstery; cherry, walnut, and cy-press tables, some with *pieds de biche*, doe or stag feet; and cherry

Armoire, lower Louisiana, possibly New Orleans, 1750–1800. Mahogany primary; Spanish cedar secondary; cornice is replacement. Louisiana State Museum, New Orleans.

learned from them. Some furniture was probably made by slaves. In the estate inventory, made July 13, 1769, of Jean Baptiste Prevost, who had been the agent of the French Company of the Indies, and therefore a man of status and means, there are two slaves listed as cabinetmakers on one of his plantations. One was Joiau (Jewel) Joseph, a Negro aged forty-five years. The other was a mulatto named Jannot. The latter was the most highly valued among all the slaves. In addition, there was a long list of over a hundred specialized cabinetmaking tools including twenty-two chisels and eleven different planes. In the succession sale in 1758 of the estate of Claude Joseph Villars DuBréuil, the

and walnut chairs with cane seats. Prevost owned "a large mirror with a crest, in a gilt frame," "a marble-topped table on a gilt pedestal," "an inlaid marqueterie table," a sofa, a settee, quantities of chairs, a walnut bedstead with roebuck feet, a day bed *(lit de repos)*, pier mirror, an armoire of red baywood, a walnut armoire, a cypress armoire, another armoire of walnut, and a variety of other goods. Some of these may have been fashioned in this country. Still another French official, Chevalier Jean de Pradel, had a handsome plantation house erected for himself on the west bank of the Mississippi, opposite New Orleans, in 1750–1751, and furnished it with large mirrors, marble tables, tapestries, a large sofa, and armchairs. In 1754 he could write with some pride that his home was "without contradiction the

Detail of mahogany armoire; pin-type hinge with door removed.

most beautiful and best furnished in the country and could pass for a small and beautiful chateau in our provinces." Pradel purchased much of his furniture and fabrics in France, and it is probable that men such as DuBréuil and Prevost did likewise. The imported items could have served as models for locally made examples.

From among this variety, armoires, or wardrobes, have survived in greater number than any other type of furniture. They belong to an essentially continental tradition—there is the Spanish *ropero*, the German *Schranck*, and the Dutch *kas*—and provide excellent and flexible storage space.

The mahogany armoire, previous page, has curve-shaped upper panels, which reflect the French rococo taste. The panels are bordered with a triple-molding or beading. As with most Louisiana armoires, there is little or no carved decoration, and the beauty of the piece is in the quality of the polished, fine-grained hard wood. This is in contrast to the often elaborately carved examples found in France, where the woods are more frequently softer or coarser-grained. (A number of the armoires that have survived in Louisiana are cypress.) Comparable examples in Canada usually have carved decoration but are most often of pine. There is evidence that armoires quite similar to the Louisiana ones were made in some of the French-owned islands in the West Indies. In the example shown here, long pin-type hinges, left, are used. This makes it possible to lift the doors off easily. The original scalloped skirt, seen in the side view, had a beaded edge that flowed into the curve of the short cabriole leg. The front feet are scrolled, very French, and rest on a small support; the back feet are shaped with small "toes." The pegged construction is undisguised. The cornice and part of the skirt are replacements, but a cornice that is removable and fits over the carcass is typical. The secondary wood is probably Spanish cedar. The back panels were left rough-hewn. A typical interior has four shelves and a belt of three small drawers attached to the bottom of the third shelf.

The armoire, upper right, must be typical of the kind found in dozens of households in French Louisiana. The patterns of the fine-grained walnut surfaces are essential to the design of this austerely simple casepiece. The doors with recessed panels project slightly from the frame. As often occurs, the center panel is in fact attached to the left door. Thus, of the two escutcheons, only one is functional, a canny and economical way to make the armoire more secure. The corners of the frame are chamfered. The inner curve of the legs flows into the rhythmic scallops of the skirt. The restrained and curved cabriole legs with hoof feet are particularly delicate. If tables and bedsteads had carved feet of comparable lightness it is no surprise that few have survived. The secondary wood is cypress. The cornice is a replacement. There is no precise way for dating this piece or this group, but insofar as can be judged, they were probably made between 1760 and 1790.

On the bottom of this armoire, in chalk and in an eighteenth-century script, the name "Glapion" is written, right. This is very possibly the name of the cabinetmaker. It has not yet been possible to trace this family back to the eighteenth century, but Gibson's 1838 *New Orleans Guide and Directory* lists Celestin Glapion, a free man of color, as a carpenter at 179 St.

Ann Street. An ancestor of his may have made this armoire. Until very recently there were practicing cabinetmakers in this family, and there appears to be a long tradition of skilled craftsmen in it.

The desire of the colonists on the Eastern Seaboard in the South to keep up with the fashions in the mother country is as manifest in their choice of silver as in their choice of furniture or architecture, although this judgment is admittedly based on a small number of surviving pieces.

After the British triumphed in the siege of Charleston in May 1780 they pillaged the countryside. It is estimated that when they evacuated in 1782 they took with them loot valued at £300,000 sterling. Silver was loaded into 500 rice barrels. It is not known how many pieces were confiscated, how much was made by local silversmiths, how much was later melted for pieces in newer fashions, and how much might still turn up someday in England.

Some of this silver would have been purchased abroad, but some would have been made in the city. Records indicate that there were twenty silversmiths working in Charleston by 1750 and thirty-five by 1775. Some of these men imported goods from London, including jewelry, and seem to have specialized in smaller items and in repair work. James Alexander Courtonne, for example, advertised in 1751 that he could "sell, make and mend all sorts of jewellers work, diamond and motto rings, and small silver plate in the neatest and most fashionable manner." He also bought wooden handles for tea and coffee pots from Thomas Elfe. The advertisements of Charles Harris are considerably more ambitious and suggest that some craftsmen made a wider range of objects. In 1768 he stated that he "Makes and sells all sorts of new fashioned bottle stands, table-spoons, feathered on the handle, dish stands, cruet frames after a new fashion; pepper coasters, ink stands, mugs, tankards, fluted & plain turin ladles, punch Ditto out of Dollars, rings, buckles, buttons, all warranted sterling." This ad is also interesting for the reference to feather-edged work, an early date for this new fashion, either in England or in America.

Armoire, lower Louisiana, possibly New Orleans, 1750–1800. Walnut primary; cypress secondary; cornice is replacement. Louisiana State Museum, New Orleans.

Detail of walnut armoire. On the bottom, in chalk, in eighteenth-century script, "Glapion."

Daniel You. Pair of silver dishes, Charleston, c. 1745–1750.
Marked: "DY" in capitals, a pellet within the "D," all within
an oval; twice on the face of plate. Wadsworth Atheneum.

A pair of dishes of a rare and unusual form, above, bear the initials DY in capitals. They are the work of Daniel You. Each is formed of three large and three small shells alternated and attached to a central flat plate. A cast pineapple finial is in the center of each, and each is supported on four legs with scroll feet. The natural curved shapes of shells have long attracted artists and craftsmen, and proponents of the rococo showed a special partiality to this form. The scroll feet are similar to those seen on French and English furniture. It is not known when Daniel You first came to Charleston, but he is known to have been working there from around 1743 through 1749/50.

Thomas You is believed to be the son, or relative, of Daniel You, for he advertised in 1756 that he "carries on the business." Later he had a shop under the evocative "Sign of the Golden Cup" (the sign itself must have been an attractive object), first in the Beef Market Square, then on Meeting Street, then on King Street. He fashioned a wide variety of objects and also cleaned and polished his customers' plate. He seems to have had a busy and prosperous career in the years between 1753 and 1780. Sugar dishes and bowls were listed among the articles he could make, and an elegantly simple example of his skill, below, is now owned by the Charleston Museum. You also advertised that he did engravings on copperplates, and in 1766 advertised that he had finished a plate of the "West Prospect of St. Philip's Church." He was one of those placed on a prison ship in the harbor in 1781.

A coffee pot with gracefully rounded bottom, tapered body, and curved flat dome with finial, above right, bears the mark of Alexander Petrie, a silversmith who worked in Charleston from around 1745 to his retirement. The curved spout is adorned with acanthus scrolls. It was probably made around 1755 when plain, unadorned surfaces were popular in silver pieces.

Petrie was among those craftsmen who had successful businesses, invested in property, and rose to the rank of "Gentleman." In his death notice in 1768 he was described as a "Silver Smith, who had acquired a handsome Fortune, with a fair character, and had some Time ago retired from Business."

Listed in Petrie's inventory after his death was "Abraham, a negro man Silversmith valued at £400." Abraham must have been an able craftsman, for at the "Public Outcry" or auction, another silversmith, Jonathan Sarrazin, purchased him for more than twice the value, £810, an unusually high price for a slave. There are other occasional references to Negroes as silversmiths. John Paul Grimké in 1771 offered a reward for a runaway slave, Joe, who was sixteen, and "very arch and sensible, and wrought at the silversmith's trade many years." In the eighteenth century it seems to have been a fairly common practice to apprentice or train Negroes at trades. Their owners then either had them work for themselves, or could rent their services out. Some must have allowed their men to work in shops of their own, and thus set up competition with white workmen. In 1755 the legislature passed a law which read in part, "And no master of any slave shall permit or suffer such slaves to carry on any handicraft trade in a shop by himself, in Town, on pain of forfeiting *five pounds* every day. Nor to put any negro or slave apprentice to any mechanic trade of another in Town, or forfeiture of *one hundred* pounds. PROVIDED, that nothing in this act shall be construed, to hinder any handicraft tradesman in town, from teaching their own negroes or slaves the trades they exercise, so that they constantly employ one white apprentice or journeyman, for every *two* negroes that they shall so teach and thenceforth employ."

The home of James Geddy II, with its adjacent silversmith shop, has been re-created and is now on exhibition in Colonial Williamsburg. Geddy was the son of a gunsmith of the same name, and took over the family shop in 1760. In his advertisements he identified himself as a goldsmith, who had on hand "a neat assortment of COUNTRY MADE GOLD and SILVER WORK" along with "a small, but neat assortment of imported JEWELRY." As in Charleston, the silver and goldsmiths made their own wares and handled a variety of imported merchandise. Several spoons bearing his mark of I.G. were among the miscellany of objects found in the archaeological investigation of the property.

Thomas You. Silver bowl, Charleston, c. 1753–1786. Marked three times:
"T.Y." Charleston Museum.

A saucepan, lower right, though unmarked, is believed to be James Geddy II's work as well. It descended in the family of Colonel William Preston, a member of the House of Burgesses, and there is a record of an account between the Colonel and Geddy in 1771–1772. In England regulations concerning silver were strict, and each piece usually bears marks indicating the town, the date, the quality, and the maker. No assay office was ever established in the colonies; later, in Baltimore, between 1814 and 1830, there was an official assay office. Therefore, American-made silver usually bears only the maker's mark, and the quality had to depend upon the integrity of the silversmith. In some cases, such as this one, silver was left unmarked. Mutual trust sufficed.

In silver, as in furniture design, there was a move toward more elaborate surface decoration in the 1750s and 1760s. A teapot, following page, made by a Baltimore silversmith, Gabriel Lewyn, exemplifies this taste. A complex pattern of tendrils, flowers, and scrolls, in repoussé, or raised relief, flows around the curves of the pot and fairly hugs it. Rather than the simpler ovoid or rounded and cylindrical shape seen in the coffee pot or the saucepan, a double-curved form is used, that of an inverted pear. The pot has been set upon a high foot that was separately

Gabriel Lewyn. Silver teapot, Baltimore, c. 1768–1780.
Marked: "GL" in rectangle five times on bottom. John
Marshall Phillips Collection, Yale University, New Haven,
Connecticut.

cast, then applied to the body. Formal gadrooning, similar to patterned molding on furniture, is used to decorate the base of the foot.

Among the many smaller pieces made by the colonial silversmiths were the wristbands and armbands sometimes given to the Indians at times of ceremonials, conferences or treaty signings, and gorgets, worn by military men and also sometimes given to the Indians. A fairly recent discovery is a pair of silver wristbands, above right, which were found in the tomb of an Indian chief in Alabama. The engraved inscription reads A GIFT OF HIS EXCELLENCY HENRY ELLIS ESQR 1760. Ellis was the second royal governor of Georgia, serving a fairly short term from February 1757 to November 1760. He made particular and earnest efforts to conciliate the Indians and was especially successful with the Creeks, whose friendship was important to the British during the French and Indian War. These wristbands, of thinly wrought metal with openings for leather ties, are thought to have come from a Creek mound.

Since the wristbands are unmarked, it seems probable that they were made in Georgia, by one of the few silversmiths working in Savannah at that time. The name of Adrian Loyer has been put forth as a possibility, since he was paid by the town council for making the court seal on December 9, 1756, and thus had some experience performing official commissions.

Gorgets were moon-shaped pieces of silver which were worn on a chain about the neck of officers in full uniform. They originated as a piece of armor defending the throat, but by the eigh-

teenth century they seem to have been largely ornamental. A gorget with "Col. C. C. Pinckney 1776" and thirteen stars engraved on it is shown at lower right. It has the mark I. VANALL in a rectangle. The only direct records of Vanall, a Charleston silversmith, are from the period 1749–1752, and he probably died around 1756. Pinckney must have acquired this as a plain gorget and had it inscribed with his name and rank, perhaps when he was advanced to colonel in 1776. The stars could have been added at the same time or still later as a memento of the American victory in the war.

The German settlers in Piedmont North Carolina were initially as faithful to their national traditions in the craft products they created as were those of the dominant English community. When the German Moravians established their settlements in the Wachovia tract at Bethabara and Salem, they fully intended to create communities which would be centers of businesses and trades. They planned to be as self-sufficient as possible and to provide services to the area in order to have additional income. They brought with them tools, equipment, and knowledge, so that soon tailors, coopers, millwrights, shoemakers, blacksmiths, and others were hard at work. A supervisory committee, the Aufseher Collegium, controlled and supervised the number and kinds of shops and the apprentice system; in its early years the Wachovia settlement had a tightly run communal system.

Fortunately for the potter Gottfried Aust, a Silesian-born artisan, there was good clay in the area. He soon had a busy shop, with three or four pottery wheels in operation. In the years between 1755 and 1788 he and his apprentices turned out a variety of wares: cream pots and cook pots, porringers, pint and quart mugs. They also made tiles for the Central European tile stoves preferred by the settlers.

In 1773 an order was issued that all craftsmen must display signs for their shops so that even the illiterate could identify the services or wares available. In response to this, Aust created a large plate, page 112 above, which is twenty-two inches in diameter, with loops or lugs at the back so it could be hung outside the shop. It is of earthenware with slip decoration. The background is the reddish color of the clay, the slip decoration is in green, yellow, and white. The ornament provides a sample of the kinds of decoration he could do. His name and the date are formed in clearly outlined letters and numbers. These are bordered and embellished with calligraphic scrolls and swirls. A circle with a compass-drawn floral pattern, and a diamond made of little diamond shapes, form major punctuation or spacing marks. The center is filled with a freely drawn flower and a bird. In general, Aust's work shows a close relationship in design and in finish with traditional German work of the period.

Aust's pottery was purchased by merchants who came from some distance and then sold the wares in their area. Several pieces believed to be by Aust have descended in a Rowan County, North Carolina, family, who lived about fifty miles from Salem. The slip decoration on one of these, page 112 below, is simpler than on the plate sign. A white slip base covers the earthenware; the decoration is in brown and green slip. The center motif is made up of lines and squiggles springing from a base, alternately dripped in firm and smudged lines, giving a curious suggestion of depth.

The potters in Bethabara and Salem were not the only potters in the back-country, for there were probably other German potters in the Piedmont as early as the 1740s, and it is believed there were English-born potters working in Randolph County, North Carolina, in the 1750s. Other utilitarian wares were made occasionally elsewhere, as we have seen in Virginia. However, the English and European manufacturers of porcelain and earthenware increased their production tremendously in the eighteenth century and dominated the market for ordinary tableware and fine decorative objects in the seaboard colonies.

Legally and politically, the eighteenth century was a man's world. The same was true of most of the arts. Clever women exerted influence indirectly if not directly. Some must have shared in decisions about house plans. There were the rare women painters, such as Mrs. Johnston in South Carolina; or those who knew something of their husband's professions and carried on after their deaths, as Mary Roberts, wife of Bishop Roberts, did. Certainly women cared about the ambience of their homes, but it was often the man, if Miles Brewton and Peter Manigault are typical, who took charge of ordering the plate, silver, and furniture.

If a woman were artistically inclined, loved form and color, had manual dexterity, and also had the time and wished to produce something relatively permanent, her major avenue for satisfying this inclination was in needlework and embroidery. Virtually every woman was taught to sew, and throughout their lives most women were responsible for doing or supervising all the "plain" sewing for their households, putting together everyday clothing and underwear, making sheets, pillowcases, towels, and

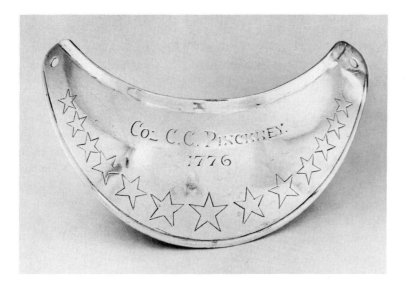

John Vanall. Silver gorget, Charleston, 1749–1752. Marked: "I. VANALL" in rectangle. "Col. C. C. Pinckney/1776" and thirteen stars added later. Charleston Museum.

Silver bracelet, found in the tomb of an Indian chief in Alabama. Inscribed: "A GIFT OF HIS EXCELLENCY HENRY ELLIS, ESQ. 1760." Private collection.

the like. She also had to know how to mark or do neat lettering or initialing, usually in cross-stitch, to identify household fabrics. More complex work was required for decorative hangings, coverlets or bedspreads, or needlework pictures.

Little girls began by making quite simple so-called marking samplers with letters of the alphabet and numbers. Then, if she liked it or was under the tutelage of someone who forced the discipline upon her, she would go on to the "fancy sampler" and more difficult stitching. The most elaborate work was probably done by women who had the leisure and materials—more often than not imported threads and fabrics—as well as the aptitude.

Nine-year-old Elizabeth Hext of Charleston must have been an unusually persevering and capable young woman to have completed the detailed sampler, page 113, in 1743. The grid of the fabric provides the basic structure for a sampler, the rows straight as a pulled thread. Dark lines of diamond patterns are used to divide the whole into sections. Interspersed within the rows of diamonds and alphabet, which is done in capitals of several sizes and in lower case, are several of those moralizing mottoes meant to prepare or inure the child to the death and judgment that would come sooner or later—perhaps sooner in a world where diphtheria, smallpox, measles, miscellaneous fevers and agues or death in early childbirth were too-familiar household events. One of these reads "Remember Man That Die Thou Must and after Come/To Judgment Just." Despite the dour messages she wrought in the cloth, she ends up with a rollicking verse that gives her name and place—establishing her identity in a way which children at a certain age love to do: "Elizabeth Hext is My Name Carolina is my Nation/Charles Town is My Dwelling Place and Christ is My Salvation." Then, "This Sampler Was Ended in the/Ninth Year of Her Age 1743." Miss Hext married when twenty or twenty-one and died at age thirty-five.

Several examples of white coverlets embroidered with white

Gottfried Aust. The sign of the potter, Salem, North Carolina, 1773. Earthenware slip-decorated plate. Old Salem, Inc., Winston-Salem, N.C.

Attributed to Gottfried Aust, w. 1755–1788. Earthenware plate with slip decoration, Salem, North Carolina. Old Salem, Inc., Winston-Salem, N.C.

yarns made by women in the South have survived. These were called "white work," as were several other techniques of working white on white. The central motif of one is shown at upper right. A variety of stitches is used to define the floral spray—trellis, buttonhole, diaper, and checker, among others. Within each flower or leaf form several textures or patterns are introduced.

Designs for coverlets such as this might have come from a variety of sources, some copied or modified from English or French chintzes, some borrowed or copied from friends. Drawing masters, such as William Dering, may have done designs. Occasionally a tutor, as in the case of Philip Fithian, who taught the Carter children, was asked to draw designs. On a cold winter night he noted in his diary, "Evening at Miss Prissy's Request I draw for her some Flowers on Linen which she is going to imbroider, for a various Counterpane." Then again, "I drew, this afternoon more Flowers for Miss Prissy." Some women may have drawn their own designs. They had to be outlined in the flat in order to be applied to the cloth. In this pattern all is curves, as compared with the strict geometry of the sampler. It is possible to identify holly leaves at the base of the spray in this coverlet, and the leaves of the sweet gum near the middle. The

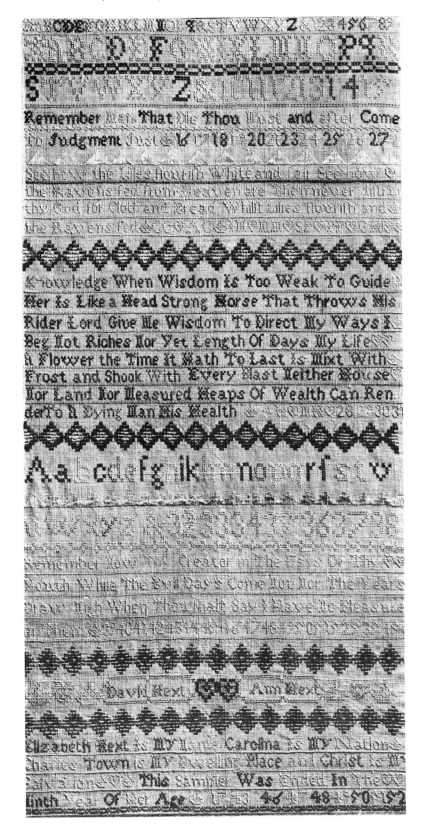

two major flowers near the top appear to be abstracted rendering of the carnation. It is just possible that this very excellent design was partly drawn from nature.

According to family tradition, the spread was made by Martha Hall, whose home was on a plantation in North Carolina, and the fabric is believed to have been grown and woven there. She married Benjamin Waller of Williamsburg in 1746. The finished coverlet is said to have first been used at the christening of her grandson, who was born in 1774.

Fewer embroidered or needlework fabrics seem to have survived from the Southern colonies than from the New England or middle colonies. This may be because, in a warm climate, less time is spent at indoor activities, or it may be that Southern women had more servants who did the basic sewing, and therefore they did not develop these skills as fully. Perhaps more decorated fabrics were imported—in North and South alike enormous quantities seem to have been purchased by the colonists. Or it may be those Southern familiars, hot, humid weather; hurricanes and floods; war and fires; or just plain wear and tear that have caused this seeming imbalance.

THE NEW NATION was self-consciously conceived. The Constitution, forged by delegates from all thirteen of the rebelling colonies and effective in June 1788, was an amalgam of legal and political concepts, some idealistic, some rational, some traditional, and some the result of pragmatic compromise. Certain ideas were borrowed from Roman antiquity, but they were put together in a new way, in a new setting, and under new circumstances. Differences among delegates were not necessarily manifested along regional lines of North and South, but were often differences between those who felt a central government should be strong and those who wished to give more power to the states. In forging the extraordinary document that is the American Constitution Southerners such as James Madison, George Mason, and George Washington were among the political leaders. Thomas Jefferson was in Paris representing the young nation in France, but his ideas played an important role. And in the decades up through 1824, four of the first five Presidents of the United States were from the South.

Political leadership does not necessarily mean leadership in the arts—quite the contrary all too often—but in these decades Jefferson particularly, and Washington and Madison to a lesser degree, found time to take an interest in the arts and felt some responsibility for encouraging or patronizing the arts, as did some other officials. It was a responsibility which philosophers of the Enlightenment felt men in public life should bear. In the everyday world of the arts, as in politics, a wide variety of factors affected development. There were those who sought ideal and public art. There were practical problems. Private tastes, new fashions, and a conservative appreciation of the past all had their influence.

When the genial Marquis de Chastellux, who had served under Rochambeau with the French forces in America, left the shores of America in 1783, he wrote a long letter to the president of William and Mary College on "The Progress of the Arts and Sciences in America." It was a discursive, thoughtful treatise in which he perceptively touched upon problems and circumstances which might affect the development of the fine arts in the new United States. His point of view was that of the educated European caught up in the optimistic concepts of the Enlightenment. His ideas on the arts were partly derived from late Renaissance artistic theory in which the fine arts were defined as architecture, painting, and sculpture, and in which it was assumed that the contemplation of such art would be morally and spiritually uplifting, theories familiar to some artists, artisans, and patrons but which, in the middle years of the eighteenth century, were not in fact very influential in Europe or the American colonies. Chastellux, something of a reforming French *philosophe*, found these ideas attractive and hoped they would prevail, so that the arts could be used to foster "that national pride, so necessary to the preservation of liberty."

Chastellux's letter was appended to his *Travels in North America*, published in 1786. An English translation came out in 1787, so his ideas and impressions had fairly wide currency. Even before publication, the letter was apparently circulated, for Jefferson knew of it as early as 1784 and encouraged Chastellux to publish it. The letter, per se, probably did not have a profound influence, but the thinking he expressed was gaining favor on the Continent and was shared by a number of leaders of the new Republic.

One of the problems that disturbed and preoccupied Chastellux was the role of cities in the new nation. He really hoped that America could remain essentially rural. Still, he wondered how the arts would flourish in the new democracy, for he noted sadly that the fine arts had had their most brilliant periods in the past under great patrons and when there was great inequality of wealth, such as under Augustus or under the powerful Roman popes. He wondered whether they could flourish in an essentially rural country: "There is one circumstance, however, which we have not yet touched upon, and which seems indispensable, both for their preservation and for their establishment. The arts, there can be no doubt about it, can never flourish, except where a great number of men are assembled. They must have large cities, they must have capitals. America possesses five such which seem ready to receive them. You can yourself name

"Virginia Capitol in 1830." Engraved from a drawing by William Goodacre, and published from 1831 until 1861 in editions of Hinton's HISTORY AND TOPOGRAPHY OF THE U.S. *The side entrance shown here replaced an earlier one and was itself replaced by the entrance seen on photographs after 1865. Valentine Museum, Richmond, Virginia.*

the first degree awarded in 1798. South Carolina was not far behind, with its university at Columbia chartered in 1805 and the first degree given in 1806. In time each of these institutions, and others, were to erect buildings that would stand as symbols of learning.

In truth it would be a long while before these capital cities or these universities and other schools served as genuine centers for the encouragement of the arts. Still, there was hope and optimism. The very names of some of these capitals and university communities were selected to evoke a sense of the history of the new nation and the role of these places: Columbia, Raleigh, Athens. The wish that the arts could serve the new nation, and that the nation and the states could be patrons of artists and thus foster a native tradition, runs through the story of artistic efforts both North and South during the first half of the nineteenth century. The South was more rural than the North and, though Baltimore, Charleston, and New Orleans, as well as other small cities in the South, provided patronage for the arts, they could not completely rival the established and growing commercial centers of New York, Philadelphia, and Boston.

them: Boston, New York, Philadelphia, Baltimore, and Charleston. But these are seaports, and commerce, it cannot be denied, has more magnificence than taste; it pays, rather than encourages artists."

Because Chastellux was skeptical of the "magnificence" rather than "taste" of the commercial centers, he encouraged the founding of capitals that would each "be the seat of government, but not a commercial city." He suggested that these be located in the center of each state so as to be accessible to all the citizenry, that a university be established at a small distance from each capital, and that "this capital and its annex preserve, like the sacred fire, the true rational spirit, . . . that spirit which allies itself perfectly with liberty and public happiness." It was for reasons such as these that the founding fathers saw fit to establish a national capital city, Washington, in 1790. In Virginia the move from Williamsburg to Richmond was proposed in 1776 and made in 1780. In South Carolina work began on a new State House in Columbia in 1788, where the capital had been changed from Charleston. The legislature of North Carolina occupied a building in Raleigh in 1794, having met in a succession of places during and after the Revolution. Other new capitals were to follow. The moves were motivated by the desire for more central locations, in order to give the up-country people easier access to the legislative bodies. In each case there was probably some maneuvering among land speculators before a specific site was selected. Progress was halting, legislators were not always enthusiastic, but gradually new buildings were created. These provided the space necessary for government functions, and also served as symbols, focal points, "temples of democracy."

Georgia and North Carolina took the lead in establishing state-chartered universities. The University of Georgia, at Athens, was the first. It was chartered in January 1785, though the first degree was not awarded until 1804. The University of North Carolina at Chapel Hill was chartered in December 1789, and

Symbols of a New Nation.

Virginia, with Jefferson as prime mover and skillful force behind the scenes, led the way in creating architecture for a new capital. Jefferson, son of a surveyor, had early developed a love of architecture and a practical knowledge of building as but two of his many interests. When Chastellux visited Jefferson at the latter's home at Monticello in 1782 he had found him the "first American who has consulted the Fine Arts to know how he should shelter himself from the weather." And he marveled that one who had never seen the shores of Europe should be familiar with such a wide range of subjects. At that time Jefferson's own house was unfinished, but enough was there to show Jefferson's imaginative use of space and familiarity with "Italian" or Palladian ideas. Jefferson had studied the books on architecture by Andrea Palladio, Robert Morris, and James Gibbs, and admired the classical buildings they depicted.

Before the move to the new capital of Richmond in 1780 Jefferson had already made sketches for two governmental buildings. He hoped there might be a pair of Roman temples on the site he favored, Shockoe Hill, which overlooked the river and the town. It would have been a remarkable plan. However, the war was still on, the British came through Richmond, and all plans were suspended, not to be taken up again for four years. By that time Jefferson was in Paris as American minister to France. It was decided that the state could afford only one building, and the group appointed to see the project through, the Directors of the Public Buildings, drew up a list of needs and a rough plan. But they floundered, and wrote to Jefferson, asking him to consult an able architect, and to suggest a design that would "unite economy with elegance and dignity."

Jefferson's interest in ancient art had led him to become acquainted with Charles-Louis Clérisseau, architect, scholar, and author of a book on classical architecture, *Monuments de Nîsmes*, and he had no hesitation in naming Clérisseau as his consultant, although he did not immediately send plans. The directors plunged ahead, lest critics should decide Richmond wasn't the best place for a capital after all. Foundations for a building 148 by 118 feet were laid, with the thought that it might have a series of square rooms around an atrium. This was not the Roman temple Jefferson had been dreaming about, and he tactfully wrote back saying that, rather than ask an architect to draw up a new plan which might not be of a pleasing form, they might better select a known and time-tested building and use it as a model. The building he suggested was the Maison Carrée, in the South of France, "erected at the time of the Caesars, and which is allowed without contradiction to be the most perfect and precious remain of antiquity in existence." It was a design that had "pleased universally for nearly 2,000 years." Clérisseau had studied it at firsthand. Jefferson was familiar with it because it was shown in Palladio. He and Clérisseau had the wisdom to have a model of their adaptation of the Maison Carrée made and shipped it to Virginia to give a clear and tangible idea of what was being proposed. The builder, Samuel Dobie, was able to make minor changes in the foundation, and by October 1786 the walls to the top of the principal story were up.

In adapting the design of the Maison Carrée, Jefferson and Clérisseau simplified it, substituting the Ionic order for the Corinthian and, in a final plan, eliminating pilasters on the side, making it easier to introduce windows. It was also decided to make the portico two columns deep, both for reasons of economy and so as not to darken the interior.

In October 1788 the legislature began to use the building, though it was then no more than four walls of unstuccoed brick with a high parapet and a flat roof; it was months, then years, before Jefferson's temple was finished. The model helped to fix the vision of what would be. Samuel Dobie drew working plans and made some changes, including the reintroduction of pilasters. A variety of other changes, important and unimportant, were suggested, and some made. It was decided to eliminate the front steps, since they would darken the offices beneath. Finally, in 1798, it was completed, stuccoed, and whitewashed. Houdon's statue of Washington, dignified, erect, of a modern and still-living hero, was placed in the central salon. Jefferson, now back home in America, familiar with France and England, and with the original Maison Carrée (which he had not seen when he sent over plans and model), thought a few corrections should be made. Nonetheless, he was proud. It was a building of "first rate dignity." And so it was and is. An engraving, left and opening Part III, published in 1831, shows how it looked then, a little stark in an unlandscaped setting, but bold and important in its eminence. The side stairs shown replaced earlier ones. It was not until after 1865 that the front steps were added.

Jefferson's respect and love for the antique in architecture are manifest in his choice of a Roman temple as a model for a modern building. In so doing, he and his fellow Virginians could suggest that they, too, were building for the ages—not just structures, but forms of government. It was an experiment in using architecture itself as symbol, though they did not phrase it as such. By selecting and modifying an ancient building, they made a confident statement on the future of the new federated states.

Part of the success of the Virginia Capitol is its relation to the site. It perches over the city and the river, not on the very top of the hill, but high enough to dominate and to provide a vista, low enough to be somewhat sheltered. Jefferson had built his own home on a little mountain, "Monticello." In 1791 he made a rough sketch of the contours of the land along the Potomac that had been selected as the site for the new Federal city and noted the hill where the nation's Capitol might be placed. He provided the engineer, Pierre Charles L'Enfant, with a sheaf of European city plans in order to suggest ideas to the Frenchman who had been chosen to create a design for the new city. He maintained an active interest in the plans and building of the President's house and in the early construction of the Capitol, helping to shape buildings that are now so well known as symbols they almost aren't seen. People speak of "the Hill'—the site that Washington, Jefferson, L'Enfant, and their colleagues selected years ago—and mean the whole complex of the nation's legislative machinery.

The first building erected in 1794 in Raleigh, North Carolina, as a statehouse was evidently a plain brick building, which did not especially please the legislators or townsmen. In a burst of patriotic fervor following the War of 1812, the North Carolina legislature decided they should improve their Capitol by placing in it a figure of George Washington, now dead, and the cherished hero of the new nation. In 1815 the governor consulted a wide circle of acquaintances, and finally took Jefferson's advice, who was by then retired and living at Monticello. As with the Virginia commission to Houdon, there were no sculptors working in America whom Jefferson felt capable of creating an appropriate monument. He recommended the Italian Antonio Canova, "for 30 years, within my own Knowledge, he has been considered by all Europe as without a rival. . . . As to the style or costume, I am sure that the artist, and every person of taste in Europe would be for Roman. . . . Our boots and regimentals have a very puny effect." The sage of Monticello went on to recommend that Canova might use a bust that had been done by another Italian artist, Giuseppe Ceracchi, and even told the governor where one of these might be found in Italy.

The bust of Washington used by Canova, and taken from a terra-cotta model by Ceracchi, may be the one shown on the following page. Ceracchi was an enthusiastic sculptor of republican principles who had come to America in 1791–1792, and again in 1794–1795, trying to persuade someone—Congress or public-spirited citizens who might set up a lottery—to subsidize a large monument to Liberty. In the process he made individual terra-cotta busts of over two dozen of the founding fathers, including the patient Washington. The funds were simply not available, and the whole idea fell through. It may have been too grandiose a concept to appeal to the American public, even if they had had the money.

While Ceracchi was in the United States, the terra-cotta model for Washington was seen by a number of his acquaintances, who are supposed to have found it a good likeness, especially the expression of the mouth. Following the dictates of the neoclassic, Ceracchi rendered the hair of the hero in the "timeless" style of ancient Rome. There is no record that this disturbed Washington's compatriots, nor is there a record that it was enthusiastically accepted. The likeness of Washington which

Giuseppe Ceracchi, or based on his work. Colossal bust of George Washington. c. 1792. Marble. Carolina Art Association/Gibbes Art Gallery, Charleston, South Carolina.

most appealed to his contemporaries was that done by the painter Gilbert Stuart. The bust shown here is larger than life, or colossal, and was either done by Ceracchi or by someone else at Signora Ceracchi's behest, after they returned to Italy. Canova may have acquired this bust and used it as a model for the North Carolina statue (or he may have used another version). Still later, this bust was acquired in Rome in 1820 by a scion of a South Carolina family, John Izard Middleton, and brought to America. It is one of four versions that has found its way back to this country.

Canova worked on his full-scale statue of Washington for more than a year, completing it in March 1821. It was delivered to Raleigh in December and greeted with much ceremony, having been carefully transported by steamboat and specially built

carriages. There was a procession and an official address. It excited "deep" and "powerful interest." It later burned, but we know how it looked from an engraving, right. The seated general (in antique dress) was shown writing his Farewell Address. In the flowery language of the time, the artist was described as a Praxiteles, a Phidias, and a Michelangelo. There was a hint of criticism in the newspaper account, which reported that some objected to showing an American general clothed as a Roman and sitting in a Roman chair. The paper explained, although it did not defend the reasons for the choice, "it is consonant to the present taste, and Canova, a Roman himself, has been so long accustomed to the classical costumes, that it would have been difficult for him to have done justice to the subject in any other garb." If Canova, the most celebrated sculptor of the time, saw fit to so show their hero, they would accept it. (The recorded comments of more than one later visitor indicate that the unrecognizable Roman guise bewildered and did not please. Still, all acknowledged the artistry, and the effect of the whole.)

The statue was on a high pedestal, and the four scenes below, at eye level, were in contemporary dress, showing the surrender of Cornwallis, the resignation of Washington at the close of the war, the "Hero, like Cincinnatus, holding the plough, on his return to private life," and Washington accepting the presidency of the United States. These were done by Tranatanove, Canova's assistant.

The newspaper reporter thought the statue and pedestal to be "finished with a boldness of outline, and a delicacy of taste, which rank them with the choicest specimens of antiquity."

But what really was important to the journalist and to Colonel William Polk, who gave the address, were the memories of Washington and his virtues, described in great detail, which the statue evoked, and the pride of North Carolina in having offered their "sister states an example worthy of imitation." Because of these he hoped that the arts would be encouraged. Polk waxed eloquent in the last paragraphs of his talk: "The record of such virtues should be transmitted to posterity by every means the Muse of History, of Painting, and of Sculpture can employ. . . . May we not, then, fellow-citizens, indulge the hope, that this beautiful specimen of the arts, besides its moral effects in holding up to the imitation of our youth the great qualities it commemorates, also refine their taste, and awaken their latent energies of genius—that while it inculcates the virtues that render life useful to our Country; it may diffuse a relish for the arts that embellish society, and call forth a display of the varied powers of man's ingenuity."

This was the evocative public art Chastellux had called for almost forty years earlier, and the values and ideas he hoped would be inspired by it.

In order to receive the statue, the North Carolina legislature employed William Nichols, an English-born master-builder, to improve and refurbish their statehouse. He was instructed to add another story and to convert the cupola to a dome. This he did, and the appearance of the Carolina State House as remodeled can be seen in a painting by Jacob Marling, following page, done sometime between 1821 and 1831. The architect added the third floor and wings to each of the long sides, making the building a Greek cross in plan. Each arm of the cross was given a pediment. Inexpensive stucco was used to help create the illusion of a heavily rusticated arcade on the ground floor in the front. The walls of this arcade were spattered with paint to make it look like gray granite. The technique of painting "false granite" is a variant of those used for creating patterns of graining or marbleizing. Ionic pilasters were applied under the pediments to create a more monumental effect. As requested, the cupola was turned into a dome; a rotunda lighted by oculi above was cut from the ground up and the Washington statue placed in it.

Nichols's building was a success, and he went on to receive the commission for the Alabama Capitol, then in Tuscaloosa, in 1827, and the old Capitol at Jackson, Mississippi, in 1834–1838. Both had virtually the same plan. The Alabama building was described as economical, "spacious, convenient, durable and imposing." The Mississippi Capitol, in which the architect used Greek orders and details, is the only one of the three that still survives.

Joseph Marling (died 1833), who did the painting of the North Carolina State House, came to the new capital city sometime after 1813. His origins are unknown. He painted portraits and miniatures, and he and his wife helped to foster the cultural and intellectual life of the little capital. He was director of the short-lived North Carolina Museum, which apparently had a small collection of paintings, including a few of his own. There was a reading room and miscellaneous displays, "natural and artificial curiosities, sketches, maps . . . rare coins and books." He advertised from time to time as a painter of portraits and miniatures. Several of these, including portraits of legislators,

Antonio Canova. Statue of Washington, formerly in the Old State House, Raleigh, North Carolina. c. 1821. Engraving.

GIORGIO WASHINGTON

Alla grande Nazione degli Stati Uniti di America

Antonio Canova D.D.D.

Jacob Marling. "First North Carolina State House." c. 1821–1831. Oil on canvas. North Carolina Museum of History, Raleigh.

have survived. His wife taught painting and drawing at the Raleigh Academy.

Marling's painting of the Capitol has a pleasing lightness and brightness of color. The yellow stucco building, with its gray rusticated base, stands out in the somewhat barren landscape setting. In the foreground are two men, perhaps legislators, standing and in conversation with each other. Three Negroes are shown, two children playing, and a woman who stands watching. Other small figures are shown as if moving about the scene. This painting is one of a group of what was becoming an increasingly popular genre, the portrait of a place. These are not pure landscape, but rather views of specific places. In the new country these seem to have contributed to a sense of identity and perhaps to a sense of permanence. There were a few other artists

who briefly visited Raleigh in these years, but Marling was the only one who established a permanent residence.

The new capitol, with the light shining down on the Washington statue in the central rotunda, was the pride of the state and a sight to see. A lithograph, not wholly accurate, right, shows three visitors, a dignified couple, the man clearly absorbed in contemplation, and a child, who seems to be tracing letters at the base. The artist of the lithograph couldn't quite bring himself to reproduce the Romanlike head of Washington, so he has substituted the familiar visage from Stuart's painting. Light bathes the head. The neoclassical taste had so influenced everyday fashion by the mid-1820s that the gentleman shown has a haircut that echoes the antique, and the lady a dress vaguely Greek.

The governor of North Carolina had also been authorized to

purchase two full-length portraits of Washington. For these he decided upon Thomas Sully, an artist who had come to America from England with his actor-parents in 1792, at the age of nine. He grew up in Charleston and learned painting from his brother-in-law, Jean Belzons, a French miniature painter now virtually unknown, and his own brother. He began his career in Norfolk and Richmond; by 1818 he had been settled in Philadelphia for a decade.

Sully first made the North Carolinians a copy based on one of Stuart's paintings, and this hangs in the capitol at Raleigh today. For the second, he proposed a more ambitious original "historical Portrait" showing an incident from the Revolutionary War, and estimated the size would be 10 feet by 8 feet. His offer was accepted. After he had spent time on preparatory sketches, he wrote again, asking for the exact size of wall space available. He was told that it was 10 feet by 9 feet 2 inches, an area only slightly larger than his own original estimate. By the time he received the reply, probably no more than two weeks after his query, he had in fact already commenced work on a considerably larger (12 feet 2½ inches by 17 feet) painting. When the painting, following page, was finished in December 1819, the state of North Carolina understandably asked him to annul the contract since it was too large for the space. In January 1820 the artist amicably agreed.

It is possible that, once launched on the project, Sully had the idea of first taking the painting on exhibit. This was frequently done by artists and was a way for them to attain wider fame, and more money, than from commissions. In April the painting was on view in Norfolk. William Dunlap, the first historian of American art, was in the city at the same time. He found the "horses are admirable. The whole composition grand. The distances sublime." Sully tried to catch, and heighten, the effect of the cold winter night in 1776 when Washington's forces crossed the Delaware, surprised the Hessian troops, and won a decisive battle at Trenton. Washington, on a white horse, and three aides, one on a rearing horse, are on the right. To the left are the troops, the river, and a cold gray sky. Although Sully also exhibited the painting in Washington and Boston, it did not meet with widespread approbation. When Dunlap wrote about the picture later, in his 1834 book, it was with some bitterness about the lack of public appreciation of the painting: "Unfortunately, Washington's portrait was not acknowledged a likeness. . . . If it was an old instead of a modern picture, the winter landscape alone would stamp it as a jewel; but in old pictures one good part redeems—in the modern, one faulty condemns." Sully seems to have shared this bitterness, and felt he had not realized his investment in time and materials. The painting ultimately passed through several hands, lay rolled up for many years, but now is proudly on display at the Boston Museum of Fine Arts.

There was a frenzy of patriotic fervor when General Lafayette, who had been barely twenty when he first came to help the American cause in the Revolution, visited America in 1824–1825 after an absence of over forty years. He was a venerable but obviously healthy and spry sixty-seven, for he made an incredible triumphal tour of the new nation, during which he traversed the whole of the South. At each stop he was received with great ceremony, troops and notables often escorting him from one point to the next. Artists were regularly called on to decorate halls and banners, to paint transparencies which were put in windows, to build temporary arches, and some to paint portraits and miniatures.

In Raleigh a newspaper account reveals that a major part of the ceremony took place at the east front of the Capitol, "opposite Canova's celebrated statue of Washington," and full advantage was derived from the setting. There Lafayette, the hero of the Revolution, and the virtues of liberty under the freedom of the Constitution, were lauded. He saw old soldiers "whose furrowed cheeks are bedewed with tears . . . impatient to clasp you to their hearts."

After the address and Lafayette's response he "was then introduced . . . to that chef d'oeuvre of the Roman Artist, the Statue of Washington. This was indeed an interesting scene, and we were fortunately so situated, that we heard the enquiries and remarks and witnessed the feelings which it elicited. We were

Statue of George Washington, formerly in the Old State House, Raleigh, North Carolina. Before 1831. Lithograph. North Carolina Museum of History, Raleigh.

Thomas Sully. "Washington's Passage of the Delaware." 1819. Oil on canvas.
Museum of Fine Arts, Boston, Massachusetts.

gratified to have the General observe, that the likeness was much better than he expected to see. He seemed deeply interested in examining the historical designs on the pedestal, and expressed his approbation of the exquisite workmanship of the whole." Toasts were later drunk to Washington, Lafayette, North Carolina, Congress, "our country," "departed heroes and Patriots of our Revolution," Greece, South America, France, the President, James Monroe, and the new President, John Quincy Adams, and still others.

In 1831 the Capitol of North Carolina burned, "a sheet of blinding, hissing flame." A spectator reported that he heard "amidst the almost breathless silence of the stupified multitude around it, the piteous exclamation of a child, 'poor State House, poor Statue, I so sorry.'" North Carolina's prized statue was mutilated and defaced, never to be repaired. In the 1820s it had been one of the best-known works of art in America. It has been suggested that this statue played a leading role in making monumental marble statuary acceptable and desirable in this country.

Because of its success, other sculptors could more easily get commissions. The state of North Carolina soon built a new Capitol, chiefly the work of the New York firm of Town and Davis, a building that still survives.

Lafayette belonged to the pantheon of American heroes before his visit in 1824–1825, but the visit cemented his position. Edward F. Peticolas of Richmond painted the hero in a full-length portrait, right, against a dramatic classical setting, by a swirl of bright red drapery. The full, but not stout, figure suggests the general's age. During his travels a perceptive Charlestonian woman described him: "He is . . . a good deal infirm from age though his appearance from the colour of his wig and the brilliancy of his eye is altogether youthful." Peticolas has caught his youthfulness. The insignia hanging from his waist may be the eagle of the Society of the Cincinnati—he and other French officers had been made members, and during the trip he was honored by its members on several special occasions. The Masons, too, frequently honored him. (It is not clear how often

Lafayette sat for the portraits painted of him during this trip; in some cases he gave only one sitting, and the artist, with the aid of engravings, made a complete portrait later.)

Edward F. Peticolas worked as an artist in Richmond from 1805 until 1840. During this period he made three extended trips to Europe, for around four years between 1815 and 1820, again in 1825, and for the last time in 1830–1833. His father was a miniaturist, and a drawing and music teacher, who had come to America from Santo Domingo after slave insurrections in 1790. Edward learned to paint from his father and had some lessons from Thomas Sully. William Dunlap visited Peticolas in Richmond in 1821 and found "His style was chaste, his coloring clear, and I felt that he deserved all the employment of that city." The comment was apt. The reds, greens, pale yellow, umber, and ocher tones in this painting have clarity and liquidity. Details are suggested and described rather than precisely rendered. Vistas open up the composition. There is a spacious, uncluttered quality that may owe something to familiarity with the work of the English painter Sir Thomas Lawrence. From the little information available on Peticolas it appears that he was a modest, retiring, even reclusive person, and may not have had many patrons. His last years were plagued by rheumatism and he painted little after 1840.

In Charleston the city commissioned a miniature of Lafayette, following page, by Charles Fraser, who by this time had a secure place and near-monopoly on miniature painting there. Using predominantly blue tones, the artist, working in very small scale, has implied the heroic by suggesting a classical setting, and opening up a vista to the right. After laying in flat areas of color the artist built up the definitions of form by a stipple technique, using short wavy lines over most of the surface and tiny dots in the flesh tones. The blue-ribboned insignia is that of the Society of the Cincinnati.

The state capitol buildings, and the statues and paintings of Washington and Lafayette, were among the most obvious of the works of art created to provide imagery and inspiration for the nation. Some efforts were genuinely successful, others forced or abortive. Some caught the mood of the country—the North Carolina Washington was popular even if there were doubts about the validity of the antique form. Other heroes gradually emerge. Jackson, Clay, Calhoun, and Daniel Boone are among those especially honored in the South. These efforts did not, could not, in themselves lead to a new, different native tradition—this is more the kind of burden placed upon the arts by theorists and academicians than by artists who learn and know the traditions of their crafts and grow from these. In the early years of the nineteenth century, however, there are the beginnings of national, and regional, iconographies—the state capitols, the country courthouses, the city halls, that give a sense of place: the images and figures that come to mind when we think of the history of the nation.

Architecture

Those who built houses and public buildings in the South in the years after the Revolution and up to the 1820s made a variety of choices. Some carefully and skillfully followed the latest taste as it came from England and France. Others used familiar and traditional plans, but adhered to the new taste in choice of door, window, and interior trim. Several typically Southern building types, such as the "Charleston single," and a number of characteristic New Orleans and lower Mississippi Valley houses and cottages evolved during this period. And some of the great co-

Edward F. Peticolas. "The Marquis de Lafayette." 1824. Oil on canvas. Valentine Museum, Richmond, Virginia.

Charles Fraser. "The Marquis de Lafayette." 1825. Watercolor on ivory. City Hall Council Chamber, Charleston, South Carolina.

lumnar mansions of the South—a type used perhaps more often than is justified as symbol of the antebellum South—were erected during these years as well.

Harbingers of a new taste for the neoclassical can be found in the American colonies in buildings and objects created before the American Revolution, as in some of the interior decoration in the Chase-Lloyd house in Annapolis. With growth and prosperity after the Revolution the new taste held sway, a taste that is especially reflected in details and sometimes in room shapes. Because this taste coincides with the founding of a nation of federated states, it is now usually called the Federal style in this country. In some ways it represents a modification and continuation of the preoccupation with ancient Roman forms that had gripped the minds of artists, architects, and designers since the Renaissance. In other ways, in a fresh awareness of specific ancient monuments, and a greater interest in the specifics of the history of art, it represents the beginning of a new historicism, which was to play a vital role in the arts throughout the nineteenth century.

The mid-eighteenth-century discovery in Italy of the ancient and buried towns of Pompeii and Herculaneum was an important factor in stimulating a renewed interest in the antique, though very little was excavated and known about these sites until con-

siderably later. Other, more accessible sites were studied, uncovered, drawn, and discussed by artists, scholars, and dilettantes. These included the Roman ruins of Diocletian's palace in Dalmatia, in present Yugoslavia, and those in the Near East at Baalbek and Palmyra. Jefferson's friend Clérisseau had studied the still-surviving Roman ruins at Nîmes in southern France. And there were always the remarkable ruins of ancient Rome in that great city. (In the eighteenth century some of these were still half buried under the layers of civilization there.) Ancient Greek ruins were also being scrutinized anew. Scholars and artists were beginning to discriminate more carefully among the "ancients," and to see the differences between the style of the Greeks and that of the Romans. They realized there was no monolithic or consistent single system, but that there was much variety in decoration, in proportions, and in some shapes and plans of buildings.

The architect in England most responsible for introducing new-old classical forms at this time was, as previously discussed, Robert Adam, who had traveled in Italy and Dalmatia, and published his book on Diocletian's palace in 1764. Much of his work was in remodeling older country houses, so that some of his most famous creations are interiors, where he concerned himself with the ornamentation and decoration of walls, ceilings, mantels and

*William Birch. "Montebello,
the Seat of Genl. S. Smith,
Maryland." c. 1812–1828.
Engraving. Montebello was built
about 1799, probably designed by
General Samuel Smith (razed
1909). Baltimore Museum of Art.*

fireplaces, door and window frames, and the skillful reordering of room shapes. He frequently designed furniture and related objects for his clients as well. In his designs he moved from the generously proportioned moldings, door and window frames of the mid-Georgian to more delicate and attenuated forms. He soon abandoned the naturalistic curves and playful qualities of the rococo, introducing instead thin, restrained forms derived from the antique, such as swags and urns, festoons of bellflowers and husks. The fan, the oval, and the ellipse were favored shapes, the geometric basis of a design was usually clearly defined, and a variety of geometric forms were used in patterns.

Adam and other architects responding to similar impulses favored more variety in room shapes; oval rooms or oval-ended rooms were popular. More thought was given to convenience. Such amenities as a second or back stairs, closets, and pantries were introduced. On the exterior the trim around doors and windows was simplified and restrained. A favorite device to give surface elegance was the placement of an arched window within a larger slightly recessed arch on the wall, thus creating discreet accents upon wall surfaces.

One of the earliest houses in America in which the new taste was manifested throughout, not just in the interior as in the pre-Revolutionary Chase-Lloyd of Annapolis, was the William Bingham house in Philadelphia, built in 1788 (long since destroyed). Another Philadelphia house, the Woodlands, was completely remodeled in the new style in the same year. Near Baltimore, General Samuel Smith built a mansion, Montebello, for himself around 1799. Though it is now destroyed, it is clear from the engraving, above, and the plan, right, that it was a thoroughly

Plan of Montebello. Maryland Historical Society, Baltimore.

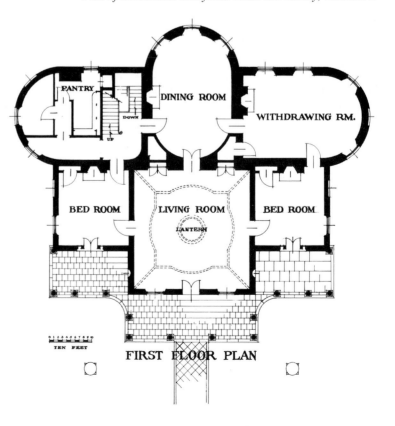

FIRST FLOOR PLAN

House on Fell Street, Baltimore, Maryland, c. 1787.

for a year or more around 1772, and so could have known first-hand the new taste of England and Europe. During the war he distinguished himself as a soldier, and after the Revolution grew wealthy as a merchant and through land speculation. His duties and business took him to many parts of the new country so that, if he had an eye for architecture, as he seems to have had, he would have been familiar with what was being built and discussed by men who shared this interest. His career ultimately combined forty years of service in Congress and a period as mayor of Baltimore in his old age.

Montebello is exceptional in being so completely Adamesque in plan. The Joseph Manigault house, built between 1790 and 1803, and the Nathaniel Russell house, built before 1809, both in Charleston and both still standing, are also among the great houses in the South where the Adamesque is expressed in the plan: both have projecting bays and curve-shaped rooms. The ornament in both is graceful and delicate. More typically, the new taste was taken up by those who introduced the characteristic elements of trim and proportions, but who made only slight modifications to basic plans and elevations. Traditional or vernacular forms undergirded the outward changes.

Baltimore experienced tremendous growth in the decades immediately before and after the Revolution, and became the third largest city in the new nation during the lifetime of the Revolutionary generation. In 1752 there were about 300 inhabitants, and by 1776, 6,755. Baltimore had become larger than Annapolis. This growth came about as the land to its north and west was settled and cultivated. Just before the Revolution wheat had become a major crop in Maryland. The grain and produce from these new farmlands were brought to Baltimore by wagon and boat, the grain milled there, and then exported to the West Indies and Europe. In the first Federal census of 1790, 13,503 inhabitants were recorded, including 1,255 slaves and 323 free blacks. The names of a group of streets laid out during this expansive period reflect a patriotic pride in the struggles and accomplishments of the Revolution. Lexington, Saratoga, and Eutaw commemorate important battles. Greene, Paca, and Fayette commemorate, respectively, the commander of the Southern campaign, the Maryland signer of the Declaration of Independence, and the well-known French officer. By the early 1830s Baltimore had over 70,000 people. The new country had rejected English rule, but this did not mean that English culture or taste was rejected. Baltimoreans shared and kept pace with changes from abroad and were among the tastemakers of the new republic.

This period of expansion saw the birth of the Baltimore row house, a type that was and still is characteristic of the city's street vistas. The earliest were similar to those already familiar in nearby Philadelphia, but during the late eighteenth and early nineteenth centuries the type became even more dominant than they were there. The first houses in Baltimore had been of wood, but by 1799 fire had become such a menace that the city enacted an ordinance prohibiting the erection of wooden buildings in the central sections of the city. Local brickmakers increased production, and since there was good clay in the region, brick was soon a cheaper building material than wood. The earliest row houses were usually built in groups of two or four, but

Adamesque building. It was a compact, stuccoed house with oval ends to the two-story main block, and a projecting one-story block on the front. A balustrade surmounts each. The long, elegant windows had only the most reticent trim, while French windows on the front were recessed in shallow arches. Closets of several shapes must have made it a convenient home. The oval dining room was apparently the most elaborately decorated room in the house.

General Smith is known to have designed his own townhouse in Baltimore in 1796 and it is probable that he designed Montebello as well. As a young man he had traveled in Europe

later speculators and builders built groups of eight or more at a time, sometimes as many as twenty.

A house on Fell Street in Baltimore, left, built around 1787 by a shipbuilder, is a typical example of a Baltimore townhouse of the Federal period. Many of these houses, designed for middle-class occupants, were one-room wide, with an entrance hall on the side. (The later and less expensive versions, meant for working-class housing, usually lacked separate entrance halls.) The exterior of the Fell Street house is notably restrained. The windowsills project slightly. The flat-arch trim over the windows is flush with the surface and so forms only a very subtle accent. (A "flat arch" seems a contradiction in terms. The bricks are set on end and cut to make them slant. This suggests the arch form, but the line over the opening is flat.) The trim around the arched door is also flush with the wall and equally subtle. It is this very restraint that characterizes the new style in its urban expression.

The interior trim on Baltimore townhouses was more elaborate. The door frame and chair rail, right, from a house on Thames Street, a house that was similar in exterior appearance to the Fell Street house, built around 1790, show the delicate, classical, essentially geometric ornament favored by this taste. Ribboned swags are used on either side of a central motif composed of a bird and formal scrolls on the "door cap" or frieze of the entablature of the door frame. Small trophies of crossed torches and quivers are placed above each swag. There is a row of small rosettes directly below, and a double row of gouged fluting is above. At either end, over the capitals of the pilasters, are ovals with human figures shown inside. Most of this applied ornament was of plaster or stucco. These forms could be combined in different arrangements. The pilasters on the sides of the doors are stylized and are slim in proportion.

A number of craftsmen specialized in making ornaments of the kind seen here, including John Rawlings, mentioned earlier. Joseph Kennedy and Thomas Littlejohn advertised in 1790 that they could do stucco work and plastering, and listed the houses where Kennedy's work could be seen. Kennedy was from Dublin and advertised that he had been "regularly bred under as good workmen as any in Ireland."

In Charleston the most typical urban dwelling built in the first two or three decades after the Revolution was the Charleston single, as it is proudly identified locally. This is an ingenious combination of a narrow, urban house with a two-story porch or "piazza" and an adjacent garden. The piazza and garden are screened from the street—the piazza by an entrance door, the garden by a high wall. You can walk along some Charleston streets and barely be aware of the open, airy verandas and verdant gardens beyond the street-level door and wall, so skillfully protected are they. The second stories of the piazzas are open on the street end, but above the eye level of a passerby. The residents have the best of both worlds, a convenient urban home and a private garden sanctuary. From the upstairs piazzas they can, if they wish, unobtrusively observe the ever-changing life of the street as well as catch whatever breezes there may be. Most of the porches are canted to catch the prevailing winds from the harbor.

The Charleston single seems to have evolved from earlier building types, but by the post-Revolutionary years had become peculiar to Charleston. Certainly no other city has as many comparable examples. In its typical or evolved form, as seen at 123 Tradd Street, following page, it is a narrow house, one room wide. There are only three bays across this narrow front, which faces the street. The significant difference from other traditional urban row houses is that, as here, the entrance to the interior is on the side, which is five bays deep. The double or two-storied piazza is on this side, and thus one reaches the entrance to the

Door frame and chair rail from first-floor front rooms of a house on Thames Street in Baltimore, Maryland, built c. 1790.

A typical Charleston single house, 123 Tradd Street, Charleston, South Carolina, c. 1800.

house through the closed street-level entrance to the piazza and the corridorlike open piazza itself. In a sense this is an adaptation of the old Mediterranean pattern of reaching the interior through a sheltered outdoor walkway or enclosed patio.

Inside there is a central stair hall and entrance opening between the two ground-floor rooms. The first two stories have essentially the same plan. The typical Charleston single usually has an inside back wall chimney. The roof is hipped. The door at 123 Tradd, which closes off the piazza from the street, has the slender proportions and delicate ornament characteristic of the Federal period.

What is remarkable in this vernacular type—there are rows and rows of them in Charleston—is the way the sidelong double piazza was built as an integral part of the house. These piazzas seem to have evolved locally from the different kinds of balconies and country porches we have already seen. Recent scholars do not believe they represent a direct importation from the West Indies or from Europe. In the post-Revolutionary period a number of such side piazzas were added to earlier Charleston houses.

There are earlier examples of the single house in Charleston. The prototype seems to be in traditional row houses or paired dwellings in which there were two entrances, one on the front,

which may have been primarily for business purposes, and one on the side, for the family. Thus came about the practice of having a side door away from the street, with the central hall facing the door. Once firmly established as an urban type in the 1790s and early 1800s, the form continued to be used. Later singles, built between 1820 and 1860, more often are only two bays wide, have a gable roof rather than a hipped roof, with the gable facing the street. The door trim to the piazza and the columns are heavier in proportion, in the Greek mode.

When the noted architect Benjamin Henry Latrobe visited New Orleans in 1819 he described several of the urban buildings surrounding the square in that city as "entirely French. A lower story divided into and let as stores; an entresol in which the shopkeepers live, or which is let to other families. Then a handsome range of apartments surrounding a court of 30 by 24 feet. The appearance externally of the house is very good. . . . In the interior, the court gives light to all the stories but is reserved only for the use of the principal story and is entered by a porte cochere."

The group of buildings Latrobe was describing has now disappeared, but a few similar ones survive. One is at 517 Decatur Street, near the river, built in 1795, after the great fire of 1794, and shown here, lower right, in a watercolor of 1852. The building is flush with the sidewalk; the overhang was added later.

On the ground floor are three doors which open to the commercial quarters. The almost square windows at the middle level represent the entresol (the area between the floors), a comparatively low-ceilinged area where the shopkeepers lived, or which was used as storage. The "principal story" is the third floor, which would be residential. The high-ceilinged rooms open to the balcony, or gallery, as it is often called in New Orleans. In other examples of this type of building, such as the 1806 Absinthe House, large fanlights above the ground-floor doors serve to light the entresol.

As Latrobe indicated, most New Orleans urban houses had a porte cochere or carriage entrance on the side, frequently closed by a large, arched doorway. On the interior, away from the street, is a courtyard or patio, often with a tree and some planting, used by the residents. A stairway from an open, arcaded vestibule in the courtyard usually leads to the living quarters above. Here, too, the family or living area is closed off from the street. This arrangement provides privacy and serenity just a few feet away from urban bustle in a manner somewhat similar to that of the Charleston single.

New Orleans, as laid out by the French, provided for deep lots, the majority of which are 120 feet in length. Therefore, in the older townhouses there is usually a side wing at the rear of the main house, extending along the courtyard, which is two or three stories and has galleries on the side facing the courtyard. This was called the *garçonnière*, or service wing, where the younger members or the servants of the household had their rooms.

Except for the Ursuline Convent mentioned earlier, no building from the French period of rule survives in New Orleans, though the lot shapes affected the plans of all subsequent buildings in the original section of the city. During the years the Spanish ruled, from 1768 to 1803, before the area was retroceded to the French (who promptly sold the whole territory to the United States), many French building traditions continued. The Spanish introduced flat roof terraces, but since these were not suitable for the rainy weather, in time virtually all were covered over with pitched roofs. As the new wave of "foreigners," the Americans, moved in, the French and Spanish populations continued to live in the old quarter and in newly developed sections, or faubourgs, downriver, as did the people of African descent associated with them. Thus the city was divided between the older Creole populations and the newer "Americans" who tended to settle upriver from the original city or quarter. (Creole is used in New Orleans by white people to denote white people of colonial French or Spanish descent, by black people to denote those descended from the black people of the French and Spanish colonial periods—some with mixed black and white ancestry—and by both races to denote the whole mixed heritage of French, Spanish, African, and even "American" traditions, plus the special circumstances of Louisiana—such as "Creole" food.)

Small cottages are also characteristic of New Orleans urban settings, familiar to New Orleanians but not always mentioned or pictured in the more romantic descriptions of the city. Among the earliest surviving examples are several dating from around

E. Surgi and A. Persac. *"A New Orleans Urban Cottage."* 1869. Watercolor. Built c. 1820, now demolished. New Orleans Notarial Archives.

"A New Orleans residence-store with entresol." 1852. Watercolor. Built in 1795 at 517 Decatur Street, New Orleans, Louisiana. New Orleans Notarial Archives.

the 1820s, located in the downriver Creole faubourgs, though there were no doubt many built before that time. An excellent example is shown in a watercolor of 1869, previous page, upper right. It is one and a half stories, and is set flush against the street with a sheltering overhang. Some cottages, as here, had hipped roofs, while others had gable roofs with the sloping side facing the street. The fanlights above the doors and windows represent a modest adaptation of the neoclassical taste. (More typically, these cottages had a door on either side and two shorter-length windows in between.) Many were of timber frame with brick as fill. The soft brick was usually stuccoed over, often in soft pastel colors, as shown here. The usual plan for such cottages was four rooms of the same size, arranged in a square, plus two smaller rooms at the rear which flanked a recessed "cabinet gallery." There is no hall or corridor, reflecting the economical and time-honored Mediterranean and French enfilade arrangement.

Latrobe, in his 1819 notes, described these cottages in considerable detail: "New Orleans, beyond Royal street . . . retains its old character without variation. The houses are, with hardly a dozen exceptions among many hundred, one-story houses. The roofs are high, covered with tiles or shingles, and project five feet over the footway, which is also five feet wide. The eaves therefore discharge the water into the gutters. The higth [sic] of the stories is harldy ten feet, the elevation above the pavement not more than a foot and a half; and therefore the eaves are not often more than 8 feet from the ground. However different this mode is from the American manner of building, it has very great advantages both with regard to the interior of the dwelling and to the street. In the summer the walls are perfectly shaded from the sun and the house kept cool, while the passenger's [sic] are also shaded from the sun and protected from the rain. . . . These one-storied houses are very simple in their plan. The two front rooms open into the street with French glass doors. Those on one side are the dining and drawing rooms, the other chambers. The front rooms, when inhabited by Americans, are the family rooms, and the back rooms the chambers. We derive from the English the habit of desiring that every one of our rooms should be separately accessible, and we consider rooms that are thoroughfares as useless. The French and Continental Europeans generally live, I believe, as much to their own satisfaction in their houses as we do in ours, and employ the room they have to more advantage because they do not require so much space for passages."

One of the best surviving examples of the small Creole house or cottage, 1436 Pauger, upper right, is located on an odd-shaped corner, and built in 1820. It has a hipped roof with an outward cant which overhangs the street. Flat tiles cover the roof. The walls are stuccoed. The shutters are vertical board, diagonal on the inside, fixed with strap hinges.

Latrobe identified these cottage dwellings with the French and continental population of the city. They seem to represent a vernacular form familiar to those of European, as opposed to American or Anglo descent. It is no surprise, then, that the virtual prototypes can be found among the unpublished drawings which the sixteenth-century architect Sebastian Serlio prepared for what was to have been Book VI of his architectural treatise. In the drawing at the right, Serlio showed dwellings for poor city artisans of the sort that would be situated near markets and fairs. The façades have four openings, two doors and two windows, in an arrangement similar to that found in many New Orleans cottages. They appear as if flush with the street or lot line. It is possible that Serlio showed a form of simple cottage dwelling already familiar to urban France in the sixteenth century, a type which the French continued to build in Louisiana.

The New Orleans cottage at the right was built by a free man of color, Jean-Louis Dolliole. He was a builder, entrepreneur, and something of a social leader in the small community of *gens de couleur libres* that was an integral part of the social fabric of New Orleans. Though the small cottages of the type shown here were built and lived in by both whites and free blacks, it has been shown that quite a few were built, lived in, and sold by free people of color.

As a class, free people of color in New Orleans, and elsewhere, had in their number tradesmen and craftsmen, including builders, masons, carpenters, and blacksmiths. Their exact contribution to the arts is hard to measure, as is that of many anonymous craftsmen, white and black. In Louisiana, at least from the inception of the French *Code Noir* (Black Code) in 1724, free people of color had a definite, if limited, legal status, which was also recognized during the Spanish period. The Americans continued to provide legal protection, though free blacks were sometimes subject to harassment and discrimination. In 1771 only ninety-nine citizens in this category were recorded as living in New Orleans. By 1830 there were around 8,000 free people of color in the city and its suburbs; the total population of the city being over 30,000. Despite difficulties, many became property owners, small tradesmen and craftsmen, writers and musicians. A number of free people of color were manumitted slaves, others had migrated to New Orleans from France, or from the Spanish and French colonies in the West Indies. Almost 2,000 arrived in New Orleans within a two-month period in 1795, after the slave uprising in Santo Domingo. Some owned a few slaves and were ambivalent in their attitude toward slavery, some bought the freedom of their slaves or of slaves who were relatives. The tensions and polarizations of the pre–Civil War period made their situation increasingly troubled. As a group they had a special, and sometimes difficult, status between free whites and black slaves. Others of similar status in other parts of the South, including rural Louisiana, had similar problems and triumphs over adversity.

The most important buildings of the Spanish regime in New Orleans are the two large paired buildings facing the original Place d'Armes, now Jackson Square. These were designed to house the Cabildo, or governing body of the city, and to serve as a rectory, Casa Curial, for the cathedral, and are now called the Cabildo and Presbytere. The latter took a long time to complete and was never used for its original purpose, the space instead was rented out to others. Both now house the Louisiana State Museum. They stand on either side of the Cathedral of St. Louis, which in its present form represents a rebuilding in 1850. An 1845 lithograph of the square, page 134, shows how the group looked at that time. (Mansard roofs have subsequently been added to both buildings.) A detail of the arcade, page 135, suggests the scale and the boldness of articulation. To walk under

Dolliole-Clapp House, 1436 Pauger Street, New Orleans, Louisiana, 1820.

the arcade is to be reminded of the many arcaded streets in Spain, echoing with the sound of footfalls.

The property on which the Cabildo stands was set aside for government use by the French in their original plan. After the Spanish took over, a simple structure was built in 1769 to house the Cabildo. This was destroyed in the disastrous fire of 1788, and the council met in temporary quarters, called Government House, for several years, until that building, too, was destroyed by a fire in 1794. There had been discussion of building a more imposing structure for government use, and a related rectory, after the 1788 fire, and Don Gilberto Guillemard, a Frenchman who had long served in the Spanish military, had drawn plans. (The mixed background was not unusual. The Spanish governor in 1794, François Louis Hector, Baron de Carondolet, was also a

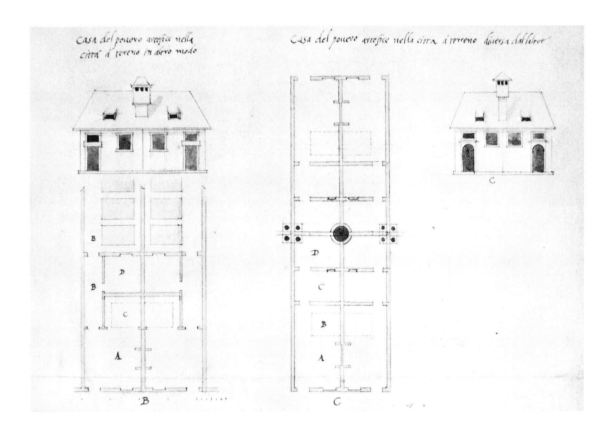

Sebastiano Serlio. Drawing of a dwelling suitable for poor city artisans, plate XLVIII, B & C, in the manuscript of his proposed book, "On domestic architecture: different dwellings from the meanest level to the most ornate palaces," c. 1547–1549. Avery Library, Columbia University, New York, N.Y.

Frenchman, a nobleman, in the Spanish service. The second Spanish governor had the unlikely name of O'Reilly. Other governors, including Bernardo de Galvez, who supported the Americans during their Revolution, and Esteban Rodriguez Miro, who followed him, were natives of Spain.) Guillemard made new designs for the Presbytere in 1791, and after the fire of 1794 reworked these. Part of the walls of the old French *corps de garde* of 1751 were still standing, and he incorporated these into the side wall of the Cabildo.

In both buildings there is an arcade of nine bays, open on the ground level and glazed on the upper level. The three central bays are incorporated into a slightly projecting pavilion crowned with a pediment. Engaged pilasters and columns articulate the surface. A balustrade surmounted the roofs. The designs show a strong similarity to the Casa Real built in 1781 to house Spanish

government offices at Antequera, Mexico, and to public buildings elsewhere in Mexico, such as at Mérida in the Yucatán. The large elliptical windows on the second level are boldly conceived, and represent another manifestation of the neoclassical; here the relation to the earlier traditions of the late Renaissance is also very close. The wrought-iron railings in front of each of the windows on the upper level are particularly fine, a play of circles, scrolls, and angular forms. They are the work of Marcelino Hernandez, a native of the Canary Islands. Much of the cost of the two buildings was borne by the private contributions of Don Andres Almonester y Roxas, a man of wealth who was responsible for a number of philanthropic projects in New Orleans at this time.

Of visitors who commented on these buildings and their effect, Latrobe, as ever, was most perspicacious: "Altho' in detail

Thomas Williams. "View of the Public Square (now Jackson Square), New Orleans, with the City Hall, Cathedral, and Court House." 1845. Lithograph. Louisiana State Museum.

VIEW of the PUBLIC SQUARE NEW-ORLEANS, with the CITY HALL, CATHEDRAL and COURT HOUSE.

these buildings are as bad as they can be, their symmetry, and the good proportions and strong relief of the facades of the Two . . . and the solid mass of . . . [the Cathedral] produce an admirable effect when seen from the river or the levee."

The history and use of the buildings are intimately tied up with the complex political history of the times, for they were designed to serve symbolic and ceremonial purposes. After Spain retroceded Louisiana to France in the second Treaty of San Ildefonso of 1800, a settlement of the Napoleonic Wars, Napoleon nurtured the idea of restoring France's empire in the New World. However, his plans for control of the Caribbean went awry, and fearing that the British might gain control of the area, Napoleon decided to negotiate with the Americans. In the spring of 1803, the Louisiana Purchase was concluded in France by Robert Livingston and James Monroe. The area of the United States, under Jefferson's presidency, was thus more than doubled in what has rightly been called one of the best real estate deals in history.

The ceremonial transfer of powers that resulted from this series of negotiations took place in the Cabildo and in the square in front, the Place d'Armes. The new French prefect, Pierre Clement Laussat, arrived in New Orleans in March 1803, and in November of the same year the Spanish officially delivered Louisiana to Laussat. Less than a month later, William C. C. Claiborne, who was then territorial governor of Mississippi, and General James Wilkinson, represented the United States and formally exchanged documents with Laussat. When these were signed, the officials of the two nations stood on the balcony of the Cabildo overlooking the square while, simultaneously, the French flag was lowered and the American flag raised. Troops from both nations took part in the ceremonies. Afterward Frenchmen, Americans, and Spaniards took part in a gala celebration and soiree.

The skill of Claiborne, who was inaugurated as governor of the New Orleans Territory in October 1804, helped the divergent peoples of the populace in forming an effective government, and in 1812 Louisiana became the eighteenth state to join the Union.

The arcade of the Cabildo, Jackson Square, New Orleans, Louisiana.

After Jackson's army vanquished the British in the Battle of New Orleans, which ended on January 8, 1815, the first celebrations were wild and exuberant. Then on January 23 there was an elaborate ceremony, which took place in the square fronting the old Cabildo. It was planned and arranged "entirely by the ladies." A temporary triumphal arch was erected, covered with entwined laurel. Young girls in white, standing by eighteen festooned pillars, represented the states. Large banners especially honored those regions whose troops had been conspicuous in the fray: Louisiana, the Mississippi Territory, Tennessee, and Kentucky. As General Jackson and his officers proceeded along the triumphal way, laurel wreaths were suspended over the general's head and flowers strewn in their path. All entered the chapel and a "Te Deum" was sung.

Though the Battle of New Orleans took place after a peace treaty had been signed—December 24, 1814—neither British nor American troops knew this. Moreover, the treaty may never have been ratified—as it was on February 17, 1815—if the battle had not ended as it had. It was a vital last phase of the War of 1812, lifting the morale of the nation. It also "marked the completion of the political Americanization of Louisiana," and from that time on, whatever the differences between the Creole and American populations, both groups actively participated in the political life of the young Republic. This event served to catapult the forty-eight-year-old Jackson into national fame and was a major stepping-stone on his way to the presidency. To the nation, and to New Orleans, he was a new hero and symbol of vitality and strength. The square where the victory was celebrated now bears his name.

A few years later, the city fathers outfitted several rooms of the Cabildo for the use of General Lafayette when the venerable hero visited New Orleans in December 1824. The council room became a parlor, the powder magazine a dining room. It was the perfect site. The equipage of state drew up to the square as the

Homeplace, near Hahnville, Louisiana, built c. 1800. The front staircase was added later.

cathedral bells rang and the crowd surged. Lafayette was formally received by the mayor under a triumphal arch erected in the square, then escorted to his quarters, called *la maison de Lafayette* for the occasion. From the balcony he waved to the crowds and reviewed troops which paraded below.

The square and the buildings flanking it have proved to be one of the most effective planned urban spaces in America. The area is small enough to be intimate, large enough and formal enough to use as a setting for public occasions.

Jackson Square with its attendant buildings is still the major focus and symbol of the city of New Orleans. Rows of townhouses and closely spaced cottages are still an important aspect of the urban scene there. As we have seen, during the late colonial period a third type of structure, the "typical" Louisiana and lower Mississippi Valley plantation house, had evolved, a form wonderfully suited to its setting. The perceptive eyes of Latrobe again provide a contemporary description of such a plantation house. The particular one he was describing was located near the site of the Battle of New Orleans, a site he visited in February 1819: "The house itself is one of the usual French plantations of the first class and I think, by far the best kind of house for the

climate, namely, a mansion surrounded entirely by a portico or gallery of two stories. The roof is enormous."

Latrobe was not the first to observe what, by the late eighteenth century, had become the familiar form of plantation houses of lower Louisiana and of the lower Mississippi valley. In 1803–1805, C. C. Robin, on a visit to Louisiana, was impressed by the way the builders had adapted their houses to the climate and by the uses which were made of the surrounding porches or galleries: "The heat of the climate makes galleries around the houses a necessity. All of them have one, some around all four sides of the house, others on two sides only, and rarely, only on one side. . . . The galleries are usually eight or nine feet wide. These wide galleries have several advantages. First, they prevent the sun's rays from striking the walls of the house and thus to keep them cool. Also, they form a convenient and pleasant spot upon which to promenade during the day (one, of course, goes to the side away from the sun), one can eat or entertain there, and very often during the hot summer nights one sleeps there. In many houses the ends of the galleries are closed, to form two additional rooms."

The comments of visitors who came through the South give us contemporary insights and impressions that would otherwise be lost. Still another, the Englishman Thomas Ashe, described his impression of seeing the succession of plantations in their settings as he traveled down the river. (Nowadays only a few survive; chemical plants and a scattering of miscellaneous buildings have replaced them.) In 1806 Ashe wrote: "It is, perhaps, the most interesting stretch of fresh water navigation in the world . . . the country to New Orleans is settled the whole way along the river, and presents a score of uninterrupted plantations in sight of each other, whose parts to the Mississippi are all cleared, and occupy on that river from five to twenty-five acres, with a depth of forty; so that a plantation of five acres front, contains two hundred. . . . The houses of a parish, which are built with all the embellishments of the French, in the West Indies style, are not crowded together, but are separated by groves and gardens, which give them a charming effect, and an extent to one settlement of several miles. The inhabitants who, for the most part, are French, live perfectly at their ease."

Among the few surviving plantation houses is the Homeplace, left, near Hahnville. The great sheltering roof and the wide galleries described in the traveler's descriptions can be seen here. It was built about 1800 for Louis Edmond Fortier. Stuccoed brick piers support the gallery, while slender wooden colonnettes support the roof. The ground-floor walls are masonry, the upper are frame. The dining room on the ground floor is paved with black and white marble. The other rooms on the ground level included two for wine storage, a pantry, and two chambers. Each has access to the lower gallery, and some of the rooms, not all, to each other. The galleries were the corridors. The front steps shown here originally did not exist. Instead, sheltered staircases inside the gallery, at the right front and the left rear, led to the second level. An old photograph, right, shows one of these gallery staircases. There is a narrow service stairway inside. The second floor had a reception room and a variety of different-sized chambers. Again, each opens onto the gallery, and some onto each other. This represents the same economical use of space that Latrobe had remarked upon as characteristic of the French townhouses and cottages of New Orleans. Nor is there a concern for precise symmetry in the spacing of the door openings. As early as 1806 Thomas Ashe identified this characteristic Louisiana form as "West Indian," and there are indeed common features between these and some West Indian or island structures. As suggested earlier, buildings of this general type found in French Louisiana (and in French settlements along the upper Mississippi) are related to French prototypes. Those in the West Indies may also have roots in this common source. Moreover, similar climatic problems may have suggested similar architectural solutions.

The roof of the Homeplace is hipped, with a slight outward cant to the eaves. Another typical configuration was a double-pitched hipped roof, the break occurring fairly high. Such a great spreading roof is seen at Destrehan, following page, completed in 1790. It was originally built for Robert Anthoine Robin de Logny between 1787 and 1790, and in its original state had brick piers and wooden colonnettes. The general plan is similar to Homeplace. In 1823 two side wings, or *garçonnières*, were added by De Logny's son-in-law, Jean Noel d'Estrehan de Beaupre, to accommodate his family of fourteen children. Around 1840 there was an extensive remodeling, in order to make the grand old house up to date—this meant in the new Greek taste. Therefore the colonnettes and piers were encased in great Tuscan columns. (During a recent examination the colonnettes were found to be intact inside.) The door and window frames and mantels were also changed to fit the same "modern taste." With the addition and changes in style, Destrehan represents a half-century of Louisiana architecture.

Destrehan is one of the best-documented colonial structures in Louisiana. The original building contract, in French, is filed in the archives of St. Charles Parish. Drawn up on January 3, 1787, it provides a description of what we now recognize as the vernacular colonial Louisiana plantation house, and is equally important because it records the role of a free man of color who was a builder. The beginning, here in translation, is formal and legal. "Before us Jacques Masicot, sub-lieutenant of the Armies, Judge and Commandant of St. Charles Parish of the Germans, there residing, have appeared in person Mr. Robert Anthoine Robin de Logny, Lieutenant of the Armies of His Majesty and planter dwelling in the said Parish, and Charles, free Mulatto, who have agreed to what follows: To wit, that the said Charles,

Outdoor staircases leading to first floor of Homeplace.

Destrehan plantation house, St. Charles Parish, Louisiana, completed in 1790, extensively remodeled in 1840.

Benjamin Henry Latrobe. "Complex of buildings on sugar plantation in Louisiana." 1818–1820. Pencil drawing. Maryland Historical Society.

Carpenter, wood worker and mason by his trade, obligates himself to construct for the said Sieur Robin de Logny, a house of sixty feet in length by thirty five in width, including the semi-doubles, raised ten feet on brick piers with a surrounding gallery of twelve feet in width, planked top and bottom, five chimneys which shall be contracted in the said house, two of which double and one single. . . ."

The contract goes on to spell out more details "according to the plan which he has in hand," and the method of payment. Charles was given one Negro and a cow with her calf at the signing of the contract. He was to be paid fifty quarts of rice in chaff and fifty quarts of corn in husk during the course of the building, and one hundred piastres at the end. Moreover, Sieur Robin de Logny was to provide Negro craftsmen to perform certain tasks—two "wood squarers" or hewers, three other workmen, and a skilled mason. All materials for the house were also furnished. On April 22, 1790, Robin de Logny and Charles once again appeared before Masicot to signify that the task was completed and all obligations discharged.

Robin de Logny unfortunately died only two years after the house was built. The inventory of the estate reveals a full complement of outbuildings such as was once familiar on these plantations. These included a separate kitchen with galleries front and rear, a storehouse, a dovecote or *pigeonnier*, a coach house, "a negro camp composed of nineteen cabins, good as well as bad," a mounted bell, nine pairs of vats, which would have been used in processing indigo, and still other sheds. The yard and garden were enclosed by stakes.

The original interior trim at Destrehan is gone. At Homeplace the surviving trim has the crispness and neatness characteristic of the neoclassical—patterns of gouge work, fluted pilasters on mantels, neat rosettes—all with a French nuance. A surviving carved mantel of the 1820s, right, from Armant plantation in Vacherie, now destroyed, shows how completely the neoclassical taste in interior decor had gained favor by that time. Slim fluted paired columns are on either side. In the panels above, combinations of fans, circles, and ovals are arranged in symmetrical patterns, all in gouge work.

The reason for the presence and prosperity of these plantations was the rich bottomland, which was used increasingly to grow sugar cane. In the 1780s indigo was the major crop in lower Louisiana, but by the beginning of the nineteenth century, sugar rapidly displaced it. The Jesuits had attempted to grow sugar cane in the 1740s, with little success. Around 1757 DuBréuil, the builder and contractor, introduced plants from Santo Domingo from which he succeeded in making fine raw sugar, but his experiments terminated when he died. Two Spaniards, Solis and Mendez, then tried Tahitian seed cane, growing sugar primarily for syrup and tafia (a rumlike drink). In 1795 Jean Etienne de Boré (son of a titled Norman family married to a d'Estrehan) improved the techniques for granulating sugar in his mill and drying shed. From that time on sugar became the important commercial staple crop for southeastern Louisiana.

At one time large building complexes used for grinding and processing the sugar were among the important outbuildings on the large plantations in lower Louisiana. These fall into the category of early industrial, or agribusiness buildings, more than into that of simple farm buildings. Latrobe drew one of these complexes, dominated by a large rotunda, lower left. C. C. Robin reported that the earliest grinding mills for sugar were built in hexagonal or octagonal form, until a planter named De Gruise found these angular buildings both displeasing to the eye and wasteful of material. According to this tradition, De Gruise heard of the central market in Paris, Les Halles, which was circular, and so had his mill constructed as a rotunda, apparently setting the fashion for sugar mills. Unfortunately, so far as I know, none of these round grinding mills survive.

During the reign of the French and Spanish powers in the lower Mississippi Valley the building traditions of these countries were adapted to the climate and to the circumstances of the inhabitants. In the country and the suburbs the galleried, or "West Indian," house became common. In the city the very French townhouse, which often combined commerical quarters at ground level with residential quarters at the upper level, and with the main entrance to the residential area on the interior courtyard, became a familiar and typical genre. So, too, the cottage fronting the street. With modifications, these basic types were to persist for some time. The taste for the neoclassical was adapted to these forms and is seen in the trim of doors, windows, chimney-pieces, and in some proportions. The next generation of builders was to adapt these types entirely to the new fashion for things Greek. During the late eighteenth and early nineteenth centuries this choice of neoclassic details, proportions, and also features such as selection of wall colors or types of wallpaper, provided a common denominator among American build-

Mantel from Armant Plantation in Vacherie, Louisiana, c. 1820. The original house was destroyed but the woodwork saved. Private collection.

ings of varied plans, whether located in urban Baltimore, rural northern Alabama (where settlements were just beginning), upstate New York, or the lowlands of South Carolina.

Revealing indices of buildings thought architecturally important, and of the social status of their owners, could be made if one were to examine all the places Lafayette is known to have stayed during his 1824–1825 tour. The Cabildo in New Orleans was one, and the Verdier house in Beaufort, Cragfont in Tennessee, and the Richard Richardson (Owens-Thomas) house in Savannah are among others. His journeys took him to many of the major towns and cities. He saw the diversity of the countryside,

John Mark Verdier House, 801 Bay Street, Beaufort, South Carolina, built c. 1790.

noted the rich bottomlands along the coasts and the rivers, and the rolling upland country. He traversed the lands west of the Alleghenies and in fact visited virtually the whole of the settled parts of the United States.

The John Mark Verdier house in Beaufort, South Carolina, above, was built around 1790 by a young merchant and factor. In 1825 it must still have been considered one of the finest houses in the prospering community of Beaufort.

The house is at once conservative and in the newest fashion. The basic elevation of a five-bay house, on raised basement, with a double portico, is reminiscent of the Miles Brewton house of 1769, and even of Drayton Hall of around 1738, both rooted in English traditions. Originally derived from bookish sources, the house with raised basement and projecting portico, sometimes two-story, sometimes one-story, had proven itself especially suitable to the lowland Carolina climate by the 1790s. A central hall, with stairway to the rear, is characteristic of some of this genre. It is one of several variants of elevation and plan that were selected out, so to speak, and repeated enough to become a vernacular in the South—examples can be seen from South Carolina to Kentucky and Tennessee.

The detailing of the doorway, the narrowness and attenuation of the columns of the portico, and most especially the panel-

ing and ornamentation in the interior, such as in the upstairs drawing room, lower right, bespeak the neoclassical, somewhat similar to the plaster work found in Baltimore interiors.

Beaufort looks out over the waters of Beaufort River and the low-lying islands beyond. The Verdier house is on Bay Street, ideally suited to catch the sea breezes. It is of wood, as were a number of the Sea Island houses and plantations. The raised foundation is of tabby, a cementlike material made from oyster shells, sand, and a lime secured through the burning of oyster shells. The Verdier house is two rooms deep. Some of the other Sea Island planters' houses are T-shaped in plan, being only one-room deep across the front, with rooms in the stem of the "T" extending back beyond the entrance hall area. In such houses every room has cross-ventilation.

Beaufort is situated on Port Royal Island, one of the Sea Islands near the coast, and near the area where Ribaut first tried to establish a settlement. The town of Beaufort was established in 1711 and began to be more secure after the Yemassee War and the establishment of the Swiss in 1733 in nearby Purrysburgh. Rice, then indigo, were the major crops in the pre-Revolutionary years. There was strife in the Beaufort area between the Patriots and Tories, and recovery after the war was slow. In the early 1790s a new product, an especially fine, long-fibered strain of cotton, was introduced from the Bahamas. This Sea Island cotton was the basis for a new era of prosperity, which lasted until the war began in 1860.

Integral to the new cotton economy that made houses such as Verdier's possible were mule-driven wooden presses. A photograph taken in the late 1930s, right, shows one of these structures, like the sugar mill, characteristic of a growing agribusiness. The center shaft is in fact a great wooden screw, and was used to ram the cotton into the wood forms, thus creating bales, which were then packed and shipped. The example shown here was in Edgecombe County, North Carolina. The basic necessities of function in this case dictated the form. There is nonetheless a pleasing combination of pyramidal forms and a warm rusticity lent by the shingled roofs. Originally this press was found under a larger shed, which protected the cotton that was about to be baled, as well as the timbers of the press, from inclement weather.

There is a family tradition that a ball honoring Lafayette was held at Cragfont, near Gallatin, Tennessee, in 1825. It is one of the first late eighteenth-, early nineteenth-century structures of native gray limestone to be found in middle Tennessee. When the French naturalist F. A. Michaux saw the house as it was just before it was finished, in 1802, he found it "very elegant for the country." The house, following page, sits on a high hill, commanding a view of a rocky valley below. It is a five-bay house, two rooms deep, with a central hall. Great chimneys are on either

An early cotton press. Edgecomb County, North Carolina.

Detail of woodwork, Verdier House.

Cragfont, near Gallatin, Tennessee, built 1798–1802.

end. There is a long addition at the rear, flanked by a two-story gallery on either side, making for an overall T-shaped plan. It is believed that the first story of this wing was constructed at the same time the front portion of the house was built, and that the second story and a two-story smokehouse at the end of the "T" were added before 1825. (Smokehouses, for curing meat, either attached or in a separate building, are found as frequently in Tennessee and Kentucky as dovecotes in Louisiana.) There is a spacious ballroom on the second floor of the wing.

Large iron stars are spaced evenly across the front. Though decorative in appearance, they are utilitarian in purpose, since they are attached to iron tie rods which serve as braces in the thick stone walls.

The fine Georgian detailing, the proportions, and the rather austere appearance are reminiscent of Pennsylvania fieldstone houses and of masonry structures in Maryland and Virginia. According to Michaux, the carpenters were brought from Baltimore, a distance of almost 700 miles, by General James Winchester, for whom the house was built. They would have done the trim and interior structure. A craftsman named Frank Weatherred is believed to have done much of the interior wood and cabinet work, such as the large chimney-piece, mantel, and dado in the

parlor, right. The chimney-piece and the risers of the stairs, page 144, are painted with a greenish sponge and line pattern that is far livelier than most false-marble patterns. The crisp geometric stenciling seen on the walls, in dark green and red, has been reproduced from a faded surviving section. It was originally designed by an itinerant artist.

When Michaux came through this area in 1802 there were still considerable sections of the land covered with what seemed like a forest of tall reeds or cane. Most of the inhabitants lived in "good log houses." As plantations were formed, land was cleared and the cattle and pigs gradually destroyed the once impenetrable canebrakes. Nearby Nashville, established for fifteen or sixteen years, could boast of seven or eight brick houses and about 120 wooden houses "built with planks." It was a regional trading center, getting supplies from Baltimore, Philadelphia, and New Orleans, and shipping produce to the latter city.

General James Winchester was a Marylander who, along with his brother, distinguished himself in the Revolutionary War, serving with General Greene in the Southern campaign. In 1785 both he and his brother moved to middle Tennessee, which was then the Mero district of North Carolina. He served the district as a military leader in the campaigns against the Indians and as a political leader. (His brother was scalped in 1794.) When Tennessee became a state in 1796 he became speaker of the state senate. Farming, milling, and commercial transactions (no doubt land speculation) contributed to his wealth. He and his wife had fourteen children, some of whom were given classical names: Marcus Brutus, Lucilius, and Valerius Publicola. He named a nearby village Castalian Springs, for the Castalian Spring on Mount Parnassus: this classical heritage was part of the mental baggage brought to the frontier. Winchester, the lawyer John Overton, and Andrew Jackson were the founders of Memphis in 1819, after Jackson and General Isaac Shelby had negotiated a treaty whereby the Chickasaw Indians ceded all their claims east of the Mississippi. The new town, situated on America's great river and "American Nile," the Mississippi, was named after the ancient Egyptian city. Winchester's son Marcus was the first mayor.

Michaux described Lexington, Kentucky, as the "oldest and most considerable" town in the new states beyond the mountains. (Kentucky became a state in 1792, having previously been a part of Virginia.) Lexington was the site of a camp of hunters who heard the news of the Battle of Lexington in Massachusetts in 1775, and named the spot for it immediately. A permanent settlement was not established until 1779, when a small fort was built, and the town was laid out in 1781 by order of the Virginia Assembly. By 1806 it was described as one of the two largest inland towns in the United States, with upward of 300 houses, "principally built of brick, in a handsome modern manner, and many . . . furnished with some pretensions to European ele-

Interior of parlor, Cragfont, with "false-marble" patterns on chimney-piece and stenciling on walls.

Stair risers at Cragfont, with sponge and line patterns.

Hopemont, known as the Hunt-Morgan House, Lexington, Kentucky, built 1814.

gance." By 1826 it had earned the encomium of "Athens of the West." Transylvania Seminary, moved there in 1788, had one of the best college libraries in the country for its time. (In 1798 it became Transylvania University.) Several churches flourished. In little more than three decades Lexington had passed from a frontier fort to a community with "an air of leisure and opulence," a center where the latest publications were available, and a community that had "taken the tone of a literary place." The rich soil of the bluegrass country, where hemp, tobacco, and wheat flourished, was the basis of the area's economy.

Hopemont, or the Hunt-Morgan house, lower left, is one of the most notable of the surviving brick houses of this early period in Lexington's history. It stands on a corner of Gratz Park, not far from the site of Transylvania University, a capacious two-and-a-half-story structure. It was built in 1814 for John Wesley Hunt, who is reputed to have become the first millionaire of the bluegrass—he manufactured hemp. (The products of hemp manufacture were vital to the cotton growers to the south and west, who used them for baling cotton.)

An important and inviting feature of the house is the wide, double-doored main entrance, right. The doors are surrounded by a beautiful leaded fanlight with side lights. Running bead moldings enframe the major sections. The architect-builder and the craftsman are unknown. The design of the doorway bears a close resemblance—although it is of larger proportions—to Plate 32 in Asher Benjamin's *American Builder's Companion*. It is very possible that this handbook was available and used. Hunt was from New Jersey, and it is also possible that some of the workmen came from there, or from Virginia or Maryland—even perhaps from England or Ireland—where lovely comparable doorways are to be seen. The presence of reeded or running bead moldings rather than articulated formal architectural orders bestows a provincial accent. This is but one of a number of such sparkling doorways which graced houses in central Kentucky built in the second and third decades of the nineteenth century.

The main entrance of the Hunt-Morgan house presents a formal, hospitable face. The side elevation, fronting the street around the corner, reflects attention to convenience and service. There was originally a smaller doorway that led from the street directly into Mr. Hunt's office. There still remains a second entrance along the walled street which opens into a service court. The floor plan is close to what Latrobe would have identified as a French or European plan, with a rectangular entrance hall from which other rooms open off, rather than there being a long central passage.

The giant columns of a projecting portico dominate the entrance to Auburn, following page, a house built in Natchez in 1812 for Lyman Harding by the architect-builder Levi Weeks.

Here are the great columns that have become a symbol of the antebellum home of the Deep South. (Not all homes were so grand, nor were all graced with columns. The great house with giant columns, as symbol, is perhaps as much a product of the post–Civil War imagination, South and North, as of the prewar period. In both North and South such columnar houses enjoyed a vogue from around 1810 through the 1860s. Perhaps more were built in the newly developing rural areas of the old Southwest,

Entrance hall of Hopemont with leaded-glass fan-shaped door.

but a number of Southerners turned to the Gothic and other styles when those tastes were introduced.) Weeks was clearly conscious of introducing a new level of grandeur into the region. In September 1812 he wrote with pride to a friend in Deerfield, Massachusetts: "The brick house I am now building is just without the city line and is designed for the most magnificent building in the Territory. The body of this house is 60 by 45 feet with a portico of 31 feet projecting 12 feet supported by 4 Ionic columns with the Corinthian entablature, the ceiling vaulted, the house two stories with a geometrical staircase to ascend to the second story. This is the first house in the Territory in which was even attempted any of the orders of Architecture."

The scale of the house (originally only five bays wide; two wings of two bays each were added later) and the giant portico were new to Natchez, which was then part of the Mississippi Territory, an area comprising the present-day states of Mississippi and Alabama. Before the building of Auburn many of the structures in Natchez were similar to those found in and near

Portico and central block of Auburn, Natchez, Mississippi.
Designed and built by Levi Weeks in 1812 for Lyman Harding.

New Orleans, and along the lower Mississippi, "impressing a visitor by their likeness to buildings seen in smaller West Indian Towns, the houses all with balconies and piazzas." The traveler who so described the houses in Natchez in 1808 found the population of the town a motley mixture of Americans, French and Spanish Creoles, mulattoes and Negroes, with occasional visiting Indians.

The early history of Natchez encapsulates in part the story of the contending forces who played out their political ambitions in this region. Situated on a bluff overlooking the Mississippi, Natchez had originally been the center of an agricultural community of the Natchez Indians. In 1716 the French established Fort Rosalie there, and a community of 700 or so French made a small colony. The Indians, apparently oppressed by the demands for land, massacred virtually all of the French males there in 1729. The latter retaliated, but the community languished until after 1763. In the settlement that followed the French and Indian

War, France ceded to the victorious English all its claims east of the Mississippi except New Orleans. At the same time it gave control of French holdings on the west side of the river, and New Orleans, to Spain. Spain in turn ceded Florida to England. The English then set up two territories in this southernmost part of the continent, East Florida, or old Spanish Florida, and West Florida, which comprised the land gained from France. Both Natchez and Pensacola were part of west Florida—Natchez its western outpost and Pensacola its capital. The British made land grants to some of their war veterans, who settled in the region, and as the tensions of the Revolution increased, some Tories moved to the region. In Natchez and in the "Florida parishes" of Louisiana one can still be made aware of this remnant of Anglican heritage.

During the Revolution, however, the Spanish in New Orleans took the opportunity of weakening the English, and the Spanish governor of New Orleans, Don Bernardo de Galvez, occupied several British posts, including that at Natchez. By 1782 the Spanish had gained all of west Florida. It was during the short Spanish period of governance, from 1779 to 1798, that the town of Natchez was laid out in neat squares on the high land above the river. However, ambitious, adventuresome citizens of the new United States were increasingly attracted to the rich alluvial lands of the region and desired greater access to the use of the river. Through a treaty with Madrid in 1795 Spain agreed to withdraw below the thirty-first parallel (the line that still defines the northern boundary of the Florida panhandle); thus Natchez and the surrounding area became a part of the new Mississippi Territory in 1795 (although the Spanish did not leave until 1798). Cotton had become the most important crop in the Natchez region by the mid-1790s. Versions of the new Whitney cotton gin—invented on a plantation near Savannah in 1793 by the Massachusetts-born Eli Whitney—were in use as early as 1796. The subsequent development of Natchez, its planters, merchants, and bankers, and its ties with Northern banking and English cotton manufacturers, is a study unto itself.

Both the owner of Auburn, Lyman Harding, and the architect, Levi Weeks, identified themselves as "Yankeys" who had come to Natchez, Harding around 1800, Weeks in 1809. Both were born and educated in Massachusetts. Harding had come to Natchez by way of Maryland, where he studied law, and established himself as a lawyer and planter. Weeks came by way of New York City, Cincinnati, and Lexington. He had gained his skills as carpenter and builder under Jonathan Warner in Williamsburg, Massachusetts, and as an architect in partnership with his brother in New York during the years 1798 to 1803.

Auburn represented the latest fashion in Natchez because of its "orders of Architecture"; that is, the giant or two-story columns, here of Ionic order, of the temple-front portico, which, it can be shown, were taken from Abraham Swan's *Collection of Designs in Architecture*. The tall columns and the great pediment of Auburn have the height associated with neoclassical Federal, yet there is a certain fullness of detail that is reminiscent of mid-century Georgian. In the eighteenth century the use of the giant order on porticoes was relatively rare—famous mansions such as Drayton Hall, the Miles Brewton house, or Shirley in Virginia had less grandiose double porticoes. The porticoes of St. Philip's

Church in Charleston probably had the first giant columns in what is now the United States. Governor Sharpe's mansion, Whitehall, in Maryland, built about 1764, a Palladian design, seems to have been the earliest domestic house to have such a portico. With the new century there came a number of houses, North and South, on which the giant order was used. The most obvious is the President's House (as the White House was originally called) in Washington, designed in 1792, though the familiar north portico as we know it today was not finished until 1829, after the burning by the British in 1814 and the subsequent rebuilding. The giant order of the Jumel-Morris mansion in New York, which was remodeled in 1810, is yet another example of the growing vogue for pretentious porticoes.

If Auburn was the first home whose façade was graced with a giant portico of a classical order in the Mississippi Territory, it was not the last in that or neighboring regions. Natchez itself has eight or more other mansions with similar porticoes, and there are still other examples in Kentucky, Tennessee, Mississippi, Alabama, Georgia, and Louisiana.

The vogue for such great columnar porticoes continued in the South and North well into the 1860s. The handling varies. The examples just mentioned fall into the late-Georgian, Federal category. Many buildings identified as Greek Revival have great columnar porticoes, though that most austere of Greek orders, the Doric, was not widely used in the South, and the term Greek Revival is sometimes used indiscriminately to describe anything with columns. Present-day architectural historians have wrestled with the problem of accurate terminology to describe the generously proportioned, columned structures often built in the middle and Deep South before the Civil War, and which usually represent a skillful amalgamation of traditional Palladian plans and classical details derived freely from either Roman, Greek, or Renaissance sources. The period term "antebellum" is widely used in the South when referring to buildings erected from 1812 to 1865. Because that term has come to imply a romanticized vision of the period, and because buildings of several different styles were built, it is not particularly helpful. In 1811 the Philadelphian architect Thomas U. Walter used the phrase "our columnar architecture" in a lecture. It is an uncomplicated term that suggests the widespread and satisfying use of columns at the time in which he spoke.

Natchez is especially interesting because these columned mansions or villas are scattered in and around that small city, or large town. They represent everyone's stereotype of the Southern plantation "big house," when in fact they are not on the main plantations. Especially by the 1820s and after, much of the land owned by the rich merchants and planters of Natchez was situated across the river in Louisiana or even in the slightly distant rich bottomland of the Mississippi Delta, upriver from Natchez between the Mississippi and Yazoo rivers. A more modest overseer's house and the cabins of the Negro workers might be on the actual plantations.

Levi Weeks, the architect of Auburn, is known to have owned eleven architectural design or pattern books at the time of his death. A careful study of the mansion has shown that he put these and others to good use in a rather free and inventive way. The Ionic capitals on the portico are from William Pain's *British Palladio*, as are parts of the idiosyncratic door frames of the front entrances, particularly the interesting ellipses of reeded drapery, and a spiral or freestanding circular stairway, below. The latter has all the sinuous elegance associated with the Federal style. Other features, such as some of the doorways, are a little old-fashioned in proportion and detailing and have been shown to derive from William Salmon's *Palladio Londinensis*, first published as early as 1734. In details the house embodies a somewhat curious melange of bookish elements. In plan it is refreshingly open and spacious. It is symmetrical in layout, and on both the ground and upper floor there is an entrance hall across the front, flanked by small rooms on either side. An arched opening

Stair hall in Auburn.

The Briars, Natchez, Mississippi, built c. 1818.

in each case leads to a barrel-vaulted back hall at right angles to the entrance hall. The ceilings are high, the ventilation excellent. When Latrobe's daughter Julia came down the Mississippi with her father in 1820, they stopped at Natchez and walked out to Auburn, a mile from the center of town, to visit Mrs. Harding. To Julia the house was "a perfect castle, and is furnished in a magnificent manner." Auburn is grand, but in 1820, before the wings were added, it was not all that large. The setting, the imposing portico, a certain spaciousness and openness contribute to a palatial feeling.

If Auburn in many ways represents everyone's idea of the quintessential great antebellum Southern mansion, another more modest Natchez residence has been rightly described as the "quintessential example of the planters' residences of the lower Mississippi valley." This is The Briars, above, built around 1818. This less pretentious structure can be taken as representative of many one-story, slightly raised and galleried houses found in the Deep South. It is one room deep, therefore easily ventilated. There is a sheltering gallery across the front and a loggia at the back, the latter set between two small rooms. The detailing is fine. The door enframement, the delicate fanlight, the window frames, especially those of the arched dormer windows, all show a knowledge of the neoclassical. In the 1840s it was the

home of the Howell family, and it was here that Varina Howell married Jefferson Davis in 1845.

For visitors from outside the South, fed on the stereotype of the great columned mansions, there is sometimes a sense of disappointment when they come upon one of these low, less grand houses and are told it is a plantation (farm) house. Related examples are found in the towns; Natchez itself has several. The storybook image of the old "aristocratic" and extremely feudal South does a disservice to the diversity that was, and is, to be found there, be it in architecture or in its people.

One of the pleasures of studying the architecture of the American South, as elsewhere, is the variety of texture to be found in any given place. Skillfully conceived buildings created by architects fully aware of their role as designers often stand in close proximity to vernacular structures created by more modest builders and craftsmen. The latter are often quick to observe the work of the tastemakers and then adapt their traditional methods and plans to the new modes, most especially in the handling of trim and also in the modification of proportions. The successful, self-conscious, architect-designed house can give structure and punctuation to a harmonious and pleasantly repetitive cityscape.

The Richard Richardson (Owens-Thomas) house in Savannah, below, is such a house. It stands at the corner of Oglethorpe Square in Savannah, commanding the attention and admiration of all who pass by. It is probably fair to say that here, as much as in any single house of its period in America, one senses and enjoys the work of the architect; his name was William Jay. All architecture, all buildings, are best understood by experiencing them, by walking in and about them, in order to feel and sense the proportions, the interplay of shapes and forms, the weight and texture of the surfaces, the colors and tones, the changing effects of the light. This is certainly true of the Richardson-Owens-Thomas house. Boldly conceived, it is full of complex subtleties. The commanding Ionic portico bows out in an undulating curve and is placed on a raised basement. The entrance door itself is placed within a shallow niche, the portico and entrance together creating a subtle play of curves. Equally remarkable is the side veranda, following page, supported by four large cast-iron acanthus leaves and with a roof topped with a Greek anthemion cornice.

The interior is bold and ingenious. On the outside wall of the dining room there is not an ordinary window, but rather a sky-light set above a shallow niche, and in a projecting curve above this niche there is a bold Greek fret design of amber glass through which light shines. In several cases there are interior lights or windows between rooms. Gilt-capped Corinthian columns frame the stairway, which divides at a landing to form double stairs to the second floor. Inlays of brass are used in the mahogany rails and treads of the stairs. The balusters are of wrought iron. The whole is elegant and sumptuous. Upstairs, part of the hall is literally a gently curved bridge spanning the lower staircase, a curious but well-designed feature that may be unique.

The Richardson-Owens-Thomas house has all the qualities of the finest English homes of the Regency, with chaste and elegant details inspired by both Greece and Rome. It is a style that serves as a transition between late Georgian and the Classic Revival. The evidence suggests that the initial designs were done in England. William Jay grew up in the lovely English city of Bath, with its array of townhouses around or along a succession of crescents, squares, and terraces. His father was a famous Nonconformist clergyman. He left for London in 1807, at the age of fourteen, to serve as an apprentice to an architect-surveyor.

The Owens-Thomas House, Savannah, Georgia, completed 1819. Designed by William Jay for Richard Richardson.

Side veranda, Owens-Thomas House.

There is no explicit record showing that Jay knew John Soane in London, but again and again one sees the affinity of Jay's work to that of the distinguished London architect. Within two years Jay had submitted designs that were shown at the Royal Academy, one in 1812 for a Grecian casino. By 1815 he had an office of his own, and in 1817 a design of his for a church in Savannah (unidentified) was shown at the Academy. By this time he had connections in Savannah, since his older sister, Anne, had married Robert Bolton of that town in 1810. Bolton's sister married Richard Richardson, a native of New Orleans and an important citizen and banker in Savannah in 1811, and it was he who commissioned Jay to do a house. This was begun in 1816 on the site of an older house, and since William Jay did not himself arrive in Savannah until December 1817, it is generally assumed that the initial designs were created in London and sent over. There is an inscription incised on the masonry foundation that reads: *Began house* A.D. *1816—Finished June* A.D. *1819—J. Retan*, confirming the name of the builder and the dates. Unfortunately Richardson's wife died in 1822 and, shortly after, he sold the house. It was purchased by a member of the Owens family in 1830 and remained in the Owens and Thomas families until 1951, when it was bequeathed to the Telfair Academy of Arts and Sciences in Savannah. Since it is and was one of the finest houses in Savannah and in America, it is no surprise to learn that those who helped to plan the Marquis de Lafayette's visit to that city in 1825 selected, with unerring taste, this house as the temporary residence for the old hero.

Jay spent seven years in America, where he worked in Georgia and South Carolina. In addition to the Owens-Thomas house he built several other private dwellings, a bank, church, and theater, some of which have been modified or destroyed. (The recently restored Scarbrough house in Savannah is another of his masterpieces.) His work provided a model of urban elegance, and no doubt this restrained masterpiece, with its high basement, influenced the proportions and chaste but elegant townhouses that form the still-surviving nineteenth-century cityscapes of Savannah. His influence was also directly felt upriver in the growing town of Augusta. His last years in America were spent in Charleston, where he helped to found the South Carolina Academy of Arts in 1821.

Jay left America in 1824. A national depression had begun in 1819, then in 1820 a yellow fever epidemic and a disastrous fire struck Savannah; for a few years there was little new building in either Savannah or Charleston. The years following the War of 1812 to the time of Jay's departure had been years of rapid growth in Savannah. Georgia, and Savannah, had developed slowly in colonial times, and by 1794 Savannah was still only a small town of 2,500 souls. Eli Whitney's cotton gin—which could do the work that it had previously taken a horse and fifty men to do—brought new prosperity. By 1818 it was the sixteenth largest city in America, with a thriving shipping business. Buckskin, rice, cotton, and timber were major exports. A twice-weekly steamboat service was inaugurated between Savannah and Charleston in 1817, and in 1819 the *Savannah* left that port to become the first steamboat to cross the Atlantic. Jay was fortunate to be in Savannah during these prosperous years, and Savannah fortunate to have him. When he left the city for Charleston in 1821, after the fire, he described it as "a Niobe of cities, a chaos of Ruins . . . She was rising a model, she had fallen a monument." It was a decade before prosperity and growth returned. Railroads were among the factors which contributed to the new flourishing.

The citizens who moved westward in increasing numbers after the Revolution took their religion with them, establishing new parishes and churches as they settled. Catholics from Maryland joined the trek to Kentucky, and in 1808 the Vatican created the Diocese of Bardstown, in Kentucky. Catholics were in a minority in the newly declared United States but, perhaps because of the French role in the Revolution, the church was able to establish the Diocese of Baltimore in 1789, which originally included all thirteen states. As the country grew, new dioceses were gradually named. The Bardstown See had jurisdiction over Kentucky and Tennessee. The small church of St. Thomas's in Bardstown, right, built in 1816, is the oldest Catholic church in the region, the oldest structure there in the Gothic taste, and, though it represents a modest, tentative essay in that style, one of the earliest buildings in the Gothic taste in the United States. The pointed arches and niches on the facade and the parapet echo, in an extremely simplified way, the façades of the great European cathedrals—a reminder of the long years when the Catholic church dominated Europe. Its immediate model is clearly St. Mary's Chapel in Baltimore, where there is the same tripartite façade with parapet and round window. The latter was built in 1806 by the French-born architect Maximilian Godefroy. The Gothic style had survived only here and there in England and Europe, mostly in church and collegiate designs, during the centuries dominated by the classicizing ideas of the Renaissance. Interest in it had been rekindled during the nascent romanticism of the eighteenth century, and with the growing knowledge of architectural history in the nineteenth century, the Gothic increasingly became a symbol of the romantic past, sym-

St. Thomas's Church, Bardstown, Kentucky, 1816.

Shaker Meetinghouse, Pleasant Hill, Kentucky, 1820. Designed and built by Micajah Burnett.

bolizing the continuity of the church and of institutions of learning. In St. Thomas's, Bardstown, and St. Mary's, Baltimore, the choice of Gothic strengthened identity with the Catholic church. In 1841 the Bardstown diocese was moved to the larger community of Louisville.

The religious freedom made possible by the separation of church and state in the new United States allowed a variety of religious sects to flourish. The young country, with its open frontiers and optimistic constitutional government, also attracted a variety of experiments in Utopian community life. It has been estimated that during the nineteenth century as many as a hundred different "model" communities were created in America—an indication both of the spiritual upheavals and economic insecurities in Europe and America, and of the driving optimism that led people to feel new solutions could be found. Among these were the pietistic, celibate Shakers. They established flourishing

agricultural and craft communities in the Northeast—New York, New Hampshire, Connecticut, Maine, and Massachusetts—and a number of Western settlements in Ohio, Indiana, and Kentucky. The buildings of one of the latter, Pleasant Hill in Kentucky, have now been lovingly restored, and in the quiet, ordered rural ambience one can imagine something of the nature of the hardworking, disciplined, but joyous life founded in religious zeal and a belief in Christ's Second Coming that seems to have characterized this sect. Their rigid codes of behavior meant that most buildings had separate entrances for men and women, and separate stairways leading to sleeping quarters, the women on the right, the men on the left. Their emphasis on order, cleanliness, efficiency, and economy meant that their buildings, and the interior furnishings, are characterized by a simplicity of form and economy of line that have long attracted twentieth-century designers, architects, and theorists.

The Meetinghouse at Pleasant Hill, left, built in 1820, exemplifies this austere taste and sense of order. There are evenly spaced windows, spare door and window frames, two doors, pairs of stair-steps, and street entrances, two chimneys, two side entrances. The Meetinghouse is white; all other frame buildings in the village were red or yellow. A visiting Virginian described it in 1825: "The church is a frame building underpinned with superior neatness in stone; it is about sixty feet long and proportionately wide, plastered and white washed, with cupboards, &c painted blue, in the neatest conceivable style." Worship services, which involved songs, spirited dances, marches, and prayers, were held in the large room on the first floor. Living quarters for the ministers, elders, and eldresses were on the second floor. The architect-builder was Micajah Burnett. He came as a child to Kentucky from Virginia with his parents in the 1790s. His parents accepted Shaker beliefs and joined a small Shaker community in 1808; their four children are recorded as "believing" in 1809. Burnett became the master-carpenter, architect, and town planner of Pleasant Hill in the years between 1813 and 1840.

There is no record of how he obtained his training, but he mastered intricate structural methods as well as basic masonry and carpentry techniques. The ceiling of the first floor of the Meetinghouse, for example, is suspended by a complex system of white-oak framing in the attic, thus eliminating the need for interior supports in the large ground-floor room. He was also responsible for the installation of a public waterworks in the village, completed in 1833. Each house and barn had running water. It was one of the first public waterworks west of the Allegheny Mountains.

Burnett designed and built twenty-three of the surviving buildings in the restored village of Pleasant Hill. The largest building is the Center Family house, a large limestone structure that took ten years—from 1824 to 1834—to build. The central hall, below, shows the neat, orderly interior arrangement, with the rows of pegs used to hang chairs, clothing, and utensils. The arched doorways seen on right and left are a concession to fashion. Burnett is known to have had a large library, and he no doubt learned some of his techniques—there are graceful spiral

Central hall of Center Family House,
Pleasant Hill, Kentucky, completed 1834.
Designed and built by Micajah Burnett.

Bethesda Presbyterian Church, Camden, South Carolina, c. 1820. Designed by Robert Mills.

body of the church," was placed between the two front doors. And, as the architect Robert Mills described it, "The interior is arranged so that the floor and pews rise as they recede from the pulpit, giving many advantages to the audience, both in hearing and seeing." Here, as much as in any single Protestant or Nonconformist house of worship, the building was designed to foster the hearing of the Word. To do so there must have been close cooperation among the pastor, the congregation, and the architect. We know little of the Reverend John Joyce but, fortunately, much is known about the architect, Robert Mills, who here, as elsewhere, proved himself a skillful architect, well able to adapt his designs to specific needs.

Robert Mills was a man of prodigious talents and interests. Problems of inland navigation and the development of canals, the potential of railroads, the solution of the problem of slavery through the establishment of a colony in Africa, prison reform, care of the insane, possible restitution to Indians are among the problems to which he addressed himself. Architecture he found to be "the most difficult, important and interesting of all branches of study." He was concerned to combine good design with the needs of each commission. He knew and understood mechanical and hydraulic engineering and fundamental principles of masonry as well as how to draw the five orders of ancient architecture and to make a good wash drawing. He is best known as the designer of the great Washington Monument in the nation's capital, and for his role as Federal architect from 1836 to 1852, during the latter years of his life. He served seven Presidents and was responsible for, among others, the U.S. Treasury Building and the old U.S. Patent Office. These are sober, strong buildings that symbolize the nation's strength and stability. Somewhat less well known are his many buildings in South Carolina and other parts of the United States.

Mills stated that he had "the honor of being the first native American who directed his studies to architecture as a profession." Through a series of rather remarkable circumstances, and because of what must have been his own precocious talents, he worked with or had contact with virtually all of the most important architects in this country before he reached thirty. He was born in South Carolina and during his youth in Charleston knew James Hoban, the Irish architect who did the winning design for the President's House. In 1800, at nineteen, he went to Washington and there was employed as a draftsman by Hoban, then working on the U.S. Capitol. Through Hoban he met Jefferson, who invited him to Monticello, where he did occasional plans and elevations for Monticello and was allowed to study in Jefferson's library, at the time the best architectural library in the country. Sometime in late 1801 he made an architectural tour of New England and, armed with an introduction from Jefferson, met Charles Bullfinch, one of the most distinguished practitioners of the English Adam style in Boston. In 1802, again with the thoughtful help of Jefferson, he met Benjamin Henry Latrobe, who had only recently come to America to practice his profession. Mills joined Latrobe's office in 1802. Though almost immediately Mills began to do some designs on his own, and there were a few interruptions, he was with Latrobe until 1809. Here he shared in Latrobe's work on the U.S. Capitol, the Baltimore Cathedral, the Philadelphia waterworks and the Chesapeake and

staircases in the more worldly Trustees' house—from these. In style, the buildings by Burnett at Pleasant Hill are conservative, an austere version of Georgian.

According to tradition, the "peculiar views" of the Presbyterian pastor, Reverend John Joyce, were responsible for the unorthodox, and very Protestant, arrangement of the entrance doors and interior of the Bethesda Presbyterian Church in Camden, South Carolina, built around 1820, above and to the right. The temple-like portico at the front is graced with four Doric columns; the spire, however, is at the rear, as are the main entrances. There are four in number, two at ground-floor level, two at gallery level. They are reached by the unusual crisscross stairs. There is a window at the central landing. The landings and openings were apparently meant to represent nothing less than the Biblical "five porches of Bethesda," the image of the House of Mercy so dear to Nonconformists. The entire arrangement is sheltered by an unorthodox three-columned porch.

On the inside the high pulpit, "standing well forward into the

Delaware Canal (the last two were essentially engineering projects), and in various private commissions. Schools of architecture did not exist at this time, but if they had, it would not have been possible to name a better faculty to one than those with whom Mills worked. In these years he became acquainted with the basic architectural literature—pattern books and theory—becoming learned in both the techniques and tradition of his profession; he saw many of the best-designed buildings in the country, and had tutelage and practical training in design, construction, and engineering. He was later to write: "Books are useful to the student, but when he enters upon the practice of his profession, he should lay them aside and only consult them upon doubtful points, or in matters of detail or as mere studies, not to copy buildings from." Rather, he saw the architect's need to analyze each commission in terms of the object or purpose of the build-

ing, the appropriate means of construction, and the situation or site. A study of his buildings reveals how skillfully he practiced what he preached.

Buildings and monuments designed by Mills were built from Connecticut to Florida, from Savannah to Arkansas. The largest number, however, are in South Carolina, his native state. Among his earliest designs were proposals submitted in 1802 for the newly established South Carolina College (now the University of South Carolina), done when he had just begun work in Latrobe's office. His earliest completed work was the 1804–1806 Circular Church in Charleston, unfortunately destroyed in 1861. He worked on his own in Richmond and Baltimore; it was in the latter city that he designed the first monument erected to George Washington. In 1820 he moved to Charleston and from 1820 to 1830 he was "civil and military engineer of the state." As

Rear entrance of Bethesda Presbyterian Church.

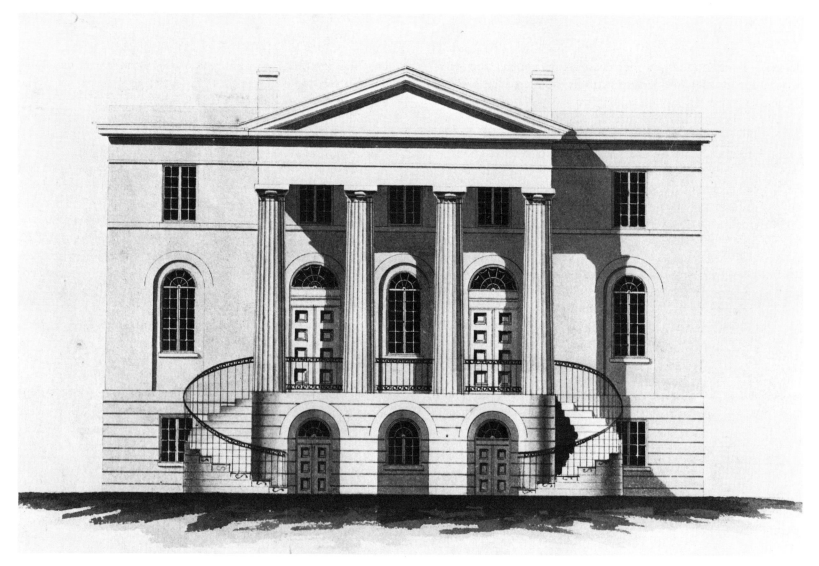

Robert Mills. "Fireproof Public Offices Charleston, South Carolina."
Rendering, ink and wash on paper with 1828 watermark. Built 1822–1826.
Papers of Robert Mills, South Carolina Historical Society, Charleston.

such, he was responsible for designing a comprehensive scheme of inland navigation linking and developing the rivers and canals, and had charge of the public buildings of the state. These included a number of courthouses and jails, which were built to his design. During this time he produced two studies, the richly documented and descriptive *Statistics of South Carolina* of 1826 and *The Atlas of South Carolina from Actual Survey*, of the same year.

His best-known South Carolina building is the "Fireproof Building," built in Charleston from 1822 to 1826, seen above in his own ink-and-wash rendering. It is, as he himself described it, "designed in the simple Greek Doric style, without any ornament, except that afforded by the porticos which face each front." Mills's career crested at almost precisely the same time as the preference for the Greek over the "Roman and mixed styles" reached its peak in this country and Europe, so that some of his finest buildings, such as this one, are predominantly in the Greek Revival style. True to his principles, this is not a pattern-book reproduction of the form. He uses the chaste Greek Doric columns, and an austere and "simple" treatment of the exterior,

but the design is carefully adapted to the particular requirements of the commission, which was to provide secure and fireproof facilities for public records, and well-lighted working space for public officers serving the different state agencies. There are eight different entrances, so that individual offices could be reached with a minimum of effort. Each individual room was so designed as to receive light and air from the outside, and air circulates through each room into one of the double halls found on each floor and up and out through a central skylighted circular staircase. The City Council explicitly requested that the building be fireproof since Charleston had suffered devastating fires. It was the kind of technical problem that engaged Mills's mind. The selection of the site was in itself important. Though in the center of an urban area, the building is on a square and the stipulation was made that no large structure was to be built within thirty feet of it, thus providing a spatial air brake. In the interior the construction is such that there are varying degrees of fireproofing. Of twenty-four rooms, only four are absolutely safe, with masonry walls and without fireplaces, areas meant for the storage of irreplaceable records. There are sheet-iron interior shutters. Though there are fireplaces in other rooms, the lower two floors are otherwise secure from fire. This seems to have been in accord with Mills's original plan.

The building as it was completed, and as it now stands, is not exactly like the rendering. An old photograph shows that the pediment and low parapet, as well as the curved stairs, were apparently damaged or destroyed in the 1886 earthquake, for they have subsequently been replaced with slightly altered features. Other changes seem to have been made in the course of the building, with or without Mills's consent. During construction Mills was busy gathering materials for his *Atlas* and *Statistics*, as well as with other building projects such as the Asylum for the Insane in Columbia; the day-to-day work was done largely under the supervision of a local architect, John George Spidle. The columns in the completed building were left plain, and the short attic windows Mills had drawn were lengthened and the horizontal string course eliminated. These changes seem to have been in the interest of economy or convenience, or both. The building is still an austere and impressive structure, light, airy, and convenient to work in. It now houses the invaluable documents and offices of the South Carolina Historical Society. Here, as in his other buildings, Mills's purpose was "to produce as much harmony and beauty of arrangement as practical. The principle assumed and acted upon was that beauty is founded upon order and that convenience and utility were constituent parts." Whether the architectural problem was one of accommodating a minister's desire to have his congregation seated so all could see

and hear the Word, providing clean and attractive surroundings for the mentally ill, or efficient and fireproof space for public offices and records, Mills combined his knowledge of engineering with a sure familiarity of the great architectural traditions, and created buildings that were, and still are, both serviceable and handsome.

The builder of the Pentagon Barracks in Baton Rouge, below, used large, unfluted Doric columns to give definition and character to this group of buildings, completed in 1825. The complex consists of four two-story brick buildings, which served as barracks for the U.S. Army. The fifth side of the pentagon, which faces toward the Mississippi River, is open. It is not known whether or not there was a building, or buildings, in this space. The Pentagon Barracks replaced an older star-shaped earthen fort. In creating the complex the builders retained for the military a masonry image of the old five-sided shape that had so long been typical of fortifications. The four barracks buildings, with their colonnaded open walkways at ground level and verandas or galleries on the second are, in essence, an adaptation to institutional life of the basic scheme developed for Louisiana plantation houses. The choice of giant Doric columns, as opposed to what might have been piers and colonnettes, shows the builder's awareness of the new appreciation of monumental columnar forms. They are in fact Roman Doric, but have a bold and chaste quality associated with the Greek taste. During the Mexican War of 1846–1848 General Zachary Taylor's forces used this as a home base; later both Confederate and Union troops were

Pentagon Barracks,
Baton Rouge, Louisiana,
completed 1825.

Charles Peale Polk. "Mrs. Elijah Etting" (née Shinah Solomon). 1792. Oil on canvas. Signed and dated lower left: "C. Polk pinxt/1792." Baltimore Museum of Art.

housed here. In 1886 the old barracks buildings had served their usefulness and were turned over to Louisiana State University. They are now used by the Louisiana state government.

Painting

However much there was a wish to create art for the new nation and the new states, the fact remained that most painters depended upon private patronage. The fact also remained that the work of "face" or portrait painters was in greatest demand.

On a national level, Charles Willson Peale and Gilbert Stuart were the best-known artists. Peale made his home in Philadelphia, but he and his painting progeny, and relatives, traveled to Washington, Baltimore, and other Southern cities to find or to accommodate sitters. Stuart, a truly excellent portrait painter, focused his attention on the first President and other people of note while the new nation's capital was still in Philadelphia. He made numerous copies of these portraits for sale. Many other

artists as well survived by making copies of Stuart's paintings of Washington for statehouses, courthouses, and city halls throughout the land. Stuart later moved to Boston. John Trumbull and John Vanderlyn had uneven careers as painters. They executed portraits for bread and butter but tried—and succeeded only in part—to gain lasting fame through their efforts at painting heroic and dramatic subjects. The brightest star on the American artistic horizon in the early nineteenth century was Washington Allston. Born in the district of Georgetown, South Carolina, in 1779, he went as a boy to Newport, Rhode Island, then enrolled at Harvard in 1796. He later studied abroad for a number of years, mingling with major artistic and literary figures in England and Italy. Though he had friends from South Carolina, his adult artistic career was spent either in or near Boston or in England. He was the first great romantic painter of America. Only a few early works were done in Carolina, when he visited there before first going abroad in 1801. Yet he never forgot those childhood experiences which stimulated his romantic sensibilities. He later recalled that he had "delighted in being terrified" by the tales told him by the Negroes, that he had made drawings in Carolina as a child of less than six years, and that he had played at making landscapes out of sticks and roots of old trees. He had rare insight into the world of his own imagination.

Considerably more modest in accomplishment or aspiration were artists who practiced their skills in the South in the early years of the new Republic. One of these was Charles Peale Polk, nephew of Charles Willson Peale. Orphaned as a child of ten, he went to Philadelphia to live with his uncle, and from him learned his craft. In 1791 he settled in Baltimore. The portrait of Mrs. Elijah Etting (née Shinah Solomon), left, was done in the following year. Something of the modeling, particularly of the eyes and facial features as well as the pose, recalls the work of his uncle. The sweep of line in the flow of the drapery, and most especially the manner in which the sprig of jasmine at her breast seems to lie atop the painting rather than being integrated as a part of her ensemble, are characteristic of Polk's slightly amateurish manner. The same is true of the leaf patterning on her scarf. It is almost as if the artist cannot resist the sharp delineation of these surface patterns. Similar floral patterns occur in his other paintings.

In this case one senses or imagines a friendly and easy rapport between subject and sitter, since she appears as a warm, generous, and benign woman. She was the widow of Elijah Etting, a Jewish general merchant who came to America in 1758, settling in York, Pennsylvania, which was then something of a frontier community. Her parents had come from London a few years earlier. Her husband became a respected citizen, general merchant, and Indian trader, and helped to supply the Revolutionary Army with blankets. As a young matron a visitor in 1773 described her as "always in good spirits, full of frolic and glee, and possessing the talent of singing agreeably," and her husband as "much less brilliant" but "always good-humored and kind." Her husband died in 1788. Two years later she moved to Baltimore with her brood of five surviving children. She ran a boardinghouse for a time and was active in Baltimore community affairs. Despite her cares and sorrows, to judge by this painting, she seems to have carried her sense of joy into mature middle age.

Her progeny were to play important roles in the histories of Philadelphia and Baltimore. Her son Solomon, for example, was active in promoting passage of a bill allowing Jews to serve in public office—hitherto forbidden. He was subsequently one of the first Maryland Jews to serve on the City Council of Baltimore, and was later its president.

Charles Peale Polk frequently had difficulty supporting himself with commissions. In order to earn extra income he made copies of portraits of that pantheon of American heroes, Washington, Lafayette, and Franklin, and occasionally did small profile portraits in gold leaf on glass, or *verre églomisé*, a popular technique at the time. After 1818 he gave up an artistic career, supporting himself afterward as a clerk in Washington. Even the highly skilled Gilbert Stuart found it easier to make copies of his own portraits of Washington than to constantly secure new commissions. Polk's uncle, Charles Willson Peale, earned money through his museum as well as from portrait commissions. Talented artists like Washington Allston spent much of their artistic life abroad, as did Benjamin West and John Singleton Copley. Given this picture of a poverty of patronage, even for portraits, it is all the more surprising that new discoveries of paintings executed in the early Republic continue to be made. Among those which have come to light recently, for example, is a group of ten paintings done around 1791 of members of the Archer Payne family of Goochland County, Virginia. Nothing is known of the artist except the family tradition that he was considered a talented painter when sober. Even such part-time artists contributed to the artistic life of their communities.

A painting recently acquired by the Maryland Historical Society, below, shows Mrs. Thomas Everette (Rebecca Myring, 1787–1833) and her five children. It may have been done shortly after she became a widow, for it is recorded in her will that the

Joshua Johnson. "Mrs. Thomas Everette [née Rebecca Myring] and Children." 1818. Oil on canvas. Maryland Historical Society, Baltimore.

Jacob Frymire. "Mrs. Marquis Calmes" (née Priscilla Heale). 1806. Oil on canvas. Signed on reverse (has been relined): "Restored/March 1932/Painting by G. Frymeier/April 7th 1806." Chicago Historical Society.

been identified as one of the few known American black painters in the period before the Civil War, and the first to whom a number of works can be attributed with some confidence. It was not easy for a person of Negro blood to enter the ranks of highly skilled crafts, though this was perhaps a little easier in the first quarter of the nineteenth century than later, when race relations became tenser. Therefore, we can only guess that Joshua Johnson, portrait painter, might have felt a compulsion to draw and paint, had a difficult time securing the training he wished, and had some open-minded patrons. On December 19, 1798, an artist of this name placed an advertisement in the *Baltimore Intelligencer* announcing his services as a portrait painter who could give "precise and natural likenesses" and then adding: "As a self-taught genius, deriving from nature and industry his knowledge of Art: and having experienced many insurpassable obstacles in the pursuit of his studies; it is highly gratifying to him to make assurances of his ability to execute all commands, with an effect, and in a style, which must give satisfaction."

Johnson's reference to "insurpassable obstacles" suggested his achievement had been more than ordinarily difficult.

Still another artist who might qualify as a "self-taught genius," who gained skill in his craft by dint of "nature and industry," is Jacob Frymire. In fact, it is probable that the paths of Charles Peale Polk, Joshua Johnson, and Jacob Frymire crossed from time to time, as they sought patrons in Maryland and Virginia.

Frymire was born in Lancaster County, Pennsylvania, sometime between 1765 and 1774, and died a farmer in 1822. From 1807 through 1818 various legal records identify him as "limner" or "painter." The term "limner," to mean portrait painter, goes back to the sixteenth century. (Its earlier usage implied an illuminator of manuscripts.) By the nineteenth century it sometimes seems to have been used to identify an artist of less pretension, one whose skill depended more on line than on facile modeling with color. Frymire might have learned his trade from Lancaster-based Jacob Eichholtz, or from the elder Peticolas, who also lived in Lancaster before 1804, when he and his family moved to Richmond. Frymire's earliest known paintings date from the 1790s. He appears to have spent much of his early career traveling as an itinerant painter, visiting various towns in Virginia, including Winchester, Alexandria, and Warrenton. In 1806 he ventured into Woodford County, in central Kentucky, and is thus one of the first-known artists to have worked there.

In Kentucky he painted Marquis Calmes IV and his wife, Priscilla Heale Calmes, left. Calmes had been involved in land speculation in Kentucky before the Revolution, then served as a second lieutenant in that war. By 1783 he and his wife had settled in Woodford County where he became a wealthy landowner active in local affairs. She is shown in a typical Frymire composition—the subject close to the picture plane, the head placed high within the picture. She looks directly out at the viewer, plain, somber, even severe, her mouth closed in the slight grimace that is often characteristic of this artist. The lace cap and collar appear to be freshly starched. The ribbon, possibly grosgrain, is explicitly delineated. The cut of her high-waisted dress shows that she was well aware of the latest fashion. The two fluted bowls she holds are equally modern for the time; they

painting was done by J. Johnson and the date of execution 1818. Her husband died in 1817. She sits somber and upright on a sofa, wearing a black dress trimmed with a white lace collar and a white cap and holding her baby. The other children stand rather stiffly alongside. The erect stances, the rather tubular arms, and even the sofa with clearly delineated brass upholstery tacks are similar to those seen in a group of paintings whose subjects are mostly members of Maryland and Virginia families.

Mention of this painting in Mrs. Everette's will is important, since it is a contemporary legal document connecting a specific painting to an artist whose name is known chiefly through printed references. A Joshua Johnson, or Johnston, is listed in virtually all the existing Baltimore directories between 1796 and 1824 as a portrait painter or limner. Among these, the 1817 directory had a listing for "Free Householders of Colour," and he was recorded as a "portrait painter, Nelson St." Johnson thus has

appear to be porcelain and seem emblems of the hospitality that the artist found in this frontier home. The Windsor chair is the sort made and used in Pennsylvania and elsewhere in the middle years of the eighteenth century, and might have been brought with the family from Virginia. There is a wealth of social history in this straightforward painting.

One other important detail in the painting is the miniature she wears on her dress showing, in reverse, a seated figure who looks somewhat like Mrs. Calmes. It was popular in the late eighteenth and early nineteenth centuries for miniature paintings, usually of a loved one or close relative, to be worn as jewelry. Frymire, like the elder Peticolas, is known to have painted small oval miniatures.

The history of the portrait miniature, paintings of figures in dimensions smaller than nature, really begins in the sixteenth century, though there are earlier roots. The term "miniature" as used today entered common usage in the eighteenth century. Though some artists worked in both large and small scale, others made a specialty of these exquisite small works executed in gouache or watercolor on ivory, or occasionally on vellum, which had been the earlier practice. In the Peale family, for instance, Charles Willson Peale learned the technique, which he taught his younger brother James. The younger brother then tended to specialize in this genre.

The "golden age" of the American miniature has been said to be the two decades spanning the end of the eighteenth and beginning of the nineteenth century. Among the most distinguished practitioners of this art in America were Edward Greene Malbone and Charles Fraser, both of whom worked in the South. Malbone was born in Newport, Rhode Island, in 1777 and had begun painting miniatures by 1794. Then he was frequently on the move and painted numerous miniatures in various cities: Boston, New York, Philadelphia, and, of special interest to us, Charleston and Savannah. Because of ill health, he went to Jamaica in 1806. He died the following year in Savannah. Fraser was a native of Charleston, born in 1782, and except for some trips to the North, lived his entire life there. His desire to be a painter was stimulated by his meeting with Washington Allston and Malbone in Charleston in 1800, on their way to London. Fraser studied law and practiced for a decade or so, from 1807 to 1818, but gave it up finally for a career in art. As we have seen, some of his earliest works were sketches he made of the country houses and churches around Charleston. He painted larger portraits as well as landscapes, but some of his finest work, and most superb characterizations, are found in miniatures. In 1857 a one-man show was held in Charleston, honoring the then venerable artist, who died in 1860.

All the young and healthy beauty and vigor of Eliza Izard and Thomas Pinckney, Jr., are captured in the pair of portrait miniatures by Malbone on the right. The background in each is composed of a softly fluid system of cross-hatching, which sets off the figures. Delicate washes are used to shape shadows and model the figures. The notation in the case of the portrait of Thomas Jr. reads "T. Pinckney Feb. 1802. Painted by R. G. Malbone of Newport," while that of Eliza Izard is signed "Malbone 1801." The two were married December 27, 1803. Portrait miniatures, because of their small scale, have a special

Edward Greene Malbone. "Miniature of Colonel Thomas Pinckney, Jr." 1802. Ivory on gold locket. In ink on case: "T. Pinckney Feb 1802, Painted by R G Malbone of NewPort." Carolina Art Association/Gibbes Art Gallery; Charleston.

Edward Greene Malbone. "Miniature of Mrs. Thomas Pinckney, Jr." (née Eliza Izard). 1801. Ivory on gold locket, red leather case. On lower right, scratched: "Malbone 1801." Carolina Art Association/Gibbes Art Gallery, Charleston.

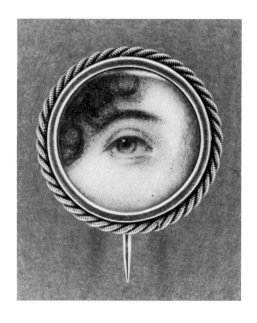

Edward Greene Malbone. "Miniature of Mrs. Maria Miles Heyward's Eye." 1802. Watercolor on ivory. Unsigned. National Museum of American Art, Smithsonian Institution, Washington, D.C.

stone. Fraser uses a neutral background, with darker shading at the base and lighter in the upper portion. As can be seen from the stamp in the case, this is one of the 314 of his works included in the 1857 exhibit. Such cases made it possible to carry about a miniature, somewhat as photographs of loved ones are now carried in billfolds.

The infirmities of old age are caught in Fraser's portrait of H. F. Plowden Weston, right. An inscription on the back indicates the sitter was eighty-five years and six months old when painted in May 1824. There is no flattery in this depiction, yet somehow the artist conveys a sense of respect, even affection, for the possibly acerbic and determined white-haired man who sits on his red chair. Weston was a merchant and planter who lived near Charleston, and Fraser had very probably known him all his life. There is here as much realism as any artist might hope to achieve before the age of photography.

One of the mechanical devices that several artists used to make quick and correct likenesses was the physiognotrace, a cumbersome device invented in 1786 by Gilles-Louis Chrétien, with which one could take an exact profile. Charles Balthazar Julien Fevret de Saint-Mémin (1770–1852), a member of the lesser French nobility and a refugee from the French Revolution, did 800 or so such profile portraits during his sojourns in America between 1793–1810 and 1812–1814. He and his parents fled to Switzerland in 1793, then came to New York with the intent of going to Santo Domingo where his mother owned an estate. The slave uprising there prevented this, so he determined to earn his living through his art, an interest that had heretofore been a pastime. He built his own physiognotrace with

intimacy, worn as jewels by some, but carried about or only gazed at privately by others. It is possible that the young couple exchanged these at some point before their marriage. In 1802 Malbone also painted a tiny miniature that represents a delightful and typical conceit of the period—the beautiful and alluring eye of Maria Miles Heyward, above. What was the occasion, and who was the recipient of this, surely, very private image?

Fraser captured on ivory a wide variety of the citizens of Charleston, young, middle-aged, old, each remarkably individual. His study of Judge Thomas Waties, below, painted in 1820, shows the mature, sixty-year-old lawyer, seems to catch something of the "moral and intellectual endowments" and "benign qualities of his heart" that are described on the judge's tomb-

Charles Fraser. "Miniature of Judge Thomas Waties." 1820. Watercolor on ivory. Signed, lower right: "C.F./1820." Label of 1857 Fraser Exhibition inside cover of case. National Museum of American Art, Smithsonian Institution, Washington, D.C.

was both a connoisseur of art and an amateur lithographer. Perhaps because Saint-Mémin shared with Rogers and Murray interests in things artistic and mechanical, this small painting is more fully developed than most of his work.

Saint-Mémin's semimechanical drawings of a host of America's leading citizens during the early years of the Republic, including Jefferson, Meriwether Lewis, and John Marshall, provide an invaluable record. His profile studies were right for the time not only because they were quick and less expensive, hence appealing to a rising middle class, but also because they recalled antique medals and hence had a neoclassical quality. After the collapse of Napoleon's Empire in 1814 the Saint-Mémin family returned to France, and his last years were spent as conservateur of the museum in Dijon.

The process of Americanizing New Orleans—a process still happily not completely achieved—had only begun during the American Revolution and afterward. At that time the "Kaintucks" and other Americans began coming into the city and settled into their own neighborhoods separate from the Creole community,

the help of instructions in an encyclopedia. In most cases he made an exact profile of his sitters on red paper (they have now faded to soft pink), and then drew in the features and clothing with black and white chalk. Using yet another mechanical device, a pantograph, he later reduced many of these to small scale and made engravings of them. Working first in and around New York and Philadelphia, Saint-Mémin in 1803 set himself up in the new Federal city of Washington. He subsequently spent most of the next four years in the South, visiting or living for a time in Baltimore, Annapolis, Richmond, and Charleston.

Though skill was needed to complete his profile outlines with interior chalk drawing he often signed these "St. Mémin fecit" or "fᵗ," implying the work as "made" in a fairly mechanical way. An exception is a particularly fine watercolor, right, which is signed "St. Mémin pinx"; that is, painted. The subject is a young Baltimore girl, Harriet Rogers, who was about seventeen when the watercolor was done in 1806. Her profile portrait dominates the small composition, which is done largely in soft tones of brown wash. (Though larger than most, by its small size, 7 by 5¾ inches, this qualifies as a miniature.) Her brown dress is in the fashionable Empire cut and her hair is piled at the back and bound with a fillet of three braids. She could almost have come off an ancient cameo. The artist devoted more than usual attention to the background, in which he shows a Baltimore landscape and her home, Druid Hill, a Federal-style mansion with columnar portico built 1797–1801 by her father, who was something of an amateur architect. In 1807 Harriet Rogers became the second wife of John Robert Murray, a wealthy New Yorker who

Attributed to one of the Salazars. Probably Louise Duralde. c. 1790–1800.
Oil on canvas. Private collection.

Spanish rule.) It is believed to be of Louise Duralde, a young woman of Spanish descent, and until recently was owned by descendants. The oval format, the upright posture, the delicate, soft-edged modeling are characteristic of the group. She is shown holding flowers, a typical attribute of a young woman. Mademoiselle Duralde (1781–1864) married Joseph Soniat du Fossat on September 22, 1801. The portrait may have been taken a few years before that date.

Part of what we know of the Salazars comes from legal records. The family was among those whose houses were destroyed in the great New Orleans fire of 1788 and consequently allowed by the cathedral's kindly curate, Père Antoine (Padre Antonio de Sedella), to erect small cabins in the Presbytere gardens. Père Antoine as a result became involved in a dispute with the Spanish officials and some of his responsibilities were taken from him. In 1789 Don José and others filed a petition protesting the high rents established by the less generous and more businesslike new authorities.

Père Antoine was both a much-loved and controversial figure in New Orleans. He first came to Louisiana in 1780, or 1781, a Spanish Capuchin priest from Granada. He was well liked by the French Louisianians, and though ousted by the Spanish in 1790 because of a feud with the bishop, he managed to return in 1795 as the pastor of St. Louis Parish Church, where he remained for the rest of his life. He was regularly embroiled in disagreements with the church authorities yet was much beloved by the people. At one point he was "elected" as parish priest by the local board of wardens, in defiance of the church hierarchy. He performed over 3,500 marriages and probably buried as many parishioners. His home was a humble hovel behind the cathedral. In his old age he was a familiar figure in his coarse brown robe and bare feet. When Lafayette visited the city the old priest welcomed the old soldier with open arms. When Père Antoine died, all businesses in the city were closed, and even the Masons accompanied his cortege.

Edmund Brewster, an artist from Philadelphia, announced his presence in New Orleans on April 6, 1819, with an advertisement in the *Louisiana Gazette*, in which he said that among the specimens of his work on view was a "full-length portrait of General Washington, executed by him since his arrival in this city." It was apparently this painting that was purchased by the New Orleans City Council on April 17, 1819, for $200, to be placed in the Session Hall of the Council. It is a copy of Stuart's "Lansdowne Washington," which had long served its purpose as an icon of the new country—and helped many a struggling artist to earn a living.

Far more successful is Brewster's full-length portrait of Père Antoine, right, showing the beloved father at seventy-four, aged but unbowed. There is a sense of authority in this hollow-cheeked figure, shown against a dramatic architectural setting of receding arches. (The latter may be imaginary.) Brewster is recorded as being in New Orleans in 1819, 1822, and 1824, and was back in Philadelphia by 1839. Most of his work seems to have been lost. This portrait has great presence and intensity. From it, too, one can sense why New Orleans, with its French and Spanish inhabitants and "popish" beliefs, seemed a very exotic place to visitors from the North and East.

on the upriver side of present Canal Street. The first artists about whom we can piece together information are a man of Spanish descent, Don José (or Joseph) Salazar de Mendoza, a native of Mérida, in the Yucatán Peninsula of Mexico, and his daughter. The family arrived in Louisiana around 1782, and José died in 1802. Most of their work was done during the years of Spanish control. The daughter, Francisca, signed at least one painting; a complete study of the work of the two Salazars is still to be done. One of two well-documented paintings by José is a 1796 full-length portrait of Don Andres Almonester y Roxas, the wealthy businessman and philanthropist who financed the building of the Cabildo in New Orleans. It is replete with heraldic emblems and lengthy scroll, in the Spanish baroque tradition.

The charming portrait of a young Creole girl, above, in her beautiful blue dress, is one of several attributed to the Salazars. (All depict members of families prominent in Louisiana under

Père Antoine, with his gaunt features and picturesque appearance, was an appealing subject; another artist who worked on a rendition, apparently a large watercolor, of the aged priest was John James Audubon, not then famous. He made reference to it in his diary on October 25, 1821, when he had just returned to New Orleans after a summer in the Louisiana and Mississippi countryside: "Since I left Cincinnati Oct. 12th 1820 I have finished 62 Drawings of *Birds & Plants*, 3 quadrupeds, 2 Snakes, 50 Portraits of all sorts and My Father *Don Antonio*." Audubon had come from Kentucky in 1820 and spent most of three years in the Deep South, gathering material for a projected book, in which he hoped to depict the birds of America in their actual lifesize. He had begun this project during his eleven-year sojourn in Kentucky where he eked out a living as a storekeeper. Financial failure persuaded him to try his all in gathering material for the book; hence the trip south. He earned money in a variety of ways—making portrait drawings, teaching French, and giving dancing lessons. From the few references in a journal he kept at irregular intervals, it sounds as if Audubon's study of Don Antonio was to be a major picture from which he hoped to have an engraving made—thus getting extra income from its sale. On October 31, 1821, he noted, "Joseph at Work Preparing Father Antoine Coat." Joseph Mason was the young assistant with Audubon during this period whose task it was to paint the plant settings for Audubon's bird studies. Again, on the thirty-first Audubon noted, "Spent some time at Work on Father Antoine." And on November 2, "Rec^d the Visit of *Brewster* the Painter, the good Man Very sorry to see My *Father* Antonio—fearing an Engraving after it—I determined to have My Drawing framed although it Cost Me about 30$ having some Hopes that it Would procure me some Pupils of Note—." This was apparently none other than Edmund Brewster, who had perhaps already begun his large oil of Père Antoine and didn't want competition from Audubon. Again on the tenth, "Called on Mr. Hawkins who visited me to see father Antoine's Drawing—Concluded to have the Engraving he Wished Me to Copy for not exceeding 50$ wishing it could be done as soon as possible." No further references to this appeared in the diary and the engraving project must have fallen through. One of Audubon's biographers reported that Audubon later worked with another artist, a John Stein, and that together they did a full-length portrait of Père Antoine that was sent to Havana. A preliminary effort to locate this has been of no avail.

Audubon's occasional journal notes during these Louisiana-Mississippi years provide flashes of insight into the friendly, yet edgy and competitive, relationships among some of the artists attracted to the Crescent City at this time. He met and knew "an Italian, painter at the Theatre," possibly Fogliardi. They showed each other drawings and Audubon was offered a chance to paint with him at the theater, but declined. John Wesley Jarvis, the eccentric New York painter, was in town and they visited together several times. The portrait business was not good in New York. Audubon saw a portrait of Jackson by Ralph E. W. Earl and criticized the other artist's work, *"Great God* forgive Me if My Judgment is Erroneous—I Never Saw A Worst painted Sign *in the Street of Paris."* He noted visits with the miniature artists Duval and Collas. There are several references to a

Mr. Sell (Sel), a virtually unknown painter who seems to have worked in New Orleans and later in Alabama, and to a Mr. Jamy (Jeannin?)—who, like Mr. Stein, seems unidentifiable. Several times he met the artist Basterot, a teacher of painting and drawing who had done a religious painting in St. Louis, and who offered Audubon a chance to work on a proposed panorama of New Orleans; Audubon decided to concentrate on his beloved birds. Audubon was most impressed, and most insecure, with the New York painter John Vanderlyn, who had studied and

Edmund Brewster. "Père Antoine at Age Seventy-four." 1822. Oil on canvas. Signed and dated: "Peint par Edmund Brewster le 6 Septembre 1822." Archdiocese of New Orleans, on loan to the Louisiana State Museum, New Orleans.

Unknown artist. "Jean Baptiste Wiltz." Oil on canvas.
Louisiana State Museum, New Orleans.

which each one-upped the other, the relations between the two men were apparently friendly. Vanderlyn gave Audubon an engraving of Ariadne which the latter dutifully studied and copied in order to improve his drawing skill. (According to French neoclassical standards, you had to study from the antique in order to truly learn to draw.)

One of the reasons Audubon came south was to see, collect, and draw the rich variety of ornithological life to be found in the lower Mississippi Valley. His journal is full of notes about these: "This morning . . . I had the pleasure of remarking thousands of purple martins travelling eastward," or "Three immense flocks of *Bank Swallows* . . . past over Me with the Rapidity of a Storm," or he might note as many as twenty different kinds of birds to be found at the market on a single morning.

Audubon hunted or bought birds in order to paint and describe them. Then, as now, others hunted simply for pleasure or for food. The pleasure and complacent pride of the hunter are recorded in the painting on the left of Jean Baptiste Wiltz. Wiltz is believed to have come from Mobile, Alabama, so this may have been painted there, or in nearby Mississippi or Louisiana. Audubon may have known the unnamed artist. The setting is a grassy swamp, typical of the wetlands of the Gulf Coast. Though the picture is hardly action-packed, Mr. Wiltz, a veteran of the siege of Mobile during the Revolution, is shown in the act of cocking his fowling musket, preparing for yet another shot. Three birds have fallen. A potentially limitless number of victims are shown streaming in orderly fashion across the sky. As with so many artists who seem to have plied their trade in the South in this period, this one is neither blatantly naïve nor amateur, nor thoroughly accomplished. There seems to have been an infinite variety of skill and ability, including artists who had developed certain specialties. In portraiture, they all appear to have had the same aim of creating a realistic likeness. Some were more modest about their abilities and identified themselves with the slightly old-fashioned term "limner." The latter tended to use less modeling or shading and their paintings are more linear, as if done within outlines and in the flat. The differences are often a matter of degree. No matter how distant the area in the South, the flow of commerce along the great waterways seems to have kept the people in touch with changing ideas and fashions. There were relatively fewer artists who can be categorized as folk painters. (In fact, there are very few nineteenth-century references where the term "folk" is used to describe a painter. This is more a late nineteenth- and twentieth-century designation, still little employed by the artists themselves.)

In the portrait of Mr. Wiltz there is an occasional awkwardness in the rendering, particularly of the hands. The artist also employs shadow and modeling sparingly, but understands their use. There is something about the boldly placed central figure, and the depiction of the setting as if at some distance in the background, that suggest the work of a theater or stage painter, although this is only a hypothesis.

In 1818, New Englander Samuel F. B. Morse decided to try Charleston. Morse was twenty-seven years old, and had already spent four years in London under the tutelage of Benjamin West and Washington Allston. There he enjoyed a certain success with two complex history, or heroic, subject paintings. On his return

showed in Paris, and was exhibiting a collection of his paintings in New Orleans. Audubon brought his portfolio of bird drawings and asked for advice. (Audubon was never quite secure about his ability and never really mastered oil painting.) "He spoke of the beautiful Coloring and Good Positions and told me that he would with pleasure give me a Certificate of his having *Inspected* them—Are All Men of Talents fools and Rude purposely or Naturally?" Then, Vanderlyn imperiously told Audubon to put his drawings down and wait. After more than thirty minutes the New York artist returned with an officer friend, "the Swet ran down My Face as I hastily open[d] My Drawings. . . . Vanderlyn took up a Bird Look[d] at it already put it down and said they Were *handsomely done.* I breathed. . ." Then "I with My Eyes *half Closed* (as you know the pretended Juges of our Day Look at Painting) saw a great Deffect in One of his figures of Women." Vanderlyn duly wrote his "Opinion in Writing" certifying Audubon's ability and accuracy and hence a recommendation that Audubon would be suitable "as a Draftsman in any Expedition to the interiors of our Country." After this initial meeting in

to Boston he found few patrons interested in the "intellectual branch" of the arts, and also that Gilbert Stuart had garnered most of the portrait commissions. Business in the countryside was no better. Relatives and connections suggested Charleston. The moment was propitious, for at that particular moment there were only a few artists working in the city. Charlestonians were not at first interested, but after seeing a portrait he had completed of his uncle, commissions flowed in. He soon raised his standard price from the $15 he had charged for a portrait in rural New England to $60 or more. Several patrons were willing to pay for grander portraits. One of these was Colonel William Drayton, right. The successful thirty-two-year-old lawyer is shown seated, his hand resting on a large open book. The great columned portico and the light-colored sky lend drama, dignity, and a sense of connection with the classical past. Morse had so many commissions during his first winter in Charleston—more than eighty—that he took this and several other of the large portraits back with him to Massachusetts to finish during the summer. He had developed the head and captured the general proportions and posture, but completed much of the background and setting, as well as other details, when he had more time.

So successful was he during the early winter months of 1818 that he returned for three more winters, arriving each year around November and staying till June. Among his most satisfactory commissions were those from John Ashe Alston, a perceptive and knowledgeable patron of the arts who lived on a plantation near Georgetown (no kin to Washington Allston). Unfortunately most of the nineteen portraits Morse painted of members of the Alston family are lost—some in a fire. Of these, the most admired was a six-foot portrait of Alston's daughter Sally. A surviving description indicates that she was shown standing amid the ruins of an abbey beside a fawn. Morse took it to Massachusetts for exhibition and the *New England Galaxy* praised it at length. The article was in turn quoted in full in the January 11, 1820, issue of the Charleston *Courier*. The picture was lauded for the air of innocence, sweetness, and unaffectedness of the sitter, and for the imaginative setting. "Mr. Morse has dared to construct . . . a background of poetical and new materials. The whole canvass is covered with the ruins of a venerable architecture—Gothic—crumbling—and falling; encumbered with ivy, and festooned with the luxuriance of nature. . . . We . . . have long wanted, somebody who should have the courage to introduce the romantic irregularities of the gothic—and abandon the tame unmeaning, straight graceful colonades of Greece."

Romantic irregularities of the Gothic, indeed. Most of Morse and Alston's contemporaries in America had barely taken up the chaste, austere Greek taste, and knew little of the esthetics of the romantic and picturesque, with its fancy for the irregular and a nostalgia for the Gothic or medieval past. There is a common romantic element in the nostalgia and historicism felt for ancient Greece and the Gothic Middle Ages, but knowledge and taste for the latter had just begun to gain ground in the 1820s. Alston, a Charleston patron, Morse, and the anonymous critic were well ahead of their compatriots.

The New England critic also used his column to excoriate Americans, North and South, for not patronizing their own art-ists, so that a Morse had to go south, and a Washington Allston had had to go to England. This was a lament more often expressed by artists than members of the fourth estate. Robert Gilmor, Jr., in Baltimore and John Ashe Alston of South Carolina were exceptions in their generous patronage of American artists.

Even though Morse had not yet invented the telegraph, the news of his success in Charleston reverberated rapidly among artists, and during his second winter there were at least thirteen others trying their fortunes there. In the third winter he would write that "the city fairly swarms with painters." Morse maintained his supremacy, although he and others suffered a paucity of commissions because of the panic of 1819. Conditions were no better during his fourth winter, the winter of 1820–1821. Cotton prices had dropped and the economy was faltering. Some families were moving west to more fertile lands.

While Morse was in the city he formed friendships with other artists, especially Charles Fraser and the amateur sculptor John

Samuel F. B. Morse. "Colonel William Drayton." 1818. Oil on canvas. The White House, Washington, D.C.

Matthew Harris Jouett. "Hon. Patrick Henry Darby of Princeton, Kentucky." 1821–1825. Oil on panel. J. B. Speed Art Museum, Louisville, Kentucky.

Stevens Cogdell, who was a lawyer by profession. During the winter of 1818–1819 they, along with the painter Alvin Fisher from Boston, met once a week to draw from plaster casts, a discipline Morse had learned in England.

From time to time modest efforts to establish some sort of organization to promote the arts had rippled the surface of life in Charleston: an exhibition at the college in 1791, an exhorting article or two in the newspapers, another exhibit in 1816 at the South Carolina Hall. In the early winter months of 1821 Cogdell, Morse, and others formed the South Carolina Academy of Fine Arts, hoping to create an institution where artists might receive some training, and where exhibitions might be held. Joel Poinsett, the diplomat, who was at that time primarily involved in the movement for improvements of the river and road systems of South Carolina, was named president. Cogdell was secretary and treasurer, and Morse and the architect William Jay were among those on the board of directors. The economic situation was not propitious and they ran into difficulties almost from the beginning, when the site they selected was opposed by a nearby resident. They did succeed in erecting a building in the classical style, and they did manage a number of exhibitions, borrowing from the fairly rich store of paintings (mostly, but not all, portraits) owned by Carolinians. By 1830 the organization was in

disarray, a newspaper published a satirical obituary, and by 1835 the building was sold to meet all debts. In 1838 there was a short-lived Academy of Arts and Design founded in Charleston, and in 1858 the Carolina Art Association was formed. The collection of the latter was destroyed in the great fire of 1861 and the organization was not revived until 1895.

There was virtually no artistic community in Harrodsburg or Lexington, Kentucky, to nourish the spirit of Matthew Harris Jouett (1787–1827). Tradition has it that he was skillful at drawing as a child and as a youth, but his father hoped for a more substantial career for his son. After study at Transylvania University around 1803–1807, Jouett read law, then enlisted and fought in the War of 1812. It was in 1815 that he finally decided upon a career in painting, and was already partially self-taught. He was good enough to receive $25 each for his portraits. In 1816 he determined to go east and sought out Gilbert Stuart, in Boston, who affectionately called him "Kentucky." Jouett spent July through October in Boston and made copious notes of his conversations with Stuart. These shed light not only on Stuart's technique, but on Jouett's, who followed many of his master's precepts. Stuart felt, for example, that "Drawing the features distinctly and carefully with chalk is a loss of time. All studies to be made with brush in hand. Nonsense to think of perfecting oneself in drawing before one begins to paint."

Jouett's portrait of Patrick Henry Darby, left, of Princeton, Kentucky, has the painterly, soft-edged quality characteristic of Stuart and his pupil. The florid flesh tones, too, have a warmth and translucency that Stuart would have liked. ("Flesh is like no other substance under heaven, it has all the gaiety of a silk mercers shop without the gaudiness or glare and all the soberness of old mahogany without its deadness or sadness.") It is a strong portrait of an obviously vigorous man. Darby was the zealous editor of a newspaper, *The Constitutional Advocate*, in Frankfort, Kentucky, from 1821 through 1825, much involved with the tempestuous politics of the frontier. Jouett's own career was cut short by an untimely death in his fortieth year. Despite a relatively short life, he is believed to have painted over 300 portraits and is thus the preeminent painter of early Kentucky. When Lafayette visited Kentucky on his triumphal tour, he sat for Jouett; and a full-length portrait based on this study and a painting by Ary Scheffer was purchased by the state. During his last few years he traveled south to Natchez and New Orleans and painted subjects there as well.

After Jouett's death a mournful laudatory poem was published by a local bard, expressing awe and appreciation of the artist's special gifts and the pride of the frontier populace in the accomplishments by one of their own:

> He was, indeed, Death's harmless foe,
>   For by his pencil's art
> With magic triumph high he soared
>   Above the spoiler's dart.
>
> He bade the living sweetly feel
>   When life's brief sun was set,
> Their pictured poems would still shine on
>   And show them living yet.

Jouett! thou wast to us a pride,
    For cradled in the world,
In our own woods, thy sail took wing,
    Thy opening genius smiled . . .

(The important role of portraits as a means of preserving the image of a departed loved one, suggested in this poem, was perceived as almost magic by at least one black slave sometime in the late eighteenth century. He was Olaudah Equiano, or Gustavus Vassa, who later was active in antislavery work in England. One of his memories was of being brought to a house in Virginia and seeing "a picture hanging in the room, which appeared constantly to look at me, I was still more affrighted, having never seen such things as these before. At one time I thought it was something relative to magic; and not seeing it move, I thought it might be some way the whites had to keep their great men when they died, and offer them libations as we used to do to our friendly spirits.")

Chester Harding. "The John Speed Smith Family, Richmond, Kentucky." c. 1819. Oil on canvas. J. B. Speed Art Museum, Louisville, Kentucky.

Attributed to Nathan and Joseph Negus. "William McIntosh." Before 1823. Oil on canvas. Alabama Department of Archives and History, Montgomery.

with his brother as chairmaker and learned something of decorating and gilding, then was a house painter and sign painter. It was not until a stay in Pittsburgh that he met up with a painter named Nelson, "one of the primitive sort. He was a sign, ornamental and portrait painter." Harding aptly describes the fierce excitement that can overtake someone when absorbed in learning a new artistic skill:

"I saw his portraits and was enamored at once . . . At length my admiration began to yield to an ambition to do the same thing. I thought of it by day, and dreamed of it by night . . . I got a board; and, with such colors as I had for use in my trade, I began a portrait of my wife. I made a thing that looked like her. The moment I saw the likeness, I became frantic with delight: it was like the discovery of a new sense; I could think of nothing else."

Harding moved to Paris, Kentucky, in 1817 and enjoyed three years of economic and artistic success there and in St. Louis. A large painting of the John Speed Smith family of Richmond, Kentucky, previous page, is believed to be a work by Harding at this period. Warm red tones in the curtains and in the patterned rug or floor cloth enliven the composition, the case of lawbooks shown behind the colonel suggests his profession as lawyer and role as the elected representative of Madison County in the state legislature. Harding was impressed with the elegance of dress he found among the "tip-top society" of the frontier. "Many fine young gentlemen, all so elegantly dressed, with ruffled shirts, rings on their white and delicate fingers, and diamond pins in their bosoms." He shows the colonel as one of those stylish gentlemen with white ruffled shirt, gold fob, and tan-and-black boots. His wife and daughter wear fashionable white and beruffled dresses; the daughter, however, is comfortably barefoot. The fine rendering of the three chairs suggests an artist familiar with cabinetwork. One of the reasons for attributing this painting to Chester Harding is the close similarities between it and one of Mrs. Green Clay, mother of Mrs. Smith, the former known to be by Harding. Mrs. Eliza Lewis Clay Smith, shown here, was a member of the distinguished Clay family and sister to Cassius Marcellus Clay, who would later obtain fame and notoriety as an abolitionist.

After three years in the upper South Harding returned to the Eastern Seaboard, and for a time his reputation eclipsed that of Stuart in Boston. In 1823 he went to England, and there his skill, and forthright charm, brought him commissions from the aristocracy, who were apparently delighted with this characteristic rough diamond from the New World. After his return to the United States in 1826 Harding painted many of the nation's political and social leaders. One of the tragedies of his old age—he died in 1866—was that two of his sons fought for the Union and two for the Confederacy.

Full-length portraits often served as advertising for an artist who was traveling and hoping to get new commissions. It is just possible that the artist who painted the portrait, upper left, of the half-Indian, half-Scottish–American, William McIntosh, in the early 1820s, wished to attract further patronage through it. McIntosh's garb tells something of his role—ultimately tragic—as a go-between for the white Americans and the Creek and Cherokee Indians. He wears the ruffled shirt of the white man,

It was the rumor that Jouett, in Lexington, was getting as much as $25 a portrait that prompted Chester Harding (1792–1866), then in Pittsburgh, to join his brother in Paris, Kentucky. Harding, too, was self-taught. In his engaging *My Egotistigraphy* he records the story of his early life in Massachusetts. He then developed his talents during an itinerant period when he had several jobs requiring manual dexterity; for a time he worked

but his colorful robe, sash, moccasins, and leggings represent adaptations of Indian practices—with perhaps some tailoring by a Scottish hand. McIntosh was a Creek Indian chief, son of William McIntosh, who was a captain in the British Army and agent to the Creek Indians, and a Creek mother, born in the land of the Creek Nation (possibly in what is now Carroll County in western Georgia, or Russell County, Alabama). During the War of 1812 the younger McIntosh, as leader of the Lower Creeks, was friendly to the Americans. As a reward he was made a brigadier general and served with Jackson in the campaigns against the Seminoles in 1817–1818.

This painting was probably done by Nathan Negus in the early 1820s. In correspondence, Negus wrote to his family that he had journeyed to Indian Springs where he painted the full-length portrait of McIntosh and a smaller one of his daughter.

(McIntosh's wife was a Cherokee.) At that time Nathan and his brother Joseph were temporarily established in Eatonton, Georgia. Joseph specialized in ornamental and room painting, while Nathan did portraits and miniatures. They had come from Petersham, Massachusetts. Joseph had preceded his brother south in the fall of 1819 and Nathan joined him in September 1820. Sometime in 1823 Joseph died. Nathan Negus is known to have been in Mobile, Alabama, in 1824, and also visited Pensacola. He set sail for Massachusetts in 1824. His career was cut short by death in July 1825. Though a fairly long list, based on journal entries, can be made of portraits, miniatures, and ornamental works done by these two brothers between 1819 and 1822, few identifiable examples survive.

McIntosh lived only a few years after this portrait was done. In 1825 he signed a treaty for cession of the Creek lands. On

Ralph E. W. Earl. "The Ephraim Hubbard Foster Family." c. 1824. Oil on canvas. Cheekwood, Fine Arts Center, Nashville, Tennessee.

John R. Martin. "James Lafayette." c. 1824. Oil on canvas. Valentine Museum, Richmond.

April 30, 1825, the Upper Creeks took revenge, killing him and burning his house on the east bank of the Chattahoochee River. He has been described as "tall, finely formed and of graceful and commanding manner," something of which can be seen in Negus's fine portrait of this man who was caught between two cultures.

Ralph E. W. Earl (1788–1838) established his reputation in Nashville, Tennessee, with a full-length portrait of General Andrew Jackson at the Battle of New Orleans. He had come to Nashville in 1817 to paint the general's portrait. In 1818 he married Jackson's niece, and from that time until his own death in 1838 he was an intimate friend of the Jackson household. He was also the self-stylized "King's painter," for he did numerous portraits of the soldier, hero, President, and statesman. His career before this association was much like that of the other artists here. Earl was the son of the New England painter Ralph Earl, and so was able to learn the rudiments of his craft at home. He spent the years 1809–1815 in England, during which time he made a journey to France. However, despite his years in Europe, rather like his father, he retained a fundamental provincialism. Between 1815 and 1818 he was among those artists who traveled the river routes and country roads that took him into Georgia, Alabama, Tennessee, and along the Mississippi. His uncomplicated ideas of picture making and composition can be seen in the group portrait of Mr. and Mrs. Ephraim Hubbard Foster and their children, done around 1824, previous page. It is a good closed composition, with father and older sons seated as a group on the left, the mother and younger children on the right. Both groups face inward on their fine gilded chairs toward where little Jane Ellen Foster stands and steals the scene. She wears a cool white gown and soft red leather shoes, but the prize is her extraordinary tartan and feathered mobcap. The father, Ephraim Hubbard Foster, is shown here in a scene of domestic tranquillity. There is no effort to remind the viewer that he had been Jackson's color-bearer at the Battle of New Orleans or the general's secretary during the Creek War of 1813–1814.

The military accomplishments of the slave, James Armistead Lafayette, were the reason for his emancipation by the General Assembly of Virginia after the Revolution. The young black slave had been allowed by his master, William Armistead, to enlist in 1781 and was assigned to service with General Lafayette. Before long he was performing important espionage services behind the lines, obtaining information about the plans and movements of the British. In 1784, when Lafayette was again in Richmond, he wrote a testimonial for James, attesting to the latter's "essential services" in collecting and faithfully delivering intelligence from the enemy. After his emancipation, James, who had taken Lafayette's name out of affection, bought forty acres in New Kent County, married, raised a family, owned some slaves, and lived an exemplary life. He became something of a local celebrity in his old age.

It was either in 1824, or a few years earlier, that the painter John R. Martin painted the old freeman's likeness, left. It is a straightforward portrait, showing the dark and furrowed face of the former soldier in his brass-buttoned uniform. When Lafayette, who disliked the institution of slavery, visited Richmond in October 1824 he greeted his fellow-soldier with affection. "The black was recognized by him in the crowd," according to a local newspaper account, "called . . . by name and taken into his embrace."

The artist John B. Martin (1797–1857) had come to America from Ireland in 1815. He first studied engraving in New York City but then settled in Richmond for the remainder of his life. His two chief means of livelihood were as a portrait painter and as an engraver and lithographer. The portrait of James Armistead Lafayette is traditional in every way, unusual for the time only in that the subject is a black person rather than a white.

One of the few genre paintings to survive from this time is that of *The Banjo Man*, right, by an unknown artist. It is believed to be the painting offered for sale under that title in a lottery listed in the *Virginia Patriot* of January 13, 1816, and to represent a slave named Sy Gilliat, known also as Cyrus, Simon, or Simeon Gilliat. He lived in Williamsburg from around 1740 to 1790, and in Richmond from 1790 to 1820. Gilliat was, according to tradition, a body servant to Lord Botetourt and official fiddler at state balls. Later he and his assistant, "London Brigs" (Gilliat with his fiddle or banjo, and Brigs with flute or a clarinet), were popular as musicians at parties. The genre scene shown here shows the Negro servant as his white patrons knew him, cheerfully playing his banjo for a children's party in a parklike or wooded setting.

A watercolor, following page, depicting a group of blacks dancing and playing music shows a more intimate picture of what slaves did when relatively unobserved by their masters, one of the few visual records of Negro life at this time. Now owned by the Abby Aldrich Rockefeller Folk Art Collection in Williamsburg, it has been widely published and discussed. It was found in Columbia, South Carolina, and is believed to have been painted on a plantation located between Charleston and Orangeburg. In the background the mansion house, various service

Artist unknown. "Sy Gilliat, or The Banjo Man." c. 1810. Oil on canvas. Valentine Museum, Richmond.

buildings, and the rows of slave cabins can be seen. The paper bears an English watermark that can be dated between 1777 and 1794, and the costumes date the painting similarly.

It has been guessed that the dance reflects a survival of African traditions, though the particular significance of the stick or cane and the scarves is not known. The stringed instrument is a molo, and the drum similar to a Yoruba instrument called a gudugudu. The dance may also be of Yoruba origin. The artist or draftsman remains equally unknown. It must have been someone who wanted to make or have a record, the motivation behind so much painting and drawing in early nineteenth-century America.

Life at an Indian village and trading post in the Chattahoochee/Apalachicola River in Florida is suggested in a remarkable and little-known painting, right, by yet another unknown artist. It represents the adventurous Indian trader, William Augustus Bowles, and his confreres among the Lower Creeks. There may be more than a little theater and propaganda in this bountiful scene. In the foreground Bowles is shown speaking to several Indians, one of whom is dressed as a chief with red cloak, feathered headdress, beaded leather moccasins, and wearing a silver armband. Plows, shovels, carts, and animals grazing in the extensive scenic background all suggest productive agriculture. On the right an Indian is lowering a basket filled to overflowing with yellow corn, symbol of the New World's bounty. Below are turnips and potatoes, more products of the land, in what in itself is

a well-done still life, redolent of the Jacques Le Moyne image of the Southern Indian.

It has been suggested that Bowles may have been the artist, and this is a very real possibility. Bowles, born on the Maryland frontier of British parents, seems to have learned to draw and paint as a child, becoming a talented amateur. His father had come from a London family of book, map, and print sellers, and a cousin, Carington Bowles, published several books on drawing, perspective, and other arts in the 1780s and 1790s, at least one of which went through eighteen editions. Throughout William Bowles's colorful career there are several references to his painting portraits—in and near Savannah, for example—or of doing scene painting. As a youth of thirteen, Bowles joined the British forces at the beginning of the Revolution. Deployed with troops to Florida late in 1778 he got into a row, or some mischief, that led to his abrupt dismissal without benefit of court-martial. Left to his own devices, he joined up later with a party of Lower Creeks in Pensacola and lived with them for several months. It was a decisive experience, and his fortunes were periodically involved with them for the rest of his adventuresome life. He was reinstated in the Army, and later returned to the Creek Nation, where he was engaged in a variety of intrigues. He was supported by wealthy British merchants in an effort to break the monopoly of the firm of Panton, Leslie and Company in their trade with the Creeks. In 1790 he went to England with a delegation of Creek and Cherokee Indians, and during this time he frequently wore Indian dress himself. Subsequently he was part of a scheme to drive Spain out of Florida and Louisiana. Incarcerated in Madrid, then sent to the Philippines (whence he escaped), by September 1799 he was once again in Florida. He was seized in 1803 at Tuskegee, and died in a military hospital in Havana in 1815.

Complex, talented, an excellent linguist, at various times in his life Bowles was soldier, artist, actor, musician, diplomat, chemist, hunter, lawyer, and Indian chief.

The painting probably was done in the 1780s or 1790s. Much

in it may be idealized, but the suggestion of the round of agricultural activities basic to the life of Indian communities has a ring of truth. For almost a decade Bowles had made his home, off and on, in the village of Chief Perryman, a village situated just above the forks of the Apalachicola River, and he knew the life well. The artist has tried to show that all was not war, council meetings, and intrigues.

The land itself and the places people lived were also subjects for the artist's brush. In some cases the painting of landscapes and views seems to have been a private pleasure for the artist,

Artist unknown, possibly William Augustus Bowles. "William Augustus Bowles at His Trading Post on the Chattahoochee River in Florida, with Members of the Creek Nation" c. 1790. Oil on canvas. Museum of Early Southern Decorative Arts, Winston-Salem, N.C.

*Thomas Coram. "View of Road Along River at Mulberry
Plantation, South Carolina." Oil on paper. Carolina Art
Association/Gibbes Art Gallery, Charleston.*

others specialized in urban views, and some few were able to earn an income from their paintings of landscapes.

The small and unpretentious painting, oil on paper, above, by Thomas Coram, catches the flavor of the low country landscape near Mulberry plantation, in South Carolina, with its expanses of water. This is one of a group of three scenes of Mulberry (the view of the house and cabins is on page 1, the other is of the river in front of the house). They may have been done as studies for engravings or larger pictures never executed, or may have been done simply for pleasure. Coram had come to Charleston in the 1770s and earned his living primarily as an engraver. Visiting cards and cards for tradesmen were among his wares; he also did engraving on silver, on watch cases, and on brass plates for doors, so working on a small scale was natural to him. That Coram was able to work on a larger scale is attested to by one of the four religious paintings he executed in this country. Designed for the chapel of the Charleston Orphans Home, it is a competent rendition of Christ blessing the children, an appropriate subject for the setting. The painting is now in the custody of the South Carolina Historical Society. According to Charleston tradition, he learned oil painting from Henry Benbridge. Coram died in Charleston in 1811, a "dear respected" figure.

The sense of a specific place is the predominant characteris-

tic of a number of views, or landscapes, painted by Francis Guy (1760–1820) during the early part of his twenty-year residence in Baltimore. A particularly fine example is his view of Jones Falls at Baltimore Street bridge, right, done around 1800–1805. The outlines of the buildings and the bridge are sharp, precise, and clear. Tiny figures are barely noticeable but, when seen, lend a quiet sense of animation. There is a fisherman in the foreground, two boys in a boat to the left, a man lifting objects on the wharf, several figures on the bridge, and two more in the boat near the right. The whole is suffused with light. The largest building, near the center, was built in 1785 as the first German Reformed Church, and became the Christ Protestant Episcopal Church in 1796. The even more austere structure on the extreme left is the First Baptist Meeting House of 1773. The Baltimore Street bridge was built in 1773 and replaced in 1808.

Given the clarity and readability of this fairly precise perspective view, it is no surprise to learn from the reminiscences of Rembrandt Peale, who had known Guy, that the latter sometimes used a special method for getting his views direct from nature: "He constructed a tent, which he could erect at pleasure, wherever a scene of interest offered itself to his fancy. A window was contrived, the size of his intended picture—this was filled up with a frame, having stretched on it a piece of black gauze.

Regulating his eyesight by a fixed notch, a little distance from the gauze, he drew with chalk all the objects seen through the medium, with perfect perspective accuracy. This drawing being conveyed to his canvas, by simple pressure from the back of his hand, he painted the scene from Nature, with a rapidly-improving eye, so that in a few days his landscape was finished, and his tent conveyed in a cart to some other inviting locality."

From time to time in the history of art various artists have employed structured "view-finders" such as that utilized by Guy. The Dutch painter Vermeer, for example, is believed to have used a device called a camera obscura. Guy, with his chalk on black gauze which was later pressed against the canvas, was using his own variation of pouncing, an old technique for transferring preparatory sketches or designs to a surface.

Among the surviving paintings by Guy are some views of country houses and estates in the vicinity of Baltimore, several in an oval format. These were probably commissioned by the owners, who had a pride of place. They are not only attractive as works of art but are now superb documents.

Francis Guy, to judge by the records that survive, was something of an eccentric and, in his later years, intemperate. He was born and grew up in the Lake District of England. His grandfather is believed to have been an eminent glass painter and stainer. (He may have learned his pouncing technique from this grandfather.) Guy is supposed to have early developed a taste for "the beautiful in art and nature" and also to have done landscape sketches in the Lake District as a boy. He would have been growing up during the years when the Reverend William Gilpin was writing his illustrated travel books on the Lake District and elsewhere, and his essays on Picturesque Beauty, Picturesque Travel and on Sketching Landscape, works which are seminal to the whole romantic movement and to the development of the picturesque in architecture. However, Guy's early Baltimore works relate, rather, to a slightly earlier tradition, the topographical view, or *veduta*, made popular by English collectors of Canaletto and others. There may just possibly be a more direct connection between the work of Guy and another Lake District artist, John Warwick Smith, who was associated for a time with

Francis Guy. "Jones Falls at Baltimore Street Bridge." c. 1800–1805. Oil on canvas. Maryland Historical Society, Baltimore.

George Beck. "View of Baltimore from Howard's Park." 1796.
Oil on canvas. Maryland Historical Society, Baltimore.

the Gilpins but whose work was always more precise. He, too, used an oval format on occasion.

Guy's father was not partial to the idea of having an artist for a son, so he was first apprenticed to a tailor. He ran away to London and there invented machinery used in the calendering (squeezing or pressing) or glazing of silks and calico, and was involved in this and the related trade of silk dyeing. "A gang of swindlers," possibly creditors, caused him to emigrate to America in 1795, and he first set up a silk-dyeing business in Brooklyn, moving from there to Baltimore around 1798. In 1800 he first appears in the city directories as a landscape painter and is

listed as such until his departure in 1817, when he returned to Brooklyn. He died in 1820.

Guy's work was uneven in quality. Rembrandt Peale says that he later "manufactured" large landscapes with vigor and then raffled them, as many as forty at a time, and another critic said that he sometimes "painted too much by the square yard." We do not know how many landscapes, or views, he produced in his years in Baltimore, but twenty-one are now recorded. They are among the beginnings of landscape painting in the United States.

George Beck (1748-49–1812), another landscape painter,

came from England in 1795, arriving in Norfolk, Virginia. From there he went to Baltimore and, after two years, to Philadelphia. He stayed in that city for six years and then moved west to Lexington. Beck's artistic career began in England; there are records of his exhibiting landscape views at the Royal Academy in London from 1790 through 1793. According to a "Memoir" published about Beck in *The Port Folio* of August 1813, he had made a sketching and painting tour through the western counties of England and Wales. In this he would seem to have adopted the fashion for travel being popularized by Gilpin, soon taken up by professionals and talented amateurs alike. The success of the "spirited productions" that resulted from this trip gave him the idea of going to America. His success in Baltimore was such that his wife, who had also exhibited at the Royal Academy, came across the ocean to join him.

Beck's view of Baltimore from Howard's Park, 1796, left, owes something to the older topographical tradition, with its well-lighted, yet fairly precise view of the city in the middle distance. The foreground, with irregular rocks strewn in the center, the dark tree and bushes on the left, and the dominant grouping of trees on the right are here used to create what Gilpin would have called Effect—a greater force and effect created by the "strong opposition of light and shade." (Beck and Gilpin also borrowed from certain seventeenth-century baroque methods of composition.) This painting was acquired by the distinguished Baltimore collector Robert Gilmor, Jr.

George Washington was also one of Beck's patrons. In his Household Accounts he noted on January 30, 1797, "P'd Sam'l Salter in full for two paintings by Beck. . . ." Also, in a list of furnishings of the Executive Mansion in Philadelphia, written by

Thomas Doughty. "View of Baltimore from Beech Hill, The Seat of Robert Gilmor, Jr." 1822. Oil on wood panel. Baltimore Museum of Art.

UNDER MY WINGS EVERY THING PROSPERS

*J. L. Bouqueta de Woiseri. "A View of New Orleans Taken
from the Plantation of Marigny." Oil on canvas. 1803.
Chicago Historical Society.*

Washington in 1797, is found "In the Green Drawing Room . . .
2 Landscapes—1 Representing a view of the Passage of Poto'k
thro' the blew mountains at the confluence of that River with the
Shan'h—the other at the F[ederal] city—cost me with the
frames 30 guineas 52-10-1." These two paintings, the second of
the Falls of the Potomac, are now on display at Mount Vernon.
They are even more "picturesque" than the view of Baltimore,
almost too much so in that the artist was not completely effective
in rendering in perspective the rough drama of the whitewater
rapids shown in both. Washington here, as with other objects
chosen for his home, showed perspicacious taste. Though his
zeal for the arts did not match that of Jefferson, he kept abreast
of trends and was a conscientious patron, a role he felt to be part
of his responsibility as a leader of government.

During his later years in Kentucky Beck apparently did little
painting; he was often in ill health. Both he and his wife taught
school for a while; he translated classical poetry and wrote original poems.

In 1822 Robert Gilmor, Jr., commissioned at least two paintings from Thomas Doughty (1793–1856), at that time a young

self-taught Philadelphia artist just beginning to establish himself. One of these is the *View of Baltimore from Beech Hill, The Seat
of Robert Gilmor, Jr.*, previous page. Doughty, like Beck, uses a
deep foreground with imposing trees on either side, but here the
effect is serenely natural. There is no feeling of an attempt to
heighten nature; rather that the luxuriant view was carefully selected and then rendered fairly realistically. The large building
in the middle distance is Benjamin Henry Latrobe's magnificent
domed Baltimore cathedral.

Doughty completed this landscape only two years after he
had taken up painting as a full-time profession. He also seems to
have had a talent for drawing and painting as a child, but started
out in the leather business. His brother, twenty years his senior,
was a naval draftsman and apparently encouraged him. As a
youth in Philadelphia he knew of the Peales and other artists,
and could have learned about the possibilities of a painting career
by observing them. From them, too, he might have gained some
of his enthusiasm for nature. At this time Charles Willson Peale
and his family were putting most of their efforts into the exhibitions of natural history in their museum in Philadelphia. A little

later, from 1810 to 1833, Thomas Doughty and his brother published in Philadelphia what is probably the first sports magazine in the United States, *The Cabinet of Natural History and American Rural Sports*. In it are many articles on natural history, and moving tributes to both Charles Willson Peale and William Bartram. In this and other of Doughty's paintings of this period there is a sense of the freshness of the natural landscape—the grasses and trees are touched by light fresh breezes, moving clouds create a soft dappling over the land. At the same time Doughty was aware of, and learning the artifices of, picture making. The two paired figures in the foreground, added for interest, are similar to figures in paintings by Guy. Also, Rembrandt Peale noted that Doughty had copied European landscapes from Gilmor's collection, which included landscape paintings by Jan Wynants, Nicolas Poussin, Jacob Ruisdael, Albert Cuyp, Salvator Rosa, and others. Gilmor collected paintings, drawings, prints, coins, medals, and manuscripts, and was an important patron in the early Republic. His library "finished in the Gothic style," where much of his collection was housed, was an inspiration to artists.

Thomas Cole, the well-known landscape painter, and Thomas Doughty were among American artists who were encouraged by him and whose paintings he owned.

At least three works by Beck, one an *East View of Baltimore*, now lost, were published as aquatints by the English firm of Atkins and Nightingale. These were part of their series on American cities, whose growth and development were a point of pride for local citizens and a source of curiosity to Europeans. Another professional artist who embarked on a series of paintings and watercolors that was published as aquatints was J. L. Bouqueta de Woiseri. The earliest of these is an 1803 painting of New Orleans, left, showing the still-pastoral edge of the city as well as the bustling port full of sailing vessels. On the far left there is a glimpse of the formal French gardens of the plantation of Bernard de Marigny. De Woiseri also did a watercolor of the same view, which was probably the first version, and published prints of it, the latter dedicated to Thomas Jefferson. The painting was more than a little political in intent. A flying eagle is shown above, grasping in its beak a long star-studded ribbon that pro-

Joshua Shaw. "Landscape with Deer, North Carolina." c. 1819–1820. Watercolor on paper. Corcoran Gallery of Art, Washington, D.C.

John James Audubon. "Carolina Chickadee." May 3, 1822.
Watercolor on paper. New-York Historical Society, New York.

claims "Under My Wings Everything Prospers." The artist was appealing to the new American constituency of this southern-most of cities. He is a painter about whom we ought to know more. Apparently of French origin, he was by 1804 in Philadelphia, where he reported he had lived in New Orleans for several years. He identified himself as a "designer, drawer, geographer and engineer," and would seem to be one of several French artist-engineers who found his way to New Orleans. He is recorded as living in New York City from 1807 to 1811. There is a

print by him showing views of Philadelphia, New York, Baltimore, Richmond, and Charleston, all on one plate. Watercolors of Boston and Philadelphia are also known, and one of Richmond is attributed to him. Thus he traveled in both North and South, contributing to the artistic life of these cities.

According to John Sartain, Joshua Shaw, "a landscape painter of excellent talents," was "the best artist in his branch in the United States" during the first twenty-five years of the latter's career in this country. A rare watercolor of his, *Landscape with Deer*, previous page, is identified on the back as a scene in North Carolina. It shows some unknown woodland stream he must have come upon during a tour he made through the South in 1819 and 1820. As Sartain aptly noted, "his touch was firm, his tints pure." Here is the world of nature undisturbed by man. During this trip south Shaw was both gathering materials and soliciting subscriptions for his *Picturesque Views of American Scenery*, published by John Hill in Philadelphia in 1819 and 1820. William Dunlap crossed paths with Shaw—Dunlap did not particularly like him—in Norfolk, Virginia, during this time. On one occasion he noted in his diary, "Shaw came in, just return'd from Savannah, Augusta, etc and represents the South as a paradise of riches. He says he obtained more subscribers to his work in Savannah, and that after the fire than any place in yᵉ U.S."

Shaw's work on *Picturesque Views of American Scenery* stressed the rural, natural scenery of America. As an Englishman who had exhibited in the Royal Academy as early as 1802, but had only come to America in 1817, he saw and proclaimed the potential of the American landscape as a subject for the artist. "In no quarter of the globe are the majesty and loveliness of nature more strikingly conspicuous than in America," he wrote in the introduction to his book. Then, "The vast regions which are comprised in or subjected to the republic present to the eye every variety of the beautiful and sublime . . . Striking however and original as the features of nature undoubtedly are in the United States, they have rarely been made the subjects of pictorial delineation . . . America only, of all the countries of civilized man, is unsung and undescribed."

Guy with his views in and around Baltimore and in his very productivity, Beck in his more dramatically organized compositions, Doughty in his feeling for the natural world as he saw it, men such as Bouqueta de Woiseri and Beck (and the Birches of Philadelphia) who did urban views that were the basis for engravings, patrons such as Robert Gilmor, Jr., and George Washington, and those subscribers in Savannah and elsewhere who were interested in Shaw's publication, all helped to lay the foundations for landscape painting in America. Joshua Shaw, and the engraver John Hill, by publishing their *Picturesque Views*, made this subject matter available to a wider audience, roused an interest in the special characteristics of American scenery, touching upon a sense of national pride. The title of their book shows an awareness of the ideas of Gilpin and others on the special virtues of rough and rugged beauty. Gilpin had discerned these qualities in the rural, and rugged, areas of Wales, Scotland, and the Lake District of England. He also saw greater picturesque beauty in a rough ruin than in a smooth building: ideas Morse and his patron Alston in South Carolina had responded to when they created that romantic setting for the portrait of Sally Alston.

Side by side with the growing esthetic appreciation of the beauties of the natural landscape was the growing scientific understanding of the flora and fauna of the United States, increasingly being studied by naturalists—the word scientist had not yet been invented. Among these, John James Audubon was considered something of an outsider. The story of his career is well known. He was born in Santo Domingo in 1785, the son of a French officer and a French maidservant, and raised by his father and stepmother in France. He came to America in 1803 to take up life on an estate of his father's near Philadelphia. A hunter and sportsman, he further developed his interest in birds and the world of nature that had fascinated him since childhood. Philadelphia at that time was a lively center of scientific inquiry, and Alexander Wilson was beginning work on his *American Ornithology*, a pioneer study with cramped but accurate engravings done by Alexander Lawson, which came out between 1808 and 1814. Audubon returned to France for a time, but by 1808 was back. With a partner he started a business venture in Louisville, married, and was involved for over ten years in several essentially unsuccessful enterprises in Kentucky, then obtained work in Cincinnati in the Western Museum. Somewhere along the line a dream grew to do a book which would show directly, in lifesize, the appearance and character of the birds of the country that had become his home.

The journey south in the fall of 1820 was in pursuit of this goal. Here were the great flyways of migrating birds, here—in the woods and rolling hills, in the swamps, along the great Mississippi, in its streams and tributaries—were to be found all manner of land and seabirds. The dream began to materialize in the years he spent in and around New Orleans and Natchez, observing, collecting, drawing, and redrawing.

Until the summer of 1822 Audubon was accompanied by young Joseph Mason, who did the plant settings. It was a felicitous collaboration, the first of several. The original watercolor of the *Carolina Chickadee*, left, shows these tiny creatures that blend so well with their surroundings. As scientist, Audubon here succeeds in presenting two views of the bird, one from above and one from below, so that the characteristics of the plumage are easily recognizable. As artists the two have created an austere and delicate composition appropriate to the scale of these birds. The plant is the rattan vine, or supplejack; the watercolor was done on May 3, 1822, when Audubon and Mason were in Natchez, Mississippi.

In 1824 Audubon made a journey to Philadelphia, hoping to get support for his project. Rebuffed by some of the older scientists loyal to the memory of Alexander Wilson, he sailed for England in 1826. After some difficulties he finally made contact with Robert Havell, Jr., with whom he was to work over the next eleven years bringing his monumental plan to fruition. In England, too, he began to get the recognition he sought and deserved. During this eleven-year period he was to cross the Atlantic at least four times in order to make more paintings for his book. In America he traveled as far south as the Florida Keys, as far north as Labrador, and as far west as Texas in his search for varieties of birds.

After Mason's departure from Louisiana, Audubon painted the settings himself, and was perfectly capable of doing so. How-

John James Audubon. "Mourning Dove." c. 1825. Watercolor on paper. New-York Historical Society, New York.

ever, the pressure to complete the task was such that he called on several other collaborators. There was a particularly warm and friendly relationship with Maria Martin in Charleston, sister-in-law and later wife of the Reverend John Bachman, a naturalist who did much to encourage Audubon in his work. In 1824 he met the German-Swiss artist George Lehman, from Lancaster, Pennsylvania, who did habitat settings for him, especially in Florida and South Carolina.

Audubon's watercolor studies are infinitely varied, as are the birds he drew. They range from restrained, fragile, and elegant designs like the *Carolina Chickadee* to denser and more painterly compositions such as that of the *Mourning Dove*, above. Here he

John James Audubon and George Lehman. "Louisiana Heron."
Painted in the Florida Keys, spring 1832. Watercolor on paper.
New-York Historical Society, New York.

has placed two pairs of the doves within the luxuriant foliage of the silky camellia, or *Virginia stewartia*. In order to achieve exact renderings Audubon, after observing creatures in the wild, wired-up freshly killed specimens in naturalistic poses, and with the aid of mechanical dividers, traced the lifesize outlines in pencil. All his views are directly at eye level, giving a sense of immediacy. The foliage was then filled in or developed. His basic medium was watercolor, but he often added pastel, crayons, inks, or oils to heighten the realism of his subjects. The *Mourning Dove* is probably wholly a composition by Audubon done around 1825 in Louisiana.

Landscape settings of some complexity were devised by George Lehman, particularly for larger water birds such as herons, egrets, and yellowlegs. In the watercolor of the *Louisiana Heron*, done in the Florida Keys in the spring of 1832, above, the flamboyant blue plumage of the bird is shown against the waving royal palms and dense tropical shrubs of the watery swamplike setting.

Audubon's remarkable work served to awaken Europeans,

and Americans, to the abundance and diversity of nature's creatures in the New World. It was a little over a century since Mark Catesby had delineated some of the birds of America, a century in which the majority of the European settlers and their descendants had been so busy claiming and clearing the land that few had taken the time to appreciate its natural wonders. Audubon's work coincided with the development of natural history into a discipline of more exact study. It was a time when the amateur enthusiast and the more dedicated professional still spoke much the same language. (Audubon, like a number of artist-naturalists of his generation, sometimes wrote with great sensitivity and evocative power.) Americans were just beginning to look upon the woodlands and rural places as a source of spiritual and esthetic inspiration and solace, and as places of recreation. Artists, here and abroad, were turning to the land itself as subject for their painting.

That most professional of architects, Benjamin Henry Latrobe, was also a talented amateur watercolorist, as sketches from his earliest years in Virginia show. These sketches reveal him also as a knowledgeable and talented amateur botanist, geologist, entomologist, man of sensibility, capable topographer, and cogent observer of people. During the first months after his arrival in Virginia in 1797 he was visited by the directors of the Dismal Swamp Canal Company to examine their floundering enterprise. The watercolor he made while there, below, and his comments, illustrate that mingling of scientific observation and delight in the experience of seeing characteristic of some of the best men of his age, as well as his continuously acute response to the American scene. The colors are the softest of muted warm beiges and blues; the tall cane that once was so common across much of the South is shown here as if shaped into an extraordinary arch. In his journal Latrobe provides a word picture: "The Canal . . . then takes a gentler turn to the right and under an arch of Canes shows at once the entrance into the Lake. The first view of this magnificent sheet of Water through so narrow and so singular an opening cannot well be described. The Lakes of Switzerland and of Westmoreland in England, have a character of Magnificence and intricacy, depending upon the Lofty mountains with which they are overhung and the infinite variety of forms and of objects that crowd upon the eye. . . . But upon opening upon Drummond lake . . . one immense object . . . fills the eye . . . . It absorbs or expells every other idea, and creates a quiet solemn pleasure, that I never felt from any similar circumstances."

Latrobe was sufficiently interested in the art of sketching that he produced an informal manuscript, "Essay on Landscape," for a young woman of his acquaintance in 1797–1798. This starts out much as many of the English handbooks that were being published at the time. The second portion of it, however, is far less formal and structured, and is like a long letter or rambling essay describing his own ideas about nature, the Great Chain of Being, and his experiences when drawing and sketching. In it he uses his own sketches of American scenery. A freely rendered, yet surely accurate, depiction of a group of trees near the James River canal locks, following page, showing a block of weather-worn granite on the right, sets him off on another train of thought: "When I see in every part of our earth, such a confused and disordered state of materials as is every where exhibited, such a jumble of finished workmanship as appears in all our chrystalyzed rocks, mingled with the wreck of ancient forests, and the petrified remains of sea and land animals, I could fancy myself imprisoned within the Walls of an old Cathedral, such as Europe every where exhibits— . . . Every attempt to clear a way through the ruin, bares the bones of some being that had once life like myself, and I puzzle my imagination to discover or invent his history. The World, indeed, is a great cemetery; everything is composed, and is upheld by decomposition, and destruction of something else; and the gay tapestry of every spring, veils the murders of all the preceding seasons!"

Benjamin Henry Latrobe. "Entrance to Lake Drummund from Washington Ditch, Dismal Swamp." June 9, 1797. Watercolor on paper. Papers of Benjamin Henry Latrobe, Maryland Historical Society, Baltimore.

Benjamin Henry Latrobe. "Group of Trees Near the James River Canal Locks." 1797–1798. Watercolor on paper. Virginia State Library, Richmond.

Sophomoric, perhaps, yet immediately before this he had briefly noted the comparative suitability of Potomac and James River granite for constructing regular walls. It was half in jest that the British writer Robert Southey wrote of the new taste for travels: "While one of the flocks of fashion migrates to the sea-coast, another flies off to the mountains of Wales, to the lakes in the northern provinces, or to Scotland; some to mineralogize, some to botanize, some to take views of the country,—all to study the picturesque, a new science for which a new language has been

formed." Art, science, literary response, religious feeling, historical association were experienced together; it was a part of a new way of seeing. Latrobe's musings on landscape painting were only for his young friend. His son, however, composed the text for a popular drawing book in 1827–1828, in which some of the father's methods and ideas are incorporated. Thus Latrobe indirectly helped in shaping American traditions of landscape drawing.

The results of a sketching trip in 1808–1809 led John Izard Middleton (1785–1849) to publish, in 1812, a serious work on archaeology, *Grecian Remains in Italy, A Description of Cyclopean Walls and of Roman Antiquities with Topographical and Picturesque Views of Ancient Latinum.* He has been identified as the "first classical archaeologist in America." In his introduction Middleton modestly said that his work as an artist was perhaps more important than his work as a scholar, and that he wrote the book because he had made accurate pictures. Later photographs of some of the sites attest to his claim. Unfortunately, his book came out in London during the American War of 1812 and when England was also involved in the Napoleonic Wars; hence it was soon forgotten, and the plates, unacknowledged, copied later by others.

Middleton was a privileged son of South Carolina's aristocracy who inherited his mother's fortune. He was among those artistic and literary Americans who spent much of their lives abroad. Though he was entranced with classical ruins, they were not the only subjects he sketched. His *View from My Window at the Hotel Sibella, Tivoli,* lower right, was done in 1808. This is a hill town with its blocky stone and stuccoed buildings clustered irregularly along either side of a stream, here and there a tower or spire rising above the other buildings. Beyond the workers at their tasks, the waterfall, and the rooftops, the mountains rise in the distance. This seemingly ageless, vernacular architecture of the hill towns of Italy was to serve as model and ideal for the architects of the next generation who designed country villas in the Italianate style. Its charm had earlier been discovered by baroque painters and was now being admired by literary and artistic men such as young Middleton in search of views.

In his sketches the artist-scholar used the "mechanical process of the camera obscura," in order to ensure the accuracy demanded by the antiquary in him. He then retouched them on the spot and "gave that grace of detail which it was impossible to attain while the paper was under the lens." Middleton's watercolor of what he identified as the Temple of Neptune at Paestum, upper right, a Greek classical temple, is rendered with meticulous accuracy. The retouching to give "grace of detail" probably included the grazing goats, the rocks and plants, and the small but resolute figure on the left who could be an antiquary acquaintance of his. The temple is now believed to have been dedicated to Hera and dates around 460 B.C. This watercolor was made in 1819, during a trip he made to southern Italy. Interestingly, Middleton's relatives on his mother's side, Mr. and Mrs. Ralph Izard, had visited the ancient Greek colonial site of Paestum in the company of the painter, John Singleton Copley, in 1775, almost a half-century earlier. They may have been the first Americans to see a Greek temple. The ancient style was becoming the newest fashion in the 1820s.

John Izard Middleton. "Temple of Neptune." October 1819. Watercolor on paper. Carolina Art Association/Gibbes Art Gallery, Charleston.

John Izard Middleton. "View from My Window at the Hotel Sibella, Tivoli." 1808. Watercolor on paper. On back: "Veduta dalla ma fenetre all albergo della Sibella, Tivoli, 1808." Middleton Place, near Charleston.

Trade card of William Camp, cabinetmaker and upholsterer in Baltimore, 1802–1819. Baltimore Museum of Art.

Products of Craftsmen

The printed label of a cabinetmaker and upholsterer in Baltimore, above, shows six different pieces of furniture. Three of them, a "Lady's Cabinet and Dressing Commode," a "Lady's Work-Table," and "A Side Board with Vase Knife Cases" are elaborately decorated and have intricate structures, with tambour closings, a variety of drawer sizes, some with interior divisions, a pop-up worktable on one, special urn-shaped knife cases on another. Decoration includes swags of fabrics, what appears to be inlay or painted ornament in ovals, baskets of flowers, strings of bellflowers, carving and grooving, and different textures of veneered woods juxtaposed. The forms themselves are decorative. The center portion of the sideboard curves in serpentine fashion, the worktable is kidney-shaped. The two chairs and the pier

table are delicate, fragile, and embellished. The knowledgeable student of furniture will quickly recognize that most of these were copied directly from plates published by Thomas Sheraton in his *Cabinet-Maker and Upholsterer's Drawing Book,* first issued in forty-two separate numbers dating from 1791 to 1793. Sheraton's plates are only one of several English publications in which designs reflecting the neoclassical taste in furniture were printed. Equally important were the trade book by Thomas Shearer, *The Cabinet-Makers' London Book of Prices,* published in 1788, and *The Cabinet-Maker and Upholsterer's Guide* first issued by George Hepplewhite's widow in 1788, with later editions in 1789 and 1794. Each of these books represented the prevailing taste as practiced by the large number of cabinetmakers then working in London. Many of the craftsmen had been influenced by the seminal designs of the architect Robert Adam, who also designed furniture, and by the enthusiasm for ancient Rome sparked by French, English, and European antiquarians and dilettantes.

The advertisement of William Camp of Baltimore therefore represents another case of direct transmittal of English design and craft concepts to American shores through the printed page. The new taste for light neoclassical ornament was coupled with the introduction of a wider variety of furniture forms. There was a greater emphasis on technical innovations, which made for greater convenience. William Camp is known to have been listed in Baltimore directories from 1802 to 1819. He also advertised in local newspapers and in these, from 1817 to 1823, he referred to his furniture manufactory and warehouse. He had one of the largest establishments in the city.

Several finely made pieces of furniture coming from Camp's shop have recently been identified. Closely related to these, and very probably by Camp, is a lady's writing desk-dressing table, far right. It is ornamented with urns, garlands, cornucopias, and *verre églomisé* decorative panels. The large eagle at the top was not in the printed source, and suggests the pride of the new Republic in its chosen symbol, selected by the founding fathers in 1782 to represent the United States. Also without English precedent, so far as I know, is the use of female figures personifying Commerce and Industry on a lady's desk and dressing table! These three symbols would be more appropriate as emblems of state. There was good reason for the choice, however. This piece was made for Mr. and Mrs. Solomon Etting of Baltimore. He was the son of Elijah and Shinah Etting—the latter the subject of a painting by Charles Peale Polk, page 158—and prospered in shipping and commerce. She was his second wife, born Rachel Gratz of Philadelphia, daughter of Barnard Gratz. The latter and his brother Michael were among the "merchant venturers" who were instrumental in opening up trade and settlements in Kentucky and other territories west of the Alleghenies. Thus as members of two American Jewish families who were prospering in the new country through commerce and industry, they had every reason to choose such emblems for their home. This dressing table, though based on easily identifiable English sources, is different from its English counterpart both in actual appearance and in the particular circumstances of its creation.

Though the technique of *verre églomisé* was known and used with some frequency in decorating mirrors and clocks, in the

President's desk, probably originally made for the House of Delegates Chamber in the Maryland State House, by John Shaw, Annapolis, 1797–1800. Mahogany and yellow pine, with satinwood and holly inlay. Museum of Fine Arts, Boston, Massachusetts.

Lady's dressing table, attributed to William Camp; Baltimore, c. 1800. Mahogany and satinwood, with inlay and painted decoration. Maryland Historical Society, Baltimore.

United States it is only on Baltimore furniture that such glass panels with painting in reverse are found with any frequency at this period. The recent discovery of the signature "Mitchell" on a panel similar to those found here suggests a craftsman who specialized in this technique. Thus the maker of the dressing table may have, as was often the case, contracted out some of the work, or purchased from colleagues elements of the final form.

An essentially flat and abstracted representation of the American eagle is appropriately found on the desk, upper left, made by John Shaw of Annapolis for the President of the Maryland House of Delegates, 1797–1800. The eagle's breast is the shield of state. In one claw it holds the olive branch of peace; in the other, the arrow of war. Satinwood and holly inlay are used to contrast with the dark mahogany. Shaw's career is exceptionally well documented. He was a Scottish-born craftsman who came to America in 1764. More than many craftsmen he affixed labels inside furniture from his shop. A number of records of payment, in account books both public and private, help further to document his work. He is known to have imported and sold certain items such as looking glasses and backgammon tables as well as doing individual commissions. Several apprentices and journeymen were associated with his shop at various times, and his products show a consistently high level of craftsmanship. In style his work is based closely on English models, some still embodying late-rococo (Chippendale) features as well as reflecting the new Adam-Hepplewhite concepts.

Rebeccah Foster. Quilt, made in Tennessee, 1808. In lower oval, underneath verses of a poem: "Rebeccah Foster/Nashville October 5/1808." Private collection.

The eagle was a particularly popular, almost ubiquitous, decorative symbol during the early Republic. It is frequently found in smaller oval inlays on furniture. In conjunction with stars representing the number of states in the Union, this may be a clue to dating, though not absolutely so. The eagle appears, for example, on a quilt from Tennessee, above, the earliest known from that state. The eagle and the other colored leaf-scroll motifs were appliquéd to the white surface by Rebeccah Foster of Nashville, who signed and dated her work October 5, 1808. There are seventeen stars above the eagle, one for every state through Ohio. Likewise the names of each state are given in each of the seventeen links of the chain that frames each oval. The words of a patriotic poem are stitched in the top and bottom of these two ovals. The ladies were every bit as patriotic as the men.

A slight variation on this theme is found in the eagle represented on the pediment of a corner cupboard, far upper right, the work of an anonymous Carolina cabinetmaker. Here the eagle grasps Masonic emblems—the compass, the square, and the

level—in its claws, and a set of scales, associated with justice, is as if suspended from its back, reminding us again of how intimately Masonic ideals and those of the new nation were associated in the minds of many. It has been suggested that the owner may have been a member of the Halifax, North Carolina, Royal White Hart Lodge, the only Freemason society in the region. Here there are fifteen stars closely crowded together, suggesting a date between 1792, when Kentucky entered the Union as the fifteenth state, and 1796, when Tennessee became the sixteenth. This is one of a group of thirty different pieces of furniture that has been recognized as coming from the same cabinetmaker's shop. They have in common certain characteristic methods of construction and decoration. In several, the design, as here, is achieved by an inlay of putty rather than of wood. Bone is also used as inlay. Raised relief carving and black-painted designs recur. A number of the pieces are of walnut, at least two are of pine, and in several cases walnut is used generously as one of the secondary woods. All of the pieces were found

in or have histories associated with the upper Roanoke River basin of northeast North Carolina, inland from the Albemarle Sound. By the late eighteenth century Halifax was the center of commerce in the area, with a number of active craftsmen, including two silversmiths. Yet it was far from being a Charleston or a Baltimore. The work of this unknown cabinetmaker is provincial, yet individual. In form, virtually all of his pieces are *retardataire*, with scroll pediments and bracket feet, for example, that were more popular in the 1760s than in the 1790s. The interpretation and adaptation of decorative motifs is highly individual. The flat pierced and lobed finials found on several of the pieces, such as that seen on another corner cupboard in the group, left, would appear to be a free interpretation of an anthemion motif like the one found in the center of a pierced pediment, just below the urn finial, on a desk and bookcase by John Shaw, below. By the same token, the boldly carved oval paterae on the doors of the cupboard have a relationship to the veneered oval and circle forms, and paterae, seen on much neoclassical furniture. This is not a one-to-one relationship. Rather, the cabinetmaker in or near the rural community of Halifax had some awareness of changing tastes and trends but did not feel bound to follow these in every way. He knew about the new popularity of inlay, of the eagle as emblem, of pierced decoration, and of oval fields within rectangles, for example. But he put these together in his own vigorous, individual, and conservative

Desk and bookcase, attributed to George Sharrock, North Carolina, 1780–1802. Walnut primary; poplar secondary. Private collection.

Pediment of a corner cupboard, attributed to Swisegood group of cabinetmakers, probably the work of John Swisegood, North Carolina, c. 1820–1825. Walnut with light wood inlays. Private collection.

manner. It may be that this cabinetmaker was European in origin; this is suggested by some of his methods of construction, and might account for some of his choices.

The tremendous amount of research that has been done during the past four or five decades uncovering the work of skilled artisans in the South has in particular brought to light new information about this period of the early Republic, when there was growth and expansion to the South and West. There have been checklists of cabinetmakers and silversmiths made up from legal and newspaper records, such as Will Theus's *Savannah Furniture, 1735–1825*, published in 1967. Special exhibits have featured furniture from certain areas; for example, "Early Furniture of Louisiana" held at the Louisiana State Museum in 1972, "Kentucky Furniture" shown at the J. B. Speed Art Museum in Louisville in 1974, or "Furniture of the Georgia Piedmont Before 1870," organized by the distinguished collector Henry D. Green, at the High Museum of Art in Atlanta in 1976. In 1968 the Houston Museum of Fine Arts organized a show on "Southern Silver," and there have been specialized exhibitions such as that on "Natchez-Made Silver of the Nineteenth Century" held at the Anglo-American Museum in Baton Rouge, in 1970. The editors of *Antiques* magazine have encouraged research and published much new material, particularly in special regional issues such as those on Tennessee and Kentucky in September 1971, November 1947, and April 1974, or those featuring individual cities. From its opening in 1965 there has been a steady output of research from the staff of the Museum of Early Southern Decorative Arts in Winston-Salem, especially concerning the work of artisans in the eastern and upper South before 1820. They have a superb collection of study photographs, and since 1975 specific results of research have been published in their *Journal*. Thus our knowledge of the material culture of the early South is ever-expanding. However, although a vast amount of individual data has been accumulated, it is not yet possible to synthesize it all, to define and make all the correct interconnections, or to describe the character of broad patterns.

Painted chest, attributed to Johannes Spitler, probably made in eastern Shenandoah County, Virginia, early nineteenth century. Private collection.

In the case of furniture of the Federal period, for example, it is probably fair to say that, in general, English fashions prevailed in the American South, but there are a number of interesting variations—in some cases representing the individual work habits and particular idiosyncrasies of taste of individual craftsmen, in other cases the variations may be because of the diverse cultural heritages of the inhabitants. Insofar as one can judge, there seems to be more variety and individuality in American furniture of this period than is true in England, although very little is known about individual cabinetmakers outside of London, or of regional differences in furniture there. This may be because of the peculiar circumstances of the changing life on the American frontier. Craftsmen in small communities worked in partial isolation. A strong sense of individuality is often characteristic of their work.

Thanks to recent research many of these craftsmen have now been identified, some literally by name and some by the common characteristics of their work. Only a few can be mentioned here. When the name of a given craftsman is known, legal and other records help to piece together information about that person's life, the kind of property he owned, the social and economic mobility he experienced, his relationship to other craftsmen, the sources of supplies, etc., and the texture of everyday living in the whole community becomes more tangible. Not many interconnections among these craftsmen have been made yet, but here and there a more detailed picture emerges.

Information has been gathered about the work of three closely associated cabinetmakers who worked in Davidson County, North Carolina: Mordicai Collins, John Swisegood, and Johnathan Long. In their work an idiosyncratic characteristic is a partiality for reeded accents, such as the reeded inverted fan plinth and reeded rosettes on the pediment of a corner cupboard, page 192, upper left, probably the work of John Swisegood. Another identifiable group of North Carolina craftsmen is that of George Sharrock and his relatives, also from the Albemarle region. Some of their work is extremely austere, as seen in the pediment of a desk and bookcase, page 192, lower left. The plain comb finial is one of the decorative and constructional ele-

ments that helps to relate this piece to others from this group. The carved finial appears to represent the simplification of complex pierced work seen in more sophisticated urban examples.

On a tall case clock believed to have been made in the North Carolina Piedmont, following page, we see both strong individual choice in ornament and a relationship to other German-Swiss artisans and their traditions. The basic form of the case is fairly

Gravestone of Daniel Wagoner, died October 12, 1827. Bethany churchyard, Davidson County, North Carolina.

Detail of hood, tall case clock.

Detail of case, tall case clock.

Tall case clock, probably by a cabinetmaker in North Carolina Piedmont, c. 1780–1800. Walnut and yellow pine, with light inlay. Museum of Early Southern Decorative Arts, Winston-Salem, N.C.

traditional, but the inlay decoration on the pediment is used to form a face, which is downright eccentric. We know that, especially in the larger urban centers, certain kinds of inlay, such as shell patterns or oval paterae, or the narrow strips and bands called stringing, were made by specialists. In other cases craftsmen seem to have made their own, as must have been true here. The introduction of a "face" motif on a clock pediment appears to be sheer whimsy, a private joke perhaps, with, as far as I know, no precedent—unique in the correct usage of that word.

Other forms or symbols are more familiar and help to connect this clock with the work of fellow craftsmen in the region. The moon and the sun, abstractly represented in the center of the trunk, is unusual, and an individual interpretation; yet these are symbols traditionally associated with the inexorable cycle of time. At the base of the trunk, within a circle, is a dark and light, rotating-lobed, crosslike symbol, the fylfot. This is a variant of ancient symbols, such as the swastika, which appear in a variety of cultures, perhaps derived from or related to sun signs and often signifying well-being or good fortune. The fylfot appears among objects created by members of the German-Swiss populations of Piedmont North Carolina and in the Shenandoah Valley of Virginia. As a familiar shape its exact meaning may have been

lost to some of the craftsmen who used it; however, its recurrence on a whole group of gravestones in Davidson County, North Carolina, suggests an association there with hope, rebirth, and the cycle of life and death. The shape of one such gravestone, page 193, below, is remarkably similar to a furniture pediment; and the chevron molding also parallels furniture forms.

The fylfot motif appears again on a painted chest, page 193, above, believed to have been made in eastern Shenandoah County in Virginia. Here much of the painted decoration—the semicircular quadrants, and the broad bands at the base of each quadrant, the barber-pole verticals and the painted shapes of scroll pediments in the center panel—is as if enlarged from inlay and stringing patterns. The craftsman of all three of these objects, as they fashioned individual pieces, drew both upon forms and symbols familiar to them from their German-Swiss heritage and upon the decorative elements found in neoclassical furniture ornament.

The thin, curvilinear stringing on the clock, for example, has its counterpart in other neoclassical work, but the terminals of hearts on the pediment and tulips on the trunk have parallels with motifs on the painted paper documents popular among these same German-Swiss communities, particularly in the years

Attributed to "Stony Creek artist" of Virginia. Birth record of George Lantz, born in Shenandoah County, Virginia, in 1788. Watercolor on paper. Private collection.

around 1780 to 1830, as in the birth record, below, prepared sometime after 1788. Here the major texts are enclosed in heart shapes. Tulips, pansies, leaf lobes, and small roses embellish the border and open spaces. It is a record of birth and baptism, a *Taufschein*. These decorative records were not necessarily made at the time of baptism but may have been made some years later—sometimes even as late as the marriage of the subject— and then presented to the individual. They represent the art of the calligrapher, sometimes a scholarly and pedantic art. A number of documents by the hand of the artist shown here have been found; several of them were done for a family belonging to the Reformed Zion Congregation, Stony Creek, near Edinburg in Shenandoah County. He has thus been identified as the "Stony Creek artist." His impeccable German, plus his steady mastery of English spelling, suggest he might have been a teacher.

The discovery of a variety of different objects fashioned by Swiss-German peoples of the Carolinas and Virginia is relatively new. Products of the craftsmanship of the German population in Pennsylvania have long been well known, as have those of the tightly knit community of Moravians in Salem, North Carolina.

Until recently it has been assumed that the other German-Swiss communities in the South were so quickly assimilated by the dominant English-speaking culture that no artifacts remained exemplifying their original European heritage. To date, most of what has been found was executed before 1830. In many cases these objects show close parallels with work done in Pennsylvania, which is only natural since so many of the German-speaking settlers in the back-country of Virginia and North Carolina had come from there.

The settlers in the German-Swiss communities in South Carolina included both those who had come directly from Europe and those from Pennsylvania. They were concentrated in the area known as the "Dutch Fork" (the term Dutch a mispronunciation of "Deutsch," that is, German), an area between the Broad and Saluda rivers, slightly north of the central area of the state. A concrete example of the direct cultural ties among the German-Swiss communities of the "Dutch Fork" in South Carolina and those in North Carolina and Pennsylvania is found in the work of another calligraphic artist, the so-called *Ehre Vater* artist. He has been given this appellation because many of the decorated or illuminated documents from his hand begin with the phrase or motto *Ehre Vater und Mutter* (Honor Father and Mother). Obviously he was a well-traveled person; *Taufscheine* by his hand have been found for subjects living in at least five different counties in Pennsylvania, from several communities in North Carolina, in the Salem-Wachovia area, and even from the Niagara peninsula of Canada. Several subjects in the Dutch Fork of South Carolina were recipients of his work. An example is seen opposite. Here the beautiful Gothic lettering (identified as fraktur, for its broken angularity) of the motto *Ehre Vater und Mutter* is used as the crown or masthead. The more detailed information about Maria Margaretha Hausihl, who was born in 1787 in Newberry County, South Carolina, is recorded below,

Chest of drawers with bowfront, Lexington, Kentucky, c. 1810–1829. Twice in script on the inside bottom of the top drawer: "Made by Elisha Warner." Cherry with light wood inlay; white pine. Anglo-American Art Museum, Louisiana State University, Baton Rouge.

Designs for "Dressing Drawers" from Hepplewhite's THE CABINET-MAKER AND UPHOLSTERER'S GUIDE, *3rd edition (London, 1794). Henry Francis duPont Winterthur Museum, Winterthur, Delaware.*

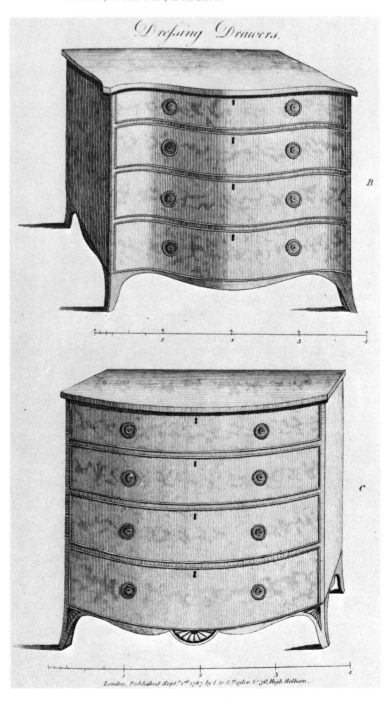

followed by a prayer to Jesus, written in a cursive script. This is flanked on either side by stylized parrots, female and male, perched upon flowery sprigs. It is thought that the artist may have been an itinerant parochial schoolmaster of the Lutheran or Reformed confession.

It comes as no surprise to find furniture made in Baltimore or Charleston that conforms closely to English fashions, nor to discover that the work of somewhat isolated craftsmen in the Albemarle region, in the Shenandoah Valley of Virginia, or in Piedmont North Carolina, shows individual and retardataire characteristics. The latter might also be expected of the craftsmen in Kentucky and Tennessee. This is not necessarily so. An elegantly shaped, discreetly decorated bowfront chest of drawers, above, closely parallels the designs of two desks shown in Hepplewhite's *Designs from the Cabinet-Maker and Upholsterer's Guide* of 1794, left. Here the Kentucky cabinetmaker, if he was working directly from the plate, created his own subtle variation. The simple, rounded, curved form is similar to the chest shown on the lower half of Hepplewhite's plate, while the single long curve of the apron at the base is closer to that shown on the upper portion. The flaring French legs conform to those in the engravings. There is a narrow band of inlay on the top; at its edges tiny diamond designs have been burned into the wood. Each drawer is likewise discreetly outlined with a thin band of

Corner cupboard, probably from Green County, Kentucky, early nineteenth century. Cherry and poplar. Private collection.

inlay, each with a tiny burned design on the outer edge. The simple, clearly defined lines of the whole serve to stress the richness of the wood itself.

Awareness and interest in what is new are not so much influenced by the actual distance from a center of changing taste as by the psychological distance. If he wished to, a cabinetmaker in Kentucky could be "closer" to London, or Baltimore—either because he had recently come from there or because he kept up with the trade—than a craftsman in a relatively isolated rural community not far from the shores of the Atlantic. On the inside bottom of the top drawer of this chest there is twice written, in ink, "Made by Elisha Warner." He was in Lexington sometime after 1810, and in the 1818 city directory was listed as a wooden-clock and cabinet maker. At the time of his death in 1829 his estate brought $56,000. This was apparently in addition to what he called his factory and cabinet shop, which he gave to his half-brother, but included about ninety clocks, a variety of furniture, plus real estate, making him one of the most affluent cabinet-makers in the region.

Many among the populace of Lexington, "the Athens of the West," were obviously anxious to keep pace with the latest fashions and ideas. Another cabinetmaker, Porter Clay, advertised in 1805 that the "newest and most elegant fashions" could be had on the shortest notice, because of "the many sources of information which he has had in his line of business" and "the regular correspondence which he has kept with all the principal Cabinet-Makers both in Philadelphia and New York." Would that we could see the nature of this correspondence. Another craftsman reported he had come directly from Baltimore and had "complete knowledge of the newest fashions." The ways of keeping pace were varied.

The primary wood of this chest is cherry, which was available in abundance in Kentucky and Tennessee in the early nineteenth century. The naturalist François André Michaux, in describing the places where the wild cherry grew—his information was gathered before 1803—wrote, "But it is no where more-profusely multiplied, nor more fully developed than beyond the mountains in the States of Ohio, Kentucky and Tennessee. On the banks of the Ohio I have measured stocks which were from 12 to 16 feet in circumference, and from 80 to 100 feet in stature, with the trunk of an uniform size and undivided to the height of 25 or 30 feet. . . . The perfect wood is of a dull, light red tint, which deepens with age. It is compact, fine-grained and brilliant, and not liable to warp when perfectly seasoned . . . Among the trees which grow east of the Mississippi, it is the most eligible substitute for Mahogany." He further states that planks were "sent from Kentucky to New Orleans, where they are also employed in cabinet-making." The fine quality of the native cherry and walnut was something which impressed foreign visitors to the region. Still another traveler, in 1808–1809, commented on the furniture being fashioned in Lexington as "in as handsome a style as in any part of America, and where the high finish which is given to the native walnut and cherry timber, precludes the regret that mahogany is not to be had but at an immense expense." A distinguishing characteristic of much of the Federal furniture of Kentucky and Tennessee is the rich glowing reddish tones of cherry wood.

Sugar chest, from Kentucky. Cherry with light inlay; poplar. Private collection.

some Baltimore furniture. This piece is of cherry. Large plain pieces of wood such as this come from those tall, thick wild cherry trees.

Frontier cabinetmakers adapted traditional forms of furniture to their own special needs in the creation of the varied sugar (and meal) chests or desks found with great frequency in Kentucky and Tennessee and also, apparently, occasionally in Missouri and in the Carolinas. They are mentioned in contemporary inventories. This unusual form is, so far as I know, indigenous to the South and seems to have been invented there. Some are quite simple, being boxlike arrangements on legs, while others are elegant and highly finished. Sugar was a precious commodity; individual loaves or cones cost as much as $27 in 1812 and came either from New Orleans or the West Indies. Some are very similar to cellarettes in appearance, but deeper. They often open from the top and have several compartments inside, with a drawer below the upper compartment. The fine inlay on the chest at the left makes it attractive enough to be placed in a dining room.

A number of these storage pieces were made to appear as desks, some even with simulated false drawers outlined in inlay on the exterior, and with nonfunctional pulls. An example of the desk-type sugar bin is shown below. The slant-top opens to the storage spaces inside. It is walnut. The compass and rule were

Sugar chest, from Kentucky, early nineteenth century. Walnut with light wood and cherry inlays; poplar. Private collection.

The special qualities of frontier life made it possible for the urbane and aware person with ties to other areas and the rural, isolated pioneer farmer and woodsman to exist side by side. These seemingly disparate qualities could, in fact, be embodied in one person. Andrew Jackson is a prime example. One has only to see the log house at Hermitage, near Nashville, where Jackson and his Rachel first lived, and the "Mansion House," which they built in 1819 (added to in 1830 and subsequently remodeled after a fire in 1834), to sense this mingling of what might seem different ways of life. By the same token, not all furniture for this region shows the close kinship with English, Maryland, or Philadelphia models that the Elisha Warner chest does.

A cherry corner cupboard, left, reveals again the conservative yet strongly individual characteristics that seem to typify backcountry furniture in the South during this period. There is the delight in inlay—an undulating vine with sinuous leaves grows out of two small jugs. Curiously isolated bell-flower pendants descend from joined arches on the upper panels. At the skirt is a dot-and-dash inlay and a fan. Several of these features, especially the undulating vine, the dot-dash, and fan, are found on other Kentucky pieces believed to have originated in Green County. The dot-dash inlay, incidentally, is very similar to that found in

Sideboard from Upper Valley of Virginia. Mahogany and mahogany veneer with light and dark inlays; yellow pine. Museum of Early Southern Decorative Arts, Winston-Salem, N.C.

Sideboard, possibly from Georgia or Alabama, early nineteenth century. Cherry and yellow pine. Private collection.

given great play by the craftsman who obviously enjoyed laying out the inlay patterns used to decorate the surface. The curious attenuated cabriole legs, which occur on a number of Kentucky pieces, particularly some from Mason County, are similar to those found on a chest of drawers in which the inscribed signature of P. Tuttle is found, though this sugar chest is not necessarily his work. Peter Tuttle was born in Prince William County, Virginia, and arrived in Mason County, Kentucky, sometime before 1810. He later worked in both Fleming and Nicholas counties in Kentucky, and died in Missouri in 1859, possibly a restless soul who sought, or was forced to seek, the challenge of ever new frontiers.

The accoutrements of hospitality were essential to Southern living, and sideboards and cellarettes were popular. Few, if any, American-made sideboards were as ostentatious as the Sheraton design reproduced on the lower portion of William Camp's trade card (page 88). Nonetheless, they were skillfully designed and meant to be showpieces. A number of Charleston cabinetmakers advertised these among their wares in the 1790s, mentioning "Elegant sideboards," or "Sideboards of different patterns," or "Sideboards plain and inlaid." These descriptions suggest the popularity and diversity of sideboards made in Charleston and throughout the South. Some Southern sideboards are beautifully serpentine in shape, some bowfronted, many have inlay of one kind or another, some with only thin stringing, some include leaf and floral motifs, others show a lavish bravura display. Inlays and mahogany veneers are used to embellish a Virginia example, upper left, with a serpentine front. A generous use of wood is exemplified here as the main body of the piece is also mahogany, while yellow pine serves as the secondary wood. A distinctly country cousin, dignified, plain, self-sufficient, is a cherry sideboard, lower left, found in the area between Eufaula and Ozark, Alabama. Little documentation about furniture-making in Alabama seems available, and it is not certain whether this simple but well-built piece originated there. However, especially after the War of 1812, wagon trains of settlers made their way from the Carolinas, Virginia, and Georgia into sections of what are now Alabama and Mississippi, caught up with "Alabama fever," a desire to find new land on what was then the Southwestern frontier. One of the routes was the Old Federal Road that led into south Alabama. After initial settlement came home-building and furnishing. This modest piece may have been fashioned by one of these intrepid settlers.

The design of a cellarette, right, though believed to have come from still-rural Piedmont Georgia, has a great deal of sophistication, with its fine proportions and restrained inlay. A cellarette is a storage box for bottles of wine and liquor. Those shown in English design books tend to be octagonal or elliptical in shape, some brass-bound and mounted on stands. A few of this type have survived in Charleston. Some of the American ones, as here, are essentially a box on a frame. It is a relatively rare form in American furniture, and those known are, more often than not, believed to be Southern in origin.

As mentioned earlier, the headboards of many beds probably from Charleston are removable; rather than being tenoned in between the headposts, there are slots. This was apparently done so that the headboard could be removed during the hot summer months, the bed moved out from the wall, and every opportunity taken to catch a fugitive cooling breeze. The bed on the following page is shown without the headboard and with fabrics, including protective mosquito netting, which was used throughout most of the Deep South for "summer dress." (It was also customary to place cool rush matting on the floors.)

The tall posts are reeded and have straight-lobed broad-leaf carving at base and top. Bending heads of grain, interpreted as rice, and leaves are shown at the swelling below the reeding. A number of such "rice" beds have survived, most with a history of ownership in or near Charleston. If meant to depict rice—and there is no reason to doubt it—such carving represents an extraordinary tribute to the crop that continued to support many citizens. We have no idea which of the many craftsmen who worked in Charleston at this time might have originated this motif. In the 1790s there were at least sixty-three cabinetmakers known to be working in Charleston; by 1810 there were eighty-one, an all-time high for that city. The bed is mahogany throughout. This, too, is typical of Charleston workmanship, where mahogany was readily available. Such mahogany bedsteads were listed among the possessions of people of moderate means as well as the wealthy. This particular bed was owned by members of the Middleton family.

Most craftsmen and their patrons thought in terms of wooden beds such as the one shown here, though some were, of course, considerably simpler. However, the architect Robert Mills,

Cellarette, from Georgia Piedmont, 1790–1800. Mahogany and southern yellow pine. Private collection.

Bed, with headboard removed, from Charleston. Mahogany throughout. Middleton family history. Middleton Place, near Charleston.

whose acute and creative mind saw the great potential in new uses of iron for construction, and who hoped to solve some of the eternal problems of fireproofing, sketched out in his diary the plans for a single iron bedstead which he thought suitable, safer, and more durable, for a hospital in Baltimore. Though the idea did not bear fruit at the time, it is surely one of the ancestors of the many brass beds of the mid-nineteenth century.

When Hepplewhite or Sheraton or other arbiters of taste discussed or illustrated beds they discussed the "bed furniture," or fabrics and hangings, and illustrated these as well as the beds themselves. The fabrics were frequently valuable, and were an integral part of the total appearance. While white, as shown here, was probably preferred for summer in the South, more colorful fabrics and hangings were used in other seasons.

With quilts and fine counterpanes we are again in the world of feminine creativity. There are fashions in the designs of these as in other objects, even though some of the techniques are age-old. Geometric patterns appear to have gained in popularity during the nineteenth century. It is recorded that the women in a Maryland family cut, pieced, assembled, and quilted the coverlet below while their men were away during the War of 1812. The seemingly simple pattern of diagonal darks animated by a "pinwheel" movement was created by piecing eight triangles into squares alternately with plain squares in a ticktacktoe pattern. These larger squares were in turn placed between plain squares in alternating rows, thus creating the longer diagonals. The stitching of the bottom and top layers together is done in varied circular and floral patterns, the border in the "Princess Feather" pattern, and these portions stuffed. Altogether it represents precision planning and execution. The esthetic appeal of repeating, "op," patterns and colors has recently come into its own, and with it a new appreciation of quilts as esthetic objects. Though not much was written about the esthetics of form and colors in quilts at the time they were created, these were certainly problems to which the creators addressed themselves. In so doing they kept alive the age-old delight in abstract pattern that can be seen in the long history of such forms—in basketry and floor patterns, needlepoint and bargello work, and mosaics, to name a few.

The majority of the quilts and bed-hangings that have survived for a century or more are of cotton, linen, or silk. Fewer examples of wool, subject to the depredations of moths, are extant. "Bed ruggs," coverlets of rough woollen materials—the usage goes back to the sixteenth century—are mentioned in estate inventories of the eighteenth and early nineteenth centuries in America, though relatively few are known. This rare Southern rug, following page, was probably made between 1770 and 1820. The foundation of the rug is a woven twill and the surface pattern was created with embroidered knots of wool. Since it is more common for the knots to be woven this is a rare example on a number of counts. The well-defined patterns in dark and light blue, salmon and pinks and tan are set against a ground of natural wool. There is a long history of ownership in a Loudoun County family in northern Virginia.

Clothing, linens, and blankets were stored in a variety of ways—hung from pegs or hooks, placed in chests, in drawers, or on shelves. Our familiar coat hangers were sufficiently new in 1845 that Thomas Webster felt it necessary to explain them in some detail as an "apparatus . . . consisting of a handle and cross-piece . . . The cross-piece goes into the arm holes. . . ." The clothespress and related wardrobe seem to have been a more familiar type of furniture in the South than in the North. Examples have been found with some frequency in Charleston, and also Virginia, Maryland, Kentucky, and elsewhere. Most found in these states stem from English models and usually have an upper portion with shelves or sliding trays for holding folded clothes or linens, behind cupboard doors. The lower portion then has two to four drawers—sometimes two wide drawers with two smaller ones above. A slight variation of this is seen, following page, on one of the handsomest of all of this genre. Here the lower portion is also closed off by doors. Magnificent mahogany veneering in patterns of large ovals and squares enhance the outside. This is one of the few Charleston pieces in which a label

has survived. Robert Walker was the cabinetmaker from whose shop this came. In addition to advertising his wares, he noted that "Orders from the Country speedily and carefully executed in the neatest manner." Despite the growth of back-country settlements, Charleston remained a major social and commercial center of South Carolina. Robert Walker (1772–1833) came to Charleston as a young man and was established in business by 1799. He appears to have been a productive cabinetmaker in the city for the next thirty years, selling not only finished furniture but dealing in "Mahogany Boards, Plank Veneers" and rarer woods such as satinwood and holly, which were used for veneers and inlays.

The Louisiana or lower Mississippi Valley counterpart of the clothespress continued to be the armoire, with the entire interior enclosed behind two long doors. Inside were several shelves with a belt of three small drawers usually placed slightly below the center. Though dating is difficult, the essential forms of those probably made in the early nineteenth century remained close to

Pieced and stuffed-work quilt, Maryland, c. 1812. "Pinwheel" pattern, "Princess Feather" quilted border. National Museum of American History, Smithsonian Institution, Washington, D.C.

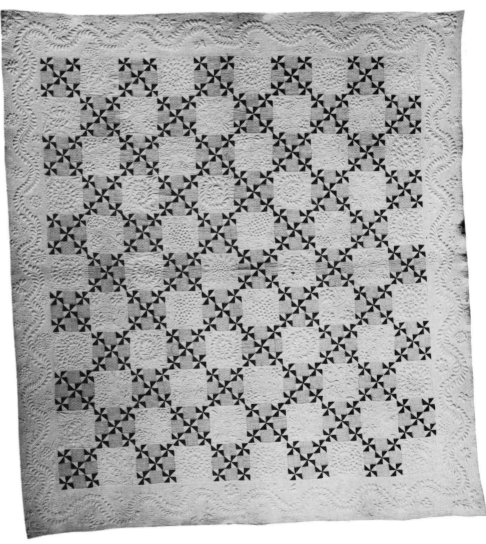

Wool bed rug, probably northern Virginia, 1770–1820. Association for the Preservation of Virginia Antiquities, John Marshall House, Richmond.

Clothespress, by Robert Walker, Charleston, before 1810. Veneered with flame mahogany in patterns of ovals within squares. Charleston Museum.

those made earlier. Delicate cabriole legs and scalloped skirts were retained, as in the wardrobe, far upper right, but here the cabinetmaker embellished virtually every available surface on the front with inlay—interlocking ellipses, ovals, barber-pole stripes, an urn with vine, and a succession of swags, all very neoclassical, and handled with the freewheeling exuberance seen in some Kentucky pieces.

In an armoire, or wardrobe, far lower right, that probably dates from just a few years later, one can see and sense the shift in taste that was beginning to take place. We see it in the bolder, larger scale, and in such a detail as the brass lion paw feet. This shift is identified in England and France as the Regency and Empire styles respectively. They represent a move toward a more literal interpretation of classical models. In England one can identify Regency beginnings in some of the drawings included in Sheraton's 1803 *Cabinet Dictionary*, where he showed a

Inlaid armoire, from Louisiana or Mississippi, 1770–1810. Mahogany, satinwood, cypress, and other woods. Private collection.

Armoire, from Louisiana. Mahogany with mahogany veneer, and cypress. Private collection.

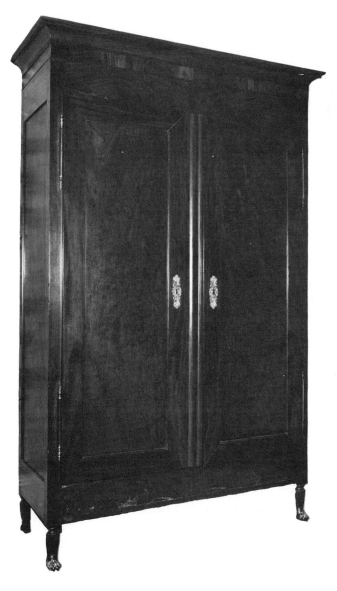

"Grecian" dining table and two "Herculaneum" chairs, the latter with lion paw feet. Gradually the lighter forms of the neoclassical gave way to more monumental and sometimes much more sculptural forms.

This new taste is clearly exemplified in a sideboard at the Hermitage in Tennessee. It is apparently the same sideboard listed in a May 16, 1821, account, both on following page, now in the Jackson Papers at the Library of Congress, which records a long list of furniture and household equipment purchased by Andrew and Rachel Jackson from François Seignouret in New Orleans. As can be seen, Seignouret supplied not only the furniture—bedsteads, a press, sideboard, chairs, washstand—but related items. The latter include mattresses, mosquito bars, counterpanes, carpeting, and bordering for the carpets. There are references to Seignouret as "upholsterer" as early as 1812. Similar references to this establishment continue through 1852 in various city directories, newspapers, and journals. In most, such as

Sideboard, purchased by Andrew Jackson from Mr. Seignouret in New Orleans, May 16, 1821. Mahogany and other woods. Ladies' Hermitage Association, near Nashville, Tennessee.

Page from account book of Andrew Jackson, May 16, 1821. Andrew Jackson Papers, Library of Congress, Washington, D.C.

Paxton's 1822 *New Orleans Directory,* or an 1852 ad in *De Bow's Review,* François Seignouret, or the firm of F. Seignouret and Co., is listed as an upholstery and furniture store or warehouse. They also imported wines. The listing in Jackson's accounts provides insight into the upholsterers' business in this period. Both fabrics connected with furnishing, and furniture, were handled. Of the latter, some appear to have been made on the premises, which was a three-story building in the old section of the city. Some work may have been contracted out, and some objects were apparently imported from Seignouret's native France.

This large order of furniture and fabrics shows the role of New Orleans and its merchants as purveyors of what was considered fashionable and finest throughout the lower Mississippi Valley. Jackson, however, did not neglect to patronize local craftsmen. A pair of sugar tongs, page 208, bearing the initial "J" belonged to Jackson and is still at the Hermitage. They bear the mark of Joseph Thorp Elliston (Nashville, 1798–1856). The neat bright-cut design is the equivalent in silver to discreet inlay decoration on furniture. Elliston was both silversmith and watchmaker. From 1814 to 1816 he was mayor of Nashville and was no doubt a political acquaintance of Jackson's. Elliston was also a member of the commission established to build the state capitol.

There is also a presidential association with the sofa made by William King, Jr., far right. The curved and sculptural lines were identified at the time as Grecian. King is recorded as working in

Georgetown, part of the District of Columbia, from at least 1801 to 1834. His shop, as was the case of so many cabinetmakers, was in his dwelling house. According to family tradition, this sofa is a full-size "sample" that King made before he made a set of twenty-four chairs and four sofas for "The President's House" in 1818; the sample was retained by King's family. The reconstruction of the White House, after its burning by the British in 1814, was nearing completion when Monroe took office. King's chairs and sofa were for the still-uncompleted East Room. The original charge for each chair was $33, and for each sofa $198, though King made deductions because the "Covers," or fabric, and varnishing were not complete. The King furniture remained unused in the unfinished East Room until Jackson's administration, when it was finally properly covered. Most of the set apparently left the White House in 1873 when a later administration made another renovation.

Though King, William Worthington, and several other local craftsmen received commissions, it was felt that other articles appropriate for the residence of the President simply were not available in the United States. Therefore, additional furniture, clocks, candelabra, decorative vases, and bronzes were ordered by President James Monroe from France. Ultimately, there was a public furor over this, and over the handling of the furniture fund. This was a contributing reason for a special law passed by Congress in 1829 prescribing that furniture "purchased for use in the President's House shall be as far as possible of American or domestic manufacture."

The silversmith Charles K. Burnett was one of the American craftsmen who provided work deemed suitable for the President's House during the Monroe administration. He was involved with the plans for the furnishings, and at one point served as witness to an inventory and valuation made of Monroe's own household furniture. A classically shaped covered sauce dish with curling handles, following page above, stands testimony to his skill. The body is based on the ancient form of the Greek drinking vessel, the kylix, and helps to demonstrate how pervasive the taste for things Greek had become. Burnett worked in Alexandria, Virginia, from around 1790 to 1800 and was working in Georgetown from about 1800 to 1849. Thomas Jefferson was also among Burnett's clients and at Monticello today there is a sugar bowl by Burnett that Jefferson gave to Camille Franzoni, wife of the Italian sculptor who came to work on the Capitol. Burnett also made a number of gorgets that were distributed by the government to, among others, members of the Choctaw tribe in Neshoba County, Mississippi, and the Alabama tribe in Texas.

The basic urn shape of a covered sugar dish, following page below, from the Baltimore establishment of Samuel Kirk (1793–1872) is classical. However, the use of abundant repoussé decoration, which includes a fanciful landscape and floral motifs, can as easily be read as late rococo exuberance or, probably more correctly, as prescient of later Victorian ornament. The state of Maryland required the use of an assayer's mark indicating the year on silver between 1815 and 1830; thus this can be dated 1828. Kirk came from Doylestown, Pennsylvania, and served his

Sofa, made by William King, Jr., Washington, D.C., 1818. Mahogany with mahogany veneer. Private collection.

Charles A. Burnet. Silver sauce dish, Georgetown, District of Columbia. c. 1815–1825. Marked: "C*A*B" in Roman capitals twice on bottom of foot. Private collection.

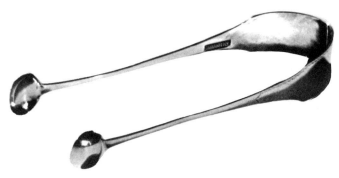

Joseph Thorp Elliston. Silver sugar tongs, Nashville, c. 1810. Marked: "ELLISTON" in rectangle. Ladies' Hermitage Association, near Nashville, Tennessee.

Samuel Kirk. Covered silver urn or sugar dish, with Baltimore assay mark for 1828. Collection of Samuel Kirk and Son, Baltimore, Maryland.

apprenticeship in Philadelphia. His ancestors apparently include English silversmiths of the late seventeenth century. He opened his own shop in Baltimore in 1815, working with a partner, John Smith, until 1821. He was on his own until his son joined him in 1846. The firm still exists. In the 1820s Kirk developed pieces in which repoussé work was used lavishly, work that has since been characteristic of many of the firm's products. Unfortunately, the early records of the firm were destroyed by fire, so it is impossible to trace the activities of Kirk in any detail, and it is difficult to arrive at any conclusion concerning his choice of this kind of ornament. Among both English and French silver of the first two decades of the nineteenth century there are examples of rich ornament, some Bacchic in the use of grape and grape leaves, but few rival Kirk. The urn shown here, ostensibly designed for sugar, was very probably more ceremonial, or emblematic of status, than strictly useful, but neither the patron nor the occasion for which it was made is known. We do know that Kirk's patrons included General Lafayette, who on his famous visit found time in 1824 to commission, or acquire, two goblets which he gave to one David Williamson. The beautiful Elizabeth Patterson Bonaparte was another of his patrons. There is much that is not known about Samuel Kirk and his work, but the examination of any single piece from his shop reveals the hand of consummate craftsmen in metal.

The crafts of metalworker and cabinetmaker are combined in a remarkable center, or library, table, right, that has a history of ownership in Georgetown, South Carolina. Simulated drapery or swags of brass are attached to the tabletop, brass plinths support the central columnar supports, and the paw feet are likewise of brass. It is an unusually stylish piece. Relatively little has been uncovered about the work of brass founders and their products. However, several groups of brass andirons have been found, all with interrelated structural elements and all with histories of ownership by families in or near Charleston, South Carolina. Though it has not been possible to establish a one-to-one relationship between existing documents concerning brass founders and this group of objects, it is probable that brass founders who practiced their trade in Charleston fashioned these. The plinths below the columnar center supports on the table shown here—which more probably originated in Charleston than the smaller community of Georgetown—bear a marked similarity to the bases of two of the pairs of andirons, and in fact appear to be parts of andirons adapted for use on the table. Some of the mystery of this handsome table may thus be solved, though the names of the makers, the patron, the occasion of the commission, or its original use are still unknown.

Metalwork of a different order was involved in the creation of a large, 5 foot 1 inch iron weathervane, right, that has served as a landmark in Camden, South Carolina, since 1826. This is a profile "likeness," considerably after the fact, of the Catawba Indian chief, King Haiglar. According to the well-established town tradition, this was made, or supervised, by a Frenchman, J. B. Mathieu, in 1826, and was placed on the summit of the market steeple. Mathieu advertised his "portrait likenesses" in Charleston in 1806 and lived in Camden from 1815 to 1834. There he advertised more modestly "Profiles at J. B. Mathieu's 50¢ warranted likenesses." Haiglar's role in the events of Camden, then called Pine Tree Hill, had taken place more than a half-century earlier, in the 1750s. He had a close relationship with the leading Quaker in the community, who became colonial agent for dealing with the Catawbas. Tradition has it that the

Iron weathervane of Catawba Indian chief, King Haiglar, Camden, South Carolina. Designed by J. B. Mathieu, 1826.

Library table, Charleston, c. 1815. Mahogany throughout, with brass ornamentation. Private collection.

Quaker once rescued Haiglar from torture by an Indian war party, and that the latter was subsequently responsible for warning the white man of a Cherokee Indian attack, thus saving his life. Haiglar and his fellow Indians joined the British against the Cherokees in 1759–1760. In 1763, however, Haiglar was cut down by a Shawnee. By the time his valiant deeds were memorialized in an iron effigy he was already a romantic figure of the past, and his fellow Catawbas reduced in number by war and disease. As changes in buildings in Camden have taken place, the weathervane has been moved from spire to spire, always being retained as a landmark. It now graces the current City Hall. Along with it has gone a town clock, with four dials, each facing in a different direction. According to tradition, the bell of this clock—which was cast in Philadelphia in 1824—served as a market bell, fire alarm, and to mark the 9 P.M. curfew before the Civil War. A Camden silversmith, Alexander Young, and then his son, served as keeper of the clock for a period of seventy years. Young was also the silversmith who made the silver trowel used by Lafayette in 1825 when the latter laid the cornerstone of the monument to General DeKalb, the Revolutionary War hero. Robert Mills was the designer of the monument, which still stands in front of Mills's Bethesda Presbyterian Church.

PART FOUR

The Sense of Separation

1825–1860

DURING THE YEARS between the inauguration of John Quincy Adams in 1825 and the Civil War brought on by the secession of eleven Southern states in 1860–1861, there was a growing sense of separation between the Northern and Southern parts of the young Republic. The South depended more on single cash crops, many white people depended upon black slave labor, and the region was essentially more agrarian. In the North, crops were more diversified; commerce and then industry gained in importance. As the nation grew in numbers, wealth, and size, the divisions developed. The first major rift occurred as early as 1817–1821 in the political debate about the status of slavery when Missouri wanted entrance to the Union, a debate which also had to do with party rivalries. New disagreements on the tariff policy, the role of the Second Bank of the United States, and other issues arose. Least defensible and most emotional was that of slavery, the tragic and "peculiar" institution that had become an integral part of large-scale cotton, sugar, and rice production in the South. Small farmers, who in fact were in the majority, probably did not profit from it, yet in the end they supported the system. So did others in the upper South who were involved in the domestic trade of slaves, the sale of surplus slaves from areas with worn-out lands to those opening up new country farther south and west. From the 1850s on, debate over these issues became more and more emotional, ultimately irreconcilable.

This further spread of white settlers westward meant occupation of lands once lived on by Indians. Jackson's campaign against the Seminoles in Florida in 1817–1818 marked a new phase in a continuing process. Though it aroused an international furor, the action laid the way for the acquisition of Florida in 1819. A series of skirmishes and maneuvers between whites and Indians led to the passage by Congress of the Indian Removal Act of 1830 and a series of treaties with the Indians in effect confirming this. Members of the Five Civilized Nations, the Creek, Seminole, Chickasaw, Choctaw, and Cherokee, were forced by the Federal government to remove to the Oklahoma Territory; many died en route, but upward of 100,000 survived. Settlers from the eastern and upper South, as well as from the North, poured into the vacated territories in Georgia, Alabama, and Mississippi, took over Indian agricultural areas, cleared other land tree by tree, planted their crops, and built their homes and towns. In the South more than the North, the centers of population shifted from the Eastern Seaboard to the lands beyond the mountains and to the new Southwest. These were flush times.

Tumultuous as some of these events were, they were background and setting for, rather than formative influences on, the visual arts. Architects, painters, and craftsmen, North and South, were in touch with each other, sharing the same ideas, on the very eve of the war. In all too many cases the war interrupted or cut off these contacts and arrested artistic efforts.

The artistic forms and choices favored in the South paralleled and were similar to developments and changing moods in Europe and England. A fresh understanding of history, and new attitudes toward it, changing concepts of nature and a new appreciation of it, and the changes wrought by technology, the steam engine, the steamboat, the telegraph, the railroad, the development of the factory system, all affected the way people felt about the world in which they lived, and these affected the arts.

In the South the acquisition of new lands gave tremendous impetus to building. There was great opportunity for architects and craftsmen in the just-opened territories, and the works of architects and builders of this generation shaped the appearance of the man-made environment of much of the South, especially the Deep South, and have had a profound effect on the perception of that mysterious and complex entity, "the South," ever since. Certainly for this time in the South, architecture was queen of the arts, providing the outward form of the symbols of state, religion, and home. If men and women knew little or nothing of the visual arts, they still probably knew something of architecture and building.

Taste in Europe and America shifted from the more delicate neoclassical to the bolder, more austere Greek. The enthusiasm

Old Capitol, Frankfort, Kentucky, 1827–1833. Designed by Gideon Shryock.

for the Greek was partly inspired by a sharper perception of history, and therefore of the arts of successive historical periods. Threads of pessimism, such as the tragic aftermath of the French Revolution, colored political, literary, and social thought, creating a romantic nostalgia for these earlier times. Thus the Greek taste was embraced not only for its purity and clarity, or for its references to Greek democratic traditions, but because it suggested an earlier ideal and purer civilization. The art of the Middle Ages also became more precisely understood, and the religious and chivalric art of that period was taken up with enthusiasm, particularly for church architecture. Some Southerners were very much in step with these new literary and artistic

moods and shifts in taste. The only two early state capitols in the United States in the Gothic taste were built in the South—in Georgia and Louisiana. Though the handling was tentative, they nonetheless represented avant-garde choices and a willingness to experiment. Unknown architect-builders in Columbus, Mississippi, created five mansions in which basic plans for a columnar house were combined imaginatively with Gothic colonnettes and tracery in wood: a combination only to be found in the mid-nineteenth century in the Deep South. A new fashion for the Italianate was picked up with promptness in some quarters and skillfully adapted to the Southern setting. The verandas, balconies, and loggias of the Italianate began to replace the great classical porticoes of the Georgian, neoclassical, and Greek. Not much modification was required, for the new taste was handled in a conservative way, and practical matters, such as need for shade and ventilation, were not forgotten.

Painters who sought recognition often did not find it easy in the agrarian South, and some had a difficult time earning a living. The craft of portraiture nonetheless flourished, perhaps as never before, and men of skill sought and found customers in the small towns and cities widely scattered throughout the South. The bourgeois quality of much of this portraiture is a fairly reliable index of the values and status of the majority of the population and its leaders. The new art of photography spread across the South and the North within a few years after its introduction. There were serious attempts, not always successful or brought to completion, to make the particular qualities of the landscape and life of the South the themes of paintings. The number of individuals who became patrons of the arts was still relatively small.

The state capitals, with their capitol buildings as centerpieces, as well as some of the county seats, laid out so that the courthouses were given prominence, provided commercial and cultural centers of sorts, yet genuine cities were few. The communities where colleges and universities were situated were only beginning to nourish the arts. Still, a small but growing number of sculptors sought and found public patronage in the South.

As is so often true, styles in objects such as furniture and silver paralleled those in architecture. As in architecture, craft traditions were beginning to be modified by new technology and mechanization. The role of individual craftsmen in any given community or area was perhaps less important than it once had been; yet the era of handcraftsmanship was far from over. Town and city directories record surprisingly large numbers who plied their trades in places such as Baltimore, Louisville, Lexington, and New Orleans. Recent research has revealed a remarkable and distinctive Southern tradition in utilitarian pottery with alkaline glazes. This tradition may have been established by one man or by one family in western South Carolina. Its spread westward in the South parallels the major east-west spread of population that took place in the Deep South—from the Carolinas into Alabama, Mississippi, and Louisiana, and farther into Texas, a population movement that meant continuity of kinship and shared values between the older settlements and the newer ones of the interior. These ties helped to create unity within the South when the area launched its ill-starred attempt to secede.

Architecture

The building, left, that served as the legislative center for the state of Kentucky from 1830 to 1910 nestles at the base of spectacular hills at the edge of the small city of Frankfort. It was designed so that a visitor would catch a view of its pristine and elegant façade of six beautifully proportioned Ionic columns across a temple front as he descended into the valley. This Old Capitol at Frankfort was the first major work of the young Kentucky-born architect Gideon Shryock, and is the first of thirteen capitols in the United States in the Greek Revival taste. The façade is Greek Ionic at its most classic. In his own description of

the Capitol, which he wrote for a Philadelphia publication in 1833, Shryock described it with the precision of the specialist: "The front elevation presents a dexastyle portico of the Ionic order, the proportions of which are taken from the temple of Minerva Polias at Priene in Ionia." The façade is indeed a fine but simplified rendition of the Temple of Athena (Minerva) at Priene, built about 334 B.C., and includes the low steps, the well-formed torus-scotia-torus of the column bases, the deeply fluted columns, and the well-defined volutes of the Ionic capitals. Since Shryock traveled little farther than Philadelphia he would only have known of this most classic of Ionic temples from books or from his mentor in that city, William Strickland.

Once beyond the elegant temple front here, as in virtually all Greek Revival buildings, the architect of necessity had to create space suitable for the use—no one was building interiors for the worship of Greek gods and goddesses. Dignity, substance, and even drama can be imparted to halls of democracy by a skillful architect. Shryock achieved all of these in his well-proportioned rooms, and most especially in the spacious stair hall lighted from the dome overhead, below. The staircase is built within a cir-

Stair hall in Old Capitol.

University of Georgia Chapel, Athens, Georgia, 1832.

cular wall, or rotunda, and the two sides curve upward unsupported. Esthetically, it has the purity of line that was associated with the Greek taste, but its sinuous curves would never have been found within an ancient Greek temple. The combination of rotunda and dome had been used in the North Carolina statehouse where the statue of Washington was so proudly displayed. It was also used in the Pennsylvania Capitol at Harrisburg, which was built slightly earlier, at a time when young Shryock was in Philadelphia studying with Strickland. However, neither has the combination of rotunda and stair hall as designed by Shryock.

The Capitol was the pride of the region even before it was completed. The locals were not above superlatives. "When completed, it will be, though not the most costly, yet the most magnificent edifice which has been erected in the western world." They had come a long way. The first Kentucky legislature met in a two-story log building in Lexington in the summer of 1792. In December of the same year Frankfort was selected as the site of the capital. Between 1793 and the erection of Shryock's building the legislature met for a time in a log and weather-boarded structure, in two successive capitol buildings, both of which burned, and in a seminary, which also burned. Sessions were being held in the Methodist church when the building of a new capitol was authorized in 1827 and a premium of $150 offered for the chosen plan.

Gideon Shryock, son of a contractor and builder, learned the rudiments of his craft from his father. At the age of twenty-one it was decided he should go to Philadelphia to study with William Strickland, architect, engineer, and former pupil of Latrobe. During the years Shryock was there, Strickland was engaged in building the Second Bank of the United States. Here the latter adapted the austere Doric of the Parthenon to the commercial function of a bank—the interior is vaulted and well lighted, the room designed to suit the needs of the institution. Intimate knowledge of this and other buildings in and around Philadelphia, training in draftsmanship, a wider knowledge of architectural books, all helped to stretch the mind and experience of the Kentuckian. On his return he set up practice in Lexington, but moved to Frankfort when his plan won the commission for the new capitol.

Local stone was quarried from the nearby riverbanks, the gray limestone known as Kentucky marble. Local convicts did much of the stonecutting. The keeper of the penitentiary invented an ingenious eight-armed saw with sixteen blades, powered by steam, which was used for the initial blocking, then each piece was polished and precisely finished to measure. In his later description of the completed building Shryock described the interior of the dome as "finished with raised pannels and ornaments in stucco superbly executed, and produces that pleasing magic effect usual with such a vast concave in such a situation." The plasterwork (the ceilings in both the legislative chambers were and are richly ornamented with square sunk panels) was done by a black craftsman, Henry Mordecai. The whole was completed in two years.

The patrons who commissioned public buildings, such as capitols, academic structures, and churches, as well as hotels, market halls, and commercial buildings, often looked to their architects and builders for designs that would serve as symbols of their function and thus as landmarks or centerpieces of a street or a neighborhood. Shryock certainly succeeded in doing this for the Kentucky legislature.

When the Georgia committee, the Senatus Academianus, charged with the responsibility of founding a university for the state after the Revolution, finally decided on a site for their seat of the Muses, they named it Athens. At that time it was possibly the northernmost town in Georgia, adjacent to the Cherokee Nation. The charter for the University of Georgia is the oldest for a state university, and was granted by the legislature in 1785. The committee, however, did not meet until 1799, and it was not until 1801 that the beautiful and healthful site in the hills of the Piedmont, a site which Governor John Milledge gave to the state, was selected. Commencement exercises were held in 1804. The first buildings were in the late Georgian taste, and it was 1832 before a building in the style worthy of the name of the little college town was erected. Even the Demosthenian Hall, built in 1824 and home of a literary club, was still in the late Federal style, crisp and attractive though it is. In the 1830s the earliest buildings had become too small to accommodate the growing number of students, and the cry went up for a new chapel. In 1832 the new edifice, left, was completed at the cost of

$15,000. It is dignified and austere, with six Doric columns across its temple front. The proportions and details of the portico are based on that most perfect and best-known of all Greek temples, the Parthenon. The Trustees were satisfied that it was "apparently correct in the proportions . . . certainly elegant in its exterior appearance, and convenient in the interior." There is an appropriate pedantic correctness in the placement of the six columns of the portico, for the two end columns are placed closer together. This was done by the Greeks to make the spaces between the end columns of a peripteral temple (with columns all around), which were silhouetted against the light, appear equal to that of the others. In this case such placement was not really necessary since the front wall of the building extends beyond the front columns and there is no void. The chapel remains one of the handsomest and most impressive structures in the serene tree-lined old central quadrangle of the now-sprawling University of Georgia campus.

The circumstances that prompted the legislature of Georgia to build their capitol, following page, at Milledgeville in the Gothic taste are not clear. As elsewhere, there were steady pressures to move the legislative center westward and up-country, away from the Eastern Seaboard, as the population center shifted. Augusta had served as the temporary capital in 1786, then Louisville was founded to serve this function in 1794. Still considered too far east, a new town was laid out at Milledgeville in 1803. It was on a grid plan with broad, spacious streets and a central square of twenty acres for a statehouse. The legislative act of 1805 authorized the creation of a building to cost $60,000. By November 1807, the statehouse was sufficiently finished for the legislature to meet there.

The first phase of building was completed in 1811. Funds for the addition of a north wing were appropriated in 1828. Still further repairs and improvements of the south wing "to complete the symmetry and appearance of the whole building" were made in 1834 and 1835. Whether the earliest portion was Gothic in appearance is not certain. By 1829, however, the statehouse was described as standing "on an eminence, three-fourths of a mile from the river, exhibiting a tasteful appearance of Gothic architecture." (The present structure is a replica built after a fire in 1941.) The majority of buildings in the Gothic style in the early nineteenth century were churches, though Latrobe had built a bank in Philadelphia in the Gothic taste and Strickland a precociously Gothic Masonic Hall, completed in 1808. Romantic literary associations, such as the ideas inspired by Sir Walter Scott's novels, may have prompted the design. Certainly Scott's chivalric tales were immensely popular in the South at this time. The Gothic style, like the Greek, was seen as having a venerable history. Hence if chosen for a building design, an intent was to suggest the permanence and dignity achieved by such venerability, and to establish a connection with the long history of man's institutions. The original architects were a Mr. Smart and William D. Lane, but little is known of them or of those responsible for the 1828 enlargement. We do not know who among the legislators, architects, or builders decided to use the Gothic style.

It was a bold and imaginative decision, and showed a willingness to follow new tastes. To judge from the prints, the effect

was of flatness and crispness, with pointed windows and crenellations as symbols of the style. A number of early nineteenth-century Gothic revival buildings in this country and in England have a similar quality of "thinness," as if the Gothic is only skin deep, a surface application. (The floor plan of the Georgia Capitol, with two projecting wings, was based on an earlier tradition.) Though Gothic was increasingly felt to be "right" for churches, domestic cottages, villas, and colleges, the state or municipal building in the Gothic style never completely appealed to American tastes. Among the few contemporary comments on the Milledgeville Capitol, there was a noticeable lack of enthusiasm. An English visitor in the early 1830s, who saw Milledgeville on a hot day when he was suffering from a fever, described the State House as "a brick building, which some blockhead of an architect has recently thought proper to *Gothicize.* The accommodation within is plain, but sufficient." Another visitor to Milledgeville a decade later was more sympathetic. "When within five or six miles of Milledgeville, we approached the ridge of a hill, from whence a fine prospect of the town, and the rich valley in which it lies is to be had. . . . We had seen nothing in the South, indeed, so beautiful, as a landscape. . . . The town in its centre appeared to add greatly to its richness; the State House or Capi-

tol, the governor's residence, some few churches with spires, and a pretty cluster of white dwellings, surrounded by gardens, made up a charming picture." On closer examination the next day, however, the visitor found, "the Capitol, or State House, seemed to us less perfect in a near view than at a distance; it being a large white Gothic structure, in bad taste and heavy proportions, though forming a very striking object in the remote picture of Milledgeville." The only other state capitol in the Gothic taste in the United States before the Civil War was in Louisiana, built from 1847 to 1852. (In late 1835 the capitol in Jackson, Mississippi, was begun according to a Gothic design, but rejected by the legislature before the high basement was completed.) The example of Georgia did not set a trend. The little-known capitol is nonetheless important because its builders were venturesome, even avant-garde, in their choice.

Churches and statehouses were often built with towers and spires, punctuations to enhance the skyline of a town or city, symbols of the public role of church and state. In 1835 a different sort of noble-looking building was begun in New Orleans, whose silhouette became a familiar and prominent landmark until it burned in 1851. This was the St. Charles Hotel, page 221, in the American section of the city, crowned with a dome that was variously compared with that of St. Paul's in London, St. Peter's in Rome, and less accurately, with the Pantheon in Rome. The Swedish novelist Fredrika Bremer wrote: "I went on shore, and up to a magnificent building resembling the Pantheon at Rome, shining out white, not of marble, but of stucco." The Englishman J. S. Buckingham, who had obviously traveled extensively, waxed enthusiastic when he saw it in 1839–1840: "The St. Charles . . . is not only the largest and handsomest hotel in the United States, but, as it seemed to me, the largest and handsomest hotel in the world. At least I remember nothing equal to it in any country that I have visited. The City of London Tavern, the Albion, the Freemason's Hall, the London Coffee House . . . the Clarendon, and Long's Hotel, in London, are all inferiors to it, in size, cost and elegance. Neither Meurice's, nor the Hotel de Londres, nor the Hotel Rivoli, nor Hotel Wagram in Paris, can compare with it; and even the Astor House at New York, the Tremont in Boston, and the American Hotel at Buffalo, all fall short of the St. Charles at New Orleans."

This was not the first, or the last, hotel to be described in superlatives. It was nonetheless high praise. The New Orleans hotels of this era were among the finest.

The creation of the St. Charles Hotel grew out of the circumstances in New Orleans at that time, and of the particular backgrounds and skills of three architects. These architects helped to shape not only the appearance of New Orleans, but of Louisville, Mobile, Memphis, and Baton Rouge.

The 1830s and '40s were boom years in New Orleans. The annexation to the United States and, even more important, the introduction of steamboats after 1811, meant that New Orleans was, for a time, the great commercial center for the trade of goods for the whole Mississippi Valley. By 1840 the population was over 100,000 and the city rivaled Boston as the fourth largest city in the United States. They were surpassed only by New York, Philadelphia, and Baltimore. Cotton, corn, flour, sugar, molasses, pork, rice, rum, tobacco, and whiskey were transported down the river; many of these products were then transshipped to Europe and to other American ports. The value of the goods handled in the New Orleans port was probably exceeded only by the cities of London, Liverpool, and New York. During these flush times the city attracted a tremendous semitransient population, largely merchants who came to do business during the comfortable fall, winter, and spring seasons, but who left during the hot summer months when diseases frequently raged. It has been estimated that in 1835 there was a transient population of between 40,000 and 50,000 people.

It was this prosperity that inspired a group of Irish-American businessmen to form the Exchange Hotel Company for the building of a new and larger hotel. The *New Orleans Bee* of December 11, 1834, reported: "One hundred and fifty thousand dollars were yesterday subscribed for the purpose of erecting a hotel similar to that of John Jacob Astor's in New York." This is a significant reference, since it shows that from the beginning the promoters had a specific prototype in mind. New Orleans merchants saw themselves as friendly rivals of their confreres in New York and intended to match the accomplishments of the growing city on the Hudson. Some of their knowledge of the hotel being built in New York might have come from two young

architects who had moved south in October 1834, first doing business in Mobile, and then establishing themselves in New Orleans. These were James Gallier and Charles Dakin. Gallier was to become the architect of the St. Charles (Exchange) Hotel, though James Dakin, Charles's older brother, may also have had a role.

James Gallier, and Charles and James Dakin, were important and influential architects in the South in the 1830s and 1840s, although Charles Dakin died in 1839. All three came from New York, where their careers had been intertwined with those of Ithiel Town, Alexander Jackson Davis, and Minard Lafever during a rich and seminal period in the history of American architecture. Their histories demonstrate the close interconnections among the relatively few men who were professional architects at this time. They shared ideas and developed rivalries. There were close ties between New York and the South. James Dakin, and possibly also Gallier, had made important contributions to architecture and architectural ideas during their short New York careers.

James Dakin was born in New York State in 1806. His father died when he was thirteen, and his mother when he was nineteen. He seems to have learned the rudiments of carpentry and building from his guardian. By 1829 he was off to New York City to try his fortune.

In that same year, Ithiel Town, an established architect and engineer, formed a new partnership with the young and talented Alexander Jackson Davis. Town was a businessman, the possessor of a large and important architectural library; Davis, a talented draftsman. Their firm, Town and Davis, was to become one of the most important architectural establishments in the United States. Dakin was taken in as an apprentice, and in this environment matured rapidly as a designer and draftsman with a sound knowledge of construction. It has been shown that some of the important early buildings of the Town and Davis firm were the work of their young colleague. In fact, in May 1832 James Dakin was made a full member of the firm, which became Town, Davis, and Dakin. In this same year or before, Dakin had made contact with some New Orleans merchants and completed designs for them. Also, while in New York Dakin provided a number of the drawings and designs for Minard Lafever's 1833 *Modern Builder's Guide* and 1835 *Beauties of Modern Architecture.* These books were important in further disseminating information and specific details or models in the Greek Revival taste to builders and architects throughout the country.

In November 1833 James Dakin withdrew from Town and Davis and set up on his own. In that same year he employed his younger brother Charles as a draftsman. One of the finest products of the new firm was the exquisite design for the Bank of Louisville, done in 1834. Though the bank was long thought to be the work of Gideon Shryock, the original drawing, by Dakin, page 226, has now come to light. Shryock was the supervising architect during the latter part of the construction. The Louisville businessmen had apparently gone to New York to secure a design for their bank and selected James Dakin. He produced a pleasing scheme in which he made use of Greek motifs, patterned on no particular building. The bank has recently been restored for the use of the Actors Theatre in Louisville.

James Dakin thus seems to have had a good business in New York during the two years, 1833–1835, that he practiced on his own. Already some of his clients were from the South.

In April 1832 James Gallier, just a few months before his thirty-fourth birthday, arrived in New York on a ship called the *Louisiana*. Gallier had already had a varied career in the building trades and in architecture. Born in Ravensdale, Ireland, in 1798, he was apprenticed to his father, a builder, at the age of fourteen. When a depression hit in 1812–1815 he went to Dublin to learn architectural drawing. In 1816 he was in Liverpool and Manchester and helped to design a cotton mill. By 1822 he was in London and there was "clerk of the works" for the architect William Wilkins. For a period he and his brother were in business together, doing joiner's piecework for various builders. Again in 1826 he was with Wilkins. At this time he studied books on engineering, steam engines, and architecture. Through a friend who was a bookseller his "Knowledge of life and the ways of society became much enlarged." During these years in London he would not only have known Wilkins's work, but those of Nash, Soane, and others. Wilkins, with his design of Downing College, Cambridge, had in effect inaugurated the Greek Revival in England in 1806–1811. He had also designed a Gothic screen for King's College, Cambridge. But life must not have been easy for Gallier. He perceived that he "could never reckon upon any great success in London without the patronage of peo-

ple in high station; and as with such people I had no influence, I saw it as hopeless to expect much success in that direction." Then, filled with the hope that propelled generations of emigrants and "having heard that any person well acquainted with the practice of building, as well as having a fair Knowledge of architecture as art, could scarcely fail of success in the United States of America, I therefore came to the conclusion that *there* lay the proper field for my labours."

In New York Gallier obtained work in May 1832 with the firm of Town, Davis, and Dakin—meeting James Dakin for the first time. In 1833 Gallier was briefly a partner with Minard Lafever, and he, too, contributed at least one design to Lafever's books. Gallier's New York career has not yet been studied. We know he delivered a series of lectures on architecture. In these he showed himself familiar with the history of architecture as it was then known, taking his listeners through a course beginning with ancient Egyptian times, and with references to Baalbek, the Temple of Solomon, even something on the Chinese. As was typical for the 1830s, he expressed admiration for the Greeks to whom "we are indebted for the purest and best canons of architecture that the world has ever seen." He had done his homework well. He knew Serlio's work of the Renaissance as well as current literature, mentioning the ideas of the rationalist architectural critic Laugier. Another Gallier project was the publication of *The American Builder's General Price-Book and Estimator* in 1833, a

Floor plan of first floor of St. Charles Hotel. Historic New Orleans Collection.

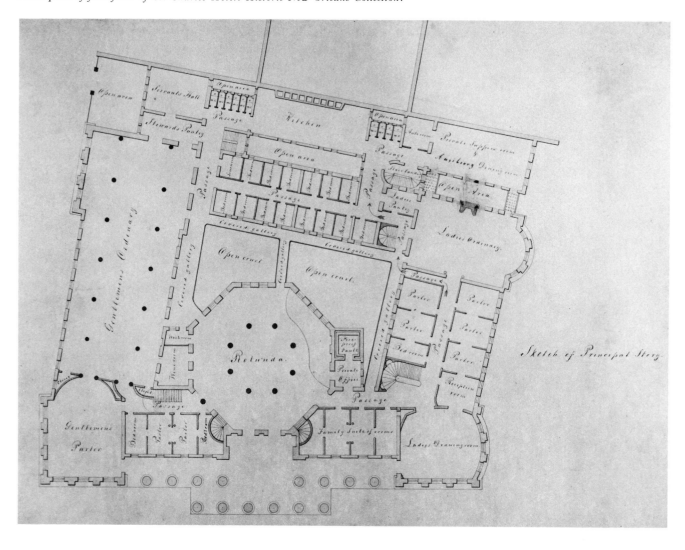

"St. Charles Exchange Hotel, New Orleans, La." Engraving. Designed by James Gallier and Charles Dakin, 1835–1838. Louisiana State Museum, New Orleans.

comprehensive guide to pricing, techniques, and measurements, concerning all aspects of the building trade—bricklaying, masonry, stonecutting, plastering, carpentry, joiners' and plumbers' work. From this it is clear that he knew something of the whole range of building practices. Both these endeavors helped to put his name before the public, but apparently little more. "It was then intimated to me by persons who had been to the South, that New Orleans would be a much better place for me to settle in than New York, if I could only bear the climate. . . ."

Gallier was correct in his decision. He and young Dakin, who had accompanied him south, quickly established a reputation in Mobile and New Orleans and soon had several important commissions in hand, including a colonnaded row house, an Episcopal church, and an arcaded public bath. In New Orleans their clients were primarily among the Americans. The rivalry between the older Creole community and the newer American sector was such that in 1836 the legislature agreed to dividing the city into three parts, or municipalities, each responsible for its own taxes, bond issues, and the like. The first was the "old" city where the French or Creoles lived; the second was the new district upriver from Canal Street which the newcomers, the Americans, were developing; the third was downriver, again largely Creole. Once a year a general council met, coordinating certain

activities. This uneasy coexistence lasted until 1852 when they were reunited.

The Irish-American merchants who were eager to build a hotel in their municipality found in Gallier and the younger Dakin men who could fulfill their ambitions. Plans were already underway when James Dakin came to New Orleans in November 1835, no doubt attracted by the news from his brother of the good business prospects. For a very brief time James Dakin joined the partnership of Gallier and Dakin, but then they decided that Gallier would go his own way, and the two brothers would form their own firm, Dakin and Dakin, which they did on December 24, 1835.

Gallier retained the contract for the St. Charles Hotel, located on the street by that name—increasingly called just that rather than St. Charles Exchange Hotel. There is strong evidence to suggest that James Dakin, during his few weeks in partnership with Gallier, was responsible for an "improved" version of the design, which might have included the colonnaded dome.

The finished product, throughout its existence, was described by all who saw it as impressive to behold. It was, it seems, deliberately planned to be bigger and better than its predecessors, in the exuberant vein that was to characterize much high Victorian design. Raised on a granite basement, it boasted a colonnaded front with projecting portico of Corinthian columns and a dome raised on a drum surrounded by a circular colonnade. Visitors were obviously given the dimensions, which they could reel off: the front, 235 feet; the depth, 195; the height to cornice, 75 feet; to the top, 185 feet. There were about 350 rooms. Some said it could accommodate 800 boarders. The gentlemen's dining room, with two ranges of Corinthian columns, could seat 500, etc. It was designed to serve a multitude of purposes. A visitor in 1844 described the entire hotel as "a small world of itself—a village."

On the ground floor there was a series of shops, facing onto three streets (it occupied virtually the whole of a city block). The inevitable cigars and newspapers were sold in cubicles near the vestibule where people came and went. The smaller entrance on the side was for ladies only. A washroom, drying room, and ironing room were among the service facilities. Public baths for both ladies and gentlemen were provided. But the center of activity from morn till night at this street level was the great barroom. Everybody could be seen here. Henry B. Whipple, the future Episcopal Bishop of Minnesota, took note of the panorama of people and activity: "From the dandy, with mustache peculiarly adapted to eating bean soup, up to the man of mind on whose brow is stamped nobility. Gamblers too may here & there be seen, men whose baggage is said to be 'a pack of cards, a bowie knife and dirty shirt.' This is a fashionable drinking depot of the American part of the city. At 11 o'clock each day a lunch is set on the table (in spacious bar room) of meats of all kinds, of fish, flesh and fowl and for a dime which buys your drink you can eat what you please. Thousands daily visit this and other similar establishments and through this corrupt fashion the temptation to drink is fearfully great. I think I saw over 500 persons in and about the St. Charles Bar Room Today. You can buy a lemonade if you choose and eat as well as those who drink strong drinks, but such are indeed scarce. The arrangements and appointments of this hotel are I think superior to anything I have ever seen. Far beyond any of the New York hotels. And the price and expense is also greater."

Here and in other great barrooms of the city all manner of business was conducted; cargoes of sugar, cotton, tobacco, and corn changed hands. The original name of the hotel was the Exchange and one of its functions was as a great commercial exchange.

On the principal floor life was less raffish. Here, as can be seen from the floor plan, page 220, was the grand entrance into the rotunda with its spiral staircase, drawing rooms, and a series of parlors. The rotunda opened onto an open and airy courtyard. The large dining room was for gentlemen, the smaller one reserved for ladies—men could enter here only if accompanying their families. The kitchen was also on this floor. The dining rooms served all "the luxuries of a tropical climate." The proprietors were "polite and attentive to their guests." Special dinners, social and political, were held here. Among those who had annual banquets were firemen's societies and the New England Society. Weekly soirees, with music, dancing, and elegant suppers, were held in the rotunda.

The upper floors were taken up with rooms. Here the numer-

ous businessmen who boarded there during the three-to-five-month winter business season stayed, some with their families, some without. Planters from the region made up another large portion of the visitors, and the remainder were more transient businessmen and travelers. Some of the latter were writers and journalists, often bent on describing life in the slave states. Their cogent comments are among the best records we have of this and other places. Fredrika Bremer was one who didn't like her room, which was cold, nor the "immense" bed, nor walking up three flights, nor the price—three dollars a day—nor eating in the great saloon where meals were served "at hours that did not suit me." Buckingham also found the style of living in the New Orleans hotels "more expensive than in the North; the cost being nearly double. Though they are well provided with furniture, table service and attendants, they are all too large for comfort, and adapted only to the American mode of living, which it is difficult to render agreeable to those who have been accustomed to the quiet privacy and superior comfort of private life in England."

The crown of the St. Charles was the dome raised on a colonnaded drum and topped by a lantern. Buckingham effectively described the inner core of the building: "The center of the whole pile is occupied by a series of circular platforms, or stories, each forming a separate rotunda, surrounded with columns at their outer diameter; and up through this ascends a spiral staircase, which extends to the very top of the building, from whence a commanding view of the city and the river may be enjoyed."

The plan of the hotel was based not directly on the Astor Hotel in New York, which was still being built when the St. Charles was going up, but rather on the slightly earlier Hotel Tremont in Boston (1829–1830), both by Isaiah Rogers. In its variety of services and accommodations the Tremont was one of the first great modern hotels in the United States. By a fortuitous circumstance the Tremont was on a trapezoidal piece of land, with angling side streets, similar to the plot on which the St. Charles was to be built. Rogers had used curved ends to the front section to disguise the transition to the angled street as Gallier was to do. In essence, Gallier flipped the design over, putting the large men's dining room on the left rather than the right. The Tremont also had a rotunda. Gallier, having been in New York, may have met the architect Isaiah Rogers, or even have visited Boston. However, this need not have been necessary because, also fortuitously, William H. Eliot had published *A Description of Tremont House in Boston* in 1830, a neat little booklet giving the plans of each floor and a series of diagrams of details.

In scale and outward appearance, the St. Charles was bigger and grander. The front of the Tremont was 160 feet long while the St. Charles was 285 feet. The Tremont had a Doric portico of four columns; Gallier used fourteen Corinthian columns for his colonnaded porch and projecting portico. The Tremont had a low dome, the St. Charles its splendid colonnaded drum and dome.

The external appearance of the St. Charles, though graced with Greek Corinthian columns, was somehow too grand, and the dome too dominant, to suggest anything but the loosest adherence to the austere Greek taste. Rather, it is in the tradition of the Italian Renaissance and its ramifications. Both Gallier and the Dakins had a good store of building images in their heads when the design was created. In Gallier's own experience Wilkins's London University, where the central section consisted of temple front on a high basement, and which was topped with a high dome, might have been a general precedent. Another obvious prototype for a great dome on a drum surrounded by columns was that of St. Paul's in London, which dominated the skyline of the old City of London in Gallier's day. Also, in the years while Dakin and Gallier were in New York, the firm of Town, Davis, and Dakin, and Dakin while on his own, did several designs which included various combinations of raised domes and porticoes. (In fact, discreet low domes had been combined with Greek temple forms since the introduction of the revival style, often to enhance the interior space and, with the inclusion of a small lantern or cupola, to provide better lighting.) One of these was the Indiana Capitol, 1831–1835, another was

Dakin's 1833 design for a hotel on Long Island, and another Dakin's 1835 design for the New York House of Detention. If, as at least one contemporary guidebook recorded, the St. Charles dome was by Dakin (presumably James), then it is easy to see how he might have evolved it. The massing and relationship of dome, colonnade, portico, and side projections were far more successful in the St. Charles scheme than in any of the examples just mentioned. This was somehow achieved thanks to the combined skills and ideas, perhaps even the clash of minds, among Gallier, the Dakins, and their patrons.

Another felicitous touch in the design of the St. Charles Hotel was the introduction of the two rounded projections on the side elevations. These helped to disguise the odd angle of the corner. On the side seen on page 221, they also gave definition to the special ladies' entrance, and seem to have given a softer, more feminine appearance to that side of the building. While the

Verandah Hotel, New Orleans, Louisiana, 1836. Designed by James and Charles Dakin. Engraving from L'ILLUSTRATION, *August 12, 1848.*

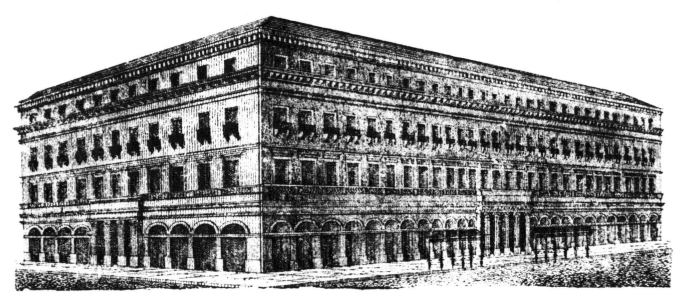

St. Louis Hotel, or St. Louis Exchange, New Orleans, Louisiana, 1835–1839.
Designed by J. N. B. D. De Pouilly and J. Isadore De Pouilly. Engraving from Pitts and Clark,
NEW ORLEANS DIRECTORY FOR 1842. *Louisiana State University Library, Baton Rouge.*

dome seems related to other Dakin designs, the skillful use of curved bays seems to relate to later examples of Gallier's work. The introduction of the curvilinear forms harmonized with the use of the Corinthian order in the columns and pilasters. That order was associated with several of the few known ancient Greek round or curved buildings; hence the combination, through a very free interpretation of Greek forms, was historically logical as well as esthetically pleasing.

Virtually everyone who saw this hotel admired it and praised it. It seems to have been successful both as a design and as a functioning building. Here life throbbed with vitality. Within its

walls appropriate settings for a wide variety of human activities were provided. It was right for its time and place. Tragically, on January 18, 1851, it burned. A second, and later a third, St. Charles was erected on the site. An office building is now replacing these. The first St. Charles spanned the years of New Orleans's headiest boom times. By 1851, though the city was still prospering, the railroads were already changing the pattern of transportation, so that the importance of the great river port in relation to the whole center of the nation was already beginning to diminish.

The St. Charles was but one of three fine hotels that graced

Orleans Cotton Press, New Orleans, Louisiana, 1833–1835. Designed by
Charles F. Zimpel. Engraving from Pitts and Clark, NEW ORLEANS DIRECTORY
FOR 1842. *Louisiana State University Library, Baton Rouge.*

New Orleans at this time. There was a quarrel among the sponsors of the St. Charles only shortly after it opened—two men of Irish and English descent clashed. As a result, the English-born Richard O. Pritchard determined to build his own hotel, and the Dakin brothers received the commission for a building that went up on a site diagonally across the street. Simple and discreet in appearance, the new Verandah Hotel (1836–1839), page 223, was a compact five-story structure. The distinguishing feature, from which the hotel received its name, was the canopied veranda or balcony projecting from the second floor and supported by iron columns. This balcony covered the sidewalk completely. Smaller iron balconies were already familiar to New Orleans, as were arcades, such as those on the Cabildo and Presbytere on Jackson Square. The idea of a walkway at ground level with gallery above was also familiar from plantation-house architecture. Here, using iron as the material, these concepts were pleasingly combined.

The canopied iron balconies extending over the sidewalk on the Verandah Hotel may have been the first in New Orleans. Later in the 1850s, such balconies became extremely fashionable; some were placed on new buildings, others added to older structures. To many people today, they are the very symbol of the street vistas of New Orleans, and they provide welcome shelter in a city where it is often hot or raining.

The dining room of the Verandah was much admired for its three elliptical domes from which chandeliers hung. Later, the two hotels were run by the same management and complemented each other. In 1855 the Verandah, too, went up in flames.

The third grand New Orleans hotel of this era was the St. Louis (1835–1839), upper left. It was the rival and counterpart of the St. Charles for the Creole, or French, part of the city. Its sponsors were Creole merchants, and its architects the French-born J. N. B. D. de Pouilly and his brother, J. Isadore. Located among the narrow built-up streets of the old quarter, the architects decided upon a discreet exterior and an inward-turning design. On three sides it was composed of a series of regular, arched granite openings, giving unity to a variety of areas and functions within. This series of arched openings—doors and windows—may have been based on the Rue de Rivoli in Paris. Though there was no open street arcade as there, much the same street vista was created. There were local precedents as well. The City Hotel, a slightly earlier hotel in New Orleans, had an arched arcade along the street façade, as did several of the marketplaces in New Orleans, and the older Cabildo and Presbytere. A relatively flat portico on St. Louis Street defined the entrance.

The interior of the St. Louis was made up of several component parts. From the beginning it was conceived of as both a city exchange and a hotel, and in fact it was built in successive phases. The glory of the exchange portion was a huge, domed rotunda that could not be seen from the street, with a gallery at the twenty-foot level; its entrepreneurs claimed that "no other public room in the country" could exceed it in grandeur and magnificence. The rotunda area was never used for a "disgusting cabaret" (a reference to the St. Charles), but for business only. Here auctions were held, often several going on at one time. To a modern eye, and to visitors' eyes, these sometimes seemed incongruous—with sales of painting, real estate, and slaves taking place simultaneously.

One visitor, seeing the rotunda no doubt in a quieter moment, felt that "the dreamy softness of the light as it falls on the mosaic pavement below makes it almost appear to be a scene of enchantment."

The other parts of the building included the hotel itself, with accommodations for 200 people, a large ballroom, dining room, kitchens, and baths. Discreet street entrances opened onto a galleried courtyard, very much in the tradition of French domestic architecture. Within the building a bank, essentially separate,

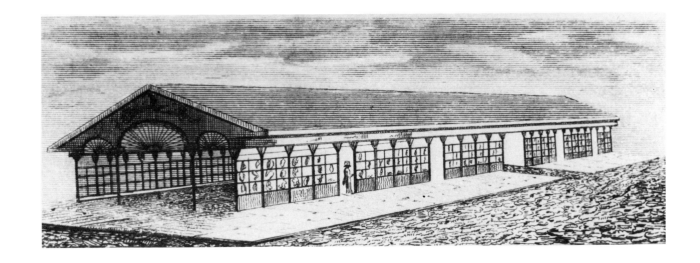

Poydras Street Market, New Orleans, Louisiana, c. 1838. Designed by F. Wilkinson. Engraving from Gibson's GUIDE AND DIRECTORY OF THE STATE OF LOUISIANA AND THE CITIES OF NEW ORLEANS AND LAFAYETTE, *New Orleans, 1838. Louisiana Collection, Howard-Tilton Library, Tulane University, New Orleans, Louisiana.*

James Dakin. "Bank of Louisville." 1834. Architectural rendering.
New Orleans Public Library.

and shops facing on to the uniform arcade were included. This complex burned in little over a year after it was completed but was immediately rebuilt, the dome even more beautifully decorated. The hotel survived into the twentieth century, becoming virtually derelict in the latter years of the nineteenth. A hurricane in 1915 served to further damage it, and it was demolished thereafter. A small section of the old wall has been incorporated into a modern hotel on the site.

Gallier, James Dakin, and J. N. B. D. de Pouilly each built other buildings in the city and in the region. Their designs give dignity and unity to public and private buildings alike; they provided models and helped to set a standard for others. Gallier was active until 1849 or so, when he turned over his business to his son, James, Jr. The senior Gallier spent long periods traveling abroad in his later years. Dakin was active in New Orleans and the region until his death in 1852. His apprentice and student, Henry Howard, was to be as productive as his mentor had been. The buildings of J. N. B. D. de Pouilly often had a subtle Gallic

quality; his productive life ended in 1875. Dakin and Gallier maintained close business and social ties with professional friends and acquaintances in New York and Philadelphia. Dakin was a founding member of the American Institution of Architects, the first professional organization of architects founded in the United States in 1837, and the forerunner of the American Institute of Architects.

The Gayoso House Hotel in Memphis, from the drawing board of James Dakin, was an elegant showplace of that city from 1842, when it was built, to July 4, 1899, when it, too, was consumed by flames. In Mobile, the United States, by Dakin and Dakin, was yet another hotel praised by Buckingham for its impressive appearance and variety of services. Elsewhere in the South new hotels were built. In 1839 the colonnaded Charleston Hotel, designed by Charles F. Reinhardt, was completed, and in Richmond the Planters' Hotel, in the Greek taste as well, was finished.

But hotels were only one of several kinds of commercial and

public buildings being erected in the growing cities of the Deep South such as New Orleans and Mobile. A sheltered arcaded walkway was used to enhance the front of one of the largest and most important commercial-industrial buildings in New Orleans of this era, the large Orleans Cotton Press, page 224, located close to the river. The design, with its central accented portion and two pedimented end units, owes something to Palladian tradition, adapted to a long street vista. It is a surprisingly esthetic design for what must have been large functional spaces on the inside. The man responsible was Charles F. Zimpel, a surveyor and builder. The Press was built between 1833 and 1835, and was 632 feet in length by 308 in breadth. It was described in the ever-expansive language of the day as "by far the largest of the kind in the world."

The Cotton Press was an integral part of the intense commercial activity of the city during the busy fall and winter season. The first of the annual cotton crop began to arrive from the hinterland in mid-August. The peak of the season was from December to March, when the waterfront was thick with steamboats, and cotton bales were piled up on the levee. There was a well-understood system of marking the bales as they arrived, then loading them in piles on the wharves, and taking them by dray to the great presses (the Orleans Cotton Press was one of several), where the bales were placed in a large steam press and reduced in size by approximately half. At the same time the cotton was classified, reweighed, and shipmarked. All of this was part of the intricate financial and mercantile transfer of property from planter, through commission merchant, to cotton broker (who handled the sales), to the next buyers. The bales were then transshipped to the North Atlantic states and abroad, especially to Liverpool in England, but also to France. Most of the shipments abroad in fact went via New York. (Among New York merchants involved in shipping out of New Orleans were Cornelius "Commodore" Vanderbilt and Charles Morgan, founder of the Morgan Line, which long plied the New Orleans–New York route.)

Still another commercial type of building in New Orleans that caught visitors' eyes, because of its appearance and because of the vibrant life, was the marketplace. Here, too, there was a tradition of arcaded walkways extending along two sides of long, low, shedlike buildings. In 1838 the newest of these, the Poydras Street Market, page 225, had pillars, or slim columns, of iron. Originally the plans had been to have an iron frame for the roof, and roofing of zinc, but delays in obtaining iron prevented this (perhaps mercifully, since the iron would have made the interior beneath incredibly hot at times), so that a wooden roof frame and slates were used. Iron was then still a relatively new building material. One of the advantages was that, with its thinner members, more light could be admitted, and it was becoming a favored material for conservatories and market and train sheds. The Poydras Market was one of the largest in the city. It extended 402 feet in length and was 42 feet wide. An elliptical center arch, and two side arches, provided esthetic nicety. The designer was F. Wilkinson, who was serving as Surveyor of the Second Municipality at this time.

It was the variety and vitality of life in the marketplaces of New Orleans which attracted and bedazzled visitors as much as the scale and quality of the buildings, which were kept clean and attractive: "The attraction is in the specimens of human kind exhibited here daily as buyers and sellers. All kinds of bipeds, fat and lean, tall and short, black and white, and all shades and sizes intermediate. The songs of the niggers, the vociferations of the street sellers, the appeals of fat market women and pretty quadroons to buy, buy: . . . The stalls grown with vegetables of all descriptions. . . . Every kind of eatable that a tropical climate will give you and money buy is here temptingly spread out before you. Game of all kinds, venison, woodcock, pheasant, snipe, plover, &c. Fish, flesh and fowl can be had in any quantity and you can see almost any kind of human specimens you may desire. . . . Shrill & bass voices, modesty and coarseness. Beauty and deformity. Vice and virtue, honesty and crime come in strange contiguity at a market scene in New Orleans."

The markets were busy every day of the week, but most especially on Sunday, a fact that disturbed more than one visitor.

All too many of the major public buildings of the 1830s and 1840s in the South have been lost to fires and other ravages of time. An excellent surviving example is the Government Street Presbyterian Church in Mobile, following page. The use of columns *in antis* here was a variation of the Greek temple theme developed in the Town and Davis office in New York at the time that James Dakin, then James Gallier and Charles Dakin, came on the scene. There is the effect and feeling of a Greek temple, yet the means are considerably simpler. Two superbly executed Ionic columns and the plain pilasters, or "pilastrades" as they seem to have been called, give the impression of a more fully developed peripteral temple. Sobriety, chastity, purity, and dignity are all words that come to mind as one sees this austere and well-proportioned structure. Originally there was also a steeple; it was blown down in 1852.

The interior, following page, which has survived with little modification, is, if anything, more successful. The services of Presbyterian worship are well served by this carefully detailed interior that is impressive yet not ostentatious. The open inside space is well lit and spacious. Every aspect of the service can be seen and heard from anywhere in the room. The focal point is the wall behind the pulpit, where the impression of a great temple front on a raised platform has been created. The sides of this front, or gate, are battered in the Egyptian fashion, similar to James Dakin's design for the Louisville bank, upper left. For the bank, Dakin used Greek motifs, although it was not modeled after a specific building, and the *in antis* paired columns are also set within slanted or slightly battered walls—the lines of the latter are derived from Egyptian pylons or gates to funerary temples. The cornice or cresting, used rather than a pediment, is topped by a fan-shaped interpretation of the Greek anthemion, surmounted on scrolls. The whole has all the qualities associated with the Greek: dignity, clarity, simplicity, and harmony of proportion. In 1841 the Philadelphia architect Thomas Ustick Walter was to say, "If our architects would oftener *think* as the Greeks thought, than to *do* as the Greeks did, our columnar architecture would possess a higher degree of originality." This Dakin achieved in what is one of the least archaeological, yet still one of the most "Greek" of designs. In the church, the front or gate, is capped with a row of anthemia similar to those on the

*Government Street Presbyterian Church,
Mobile, Alabama, 1836–1837. Designed
by James Gallier and Charles Dakin,
and erected by Charles Dakin.*

*Interior of Government Street Presbyterian Church.
Possibly designed by James and Charles Dakin,
built by Charles Dakin.*

ancient Choragic Monument of Lysicrates in Athens. Four Corinthian columns form a screen within this and support the entablature above. On the walls, the simple and well-modulated moldings of the entablaturelike cornice provide the transition to the deeply coffered ceiling. Details, such as the Greek fret along the face of the galleries, are close to those in Lafever's *Beauties of Modern Architecture;* the capitals of the Corinthian columns supporting the galleries are based on those of the Tower of the Winds.

J. S. Buckingham, who was one of the best architectural critics among the traveling journalists, found high praise for the interior when he visited Mobile in March 1839: "Of churches, the Presbyterian is the largest and most beautiful. Its exterior is not in the best taste, but its interior is unsurpassed in chasteness of style and elegance of decoration in the United States. There is a singular, but at the same time very happy union of Egyptian and Greek, in the elevated platform, answering the purpose of the pulpit; and the semi-Theban and semi-Corinthian portico, which seems to rise behind the platform, with the rich diagonally-indented ceiling, and luxurious sofa-like pews, make this interior altogether the most strikingly beautiful I ever remember."

It is noteworthy that he described the entire raised platform as "answering the purpose of the pulpit." The Word was given a superb setting here.

Gallier and (Charles) Dakin received the commission for the Government Street Presbyterian Church during 1834–1835, their first year in the South. When James Dakin came in late 1835, and when the Gallier and Dakin partnership was dissolved and the new Dakin and Dakin firm established, the latter took over its completion. Charles Dakin was in charge and lived in Mobile, while, as we have seen, James located in New Orleans. A builder, Thomas James, was chief bricklayer and contractor. It is hard to sort out the design contributions of James Gallier, James Dakin, and Charles Dakin, but the evidence here points strongly to Gallier and Dakin as designers of the exterior and Dakin and Dakin of the interior. The detailing of the latter especially relates to other designs of James Dakin. Charles Dakin, the contractor Thomas James, and the workmen obviously performed their responsibilities with great skill. Some of the "joiners work" was shipped in from New York.

A member of the congregation who seems to have had a major role in the commissioning of the church was Henry Hitchcock; he and J. E. Collins are known to have been members of the building committee, and in an advertisement for materials and workmen those interested were directed to the offices of the Mobile Steam Cotton Press Company, an establishment owned by Hitchcock. He was also the prime mover behind the building of the Barton Academy, which still stands, and of the former United States, or Government Street Hotel, the first designed by Gallier and Dakin and erected by Charles Dakin, the other by Dakin and Dakin. The latter architects also did a number of stores in Mobile as well as cotton press buildings for Hitchcock. All of these and other buildings were built or contracted for in the boom years of 1835–1837. Mobile, like New Orleans, was growing rich in the shipment of cotton and other goods. These were drawn from the fertile lands bordering on the Tombigbee, Black Warrior, and Alabama rivers. The panic of 1837 slowed, then virtually stopped, all building activity. By 1839, when the effects of the panic were still being felt, the Dakins' friend and best client, Hitchcock, died in a yellow fever epidemic that swept the city that summer. In October of the same year two great fires swept through downtown Mobile, destroying many of its finest buildings.

One of the most famous of all public buildings in the South, Tennessee's State Capitol, following page, was built after the region had recovered from the panic and depression years of the late 1830s. It was also one of the last state capitols to be built in the Greek taste, and is surely one of the finest. Dramatically situated on a hill above Nashville overlooking the city and the Cumberland River, site and building call to mind the Acropolis in Athens. William Strickland provided the design for "an Athenian building," but it was a relatively anonymous government committee which decided on the effective and imposing site.

From 1796, when Tennessee became the sixteenth state, to 1843, the legislature met at times in Knoxville, Kingston, Nashville, and Murfreesboro. The competition among these towns was resolved in October 1843; it was decided to locate permanently in Nashville. A Board of Commissioners selected and bought four acres of Campbell's Hill at the end of the same year. The act authorizing the building stated that the commissioners should "superintend the construction of the State house . . . direct the labor of the Penitentiary to the erection of same, and thereby save the people of the State from taxation." No official competition for a design was authorized or held. James H. Dakin of New Orleans, Gideon Shryock of Kentucky, and Adolphus Heiman of Nashville either inquired about the specifications or submitted plans. The commissioners appear to have moved with caution. They made inquiries among acquaintances in Northern and Eastern states, and purchased a set of plans for the newly built Capitol in Raleigh. By October 1845, a year after the decision to locate in Nashville was made, they decided to invite Strickland, whose reputation was such "That while on occasions he had displayed the utmost good taste in the buildings erected by him, he never sacrificed solidarity for show—the useful, for the merely ornamental; and that his estimates of cost were to be implicitly relied on." It was an opportune moment for Strickland, who had had few commissions following the 1837 depression. The specifications he submitted in May 1845 were clear and precise as to materials, measurements, and design, and his plans were approved in October of that year. "The architecture of the building is to consist of a Doric basement, four Ionic Porticos, two of eight and two of six columns four feet in diameter, surmounted by a Corinthian Tower in the center of the roof, the whole height of which is to be 170 feet from the summit of the site. The Porticos are after the order of the Erechtheum, and the tower from the choragic monument of Lysicrates of Athens." The basic material was to be limestone secured from near Nashville, the marble from east Tennessee. The rafters of the roof, the window frames, and sashes were to be of cast iron, the roof covered with sheet copper, and the floors flagged with stone, "so as to be thoroughly fireproof in all of its various compartments."

Strickland's choice of the Erechtheum as a model was astute. Situated on the Acropolis, it was fully described in Stuart and Revett's *Antiquities of Athens* of 1762. Of all the Greek temples

Capitol of Tennessee, Nashville, 1845–1859. Designed by William Strickland.

this is the most irregular in its massing, with its two side porticoes projecting at uneven levels. Strickland did not copy this exactly, yet by giving his legislative temple greater irregularity than one based on the "purer" Parthenon would have had, he was responding in a subtle way to the new feeling for the picturesque.

The tall tower, the top portion of which is an enlarged version of the Choragic Monument of Lysicrates, contributes to this romantic and picturesque effect. We have forgotten that from the Middle Ages well into the nineteenth century this unusual Greek monument was generally known as the "Lantern of Demosthenes," or "Candlestick of Demosthenes," and therefore was associated in the minds of those knowledgeable about architecture with the great orator, statesman, and defender of Athenian political freedom. Thus it is singularly appropriate as the tower of a capitol building of a federated state where lawyers, orators, and statesmen flourished. This association persisted among educated men, almost as if they preferred it. Strickland's mentor, Latrobe, writing in 1807, described the "Lanthorn of Demosthenes" as "than which nothing of the kind can be more beautiful." Jefferson, at some point, probably around 1799, had once suggested that the monument to George Washington be based on the "Lanthorn of Demosthenes," and recalled this proposal in a letter he wrote in his old age to his architect friend Robert Mills. The newly built second State Capitol at Raleigh, North Carolina, plans of which (by Town and Davis) the Tennessee Commissioners had secured, had a dome topped by a short cupola. In describing the latter the architect on the spot, David Paton, wrote, "Its dome is decorated at the top with a similar ornament to that of the Choragic Monument of Lysicrates, commonly called the Lanthorn of Demosthenes." The version of the monument as used on the Tennessee Capitol was on a larger scale, and was visible from a great distance, placed as it was on the great rusticated stone base.

The Capitol in Nashville was a major undertaking and the work progressed slowly. Strickland had promised the Tennessee orators that the building would be ready for occupancy by the fall of 1853, and though still incomplete, it was ready for use. Strickland lived long enough to hear the praises of the speaker of the Senate at the opening session, and to hear complaints about the continuing high costs. Guided by a sense of history, and pride in his accomplishment, Strickland requested that in the event of his death his remains be buried within the walls, a request immediately granted by the General Assembly despite their complaints, because they wished to honor "his genius in erecting so grand a work." Six short weeks later he collapsed on the post office steps and died early the next day. As planned, his remains were placed in a vault he had had cut in the east wall of the north basement portico.

Others carried on the work. For a year or so Strickland's son, Francis, was in charge. Among the commissioners Samuel D. Morgan, a wealthy Nashville merchant, was a driving force. He subsequently appointed H. M. Akeroyed as draftsman. It was Morgan apparently who directed that the interior of the library, right, be finished with cast-iron decoration in imitation of the library of Sir Walter Scott at Abbotsford. It is a fanciful, vaguely medieval, confection of iron lace utterly in contrast to the austere treatment given to the interiors by Strickland. Morgan's reason for the choice of cast iron was ostensibly practical, for he decreed that in "fitting up this apartment no materials whatever but iron will be used thus securing against the possibility of danger from fire the valuable works it is destined to contain." The choice of a room approximately replicating the galleried study of Sir Walter was sheer romanticism, fortunately also practical and fireproof. It is perhaps relevant that the plans of the North Carolina State House stated that the library there was to be in "the florid Gothic style." The citizens of Tennessee saw to it that their own regional and national heroes were honored in this library. In the center of each section of the balustrade there is a small rondel in which the head of a figure is shown in bronze against a black background. Portrayed are literary figures, well-known states-

men, and an even-handed selection of distinguished Tennesseans, an unusual mixture of notables not usually found in the same company, yet an index of those admired by the members of the Tennessee Historical Society (who did the selecting) around 1855. Included are, in sequence, Shakespeare, Joseph Addison, Dante, Ephraim H. Foster (Tennessee lawyer and U.S. Senator), Sir Walter Scott, Lord Byron, George Washington, Benjamin Franklin, Thomas Jefferson, Patrick Henry, Andrew Jackson, Daniel Webster, Henry Clay, John Milton, James K. Polk, Washington Irving, William Hickling Prescott, Felix Grundy

Interior of Library, Capitol of Tennessee, installed 1854–1859.

(skilled criminal lawyer and U.S. Senator from Tennessee), William Carroll (a governor of Tennessee), Hugh Lawson White (jurist and U.S. Senator from Tennessee), Joseph Story (distinguished New England jurist and Justice of the Supreme Court), John Bell (Tennessee Congressman and Senator), and John C. Calhoun. All of the ironwork was done by the firm of Wood and Perot of Philadelphia, who reported that they had employed a skilled German artist.

In the ceiling paintings, locally famous Tennesseans, such as the presidents of the fledgling institutions of learning, the University of Nashville, Cumberland College, and East Tennessee College, were honored alongside several Americans of national repute. The latter included the historian William H. Prescott and the poet Henry Wadsworth Longfellow. These were frescoed by two artists recently come to Tennessee from Germany, Theodore and John Wolfe Schleicher. Entering the lavishly decorated library, one is meant to feel oneself in the company of those distinguished in the world of learning and accomplishment, a world to which, the designers felt, Tennesseans had contributed and shared.

The massive chandelier of bronze and brass is decorated with twining leaves and reproductions of Tennessee flowers. This, too, came from Philadelphia, made by the firm of Cornelius and Baker. At the time it was described as a "specimen of the highest advancement of the art of designing in metal yet produced in this country."

The Tennessee Capitol was fully completed in 1859, when the last stone was set in the terrace. It was fitting that the body of Samuel D. Morgan, who had guided the building of the Capitol to completion, was also interred in the walls of this memorable structure.

The years between the building of the state capitols of Kentucky and Tennessee roughly bracket the period when the Greek taste was most popular in the United States and in Europe. The archaeological discoveries of the second half of the eighteenth century and publications such as Stuart and Revett's *Antiquities of Athens* provided the groundwork. The monuments of the ancient Greeks began to seem "purer," finer, more chaste, austere, and "correct" than the classicism seen in the buildings and monuments of ancient Rome or the Renaissance. Further impetus for the love of things Greek was given by the struggle for independence of modern Greece against the Turks, a struggle that began in 1821 and did not end until 1833, a struggle that caught the imagination of the freedom-loving throughout Europe and America. Lord Byron died on Greek soil, where he had gone in a melodramatic effort to participate in the revolution. The French painter Delacroix dramatized it in his *Massacre at Chios*. In America there was a natural identification with the aspirations of the Greeks. During Lafayette's 1824–1825 tour many a toast was drunk to the patriots of Greece, or to Greece, "birthplace of the arts and science," whose "sons have shown themselves the legitimate descendants of those who fought at Marathon and Thermopylae." Thus the Greek taste struck a responsive chord in the new Republic. This does not mean that every building in the Greek taste was seen as a symbol of democracy, or associated with those ideals. People took pleasure from the historical associations conjured up by buildings on ancient

models. It connected them with history. In the case of governmental buildings, this association was an element in the choice. Jefferson, who looked to the future as much to the past, phrased it somewhat differently. When writing to Latrobe about some problems with the building of the Capitol in Washington, a building he saw as "the first temple dedicated to the sovereignty of the people," he expressed the feeling that the style should be worthy of the purpose, thus "embellishing with Athenian taste the course of a nation looking far beyond the range of Athenian destinies." In the 1830s and 1840s, when enthusiasm for the pure, chaste lines of ancient Greece was at its height, almost any kind of building was designed with elements quoted from ancient models—banks, churches, houses, even privies. Though important, and all-important in the myths that were woven about life in the Old South many years after the Civil War, it was not, as we have already seen, the only mode of building done in this period.

The appeal of the Gothic as a style appropriate to churches gained steadily and began to rival that of the Greek. In some ways even more than with the Greek, there was the attraction of a far-off period, a period being romanticized by novelists. This general appeal was strengthened by scholarly studies, particularly those in England, of old surviving Gothic buildings, most of which were the great cathedrals, but which also included some of the collegiate structures of Oxford and Cambridge.

A new impetus to the popularity of Gothic was given by the writings of an eccentric and impassioned Englishman, A. W. N. Pugin, a convert to Roman Catholicism who saw Gothic as the architectural style in use when Christianity was at its finest and purest, and as therefore the style most conducive to Christian living. He also saw Gothic as quintessentially English. Pugin, an architect and designer as well as a theorist, published his ideas and designs in several illustrated polemical books and treatises that were widely read and influential.

At the same time a group of Anglicans in England developed an enthusiasm for the Gothic, and most particularly for the small, late-Gothic parish churches found throughout the English countryside, churches that appeared so rooted to their sites that building and setting seemed one. Many of these were irregular in massing, some had bell towers, some had the main entrance through a porch on the south side. To these enthusiasts the medieval parish churches of the fourteenth century represented the best models, for before that, they felt, the church had been immature, and after that had gradually become decadent. To these men the quality of English parish churches embodied a spirit of "sacramentality" which the church needed and lacked. To achieve this, outward and visible forms should convey, symbolize, and express abstract meaning. The Gothic church was thus seen as the embodiment in wood or stone of Christian doctrine and spirit.

In the 1830s these men formed themselves into a group known as the Cambridge Camden Society, later as the Ecclesiological Society. Ecclesiology was for them the "science" of church architecture. During the 1840s their ideas had a surprisingly important influence on the designs of Anglican parish churches in England and its former colonies, an influence that has persisted in images that, to our mind's eye, universally

Church of the Holy Cross, Stateburg, near Sumter, South Carolina, 1850. Designed by Edward C. Jones of Charleston; built in the packed earth, or terre pisé, technique under supervision of Dr. W. W. Anderson.

conjure up ideas of religion. Theirs was essentially a reform movement. They rejected the many simplifications (earlier reforms) in liturgical practices that had served to modify church architecture since the Reformation. It was perhaps an inevitable swing of the pendulum.

The parallel currents of thought about the Gothic period and the Gothic style in architecture—the scholarly publications, Pugin's polemics and designs, and those of the ecclesiologists—were quick to reach American shores. Americans selected and adapted from among them to fit their needs.

In the gently rolling "high hills of the Santee," in South Carolina, stands the rural parish Church of the Holy Cross, above.

But for the Spanish moss hanging on the trees nearby, it evokes an English medieval country church, somehow simplified. The cornerstone was laid in 1850. It is cruciform, with tall, slim lancet windows. Buttresses reinforce the sides and corners of church and tower. The entrance porch, topped by a tower, is significantly to the side—the ecclesiologists favored this arrangement. The tall, slim steeple with its caplike base soars above the church. Here is the "*height* or the *vertical* principle" which Pugin felt to be so important an element in creating the spiritual qualities of the Gothic. The steep-pitched roofs gave further emphasis to height and verticality.

At first glance, the Church of the Holy Cross appears to be

St. Andrew's Episcopal Church, Prairieville, Alabama, 1853. Design probably based on one by Richard Upjohn.

masonry covered with stucco. This is not so. It was built in an unusual French technique, terre pisé, or packed earth, and is probably the only church built in this technique in the Eastern United States. The decision to use this material and method was that of Dr. W. W. Anderson, chairman of the building committee, an inquisitive man interested in experiment, who was following up on an enthusiasm begun in his college years. While a student at the University of Pennsylvania in Philadelphia around 1810, he became fascinated with architecture. One of the books he acquired was a how-to volume by Stephen W. Johnson, published in 1806, and dedicated to Thomas Jefferson. The full and florid title, of a kind editors today would abhor, was *Rural economy; containing a treatise on pisé building, as recommended by the Board of Agriculture in Great Britain, with improvements by the author; on building in general, particularly on the arrangement of those belonging to farms; on the culture of the vine; and on turnpike roads.* The treatise therein on pisé building was in fact a translation of one by a M. Couteraux, prepared in Paris in 1791. The author had studied structures around Lyon, which were apparently based upon techniques utilized by the Romans, techniques which may have been derived from Carthage and North Africa.

The young doctor from Philadelphia came to the up-country of South Carolina to seek his fortune, and there married a well-to-do young woman who inherited a plantation. Here, around 1820, Dr. Anderson first tried the French building technique described in the book, building the wings of their house in this manner. With that success he went on to build a small schoolhouse, a loom house, a summer kitchen, quarters for the cook, and an office for himself. All were done in this rammed-earth process in which damp earth was tamped between wooden forms to brick solidity. There was a method for creating a protective outside surface for the walls. Thus when planning for building a church in what was the village of Stateburg—they had hoped to get the state capitol—Dr. Anderson persuaded his fellow members of the building committee and the architect to use the terre pisé technique. Anderson's slaves were skilled in the method and did most of the labor. The architect was a Charlestonian, Edward C. Jones, well known in Charleston in the middle years of the century. The design of the Church of the Holy Cross suggests that he and Dr. Anderson were familiar with the dictums of Pugin and the ecclesiologists, either directly or indirectly.

When the Americans formed their own ecclesiology society in 1848, an article in their very first publication spoke directly to the needs of parishes in newly settled parts of the country; it was called "Cheap Churches," and set standards and described practical ways and means to achieve them. In it the unknown authors captured the essence of the high-flown and complex ideas of the English theorists, stressing what they deemed essential for Americans. They accepted the Gothic or pointed church of the fourteenth century as the "unequalled" ideal. They also felt there should be a clear and marked division within a church between chancel and nave. The chancel was the area associated with the clergy, a roomy space "in which the service of God may be solemnly, and if not always magnificently, yet ever with all due circumstance performed." The nave was reserved for the congregation. The simplest materials used in a straightforward way were to be favored over imitations such as painting wood to look like marble. "We are bound to give God the best that we can; if we cannot give stone, we may give wood; if we cannot give gold, we may give silver. He asks no more of us than to do our best, and will reward, as such, the least as richly as the most valuable." Economy and beauty were the desired aims. Economy meant wasting nothing; beauty meant an arrangement and those accoutrements appropriate and essential to "the Church and its Service," so that building and service "may with these alone be most solemn, religious and Church-like."

St. Andrew's Episcopal Church, left, located eight miles east of Demopolis, Alabama, is a successful fulfillment of the aims just described. It is small, simple, and unpretentious, yet all the essential elements are there. The parts are clearly defined, yet unified. The roof lines of nave, chancel, and vestibule or porch are steep. That of the chancel is lower than the nave, as was considered appropriate. The exterior is sheathed with vertical boards, the joints covered with battens. The pointed arch of the entrance and the slim lancet windows again echo in a simplified way the forms of English Gothic. There are even tall, slender wooden buttresses on the outside.

The Parish of St. Andrew's was first organized in 1834 as a mission in the canebrake of what is now Hale County. There was then—it has since disappeared—an embryonic village, first called Macon, later Prairieville; twelve to fifteen families, new settlers in this fertile region of black soil, met here once a month for services. By 1852 the number of parishioners had grown and a site for church and graveyard had been obtained. In 1853 the rector reported that "a handsome and substantial Gothic edifice, in the early English style, is now being erected in this Parish, and it is hoped will be ready for consecration by the fall." It was not consecrated until 1858.

There is a strong local tradition that the design was by "Mr. Upjohn." This is plausible. Richard Upjohn was an English-born architect trained in the craft tradition, who came to the United States in 1829. His first Gothic-design church was St. John's in Bangor, Maine, completed in 1837. The church that established his reputation was Trinity Church in New York City, begun in 1841 and consecrated in 1846. It had a symmetrical design that owed much to Pugin. From this time on commissions and requests for designs poured into his office. After 1844 his church designs conformed even more closely to the English parish models so favored by the ecclesiologists. Upjohn was a devoted churchman, and he began to make it a practice to donate his services as architect to at least one church each year; a number of

these were in the South. In 1852 he issued a modest publication, *Rural Architecture*, giving complete specifications for a wooden church and group of related buildings. His purpose was "simply to supply the want which is often felt, especially in the newly settled parts of our country, of designs for cheap but still substantial buildings for the use of parishes, schools, etc." The church design shown had a steep-roofed nave, and a deep chancel with lower roof line. The entrance on the south side was through the base of a tower with spire. Vertical boards with battens and lancet windows were used to give further vertical emphasis. The modest wooden board-and-batten church, stimulated by Upjohn's model, became a characteristically American interpretation of the parish church.

St. Andrew's in Prairieville is so close in general conformation to Upjohn's model that it is easy to believe that the architect may have supplied a variant plan to the parish, though no record of this exists. Otherwise it seems that the builders studied the design in *Rural Architecture* and made their own modifications. The dimensions of St. Andrew's are smaller, and it has a vestibule or porch rather than a tower with spire. Upjohn, in his book, had specified that "all the outside wood work, except the shingles, to be painted 3 good coats of warm brown color," and the builders in far-off Alabama followed suit, painting their modest but substantial church a warm red-brown. In the interior an equally warm coloring was achieved by staining all the woodwork with a brew made from the stems of tobacco plants.

The actual construction of the church was carried out by slaves belonging to various members of the church. In charge were Peter Lee and Joe Glasgow, two master carpenters, slaves of Captain Henry A. Tayloe, a son of Colonel John Tayloe, who had the large estate, Mount Airy, in Virginia. In the interior all the carving, such as the altar rail, a prie-dieu, the graceful pointed arches in the nave, was apparently done by the skilled and expert hands of Peter Lee. In this simple, straightforward, well-built, well-designed structure the congregation acquired a place of worship fully expressing the best of the aspirations of the church-building theorists: a humble churchlike spirit, simple materials used simply and for symbolic effect, beauty in proportion, and realization of honest aims. Services were held for both white and black members of the congregation until the Civil War. There are two other equally attractive board-and-batten churches in nearby communities, the still-smaller St. John's Church in Forklands, and St. Paul's in Lowndesboro. These are but three of a number of churches in the South in which the influence of the ideas of the ecclesiologists can be clearly seen.

If Gothic was deemed especially appropriate for houses of worship for Christians, there were no such guidelines for styles for commercial buildings and banks, the latter identified as Temples of Mammon by an unidentified critic—apparently the novelist William Gilmore Simms—writing in *Harper's* in 1857. For this writer the then newly erected Farmer's and Exchange Bank in Charleston, following page, was a "fanciful little fabric, a little too ornate for such a worship," but "a bijou of a banking house." He described it as "a novelty in the architecture of Charleston, if not of the day, being Moorish in all its details, yet without reminding you of the Alhambra or the Vermilion towers. It is of brown stone of two tints, laid alternately—an arrangement which

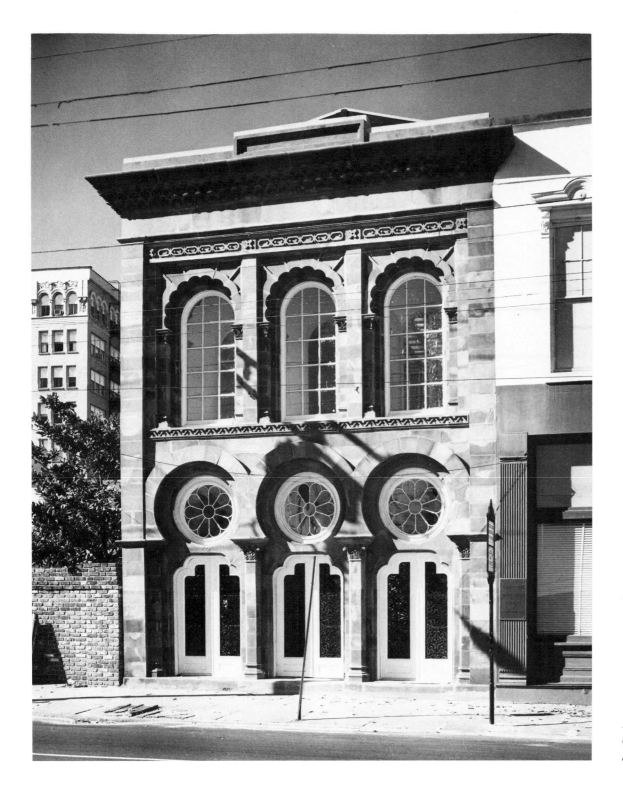

Farmer's and Exchange Bank, 141 East Bay, Charleston, South Carolina, c. 1853–1859. Designed by Francis D. Lee.

adds considerably to the effect. The interior is finished with arabesque work from floor to ceiling, and is lighted with subdued rays from the summit." Moorish was one more historical style with which the history-oriented architects of mid-nineteenth century began to experiment in order to get novel, richly colored, and picturesque effects. The critic here was able to rationalize the choice of Moorish as one of several styles he saw as appropriate for the flat, sea-level setting of Charleston: "The Grecian style is wholly inappropriate to such a dead level as that of Charleston. The skies, climate, and plain surface of the city

considered, and the light Moorish, Saracen, Italian—even Gothic—are all in better propriety."

By the 1850s the widespread enthusiasm for the Greek was beginning to pall. The esthetic of the picturesque, particularly in domestic architecture, was gaining ground and there was increasing interest in the relationship between building and setting. It is noteworthy that the critic used this argument to justify favoring historic styles other than the Greek. We witness his reasoning more fully where, in the same text, he damned with faint praise a recently built Presbyterian church in the Greek taste: "There is an objection, however, to the style, but only as it regards locality. To be altogether satisfied with the Grecian temple style, we must first satisfy the mind and eye in respect to *place*. Now, there is no getting over the absurdity of a Greek temple on a dead city level—taking a model from a mountain, designed expressly for a great elevation, and letting it down upon the plain, where it is overlooked on every side by meaner, but taller structures. . . . About the time when . . . several Greek revival buildings were conceived, the Greek was something of a frenzy North and South, though rarely a proper style for either region. But men built their dwellings, offices, and outhouses after Grecian temples; as if the Greeks themselves had ever assigned such fabrics as abodes for any but their gods, or had ever built such structures, whether for gods or men, any where but on noble eminences, looking grandly forth upon plain or sea! But we have survived these absurdities of thought and taste."

The Moorish never enjoyed the widespread popularity of the Greek or Gothic, and seems to have been more often associated with commercial buildings—perhaps recalling the crowded bazaars of ancient cities—than with low-lying settings. The identification with historical continuities of the past seems to have been a need for architects and clients in the nineteenth century. This was so both in America and in Europe. There was self-conscious pride in the progress and technological change that was taking place—new steam power was revolutionizing transportation on land and sea, and beginning to affect agriculture, and the telegraph was changing communication; machines were changing production methods, factories were an increasingly important institution. Scholarship was changing the perception of the past while technology was changing the perception of the future. The attempted reconciliation of the two in architecture, which was an increasing phenomenon of the nineteenth century, was perhaps a way of tying the strands of an expanding universe, past and present, together.

The contemporary critic was content to identify the Farmer's and Exchange Bank in Charleston as a "bijou of a banking house." The architects were identified as Jones and Lee. In July 1852 Francis D. Lee became a partner with Edward C. Jones, with whom he had served as an apprentice, and they remained partners through 1857. Lee has been given credit for the design. His long career included the designs for a number of buildings in and around Charleston, service in the Confederate Army where his technical engineering talents were put to good use—he invented a submarine torpedo—and a postwar career in St. Louis, where he had a distinguished record as an architect. On his father's side he was a descendant of the colonial painter Jeremiah Theus. Possibly his interest in form and color was inspired by this family tradition.

One of the products consistently improved during the Industrial Revolution was iron. By mid-century materials and techniques were such that cast iron was being put to use not only for decorating and for interior structural elements, but was being molded into pieces that could be applied to façades of buildings. When the store for Theo. Frois and Company's dry-goods business, right, was erected in New Orleans in 1859, this was a still-novel technique. It was one of the first two buildings for which the actual castings of the façade pieces had been made locally, a

William A. Freret. "Frois building on Canal Street in New Orleans." Architectural drawing. Built 1859; now demolished. Louisiana State Museum, New Orleans.

Louisville Water Company Pumping Station, Louisville, Kentucky, 1858–1860. Designed and built by chief engineer Theodore R. Scowden.

of cast iron on façades began to wane in the 1860s and 1870s. They represent one phase in the rapidly changing building technology of the nineteenth and twentieth centuries which eventually led to steel-frame structures and modern skyscrapers.

When the Frois building and a similar structure were completed in 1859 there was criticism because "mixed" styles were used. (The chief inspiration would appear to have been Renaissance buildings in Venice.) A New Orleans columnist felt called upon to defend the architects' freedom in the *Times-Picayune*. In so doing he perceptively linked such freedom and invention to the development of new types of commercial structures, such as stores and office buildings. At the same time he exhibited some of the ambivalent attitudes often found among nineteenth-century architectural critics because, though they favored the new, they also held great respect for historical styles. "We are a new people and there is scarcely an instrument invented in Europe, that we have not improved, or better, in most instances we have had to create so as to supply our wants. And why should we not create a new order of architecture. Admitting that churches, public edifices, should be constructed according to the time-honored rules of the art."

This was advanced thinking for 1859, for the problem of whether to use traditional architectural vocabularies for new types of buildings was one which was to preoccupy architects well into the twentieth century, and is still an open question.

"Mixed" might also have been the name of the style given to the design of the Louisville Water Company Pumping Station, left, built 1858–1860. The plan of the main building, with low wings and projecting pavilions, is essentially Palladian. The encircling columnar colonnade, with its balusters and classical figures (there is one lone Indian), also is reminiscent of the Italian Renaissance. The standpipe is the landmark-centerpiece of the group and is essentially an engineering component. It is tapered a little too much, and molded—it cannot be called fluted—in the form of a giant column, then topped with a cupola consisting of drum and small dome. Despite the classical details, Near Eastern minarets located near oases come to mind and perhaps were meant to. This monumental group was designed by the chief engineer of the Louisville Water Company, Theodore R. Scowden. The building is brick, the capitals and entablatures molded in related terra cotta. Cast iron and riveted steel plates were used for the standpipe tower, the window and door pediments, and much of the trim. This pumping station's capacity was 16 million gallons a day.

Agriculture, its related commerce, and shipping dominated the economy of the South during the first half of the nineteenth century. Manufacturing and industry were less developed, and from the 1840s on there was a growing concern among Southerners about this imbalance and its effect on the prosperity of the region. One of the strongest advocates of the need to develop manufacturing was James D. B. De Bow, the editor of *De Bow's Review*, published in New Orleans. This serious economic journal, the prewar editions of which were issued from 1846 to 1864, had, from 1848 on, the largest circulation of any magazine in the South. Conditions and techniques of the agricultural economy of

source of pride. The architect was William A. Freret, and the iron foundry responsible was the firm of Bennett and Lurges. The iron foundries employed skilled craftsmen-sculptors to make the molds and thus create multiple units of rich and complex effects. The iron pieces for the front of the Frois building (now demolished) were shaped to look like stone. The woodcarver-sculptor was A. De Frosse. The building contract indicates that a brick structure was erected first, then the façade pieces of cast iron were bolted together and secured with rods to the masonry. This technique of applying a cast-iron front to what was essentially a masonry box was the basic method of the time. In the 1850s and 1860s there was a great vogue for such buildings, believed to be fireproof. They were, alas, not, and the use

the South, of transportation, and of commerce were regularly reviewed. Concerned with the need for internal improvements, the editor also advocated practical policies such as direct trade with Europe—rather than the reliance upon New York middlemen that was often the case—and a canal through Central America. The emphasis on a more completely self-sufficient economic system grew as the possibility of secession became ever more a reality during the political turmoil of the 1850s.

In 1851 De Bow began an occasional series that he called a "Gallery of Industry and Enterprise," featuring biographies of men who were engaged in manufacturing. The achievements of Daniel Pratt of Alabama were lauded in the February 1851 issue, and views of the manufacturing town—Prattville—he had founded were shown. He had built a group of industrial mills, below, as well as "houses for the operatives," following page. The mills were tall, narrow three- and four-story rectangular blocks, with regular ranges of windows. Several still survive grouped alongside Autauga Creek. The cupolas or bell towers were functional as well as decorative, for the bells tolled the rhythm of the workdays. The interiors of the mills have been described as spacious and well lighted. The "neat residences" of

the workers appear to have been mostly of equal size, equally spaced. All were apparently in the trimmed-down, utilitarian, yet human style of the first half of the nineteenth century that has been called "corporate."

Pratt was born in Temple, New Hampshire, in 1799, and at the age of sixteen was apprenticed to a carpenter. In 1819, poor but ambitious, he borrowed money in order to try his fortune in the South, arriving in Savannah late in that year. By 1821 he was in Milledgeville, then the capital of Georgia. Here he first was associated with John Marlor, an English architect already established there. As did so many young craftsmen, he seems to have evolved from carpenter-builder to architect, and a number of fine houses in the Milledgeville area are assigned to him. In 1827 he visited New Hampshire briefly, then returned south with a new bride. The War of 1812 had stimulated textile manufacturing in New England and the building of textile factories and new industrial communities, such as Lowell, Massachusetts, and Harrisville, New Hampshire, which were based on English industrial towns. Pratt may have been aware of these even before his move south, but, given his future career, he surely observed them during his visit in 1827. In 1831 Pratt moved to Clinton,

"Mill buildings at Prattville, Alabama." Probably designed by Daniel Pratt and built by him, c. 1838–1850. Engraving from Henry Ames Blood, THE HISTORY OF TEMPLE, N.H. *(Boston, 1860).*

Office of Daniel Pratt's Cotton Gin Factory.

"Houses for the Operatives, Prattville, Alabama."
Probably designed by Daniel Pratt. Print from DE BOW'S
REVIEW, *vol. 11, 1851.*

Georgia, and was for a time a partner in a cotton gin manufacturing firm. In 1833 he struck out on his own, moving still farther west to Autauga County in Alabama, not far from Montgomery, in an area only recently wrested from the Creek Indians. Here he began the production of cotton gins, his improved product soon being sold throughout the South, often as far afield as Tennessee, Texas, and even Mexico.

In 1838 Pratt bought another and larger tract of wooded land on Autauga Creek, and within a few years had established his own small industrial community. Here in the piney woods—a site selected because of the availability of timber—and alongside the creek, which provided the water power, he built first a sawmill, then a planing mill, and in rapid succession, a flour mill (the first sizable one in Alabama), a grist mill, and then the gin factory. This enterprising and sober man soon had so much business that he established a warehouse in New Orleans, and in 1846 he established a cotton factory, producing utilitarian osnaburg and sheeting. About sixty-five uniform and equally spaced houses "neatly painted" and within walking distance of the mills were built for the workmen and their families. There were three churches, two schoolhouses, four stores, a carriage shop, and two blacksmith shops. Soon thereafter an iron foundry, a new brick flour mill, and a sash door and blind factory were built. The sale of "ardent spirits" was prohibited. Pratt's own house was similar to the neoclassical houses he had designed in the Milledgeville area, but included a large wing for a picture gallery—he was an active patron of the arts—and was landscaped with a fountain in the front and terraced garden in the back. His great-grandnephew later said that he "duplicated a New England village,

both as to its physical setting and background." After the war Pratt was one of the men responsible for beginning the iron and steel industries in and around Birmingham, Alabama.

Prattville, with the cotton mill and gin factory, probably its two largest enterprises, was one of the most developed small industrial communities, but in other places in the South industries were beginning to spring up. The September 22, 1859, afternoon edition of the New Orleans *Times-Picayune* reported to its readers with some pride that the South was now beginning to develop factories, that they were producing some of their own manufactured goods which, a few years previously, "with truth it was said that no article used, from the cradle to the grave, was of domestic production." (This was not entirely true.) The first experiments had been on a small scale, "but they have resulted so favorably that capitalists began to examine enterprises which, a few years since, they would have scrupulously avoided." The newspaper recorded 18 cotton factories in South Carolina, 35 in Georgia, 13 in Alabama, 2 in Louisiana, 8 in Kentucky, and 33 in Tennessee. There were 3 woollen factories in Georgia, 3 in Alabama, 7 in Kentucky, and 4 in Tennessee. They did not report on other industries, which were still few and far between. (Some of the largest of sugar and cotton plantations had near-factory conditions of production, but these were of raw materials, not finished goods.) As one crisscrosses the South today one can occasionally come across some remnants of these early industries—a fragment of mill housing survives in Roswell, Georgia; in Columbus part of the abandoned great brick factory of the Columbus Iron Works, built in 1857, has now become the city's Trade and Convention Center. When the war came, however, the industries were too few and too late. They could not provide supplies and matériel to match what the North provided the Federal armies.

The public architecture in the South in this period closely paralleled in form that in the rest of the country. There were strong commercial and banking ties with New York and Philadelphia in communities such as New Orleans, Mobile, and Natchez. In some cases, such as with the St. Charles Hotel, the Southern examples excelled in grandness and size the prototypes on which they were built. Occasionally, as in the critique of the Moorish bank built in Charleston, it was argued that certain styles were more appropriate for flat, low-lying settings in hot climates than was the Greek taste. This parallels the general arguments put forth by those who favored the picturesque and who put a renewed emphasis on the relationship between building and setting, but nonetheless takes cognizance of a relationship between climate, setting, and building design. The arcaded

walkways that were included in the designs of a number of public buildings in the South have parallels elsewhere, but also were singularly suitable to the South. The use of cast-iron balconies, such as Dakin introduced in the Verandah Hotel in New Orleans, may have originated in New York, but it was in Charleston, Savannah, Mobile, and New Orleans that they enjoyed the greatest popularity, particularly on townhouses, because they provided the sheltered outdoor living space so desirable in a hot climate.

In domestic architecture as well, the surface language of style seen in the South is similar to that elsewhere. The transition from the Federal to Greek, to Italianate and more fanciful styles, is often very subtle because of certain strong continuities, most especially the continued use of porches, galleries, and wide central halls. The Gordon-Banks house in Georgia, below, for example, has a close affinity to New England late Federal wooden houses. This is not surprising, since it was designed by Daniel

Gordon-Banks House, originally designed and built by Daniel Pratt for John W. Gordon in Haddock, Georgia, 1828–1830. Now in Newnan, Georgia.

Pratt during the early part of his career, when he had recently come from New England to Georgia. Begun in 1828 for John W. Gordon in Haddock, near Milledgeville, several years passed before it was completed. Gordon was a cotton planter, state senator, and a brigadier general in the Georgia militia.

This house is basically a single five-bay rectangular block with pilasters at the corners (the wings are later additions). The graceful double portico with only two giant columns is more Southern than Northern, in some ways a simplification of those on earlier colonial mansions such as Drayton Hall and the Miles Brewton house. Modified and simplified giant porticoes of this kind are found throughout the Deep South on houses built in the 1830s and 1840s. Here large-scale doors are surrounded by fanlights of equal proportion. Light pours through these into the open, spacious, roomlike central halls on both the first (right) and second floors, halls which serve as great breezeways. Much of the detail, such as the fanlight, balusters, and parts of the exterior cornice, is based on plates in Asher Benjamin's *American Builder's Companion*, first published in 1806, a handbook so popular that it was reissued several times. The later 1826 and 1827 editions were brought up to date with new plates showing Grecian elements and handrails for circular stairs. The house is, for its time, essentially conservative, late neoclassical, "columnar." The interior proportions and something of the richness of coloring project the feel of the English Regency—Pratt would have known Jay's distinguished houses in Savannah, but he uses what he might have absorbed from them in a restrained way.

Old engravings show that the house Daniel Pratt later designed for himself in his community of Prattville, Alabama, looked very much like the Gordon-Banks house. Unfortunately, it has long since been destroyed.

By a stroke of good fortune, the carved woodwork, plasterwork, and painted decoration in the Gordon-Banks home survived virtually intact and needed only a few repairs and touching up during the recent restoration. Few interiors have survived so completely. The doors and door frames, the dado, and the staircase are all painted in rich, dark colors and in graining patterns simulating maple and dark wood veneers. Gilding is used on the door frame, the capitals of the pilasters, and on the scrolled step ends. The small plaster leaves that form the outer edge of the molding of the broad arch are also gilded. The baseboards were painted to resemble marble. The rich colors used on the woodwork and plasterwork throughout the house are very different from the delicate pastels favored during the Federal period.

White-pillared, columnar houses of all kinds became increasingly popular in the 1830s and 1840s. Some were located on country plantations, the "big house" with nearby slave cabins and a cluster of outbuildings. As such they were part of an isolated, semi–self-sufficient agricultural unit, an important component of the rural South. Just as many columned mansions, perhaps even more, were located in shipping or market towns. It has been shown, for example, that the majority of Greek Revival houses in Georgia are found in towns rather than in the country, and their owners were more often merchants than planters, or landowners with other financial interests, whose plantations were located some distance from their homes. Most such mansions were in Piedmont Georgia. The university town of Athens,

appropriately, probably has more houses still standing in the Greek Revival taste than any other town in the state. Washington-Wilkes, Macon, Madison, Milledgeville, La Grange, and Columbus are all notable for their fine mansions. Despite the number of surviving pillared halls, the *Gone With the Wind* vision of pre–Civil War Georgia is far from accurate. It has been estimated that no more than 5,000 people, or less than 0.5 percent of the total population of Georgia in 1806, lived in such houses. Other towns where the planter-landowner-merchants chose to build their spacious homes in relatively close proximity to each other are dotted along the rivers and major roads throughout the South. Natchez was perhaps the richest of these communities, but others include Camden, South Carolina; Columbus, Mississippi; and Lowndesboro, Alabama, to name but a few. Whether plantation house or villa in town, good land was nearby.

These Southern mansions have come to symbolize a gracious, leisurely, chivalric way of life as well as the oppression and cruelties of the system of slavery. There is truth in both concepts, and the reality is multitextured. The proportion of people who lived in mansions was always relatively small, as was the proportion of people who owned large numbers of slaves. The statistics seem to show that three-fourths of white Southerners had no connection with slavery, and in 1850 only 8,000 landowners had fifty or more slaves. And not all mansions were columnar.

New styles were seldom initiated in the agricultural South; yet its inhabitants were surprisingly quick in responding to changes in taste. Some of the great houses that went up on the eve of the Civil War had columns, but even these show a variety of details that indicates a move away from the bold simplicity associated with the Greek–Italianate, Moorish, "bracketed," Gothic, and a variety of "mixed" styles are seen in domestic houses as well as in public buildings. Certain vernacular traditions continued strong—verandas, galleries, porches, balconies are ubiquitous. A statistical analysis of measurements of houses in selected communities in different areas would be needed to prove it, but one feels that, in general, central halls are wider and ceilings higher in Southern houses of the mid-nineteenth century than in their Northern counterparts. Usually windows and doors were carefully placed to ensure cross-ventilation. These adaptations are found in cottage and mansion alike. Certain floor plans were consistently favored even as the "styles" of houses changed. Outside staircases were a vernacular tradition in the Deep South; these are seldom seen elsewhere. Raised cottages and cottages with porches on one or more sides remained popular, though different decorative details were introduced by each generation in keeping with changing fashions.

Though large mansions were few, the exception rather than the rule, those erected were impressive and capture the imagination. The prosperity of the 1840s and 1850s meant that the "few" who could afford to build such mansions nonetheless numbered in the thousands, and they were often the political, social, cultural, and intellectual leaders as well. As architecture, many of the homes were very fine indeed, and a survey such as this can show only a small selection. As symbol, they seem to represent a way of life and convey a sense of dignity and permanence. Some were lavishly built with fine materials, careful workmanship, and ever more spacious proportions. It is also true

Entrance hall, Gordon-Banks House.

that a colonnade or great portico across the front of a fairly ordinary-sized house creates an appearance of size and dignity that is illusory. The symbol, sufficiently potent in the pre–Civil War days so that a small farmer could identify with a rich landowner, seems to have become more so in postwar days, first as a symbol of the lost cause, increasingly of a romantic era gone by. The white-pillared Southern mansion of the popular imagination did exist, but the idea that virtually all white Southerners led their lives within such halls is a myth, a wishful re-creation of the past, aided and abetted by twentieth-century writers and filmmakers.

In domestic architecture the transition from the neoclassical or Federal to what can be identified as Greek is less precisely defined than with public architecture. In a house classified as Greek Revival a "correct" rendering of the columnar details from a Greek temple might be used; or the door frames might be canted in the manner of those on the Erechtheum; yet plan and

Houmas House, on Mississippi River, Burnside, Louisiana. Built c. 1840 as major addition to an earlier building for John Smith Preston, and possibly designed by him and a local contractor.

Oakleigh, 150 Oakleigh Place, Mobile, Alabama, built for James Roper, c. 1833–1838.

elevation might represent a continuation of an already established tradition. Details such as the honeysuckle or anthemion motifs might be found as the interior ornament around doors and windows. However, there was often considerable simplification of Greek forms; plain square box columns with a simple capital caught the spirit of the austere, chaste Greek, although a far cry from the Doric of the Parthenon. The practice of simplifying and modifying high-style pattern-book concepts had long been practiced by American builders and architects. Some of the pattern-book writers, such as Asher Benjamin and Minard Lafever, freely introduced such modifications in their books, creating a kind of classical vernacular. In so doing, a recognizable idiom, having the feeling of the Greek, was achieved. The dignity and the clarity of form found in the buildings of that ancient republic were translated into a usable artistic vocabulary that, in the South, was suitable for the climate and for the aspirations of those who lived there.

In Louisiana, along the Mississippi, the transition from the colonial idiom developed by the Creoles to the grander mode that is Greek was easy enough. One sees it in the house of Houmas plantation, page 211 and above left, a house set on a great open lawn shaded by giant oaks, cool, or cooler, even on the hottest days. It is flanked by attractive *garçonnières*. Instead of pillars and thin posts there are now giant columns, unfluted and with simplified Tuscan capitals. Instead of the older Creole enfilade plan, there is a wide central hall, with equally spaced rooms to right and left. The large squared-off door frames with side lights have the angularity and plainness of the Greek. The hipped roof is lower. But the great open galleries at two levels, those outdoor living rooms so beloved by the Creoles, are still there. The belvedere on the roof serves not only as lookout, but as a kind of large roof vent, drawing hot air upward. Houmas is typical of the plantation houses along the Mississippi and in the environs of New Orleans built during the 1840s. All too few remain.

Though Creole in flavor, Houmas was one of the few sugar plantations along this stretch of the river owned by Anglo-Americans. Originally on land frequented by the Houmas Indians, and owned at one time by members of the Bringier family—Creoles who owned a series of plantations on either side—the property was purchased in 1811 by the wealthy South Carolinian General Wade Hampton. He and his son were largely absentee owners, visiting only occasionally; slaves did the work, supervised by an overseer who lived in a small house on the property. Numerous Carolinians and Virginians had moved westward seeking new lands. The artist Charles Fraser in his *Reminiscences of Charleston* written in 1854, recalled the great planters of pre-Revolutionary days, "The ruinous remains of many of their seats and mansions scattered throughout the neighboring Parishes, are melancholy memorials of bye-gone days." Their own lands depleted, the sons and grandsons of the early planters were among those buying up the rich lands of the new Southwest.

In 1840 the general's daughter and her husband, John Smith Preston, came out to Louisiana, and the larger house was built in front of the cottage, the latter becoming the kitchen at the rear. No architect is known, but there were already similar houses in the area, as well as skilled craftsmen, black and white; Preston himself was knowledgeable about the arts, and he would have had little trouble finding workmen to help him create and build the house.

The effect of a temple front is created by the portico at Oakleigh Place, lower left, built in Mobile between 1833 and 1838 for the merchant James Roper. Square brick piers, square box columns with Tuscanlike capitals contribute to this. The wide canted door frame of the main entrance is typical of those used on Greek Revival houses throughout the country. Though brought up to date with the templelike front, in essence this is a large version of the raised cottage type found on the Gulf Coast and elsewhere in the South, here with service areas on the ground floor and the main living room above. The brick walls of the ground floor are said to have been made from clay on the property. The curved outdoor staircase, though rare in that form, is reminiscent of those found earlier in the Deep South. The T-shaped plan, allowing for maximum ventilation throughout, is similar to those found in the rice country of South Carolina. Smaller galleries or porches fronting each of the two side wings provide still further sheltered outdoor space.

Considerably more correct as things Greek go is the Governor's Mansion in Austin, Texas, built in 1853, below. The portico, which stretches across the front, has a colonnade of six great fluted columns with Ionic capitals. The house is almost square in plan, with a large central hall with staircase, and two square rooms on either side, a plan found elsewhere in the Deep South. The Governor's Mansion was built by Abner Hugh Cook, a carpenter-architect who came from the Carolinas to Texas in 1841. Little is known about his background, but his skill and finesse in handling details and feeling for proportions suggest familiarity on his part, or on that of an unknown designer, with the architecture found in the more established areas of the Deep South and with the popular architectural handbooks. Cook was responsible for several other well-designed and well-proportioned houses in the Greek taste in the frontier community of Austin.

The town of Austin was laid out as the capital of the Republic of Texas in 1839, and continued as the capital of the state when Texas was annexed to the United States in 1845. The towns of Austin, San Antonio, and Waco are on an imaginary line that more or less represents the western boundary of the Old South. Beyond this line lie the scraggly hills of the Great Plains—the beginning of the West. The land in east Texas is largely blackland prairie and the climate is hot and humid for much of the year. From the time of the first colonization led by Stephen Austin in the 1820s to the Civil War there was a steady influx of

Governor's Mansion, Eleventh and Colorado Streets, Austin, Texas, built by Abner Hugh Cook, 1853.

McDonald House, originally in Cuthbert, Georgia, now in Westville, near Lumpkin, Georgia. Begun 1843, front portion including porch added a few years later.

adventuresome and land-hungry settlers into this region. The largest proportion of these were Anglo-Americans, many from the Deep South. They found the land suitable for cultivation of cotton, sugar cane, and rice and, when possible, established a way of life similar to that in the older Southern states. Mansions of the caliber of the Governor's were rare in this frontier region. A much larger number of homes were simple frame structures with a porch across the front, yet, as in many newly settled areas, as soon as elementary shelters were provided there were those who then succeeded in building more impressive and substantial structures in the current fashion.

Frontier conditions still prevailed in many parts of the Deep South in the 1830s, '40s, and '50s, wherever the lands had only recently been made available to white settlers. One such region was the upland cotton country of Georgia. The McDonald house, above, originally in Cuthbert, Georgia, in Randolph County, not far from the Chattahoochee, was built in several phases by a Scotsman and merchant named Edward McDonald. The earliest portion was erected in 1843. A few years later a second story, two front parlors, and the portico were added. Thus it became a Greek Revival house with colonnade across the front (prostyle). The colonnade gives it presence and modest grandeur. However, inside it is basically a very plain, relatively small, and utilitarian structure; the interior walls are simply sheathed with boards. Nonetheless, the house as seen from a slight distance is impressive, and effective as symbol. It is a thrifty man's Greek Revival mansion.

The McDonald house has recently been moved to Westville,

near Lumpkin, Georgia, a functioning living-history village where the sights, sounds, even smells of village life in the upland cotton country during the 1850s are suggested. Such villages were often some distance from any large city.

To reach Demopolis, Alabama, from Mobile required two nights on a steamboat in the 1840s. At least another day was involved if one wished to visit New Orleans. In this rich black belt of Alabama, an area so named because of its soil, in a territory that had daunted the French Napoleonic refugees who first tried to settle there, General Nathan Bryan Whitfield built a house, Gaineswood, lower right, that rivaled many a city mansion or country villa, North or South.

Gaineswood is a mansion of complex design and plan, upper right; this is no symmetrical Palladian scheme. There is a different-sized portico on each side: a columned temple-front portico faces north, one of two major entrances; a porte cochere is on the west where there is a second major entrance; a gracefully curved private columned porch on the east opens out from the second Mrs. Whitfield's bedroom, a low porch on the south onto an enclosed garden or parterre; and there is another porch on the southwest. The interior is equally complex, with a ballroom, following page, at the front; reception rooms are on either side of the west entrance, which leads to a spacious cross hall. The dining room and library are both beautifully lit with domed skylights. An office, conservatory, and three bedrooms are also included on the ground floor. Changes and additions were made throughout the entire period of building.

The second floor is even more idiosyncratic. There are two

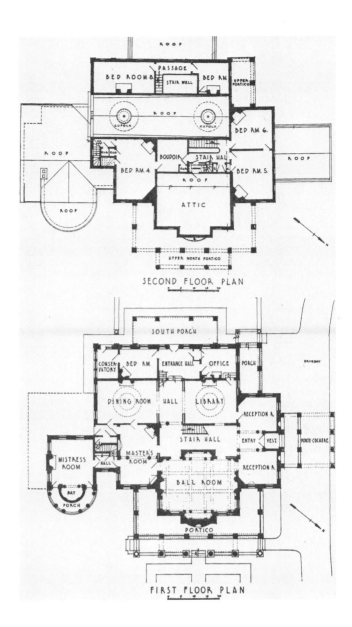

SECOND FLOOR PLAN

FIRST FLOOR PLAN

quite separate units, reached by separate staircases. The low-ceilinged bedrooms at the back were designed for the small children, those in the front for older children or adults.

Finally, on the roof, there is a "ring," apparently designed by a son. This is not a covered cupola, but an open, balustraded observatory platform where, according to tradition, members of the family enjoyed starlit musical evenings.

The many-columned porches on the outside are essentially Greek in detail—fluted Doric and square boxed columns were used. The columns, capitals, and plasterwork ornament on the inside were based on antique prototypes. In the varied façades, irregular massing, and irregular plan, however, the scheme is essentially that of a picturesque villa of vaguely Italianate flavor. Whatever may have been the original plan, this is the net effect. Moreover, the planting and landscaping, which included a meandering lane and an irregularly shaped artificial lake, were all in keeping with the informal precepts of the picturesque.

Family tradition is that the owner, Nathan Bryan Whitfield, was architect-designer and builder. There is every indication that he was an ingenious and well-informed man, with a bent toward engineering. The intricate, yet still practical design, suited to the tastes and needs of a particular family, suggests the work of a talented, perhaps slightly amateur, student of architecture. Whitfield was born in North Carolina, the son of a founder of the new university there. Before moving westward to Alabama

Below: Gaineswood, Demopolis, Alabama, 1843–1859. Probably designed by the owner, Nathan Bryan Whitfield, and built under his supervision. Left: Floor plan, from Jesse G. Whitfield, GAINESWOOD AND OTHER MEMORIES *(Demopolis, Alabama, n.d.).*

Ballroom of Gaineswood.

he served in both the House and Senate of his native state. In 1843 he purchased the land on which Gaineswood stands—his second plantation in the area—from his friend, General George Gaines, who was the Choctaw Indian factor and who had a log house there. Tradition has it that it was on these grounds that Chief Pushmataha signed the treaty by which the people of the Choctaw Nation were removed to the West. Whitfield is known to have owned Stuart and Revett's *Antiquities of Athens* as well as other architectural books. Recently it has been suggested that Whitfield may have been influenced by an early design of James Dakin for the Perry House in Brooklyn, or by two related designs published in Minard Lafever's *Modern Builder's Guide*. This is entirely possible, since Whitfield was a cosmopolitan man who made trips to Mobile and New Orleans with some frequency, as well as visits to Philadelphia and New York. He might even have known Dakin and Gallier, and no doubt discussed his architectural ideas with knowledgeable acquaintances.

The house was begun in 1834 but not finished until 1859, because Whitfield was frequently preoccupied elsewhere. His first wife died in 1846, and in 1853 there was a yellow fever epidemic. During this period Whitfield was also involved with building the parish Episcopal church, and with a plank road and drainage canal.

Much of the work of construction was done on the place, with skilled black and white craftsmen using tools and machines, some of Whitfield's invention; carpentry and plaster shops were set up on the premises. While some of the plasterwork, which is

used almost too lavishly on the interior, may have been ordered or copied from a catalogue still owned by members of the family, a slave named Sandy did much of it. The wood graining was by John Verdin of Philadelphia, who stayed eighteen months, and there is a tradition that a wandering Pole did some ornamental painting. Other elements, such as marble mantelpieces, were ordered from Philadelphia. In the ballroom there are vis-à-vis mirrors, which create seemingly magical multiple reflections and an illusion of great depth. A grandson remembered when these arrived from France and how he caulked the seams of the box they had come in to make it into a boat. Ionic and Corinthian columns and pilasters are used throughout the ground floor to accent alcoves and halls.

An artesian well supplied water and a smokehouse and packing house were among the service buildings on the premises. Records indicate that the three annual killings of pork averaged 30 to 40,000 pounds of meat. The Whitfields lost much of their fortune during the Civil War and for a time the mansion was left derelict. Several owners from 1896 onward helped to rehabilitate it. Now the house has been restored and is open to the public. It has not yet been possible to recapture the effects of the landscaped setting, though plans are afoot to do so.

The plantation house with the improbable name, Rattle and Snap, right, appears today much as it must have when completed in 1845. It was apparently given this name by William Polk, a Revolutionary War veteran entitled to a land grant, when the governor of North Carolina threw dice to decide which tract went to which veteran. William Polk was a North Carolinian appointed surveyor-general of the Middle District of Tennessee in 1784. Through land speculation he became one of the largest landowners in Tennessee. The original tract of land in Maury County, near Columbia, contained 5,648 acres. Four of Polk's sons had homes on the property, the most lavish of which was Rattle and Snap, built by the youngest of these four, George.

Ten giant Corinthian columns grace the façade with its projecting pedimented portico. Each wooden column is twenty-six feet tall; the capitals are of cast iron. The porch is recessed, and a small balcony juts out from the second floor. No architect is known, but we can imagine that owner and builder perused popular builders' guides and discussed plans and appropriate embellishments with friends and neighbors, lumbermen and suppliers. Pilasters flank the corners of this brick and stone structure. From the front, the façade can be read as the old, familiar five-bay Southern house in the Georgian taste found in the Carolinas and Virginia dressed up with giant Corinthian columns. Porches of varying shape on either side and a long L-shaped rear service wing, flanked by yet another double gallery, belie the strict symmetry of an earlier era. The cast-iron porch and balcony on the east, following page, present a charming mixture; the slim columns echo Gothic colonnettes and are decorated with vine and circle motifs as well as with the Greek anthemion and lyre. This porch appears to have been added about the time when the building was nearing completion.

The spacious rooms on the inside make possible entertaining on a grand scale.

Most of the outbuildings that were once a part of the larger plantations are now gone. One of the few surviving groups of slave cabins, the "quarters," are those, following page, which still exist at Evergreen plantation, on the west bank of the Mississippi in Louisiana. Here they stand in double facing rows with a line of sheltering oaks in between. In these simple structures the shaded porch was an integral feature. Stables, smokehouses, privies, separate kitchens, icehouses, sometimes separate offices,

Rattle and Snap, near Columbia, Tennessee, completed for George Polk, 1845.

Porch and balcony on east side of Rattle and Snap.

were among typical outbuildings. (Houses in towns often had fewer but similar auxiliary buildings.) No longer needed as patterns of living and farm techniques have changed, many of these once functional buildings have disappeared. It is therefore sometimes hard to conceive the nature of the everyday, workaday life that took place within these partly self-sufficient households. The rhythm of the seasons governed rural life from planting to harvesting. Animals had to be cared for daily. Cooking, laundering, cleaning, sewing, gardening, and butchering took place on daily, weekly, or seasonal schedules. Births and deaths took place at home, not in hospitals. Entertaining and much of education also took place at home.

Even as elegant and more varied houses were built, the log houses and log cabins that were so much a part of frontier life in the upper South continued to be built and used. Wynnewood, or Castalian Springs, right, near Gallatin in Tennessee, is a surviving example. This two-story structure is of larger scale than most and in fact was intended originally as a tavern when it was built in 1828. The front porch seen here is a later addition; originally the steps led to the open breezeway or "dog-trot." The tavern, meant to service travelers who journeyed along the old stagecoach road that led from Baltimore to the Indian Nation in Middle Tennessee, was unsuccessful. In 1834 Colonel Alfred R. Wynne bought out the other stockholders in the tavern and converted it to a residence, and members of that family lived there until 1973. It is now the property of the state of Tennessee. Snug and solidly built, it has had an extraordinarily long and useful life. Only a few structural changes were made through the years. Colonel Wynne was apparently unconcerned about external elegances in his well-wrought house, but he did indulge in a love

The "quarters," or slave cabins, on Evergreen Plantation, Vacherie, Louisiana, c. 1840–1860.

of horses and racing, a taste he shared with his friend Andrew Jackson, and he had his own racetrack on the property.

The house of the Smith family, following page, begun in 1840 and originally located on a farm north of Atlanta, is typical of many built by owners of small farms. The genre, now being called "plantation plain style" to differentiate it from its more elegant counterparts, often, as here, consists of a simple frame two-story gable-ended structure with chimneys at the end. On each floor there are only two rooms of unequal size. Additional space is provided by the lean-to at the rear, the porch with shed roof, and a small guest room on the front. In the case of the Smith house, it is believed that the porch as it now appears is the result of a late completion, or early remodeling. Porches with shed roofs across the front like this one are frequently seen. It is believed that the house was left unpainted for a time, then painted blue-gray on the outside. On the inside the simply finished, smooth board walls are a sandy yellow, the mantelpieces and baseboards black. When John Townsend Trowbridge traveled in the South immediately after the war he described the interior of a house near Augusta even simpler in finish: "I passed the night at a planter's house of the middle class. It was a plain, one-and-a-half story, unpainted, weather-browned frame dwelling, with a porch in front, and two front windows. The oaken floors were carpetless, but clean swept. The rooms were not done off at all; there was not a lath, nor any appearance of plastering or whitewash about them. The rafters and shingles of the roof formed the ceiling of the garret-chamber; the sleepers and boards of the chamber-floor, the ceiling of the sitting-room; and the undisguised beams, struts, and clapboards of the frame and its covering composed the walls." These simple vernacular houses, some of which have long since disappeared, and some of which have been modified and improved, provide a more realistic picture of the homes of a greater majority of people. Trowbridge was careful to note that the house he described "was not the house of a small farmer, but of the owner of two plantations, of a thousand acres each." In this case, it was apparently not economics that determined the choice of such a modest home, for this man could have afforded something more elaborate. This planter apparently felt comfortable in the simplest setting. He must have occupied himself with the running of the plantation, and perhaps with the pleasures of outdoor country life, and did not feel the need or desire to have a large well-finished home to proclaim his social or economic status.

The vernacular Southern raised cottage could become quite transformed with the advent of the picturesque and the development of a new tool, the jigsaw, as can be seen in the delightful Olney Ethridge cottage in Sparta, Georgia, following page. The complex patterns of the veranda railings, flat pierced posts, and pierced "frieze," plus the board and batten siding and high gabled roof edged with scalloped verge boards, create a fanciful appearance that is quite different from the staid look of earlier buildings with simple columns or posts. The taste for things picturesque and for fanciful architecture had its roots in romantic British and European ideas. The interest in the picturesque created a new enthusiasm for old rustic cottages and farmhouses, and soon architects were creating designs for country houses in a "rural cottage style." These ideas were picked up in America by architects such as Town and Davis in New York; the writings of Alexander Jackson Downing and others spread them to a much larger audience. Downing's two most influential works were *Cot-*

Wynnewood, or Castalian Springs, near Gallatin, Tennessee. Built 1828 as a tavern with open breezeway or dog-trot; converted to a residence in 1834 by Colonel Alfred R. Wynne.

Tullie Smith House, built c. 1840 on a farm north of Atlanta. Now owned by the Atlanta Historical Society.

Olney Ethridge Cottage, Sparta, Georgia, 1853.

tage Residences, Rural Architecture and Landscape Gardening, first published in 1842, and *The Architecture of Country Houses*, published in 1850. Both went through numerous editions and were widely read throughout the country. *Country Houses* described a hierarchy of building types—cottages, farmhouses, and villas. The new importance given to smaller houses perfectly suited middle-class and egalitarian Americans. In the models he provided, Downing tried to steer a course between the admirably simple and the effectively picturesque. He encouraged the use of deep overhanging roofs and verge boards to create showy patterns, but inveighed against the "frippery and 'gingerbread'" that he felt degraded rather than elevated the beauty of a cottage. The carpenters and builders who had access to the jigsaw, however, frequently indulged themselves in just such playful effects, and we have come to appreciate the freedom, inventiveness, and fantasy of the combinations they created. The jigsaw, powered by steam, made possible high-speed cutting and easy replication of a variety of shapes. In the middle years of the nineteenth century, builders, and suppliers to builders, made full use of it.

One or more unknown builders or amateur architects in Columbus, Mississippi, concocted the designs for five large houses in which echoes of the Greek colonnaded porches of the South, the Gothic, and the fanciful details made possible by the jigsaw are combined in surprisingly pleasing combinations. Only three of these remain. Of these, the Gothic concepts were most fully expressed in the Flynn house, right, one of the houses destroyed. The columns were similar to the clustered columns of the Gothic, the central arch of the low gable was like a Tudor arch, and the flat openwork scroll pattern above it echoed in a most general way the carving of verge boards on fifteenth-century manor houses. On each side was a round and then a narrower pointed arch. There were second-floor balconies as on Greek Revival mansions. On the other houses, the columns were more evenly spaced, but all were seemingly from the hand of the same designers, all probably built in the 1850s. Though borrowing freely from various traditions, they represent the imaginative use of wood to create quite new and appealing designs.

Columbus is another of those Southern towns in which planters with land in the surrounding area had their mansions. Located at the intersection of two important traffic routes—the Tombigbee River, which flows to Mobile, and on Andrew Jackson's old military highway, which went from Nashville to New Orleans—it became an important trading and educational center. Incorporated as a town in 1821, it grew in size in the 1830s after the ever land-hungry Americans succeeded in making treaties with the Choctaw and the Chickasaw and those natives ceded their land to the U.S. government. Settlers from Georgia, Virginia, and the Carolinas soon were producing cotton and corn on the rich lands. There is a house in Athens, Georgia—the Treanor or John A. Cobb house, built around 1840—with a similar, though less exuberant, giant portico on which attenuated Gothic columns are similarly used. Possibly some Georgia builder or planter moved from there to Mississippi, and there is a connection.

Cotton planters who moved into southeastern Alabama after 1832, when the Indians were compelled by treaty to move, established the trading town of Irwinton on the Chattahoochee. An inn was the first building erected. It served as a stopping place for the steamboats carrying cotton down to the port at Apalachicola, Florida. Seth Lore laid out the new town; some of the major streets are unusually wide, giving a spacious open quality. Four of them are named Livingston, Orange, Randolph, and Eufaula, the initials of which spell Lore's last name. In 1844 the town was renamed Eufaula, after the branch of the Lower Creek Indians who had lived in the vicinity. Here, too, the planter-merchants of the area built their homes side by side, most set back from the streets, each on a generous-sized piece of land. Eufaula became the major trade center for southeastern Alabama, and was a reasonably prosperous community even after the Civil War; a kind of quiescence settled over it after World War I when cotton prices declined, and it is only since the 1960s, when the Chattahoochee was dammed, that much new building has taken place. An active, self-generated preservation movement has prevented the destruction of most of the well-preserved buildings of the nineteenth century.

Flynn House, Columbus, Mississippi, c. 1850–1860. Now demolished.

Dean-Page Hall, North Randolph Avenue, Eufaula, Alabama, completed in the 1850s.

Several of the larger houses have tall cupolas or observatories at the top, which were designed so that the owners could enjoy the vistas and which give a picturesque, towerlike effect. If the windows are opened, these observatories enhance the flow of hot air upward and out, helping to cool the lower rooms. They are seen on a number of houses in Georgia and Alabama. The houses in Eufaula are four-square, with surrounding verandas on the ground floor and the observatory in the center at the top. The roof brackets, the balustrades, and the towerlike effect suggest that the builders were aware of the towered Italianate mode seen in the pattern books. Yet these are not textbook examples, but a free and local interpretation of current ideas. Dean-Page Hall, above, completed in the 1850s, is one of these. The lacy wooden tracery of the supporting shafts or "columns" of the veranda and

the window frames on the observatory inject an element of fanciful Gothic into the design. It was not easy to build mansions on this scale in this area. All the necessary supplies, such as the wood, which had to be cut and measured and seasoned, and the materials that had to be shipped in from elsewhere, took five years to collect. Five more years were needed before the house was completed.

A symmetrical plan and a variety of curved elements, such as round-headed windows and the swelling curve of the veranda, characterize Dinglewood, right, an Italianate villa in Columbus, Georgia, built in 1859 for Joel Early Hurt, and designed by the architects Barringer and Morton. Here the architects put into effect precepts found in the new publications on architecture. Calvert Vaux, in his *Villas and Cottages* of 1857, said, "The introduction of circular-headed windows, circular projections, or verandahs, and of curved lines in the design of the roof, and in the details generally, will always have an easy, agreeable effect, if well managed." Samuel Sloan, the Philadelphia architect whose publications reached a wide audience, much favored the Italian style, which he characterized by the free use of the semi-circular arch and the use of a tower or campanile. He, and his clients, liked this mode because with it one had great freedom in general design and thus "considerable room for the exercise of taste." Since most of the villas in Italy that were the general models for the new style had been erected on hilly grounds,

many of the designs were irregular in plan and outline. However, as Sloan explicitly noted, "The style is by no means incompatible with a level country, but in that case the design is more regular and symmetrical." Those Southerners who chose the Italianate mode often built their homes, as at Eufaula, Alabama, and Columbus, Georgia, on flatlands near a river, and hence could readily rationalize their love for the traditional wide central hall and a generally symmetrical plan with their quick adoption of the outward qualities of the new styles. The Italianate was also considered suitable for the villa in or near a town, for, according to the tastemakers, "It speaks of the inhabitant as a per-

Dinglewood, Columbus, Georgia, built for Joel Early Hurt, 1859. Designed by Barringer and Morton.

255

The door panels and wall of the downriver drawing room at San Francisco Plantation House, Reserve, Louisiana, c. 1856–1860. The painting was probably done by Domenico Canova.

finishing and furnishing of the interiors of their homes. Some of the finest and most varied interior painting in a mid-Victorian American house is to be seen in the plantation-villa at Reserve, Louisiana, called, since about 1879, San Francisco. The house is situated on a plantation on the east bank of the Mississippi River about midway between New Orleans and Baton Rouge. The land was purchased in 1830 by Edmond Bozonier Marmillion and a partner from a free man of color, Elisée Rilliéux, and the present house was probably built around 1853–1856 after a disastrous break in the levee that destroyed part of the property in 1852. (These levee breaks were locally called "crevasses." The river eroded the levee and flowed in, causing the land and all upon it to crumble and fall in.) The house is wide in scale, with a raised basement, and with a gallery or porch extending around three sides in the tradition of the French colonial houses, but the exterior ornament includes a variety of millwork brackets and balustrades that gives it a fanciful appearance.

Evidence suggests that initially wallpaper was applied in several rooms and the woodwork painted a pale tone. Shortly thereafter the wallpaper was removed and the house redecorated. Five of the ceilings were lavishly painted, and the woodwork was painted, grained, or marbled in a variety of ways. Thanks to benign neglect one of these ceilings and some of the painting on the doors of the parlor on the downriver side were never painted over. A recent restoration, based on meticulous research and analysis of paint layers and colors, revealed a far richer decorative scheme than had been imagined. By carefully scraping some of the overpainting away and by tracing the patterns underneath other layers—patterns still discernible under a strong raking light—the character and colors of the partially obliterated decoration could be discerned. It was then carefully restored, using the principles and techniques developed in the conservation of oil paintings.

Particularly striking is the Pompeian decoration of the door panels and wall of the downriver parlor or drawing room, left. Although the light-colored panels with their delicate floral motifs had never been painted over, the green *rinceau* vine patterns and borders set against a rich chocolate brown had been. The stenciled border above with its touches of bright red, green, and blue, and the red and blue accents on the pale yellow moldings, contribute to a rich polychrome effect. The walls of this room are a warm gold and a complex ceiling decoration completes the color scheme.

According to tradition, most of the decorative painting was done by Dominique, or Domenico, Canova, a painter who lived and worked in New Orleans in the 1840s, 1850s, and 1860s. Canova is known to have painted the designs on the dome of the St. Louis Hotel in New Orleans, and to have taught at a college not far from this plantation. According to the restorers, more than one artist was involved in the painting, but we do not know who the others might have been. Canova is supposed to have been the nephew of the famous Italian sculptor, though it has been suggested that his name may have been Casanova changed to Canova in order to capitalize on the sculptor's fame. Some of the design motifs were taken from pages of a *Manuel de Peintures* published by A. Morel et Cie in Paris beginning in March 1850. The redecoration probably took place after 1856, when Marmillion's

son of educated and refined tastes, who can appreciate the beautiful both in art and nature; who, accustomed to all the ease and luxury of a city life, is now enjoying the more pure and elevating pleasures of the country." (The reverse was true of some Southerners; they had lived in the country but now wanted some of the advantages of town life.) Design 31 in Sloan's *Model Architect* had a centrally placed observatory tower similar to those seen at Eufaula or at Dinglewood. The latter house was also very up to date in that it had an internal waterworks system and private gasworks.

Architects and their clients also exercised their taste in the

son became a part-owner after the father's death. He and his wife must have consulted with the painters before the rich decorative treatment that lends such distinction to the rooms was decided upon. The costs may have been more than the younger Marmillion anticipated. In the annual crop reports of 1860–1861 the name of the plantation as "St. Frusquin" first appears. This was French slang meaning to lose one's all. Since, in the period between 1856 and 1859 there were some bumper sugar crops, the Marmillions would have had the funds to undertake this lavish redecoration, but the costs might have left them feeling penniless. The name of the plantation was apparently changed to San Francisco in 1879, when the original term had lost its relevance or was no longer understood.

Samuel Sloan, whose *Model Architect* was published in 1852, had an eye on the prospering Southern market. Therefore he included two designs, numbers 44 and 53, in his second volume, which he identified as suitable for that region. One had a wide central hall and symmetrical plan, the other was similar to an asymmetrical design he had done for a client in Montgomery, Alabama, where the site was on a hillside. He felt "the detachment of the kitchen from the main building, the size of the ground floor, the necessity for large windows, wide doors and ample verandahs, the difference in the number of stories, and many other considerations all tend to render a design prepared for a northern mansion totally unfit for the wants and conveniences of a Southern family." Also, "The laws of hospitality, observed there, require a larger number of sleeping apartments for a family of the same number of persons, since, at many seasons of the year, the Southern householder takes a pride in converting his mansion into a sort of honorary hotel."

If it had ever been completed, Longwood, in Natchez, below, built by Dr. Haller Nutt, would have made a superb "honorary hotel." As early as 1850 Dr. and Mrs. Nutt bought land in Natchez in order to build a summer home there. They owned two plantations in Louisiana, across and upriver from Natchez, and lived in a well-appointed but architecturally unimportant

Longwood, Natchez, Mississippi,
built for Dr. Haller Nutt, 1860–1861.
Designed by Samuel Sloan.

house at the plantation they called Winter Quarters. Nutt was a successful cotton farmer who kept well abreast of the latest scientific and technical developments. His father had introduced the use of steam to the cotton gin. To judge by later letters, his wife also possessed managerial skill and agricultural know-how. Husband and wife must have pored over the various designs in Samuel Sloan's book and in 1859, if not earlier, decided upon the elaborate plan for an Oriental Villa published there, number 49. Sloan was frank in his lengthy description. The villa was in a style seldom chosen because, "a large edifice is necessary to give it proper force and expression," and it would be expensive. However, for those to whom "these objections are of little force," and who "seek for a design at once original, striking, appropriate and picturesque," this could be recommended. If the Nutts were to rival the existing mansions and villas around Natchez, such a design was a good choice.

By 1857–1858 the Nutts had built a servants' house on the property in Natchez, large enough to house the thirty-two servants who would eventually be needed for their new mansion, and in which they stayed from time to time while Longwood was being built. This still stands. Their eldest daughter attended school in Philadelphia, and Dr. Nutt must have made contact with Sloan and invited him as architect for their house—this was not the kind of mansion that could be erected simply by consulting a published design, however fully described. In January 1860 work commenced. Sloan came out for a visit in February 1860 and again in late June. In April Mr. Addison Hutton was sent from Philadelphia to supervise the work; in May two bricklayers came. In September the Nutts were in Philadelphia. In the intervals between personal visits Sloan and Nutt had a lengthy correspondence; the published design was modified to suit the specific needs of the Nutts. Sloan had prepared specifications for the different kinds of lumber needed; Nutt first purchased some white pine lumber locally and dressed yellow pine flooring in New Orleans. He set up a brickyard on the property, and the bricklayers and Nutt's slave craftsmen set to work. In Philadelphia Sloan arranged for the preparation of all the window and door frames, brackets, and other detailed finishing elements. Nutt arranged to secure still more lumber, most of it cypress, from a local sawmill. Drawings were sent back and forth. Foundations were laid. Lime was sent from Philadelphia—Sloan wanted to know if German silver would be desired for the grates. In emergencies telegrams were sent. Specifications included an iron cistern in the kitchen above the level of the bathtub, which was to be lined with copper—tinned and planished—silver-plated fixtures, pipes for gaslights, speaking tubes from dining room to kitchen, a furnace in the basement with necessary flues and registers, some silver-plated doorknobs and some white porcelain.

The two men corresponded regularly even as the clouds of war began to gather. When the brickwork was finished in March 1861, the Northern workmen who were returning home put a notice in the Natchez paper thanking Nutt and the citizens of Natchez for their courtesy "during the intense excitement through which we have just passed." At first surprised because he had not been informed, Nutt was pleased and wrote to Sloan, "It will show to Northern people that Philadelphia Mechanics

have been south and well treated and not hanged." After the Southern attack on Fort Sumter in April communication became increasingly difficult, mails were slow or interrupted between North and South. Nonetheless work continued; both men deplored the emotional intensity surrounding what they saw as acts of politicians. By August, however, all but one of the Northern workmen had returned, and building was stopped. Virtually all of the exterior was completed and the interiors of the ground or basement floor rooms were finished. For two years no communications passed between the two men, but in October 1863 they again corresponded and Sloan even hoped he would be able to make a visit if the war would abate. Nutt died in June 1864, a broken man, torn in spirit, since he had opposed secession; his plantations suffered depredations from both Union and Confederate forces. (Despite the extraordinary strength of the "Confederate legend" in Natchez today, the record shows that most of the powerful and wealthy men of Natchez at first opposed secession and the war, and did all they could to prevent what they saw as potential disaster. They somehow thought slavery and other issues could be reconciled. In the end they supported the war and gave generously of themselves and their families even though they saw the hopelessness of the cause.) Members of the Nutt family lived in the fairly spacious series of ground-floor rooms at Longwood for some time, and the property was owned by descendants of Haller and Julia Nutt until 1968. The upper floors remain to this day unfinished, just as they were when work stopped more than a century ago.

Sloan was sufficiently proud of the house and design that he published it in *Godey's Ladies Book* in 1860, and then again in his own work, *Sloan's Homestead Architecture* in 1861. Since many modifications had been made to his first plan for an Oriental Villa, he was justified in presenting this as a new and different design. In his *Homestead Architecture*, Design I, he described it as "adapted to the wants of the man of fortune in any section, but particularly suitable for the home of the retired Southern planter." He further explained, "The choice of style in this example was less a matter of caprice than the natural growth of the ground-plan adopted." As can be seen from the complex plans, right, on each floor two series of rooms were to have been built around the center octagon or rotunda, making for a sequence of private and more public rooms. It was so designed that virtually every room had direct access to either a porch or a balcony. If there was even a whiff of a prevailing breeze, it could have been found. The central rotunda on each floor was meant "not only for a thoroughfare by which all adjacent rooms could be located," but also "as a medium for light and ventilation." No practical reason, but fancy "dictated that the dome should be bulbiform— a remembrance of Eastern magnificence which few will judge misplaced as it looms up against the mellowed azure of a Southern sky." Sloan was mildly apologetic in explaining the slightly mixed style. "In addition to this, the Moorish arch employed in the balconies and the foliated drapery of the verandas will fully sustain us in the application of the term 'Oriental,' despite the Italian details of cornice and window."

Longwood, still unfinished on the inside, stands as an example of the bold and grandiose aspirations of the wealthy cotton planters along the Mississippi in the flush times of the 1850s.

Equally grandiose, if not more so, was Belle Grove, following page, formerly located on the Mississippi between White Castle and Donaldsonville, Louisiana. It was of brick, stuccoed over to imitate stone and tinted a warm roseate tone. It was built for John Andrews, a former Virginian, by the New Orleans architect Henry Howard, and completed in 1857. It was, by all accounts, one of the grandest, if not *the* grandest, of Southern plantation houses. As late as 1924 its occupants, not descendants of the original owner, lived there on a fairly lavish scale, but hurricanes and unexpected early winter freezes created a sequence of failures of the sugar crop that made support of such an elaborate home impossible. Many people still living witnessed the gradual ruin of the proud structure, which ended in a fire on March 15, 1952.

It was large in scale, the raised basement itself twelve feet high. A giant portico with Corinthian columns dominated the front. On one side stood another great portico, this with a flat roof rather than a pediment. On the other side there was a rounded projecting bay. Farther back a large one-story wing housed the kitchen and servants' quarters; to the rear on the other side was a two-story wing with library and bedroom below and two bedrooms above. There were a number of balconies, galleries, piazzas, and verandas—all four terms were used on a contemporary plan—so that every major room had access to one of these. In style it represented a synthesis of the older Greek tradition of columns and giant portico with the freer use of side porches, bays, balconies, and verandas characteristic of the Italian taste. The rusticated basement with arched windows echoed Italian town palaces. A variety of room shapes and sizes was found inside, with columns and pilasters to lend accent. The main staircase spiraled gracefully upward; there was an additional service stairway inside. The portico was reached by a graduated stairway with landing, and there were two outside stairways on the rear of the house. Romantic fantasy has it that there were seventy rooms. Depending on what one counts as rooms, there were closer to forty or fifty.

The owner was John Andrews, formerly of Virginia, who seems to have come to Louisiana around 1830 and may have first lived in an eight-room house that later became the overseer's. At least, an advertisement for the sale of the property, page 261, published sometime around 1867 indicates that the owner had resided there for thirty-seven years. In this same notice, he reported that the prewar sugar crop of 1856 sold for $97,000, and that the "very elegant, nearly new Dwelling House" had cost $75,000 in 1857.

Henry Howard, the architect, is little known outside of New Orleans, though when he died in November 1884, the New Orleans *Daily News* described him as "one of the most successful architects in the United States." He designed at least thirty-eight buildings in the years between 1848, when at age thirty he opened his own architectural practice, and 1872, when he wrote a short autobiography. During these years he also served as principal draftsman with the Confederate Naval Iron Works in Columbus, Georgia. Howard came to America from Cork, Ireland, at age eighteen, in 1836. His father had been a builder, and the boy studied at the Mechanics Institute in his native city. There were few opportunities in the building trades in New York, so he

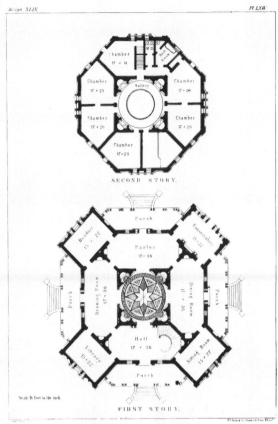

"An Oriental Villa," Design 49 in Sloan's THE MODEL ARCHITECT, *vol. II, 1852. The plan of Longwood was slightly modified from this.*

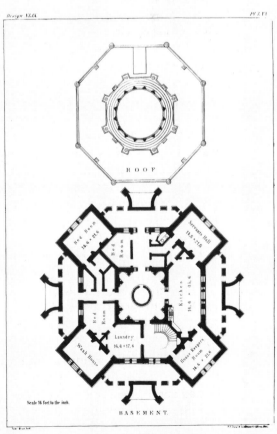

*Belle Grove, on Mississippi River between White Castle and
Donaldsonville, Louisiana, built for John Andrews, 1857.
Designed by Henry Howard. Now demolished.*

took a job with a looking-glass and picture frame-maker's establishment. In the fall of 1837 he journeyed to New Orleans, where a yellow fever epidemic was raging and, despite the depression, found work as a carpenter-joiner. He became especially skilled in "the most difficult branch of the trade, viz, stair building." Indeed, many of the buildings he designed have impressive spiral stairs. After five years he became foreman for a local builder, then upgraded his skills by studying for a time with James Dakin and with Henry Molhausen, a Prussian whom he described as a good surveyor and engineer. By the time Howard designed and built Belle Grove he had had almost ten years' experience as an architect, and several important plantation houses were numbered among his works.

Andrews seems to have fared badly during the war, and sometime before 1867 or 1868 put his property up for sale. The advertisement for it is a revealing document, giving a layout and description of all the buildings as well as elevations and plans of the house. The buildings included a storehouse by the river, a hospital, the overseer's house, twenty Negro cabins plus a two-

story brick house with accommodations for 150 laborers, the large and fully equipped sugar house, a cooperage, a steam sawmill, a blacksmith's shop, stables and corn crib, and a smoke and meat house. Among advantages of the property, the owner declared that "No part of this Plantation has been overflowed by any 'crevasse' or break in the river levee during the last 37 years," that "no case of yellow fever" had occurred "in the vicinity," and that "the society of the neighborhood is large, cultural and social."

The Civil War brought irrevocable changes to the South. Some areas were devastated, flush times were over, slavery was ended, fortunes were lost, some new fortunes were soon made. The whole agriculturally based society went through painful and complex readjustments, and whatever economic and industrial gains the South seemed to have been making were lost. The very poverty of some during the postwar years helped to preserve much of the architecture of the region, architecture which might have been swept away if there had been greater prosperity. Building did go on, however, and anyone who travels

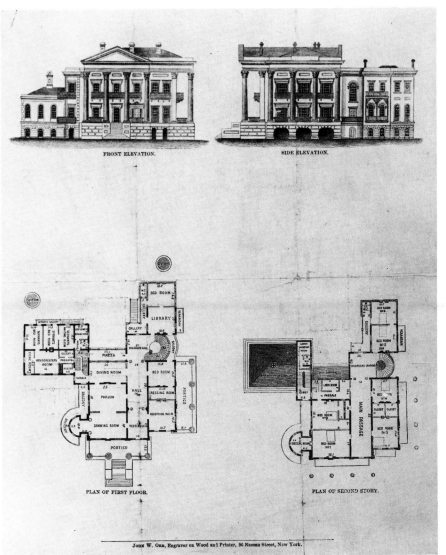

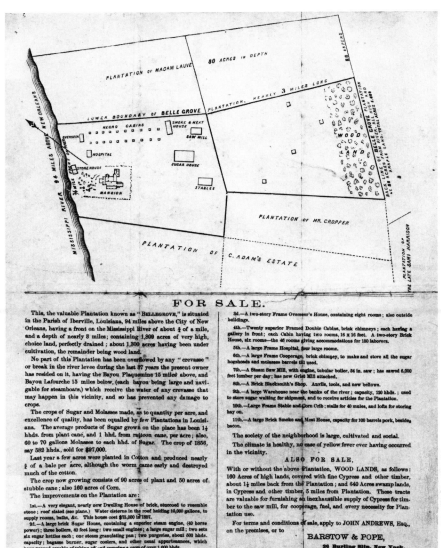

Bill of sale for Belle Grove Plantation, 1867 or 1868. Historic New Orleans Collection.

through the South with an eye for fine and interesting buildings of the 1880s and 1890s, and later, or even the 1870s, will find much to delight him, but these are outside the scope of this study.

Painting

No more than a hint of exaggeration was probably intended when the American art critic John Neal, writing in 1829, spoke of the "multitude of portraits" that could be found "in every village in our country." Neal was writing for a Boston literary magazine and if his own experience was more in the North than in the South, his observation was a shrewd assessment of fact for both regions. To judge from what survives there seems to have been a passion for portraiture, for likenesses, be they head size, bust size, Kit-Cat (less than half-length, but including head and at least one hand), three-quarter length, or whole length. Artists usually charged by size and the less expensive head and bust

sizes seem to have been most favored. Of portraits done in the South, some are large, colorful, and somewhat idealized, more are small in scale, somber in color, and remarkably plain and straightforward. On their flat canvases the artists, using different painterly styles, caught the shapes of the features, clothing, and sometimes gestures of a wide variety of subjects. There are still a large number of portraits, painted in the United States in the middle years of the nineteenth century, which need to be recorded and assessed.

One of the most sought-after portraitists was Thomas Sully. Having started out in Charleston, Norfolk, and Richmond, he settled permanently in Philadelphia in 1808. Throughout his long career, ending in his ninetieth year, he had patrons from the South and made occasional trips into the region. Several sittings must have been involved in bringing to completion on June 16, 1837, the lovely portrait of Mrs. William Crawford, née Temperance Fitts, following page, which he began on May 29, 1837. Sully's special gifts were a feeling for soft, rich colors, a fluid brush stroke, skill in creating the effects of the play of light, and

Thomas Sully. "Mrs. William Crawford"
(née Temperance Fitts). Begun May 29, 1837,
finished June 16, 1837. Oil on canvas. Alabama
Department of Archives and History, Montgomery.

an ability to flatter his sitters subtly, most especially women. All his mature talents were brought to bear in his portrait of the long-necked beauty from Mobile, Alabama, shown here in an elegantly cut gown of purple velvet and wearing a white turban draped with a veil. One of Neal's generalizations about Sully's work, stated in nineteenth-century phraseology, aptly fits this painting and reflects a feminine ideal of the time. "He had a sense of beauty, a perception of the graceful and bewitching—of that which gives a high-bred woman dominion over men. . . . His female portraitures are often poems,—full of grace and tenderness, lithe, flexible, and emotional; their eyes, too, are liquid enough and clear enough to satisfy even a husband—or a lover." The elegant Mrs. Crawford was the daughter of a judge and wife

of a judge, and it is easy to imagine that she fulfilled her role of helpmate and hostess in the legal and political circles in which she moved with skill and grace.

Something of the same sense of elegance and charm is seen in the portrait of three young Kentucky subjects, the Anderson boys, right, painted by Oliver Frazer in 1839. Frazer was a native-born Kentuckian of Irish descent who first studied painting in Lexington with Matthew Jouett. On the latter's advice he spent a short time with Thomas Sully in Philadelphia. From there he went on to Europe, where he traveled and studied for four years, and made the acquaintance of the American G. P. A. Healy, who became a lifelong friend. Frazer found the English school most congenial and, like his mentor, Sully, admired the romantic and somewhat idealized portraiture of Sir Thomas Lawrence. In the portrait of the Anderson boys Frazer uses hazy lighting in the loosely brushed background to set off the delicate features of the three serious-eyed children who are made to appear as young aristocrats.

Well over fifty portraits by Frazer have been identified. He was one of several painters in the Lexington region during the 1840s and '50s. Others included Joseph Henry Bush and Louis M. Morgan. Frazer was also only one of a number of artists who studied for a time with Sully and who spent a large part of their career in the South. Whether these artists actually studied or worked in Sully's studio as apprentices is not clear. In some cases Sully advised young artists to take lessons from Pietro Ancora, a well-known drawing master in Philadelphia. Others who received guidance from Sully included Alfred J. Miller of Baltimore; James Reid Lambdin, who spent from 1832 to 1837 in Louisville; Joseph Henry Bush of Kentucky, who also spent winters in Louisiana and Mississippi painting portraits of planters and their families; Henry James Brown, who worked in and around Lynchburg, Virginia; Thomas S. Officer, who worked in Mobile in 1835 and 1837 and so admired Sully that he took that as his middle name; and William Edward West, a native of Lexington, who spent a year in Natchez after his study with Sully, became famous in Europe for his portraits of Byron, Shelley, and Trelawney, worked a number of years in New York, then spent his last two years in Nashville. Though their styles differ, one can see in the work of each something of Sully's influence—in fluid brushwork, use of background highlights, and a tendency to idealize.

Paintings by some of these men help to reinforce the "Southern aristocrat" image; an image that had more reality in the eighteenth century than in the nineteenth. Far more of the portraits painted in the South during the immediate antebellum period are simple and bourgeois in character, and no doubt accurately reflect the appearance of the majority of the planter and merchant classes of the region.

The plain portrait of Mrs. Isaac Shelby, following page, is in contrast to that of the elegant Mrs. Crawford, though she, too, moved in political circles; her soldier husband served as the first Governor of Kentucky from 1792 through 1796, then came out of retirement to serve another term during the War of 1812. When this portrait was painted she was recently widowed, was sixty-three years old, had borne eleven children, and raised this large family at their home, Traveller's Rest, in Lincoln County. There is no pretense and little artifice here. This pioneer lady, upright of posture and clear-eyed, looks directly at the viewer. She wears her widow's weeds with dignity. We do not know why she chose to have her portrait done at this time, but it might be that members of the family, conscious of the recent death of their father, wanted her likeness to be recorded for posterity. The portrait is signed and dated "Painted by P. Henry Davenport/Danville/Ky/ 1827." Davenport was a native of Danville, Kentucky, born in 1803 and named after the Virginia patriot, Patrick Henry. He appears to have been self-taught, and his style has something of the linear hard-edged character of such artists, though it is not as flat or awkward as some. His crisp style seems singularly appropriate for his stalwart subject. He worked as an itinerant in and around Danville until 1840, after which he moved on to Illinois and Indiana.

The number of portraits of women wearing mourning dress—it is harder to identify men in black suits as being in mourning—reminds us of the frequency of early death in the nineteenth century. A poignant posthumous miniature of Felix Grundy Eakins, following page, was painted in Nashville in 1846 by John Wood Dodge. On first glance the child with a broken toy and tools cast aside could be any lively and destructive child. However, here the attributes become emblems of a broken and unfinished life, as do the wilted flowers. An urn is a traditional and popular garden or porch ornament, but it is also a symbol of death and mourning in classical art and in the imagery of mourning jewelry. John Wood Dodge was a New Yorker who specialized in miniatures, and who also exhibited dioramic paintings.

Oliver Frazer. "The Anderson Boys, Edward, John, and Benjamin." c. 1839. Oil on canvas. J. B. Speed Art Museum, Louisville, Kentucky.

Patrick Henry Davenport. "Mrs. Isaac Shelby" (née Susannah Hart). 1827. Signed and dated: "Painted by P. Henry Davenport/Danville/Ky/1827." Oil on wood. Kentucky Historical Society, Frankfort.

Another unusual mourning portrait is that of the bereaved family of Bernard Duchamp of New Orleans, right, done in 1832 by an unidentified artist. Here the wife and mother, with her five children, is shown seated before the draped portrait of the deceased husband and father, which stands on an easel. Behind them an ethereally lighted window or opening suggests the heavenly paradise where the soul will find rest. A preoccupation with sorrow and death was all too typical of the nineteenth century—one need only think of Queen Victoria in perpetual mourning after the death of Prince Albert. It also can be seen in any study of funeral practices, in endless photographs, and is reflected in the words of many songs. The fact that certain scientific achievements, such as vaccination, new methods of diagnosis, improvements in medical training and facilities eliminated some causes of death, made the ones that did occur all the more poignant. Statistics suggest that those living in the American South ran a greater risk of infection, disease, and early mortality. New Orleans, where yellow fever epidemics broke out regularly, was known as "the graveyard of the Southwest," and as early as 1840 life insurance companies often charged one percent more premium on Southern cases.

The artist of the painting of the Duchamp family mourning is not known, nor is the artist of the original portrait of Bernard

John Wood Dodge. "Posthumous likeness of Felix Grundy Eakins, Aged Three Years." 1846. Miniature on ivory. Cheekwood, Fine Arts Center, Nashville, Tennessee.

Dodge showed in New York from around 1830 to 1839, then removed to the South. His account book preserves a record of his travels. From 1839 through 1854 these included Huntsville, Alabama; Marietta, Ohio; White Sulphur Springs and Petersburg, Virginia; Nashville and Memphis, Tennessee; New Orleans, Louisville, Natchez, and St. Louis. Some places were visited several times. At some point he established the community of Pomona in Cumberland County, Tennessee, where he lived and achieved local fame as the founder of apple orchards. The little portrait of Felix Eakins is a tenderly conceived picture, and fairly unusual in its subtle imagery. Dodge and his patrons recognized this, for he charged $225 and noted it was "taken after death." His usual charges for miniatures were $75 or $100. A more characteristic posthumous portrait of a child showed the head or bust with a band of clouds below, or an angel or clouds in the background. Artists were not particularly fond of the task, but posthumous portraits were part of their stock-in-trade. Later in the century the camera would be used for many a sorrowing family to record the likeness of a child taken suddenly in death.

Duchamp, which still exists and which was done about a decade earlier. In both there is fine, controlled brushwork and a certain precision and restraint in execution suggestive of the French academic tradition. While these paintings seem to have been done in New Orleans, they may also have been painted in France when the family visited there.

Beginning in the 1820s there are records that show a small but steady stream of artists of French birth or training who were attracted to New Orleans, and who lived and worked there intermittently for a number of years. One such artist was Louis Antoine Collas, a well-traveled portraitist and miniaturist, who had already spent time in New York, Philadelphia, and Charleston before coming to New Orleans in 1822. Born in Bordeaux, he studied in Paris, exhibited intermittently in the salons from 1798 through 1832, and spent 1802–1811 in St. Petersburg, Russia, where he painted miniatures in the court of the czar. He was in New York City by 1816, and in Charleston in 1816–1818, where his subjects included members of the Alston and Izard families. He lived in New Orleans from 1822 to 1824, then he returned to the city each spring between 1826 and 1829, possibly traveling the countryside in the winter months. In New Orleans he painted both portraits and miniatures, and his subjects included members of several prominent white Creole families. The unknown subject of one of his portraits, page 267, dated 1829, is believed to be a free woman of color. She is shown seated, half-length, with light falling evenly across her features. She wears a

Artist unknown. "The Bereaved Family of Bernard Duchamp." 1832. Oil on canvas. Louisiana State Museum, New Orleans.

Jean Joseph Vaudechamp. "Antoine Jacques Phillipe de Marigny de Mandeville." 1833. Oil on canvas. Signed and dated: "Vaudechamp 1833." Louisiana State Museum, New Orleans.

until 1839–1840, arriving in November or December and staying through the winter months. At least seventy-eight portraits by Vaudechamp have been located, and this may be a small portion of the total. Some may have gone to New York, Philadelphia, or back to France along with the migratory members of New Orleans's winter population. Those that survive show an even-handed realism, fine draftsmanship, concentration on the features of the individuals, and little background detail, all traits conforming to the French academic traditions of the time. His subjects appear as eminently bourgeois citizens. One of the most expressive of his paintings is that of Madame Theodore Bailly-Blanchard, right, painted in 1832. A lively grimace animates her face and dominates the composition. The artist has effectively caught the glints of blue on the frothy sheer lace and ribbons of her mobcap. She was not a classic beauty and did not expect the artist to make her appear so, but she was probably a good companion. She was the wife of a commission merchant, and they made their home in the old section of the city. As with so many Vaudechamp portraits, details of objects such as eyeglasses are rendered with loving and precise care. If the fine draftsmanship and realistic depictions of Vaudechamp represent typical work of artists of not quite the first rank in France, and if his work also represents what the solid middle class of France desired in portraiture, then it is not surprising that the art of photography saw its beginnings in France in the 1820s and '30s as certain artistic wishes and technical accomplishments came together.

Vaudechamp's portrait of Antoine Jacques Phillipe de Marigny de Mandeville, left, completed in 1833, is notable as an ambitious attempt to show the full regalia of a young aristocrat of New Orleans. Though brilliant in coloration, it is not totally successful, since the modeling of the figure is somewhat weak. Young Mandeville was the fifth-generation member of a prominent Louisiana family. Educated at St. Cyr Academy in France, he served for a short time as a cadet and officer in the French Army. He returned to New Orleans in 1833 and is shown here in the dress uniform of a lieutenant or captain in the First Squadron of Cavalry, Orleans Lancers, of the Louisiana Militia. Gold braid and polished brass abound, though the young officer has a withdrawn and inward expression that suggests his possible indifference to the gaudy glamour. Mandeville was later to serve as a colonel in the Confederate Army, and after the war lived a quiet and private life until his death in 1890.

Mandeville's portrait is the most ambitious of known Vaudechamp paintings. Most others are closer in format to that of Mme. Bailly-Blanchard. From these it appears that many of the leaders of the merchant-planter society of New Orleans had little desire to be recorded in a grander manner, though a few had such portraits done in France. After his return to France, Vaudechamp exhibited in the salons until 1848; he died in 1886.

Another of this group of French-speaking artists who was important to the portrait tradition of the lower Mississippi Valley was Jacques Guillaume Lucien Amans (1801–1888). Born in Belgium, he studied in France, where he exhibited in the salons from 1831 to 1837. He is known to have been in New Orleans by 1836; he then followed a pattern much like Vaudechamp's, visiting the city every winter. His connection with New Orleans was to last until 1856, when he and his wife, a Louisiana woman,

yellow-and-green kerchief, locally called a tignon (from chignon), which was characteristically worn by women of black descent. Her fine lace collar, the snuffbox she holds, the attractive painted chair as well as her dignified expression and pose all suggest a woman of some standing and substance within the community.

The best-known and certainly one of the most productive of French-born artists working in New Orleans and environs in the 1830s was Jean Joseph Vaudechamp (1790–1886). He studied with Anne-Louis Girodet in Paris and exhibited with some regularity in the salons from 1817 through 1848, attaining a Third Class Medal in 1843. He first came to New Orleans at the age of forty-one, in 1831. He then returned virtually every autumn,

returned to France, perhaps because they feared the consequences of a war and civil unrest. It is very possible that his decision to come to America was influenced by Vaudechamp, for the two came over on the same ship in 1836 and 1837, and occupied studios on the same street in the latter year. At least seventy-five paintings believed to be by Amans are known, of which only a third are signed; they are somewhat uneven in quality. Aman's favorite pose was the seated three-quarter-length figure, such as that in the small version of the portrait of his father-in-law, Pierre Landreaux, following page, signed and dated 1845. Amans's work is usually softer-edged and more generalized than Vaudechamp's, but he, too, concentrated on the face and hands of the sitter to convey the personality. One senses that the strong characterization of the mature features of Landreaux was considered an excellent likeness. The face is especially well modeled, with strong shadows and contours. Landreaux was a planter in St. Charles Parish and for a time Recorder of Mortgages for Orleans Parish. The pose and style are reminiscent of the work of the French artist Ingres. Amans's subjects included General Zachary Taylor and a variety of clients in the New Orleans region. As did Vaudechamp, he seems to have sometimes stayed at a plantation and painted several members of a family.

Amans's portrait of a fellow artist, A. C. Jaume, page 269, signed and dated 1841, is one of his most sympathetic. The

Jean Joseph Vaudechamp. "Mme. Theodore Bailly-Blanchard" (née Rosa Colin). 1832. Signed and dated: "Vaudechamp 1832." Oil on canvas. Louisiana State Museum, New Orleans.

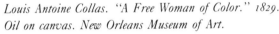

Louis Antoine Collas. "A Free Woman of Color." 1829. Oil on canvas. New Orleans Museum of Art.

edges are especially soft, so that the figure blends into the background, while a strong light is used to model the face of the sensitive young man. It is the most romantic of Amans's paintings, free and intimate, and appears to be a response to the new romantic movement. This was probably not done as a commission, but as a study for a friend; hence he may have felt able to experiment. Jaume was also from France, and was in New Orleans in 1834, 1837, and 1841, 1842, and 1843. He advertised as both a teacher and painter during these years, and his studio was just down the street from Amans. Only a few paintings by his hand have been identified.

When General Andrew Jackson, as a former President, aged and ailing, came to New Orleans on January 8, 1840, to commemorate the twenty-fifth anniversary of the Battle of New Orleans, Amans did a seated three-quarter-length portrait, a formal

state portrait with drapery and suggestions of classical architecture in the background. He made several versions of this. Another artist who used the opportunity of Jackson's visit to make a sketch was Jules Lion, a French-born free man of color. He then translated his sketch into a lithograph, lower right. The *New Orleans Bee* of January 10, 1840, described the old general as "very feeble . . . His face is emaciated, his form stooped, and the sunken eye and unsteady step give little indication of his former prowess and youthful vigor." Something of the former spirit of the old man is suggested through the rendering of the tight lips, long jaw, high forehead, and sweeping mane of hair. Jules Lion distinguished himself in lithography and the making of daguerreotypes while in New Orleans, where he lived and worked from

around 1836 until his death in 1866. In Paris he had exhibited in the salons of 1831 and 1836.

Amans and Lion were two among many artists who painted Jackson during his lifetime. He had been painted as early as 1815 by Thomas Sully and others when he first attained fame. Ralph E. W. Earl, who became one of Jackson's friends, made over thirty portraits of him. The state portrait continued to flourish. In the South, in addition to Jackson, probably the two political leaders most frequently portrayed were Henry Clay and John C. Calhoun. Copies of paintings of former leaders were also made for statehouses and city halls. The portraits of Washington, Jefferson, Lafayette, and Franklin by C. R. Parker, which now hang in the Georgia Capitol, are a case in point.

A. D. Lansot, Etienne Constant Carlin, and Adolphe D. Rinck were other artists who visited New Orleans during these years. A Frenchwoman, L. Sotta, was there during the winter of 1841–1842 and painted several memorable portraits characterized by penetrating realism; she, too, had exhibited in the Paris salons, in 1833 and 1838. American-born artists working for a time in the 1840s in New Orleans included Chester Harding, Theodore Moise, and G. P. A. Healy. The last made a copy of Amans's portrait of Zachary Taylor in the 1860s, which suggests there might have been contact between the two men in the late 1840s or '50s. We know little about the interaction among these artists, nor do we know how much, if any, contact there was between these artists and those in New York or Philadelphia, where the foreign visitors might have stopped briefly, as did Vaudechamp, on their trips back and forth across the Atlantic. In the studies of American painting most of the foreign-born artists who came in colonial times are clearly identified, but there is a tendency to forget those who came to our shores later, partly because there were so many more artists. The work of these men and their ideas, however, contributed to the artistic perceptions of their own and successive generations.

New Orleans may have attracted a larger number of artists than did smaller cities and towns, but as one begins to review the large number of portraits produced in the South during the 1830s, '40s, and '50s, Neal's statement that portraits could be found in virtually every village across the land seems true. There are some artists who traveled in several states, and others primarily associated with one area or community. Among those who traveled in various parts of the South is C. R. Parker, whose portraits from the 1830s and 1840s can be found in Louisiana, Mississippi, Alabama, and Georgia. Parker's paintings are characterized by fine, rather delicate, draftsmanship, and, as with Vaudechamp, a delight in careful rendering of fine jewelry, eyeglasses, and so on. Audubon seems to have met Parker in Natchez in the 1820s, and the two were together in London and Paris in 1828, where Parker painted the distinguished French naturalists Cuvier and Redouté. Parker was in New Orleans in 1826, then again in 1832, 1838, and 1845–1846, and is known to have visited Mobile in the spring of 1840, 1843, and 1844. Among his patrons was Mrs. John Andrews, the wife of the owner of Belle Grove plantation, described earlier.

Artists who are very much associated with one locale include Samuel M. Shaver, who worked primarily in east Tennessee, and William Bogart Cooper, associated with Middle Tennessee. The portraiture of both these men is characterized by an almost Puritan severity and directness. Thomas Cantwell Healy, the younger brother of the well-known portrait painter, G. P. A. Healy, spent most of his artistic career in the town of Port Gibson, Mississippi, competently portraying many of the citizens of southwestern Mississippi. The career of John Toole, a portrait painter who worked in Virginia—Harpers Ferry, Fredericksburg, Petersburg, Charlottesville, Richmond—is another whose work and career have been traced. His art, as did that of many, evolved from angular "primitiveness" to subtler professionalism.

William James Hubard is best known in and around Baltimore, Richmond, and Norfolk. One of his specialties was the small cabinet-sized portrait, around 21 by 15 inches, in which the

Jules Lion. "Andrew Jackson." 1840. Lithograph. Robert G. Pollack Collection, Tulane University, New Orleans, Louisiana.

William James Hubard. "Robert Gilmor, Jr." c. 1829–1831.
Oil on panel. Baltimore Museum of Art.

significant gesture has roots in this early experience. Finally he managed to break away and took up oil painting, possibly encouraged to do so by Gilbert Stuart. He returned to England for two years, then took up residence first in Philadelphia, next in Baltimore, where this painting was done. During this time he exhibited portraits of Henry Clay and John C. Calhoun, and did portraits of Andrew Jackson and John Marshall, all possibly with the intent of doing a series of statesmen. At least twenty-eight portraits from the Baltimore period alone are known. In the early 1830s he established contacts in Virginia, and settled for a time in Gloucester County. Around 1835–1837 he married, and he and his wife went abroad for a year or so. While there he did a cabinet portrait of the sculptor Horatio Greenough, and also was friendly with Hiram Powers. As did most American artists who visited Europe, he studied and copied works of old masters hanging in the great museums of France and Italy. On return he and his wife seem to have lived again for a time in Virginia. Something like sixty portraits of Virginia subjects, done before or after the European sojourn, have been identified.

By 1841 the Hubards were in Richmond, their home till the end of his life. Here he found a coterie of friends with artistic and literary interests, including Edward A. Peticolas and Mann S. Valentine and his family. Hubard's own work became more experimental, and he did several paintings based on literary and historical themes. His friendship with Valentine's eldest son, Mann S. Valentine II, was especially congenial. The latter, following in the footsteps of his father, was a merchant, and later a successful manufacturer of meat extract, but spent his free time

William Harrison Scarborough. "Self Portrait." c. 1845–1855.
Oil on wooden panel. Florence Museum, Florence, S.C.

subject full-length, seated or standing, was shown in a rather dark setting in which characteristic attributes of the sitter were included. Light plays on the features and figure of the sitter. Typical is the fine, small portrait of Robert Gilmor, Jr., above. Baltimore's distinguished collector and patron of American artists, shown surrounded by objects from his collection—Greek vases, a portfolio from which watercolors or paints are spilling out, some rolled-up scrolls, possibly maps, and sculpture in the upper right. Bodily gestures and features are acutely observed. This painting was probably done around 1829–1831, about midpoint in Hubard's checkered career.

As a boy in England Hubard was taken up by a somewhat unscrupulous manager who moved him about, demonstrating his talent for cutting likenesses or silhouettes, even taking him to America sometime before 1824. His talent or feeling for the

*William James Hubard. "Self-Portrait with
Mann S. Valentine II." 1852. Oil on canvas.
Valentine Museum, Richmond, Virginia.*

pursuing cultural interests; he wrote three books, studied and practiced archaeology, did sculpture, patronized artists, and collected works of art. In 1852 the young businessman wrote a ghost story called "Amadeus, or a Night with the Spirit," for which Hubard made twenty-eight drawings. When the book was published the drawings were not included, probably because they were too expensive to reproduce. However, Hubard painted a curious circular double portrait, above, showing the two collaborators, and figments of figures from the ghostly story in the background. The artist is shown full face and frontally on the left; Valentine is seen in profile, three-quarter length on the right, and a theatrical red drapery pulls the scene together. The whole is suggestive of the flights of fancy, love of poetry, and feeling for romance both enjoyed.

Hubard became interested in sculpture—an interest he had nourished since his days in Florence—and particularly in a scheme to cast bronze reproductions, in smaller scale, of Houdon's statue of Washington. At great cost, he succeeded, but by then war was imminent. He began experimenting with a "chemical compound" for the Confederate Army and died when it exploded. His small-scale portraits form an acute and sharply drawn record of his Maryland and Virginia compatriots. Mann

Valentine II lived until 1892. He willed the extensive family collection of paintings, sculpture, Indian artifacts, and manuscripts to what has become the Valentine Museum, a rich repository with a special emphasis on the arts and life of the city of Richmond, one of the many cultural institutions of the nation with beginnings in the nineteenth century.

James Deveaux and William Harrison Scarborough were among the artists painting in Columbia, South Carolina. Though both were in and out of Charleston, they found their principal patrons in the up-country, in and around the new capital. Deveaux (1812–1844) studied in Philadelphia for a time and is believed to have painted well over 200 portraits of Carolinians during the 1830s. He twice visited Europe, first sent by Colonel Wade Hampton for study, then again to Italy to paint copies of old masters, where he died. Scarborough (1812–1871) was originally from Tennessee and studied art and medicine in Cincinnati. By 1830 he was in South Carolina, and subsequently settled in Columbia. His self-portrait, lower left, is fairly somber, but made interesting by the well-modeled face and sometimes thick brushwork. In 1847, Scarborough painted South Carolina's famous political leader, John C. Calhoun. His reputation was established by the 240 or more portraits and miniatures he painted

Robert R. Curtis. "Osceola, a Seminole leader." 1838.
Oil on canvas. Charleston Museum.

the series of treaties by which the Indians agreed to remove beyond the Mississippi. Threatened by the Americans, he was reported to have replied that his people were accustomed to the warm air, rivers, and lakes of Florida, and especially its light wood (timber, probably pine), which was easy to fell and which burned easily. "They can not live in that cold country where only the oak tree grows." He hid the women and children in the swamps, organized the men, and harassed the whites with guerrilla tactics, precipitating the Second Seminole War. Captured under false pretenses when he came for an interview under a flag of truce on October 21, 1837, he was imprisoned first in Florida, then brought to Fort Moultrie, near Charleston. Public indignation ran high, "His handsome person, his melodious voice, his large dark eyes, his bravery and his fate, awoke a universal interest in him, and the ladies, in particular, felt an enthusiasm for the handsome Seminole chief, visited him and made him presents. But he seemed indifferent to all. . . ." It was during this time that Curtis painted Osceola, managing to capture the inward melancholy of the ill-fated man. Osceola's health rapidly declined; he ate little and would take no medicine. Within a few months he died. "The captive eagle could not live, deprived of the free life and air of his forest."

Curtis painted Osceola as a token of gratitude for Dr. R. L. Baker, who was friend and patron, and who had assisted the artist by supporting his studies in Europe. In this warm and colorful painting of a genuinely tragic and romantic subject, Curtis used all his painterly skill and knowledge derived from these studies. Osceola's clothing, a mixture of American and European textiles, calico coat, cloth turban, silver gorgets, and Indian, feathered headdress, shows how contact and trade with the white men had modified Indian dress. It is noteworthy that in South Carolina Deveaux, Scarborough, and Curtis each had acquaintances who acted as occasional patrons and were collectors; Hubard found similar encouragement in Baltimore and Richmond. Critics at the time bemoaned how little patronage there was for American artists, since most collectors still preferred a copy of an old master to an original painting by an American. This was true, yet the burgeoning interest in and support for the arts were encouraging. Unfortunately much of this came to an end as the South plunged into war.

Curtis was one of four or more artists who painted or drew Osceola. Much as modern figures who attract the public eye, however momentarily, have to pose for photographers, Osceola was asked to pose for an Army officer while still in Florida, then for Curtis and W. L. Laning, a decorative painter from Charleston, at Fort Moultrie, and for George Catlin. Engravings and replicas were ultimately made of most of these. Though it did not come to fruition, Hubard apparently planned to do a "historic painting illustrative of Indian characters," and requested sketches and information from the Army captain.

Osceola was a special case because of his celebrity. Other native and dark-skinned denizens of the American South attracted artists because they were colorful and picturesque in appearance and thus made good subjects for exhibition pictures. George Catlin, as is well known, was moved by a desire to record peoples whose way of life he saw disappearing. He also saw the commercial possibilities of exhibiting such paintings and in fact

in North and South Carolina and Georgia—a parade of solemn, serious individuals—but landscapes were also included in his oeuvre. He was in Europe in 1857, after which he hoped to establish an art gallery in Columbia, plans which fell through with the beginning of hostilities. Scarborough was encouraged in his work by the physician and collector, Robert Wilson Gibbes, who also helped Deveaux and was one of those who aided Hiram Powers to study in Italy. Gibbes's fine collection of paintings and engravings were lost in the burning of Columbia near the end of the Civil War.

In 1837 a writer in the Charleston *Courier* described Robert R. Curtis (1816–1877) as a native of Charleston "whose merits have been most strangely neglected." Few of his works are known. He was in fact a native of Germany who had come to Charleston at an early age. He studied with John Neagle of Philadelphia, knew Sully, and exhibited in the 1830s in New York. His merits as a painter can be seen in his compassionate portrait of Osceola, the Seminole Indian leader, above. Osceola opposed

supported himself for some time in this way. By 1838 Catlin had already made several journeys into the upper Midwest and the Great Plains in pursuit of his aim of painting the vanishing native Americans. In the Oklahoma Territory he met and painted members of the Choctaw, Creek, Cherokee, and Yuchi tribes of Georgia, Alabama, and Florida who had already been removed to the West. Sometime in the winter months of 1834 and 1835 he visited the Seminole Indians on the Gulf Coast near Pensacola and sketched a Seminole family drying fish on the snow-white sand dunes of Santa Rosa Island. Thus when he came to Fort Moultrie he was already familiar with the situation of the Seminoles. He did at least two portraits of Osceola, then painted several others of the imprisoned Seminoles; among those was Eematla, or King Phillip, right, described as the second chief, and an aged man. The swarthy features of the face are particularly well modeled. The old chief wears a red-and-green turban and has wrapped a gray trade blanket around his shoulders. Eematla died on the way to Arkansas with his fellow prisoners. Catlin's paintings of Western Indians are best known. His thirty-two or more paintings, plus sketches, of various members of the Southeastern tribes, though less known, are among his most fully developed works and form an important part of the history he set out to record.

A young Choctaw woman is shown below, signed and dated "P. Römer, Mobile, 1850." It may have been commissioned, but it is more probable that it was done as a picturesque subject by

George Catlin. "King Phillip, Second Chief, Seminole Indians." 1838. Oil on canvas. National Museum of American Art, Washington, D.C.

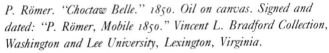

P. Römer. "Choctaw Belle." 1850. Oil on canvas. Signed and dated: "P. Römer, Mobile 1850." Vincent L. Bradford Collection, Washington and Lee University, Lexington, Virginia.

the artist whose oeuvre includes romantic subjects such as *The Bandit* and *The Bandit's Bride*. Her exotic heritage, for she must have seemed that to the painter from Bavaria, is suggested by the unusual side pose, her long, dark, loosely hanging hair, and what appears to be a trade blanket wrapped around her shoulders. All of the portraits of Caucasian subjects signed by or attributed to Römer are in conventional poses and dress. Little is known of Römer, but a number of signed and dated portraits indicate that he was active in Mobile between 1850 and 1865. He became a U.S. citizen on May 26, 1856. He appears to have been professionally trained in Europe. Contrary to the practice of some artists who visited Mobile only in the winter months, he made his home in Dog River, near Mobile, from 1852 through 1866, and most of his patrons were from Mobile or Baldwin counties.

Several other artists who worked in Alabama are associated with certain towns. William Frye, born in Bohemia, painted mostly around Huntsville. (He had emigrated to America with

*William Halsey. "Milo Parker Jewett, LL. D." c. 1847–1852.
Oil on canvas. Judson College, Marion, Alabama.*

in both North and South by the rapidly proliferating Baptists. With the beginning of hostilities Jewett left for the North and was selected by Matthew Vassar to head a new women's liberal arts college in Poughkeepsie.

Another educator who established himself in the South but could not accept seccession was Frederick A. P. Barnard. He taught at the University of Alabama, then at the University of Mississippi, where he became President and then Chancellor. He became President of Columbia University in New York in 1864 and worked long and hard to establish a course of collegiate study for women there. While still a professor of mathematics and chemistry at the University of Alabama, Professor Barnard experimented with the new art of photography, whose history from this time on parallels, impinges upon, and sometimes intertwines with the history of painting. Barnard discovered a process of accelerating the impression on a metal plate used in the making of daguerreotypes and reducing the exposure time needed, thus rendering daguerreotype portraiture more possible. By October 1841, he and a partner, Dr. William H. Harrington, had established a daguerreotype firm in Tuscaloosa, and by February 1842, the latter was in New Orleans. They were among the earliest producers of the process in the Deep South.

The first important steps leading to the development of pho-

*Unknown photographer.
"Judah Philip Benjamin." c. 1848–1850.
J. Hardy-Stashin Collection.*

the express purpose of painting the Indians, but was deflected from this.) Nicola Marschall, also from Germany, came first to Mobile, but then taught a number of years at the Seminary in Marion, Alabama, and is associated with that region. Joseph Thoits Moore, a native of Maine, painted a view of the new State Capitol in Montgomery, other architectural scenes (most unfortunately destroyed in the 1848 fire), and a number of portraits in that city. These are among the best-known artists in the region, but there are still others whose careers have not been studied.

William Halsey worked in Huntsville, Alabama, between 1847 and 1852. During this time he was commissioned to paint the portrait of Milo Parker Jewett, above, first President of Judson College in Marion, Alabama. This, too, is a realistic, bourgeois portrait, showing the young spectacled educator from New England alongside his books. The Judson Female Institute was the first Baptist academy for women, founded in January 1839. It was one of a succession of institutions of higher learning founded

tography as we know it today took place almost simultaneously in England and France in 1826, but the rapid spread of the technique of making impressions on metal plates took place after Louis Jacques Mandé Daguerre of France announced and revealed his methods in January and August 1839. Publication of the method was widespread and by November 1839 daguerreotype equipment was being sold in New York. One of the first Americans to take up the new technique was the artist Samuel F. B. Morse. At this point he had already invented the telegraph and virtually given up painting, although he was not yet prospering from the development of the telegraph. He taught literature and the art of design at New York University and gave lessons in the new technique. Barnard was one of his students, as was T. W. Cridland of Lexington, Kentucky, believed to be the first, or one of the first, professional daguerreotypists west of the Alleghenies. Interest in the new methods spread rapidly to towns and cities across the land; there were even traveling daguerreotypists who carted their equipment in wagons. By 1845 a New Orleans journalist could report that the "daguerreotype has almost surpassed the miniature." Jules Lion was the first to display "daguerreotype drawings" in New Orleans, but others soon practiced the art.

It is difficult to identify the work of individual daguerreotypists and sometimes equally difficult to identify the sitters. Judah P. Benjamin is probably the subject in the print lower left. The relation in concept to the realistic portraiture being done for painting and miniatures is clear; the focus is on the features, the interest is in fidelity of likeness, and there is no background or setting. Benjamin was Jewish, born in the West Indies. Established in New Orleans by 1828, he became a lawyer, sugar planter, politician, and then Senator from Louisiana from 1853 to 1861. He applied himself with equal brilliance to problems of international law, techniques of sugar chemistry, and the development of commerce in the South. He became a close associate of Jefferson Davis and served as Secretary of State for the Confederacy; after the defeat he made his way via the West Indies to England and had a distinguished legal career there. The daguerreotype appears to have been made around 1848–1850, and might well have been done in New Orleans.

By the 1850s new processes, using glass negatives and paper prints, superseded the earlier methods. The paper print photograph of Admiral David Farragut, right, was made with one of these techniques. The photographer was Edward Jacobs of New Orleans. He had established a studio there as early as 1844, and soon needed to enlarge it. His quarters included a gallery where busts and other works of art were shown, and a reception room for ladies. He had a variety of movable screens to be used as backgrounds. During the 1850s he was the most prominent photographer in New Orleans. Farragut's portrait was probably made in the summer of 1862, after the surrender of New Orleans to Federal forces. The photograph is in the tradition of state paintings: he appears in dress uniform, with arms crossed in a manly gesture. His admiral's hat on a table nearby is the only attribute. He was in his early sixties, and had served in the Navy since age nine and a half. Farragut was born in Knoxville, Tennessee, and spent part of his childhood in New Orleans. During his many years in the Navy he made his home in Norfolk, Virginia, and

Edward Jacobs, photographer. "Admiral David Farragut." Probably Summer 1862. Paper print. National Portrait Gallery, Washington, D.C.

lived there when not at sea. When the Virginia Convention of 1861 passed an ordinance of secession, he supported Lincoln and moved to the North. At first suspect because of his many Southern ties, he nonetheless faithfully served the Union throughout the war. Edward Jacobs practiced as a photographer in New Orleans until 1864, after which there is no further record of him in the city.

Just as there was something almost photographic in many nineteenth-century portraits done just before the invention of photography, some portraits of places show a similar desire on the part of the artist to record with precision and clarity. Little is known of the artist S. Barnard, a native of South Carolina, who

S. Barnard. "View Along the East Battery, Charleston." 1831.
Oil on canvas. Mabel Brady Garvan Collection, Yale University
Art Gallery. New Haven, Connecticut.

signed and dated a *View Along the East Battery, Charleston,* above, in 1831. He did two other views of the harbor at the same time, and apparently these are his only known works. Given the clarity and crispness of the view, it is possible the artist made a preliminary study with a camera obscura. Or he may simply have used his disciplined eye to calculate the interrelationships in the scene before him. This type of precise view of a place has roots in the great paintings of Canaletto and Bellotto, eighteenth-century Italian artists whose views of Venice, London, and Warsaw were celebrated in their time. The artist has included the varied street life—the mixed racial scene, adults strolling and gossiping, children playing, and dogs amiably cavorting. The Battery then as now was a favorite place for Charlestonians to stroll, to catch the fresh sea breezes and to watch the ever-changing quality of the

sea and the ships. Though in no way produced in the quantity of portraits, rather precise views of places seem to have enjoyed popularity as a type of painting in the 1830s, 1840s, and 1850s. The pleasure is in seeing the control of line and color, and the lively realism of detail.

Radiant light suffuses another view of Charleston, right, made in 1846 by Henry Jackson. The man-made environment of houses, mill, and wharf is a mere sliver in the study of the subtle changes in color and light on the millpond and in the sky. This painting can be classified as a precise view, but here the artist's interest and achievement were in the analysis of light and atmosphere. Henry Jackson was the son of a struggling miniature painter and restorer of paintings in Charleston. In the 1840s he was mentioned several times in the Charleston newspapers as a painter of landscapes and as an engraver. He may have had difficulty making sales, since he later took over his father's painting-restoration business.

Nicolino Calyo, a Neapolitan-trained painter, came to America in the 1830s and lived in Baltimore from 1834 to 1836. While there he did several gouache paintings of scenes in Baltimore, including the *View of the Port of Baltimore*, following page. This is a sparkling and precise view in which the light on the surface of the water and the wide expanse of sky are an important part of the composition. The life on the waterfront—loading and unloading of boats, a steamboat, and clipper ships—are all shown. On the bluff on the left is the old Marine Observatory, near the center in the far distance the domed outline of Latrobe's Baltimore Cathedral can be seen, and to the right of this the tall shaft of Mills's monument to Washington. Calyo was a well-trained European artist whose works included portraits, miniatures, landscapes, and historical scenes. He settled in New York around

1836–1837. In the 1850s he painted a panorama of the Connecticut River and exhibited this in New York, Philadelphia, Boston, and New Orleans. Panoramas were popular painterly shows, combining theater, geography, and visual journalism, first introduced in England in 1787. The earliest ones involved a circular painting placed within a circular hall so that the viewer, standing on a platform in the center in semidarkness, lost all judgment of distance and space, and felt he was *there*, in the presence of nature, an illusion of the real. These were popular in England and Europe in the early nineteenth century, and various panoramas were exhibited in New York as early as 1790. In 1830 Antonio Mondelli, a scene painter of Italian descent in New Orleans, advertised an exhibit of a panoramic view of the city and port of New Orleans in St. Louis. It is difficult to measure the effect of the theatrical showmanship and special technical effects needed to produce panoramas upon easel painting. There surely was some. The panoramas, which later moved—the paintings on

Henry Joseph Jackson. "View of Charleston." 1846. Oil on canvas. Carolina Art Association/Gibbes Art Gallery, Charleston, S.C.

Nicolino Calyo. "View of the Port of Baltimore." 1836.
Watercolor on paper. Baltimore Museum of Art.

reels of canvas—are mostly all destroyed, so detailed comparisons are not possible. Rivers and the adjoining landscapes and harbors, especially the Mississippi, but also the Hudson and Connecticut, were favorite subjects, and the wide horizontal format required for these may have contributed to the taste for the horizontal sea and landscapes, quiet in mood, rich in atmospheric effects, that were popular in the 1850s and 1860s in America and are now identified as luminist. Calyo lived and worked mostly in New York City until his death in 1884. His home in his old age is said to have resembled a small museum, with all sorts of paintings, paints, and curiosities.

Fascination with the illusion of the real, this time of an interior scene, is seen in George Cooke's monumental painting, 17

by 23 feet, of the interior of St. Peter's, right, based on a smaller painting he had done in 1828 while studying in Italy. This large view took three summers, 1845 through 1847, to complete for his friend and patron, the industrialist Daniel Pratt of Prattville. It hung in Pratt's gallery, adjoined to his home, until that building had to be torn down. It was offered to the University of Georgia in Athens in 1867 and the following year was hung on the end wall of the chapel there, where it remains, a boldly illusionistic painting that can dwarf the viewer—long affectionately called "The Painting" by students and townspeople, but little known elsewhere. In it Cooke captures with mathematical precision the great, overwhelming scale of St. Peter's, suggesting in vignettes the daily life that took place there. There are a group of clerics, a processional, barefoot pilgrims, loitering worshipers, and tourists.

Fairly large paintings of interior vistas, such as Cooke's, also appear to have enjoyed a certain popularity as exhibition pictures in both America and Europe. Probably the most celebrated example in Europe, which others then sought to emulate, was François Granet's view of the choir of the Capuchin church in the Piazza Barberini in Rome. This was so extraordinarily popular that, according to tradition, the artist made an unprecedented sixteen copies of it, one of which made its way to America. Thomas Sully, in turn, made a copy in 1821 and circulated it North and South with great success. Such paintings seemed to have been admired for their artistic effect and technical craftsmanship, and because they provided a tangible impression of grand and unfamiliar places. Cooke showed his smaller painting

of the interior of St. Peter's when he exhibited his paintings throughout America. The large version for Pratt probably would have been too unwieldy to travel.

When American artists went to Italy during this period, they did not necessarily go to study in the academies, or to look at what was current in Italy: Cooke in an article in the *Southern Literary Magazine* of May 1835 flatly declared that "no country at present is so deficient in men eminent in sculpture and painting." Instead many went to study and absorb the great art of the past, and to live a contemplative life for a time away from practical considerations. In actuality, they often had commissions to paint copies of old masters for their clients or for exhibition in America. In the time before photography and the multiple-media of today, such copies were the only way someone not frequently in Rome or Paris could know the color and scale of the

George Cooke. "Interior of St. Peter's, Rome." 1845–1847.
Oil on canvas. University of Georgia, Athens.

old masters; in the museum galleries artists from various nations, not just Americans, were to be seen making copies. During his sojourn in Europe Cooke produced thirty paintings, including copies after the Renaissance masters Raphael and Correggio, and more dramatic subjects based on works attributed to Salvator Rosa and Claude, as well as some subjects of his own choosing, such as the St. Peter's interior. While in England en route home, Cooke received a commission from the New Orleans merchant and art patron, James Robb, to do a copy of Géricault's dramatic and tragic *Raft of the Medusa*, a virtually contemporary or modern subject, and a sophisticated choice on the part of the patron. He went back to France and produced a copy of original size. When Cooke returned to the United States some of his pictures were exhibited in New York, Charleston, Richmond, Philadelphia, New York again, Washington, and Boston. In 1844 he brought his "National Gallery" to New Orleans, where he met and became friends with Daniel Pratt. Pratt at this time was building a warehouse for his gin business and thereupon had the third and fourth floors fitted out as a gallery and studio for the artist. Here, during the next five years, Cooke showed his own work, that of other Americans such as Sully, Thomas Cole, Thomas Doughty, John Gadsby Chapman, and European artists such as the Milanese, Anelli.

During his lifetime Cooke executed and exhibited a number of city views, including ones of Washington, Charleston, and Richmond, as well as scenes of Mount Vernon and Monticello. Most are lost, but to judge from a surviving view of Washington and aquatints based on others, several had a crisp clarity, with expanses of sparkling water, reflections, and atmospheric skies. It would be gratifying if these were rediscovered. Cooke wrote several essays on the scenery of the American South that were virtually invitations to artists, himself included, to paint the picturesque and dramatic scenery of the mountainous regions of the South, the Southern counterpart of the Catskills and Adirondacks. It appears to have been a task beyond his own capabilities, for his few mountain or landscape scenes that survive, such as of Tallulah Falls in Georgia and Red Sulphur Springs in Virginia, are awkward and unconvincing.

The versatile and productive Cooke, whom contemporaries identified as "distinguished" and "a true lover of the sublime in nature," also executed a number of paintings based on American historical subjects. One of the surviving subjects, *The Landing of the Maidens of Jamestown*, has a sentimental, anecdotal quality, conveying little dramatic effect. He hoped to receive a commission for one of the large panels in the rotunda of the Capitol at Washington, but failed, and was partially compensated by an 1837 War Department request to paint six visiting Indian chiefs, paintings unfortunately destroyed in an 1865 fire at the Smithsonian. Henry Clay, John C. Calhoun, and Bishop Leonidas Polk were among his many portrait subjects.

Cooke died of Asiatic cholera contracted during an epidemic in New Orleans in March 1849, just a few days after his fifty-sixth birthday. His known surviving works are uneven in quality, making his career difficult to evaluate. He nonetheless seems to have played a valuable role in the artistic life of the nation and the South, contributing to the development of landscape, history, and portrait painting, and exhibiting good European copies and American works, thus enlarging the artistic awareness of his generation.

The artist who received a commission for one of the large paintings in the rotunda instead of Cooke was John Gadsby Chapman, a younger artist from Virginia and a relative by marriage of Cooke's wife. Chapman spent the better part of four years, between 1837 and 1840, working on his huge 12 by 18 foot canvas of the baptism of Pocahontas; Cooke's daughter posed for Pocahontas. As with many in this series intended to translate the nation's history into visual epic, it looks forced. Unfortunately, it consumed much of Chapman's time and talent during some of the most productive years of his life.

Chapman (1808–1889) was a native of Alexandria, Virginia. Cooke and Charles Bird King, a painter established in Washington, encouraged him to pursue his interest in an artistic career. He went to Philadelphia and sought the guidance of Thomas Sully, who advised him to study with Pietro Ancora, the drawing master. This he did for six months, but feeling the need for still more training in order to become a history-painter, he went to Italy. Here he enjoyed the companionship of Samuel F. B. Morse and Cooke, among others, and absorbed some of the lessons of the great masters by copying their work—one such commission was from James Fenimore Cooper.

Chapman and Cooke returned on the same boat in 1831. In the years between 1831 and 1834 young Chapman lived in his hometown of Alexandria and had a studio in Washington. He established himself as a professional by exhibiting his paintings in Washington, Richmond, New York, Philadelphia, and Boston, and painted portraits, including Colonel David Crockett, President Madison, and members of the Washington family. He longed to receive one of the commissions for the rotunda and, apparently as preparation and research, he roamed the Virginia countryside, painting scenes of places associated with the history of the nation.

Whatever his motive, these landscape views reveal him as captivated by his native land. One is the exquisite small study, right, a view of Yorktown, where Cornwallis laid down his arms. An inscription on the back reads, "It is exactly between the plough and the bush in the picture and was taken on this spot by John G. Chapman in 1834." In this serene, smoothly finished pastoral scene, what was once the raw wilderness of the New World is here a cultivated, mellowed, domesticated land. It is becoming old Virginia, the signs of past wars all but obliterated. Chapman, as he shows the plowman returning from the fields, a part of the immemorial round of tilling the land and making it produce, has succeeded in transferring to his native land the sense of the past which he must have developed in Italy. Other scenes done at this time have some of the same quality, at once fresh and perceptive, mellow and elegiac.

In the fall of 1834, after the death of his father, Chapman moved to New York. It was propitious. He was elected a full member of the National Academy in 1836—he had exhibited there in 1835—and he was soon in demand as a designer of engravings for magazines and books. It was just at this time that illustrations in printed publications were becoming popular, made possible by the use of the engraved wood block to reproduce drawings. Chapman seems to have been able to work on the small scale and at the pace required for this new profession. Some of the earliest engravings, based on Chapman's paintings of Southern scenes were reproduced in *The Family Magazine* in 1836, 1837, and 1838, then for the next decade and more, he enjoyed great success as an illustrator in New York. He designed and made his own etchings and engravings for a variety of publications, periodicals, books, and the ever-popular gift volumes. James K. Paulding's *A Gift from Fairy Land*, with illustrations by Chapman, is considered one of the most beautiful books published in America during the first half of the nineteenth century. During this time he also completed the large Pocahontas.

Another project was his *American Drawing Book*, begun in 1843, copyrighted in 1847, with an expanded version in 1858. Highly regarded and apparently much used, it was also published twice in England, reissued in the 1860s, in 1870, and again in 1877. Despite these popular successes, Chapman was often, if not constantly, in debt and poor health. In 1848 he decided to go abroad for a time in order to paint at greater leisure, to get away from the pressures of life in New York, and to live in a better climate. The "time" turned out to be thirty-four years. Though life in Rome was in many ways serene, he no longer had orders for illustrations and had to seek commissions, mostly from visiting Americans. The Linton-Surget families of Natchez and New Orleans were among the patrons who bought large-size canvases. These are light-filled, highly finished figure paintings, but others of his customers wanted smaller, cheaper souvenirs and for these he was reduced to making colored engravings. The Civil War cut off the flow of visitors and by 1864 Chapman was virtually penniless. His life even in faraway Italy was profoundly affected by the American holocaust. He returned to the United States in 1889 and died eleven weeks later.

The Charlestonian, Charles Fraser, never visited Italy, yet in a miniature of his, following page, perhaps copied from a print, he captures the picturesque rural, timeless quality of the hill country of Italy. Even the colors seem right. There are muted greens and umbers, with delicate lavender and blue tints in the background. Fraser continued to produce the portrait miniatures that caught the subtle nuances of the personalities of his fellow

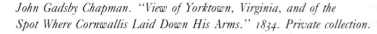

John Gadsby Chapman. "View of Yorktown, Virginia, and of the Spot Where Cornwallis Laid Down His Arms." 1834. Private collection.

Charles Fraser. "Landscape." Columbia Museum of Art, Columbia, S.C.

of these views are known, but if they were or are as vibrant and lively as the scene of *Oakland House and Race Course, Louisville,* signed and dated 1840, right, then another facet of the history of painting in America remains to be discovered. Here is recorded the colorful panorama of people and setting as they gather for the excitement of a race, in the light and shadow of a bright summer day. Just the year before, in September 1839, this course was the scene of the famous, and widely promoted, match between the stunningly handsome Grey Eagle of Lexington and Wagner, a powerful horse from Tennessee and Louisiana. The crowd, which included people from all parts of the Union, was said to have been "the largest ever up to that time seen at a race in America." It was the first Kentucky race of national importance—the account written by a New York journalist is considered one of the classics in turf literature. Henceforth Kentucky rivaled and surpassed other areas, such as Virginia, in producing racehorses. It is not known whether this painting of Oakland House and Race Course was done on commission or whether it was one "on hand" to be disposed of "on moderate terms." In the eyes of horse fanciers and Kentuckians it was a famous place worthy of being portrayed, and for this reason the painting no doubt survived while other works by these artists are little known or have been lost. It is fitting that a racecourse should be the subject of a fine painting done in the South, for in the period 1800 to 1865 the number of courses in the South far exceeded those in the North. From 1800 to 1830 there were nine important courses in the North, and forty-two in the South. From 1830 to 1865 there were twenty-one in the North and eighty-three in the South. An outdoor sporting life, and hunting, shooting, and fishing, were all-important to many Southern males.

No single artist or group of artists emerged as painters of the Southern countryside or mountains during the period from the 1830s to the 1860s. In the North, artists such as Cole and Church made their reputations by capturing something of the awesome and picturesque qualities of Niagara Falls and the Catskill Mountains, the first especially considered one of the great phenomena of the New World. In the South and what was then the West, the two natural areas that had roughly comparable qualities were the Mississippi River with its extraordinary length and diversity and the great ranges of the Alleghenies—the Blue Ridge and the Smoky Mountains. Yet both were, from a painterly point of view, extremely diffuse and, in the case of the mountains, difficult to access and not near enough to urban centers, which seem so necessary for the nurture of most artists.

The painters who created the ambitious panoramas of the Mississippi River made every effort to convey the drama and diversity of the changing landscapes and variety of human activity that took place along the great river. The descriptions and the publicity which these received both here and abroad would indicate that in many cases they achieved their goal. John Barnard, Henry Lewis, Leon Pomarede, and John Rowan Smith, each of whom produced a major panorama, all seem to have been painters of some skill and yet, because they concentrated so much of their effort on what turned out to be a short-lived interest, neither they nor the range of their work is remembered or can be well judged.

In 1842 a slim volume entitled *Georgia Illustrated* was printed

Charlestonians until just a few years before his death in 1860, but he also did 139 "Landscapes and other Pieces," few of which are known today. Here, in an imagined scene, he captures the somber quality of Italy, the Italy seen by romantic visitors who received spiritual and artistic nourishment by visiting that ancient country.

While American artists sought a sense of the past in the New World, there was a regular traffic of European artists who came to America, no doubt to seek their fortune, to enjoy the adventure and opportunities of the New World. A number of these, as we have seen, sought out the newly developing cities and towns west of the Alleghenies, in the Mississippi Valley, and on the Gulf Coast. Robert Brammer, possibly German-born, and his partner, Augustus A. Von Smith, listed as "foreign-born" when he lived in Vincennes, Indiana, from 1835 to 1840–1841, appear to have been such artists. The two men advertised in the Louisville *Daily Gazette* on October 6, 1841, as specialists in portrait, miniature, and landscape painting. In the 1838–1839 city directory of Louisville, Brammer notified the public that he would "always have on hand a number of oil paintings & views in the United States which he will dispose of on moderate terms." Few

and published in Penfield, Georgia, a community in the pied-mont. It contained a series of small, sharply etched steel engravings of "natural scenery and public edifices" based on sketches by T. Addison Richards, with descriptive texts edited by his brother, William C. Richards. In it they proclaim the beauties of Georgia, including its mountain cataracts, which "in particular features, far surpass" Niagara Falls. "The upper part of the State abounds with romantic and picturesque views. Mountains and vallies, glens and waterfalls, caverns and cliffs, with pastoral landscapes, are met with through all that region. Nor is it alone in the upper part of the State, that Nature has lavished her beauties. There are scenes of loveliness peculiar to the 'sunny South,' among the green savannas and dense forests of the 'low country.'" Though the editors extolled the beauties of Tallulah Falls

and the Nacoochee Valley they felt compelled to report that they were hard to find, hidden in the solitude of the mountains, and not along the regular thoroughfares of travel. They noted also that the few books on American scenery had been published in England. "It is therefore no small cause of gratification to the Editor of this work, that it is thoroughly and exclusively American, in its design and execution." They encouraged others to discover this area they so loved. "The pen of the artist . . . will find ample and fitting themes for their choicest delineations in Georgia." The engravings, though tiny, are charming, the essays full of poetic metaphors and relevant facts about the scenes depicted.

In May 1853, a little over ten years later, T. Addison Richards wrote an illustrated essay in *Harper's New Monthly Magazine*

Robert Brammer and Augustus A. Von Smith. "Oakland House and Race Course, Louisville." 1840. Oil on canvas. J. B. Speed Art Museum, Louisville, Kentucky.

on "The Landscape of the South." Again he described the natural scenery of the Southern states, "so inadequately is its beauty known abroad or appreciated at home," in eloquent prose, accompanied by engraved vignettes, based on his own drawings. Yet in his last paragraphs he all too graphically records why these places were so little known: "Still the Northern voyager will sadly miss the superior convenience of his own more traveled and better ordered routes: the by-ways are miserable, the people ignorant, the fare scant and wretched, and the expense of travel disproportionately great." Part of the untouched American Eden

was there, but only the most intrepid could reach it. Reason enough, unfortunately, why few artists explored the hidden wonders of the Southern hills and mountains, and why few Southern artists developed the dramatic and picturesque landscape themes so favored at this time. T. Addison himself seems to have produced more fine pencil sketches, which served as the bases for engravings, than finished oil paintings.

In one of the paintings, below, Richards caught the gentle beauty of a Southern river scene, with moss-laden oak dominating the tranquil rural setting. Here he evokes one of the many

T. Addison Richards. "River Plantation." c. 1845–1855.
Oil on canvas. Private collection.

faces of the South he described so well. It is possible that he developed only a few of his sketches into paintings. In 1843 an article in a Charleston publication noted that Richards was in the city, that his "drawings of the beautiful scenery of the Southern States are almost the first pictures which have been made from this rich storehouse of nature," and that, "From these Southern sketches, the artist designs painting cabinet pictures, and those who desire to ornament their parlors with exquisite home views will do well to commission some from his easel." Possibly he did not receive as many commissions as he hoped. He was also absorbed, with his brother, in several other publishing enterprises during the years he lived in the South.

Richards (1820–1900) was born in London but was brought to America when eleven. His father was a Baptist minister and the family first lived in New York, then moved to Charleston, and finally to Penfield, Georgia. Thomas Addison Richards was a precocious artist who published one of those many nineteenth-century guides to drawing and painting, a text on flower painting, when he was only eighteen. *Georgia Illustrated* was the first of several enterprises launched by him or his brother in the 1840s. For a little over two years they put out a literary journal, *The Orion*, for which the artist planned to travel from Virginia to Louisiana to make drawings, but publication delays dogged production. By 1845 T. Addison had returned to New York and after two years of study became an associate member of the National Academy of Design. Within a few years he was the academy's corresponding secretary, a position he occupied for forty years. His brother published the *Southern Literary Gazette* in Athens, Georgia, for about five years, beginning in 1848, and T. Addison provided some articles and sketches. In May 1853 he wrote the essays on Southern scenery for *Harper's*. Despite his obvious love for the landscape of the South, it seems to have been impossible for him to develop a sustained career with paintings of that region. He became a teacher in New York and spent many summers sketching in various parts of the country. Since his gift for words was as great as his gift for painting he used these travels as the basis for the first complete travel guide of the United States, *Appleton's Illustrated Handbook of American Travel*, published in 1857. From this one could learn all that was necessary about hotels, railroad connections, roads, etc., to get to the picturesque sites sought by painters. Richards also exhibited frequently at the National Academy of Design, and was well known in artistic circles during his long life.

The single natural phenomenon of the South that got attention comparable to the awe-inspiring falls of Niagara in the North was the great stone Natural Bridge of Virginia. Jefferson was so enamored of it that he acquired it and the adjoining land from the British Crown in 1774, treating it throughout the rest of his life as something of a public trust, keeping it unspoiled and yet available to visitors. Seeing it aroused deep feelings in him. "It is impossible for the emotions, arising from the sublime, to be felt what they are here: so beautiful an arch, so light, and springing as it were up to heaven, the rapture of the Spectator is really indescribable." He tried to persuade artists to paint it, and encouraged the French soldier-philosopher Chastellux to visit it. The Frenchman also found "this whole display of rude and formless Nature striving to achieve art's forms" a setting which

excited a "gloomy and melancholy admiration." The drawings made by Baron Turpin at Chastellux's requests were the first published views (1786) of this American phenomenon; reasonably accurate, they nonetheless fail to create the drama felt by Jefferson. Word pictures were more successful.

In 1834–1835 one of two traveling ministers recorded his impressions, first of the bridge as seen at a slight distance from above. "Observe those hills, gathering all around you in their fairest forms and richest verdure, as if to do honor to a scene of surpassing excellence. Now look at the bridge itself, springing from this bed of verdant loveliness, distinct, one, complete! . . . Look at that masonry. Is it not most like the perfection of art; and yet what art could never reach? Look at that colouring. Does it not appear like the painter's highest skill, and yet unspeakably transcend it?" He found it even more beautiful as they descended in the cool shade of the valley—on a day when it was 95 degrees—and saw it from below. "Oh, it is sublime—so strong, and yet so elegant—springing from earth and bathing its head in heaven! But it is the sublime not allied to the terrific, as at Niagara; it is the sublime associated with the pleasing. I sat, and gazed in wonder and astonishment. That afternoon was the shortest I ever remembered."

Jefferson is known to have owned an oil painting of Natural Bridge, but neither its whereabouts nor the artist is now known. Frederick E. Church, the New York artist whose painting of Niagara Falls was considered one of the great masterpieces of the time, painted a fine, yet modest view of it during a visit in 1852. The German artist Edward Beyer included a lithograph of the bridge in his *Album of Virginia* printed in 1858. This was based on a painting he made during his American sojourn from 1848 to 1857. He was another panorama and landscape painter who worked in America, and whose oeuvre is little known. The American-born artist David Johnson (1827–1908), in his painting of 1860, following page, chose a panoramic view of the bridge as seen from the nearby hills. Animals graze in a field in the foreground, the cleft in the earth where the Cedar River flows below is concealed by the dense foliage, the great limestone arch emerges from this, and beyond, the level line of the Blue Ridge Mountains suggests the vastness of the setting. The shifting light of the sun plays across the canvas. Johnson, a lesser-known figure of the Hudson River group of landscape painters, shared with them their faith in the divinity of nature, and their delight in its specific and infinite variety. In this precise yet severe landscape he caught more the pleasing than the sublime aspect of the scene, recording the phenomenon of the unusual geological formation, and at the same time portraying the semiagricultural setting of the Valley of Virginia, where open fields are folded between long mountain ranges. When Johnson died early in the twentieth century he was described as "one of the strongest and best known of American landscape painters of the middle of the last century." His work is once again becoming known.

Though no single artist or group of artists emerged as major painters of Southern scenes until after the Civil War, the number of individual paintings of Southern places that has survived can be surprising, as suggested by the diverse examples already shown. An unidentified artist named Thompson was responsible for the still, quiet, slightly naïve view of the Wetumpka Bridge in

David Johnson. "Natural Bridge, Virginia." 1860. Oil on canvas. Signed and dated: "D.J. 1860." Reynolda House, Winston-Salem, N.C.

Alabama, dated 1847, right. Though the name is very un-French, there is a slim possibility that the artist might have accompanied a French journalist who published an article in the Parisian journal *L'Illustration*, June 10, 1848. Here various kinds of boats used in American waters were described and illustrated, among them the type of steamboat used on the inland waters of Alabama, vessels that carried heavy loads of merchandise. Precisely the same scene is not shown. However, the existence of such illustrations, more probably based on drawings than paintings, speaks of the number of artist-craftsmen, foreign-born or American, who plied their trade throughout the newer regions of the United States at this time, and whose presence, however transitory, contributed to some awareness of the arts among the

populace. (The same journal, in its August 12, 1848, issue, favored its readers with sketches of the St. Charles and Verandah hotels in New Orleans and with a scene of the inside at a New Orleans bar.)

Wetumpka, located on the Coosa River near the center of the state, had been the site of a fort as early as 1714, and became an important cotton shipping port in the late 1840s and 1850s, taking on the cotton produced in the counties to the north. It was hoped that it might become a major link in a system of inland river transport going from Virginia to Mobile and the Gulf. It may be apocryphal, but an "Eastern journalist" is said to have written around this time that "Wetumpka, Ala., and Chicago, Ill., are two of the most promising cities of the West." The dreams of many a burgeoning community were dashed by changing circumstances or the politics of transportation. The city that was to become the link, the hub, among various lines of railroads in the Southeast was the little town first called Terminus in Georgia, and renamed Atlanta in 1845.

The training and skills developed by the French-born artist Hippolyte Victor Valentin Sebron were brought to bear in the canvas, *Large Steamboats at the Sugar Levee in New Orleans*, signed and dated 1853, following page. In a well-lighted painting the viewer sees, as if from slightly above, a meticulous portrait of the wharf at New Orleans. A sailing craft and the steamboats dominate the front and middle ground; in the hazy distance the buildings which line the great crescent of the river are seen. A rich and detailed picture of everyday life on the waterfront is presented: a fruit vendor with pineapples and bananas, brokers, factors, and planters, the workers unloading and loading, the draymen, the passengers on the steamboats, and the crowded setting with its barrels, boxes, bales, and hogsheads. Sebron (1801–1879), born

Thompson. "Wetumpka Bridge, Alabama." 1847. Oil on canvas. Signed and dated: "Wetumpka/From/West Side River,/Opposite/Low-water rock/A.E. [?] Thompson/pt. 1847." M. and M. Karolik Collection, Museum of Fine Arts, Boston, Massachusetts.

Hippolyte Victor Valentin Sebron. "Large Steamboats at the Sugar Levee in New Orleans." 1853. Oil on canvas. Printed inscription and signatures on front and reverse: "H. Sebron New Orleans 1853." Tulane University, New Orleans, Louisiana.

in France, exhibited with some regularity in the French salons between 1831 and 1878, and this painting, as do others of his, displays the meticulous craftsmanship and high finish of someone trained in the disciplined French academic tradition.

Sebron's style and choice of subject matter were no doubt influenced by his teacher, then colleague—the artist, later inventor of the daguerreotype, L. J. M. Daguerre. For a time the lives of the two men were closely allied. Daguerre's own experience had been as assistant to a French creator of panoramas, and Daguerre's first salon painting was of the interior of a chapel, a type of subject, along with meticulous views, that seems to have interested many artists of the early nineteenth century, although

these genres are seldom discussed in the studies that trace changes of taste from classicism to romanticism, then realism.

Daguerre began experimenting with what he called the diorama, a painterly kind of popular entertainment, in the 1820s. (This was a subtler form than the partly three-dimensional type familiar today.) His diorama pictures were shown in a complicated stagelike setting with changing lighting effects manipulated from the rear, the lights shining through the painting that had been done on fine transparent linen. He met with great success, and from 1834 on, now in collaboration with Sebron, developed and presented a complex "double-effect" diorama. This involved painting the shapes for the first effect on the front of transparent white calico, and for the second on the reverse of the same cloth in varying thicknesses of opaque gray, thus achieving gradation of tones. By manipulating colored screens and lights on the painted calico, an effect of light changing throughout a day or night could be achieved and also the effect of different scenes, for with some colored lights certain objects or figures appeared and with others, still different forms came into view. The spectators found it nothing short of magic.

The impulse to produce the illusion of the real in panoramas, and then in the complex double-effect dioramas, must have been an important underlying impulse in French art, which influenced the content and form of easel painting. The questions raised by the observation and manipulation of the changing effects of light in relation to color may also later have had some influence on the perceptions of the artists who were to become known as the Impressionists.

Five double-effect diorama pictures were produced between 1834 and 1839, and all were presented as by Daguerre and Sebron. Since Sebron is the only assistant of Daguerre whose name appeared in association with the master's, this may mean that Sebron was either an unusually able assistant or that he played a major role in developing the technique. During this time Daguerre was also increasingly preoccupied with his photographic experiments—so obsessed that he sometimes sequestered himself for days at a time. However, Sebron was not credited when Daguerre, in 1839, published his methods of producing the diorama and the daguerreotype, both of which had begun as ways to improve and enlarge the scope of painting. The diorama paintings of Daguerre and Sebron were destroyed in a fire in 1839. However, the diorama continued to be popular in Europe until about 1850. A variety of inferior competitors entered the field and the novelty of this special kind of painting, which gave esthetic satisfaction, instruction, and amusement, eventually wore off.

Sebron's career has not been fully studied. His reputation in New Orleans seems to have preceded him, for on March 31, 1847, a notice in a New Orleans newspaper reported that a painting, *The Departure of the Israelites*, by Daguerre and Sebron, "his

James G. Benton and Charles L. Smith. "'Independence Hall,' Washington-on-the-Brazos." 1852. Oil. From the Moving Panorama of Texas and California. Republic National Bank, Dallas, Texas.

pupil, of Paris," was so successful that the proprietor would extend the time of the showing. The painting may have been by the two Parisians, but it may only have been based on their technique. In the next year, on February 26, 1848, there is a reference to dioramic pictures being exhibited by Mr. Dodge, "well-known . . . as one of our most successful miniature painters." Then again in February 1849 there are references to J. W. Dodge's "grand Exhibition," and one of the subjects is *The Departure of the Israelites*. These were described as paintings "of which Daguerre is the creator." The relationship, if any, between Dodge and Sebron is not known.

The first firm notice of Sebron's presence in New Orleans is in the *New Orleans Bee* of December 15, 1851, when it is reported that he had "returned to the city after a trip through the west." Then in May 1852, announcements appear in several newspapers of an exhibition of two oil paintings, *Cataract of Niagara* and *Lower Sugar Levee*, both of which were finished in New Orleans. Sebron was described as "a modest artist" who had been in the city for the past year and who had collaborated with Daguerre on several diorama canvases.

In preparing for the painting of the sugar levee, Sebron used the traditional techniques of the academic artist. A large oil sketch and a smaller pastel study of a steamboat exist. The vantage point is very similar to that found in the earliest daguerreotypes, which are views of cities. The carefully observed differences in tonal gradations and effects of light would have been learned as a part of the discipline of preparing diorama paintings. The impersonal and seemingly nonselective—not explicitly storytelling—observations of all the activities of life on the waterfront had to be recorded by the artist's brush, for no camera at this time could have caught the immediacy of movement; yet this is partly what those who were developing cameras aimed to achieve. This is a realistic rendering of a slice of life, a type of composition rooted in the view painting of the eighteenth century, but which also anticipates an approach to subject matter found later among French Impressionists. This painting seems to crystallize the moment when the images of the camera were just beginning to influence—in ways both positive and negative—the nature and purposes of easel painting. Sebron was in New York in 1854, and returned to France the following year. During the remainder of his life he appears to have limited himself primarily to paintings of views and interiors.

By the 1850s the open lands of Texas and the gold of California were attracting the attention of the venturesome in search of a fortune, and the harbor at New Orleans, portrayed with such richness of detail by Sebron, was one of the points of departure for both these destinations. Two artists who took advantage of this enthusiasm for the West were a military officer, James G. Benton, and "the talented and well known scenic artist," Charles L. Smith of New Orleans. Together they produced a *Moving Panorama of Texas and California*, which was put on exhibit in a large pavilion in New Orleans on April 30, 1852. The newspaper announcement noted that the panorama represented "the principal battlefields of Texas, views of the old Spanish missions, and other objects of interest in that beautiful and romantic country," and also that "We can testify to the accuracy of the views of Texas scenery . . . as we happened to see the origi-

nal sketches in San Antonio some months since from the pencil of an accomplished officer of the army, Lieut. J. G. Benton."

Fortunately, a section of this panorama, the whole of which was advertised as consisting of over 10,000 square feet of canvas, has survived, previous page. It shows a one-story wood structure with a porch across the front in Washington-on-the-Brazos, where the Texas Declaration of Independence (from Mexico) was drawn up on March 2, 1836. If the whole 300-foot length of this panorama was as carefully painted as this section, a viewer would have received a bright and vivid impression of the sights of Texas and California. Action is suggested in this illustrative work that shows the delegates converging for their meeting, a meeting decisive to the history of Texas and to the United States. Accompanied by a narrative, and possibly music, the effect might have been comparable to today's documentary television or film travelogues in which artistry and showmanship are combined.

An enterprise such as this panorama involved a number of participants. In this case some of the initial drawings were done by Benton, a New Englander who trained at West Point and who studied topographical drawing there under Robert W. Weir. At the time he made the drawings Benton was in command of the San Antonio Ordinance Depot. (The California scenes were based on drawings by a Mr. Perrine.) Little is known about Smith, except that he was a New Yorker who worked as a scene painter in New Orleans from about 1830 to 1857. It was he who took the drawings and used them as the basis for paintings on a large canvas. The promoters were Messrs. Sala and Stearns, Texans who seem to have been performers and entertainers. Smith, described as "our renowned Southern artist," was responsible for two additional panoramas shown in New Orleans in 1857—"these beautiful works of art" depicted the *Creation of the World* and *Commodore Perry's Expedition to Japan*.

The artist Alfred Boisseau (1823–1901), a contemporary of Sebron, Smith, and Benton, practiced the more traditional art of easel painting. He was yet another painter of French origin attracted to the New World in the prosperous years of the late 1840s and '50s. Born in Paris, he exhibited in the salons from 1842 through 1848. In 1845 he was in New Orleans, and in 1847 he painted the sparkling composition of *Indians Walking Along the Bayou in Louisiana*, right. They are believed to be Choctaw. The vibrant blues and greens of the luxuriant setting dominate the canvas. The Indians, in their haphazardly exotic clothing, were still a familiar sight in New Orleans in the 1840s, buying and selling in the market; there were several bands of these essentially agricultural peoples living in Louisiana at the time. The mixed levels of assimilation of the white man's ways are again suggested here—the man carries an American gun, the child a cane blowgun and two darts, one woman bears her burden in a basket, Indian style, as does the other, who carries her papoose. The fabrics are all European or American, but draped or cut after their own fashion.

Boisseau seems to have been a restless individual, or felt compelled by necessity to move on for want of commissions. He executed a number of portraits in Louisiana, some rather stiff and formal, others possessing great charm. In 1852 and 1853, and possibly again in 1857, he was in Cleveland, where he advertised as artist, portrait painter, and daguerreotypist. Later he was in Montreal, and there is a painting by A. Boisseau signed and dated Alaska, 1877, a long way from tropical bayous.

Artists in the nineteenth century used the term "fancy" to describe a category of painting—compositions that might tell a story but were not intended to carry a serious message. Christian Mayr (1805?—1851), a German-born artist who seems to have spent time in the South off and on from 1838, and especially from 1840 to 1845, when he was first in Charleston, then in New Orleans, included "beautiful fancy pieces" among his works. His painting of the *Kitchen Ball at White Sulphur Springs*, following page, done in 1838, would probably have been so categorized. Here he shows the slave kitchen staff enjoying themselves at a party, all well dressed and behaving with the same degree of dignity, decorum, and spirit which a similar country party of white people would have displayed. The subject is simply a lively party, and the artist delights in the varied action of the figures as they dance, play music, watch, and gossip. The artist

also recorded with care the details of the setting—the room with open rafters, the candelabra, the baskets, and other bric-a-brac can be seen. The subjects are dark-skinned because that is what they in fact are; he neither suggests the complex problems of people in bondage nor does he demean his subjects in any way. To judge by his advertisements and references to particular paintings, Mayr was a very productive artist. His best-known painting today is the large group portrait of the members of the Charleston Fire Department, completed in 1841. During his stay in Charleston he exhibited religious paintings of *The Temptation* (Adam and Eve) and *Death of Abel*, paintings of historical subjects such as *The Crusader's Farewell* and *Captain Smith in Virginia*, as well as a variety of genre or fancy pieces entitled *Bachelor Hall*, *Dressing for a Ball*, *Saturday Afternoon*, or *The Sick Room*. His contemporaries especially admired his small-scale full-length portraits. After 1845 he made his home in New York City, and in 1849 was elected Academician of the National Academy, a signal recognition of his accomplishments as an artist.

Alfred Boisseau. "Indians Walking Along the Bayou in Louisiana." 1847. Oil on canvas. Signed: "Al. Boisseau." New Orleans Museum of Art.

Christian Mayr. "Kitchen Ball at White Sulphur Springs." 1838.
Oil on canvas. North Carolina Museum of Art, Raleigh.

Slave auctions attracted the negative attention of English and European travelers in the South, as well as abolitionist journalists who toured the South, and on a few occasions artists made this a subject of a painting. Eyre Crowe (1824–1910) was a young English artist who took time off from his developing career to serve as secretary to the novelist William Makepeace Thackeray, when the latter made a lecture tour in America in 1852–1853. Crowe made sketches and watercolors as they traveled about. In Richmond, Virginia, on March 3, 1853, he decided to observe the auction rooms, and found them a succession of "low rooms, roughly white-washed, with worn and dirty flooring, open, as to doors and windows, to the street." Buyers moved along from one

room to the next as the sales took place. Crowe moved ahead of the crowd: "On rough benches were sitting, huddled close together, neatly dressed in grey, young negro girls with white collars fastened by scarlet bows, and in white aprons. The form of a woman clasping her infant, ever touching, seemed the more so here. There was a muscular field-labourer sitting apart; a rusty old stove filled up another space. Having rapidly sketched these features, I had not time to put my outline away before the whole group of buyers and dealers were in the compartment. I thought the best plan was to go on unconcernedly; but, perceiving me so engaged, no one would bid. The auctioneers, who had mounted the table, came down and asked me whether, 'if I had a business store, and someone came in and interrupted my trading, I should like it.' This was unanswerable; I got up with the intention of leaving quietly, but, feeling this would savour of flight, I turned round to the now evidently angry crowd of dealers, and said, 'You may turn me away, but I can recollect all I have seen.' I lingered in a neighboring vacated store, to give myself the attitude of leisurely retreat, and I left this stifling atmosphere of human traffic."

Thackeray wrote a friend that Crowe had been "imprudent," and the artist later admitted to this, especially since at that time Mrs. Stowe's "fiery denunciations" in *Uncle Tom's Cabin* had raised the question of slavery to "fever-heat." His overt interest in the slave auction might have brought the wrath, and more, of the crowd upon himself and upon Thackeray.

Crowe used his sketch as a basis for a painting, below. It is a compassionate picture of the slaves as they were seated waiting for the auction; the drama is in their calm and dignified mien under trying circumstances. The white auctioneer and buyers are given secondary positions. It is a fair-minded depiction, for the artist recorded what he saw but did not embellish upon it in order to make it more dramatic than it actually was. Crowe may have done the painting shortly after his visit, or he may not have done it until 1859–1860. In 1861, when the topic had become even more timely, he exhibited it at the Royal Academy in London. Crowe much later—in 1893—published some of the sketches made during his American trip as accompaniment to his narrative, *With Thackerary in America*, and appears to have developed one or two other drawings into paintings in the years after 1853; his American work was a short episode in a long career.

John Antrobus (1837–1907) conceived a plan to paint a series of twelve pictures "representing Southern life and nature" around 1858. In this he was considerably more ambitious than other painters who worked in the South. He may have known or read T. Addison Richards's and George Cooke's appeals to artists to look at the landscape of the South, and as a newcomer to American shores sometime in the 1850s—he came from England and was in Montgomery, Alabama, by 1855—he may have decided to seize "boldly upon new subjects" and thus find an "untrodden field of art-labor" worthy of pursuit.

The first painting in the series was a large canvas, *The Cotton*

John Antrobus. "Plantation Burial." 1860. Oil on canvas.
Historic New Orleans Collection.

Picking, a scene typical of Louisiana cotton country, now unfortunately lost or unlocated. The following spring Antrobus, who had spent the winter season in Carroll Parish, along the Mississippi River in northern Louisiana, exhibited the next in his series, a large painting—*Plantation Burial*, above. The scene takes place in a heavily wooded area, in itself creating a mood of melancholy gloom. The black preacher, family, and friends are shown gathered around the coffin. On the left is a view of the Mississippi and the town of Lake Providence. On the far left a white man, perhaps the overseer, is shown at a discreet distance, and on the far right and as if deep in the woods, again at a discreet distance, the white master and mistress, all three quietly observing the Negroes as they gathered to bury their dead in their own fashion. The reporter described it as "drawn from life" and said the event had taken place at "the plantation of the late Governor Tucker of Carroll Parish." One or more sketches must have been made on the spot, then developed into a painting in the studio. In a classically organized composition, with the major figure group massed within a large triangle, the artist appears to have captured

a very private episode in the life of the slaves, at the same time recording attitudes of grief and sorrow which are universal to mankind. He has also caught the close and oppressive atmosphere of some Southern forests—a quality that could, and perhaps did, discourage artists.

Antrobus began his series at least as early as late 1858, but there is nonetheless a parallel, and perhaps an association, with T. Addison Richards. The latter wrote and illustrated another article for *Harper's*, "The Rice Lands of the South," published in November 1859. Richards described and showed scenes of the low country of South Carolina and Georgia and of the biracial life of the region. Included was an engraving showing a Negro funeral, and he wrote of the "impromptu music wondrously sweet and wild and weird, which well counterfeited on the lyric stage, would bring fame and fortune," and which could be heard at Negro funeral solemnities "celebrated, as they generally are, in the deep night-darkness of some dense old wood, made doubly dismal by the ghostly light of the pine torches and the phantom-like figures of the scarcely visible mourners." Antrobus may have gotten the idea of including a plantation burial in his series from Richards, or it may have been sheer coincidence. Insofar as is known, no more in the proposed series of twelve paintings was completed. The next we hear of Antrobus is from an item in the New Orleans *Daily Picayune* of July 9, 1861, when mention is made of a visit by the "artist-soldier" who was now a member of the Delhi Southrons and who expected to proceed "to the seat of the War in Virginia" soon. He survived the war, married a New Orleans woman, then lived in Chicago and Washington. There apparently was little market for his work in the South after the war. Around 1875 he established himself in Detroit and became a well-known portrait and landscape painter there, where he died in 1907. Throughout his career he wrote poetry and newspaper articles from time to time.

An underlying theme in the development of easel painting in the middle years of the nineteenth century is the search for new kinds of subject matter and new types of vision, as is implicit in the efforts to enlarge the scope of painting through the diorama—with its emphasis on the changing qualities of light—and the daguerreotype, and also in the essays on the special qualities of the scenery of unfamiliar areas. Old categories of religious and historic painting were losing their appeal, and the roles of the portraitist and miniature painter were being diminished. The theme of America's own history continued to attract artists who hoped to earn money and fame by exhibiting these to the public and to gain commissions from national, state, and local legislatures. Their success in selling these paintings, or in obtaining commissions, was very uneven. John Blake White (1781–1859) was a South Carolinian who had hoped for a career as a history painter and prepared himself by studying with Benjamin West in London, then found insufficient success when he attempted to paint full-time in Charleston and Boston. He therefore read law, practiced in Charleston, and served for some time in the state legislature. Having established himself, he continued to paint intermittently and offered for public view a succession of history paintings, sometimes taking as his theme near-contemporary events, such as an 1812 painting of *The Massacre of the American Prisoners by the English and Their Indian Allies at French Town, on the River Raisin*. In the summer of 1816, he tried to capitalize on public pride by painting the *Battle of New Orleans*, but sadly noted in his journal, "Offer it for exhibition, but no interest is excited in the public mind." He persisted through the years, and finally received national recognition in 1840–1841 when his painting of an episode from the Revolutionary War, *General Marion Inviting a British Officer to Dinner*, more popularly called *Marion in the Swamp*, was selected by the newly formed Apollo Association as a subject for an engraving to be distributed to its members. Through the engraving, White's painting became one of the most familiar pictures in the United States—it was subsequently used in 1861 as the image on the ten-dollar banknote issued by South Carolina.

The subject was one which had particular appeal for Americans, for it memorialized the simple, plain virtues of American soldiers under adversity, and for Southerners, one of their own. As recorded in the somewhat fictionalized biography of Marion written by none other than Parson Weems, it had become, by the 1840s, a legendary episode of the Revolution. First published in 1809, it was a best seller after that. (Parson Weems created the story of George Washington and the cherry tree.) The story as told by Weems was that Marion and his men, while camping in the simplest of circumstances on a swampy island near Georgetown, South Carolina, received, as was the custom, a blindfolded young British officer into their midst under a flag of truce. Upon the removal of his blindfold the young officer was astounded first to learn that the legendary officer, Marion, was no more than "a swarthy, smoke-dried little man, with scarce enough of threadbare homespun to cover his nakedness" instead of an officer of martial aspect, then further amazed when invited to join Marion for "dinner" and learned that all they had were some roasted sweet potatoes to eat, which were served on a piece of bark. The Englishman could not fathom why and how Marion and his men could accept such a life, with virtually no pay and "no provision but potatoes." Whereupon, the American hero, according to Weems, delivered a moving statement on the joys of liberty and freedom. The dumbfounded but impressed young officer was said to have been "so struck with Marion's sentiments, that he never rested until he threw up his commissions, and retired from the service."

The story and White's painting struck a chord of popular sentiment. Prints and naïve paintings were based on them, and the painting became one of the best known and most successful of American history paintings.

The Southern novelist and writer William Gilmore Simms repeated the story in his 1844 biography of Marion, reporting also that the story had recently had "a more extended circulation" because of White's painting and the engraving after it. Simms's fervid romantic imagination likened Marion and his militia to "Robin Hood and his outlaws," and described the dense forest setting as a place where "the sunlight came as sparingly, and with rays as mellow and subdued, as through the painted window of the old cathedral, falling upon aisle and chancel." Simms eliminated the peroration on liberty and freedom and instead emphasized the hardiness, good manners, and lack of pretension of Marion and his men—chivalrous virtues all.

One of the better artists to take up this theme again was William D. Washington, who exhibited an oil sketch for a large picture, *Marion's Camp*, following page, at the Washington Art Association in 1859. Washington's study is considerably more dramatic and atmospheric than White's appears to have been and seems to be based largely on Simms's description. The artist shows Marion's camp in the flickering light of the fire, the men in varied and casual attitudes, and Marion as a kind of Robin Hood.

William D. Washington's skill in capturing the varied light effects and his handling of such a variety of detail, even in this loosely brushed study, no doubt reflects some of his training in Düsseldorf, Germany. Washington (1833–1870) was a Virginia-born artist who grew up in Washington, D.C. He started his career as a draftsman in the Patent Office, and went to Germany to study with the German-American artist Emanuel Leutze and with the academy there. Here he received disciplined and sound technical training. He was one of a number of American artists, including Eastman Johnson and George Bingham, who studied in Düsseldorf, improving their skills and absorbing a sense of the

William D. Washington. "Marion's Camp." 1859. Oil sketch.
Oil on canvas. University of South Carolina, Columbia.

past, and who, during their time there or subsequently, sought to create American history paintings that would extol the deeds and values of the nation. After his return to America, Washington was, in 1856, among the founders of the Washington, D.C. Art Association. However, with the advent of the Civil War he removed to Virginia and later taught for a short time at the Virginia Military Institute in Lexington before his untimely death.

Edward Troye (1808–1874) was an artist who never suffered for lack of subject matter that appealed to his clients. Born into a family of artists, trained in England, Troye came to America via

the West Indies, and enjoyed a long and continuously successful career as the country's foremost painter of horses and prize livestock. Racing in the colonies had its beginings in New York City and Philadelphia, but it was in the South that it enjoyed the greatest popularity, with Virginia identified as the "Race Horse Region" and "cradle of the thoroughbred" in North America. By the middle years of the nineteenth century the bluegrass region of Kentucky had developed as the major center of breeding and raising blood horses. In retrospect, it is possible to see the signs of rising sectionalism and North-South antagonisms in a series of challenge races between Northern and Southern horses which began in 1821, and which continued until 1845. The most political of these races was that between New York's Eclipse and Virginia's Henry, held in New York on May 27, 1823—as many as 20,000 Southerners were said to have made the journey North. Eclipse was the victor, but it was a race long argued. Appropriately enough, Edward Troye painted both horses in this contest in 1834, apparently when both were retired in Virginia.

Troye settled in Philadelphia around 1828, but by the 1830s had found his métier and was traveling among the plantations of Virginia, the Carolinas, Alabama, Louisiana, Mississippi, and Kentucky, painting blooded horses and occasionally prize cattle. Most of his adult life was spent in the South. He made his home in Kentucky for several periods, taught for a time at Spring Hill College in Mobile, and owned property in Alabama. Over 300 paintings by his hand are recorded; most are of horses, but portraits and religious and historical subjects are included in his

oeuvre. His painting career extended from 1830 to 1870 and during this time he painted most of the great racehorses of the period; his reputation spread rapidly by word of mouth. The majority of his horse paintings follow the English convention of a horizontal format with horse in profile. A landscape setting with low horizon, and a touch of red in the foliage are typical of Troye's work. At times his compositions are more elaborate and include a trainer, jockey, or servant, and stables in the background. One of the artist's best patrons, and a close friend, was Alexander Keene Richards, a horse breeder who had an estate, Blue Grass Park, near Georgetown, Kentucky, and a plantation in East Carroll Parish, Louisiana. Richards wanted to improve his stock by importing Arabian breeds, and so made several trips to the Middle East. On the second of these, which began in the winter of 1855–1856, Troye accompanied him. Among the paintings completed on this sojourn is the one below, showing Richards in a desert setting, wearing a red Arab cloak and white na-

Edward Troye. "Sacklowie and Alexander Keene Richards." 1855–1857. Oil on canvas. Private collection.

Francis Blackwell Mayer. "Independence, Squire Jack Porter." 1858.
Oil on millboard. Signed and dated: "F. B. Mayer 1858."
National Museum of American Art, Washington, D.C.

tive costume with one of the three horses purchased there—probably Sacklowie. On the far right the outlines of a Middle Eastern city can be seen. According to family tradition, to avoid the heat of the day, this was painted on three successive moonlight evenings. Though the setting is exotic, the composition is typical of Troye.

During this time Troye also painted several large scenes from the Holy Land. After his return these were exhibited in New Orleans and New York, and very probably also in Canada. During the Civil War Troye stayed with friends in Woodford County, Kentucky, then apparently spent two years in Europe. In the remaining war years he lived either with the Richards family or in Woodford County. Immediately after the war he traveled frequently. Many of his patrons were in the North, but he maintained his base in the South and died on Keene Richards's estate in Kentucky.

Two of the most successful paintings of the Baltimore artist Francis Blackwell Mayer (1827–1899) were painted in 1858, and

both are of a rather special type of subject matter in that they represent concepts as manifested in everyday life rather than scenes of everyday life per se as found in more typical genre paintings of the period. One of these, above, is called *Independence, Squire Jack Porter*. The sitter was Captain John M. Porter, who had fought in the War of 1812 and who, at the time of the painting, owned a farm in Frostburg, in western Maryland. The artist shows his subject in a very relaxed pose, alone, smoking a pipe, seated on a bench on the porch of his rustic farmhouse. But the subject is much more than an informal portrait. The subject is independence, and Squire Porter exemplifies this in every gesture and in his situation. Without knowing the circumstances or way of life of this man, the viewer can—and was meant to—conjecture about him. This is a man who lives alone, not dependent upon others, or at best he and his family are independent of others. From the simple setting one guesses that he, or they, were virtually self-sufficient, raising their own crops and animals. His time is his own; he is beholden to no one. And, all important, from the inward and contemplative gaze, one knows that this man is master of his own thoughts and makes his own decisions. Executed in almost monochromatic umbers and ochers, it is an effective painting. The brushwork is soft and fluid, and the canvas is suffused with light.

Another of Mayer's paintings, below, represents states of activity, *Leisure and Labor*. The setting is a rural blacksmith shop. Again the artist's fluid brush creates a warm and here considerably richer composition of color and light: the use of cool and muted tones of blues to suggest surface textures and distance is particularly fine. The subject is less subtle, but skillfully done, and again the viewer is meant to conjecture and read into the painting ideas beyond those that meet the eye. On the left the blacksmith bends over his work, no doubt only one task in a long day at his hot forge. On the right is the leisured young gentleman, casually but smartly dressed in well-tailored clothes and riding boots, accompanied by his sleek hunting dog. He could

be son and heir to a local landowner. The broken plow along side may simply be a part of the setting, or was included to suggest further the lack of productive activity on the part of the young man.

In these two paintings Mayer succeeded in giving a certain universality to this type of subject matter. It is also possible that Mayer was expressing his own philosophical and political ideas—a desire to remain independent of heated political arguments, a respect for labor, and a disdain for the leisure class.

In a way, these paintings with "readable" subjects about the conditions or activities of body and spirit can be interpreted as nineteenth-century versions of older morality paintings—such as portrayals of virtues and vices or the fashionable and allegorical "emblems" on which paintings or parts of paintings were based in the sixteenth century. Mayer was by no means the only artist

Francis Blackwell Mayer. "Leisure and Labor." 1858.
Oil on canvas. Signed and dated: "F. B. Mayer/1858.
Corcoran Gallery of Art, Washington, D.C.

to choose such subjects, which enjoyed a certain popularity for a
time. A histrionic painting by one of Mayer's mentors, Ernst
Fischer (1815–1874), a German-born artist who worked in Baltimore between 1848 and 1858, is entitled *Anxious Moment* and
shows members of a group in a room, all expressing by gesture
and features states of anxiety—possibly they were being attacked. In the years 1844–1846 members of the Artists' Sketching Club in New York set themselves artistic problems of this
sort at their meetings, and there survives a group of drawings
made by members on such subjects as Perseverance, Speculation, and the Trying Hour. Mayer very probably was acquainted
with the Sketching Club's work, for the drawings were exhibited
during the period when Mayer was in Philadelphia and New
York studying his craft.

In 1847 he was back in Baltimore and was one of the founders
of the Maryland Art Association, the first formal organization of
its kind in that city. He studied further with Ernst Fischer, and
by 1851 had settled down to several very productive years as an
artist. In 1855 he helped to found the Artists' Association of
Mayland—another organization which provided opportunities
for artists to meet together and exhibit. The war created a hiatus
in Mayer's career. His family was torn by it. His brother served

in the Navy, on the Union side, but the family felt sympathy
with the Southern cause. Mayer himself apparently chose to
remain neutral, or independent, for in 1862 he went to Paris and
stayed there for almost a decade. After his return he settled in
Annapolis. A number of his paintings from this last period are
romanticized but accurately researched representations of life in
that city in the eighteenth century. For Mayer they represent a
seeming retreat into the past.

For some artists, watercolors or drawings were mediums as
congenial, or more so, than oils. Thomas Middleton (1797–
1863), an amateur portrait and topographical artist and a member
of the distinguished Charleston family, worked in several mediums, including engraving. In a wash drawing, above, he provides a lively rendering of an amateur musical occasion being
enjoyed by gentlemen of leisure. The setting is a room in the
home of his host and relative, Arthur Middleton, where the cumulative collection of paintings brought together by this highly
cultivated family were hung. To the left of the fireplace is a
portrait done in England by Benjamin West of an earlier Thomas
Middleton. The others portray a variety of subjects; some were
perhaps purchased in Europe and may have been originals or
good copies. There is a baroque or neoclassical history painting,

what appears to be a genre painting of a country scene, a sea or landscape, and a painting showing an interior or architectural "view." This was surely one of the more extensive private collections to be found in the South at this time. Other Southern families or patrons who had collections of comparable quality included Robert Gilmor, Jr., in Baltimore, the Valentines in Richmond, the Alstons in Charleston, Daniel Pratt in Alabama, the Linton-Surgets in Natchez, and James Robb in New Orleans. Middleton and his friends also supported efforts to establish the short-lived Academy of Art in Charleston.

Another active amateur artist was John Hazlehurst Boneval Latrobe, son of the architect-artist Benjamin Henry Latrobe. He obviously learned his skills from his versatile father. While still studying law he was the unnamed author of and did most of the illustrations for *Lucas' Progressive Drawing Book*, first published by Fielding Lucas in Baltimore in 1827. He also illustrated a number of other popular books. The Latrobe-Lucas drawing book,

dedicated to Robert Gilmor, Jr., was, along with Chapman's, one of the many how-to books in which Americans were urged to learn to draw and paint. So many books of this kind were published in America between 1820 and 1860 that this effort to make art accessible to the citizens of a democracy has been called an "art crusade." For his illustrations Latrobe used views of American scenes, "In order to give interest to the work and to stamp it with a national character." Much of the content was derived from an English publication by J. Varley, but by illustrating it with views of Maryland, Pennsylvania, and even of the Mississippi River, he made it convincing and relevant to his readers.

Latrobe, who developed into a distinguished Baltimore lawyer, often took paints and sketchbooks with him on his travels. (One of the reasons watercoloring gained in popularity in both England and America during the early nineteenth century was that much better commercially prepared paints and papers became available.) In 1832 he spent his summer holiday in Vir-

John H. B. Latrobe. "White Sulphur Springs Dining Room." 1832. Watercolor. Kennedy Galleries, New York, N.Y.

ginia, traveling leisurely by stage through Fredericksburg, Charlottesville, Staunton, then through Warm Springs and Hot Springs to reach his destination at White Sulphur Springs, which had become a popular resort. He took in all the sights—Jefferson's home at Monticello, Madison's at Montpelier, and the University of Virginia. When he arrived at White Sulphur Springs he immediately found friends and acquaintances. While there he made a series of watercolors delineating the buildings, the setting, and the pastimes of the visitors. In one of these, previous page, he shows the building used as the dining hall and stage office, a long, low structure with surrounding veranda. In a letter he described the lively scrambles at mealtimes: "Crowds collect around the dining room when the bell rings, and when they are opened there is a rush, like that at a booth at a contested election. Every man, woman, and child rush to any seat which they may happen to find, and in a very short time the food upon the tables disappears, consumed by the hungry mob. If you have a servant of your own, he must bribe the cook. If you have no servant, you must bribe one of those attached to the place, or you run the risk of getting nothing. . . . Bribe high and you live high; fail to bribe and you starve; look sharp and eat fast, you forget good manners."

Latrobe was to return to White Sulphur Springs a number of times and at some point he designed a group of buildings there known as the Baltimore Cottages. This was one of a number of minor architectural projects he was involved in as a skilled amateur. He had, in fact, initially intended to follow his father's career as an architect and had studied engineering at West Point,

David Hunter Strother (Porte Crayon). "Negro Girl with White Scarf." n.d. Ink wash drawing with white on beige paper. Private collection.

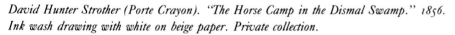

David Hunter Strother (Porte Crayon). "The Horse Camp in the Dismal Swamp." 1856. Ink wash drawing with white on beige paper. Private collection.

but was unable to complete his courses after his father died and instead studied law. Among his many civic activities, the two of which he was especially proud were his role in the American Colonization Society, which helped to establish the Republic of Liberia, and his longtime association with the Maryland Historical Society, which he helped to found in 1844 and where he was instrumental in beginning the excellent art collection.

David Hunter Strother (1816–1888), who for a time was one of the best-known writer-illustrators for *Harper's*, was encouraged in his hope of becoming an artist by his fellow Virginian, John Gadsby Chapman, and in 1836 to 1838 studied in New York under the tutelage of Samuel F. B. Morse. At the end of this time, Morse's own artistic career was at its nadir (and his scientific career only beginning to flourish), and he flatly advised the young artist to avoid the "beggary" of a life in art. Strother left New York and for over a year earned his living as a portrait painter in his native Valley of Virginia and on travels that took him as far west as Indiana. It was not a career especially to his liking, and in 1840, again encouraged by Chapman, he set out for Europe to train himself as a painter of history.

During the three years Strother spent abroad he wrote lively letters to his family, which his father had published in a local newspaper. In a sense, this began his writing career. Upon return he settled for a time in Baltimore, but was not overwhelmed with sales or commissions. It was Chapman, then the dean of American engraving, who encouraged him to come to New York to try his hand at illustration. This time success followed. After some initial commissions for illustrations for books, in 1853 he sold his first illustrated article to *Harper's*. In the same year he met Washington Irving, and Strother's adaptation of the pseudonym Porte Crayon may have been in partial imitation of the self-styled Geoffrey Crayon of Irving. For the next quarter of a century he was a regular contributor to *Harper's*, with a four-year hiatus dur-

ing the war, and all his articles were illustrated with engravings based on his drawings. He was said to be one of the highest-paid writers for that extremely popular journal. His best work was probably done before the war. His specialty was lively, witty, informative tales of travel, many about excursions into his beloved Southern mountains. He loved people, especially country types, and wrote sympathetically about them and their lives.

The drawings to accompany his articles were done on various sizes of tinted papers, with pencil and/or ink, and heightened with black and white washes. A drawing, lower left, done for an article on the Dismal Swamp in North Carolina, which appeared in September 1856, shows the rude shelters, called oddly, the Horse Camp, used by the men and mules of a lumbering company. Wood was cut and made into shingles deep within the swamp, then transported out in carts on the log road that had been built. The employees were mostly slaves, perhaps even

Marie Adrien Persac. "Saloon of Mississippi River Steamboat, 'Princess.'" 1861. Gouache with foreground figures in collage on paper. Signed and dated: "A. Persac 1861." Anglo-American Art Museum, Louisiana State University, Baton Rouge.

some escaped slaves, skilled in woodcraft, who worked at fixed piecework rates—"the provisions are furnished, the work paid for, and no questions are asked, so that the matter always remains involved in mystery."

Another drawing, page 302, shows a young black woman, and demonstrates Strother's deft handling of line and tone. As with many of his colleagues, the war affected the course of his life. He chose to fight with the Union and served his country well as topographical engineer and staff officer under several generals: this included service in his own Valley of Virginia. He was subsequently estranged from some friends and relatives, though wounds gradually healed as the years passed. In 1879 he was appointed U.S. Consul General to Mexico, where he served ably for six years.

The gouache paintings of Marie Adrien Persac, such as his precisely rendered interior of the Mississippi River steamboat *Princess*, previous page, dated 1861, suggests his technical and professional skills as surveyor, civil engineer, cartographer, and photographer. The saloon or main cabin is shown, replete with its painted floorcloth and elaborately bracketed ceiling in the Gothic taste. A large banquet table laden with food fills the length of the hall. It is a rare and unusually detailed record of the interior of one of the great steamboats of that era. As is true of many of Persac's gouaches, the foreground figures were cut out of magazines, such as *Godey's*, for the artist obviously was not comfortable painting figures. Persac, who is believed to have been born in Lyons, France, in 1823, was in America by 1851. He worked as a surveyor and civil engineer. Either as a pastime or to earn extra money, he painted a number of fresh, clear, precise views of plantations in Louisiana. He was listed in New Orleans city directories from 1857 until his death in 1873.

The silhouettist William Henry Brown (1808–1883) did not need cutout figures from magazines to create his collage pictures of watercolors and cutout silhouettes of figures, animals, and objects, for, with consummate skill, he cut his own. A native-born Charlestonian, he was one of the last great silhouette artists. In an autobiographical statement written in the third person, the artist recalled that, "from his earliest recollection, he had been gifted with a rare and peculiar talent or faculty (entirely intuitive in him) of executing with wonderful facility and accuracy the outlines or form of any person or object from a single glance of the eye, and without any machinery whatever, but with a pair of common scissors and a piece of black paper." For a period of more than thirty years he earned his living as a silhouettist. His subjects included Lafayette, done in 1825, Andrew Jackson, John Marshall, John Randolph, Henry Clay, Martin Van Buren, John C. Calhoun, Daniel Webster, and Abraham Lincoln. Such was his fame and skill that in 1845 he successfully published his *Portrait Gallery of Distinguished American Citizens*, a volume which has been reissued in facsimile at least twice in modern times.

In addition to cutting silhouettes in which significant postures and gestures were caught, he extended his art "to portraying entire family groups, military companies, fire companies with their engines and horse-carriages, sporting scenes, race-courses and marine views." During this time he traveled widely in the United States. According to the tradition of the Vick family of Mississippi (after whom Vicksburg was named), a member of their family met Brown while in New Orleans sometime in the 1840s and invited him to visit their plantation, called Nitta Yuma, which means "beartrack." Here, apparently to amuse the children and as a gift to the family, he created a group of pictures called *Hauling the Whole Week's Picking*, depicting life on the plantation. They make up a strip about five feet long, part of which is shown below. These are unusual in Brown's oeuvre in that the various pieces, such as the dog, the cart, the blankets, etc., are painted with color, rather than the whole being done in black.

While in the Mississippi Valley he also did a group portrait of a local military unit, the Natchez fencibles. One of the works of

William Henry Brown. "Hauling the Whole Week's Picking." c. 1842. Silhouette cutouts, painted with watercolors, sections of a strip. Historic New Orleans Collection.

which he was most proud was his silhouette picture of the first locomotive and train of passenger cars ever run in the state of New York, done in 1831 and showing the engine, a supply car, and two passenger carriages—each passenger identifiable. He became an aficionado of trains and in 1859 gave up his artistic career and began to work for a railroad in Pennsylvania. In his old age he retuned to Charleston, where he died in 1883.

Sculpture

An eight-month visit, which started as an ocean voyage designed to improve his health, took John Cogdell (1778–1847) to Italy and the Mediterranean in 1800, when he was twenty-two. While there he visited the studio of Canova and saw some of the great paintings of Italy; it was a visit that sparked a lifelong interest in the arts. His artistic career, as with several Charlestonians of this period, was an avocation—he had already been admitted to the bar in 1799 and was a practicing lawyer throughout his life, serving his city and state in a variety of official capacities. He was attracted to painting first, and executed portraits and occasionally landscapes for friends or for his own pleasure. He joined with Samuel F. B. Morse and others in the founding of the short-lived South Carolina Academy of Fine Arts in 1821 and served for a time as its president.

It was not until 1825 that he began to experiment with clay and modeling, and, encouraged by his friend Washington Allston, sent a cast of his first successful essay, a bust of Dr. John Holbrook, to the Boston Athenaeum. From then on he turned his efforts increasingly toward sculpture and sent examples of his work for exhibition on occasion to the Pennsylvania Academy in Philadelphia and the National Academy of Design in New York. He gave a cast he had done of General William Moultrie to Congress, where it was housed in the library and praised by the members. He was one of the few, sometimes the only, native-born American sculptors exhibiting in the 1820s. His exhibited works included busts of Lafayette and Sir Walter Scott as well as some imaginary compositions such as of Hagar and Ishmael. William Dunlap singled out for attention the marble tablet, right, which Cogdell executed in memory of his mother in 1833, and which was placed in St. Philip's Church in Charleston by him and his two brothers. The imagery is idealized and neoclassical, showing three classically draped figures around an urn, in three different attitudes of grief—allusions to the "bereaved affection" and submissive bowing to the will of God referred to in the accompanying inscription. Cogdell, the self-taught amateur, has here, in the demanding medium of marble, achieved a balance between moving and realistic images of grief and the kind of generalized, seemingly eternal, forms that his generation felt could be achieved through basing their work on the antique. Charleston was relatively rich in mortuary sculpture, a number of such tablets having been commissioned from abroad or from foreign-born artists. He learned from these, and from his travels in Italy, and up and down the Eastern Seaboard, what was considered appropriate. Though only a serious amateur, Cogdell's success was enough to encourage his fellow countrymen in the belief that America could and would produce sculptors of its own.

John Cogdell. Memorial to Mary Ann Elizabeth Cogdell. 1833. Marble. St. Philip's Church, Charleston, S.C.

Most of the American artists who aspired to be sculptors in the middle part of the nineteenth century spent the majority of their working years in Italy. There they could study the antique they admired so much, draw from the nude at the academy—a practice frowned upon at home—live cheaply, have ready access to an inexpensive supply of marble, and find the skilled and trained assistants who could execute in marble the works they modeled in clay or plaster. For this generation of sculptors the production of the clay model was considered the creative problem, the execution a technical task they would supervise, perhaps adding the finishing touches. The first two Americans to

Hiram Powers. "Andrew Jackson." Plaster model made in 1835; later cut in marble. National Museum of American Art, Washington, D.C.

achieve not only national, but international, reputations were Horatio Greenough (1800–1852) and Hiram Powers (1805–1873). Neither is Southern, nor did either work for very long in the South. Powers, however, spent from November 1834 through the fall of 1837 in Washington, D.C., and enjoyed extensive Southern patronage, particularly from the Preston family of Columbia, South Carolina, and deserves mention here. He was born in Vermont, but grew up in the thriving city of Cincinnati on the Ohio River. Here he learned techniques of modeling from Frederick Eckstein, a German-born sculptor who had come to America with his sculptor-father in 1794 and settled in Cincinnati in 1823. In his position as supervisor of the mechanical section of the Western Museum Powers developed his skill in modeling realistic wax figures. He was encouraged and helped by a wealthy Cincinnati citizen, Nicholas Longworth, who in 1834, feeling his protégé ready for broader fields, gave him money to move to Washington. Here he was able to secure sittings from President Andrew Jackson, then sixty-eight, and with it, recognition of his talents. The bust above catches the worn, rugged features of the old hero, and a sense of his stubborn determination and inward strength. In a full-length figure the aged fron-

tiersman might have seemed incongruous if shown in a loosely draped toga, but in the bust-length figure it adds to the sense of the heroic that is an integral part of the artist's concept. This figure was molded in plaster and not cut in marble until considerably later, when Powers was in Italy.

While in Washington Powers also successfully modeled John Marshall, John C. Calhoun, Daniel Webster, and others. He attracted the attention of Senator William Preston of Columbia, South Carolina. The latter, interested in the arts, introduced the sculptor to his brother, John Smith Preston, who loaned Powers most of the money needed to move with his family to Italy, which he did in 1837. Powers spent the rest of his life there and achieved international fame with figures like the *Greek Slave*, and idealized female busts such as *Proserpine*, of which Powers had at least a hundred copies made. The Linton-Surgets of Natchez and New Orleans were among those who acquired the latter. The Prestons remained faithful patrons and their houses in Columbia and in Louisiana reflected this. In the late 1840s Wharton Green of Charleston commissioned Powers to do an idealized larger-than-life portrait statue of John C. Calhoun. The head was based on the one he had done in plaster in Washington. The figure was shown dressed in a Roman toga, holding a scroll that read "Truth/Justice/and the/Constitution" alongside the trunk of a palmetto, the state tree of South Carolina. In 1850 the ship on which it was being sent to the U.S. was wrecked off Fire Island near New York, but the statue was recovered, minus the left arm. It was subsequently burned during the Civil War, and today is known only by prints and by at least one small-scale replica.

Two major equestrian statues created for America at this time were the bronze of Andrew Jackson commissioned by the Jackson Monument Committee in 1847, after Old Hickory's death, and that of George Washington commissioned in 1849–1850 by the state of Virginia. Clark Mills won the competition for the Jackson monument and carefully created the plaster models for it in his studio and foundry in Washington, D.C. Mills (1815–1883) was a native of New York State who as a young man found his way to New Orleans, where he earned his living as a jack-of-all-trades; later, in Charleston, he worked as an ornamental plasterer, there learning beginning principles of modeling. Somehow, from Cogdell or others, he became interested in sculpture and his first efforts, around 1844, were made from life. In 1845 he completed a marble bust of John C. Calhoun, for which the city gave him a gold medal. The Prestons first invited him to Columbia, then encouraged him to go to Washington before departing for Italy. While in the nation's capital, he obtained the commission for the statue of Jackson and moved his studio there. Mills succeeds in this tour-de-force, right, in showing the hero, the man of action, on a rearing horse, thus solving a major problem of establishing a balance among parts that had challenged sculptors since the time of Leonardo da Vinci. The finished bronze was achieved only after great difficulty—the horse was recast six times. Jackson was shown wearing a uniform based on the one he had worn at the Battle of New Orleans, and it was unveiled in Washington, D.C., on the thirty-eighth anniversary of that battle, January 8, 1853, amid much fanfare and to the approbation of "the shouts of thousands." The cities of New Orleans and Nashville commissioned full-sized replicas. Mills journeyed to New Orleans in 1855 to see about the pedestal to support that version, then returned in January 1856 to attend to its placement. Elaborate plans were made for the ceremony, which was held a month after the forty-first anniversary of the Battle of New Orleans, and in which various military bodies, as well as trade societies, took part. The square where the statue was placed, and still stands, the Place d'Armes, was henceforth called Jackson Square. The Nashville replica was not erected until 1880 and stands near Strickland's Capitol. Mills, whose first efforts were based on achieving verisimilitude through life works, went beyond this in his Jackson because, through stance and gesture of the rearing horse and the erect figure of Jackson, he created a heroic image.

In 1849 Thomas Crawford (1813?–1857) won the competition for the outdoor monument to General George Washington which the state of Virginia planned to erect near the Capitol in Richmond. Clark Mills was the disappointed loser. Crawford was a native New Yorker who by that time had established a reputation as a neoclassicist and had worked for over a decade in Rome. He returned to Rome to complete the commission and died before he had modeled all the subordinate figures. The design was a tripartite concept, with Washington at the top, six great past leaders of Virginia—Jefferson, Patrick Henry, George Mason, John Marshall, William Nelson, and Meriwether Lewis—on a lower level, then eagles below. Randolph Rogers finished it. It is notable as one of the most elaborate sculptural groups to be completed at this time, a significant indication of continuing public patronage of the arts in the South, and a measure of the pride of Virginia in its history and its heroes. Frederick Law Olmsted, the farmer-agriculturist-journalist, who later became a distinguished

Clark Mills. "Andrew Jackson." 1848–1853. Bronze. Lafayette Square, Washington, D.C.

landscape architect, saw the group when he visited Richmond during his tour of the Southern states in the years immediately preceding the Civil War. In Virginia he had been disturbed by what he felt was a "lack of faith in the capacity of men individually, white and black," and by what he felt had become a revolt against the generous and noble theories of Jefferson. Therefore, his comment on the Richmond monument was as much social as artistic: "The Crawford Washington Monument is much the highest attainment of American plastic art, and would be a glory to any town or country, but it points to the past. What a failure has there been in the promises of the past."

Thanks to the esteem achieved by men like Powers and Greenough abroad, and the skill of men such as Cogdell and Mills at home, sculptors began to find increasing patronage, pub-

Artist unknown, attributed to Henry Dexter. "Mary Telfair." 1860. Marble. Signed: "HD 1860 Savh Ga." Telfair Academy of Arts and Sciences, Savannah, Georgia.

lic and private. In 1858 the state of South Carolina commissioned Henry Kirke Brown (1814–1886), a Massachusetts man who had studied in Rome, to do a group of thirteen figures for the pediment of the State Capitol, a project incomplete when the war began. The finished figures were unfortunately destroyed when Sherman's troops burned Columbia. The Ladies' Clay Association of Virginia commissioned the Kentuckian Joel Tanner Hart to do a full-length portrait sculpture of their political hero, Henry Clay, in 1846, but the sculptor, who suffered from illness and often found other things to occupy his time in Italy, did not complete his curiously appealing statue until 1859. Replicas were later made for Louisville and New Orleans. Hart's Clay is utterly and completely naturalistic, showing the politician-statesman mildly gesturing, in rumpled suit, somewhat incongruous for the white marble so favored by the neoclassicists. Recently the work of Edwin Lyon, an English-born sculptor who lived and worked in New Orleans and Natchez from about 1846 until his death in 1853, has been rediscovered. Only his Natchez work is known; there are several life-sized bust figures as well as some charming six-inch wax busts. Alexander Galt of Virginia began his career by working in the small. After a sojourn of six years in Italy he came back in 1856 and received commissions from the national government and his native state. With the war, he established himself in Richmond, but much of his work was destroyed by fire in 1863.

The artist who executed the portrait medallion of Mary Telfair, left, is unknown. The portrayal was very probably sufficiently realistic to satisfy the desire for a likeness, yet the profile view calls to mind works of the antique and the Renaissance. The medallion is signed "HD [or ID or JD] 1860 Savh Ga." It is thought that it may be the work of Henry Dexter (1806–1876), a New Englander who, following the pattern, spent some time in Italy. In 1859 he conceived an elaborate scheme for a kind of national portrait gallery and set out to model the governors of every state and the President, a project which took him to each state and included a tour through the South. (If not by Dexter, this is the work of a skilled professional attuned to current international fashions.) The portrait of Mary Telfair is pendant to one of her sister of the same size, executed eight years earlier by an English artist in Rome. Mary Telfair was the sister of Alexander Telfair of Savannah, who employed the distinguished architect William Jay to design his home in 1820. His sister Mary, as the last survivor of Alexander, gave the house to the Georgia Historical Society in 1875 for use as a museum. This has subsequently become the Telfair Academy of Arts and Sciences. The mansion, since expanded, now houses an excellent collection of works of art, including some originally acquired by the Telfairs.

Sculpture, or woodcarving, was taken up purely as a pastime by Pierre Joseph Landry (1770–1843) around 1833. According to a local tradition, Landry, a veteran who had fought in the Battle of New Orleans, began woodcarving when confined to a wheelchair after an injury. What may be one of his earliest works is a self-portrait in wood, upper right, with an inscription proudly incised on the base: "Tête de P. J. Landry age de 63 ans fait par lui en 1833." It is a lively visage, the rounded forms slightly simplified and generalized, the hair skillfully stylized in clustered strands. There is no record of Landry having done other

Pierre Joseph Landry. "Self-Portrait." 1833. Wood. Incised on base: "Tête de P. J. Landry age de 63 ans fait par lui en 1833." Louisiana State Museum, New Orleans.

represents Napoleon, who died in 1821. On first consideration, this seems fanciful, for why should a retired planter in Louisiana be creating an allegorical tribute to Napoleon? However, in November 1834 the physician who had attended Napoleon during his last exile on St. Helena arrived in New Orleans and, amid an elaborate ceremony, which ended with an artillery salute of 101 guns, gave to the city a bronze replica of the death mask of Napoleon which he had made at the time of Napoleon's death. (The mask is again on view in the Louisiana State Museum after having almost been lost after the Civil War.) The doctor had only received permission from the French government to make bronze replicas of his plaster death mask after Louis Philippe came to the throne in 1830. Thus in the 1830s in France there

Pierre Joseph Landry. "Seaman's Allegory, or Homage to Napoleon." c. 1834. Wood. Historic New Orleans Collection.

carving, or any kind of drawing earlier, but from the controlled skill shown here it would appear that he possessed disciplined manual dexterity. During the next few years he carved a number of storytelling or allegorical figures. One of these, right, has been called Seaman's Allegory. On the left is a young, vigorous youth in uniform carrying what may be a dispatch box, on the right a kneeling, weeping woman. Around the base are stylized waves and a small boat with two figures. The young man is shown beneath a tree with large stylized leaves—perhaps to suggest the evergreen *Magnolia grandiflora* common to Louisiana—while she is beneath a drooping tree suggestive of the weeping willow. The allegory, or simple story, has been thought to be of a lover or husband long absent, possibly lost at sea, though there is no hint of a shipwreck. The two trees are conjoined in a broad curve at the top, giving unity to the whole, and no doubt a device to give strength to the piece and to prevent splintering. The execution is partially stylized, narrow gouges being used to suggest the bark of the trees, the branches and leaves of the willow, and the surface of the sea.

More enigmatic still, and subtle and skillful from a conceptual and craftsmanship point of view, is the figure of a man with silhouetted tricorn hat which can be seen in the negative space between the two tree trunks. There is a local tradition that this

was a rekindling of enthusiasm for Napoleon, an enthusiasm shared in New Orleans. Stimulated by this "French craze" the main street of a new subdivision in New Orleans was named Napoleon Avenue, and neighboring streets were named after the places of his great victories: Milan, Austerlitz, Berlin (now General Pershing Street), Marengo, and Constantinople. Given this preoccupation and enthusiasm for Napoleon in the mid-1830s, it is very possible that the old military officer, Landry, who had been born in France and lived there until he was fifteen, may, in this carving, have created a private and allegorical tribute to Napoleon, rather than a seaman's story. The water at the base may be meant to suggest the island of St. Helena. The young man on the left under the tree—which always has green leaves—may represent the principle of life, while the figure on the right, weeping and placed under a tree that is a traditional emblem of sorrow and death, may represent death and dying. The figure represented by the negative space—ethereal or spiritual space—possibly represents the spirit and memory of Napoleon that would long outlast his temporal life. (The figure is tall and slim, not short and stout like Napoleon in his later years.) It is possible that Landry drew his imagery from some popular print, or he may have invented it himself.

Though Landry's work has qualities of the naïve or self-trained artist—his work shows no relationship to the then-current academic international neoclassical taste—he himself was probably an informed and complex man. At the time of his death his estate inventory showed he owned a library of 266 volumes, including history, science, and literature. He was a successful plantation owner; the value of his property was over $24,000. His other surviving works reflect his complex mind. Among these are a large, multipieced *Wheel of Life*, which he completed in 1834, showing nine stages in the life of man, an allegorical figure of Louisiana, and a depiction of Andrew Jackson and Louis Philippe, which commemorated the 1836 settlement of a Napoleonic debt (by France), as well as religious representations including the Holy Family with Joseph as carpenter at a workbench, Cain and Abel, and Suzanna at her bath. Though many of his figures are in contemporary dress, there is a strong semiabstract quality about his work reminiscent of the medieval. It is possible that his style owes something to his memories of the medieval art he might have seen as a boy at St.-Malo in Brittany or at Mont-St.-Michel, which was about fifty miles from his home.

The semiabstract qualities found in Landry's work are also to be seen in the work of the artisan-craftsmen stonecutters who carved memorial vignettes on tombstones. The marble tombstone of Benjamin Jones, upper left, a fireman in New Orleans who died in 1858, shows highly stylized weeping willow trees on either side of a depiction of Jones alongside his company's fire pump. The weeping willow was an especially favored emblem on mid-nineteenth-century tombstones. The name of the anonymous stonecutter of this and similar tombstones is not known. He worked within a tradition that called for simplified or semiabstract forms such as seen here, suggestive rather than completely detailed, labor-saving, and, not incidentally, especially appealing to the modern eye.

Firemen were a special kind of hero in New Orleans and elsewhere, for they risked their lives battling the fires that so frequently ravaged the towns and cities of America. The first important fire ordinances in New Orleans were made in 1807, but it was not until 1829 that the first volunteer fire companies were established. In 1834 the Firemen's Charitable Association was founded to provide relief for needy members and for families of deceased members. Their resources were severely taxed after an 1838 epidemic but, with the aid of a special bequest, they purchased a large piece of land for the burial of their members. This became the Cypress Grove Cemetery in New Orleans (still called the Firemen's Cemetery), and it is there that this and many other firemen's tombs were placed. The sculptural vignettes on many of these, which now interest us as examples of craftsmanship, also provide a visual history of the different kinds of fire pumps and fire engines used at the time. The Firemen's Charitable Association still exists. During the nineteenth century the annual firemen's parades, held in March of each year, though suspended during the Civil War, were major social events.

A wood carving, the *Dancing Negro*, lower left, is a product of an unknown artisan's hand. It was found in South Carolina and probably dates to the middle years of the nineteenth century. The face is animated and a sense of vigor and liveliness characterizes the figure; originally it was probably painted. The purpose is unknown; it might possibly have served as a sign of some kind. A renewed appreciation of the products of artisan-craftsmen occurred among artists and collectors early in this century, when artists—feeling the academic tradition exhausted—sought inspiration from a variety of "primitive," semiabstract, sometimes naïve art forms, seeing in them combinations of form, color, design, and pattern not found in traditional Western art. This wood carving was bought by the Polish-American sculptor

Elie Nadelman in the 1920s, when he and his wife were collecting what became one of the best as well as one of the earliest collections of American artisan or folk sculpture. Thus this object is of interest not only for its own qualities but for its place in the changing history of taste.

The changing history of technology is reflected in an unusual monument to be found on the State House grounds in Columbia, South Carolina, the metal and cast-iron monument, below, dedicated to the men of the Palmetto Regiment who fell in the Mexican War in 1847, the war prompted by boundary disputes arising out of the annexation of Texas in 1845. The state of

Christopher Werner. Monument to men of Palmetto Regiment who fell in Mexican War in 1847. 1858. Cast iron. On grounds of the State House, Columbia, S.C.

Card table, probably Baltimore, c. 1830. Mahogany grained to simulate rosewood; stenciled and freehand designs imitate inlay; brass rosettes on brackets. Valentine Museum, Richmond, Virginia.

South Carolina purchased it from Christopher Werner, an ironworker from Germany who was active in Charleston from 1828 through 1870. He operated an iron foundry and made ornamental ironwork of various kinds, in particular some of the lovely iron gates still to be seen in Charleston. As with so many blacksmith shops and iron foundries, Warner employed slaves as well as white employees, and at one time had three white workers and five slaves. Despite difficulties, which included an unreasonable request to place a bronze eagle on top of the tree and a fire in his foundry just as the work was near completion, Werner and his men completed their task.

The monument was originally erected in front of the old State House in 1858. Perhaps because it was dedicated to troops who had fought under the United States flag, it suffered only minor injuries when Sherman's troops took Columbia and the old State House itself was destroyed.

There is an innocent audacity in molding and shaping pieces of iron into the image of a full-fledged tree. This was made at a time when cast iron was increasingly used for structural and orna-

mental purposes in building, and the range of its uses being experimented with and extended. Stoves, coffins, ornamental garden furniture, some sculpture, all kinds of new machinery, bedsteads, and lamps were among the many things being fashioned from iron. If an image of a palmetto tree was wanted for a monument, then iron seemed a more suitable material than stone or wood. Christopher Werner obviously accepted the challenge and achieved the desired result.

At the base of the statue the names of all who had fallen were recorded. The Palmetto Regiment had "afforded an opportunity for the military pursuit of the younger portion . . . of the state to manifest itself," and it had proven itself in virtually every action of the war. The price of their gallantry was high, for out of the original group of nearly 1,200 men, barely 300 returned. Those who did were enthusiastically received and each given a medal by the state. Of that number many were to serve in the gray uniform of the Confederacy.

Though meant to honor heroes of the past when erected in 1858, for those who were living this image of the palmetto was probably also a symbol of the proud sectionalism that was sweeping South Carolina and the rest of the South. Articles in *De Bow's Review*, for example, demonstrate again and again the militant and defensive attitudes of some Southerners at this time. Typical was a polemical essay by the ardent secessionist Colonel Lawrence M. Keitt, of South Carolina, whose anger was directed against "pious" and "patriotic" orators and clergymen of Massachusetts. The author compared the relative Northern and Southern contributions during the Revolutionary War, the War of 1812, and the Mexican War, and according to his statistics the nonslaveholding states had 22,136 troops serving in the Mexican War, while the states south of the Mason-Dixon line had 42,213. His implication throughout was that if called upon again, Southerners would not shrink from military actions. True to his word, he fought valiantly and was mortally wounded in the war that followed.

Products of Craftsmen

The proportions and bold decorations of the card table, upper left, would have been considered elegant and appropriate for a house with the proportions and austere ornament of the Greek taste. It is not strictly archaeological in form, but neither were the houses. The designers of the French Empire, English Regency, and French Restoration (Louis XVIII, the restored Bourbon monarch, was on the throne from 1814 to 1824, his brother Charles X from 1824 to 1830), all favored somewhat heavy forms and rich, clearly defined ornament deriving, in a fairly free way, from ancient models. Their American counterparts quickly took up the new fashions. In this example from Baltimore the mahogany has been grained to simulate rosewood and inlay, then further embellished with stenciled and freehand floral designs. Embossed brass rosettes are on the brackets and brass is used to cap the feet. The effect is of opulence and richness, appropriate for an increasingly materialistic age.

The sofa, or settee, lower left, also of Baltimore origin, has the strong scroll forms that were becoming increasingly popular.

In places the solid mahogany is covered with a mahogany veneer, indicating a lavish use of materials and delight in surface effects; the carving is equally impressive and rich.

Baltimore remained a center of cabinetmaking, and in 1840 an English-born draftsman, cabinetmaker, and architect, John Hall, issued a book, *The Cabinet Makers' Assistant, Embracing the Most Modern Style of Cabinet Furniture*. Though a price book issued in New York in 1834 had some illustrations, this is, in ef-fect, the first American pattern book for furniture. He favored the use of large flat scrolls as structural or decorative elements. Typical is his design for a "consol bureau," above, where such scrolls are used to embellish the front, and smaller but similar scrolls serve as feet. These could be cut with the aid of steam-driven bandsaws, and this simplified classical furniture, "pillar and scroll," therefore exemplifies another result of technological change. Hall was not original in his designs; he borrowed from a

Sofa, Baltimore, c. 1825. Mahogany and mahogany veneer. Maryland Historical Society, Baltimore.

London 1826 publication of George Smith and from a book on architecture and furniture first published in London in 1833 by J. C. Loudon. The forms he showed paralleled those being produced in New York by Joseph W. Meeks and Company, an aggressive firm with an outlet in New Orleans as early as 1830, and a network of sales connections that included Baltimore, Washington, Alexandria, and Charleston. Craftsmen have always had their own private and varied grapevines for learning about new tastes. Hall's book was certainly one way by which a simplified version of the late classical taste was spread. And spread it did. Its virtue was that the basic forms were simple, therefore readily copied and modified by craftsmen in various locales. The furniture was not too expensive and therefore available to the growing middle class. In many homes a few bold and well-designed pieces easily lent an air of dignity to the high-ceilinged rooms in which they were frequently placed.

After the first North Carolina State House burned in 1831, the legislative committee responsible for the rebuilding turned to New York and the firm of Town and Davis for their plans, and subsequently employed David Paton, a young Scottish architect, as local supervisor. For the chairs and desks needed for the Senate and Representatives' chambers, the commissioners "were

Desk for Senate chamber,
by William Thompson, Raleigh, 1840.
Mahogany. The Capitol, Raleigh, N.C.

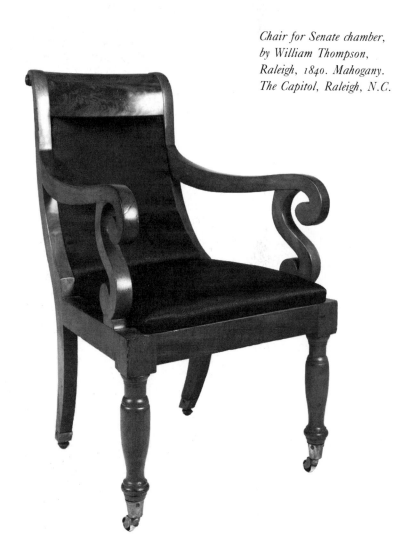

Chair for Senate chamber,
by William Thompson,
Raleigh, 1840. Mahogany.
The Capitol, Raleigh, N.C.

satisfied that they could not have had these articles made at the north, and brought here, cheaper than Mr. Thompson contracted to make them for; and for strength and durability, they are, unquestionably superior articles." The chairs for the Senate chamber, left, have the lively scrolled arm supports and curved back characteristic of the late classical. The single desks, above, were slanted for convenience and had a drawer in which papers could be kept. The supports are urn-shaped cut from flat boards, supported on inverted scrolls. The craftsman who performed so satisfactorily was William Thompson (1796?–1869), New York–born, but living in Raleigh from around 1819. From time to time he apparently went to New York and personally selected materials for his business, and in 1826 he advertised for someone who could paint and ornament chairs. As with many artisans, he seems to have acquired substantial means, for the 1860 census recorded that his real estate was valued at $7,000 and his personal estate at $16,000.

The general silhouette of the wardrobe or armoire, upper right, with its large molded cornice, is typical of the furniture favored by John Hall, the Meeks, and craftsmen of this period. It is unusual in that, on the interior, it bears the maker's stamp, lower right—D. Barjon, Jr., New Orleans. A Dutreuil Barjon is listed as a cabinetmaker in the city directories, with few exceptions from 1822 through 1858. The address, 279 Royal, is given from 1824 through 1841, then again from 1846 through 1856. Records indicate that this establishment was one of father and son. Both were apparently free people of color. The father was a native of Santo Domingo and of French descent, and is identified in his advertisements as an *ébéniste*, a skilled craftsman. An 1834 advertisement is written in both English and French, so he apparently served both the American and Creole communities. The father suffered financial losses in 1843, and an inventory prepared in connection with bankruptcy proceedings shows that "1 machine à Vapeur avec boilloire" (steam machine with boiler) and a "Scie circulaire" (circular saw) were among his possessions, indicating that the shop had the newest technology. It was not until 1857, when racial tensions were increasing and free people of color were looked upon with suspicion because it was thought they might be fomenting trouble, that one of the directories—Mygatt's—listed the identification "f.m.c." after the name of D. Barjon.

For every cabinetmaker whose work can be identified because there is a stamped or labeled piece, a bill of sale, or some other evidence, there were no doubt literally dozens working. We know of some of these because their names are listed in a city directory or there is other fragmentary evidence of their role as craftsmen. For example, in Michel's city directory for New Orleans of 1843, one of the years when Barjon was working, there were eighty cabinetmakers listed, twenty-three men who were identified as having furniture stores (Barjon, usually listed as a cabinetmaker, was given here), and three upholsterers. This was a period when the furniture trade was gradually becoming mechanized, although there were still many individually or family-operated shops where craftsmen largely used hand tools and much of the work was made to order. On the other hand, some shops made objects for display and sale, or for other merchants in their area to sell. In the 1840s centers such as New York, St. Louis, and Cincinnati were beginning to mass-produce furni-

Armoire or wardrobe, by Dutreuil Barjon, Jr., New Orleans, c. 1840–1850. Mahogany with mahogany veneer. Bocage Restoration, Louisiana.

Maker's stamp inside the armoire. Dutreuil Barjon, Jr., was at 279 Royal from 1824 through 1841, then again from 1846 through 1856.

ture and ship it to the hinterland—in some cases parts were shipped and assembled at the place of arrival. Hence, from the 1840s on, there are increasing references to furniture stores and warehouses.

In smaller communities one or two cabinetmakers might dominate the local trade for a while. This seems to have been true of the town of Milton, in Caswell County, North Carolina, tobacco country near the Virginia border. Here Thomas Day worked from the 1820s through 1859 with relatively little competition. He was a free Negro who seems to have arrived in the community, probably as an apprentice, around 1823, and who bought a lot on the town's main street in 1827. His business grew along

315

with the town, and in the 1850 industrial census he was reported as employing twelve workers and having a capital investment of $15,800. He sold some of the products of his shop wholesale to merchants in the region, and his custom orders included work for Governor David S. Reid and other prominent families in the immediate area. He also worked as a house carpenter, and among his contracts were those for the halls of two debating societies, the Philanthropic and the Dialectic, of the University of North Carolina in Chapel Hill.

Though occasionally idiosyncratic in style, most of Day's work closely follows the late classical taste of the time. A well-designed dining table, with an extra leaf for extending its length on occasion, below, was made for Governor Reid, probably in the 1850s. It is of solid walnut. The introduction of a hanging rack for storage of the leaf is unusual if not unique, and is so skillfully done that it seems a natural part of the structure, the product of an imaginative worker.

In silver, as in furniture, bolder, often bulbous forms were popular. These can be seen in the tea service, about 1825–1830, far right above and below, by the Charleston silversmith John Ewan (1786–1852). The delightful dolphin finials on each of these pieces are reminiscent of the dolphin feet seen on some

European furniture; these creatures were made legendary by the ancient Greeks and hence associated with the Greek taste. To judge by the surviving amount of silver from his shop, Ewan was one of the most productive Charleston silversmiths. In an advertisement he stated that "Persons Having old fashioned Silver Plate, Spoons, &c. which they would wish to have manufactured, may rest assured of having the same Silver returned." Thus he, like his fellow craftsmen, sometimes melted down old pieces in order to make new objects. He also sold jewelry and watches, as did many silversmiths at this time. As with furniture, local craftsmen often created some of their own stock, but also purchased finished products from manufacturers elsewhere. This practice became more common as the century progressed.

Silver pitchers as prizes or commemoration pieces were no doubt popular throughout the country at this time, but they seem to have been especially popular in the South, where they were frequently given to winners of horseraces, for prize livestock, and to commemorate special political, military, and social events. One of these, near right, was fashioned by the Tennessee silversmiths Campbell and Donigan, who worked in Nashville in the 1850s. The lines are based on traditional classical forms, with the fullness and generosity found in work of the

Extension table, by Thomas Day, Caswell County, North Carolina, probably 1850s. Walnut. North Carolina Museum of History, Raleigh.

John Ewan. Silver tea service, Charleston, 1825–1830. Mark: "J. EWAN" in Roman capitals within a rectangle on bottom. Telfair Academy of Arts and Sciences, Savannah, Georgia.

Campbell and Donigan. Silver pitcher, Nashville, c. 1855. Mark: "C & D," in rectangle with pseudohallmark, a bull, below. Private collection.

Virginia Ivey. All-white quilted counterpane, stuffed work. An inscription borders the center design: "1856 A Representation of the Fair Ground near Russellville Kentucky." National Museum of American History, Smithsonian Institution, Washington, D.C.

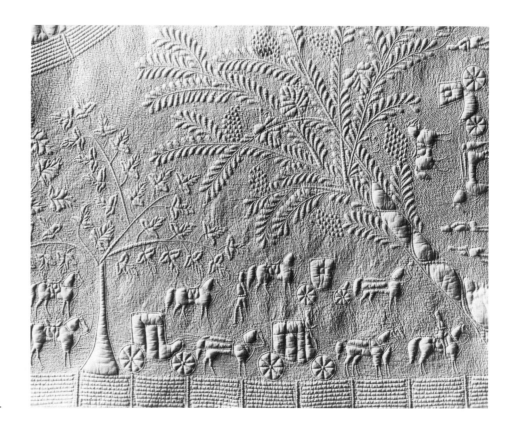

Detail of quilted counterpane.

Susan Ladson McPherson. Chintz appliqué quilt, Charleston, c. 1845–1850. National Museum of American History, Smithsonian Institution, Washington, D.C.

1840s and 1850s. There is an engraved inscription: "Premium to Locomotive, At the State Fair of Tenn. 1855." Locomotive was a much prized bull, owned by James E. Letton of Millersburg, Kentucky, and purchased from a "celebrated herd" in Kirkleavington, England. Such was this animal's fame that when a writer for the journal *American Agriculturist* visited the area he made a special trip to see this fine specimen.

A Kentucky woman, Virginia Ivey, was apparently so captivated by the annual events at the fairground near Russellville, in Logan County, not far from the Tennessee border, that she designed, stitched, and stuffed an entire quilt, upper left, representing it. On the outside edge she created the image of a wooden fence, one of those white fences that still gives the appearance of firm line drawings placed upon the landscape of Kentucky bluegrass fields. Inside, lower left, is a luxuriance of trees and a parade of saddle horses and carriages with horses. Several buildings or pavilions are shown, and in the center a tent with figures surrounded by horses, cattle, sheep, and chickens. This is bordered by a precise inscription: "1856 A Representation of the Fair Ground near Russelville Kentucky." The design is all laid out in the flat; that is, animals, carriages, and people in profile, trees and leaves with flattened salient forms defined, and

only single views of buildings shown. The concept is totally non-academic, although it never (or rarely) has been proposed that quilt designs should be anything else. The designer, as if by intuition, and knowing the limits of her own skills and the medium being used, created a flat design for a flat surface.

The creation and completion of the quilt took imaginative planning and what must have been dogged patience. The vision, memory, and delight in the events of the fair must have sustained her as she took stitch after stitch. All the excitement of a country fair is suggested, with its recollections of the warm smells of the animals, the gathering of the people, the competitions being judged, the socializing, and the gossiping. It is a charming and delightful document of social history.

Social history of a grimmer sort, not immediately discernible, is recorded in a quilt made by another Kentucky woman, following page. This was done by Elizabeth Mitchell of Lewis County, which borders on the Ohio River, in 1839. The basic pattern is a traditional geometric one sometimes called the lemon-star pattern. Within it there is a center field with pathway, gate, and fence indicated. A fencelike pattern is used for the outside border. The boatlike objects along the outer edge and those within the center field represent coffins, and, as family members died

Elizabeth Mitchell. "Graveyard Quilt" in lemon-star pattern, Lewis County, Kentucky, 1839. Kentucky History Museum, Frankfort.

their graves were moved from the quilt's border to the "grave-yard" in its center. One can only imagine that Elizabeth Mitchell was torn by grief at the death of members of her family and made the quilt to help assuage her emotions.

This, and the country fair quilt above, are exceptions to the rule, for most surviving quilts of the mid-nineteenth century have traditional geometric and floral patterns, and are not story-telling as these are. In a time when women's artistic outlets were relatively few, it is remarkable that two Kentucky women should have used quilts as a means of expressing and recording their feelings and memories, joys and sorrows.

Group memories and familial feelings would have been called up by the South Carolina woman who possessed the friendship or album quilt, right, probably made in the 1840s or '50s. Each square of such a quilt was made by a different woman, and presumably they gathered together for several hours at a time as they worked. In this case each square was made of appli-quéd pieces cut from chintz, "laid-work," and each seamstress had to, and did, measure up to the standard of the group. The result is a harmonious combination of individually varied blocks,

each of which is signed by its maker. The blocks are unified by chintz strips that form a grid, and by a wide chintz border. The final quilting, or stitching of the layers together, is done here in a diamond pattern, and that, too, may have been a cooperative effort. Thirty-six women were involved, fifteen married and twenty-one single; six were members of the Porcher family, four were Warings, three Whites, three Smiths, three DuBoses, and an assortment of Ravenels, Stevenses, and others. It was pre-sumably a neighborhood group, possibly an assortment of sisters, cousins, aunts, cousins twice-removed, and friends—one of those intricately interrelated kith and kin groups that someone who knew them all would understand but that would baffle a stranger.

The finest English chintzes were used in a colorful appliqué quilt, previous page, made by a Susan Ladson McPherson of Charleston sometime around 1845–1850. A number of such quilts have survived in the Charleston area, probably made by ladies who had the money to acquire the materials and the lei-sure to do the intricate work. The pattern is dense and free-flowing with a rich variety of floral forms laid out in vinelike

Group of South Carolina women. Friendship quilt,
appliqué chintz, c. 1840. Each square signed by maker.
Historic Columbia Foundation, Columbia, S.C.

clusters. The pattern of the chintzes from which these were cut, and the arrangement of them made here, exemplify the blossoming once again, in mid-nineteenth century, of a taste of rococo fantasies and flourishes. In the revival of eighteenth-century styles, part and parcel of the historicism that runs through so much nineteenth-century design, there is often an exaggeration and an exuberance that go beyond the prototypes, and this would seem to be true here.

Rococo revival designs seem to have been adopted primarily for objects used in the home, such as fabrics, silver, and furniture, which was also true of the rococo when it was originally popular. In furniture, an 1856 advertisement for the firm of P. Mallard, "Cabinet Maker and Upholsterer and dealer in Fancy Articles" in New Orleans, following page, shows a conjectural interior in which every article, from footstools to the bed in an adjacent room, are in the rococo taste. The text that accompanied this engraving—which was especially designed for the store—indicated that he "Has always on hand, a large stock of highly finished Furniture, imported and manufactured especially for the southern climate," and that "His extensive establishment

enables him to execute the largest orders in the shortest delay and in moderate terms." Few of the actual pieces of furniture that have come down to us and can firmly be identified as from Mallard's shop are quite as exuberantly rococo as those pictured in the ad. Prudent Mallard seems to have specialized in making and selling large bedroom sets with all the related accoutrements. In April 1861, the New Orleans banker Emile H. Reynes, a man of Spanish descent, bought such a set, the bed, night table, and dressing table of which are shown on page 323. Both the bed and the dressing table are ornamented with large cabochons within scrolls. The most explicit adaptation to the Southern climate is seen in the finials at the foot of the bed—the center section of each of these is attached to a dowel and can be pulled up so that the fine gauze mosquito netting connected to the half-tester above could be pulled out over them, making for a protective tentlike shelter on hot summer nights.

By a stroke of good fortune the original bill of sale for this set, page 324, survives. The total bill—which included some dining items worth a little over $50—was $1,108.90. The "Lit Victoria palisandre," or Victorian rosewood bed, cost $170. (The terminology here is in itself interesting, since it is an early use of Victoria, or Victorian, as an adjective—here the French usage apparently means that this type of half-tester bed was the kind used by Queen Victoria. Soon the word was used to designate all manner of fashions and behavior associated with her reign.) One of the two armoires, with mirrored door, also cost $170, while the other, with plain door, was $135. The two separate and accompanying pediments cost $32. The "Toilette Duchesse," or dressing table, was $90, a washstand $55, and the night table $30. The bolsters and two large pillows for the bed were $20, two mattresses stuffed with Spanish moss were also $20, and extra Spanish moss for the canopy or tester an additional $23. Border material, grass matting for the floor—used in the summertime when carpets were taken up—cloth for the mantel, window cornices, and cord and tassel for the bed are among other items furnished by Mallard.

The firm of Prudent Mallard was one of the best known of cabinetmakers, furniture stores, and upholsterers operating in New Orleans in the mid-nineteenth century. Mallard came from France to New Orleans, probably in 1838, when he is first listed in the city directories, and his establishment was henceforth regularly listed until 1876; he died in 1879. That his was one of the most prominent firms of this kind is attested to by the fact that in February 1846 he was paid $250 by the state of Louisiana "for furnishing and repairing furniture for the State House," and by occasional references to him elsewhere, such as a description of Edward Jacobs's daguerreotype establishment with its carpeted gallery decorated with sofas from the local firm of Mallard and Co.

Though no detailed study of the furniture and upholsterers'

Upper right and below: Advertisement of P. Mallard, Cabinet Maker and Upholsterer, New Orleans, which appeared in DE BOW'S REVIEW, *November 1856. Tulane University Library, New Orleans, Louisiana.*

businesses in New Orleans has been made, one has the impression that Mallard and his fellow craftsmen-entrepreneurs sold their goods to Southerners within a wide arc—certainly as far north as Natchez, if not Nashville; as far east as Mobile; and on occasion as far west as Galveston. Mallard was by no means the only shop making and selling furniture. In Gardner's 1859 city directory there are, in the alphabetical listing, over 80 men listed as cabinetmakers, over 70 as dealers in furniture, and 25 upholsterers. In the classified listing for the same year only one cabinetmaker had himself identified; there are 21 dealers in new furniture and 8 upholsterers. In each case Mallard was listed as an upholsterer, though in other years he is found as a cabinetmaker and as a dealer in furniture. Presumably some of the cabi-

netmakers worked for others in shops employing several men, or for the furniture dealers and upholsterers. Some cabinetmakers may also have done interior woodwork for houses and related tasks. There is no indication that there were any genuine factories producing furniture, but there were quite a few small-scale entrepreneurs, and in these the end products were partly created with aid of machines and power, and partly by hand. For furniture as with other products, New Orleans was an important distribution center, and many now anonymous craftsmen were at work in the trade.

Mallard most frequently advertised as an upholsterer. In Thomas Webster's *Encyclopedia of Domestic Economy* of 1845, a cabinetmaker was defined as one who "is occupied with the

Bedroom with New Orleans furniture. The bed, night table, and dressing table (toilette) were purchased in April 1861 by Emile H. Reynes from P. Mallard in New Orleans. Gallier House, New Orleans, Louisiana.

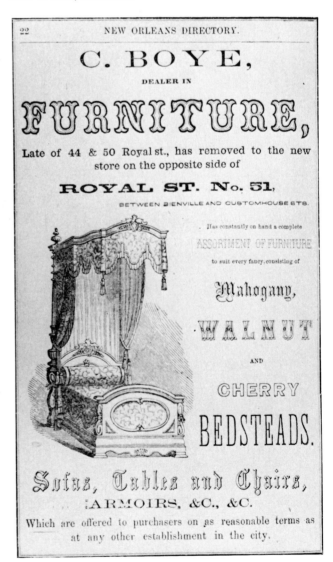

New Orleans, 14 Avril, 1861

M: E. H. Reynes

Bought of **P. MALLARD,**

IMPORTER AND MANUFACTURER OF FURNITURE,

No. 67 Royal and 80 Bienville Streets.

*Bill of sale for bedroom furniture and household equipment sold to
E. H. Reynes by P. Mallard. Gallier House, New Orleans, Louisiana.*

nicer kinds of furniture made of the finer woods, such as tables, sideboards, chairs, sofas, cabinets of all kinds, &c." He went on to define upholsterers as "concerned with certain articles of furniture that do not belong to this class, as beds and everything belonging to them, carpets, floor cloths, windows curtains, &c." He further elaborates on the complexities of the trade: "But these trades are necessarily so connected in many parts that, as far as the public is concerned, the cabinet-maker and upholsterer are now often united in the same person." He indicates that some upholsterers secure their furniture from various specialized craftsmen, such as bedstead-makers or chair-makers, while others employ work-people on their own premises.

One of Mallard's competitors was Henry Siebrecht, who was regularly listed in the directories from 1834 into the 1870s, and

who, like Mallard, was known to have made and sold fine furniture. He, too, was listed variously as cabinetmaker, upholsterer, importer, and manufacturer of fine furniture. Still another establishment, which was not as long-lived, but to judge by several advertisements was for a time one of the larger shops, was that of C. Boye. In an advertisement that he placed in an 1858 city directory, below, a fully draped bed is shown. It, too, is in the French rococo taste, a taste or style which in the mid-nineteenth century was often called Louis XIV, though the resemblance to the historical style was a free interpretation. If the engraved plate has any direct relationship to the products sold, then the quality of craftsmanship of the objects sold by Mr. Boye compared favorably with those of Mallard, Siebrecht, and others.

Furniture in the Gothic style was considered especially suitable for libraries in both Europe and America, for the association of Gothic with long-established universities, as well as with churches, was strong. The very furniture was meant to suggest the quiet and repose of well-used studies where, through books,

Advertisement in GARDNER & WHARTON'S NEW ORLEANS
DIRECTORY FOR THE YEAR 1858. *Tulane University Library,
New Orleans, Louisiana.*

Pair of bookcases, made for the study of Enoch Pratt House, Baltimore, c. 1847. Rosewood with mother-of-pearl escutcheons. Maryland Historical Society, Baltimore.

one could have contact with ideas of the past as well as the present. The distinguished merchant-philanthropist of Baltimore, Enoch Pratt (1808–1896), chose to have his study done in the Gothic taste, where the intricacy of the ceiling was matched by the somber and ornate rosewood bookcases, above. The openwork pediments with the tall pinnacles are unusual, suggestive of collegiate spires. Low relief carving at the base of the doors and around the door frames gives a rich surface and provides a sense of material elegance, a feeling for which was an important aspect of the mid-nineteenth century esthetic. It is thought that these cases may have been made for Pratt by Robert Renwick, or his firm, one of several in Baltimore which, as with comparable firms in other cities, is variously listed in the 1845 to 1850 directories as cabinetmaking shop or furniture store.

Though Pratt's career was devoted to business, he obviously loved books and libraries and had great faith in education. He was a self-made New Englander who established himself as an iron commission merchant in Baltimore in 1830, and who gradu-

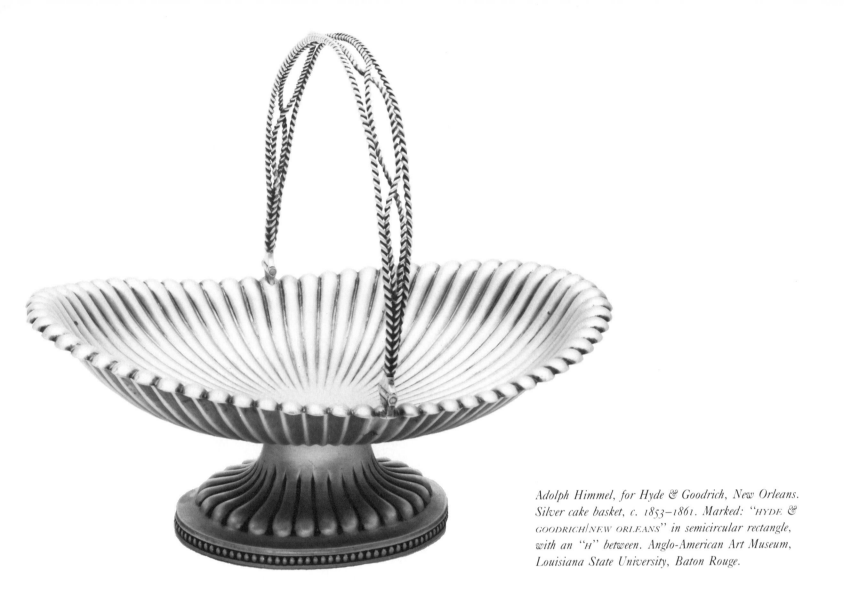

Adolph Himmel, for Hyde & Goodrich, New Orleans. Silver cake basket, c. 1853–1861. Marked: "HYDE & GOODRICH/NEW ORLEANS" in semicircular rectangle, with an "H" between. Anglo-American Art Museum, Louisiana State University, Baton Rouge.

ally developed a wide range of business and financial interests. For sixty years he was director of the National Farmers and Planters Bank. He opposed slavery, was a member of the American Colonization Society, and favored the Union during the Civil War. In his later years he devoted himself increasingly to philanthropic causes, among the most important of which was the establishment in 1886 of the Enoch Pratt Free Library of Baltimore, with initial holdings of 32,000 volumes and a generous endowment. He introduced the idea of branch libraries to make borrowing easier. Andrew Carnegie is said to have taken inspiration for his benefactions to libraries from Pratt. One would like to think Enoch Pratt's own inspiration came from long and pleasant hours spent in his study with its dark and richly carved bookcases.

An effect of material elegance, simplicity of form, and richness of surface is achieved in the design of a silver cake basket, above, fashioned in New Orleans around 1853–1861. The simple oval-shaped bowl and pedestal base have a gadrooned surface, while the handle is composed of intertwined strands of wire. As with a number of examples made and sold in New Orleans in the flush times of the 1850s, the marks on the bottom include HYDE & GOODRICH in an arc, then H, then NEW ORLEANS in a complementary arc below. Hyde and Goodrich was

a partnership firm first established in New Orleans in 1829, and was in fact a branch of the New York firm, James N. Hyde & Co. Some of the members of these two families were silversmiths, while others were responsible for the business operations of the firm which, like modern jewelry stores, handled jewelry, watches, plated ware, gold and silver, and still other objects. The families were interrelated and several moved from New York south. When first established in New Orleans most of the objects were made in New York or New England and shipped to the branch. In the 1850s there was an influx of skilled German craftsmen into New Orleans—part of the larger German immigration to America resulting in part from the political upheavals of 1848—and at least two of these men crafted pieces for sale by Hyde and Goodrich. One of them was Adolph Himmel, who marked his work with an "H." He was the craftsman who made this beautifully elegant cake basket.

Himmel is first recorded in New Orleans in 1852, when he was a partner with another German craftsman, Christopf Christian Kuchler. Within a year the partnership dissolved and both are known to have created pieces for Hyde and Goodrich. From 1855 onward Himmel seems to have been the chief local craftsman for that firm, and for its successor, Thomas, Griswold & Co., until he established his own Silverware Manufactory in

1869. At his death in 1877, Himmel's estate—all the materials in his workshop, "a lot of old silversmith tools, work blocks, hand machinery, etc."—was valued at $8,500. Himmel in his later years had as business associate a member of a New Orleans family that still operates a major jewelry store in the city. Thus there is an intertwined line of continuity of craftsmen and businessmen in association from 1829 to the present day. Because of the tradition of marking silver, the role of individual craftsmen and their relation to or part in the marketing system are considerably easier to trace than the work of craftsmen in allied areas such as furniture. In silver, as in furniture, one can see and trace the transition from family-craft-guild-based methods of production to modern methods of mass production and complex marketing systems. Nonetheless, there do still survive individual or family-run craft enterprises, only nowadays their products reach a very small percentage of the total market.

Silversmiths, when called upon to create trophy pieces, often combined realistic pictorial imagery, which was akin to the realistic imagery popular in paintings, with the floral and abstract forms more traditionally used on silver. This is true of the elaborately embellished Warfield Cup, right, in which a typical racecourse scene is shown in relief circling the base of the bowl, while the rim or gallery is decorated with an openwork rococo floral motif and the base with a floral wreath in repoussé. The bowl is inscribed: "Presented by the Citizens of Lexington Kentucky to Dr. Elisha Warfield as a Token of their Esteem for the Immortal Horse Lexington 1854." It bears the marks GARNER & WINCHESTER AND LEX. KY.

Garner and Winchester were silversmiths living and working in Lexington from 1838 to 1861, and during those years they produced some very elaborately decorated work. Little seems to be known about Winchester, but Eli C. Garner was one of two apprentices to the Lexington silversmith Asa Blanchard, who died in 1838. Blanchard willed his tools to the two apprentices and suggested that they go into partnership. The other disappeared from the scene, and Garner established what became a longtime partnership with Winchester. Garner is known to have had two mulatto sons who were trained as engravers, and one of them, George, was apparently active in Lexington for some time. It is very possible that he executed the inscription on this bowl. The person who designed the depiction of the course remains a matter of conjecture. The aid of a skilled painter such as Edward Troye may, or may not, have been enlisted. It is conceivable than an artist-draftsman from New Orleans might have provided a sketch.

The setting, though generalized, may have been intended to represent the Metairie Race Track in New Orleans, for there on April 1, 1854, the horse Lexington won the fourth race of his career in the highly touted and now legendary Great State Post Stake. Lexington was the horse representing the State of Kentucky, competing against horses sponsored by subscribers from Mississippi, Alabama, and Louisiana. The attendance was estimated at 20,000, most New Orleans business houses closed their doors, and former President Millard Fillmore was one of the judges. (The Metairie course was the scene of four of Lexington's great victories; it is now the site of a cemetery.) The pride of the Kentuckians was well justified, for in his racing career Lexington lost only one of the seven races in which he was entered, and his progeny included many famous winners. The fortunes of horses, as well as of men, were affected by the Civil War, for this prized stallion was sent to Illinois for safekeeping. After he died, back in Kentucky in 1875, his skeleton was presented to the Smithsonian Institution.

Dr. Elisha Warfield, the original recipient of this breeding trophy, was in his seventy-third year when he was awarded this cup and had at that time been involved in breeding and racing thoroughbreds for virtually half a century. He was trained as a medical doctor at Transylvania University and practiced until he was forty, at which time he retired to make what had been a part-time interest into a full-time vocation. He combined the day-to-day practical knowledge of a breeder with study and research, and many of the horses he bred, including Lexington, have since become historic. At the time Lexington won the famous Great State Post Stake he was no longer owned by Dr. Warfield, but the citizens of Kentucky were honoring the aging man not only for his achievement in breeding Lexington, but for his contributions to the breeding of thoroughbreds. Modern historians have called Warfield the Father of Kentucky Turf.

Garner and Winchester. Lexington silver bowl, Lexington, 1854. Marked: "GARNER & WINCHESTER" and "LEX. KY" in impressed rectangles. Private collection.

Attributed to Collin Rhodes. One-gallon preserve jar, Edgefield County, South Carolina, c. 1835. Stoneware; alkaline glaze inside and out; wheel thrown. Private collection.

Silver, fine furniture, and fine needlework often were made with utilitarian purposes in mind, but they also were meant to be admired and to add elegance and distinction to the environment in which they were placed. Other, humbler, objects were made with utilitarian purposes more completely in mind; yet here, too, pride of craftsmanship could and did exist.

When Robert Mills wrote his thick volume, *Statistics of South Carolina*, published in 1826, he mentioned the stoneware "pitchers, jugs, jars, etc." which were the principal items of manufacture in the Edgefield district, in the western central part of the state: "There is another village of sixteen or seventeen houses, and as many families, . . . called the Pottery, or Pottersville, but which should be called Landrumville, from its ingenious and scientific founder, Dr. Abner Landrum. This village is altogether supported by the manufacture of stoneware, carried on by this gentleman; and which, by his own discoveries is made much stronger, better, and cheaper than any European or American ware of the same kind."

Mills's statement is direct and laconic, and as a South Carolinian he could be expected to be chauvinistic about wares produced in his own state. As a man with a wide-ranging mind, and as architect and engineer, he was interested in new scientific discoveries and able to make valid judgments. Therefore his

statement that the wares produced in Landrum's pottery were in some way different from American and English wares carries weight.

Disciplined and devoted researchers and avid collectors have gathered information about, and examples of, the well-made utilitarian pottery of the Edgefield region and other Southern potteries, so that the history can be pieced together and distinctive qualities defined. The results are illuminating. The research reveals a distinctive Deep South tradition of utilitarian wares with alkaline glazes, glazes that have a glossy, transparent quality and range in tones from muted green through tans and deep browns. These glazes appear to have first been introduced in the Carolinas, and then spread into Georgia, Florida, Alabama, Mississippi, Arkansas, and Texas. The techniques were fairly widely used in the 1830s, and were still in use in some places into this century. These glazes were not, as Mills indicated, used in other

Attributed to Peter or Daniel Cribbs. Jug. Tuscaloosa, Alabama (originally called Bama City), c. 1840–1850. One-gallon capacity. Stoneware; light beige salt glaze on exterior, no glaze on interior; wheel thrown. Impressed on front: "BAMA CITY" and an "1." Private collection.

American or British wares, but they were used in the Orient. In essence, the glazes were achieved through the use of wood (plant) ashes and sand or sandy clay.

Whether or not the use of alkaline glazes began with Dr. Abner Landrum in the Edgefield district or whether they were introduced earlier in North Carolina, where the Landrums lived before moving to South Carolina, is still a matter of conjecture. Mills felt that Abner Landrum had made "his own discoveries." By this he could have meant independent invention, or discoveries through research and experimentation. If others in North Carolina or members of his family had already introduced the use of such glazes he may have improved them. The fact that he named his children Wedgwood (after the eighteenth-century ceramist, experimenter, and industrialist), Palissey (a distinguished French artistic potter of the sixteenth century), and Manises (the place where much of the beautiful Hispano-Moresque wares of the fifteenth century and later were made) suggests he had a keen interest in the history of ceramics. It is just possible that his reading might have included some of the information that had filtered into Europe about Chinese methods. Landrum was the publisher of a local newspaper, physician, and scientific farmer, as well as the guiding force behind pottery-making in Edgefield. Like Mills, he was a man with a variety of interests.

The existence of a pottery in Pottersville seems to date from 1810. In 1827 "The Pottersville Manufactory" was taken over by members of the Drake family. Subsequently other potteries were established in the Edgefield district, such as the Phoenix Factory owned by Collin Rhodes (related to the Landrums by marriage) and Robert W. Mathis, and the property operated by Lewis Miles at his Stoney Bluff plantation. In all of these, slaves were an integral part of the work force, and some were identified as turners (they threw pottery on the wheel). The work of Dave, a slave of Lewis Miles, is often signed.

The subtle olive green sometimes produced by the alkaline glazes can be seen in a one-gallon preserve jar, upper left, believed to have been made by Collin Rhodes around 1835. Most of the jugs and storage containers were sized according to capacity, and often the number of gallons the vessel held was impressed on the outside. Some Edgefield examples were much larger and held ten gallons. The jugs were used to store all manner of things: milk, molasses, cider, vinegar, and other liquids; wider-mouthed vessels were used for salted meats, pickles, lard, and even dried foods such as flour, beans, and meal. Here the potter has decorated his piece with a spray of an abstract flower and leaf form. This was done in the traditional method of trailing a white pipe-clay slip over the surface. Rhodes seems to have used these floral groups as a kind of trademark, and in a number of cases signed his work, making it identifiable and indicating pride in the finished product.

Dave, known also as Dave Potter, Dave Pottery, or Dave of the *Hive* (the name, for a time, of the newspaper Landrum published), was a slave originally owned by Abner Landrum and taught by him to read and write. Dave worked as a typesetter on Landrum's newspaper until 1831 when the latter moved to Columbia, South Carolina. Landrum's son-in-law, Lewis Miles, then became Dave's owner and Dave worked in Miles's pottery.

John M. Wilson Pottery. Jug, Guadalupe County, Texas, 1857–1869. Capacity about three gallons. Stoneware; alkaline glaze. Private collection.

The storage jars by Dave are among the largest examples of hand-thrown stoneware made in the United States in this period, some holding as much as thirty gallons. Proud of his skills and of his literacy, Dave frequently inscribed his pieces, as is the case with the jug, following page, where he wrote "LM/Oct 26. 1853/Dave." In other cases he wrote short doggerel verses and his name. Here a heavy coating of the glaze on the upper part of the jug gives a creamy-white effect, an effect created by firing in an oxidizing kiln.

The same basic techniques of glazing and firing were used on a three-gallon jug, above, made at the John M. Wilson Pottery in Guadalupe County, Texas (near San Antonio), around 1857–1869. This was apparently fired on its side so that the glaze is a

Dave the Potter. Jug, Edgefield County, South Carolina, October 26, 1853. Capacity about three gallons. Stoneware; alkaline glaze. Inscribed near rim: "LM/Oct 26. 1853/Dave." Private collection.

1850. The free and simple decoration on this well-shaped form has something of the same discreet elegance seen on Oriental wares, though it is doubtful there is any connection. It would have added an appealing note to any kitchen or pantry.

The alkaline and salt-glazed stonewares are but a few of the varieties of pottery and stonewares made in the South, and new information about the work of individual potters and potteries is still being discovered. The fact that there were three communities called Jugtown—in Georgia, North Carolina, and Alabama—and a Pottertown in Kentucky, as well as Pottersville in South Carolina, is a superficial indication of the existence of pottery-making centers. The special qualities of the alkaline-glazed stonewares of the Catawba Valley, North Carolina, area (fifty miles northwest of Charlotte) were highlighted in a special exhibition, the result of a recent study. A variety of useful and decorative wares were produced there, and in a number of cases descendants of mid-nineteenth-century potters produced wares using traditional methods well into the twentieth century.

The majority of utilitarian ceramic wares were used for storage or serving of foods—storage in outside spring houses, cold cellars, pantries, and kitchens, the latter, in the South, frequently separate from the main dwelling. A familiar type of furniture used for food storage in the South, from the middle years of the nineteenth century onward, if not before, was the food safe. These usually had a wood frame with shelves, closed doors, and tin-pierced panels all around for ventilation. They served to keep flying insects, "varmints," and children out, and gave some measure of protection to perishable foods. These vary in size; some may be five or six feet tall, some closer to waist height. A somewhat atypical example from Georgia is seen at right, in which the ventilating panels were placed in a simple low buffet or sideboard. Often, as here, the pierced-tin panels were done in patterns, making for an attractive piece of furniture. This food safe would have been appropriate for a simple dining room in an unpretentious home in town or country.

The use of "safe" to denote a chest or cupboard for protecting provisions goes back to the fifteenth century. Earlier examples appear to have had stretched cloth as ventilating panels. Pierced tin later replaced this. Nowadays these are sometimes called, variously, pie closets, jelly cupboards, and so on. In the 1818 edition of Noah Webster's *Dictionary* a safe is identified as "a buttery, a pantry," and in the 1853 edition as "a chest or closet for securing provisions from noxious animals." Catherine E. Beecher, in her *Treatise on Domestic Economy* published in 1843, page 317, speaks of "a safe, or moveable closet, with sides of wire or perforated tin, in which cold meats, cream, and other articles should be kept; (if ants be troublesome, set the legs in tin cups of water)." In the same author's *Domestic Receipt Book* she included a small engraving of a tin safe and directions for making it: "It is to be made five feet high, five feet wide, a division in the middle, and three shelves each side. Two doors in front, with a lock and key, and all the panels of perforated tin. It is very useful to preserve food in hot weather, and to protect it also from mice." In the North, where Miss Beecher lived, these safes were often placed in the cellar. In yet another book on domestic economy—a genre that proliferated in the nineteenth century—it was recommended that safes be placed in the pantry

warm tan on one side and light olive green on the other. The clouded spots, which to a modern eye give a pleasing decorative effect, were an accidental result of salt precipitating from the roof of the kiln during firing.

In general, stoneware with alkaline glazes was made in the Deep South. It is almost as if a line were drawn through North Carolina westward, as virtually no examples have been found above that line. Salt-glazed stoneware, based on well-established European traditions (salt is placed in the kiln firebox at the time of firing—the vaporization of the salt creates the glaze or glass-like coating), were made in a number of places throughout the South, but more frequently in areas above this invisible line.

The Cribbs family is believed to have come from Canton or New Philadelphia, Ohio, both centers of stoneware production, to Bama City (now Tuscaloosa) sometime around or before 1827, and established a pottery there. A stoneware jug with a loosely brushed spray of three leaves, page 328, is impressed with BAMA-CITY and an "1." These indicate the place of origin and the capacity of one gallon. It probably was made around 1840–

or kitchen entry since the kitchen itself would be too warm. This advice would have applied to the South where houses were, and are, frequently without basements. In the 1877 estate inventory of the New Orleans silversmith Adolph Himmel, a Kitchen Safe was "appraised at the sum of Four Dollars."

Another piece of kitchen furniture frequently seen in the South is the special table for making beaten biscuits, a staple of diets in the Deep South. Basically, it is a worktable topped by a thick slab of marble; frequently, as in the Alabama example, following page, there is also a cover to protect the surface when not in use. The tapered legs add subtlety to the simple, straightforward form. The biscuits, the basic ingredients of which are flour, shortening, and water or milk, are unleavened, made flaky by laborious beating of the dough with a wooden mallet or "axe," then folded again and again, until the dough is well blistered, a process that can take well over half an hour. Each cook had her own private recipe. In some cases, as here, a biscuit machine, which looks rather like a clothes-wringer, was used. The biscuits are eaten hot or can be stored, and are crisp and crunchy to taste. As early as 1855 Mary Stuart Smith, in her *Virginia Cookery-Book*, was describing them as a rarity, but they still survive. Their roots would seem to go back to the earlier hard

biscuits made for seamen, but with shortening added. These or similar marble-top worktables were used for making other pastries and candies—in Louisiana for the ubiquitous pralines.

A variety of household objects—baskets, clothes hampers, cradles, even wagons—were of willow ware. Such articles were advertised in the *Mobile Commercial Register & Patriot* of February 6, 1833, following page. They were probably made in the region, since there are men and women today who once again work in this traditional craft. These lightweight objects supplemented and complemented the heavier and sturdier furniture made by the cabinetmakers. Skill, discipline, and imagination went into their creation. The same is true of the wide range of products made in whole or in part of rush, reed, pine needles, grass, and palmetto in traditional ways by various individuals and groups of craftsmen. These include the baskets of the Moravian settlers in North Carolina, the coiled grass baskets made by Afro-Americans of the Sea Islands off the coast of South Carolina, the traditional chairs with rush and reed woven seats made by the Southern Highlanders of North Carolina, Kentucky, and Tennessee, and the traditional basketry of various Indian groups such as the Cherokee of North Carolina or the Coushatta of western Louisiana. In some cases, similar products are made today by skilled

Sideboard and food safe, Georgia. Pine with pierced tin panels. Tullie Smith House, Atlanta Historical Society.

craftsmen. The objects they fashion no doubt reflect or are very similar to the products made by their forefathers in the nineteenth, eighteenth, and even earlier centuries. Since these products are relatively fragile and were used extensively, few documented examples of the earlier periods are known or can be identified.

The painting on a chest of drawers, lower right, from North Carolina represents a simplified and stylized—somewhat naïve—version of the false graining that was a traditional art of the furniture and interior house painter. This attractive red and ocher piece is remarkable, too, in that, while the top was still wet, an inscription was drawn into the paint, probably with a stick or end of a paint brush, which reads *W. D. Evans, Kernersville, N.C. December 23rd, 1861.* Kernersville is between Winston-Salem and Greensboro. Relatively few examples of this

WILLOW WARE.

Willow ware, as advertised by Jotham Clarke & Co., Mobile Furniture Ware-House, Dauphin Street. From MOBILE COMMERCIAL REGISTER & PATRIOT, *February 6, 1833. Private collection.*

kind of painted furniture are known in the South, and documented examples are even rarer. One can only speculate on the reasons for Evans's recording his name and the place on this chest of drawers just a few days before the first Christmas during the war that embroiled the nation.

Those architects, artists, and craftsmen who lived and worked in the South before 1860 shared, in large part, the aims and interests of their colleagues in other parts of the country. Most of what they produced was surely as strongly influenced by the values and traditions of the periods in which they worked as by the particular, and varied, Southern settings, both human and physical, where they lived out all or part of their lives. Nonetheless, many of the examples shown here reveal the interaction that frequently occurs between an artist or craftsman and the place where he lived, and the traditions of that place. If produced elsewhere, these buildings or objects might not have been quite the same.

For example, insofar as I know, there was at no time a highly articulated or self-conscious attempt to create a specifically Southern architecture. There were, to be sure, a few comments by literary people like William Gilmore Simms, who suggested that certain styles, such as the Moorish, were more suitable than other styles for the flatlands of the South. Writers of architectural design books, such as A. J. Downing and Samuel Sloan, made mention of certain qualities or adaptations appropriate for buildings in the South. The ideas of both were influenced by concepts of the picturesque in which the relation of a building to its site was emphasized. Downing, for example, produced a design for "A small Country House for the Southern States." He showed a house with a projecting roof and long extended veranda, and indicated that both would afford "ample shade, so indispensable to all dwellings in a southern climate." Sloan, as we have seen, also created several designs suitable for the South. He noted not only the need for certain adaptations to the climate but the Southern tradition of hospitality which necessitated more rooms for sleeping.

However, long before these men put pen to paper, in fact, from the time of the earliest settlements, builders made adapta-

Worktable, with marble slab and cover, for making beaten biscuits, Alabama. Oakleigh, Historical Mobile Preservation Society, Mobile, Alabama.

tions of traditional designs in order to suit the climate and their pattern of living. These adaptations were noticed and remarked upon by visitors from other areas. Those who designed in the high styles often appear to have taken cognizance of the wise adaptations of the builders of vernacular structures and incorporated similar elements into their designs. Hence one can often identify buildings with an architectural Southern accent—an accent that varies by region or place, as do those of speech.

A reference to the particular environment, and an interest in the flora and fauna of the region, were shown by artists and craftsmen from time to time, as when flowers or plants were used as decorative emblems on documents, buildings, quilts, silver, or furniture. But these references appeared only occasionally. There was no consistent or conscious effort by any group of craftsmen before the Civil War to use Southern imagery on objects or buildings to indicate a sense of Southern regionalism.

Since the South was so rich in the variety of nature's living forms, it attracted the time and attention of the artist-naturalists who recorded these forms, often with grace and vitality, for scientific and didactic purposes. The prevalence of sporting paintings and sporting trophies is a reflection of the racing, sport, and outdoor life of the South.

In furniture the most explicit adjustments to the environment were made in some parts of beds: in the Carolinas beds were often made with removable headboards so as not to impede night breezes. Some Victorian beds had dowels in the bottom bedposts for support of protective mosquito netting.

In painting, some artists were concerned with creating images of the specifically Southern landscapes or with themes showing life as lived in the South. This occurred at a time when,

Painted chest of drawers, Kernersville, North Carolina, completed December 23, 1861. Tulip poplar and yellow pine. Fine Arts Museum of the South, Mobile, Alabama.

333

in the South, there was a growing sense of separateness from the rest of the country, and a desire to establish a regional identity. However, it was also during this time that a number of artists in America were deliberately seeking out American themes. Thomas Cole in New York, for example, wrote his "Essay on American Scenery," and encouraged Americans, and his fellow artists, to discover their "own land; its beauty, its magnificence, its sublimity." The desire on the part of certain artists to use Southern images in their paintings thus paralleled the efforts of other American artists to create paintings with specifically American subject matter. The efforts in this direction on the part of Southern artists bore relatively little fruit in the period before the Civil War. Later, in the 1880s and 1890s, a number of artists in the South made the landscape and the life of the region the theme of their canvases.

The war, which began with the Confederate firing on Fort Sumter on April 12, 1861, and ended with Lee's surrender at Appomattox Court House on April 9, 1865, had a profound effect on the lives of most individuals who lived in the South, white and black, artists, craftsmen, and their patrons among them. And in the "stillness" that followed Appomattox immediate efforts were concentrated on recouping losses and beginning life anew under changed circumstances.

Some areas suffered great damage during the war. Photographs of Columbia, South Carolina, for example, show a city almost totally demolished; much of that city's architectural and artistic heritage was irretrievably lost. When Sherman made his famous march through Georgia, he ravaged the countryside and destroyed virtually everything in his path. Though destruction in other communities and sections was less, they also suffered because of the economic burden of the war, because men were away, and because of the postwar economic upheavals and chaos. Fields and homes were neglected. In some situations the experience of defeat and postwar poverty limited and stifled creativity, patronage, development, and new building.

One feels as if certain communities, such as Natchez, Mississippi, were almost frozen in place from 1865 onward. In some ways this very poverty can now be seen as a boon, because many buildings and artifacts were preserved and not lost to progress or change. Yet around the edges of this small city, there are some rather handsome mansions built in the newest fashions of the 1870s and 1880s. The same is true of dozens of Southern communities that had known great affluence in the immediate prewar years. Southern cities such as Richmond, Pensacola, and New Orleans have large sections with spacious Victorian houses—an indication of post–Civil War prosperity. Birmingham, Alabama, is essentially a city that developed after 1865. Architecture is one of the most easily observable of the arts, and buildings are often an index of the creative vitality of a community. Though the South endured much poverty after the Civil War and remained largely rural until well into the twentieth century, the visual arts and crafts continued to play a role, and the people of the South continued to participate in the changing artistic interests and aspirations of the nation.

Notes on an Afterimage

For MANY PEOPLE TODAY the large house with white columns is probably the single most familiar visual image of the Old South, an image that obviously has its roots in the pre–Civil War period. It has become a stereotype, and is tied up with the broader romantic ideal of the patriarchal, hierarchical, and aristocratic life-style believed to have been associated with white Southern plantation life. Students of literature and history have studied the literary and philosophical concepts related to this broad plantation image in order to gain insight into the distinctive qualities of the South and its people. They have focused primarily on the complex web of attitudes, behavior, and ideas associated with it rather than upon the visual image itself. Therefore a brief recapitulation and a few general comments on the physical reality may be in order:

Mansions such as Drayton Hall, based on English country houses, were built in the colonial South during the eighteenth century by men of affluence. The next generation built houses on a similar scale in the newest taste. As early as the 1830s there were descriptions of such plantations in novels and essays. The references were often rather vague, but mentioned mansions with "spacious halls." During the period when the Greek Revival was at its height, the physical area of the settled South expanded tremendously and a fair number of white people enjoyed prosperity or the illusion of prosperity. In that time large, well-built homes such as Rattle and Snap in Tennessee or the Governor's Mansion in Texas were erected. Simpler structures, such as the McDonald House, now in Westville, near Lumpkin, Georgia, were built in imitation of these. On the latter, the portico across the front creates the illusion, from a distance, of a house of equal grandeur. The great mansions in this style were potent images at the time they were built, and were perceived as worthy of imitation by people of lesser means.

However, as we have also seen, Southerners shared in and followed the changing tastes of the time. Houses in the new modes—Italianate, Gothic, or Moorish—were being built on the very eve of the Civil War in such diverse places as Eufaula and Marion, Alabama; Columbus, Georgia; and Natchez, Mississippi. We have seen that William Gilmore Simms, in 1857, inveighed against the Greek style as inappropriate for the low-lying areas of the South, and proclaimed instead the virtues of the Moorish. It is also worth noting that when that great generalizer and creator of stereotypes, Harriet Beecher Stowe, who had never been to the Deep South, described a villa near New Orleans in her novel *Uncle Tom's Cabin*, published in 1852, it was an "East Indian" villa, with "light verandahs" all around, not a Greek Revival mansion. It thus appears that in the 1850s the taste for the Greek was thought of by the reasonably well informed, in both North and South, as a fashion on its way out, not as a symbol of the South.

Large private homes—and there certainly were quite a few—erected in town or country in the South during the years between 1860 and 1900 were built in the prevailing taste of the times, such as French Empire or Queen Anne. Verandas, porches, balconies, and loggias may abound, but these are not in the Greek Revival style.

The visual stereotype of the white-pillared mansion as the consistently preferred choice of Southerners therefore appears to be a late nineteenth- or early twentieth-century creation. This development can be briefly suggested:

In the 1884–1885 Cotton Exposition in New Orleans, for example, there was a display of photographs of the "homes of the planters of the interior. Many stately mansions were there, all bearing the distinguished marks of age." (Incidentally, the Alabama headquarters in this exhibit was designed in the "Mooro-Arabic" style.) In the great Columbian Exposition held in Chicago in 1893, the Pennsylvania building was copied after Independence Hall, while those of Massachusetts and New Jersey were meant to replicate or suggest the colonial home of John Hancock and Washington's headquarters at Morristown. Texas and California had buildings based on Spanish mission prototypes. Some of the buildings from Southern states were also based on earlier structures. That of Virginia was modeled on

Mount Vernon, with its giant portico. The Kentucky building was essentially late Federal in style, also with a giant columnar portico, and the Louisiana building was based on the colonial plantation type with galleries all around supported by simple columns and colonnettes. Thus certain building styles were seen as emblematic of certain areas. Each also suggested a way of life that had passed; in the selections made by the Southern states, there was perhaps more than a hint of nostalgia for the lost cause. In the Jamestown Tercentennial Exposition of 1907, similar choices were made. The Virginia building was patterned after a Georgian mansion, but with a giant portico and large fluted columns, "A noteworthy State Building illustrating Colonial period." The Louisiana building was also vaguely Federal, with a giant portico across the entire front and a projecting central pavilion.

The interest in historical buildings as symbols of the original colonies and of the Old South was related to yet another phase of historicism in late nineteenth- and early twentieth-century architecture—a phase stimulated in part by the expositions just mentioned. The revival of "early American" or "colonial" began in the 1890s and continued at least into the 1930s (variations on these themes are still being built), causing everyone to take a long second look at the nation's architectural heritage. Southern versions of this revival included both the "Southern colonial" and "antebellum." "Antebellum" was equated with Greek Revival, and the architectural revival of the mansion with columns on the front—mostly in its Greek Revival form—served to provide a visual image of "the big house," reinforcing the sentimental and literary image of the plantation house as the symbol of the Old South, particularly of the Deep South. In addition, architects and preservationists of the twentieth century first focused their efforts on the care of Georgian and "antebellum" structures because these seemed in most danger and were considered architecturally most distinguished; it is only in relatively recent times that there has been sensitive observation and concern for the vernacular and for Victorian and post-Victorian buildings.

Novels and plays, such as J. K. Tillotson's *The Planter's Wife* or H. G. Donnelly's *Carolina* (1906), were set in Southern mansions. Margaret Mitchell's immensely successful *Gone With the Wind* (1936), popularized the image. She skillfully made use of two plantation houses as symbols. Tara, the home of the newcomers, the O'Haras, was a "clumsy, sprawling building . . . built according to no architectural plan whatsoever." Twelve Oaks, the home of the aristocratic Wilkes, was a "white house [which] reared its perfect symmetry before her, tall of columns, wide of verandas, flat of roof" with "a stately beauty, a mellowed dignity."

In 1941 J. Frazer Smith published his *White Pillars*, one of a number of American regional architectural histories that came off the presses in the 1920s, '30s, and '40s. The subtitle, "The Architecture of the South," was appended to the dust jacket. The focus was on the Lower Mississippi Valley, but buildings from Kentucky, Tennessee, and Alabama were included as well as from Mississippi and Louisiana. Of the seventy-two buildings illustrated, fifty had columnar fronts or porticos. The other twelve included two Gothic churches and three interior views. Leicester B. Holland wrote in his Foreword, "This book is a survey of the habitations of man of the Caucasian race—genus North American; species, Deep Southern; variety planter—thriving luxuriantly in the first half of the last century." The image was full-blown.

In the middle years of the twentieth century the great Southern mansion also became a symbol of a poverty-stricken, decaying, and decadent South, ravished by the Civil War and the poverty of its aftermath. The postwar poverty was not the first time, nor the last, in which parts of the South experienced economic hardship and depression. The artist Charles Fraser could write in the 1850s of the neglected and crumbling mansions along the Ashley and Cooper rivers in South Carolina at that time. He was recalling handsome eighteenth-century buildings that had been abandoned and had fallen into decay because the soil of the area became exhausted and fallow, and the owners left to settle elsewhere.

In many sections of the South cotton remained a major cash crop after the Civil War, providing a reasonable support for those who worked the land and traded in the crop. But when the boll weevil crept across the Mexican border in 1892–1893, the long reign of cotton as king began to wane. By 1922 this destructive beetle had spread across the entire South, devastating the crops and causing the collapse of the agricultural system as well as of the then infant textile industry (an industry that subsequently revived and is important in the economic life of the contemporary South). Hurricanes and several unexpected freezes in the 1920s caused the loss of several sugar crops and, in some cases, the abandonment of plantation houses. The Great Depression of the 1930s followed fast on the heels of the boll weevil and other natural disasters. The mid-twentieth-century perception of a decadent South owes as much to these assaults upon the economy as to post–Civil War conditions.

The visual image of the plantation house in ruins goes hand-in-hand with that of the impeccably kept great mansion. Indeed, the book cover of J. Frazer Smith's *White Pillars* showed not a surviving plantation house in good condition but the spectacular ruins of Windsor, near Port Gibson, Mississippi, where twenty-four giant columns are all that survive of a once-grand house destroyed not by the War but by a fire in 1890. A similar elegaic mood is powerfully evoked in the work of the writer-photographer Clarence John Laughlin, whose *Ghosts Along the Mississippi*, first published in 1948, is perennially popular.

For varied and different reasons, consciously and unconsciously, exposition planners, politicians, historians, architects, novelists, filmmakers, and ordinary citizens have perpetuated the image of the romantic, columned plantation house. Historians may try to place this image within a properly defined and limited context, and new images of the South are emerging as part of rapid social change. Nonetheless, the now-familiar image of the white-columned plantation house, a symbol of the Old South, has become part of the national mythology.

NOTES

SELECT BIBLIOGRAPHY

CREDITS

INDEX

Notes

PART ONE *Beginnings,* 1560–1735

ix OR HAS BEEN: Among these many studies, four recent useful volumes, with extensive bibliographic notes, are I. A. Newby, *The South: A History* (New York, 1978); Edgar T. Thompson, ed., *Perspectives on the South: Agenda for Research* (Durham, 1967); Arthur S. Link and Rembert W. Patrick, eds., *Writing Southern History: Essays in Historiography in Honor of Fletcher M. Green* (Baton Rouge, 1965); and F. Garvin Davenport, Jr., *The Myth of Southern History* (Nashville, 1967). For an excellent brief discussion of the cultural geography of the South, see Wilbur Zelinsky, *The Cultural Geography of the United States* (Englewood Cliffs, N.J., 1973), 80–81, 118–119, 122–124.

ix REST OF AMERICA: For a summary, see Newby, *The South,* 30.

ix STATES RIGHTS: Newby, *The South,* provides a valuable summary of these complex developments, 37–182.

x 29.9 PERCENT, RESPECTIVELY: Ibid., 108. I believe these figures omit the Indians, whose populations, as members of separate nations, were not included in census figures.

x MEN ARE ASSEMBLED: Howard G. Rice, intro., *Travels in North America in the Years 1780, 1781, and 1782, by the Marquis de Chastellux,* 2 vols. (Chapel Hill, 1963), 2, 537.

x OFFICIALLY FOSTERED: See, for example, E. Milby Burton, *South Carolina Silversmiths 1690–1860* (Rutland, 1968), xiv–xvi; Lafayette C. Baker, *History of the United States Secret Service* (Philadelphia, 1868), 373.

x KNOWLEDGE WAS DISTURBING: *Antiques,* 55 (April 1949), special supplement. Report on the first Antiques and Decorations Forum held at Williams-burg, Jan. 24–Feb. 4, 1949. The most notable earlier study of Southern furniture was Paul Burroughs, *Southern Antiques* (Richmond, 1931).

xi JANUARY 1952: *Antiques, 61,* the entire January 1952 issue.

xi AND THEIR HERITAGE: For example, Allan H. Eaton's pioneer study, *Handicrafts of the Southern Highlands* (New York, 1937); John Michael Vlach, *The Afro-American Tradition in Decorative Arts,* Cleveland Museum of Art (Cleveland, 1978); and Maude Southwell Wahlman, "The Art of the Afro-American Quilt: Origins, Development and Significance," diss., Yale, 1980.

3 WORTHY OF OBSERVING: The best reference is Paul Hulton (foreword, catalogue, and introductory studies), *The Work of Jacques Le Moyne de Morgues: A Huguenot Artist in France, Florida and England,* 2 vols. (London, 1977). In the essay in this study by William C. Sturtevant, "The ethnological evaluation of the Le Moyne–De Bry illustrations," this author states, "Not only are the Le Moyne–De Bry illustrations the only ones picturing the Timucua that have survived; they are also the earliest of all depictions of North American Indian life. There are less than ten known earlier illustrations, most of which are of doubtful reliability" (p. 70). For Le Moyne, see also Stefan Lorant, ed., *The New World: The First Pictures of America Made by John White and Jacques Le Moyne and Engraved by Theodore De Bry* (New York, 1946), 5–86; Jean Ribaut, *The Whole True Discouerye of Terra Florida,* Facsimile of 1563 edition, intro. David L. Dowd (Gainesville, 1964); Hugh Honour, *The European Vision of America,* Cleveland Museum of Art (Kent, Ohio, 1975), no. 65; Joseph C. Ewers, "An Anthropologist Looks at Early Pictures of North American Indians," *New-York Historical Society Quarterly, 32* (Oct. 1934), 223–225. (It is now generally agreed that the crayon drawing discussed in this article is a copy after an engraving.)

4 OR SOON THEREAFTER: Sturtevant, "Ethnological evaluation," in Hulton, *Jacques Le Moyne, 1,* 69–71, suggests that the engravings were possibly created "by repeating, combining, and rearranging a very small number of original sketches." See also Hulton, *1,* 8–10.

5 COULD BE EITHER: I am grateful to Professor Joseph Ewan of Tulane University for his help in identifying the plants, fruits, and vegetables.

5 OF THE TIMUCUANS: Sturtevant, "Ethnological evaluation," *1,* 71. For Le Moyne's artistic style, see Hulton, *Jacques Le Moyne, 2,* 13.

5 DEVELOPED IN THE SOUTH: Hulton, *Le Moyne, 1,* 142. For the original text see Jacques Le Moyne de Morgues, *Brevis Narratio eorum quae in Florida Americae Provincia* (Frankfurt, 1591), Plate 10.

6 SOUTHEASTERN NORTH AMERICA: The best study of John White's drawings is Paul Hulton and David Beers Quinn, *The American Drawings of John White, 1577–1590, with Drawings of European and Oriental Subjects* (London and Chapel Hill, 1964). See also David Beers Quinn, ed., *The Roanoke Voyages, 1584–1590,* Hakluyt Society, 2nd ser., no. 104, 2 vols. (London, 1955), 2, 545–547.

6 THEIR HAND AT JOINERY: Quinn, *Roanoke Voyages, 1,* 329.

6 TO HAVE SURVIVED: Ibid., 495.

8 FAMINE STRUCK: Of the numerous publications about the early history of Virginia, one of the most useful, with excellent bibliography, is Edmund S. Morgan, *American Slavery, American Freedom: The Ordeal of Colonial Virginia* (New York, 1975); see also Cary Carson, Norman F. Barka, William M. Kelso, Gary Wheeler Stone, and Dell Upton, "Impermanent Architecture in the Southern American Colonies," *Winterthur Portfolio, 16* (Summer/Autumn

1981), 135–196, which refutes in part some of Morgan's hypotheses.

8 OFTEN UNBRIDGEABLE: J. Paul Hudson, "Jamestown artisans and craftsmen," *Antiques, 71* (Jan. 1957), 47–50; J. Paul Hudson and C. Malcolm Watkins, "The earliest known English pottery in America," *Antiques, 71* (Jan. 1957), 51–54; Morgan, . . . *Slavery* . . . *Freedom*, 86–87; for a summary of the nature of the archaeological digs at Jamestown that took place in the early twentieth century, see Ivor Noël Hume, *Martin's Hundred* (New York, 1982), 27–33.

8 "WANTON CITY ORNAMENTS": William Strachey, "A True Reportory of the Wreck and Redemption of Sir Thomas Gates, Knight" (London, 1625), in Louis B. Wright, ed., *A Voyage to Virginia: Two Narratives* (Charlottesville, 1964), 81–82.

8 ON THE JAMES RIVER: Ivor Noël Hume, "First Look at Lost Virginia Settlement," *National Geographic, 155* (June 1979), 735–767; also *Martin's Hundred*.

9 "NAME OF A TOWN": Robert Beverley, *The History & Present State of Virginia* (London, 1705), in Louis B. Wright, intro. and ed. (Chapel Hill, 1947), 57–58. For the concepts of town planning and the early efforts to build towns, see John W. Reps, *Tidewater Towns: City Planning in Colonial Virginia and Maryland* (Williamsburg and Charlottesville, 1973), 1–91; for the 1662 Act, 52–53. *See also* Morgan, . . . *Slavery* . . . *Freedom*, 188–191, 283–285, 287–288.

9 "CONSUME THEM ALL": Susan M. Kingsbury, ed., *The Records of the Virginia Company of London* (Washington, 1935), *4*, 259.

9 10 BY 10 FEET: Dell Upton, "Early Vernacular Architecture in Southeastern Virginia," diss., Brown University, 1980. I am grateful to Mr. Upton for reviewing portions of my manuscript and allowing me to read several portions of the draft of his dissertation. For several different early building methods apparently used or known during the first half-century of settlement, see "Houses for New Albion," *Journal of the Society of Architectural Historians, 15* (Oct. 1956), 2; a 1650 document is quoted. The study of Cary Carson et al., "Impermanent Architecture," is based on archaeological evidence, and discusses the various types of building techniques used in the Chesapeake colonies, as well as the implications this evidence presents for the changing nature of the economy of these colonies during the seventeenth century.

9 "THE PRISON HOUSE": William W. Hening, ed., *The Statutes at Large: being a collection of all the Laws of Virginia from the first session of the legislature in the year 1619*, 13 vols. (New York, 1819–1823), *1* (1823), 340.

10 "PRITTY AND CONVENIENT": John Hammond, *Leah and Richel, or, the Two Fruitful Sisters Virginia and Maryland* (London, 1656), 18, in Peter Force, *Tracts and Other Papers, 3* (1844; reprint ed., New York, 1947).

10 GABLE AND CHIMNEYS: Cary Carson, "The Virginia House in Maryland," *Maryland Historical Magazine, 69* (Summer 1974), 185–196; and Carson et al., "Impermanent Architecture."

10 "VIRGINIA BUILT": Hening, *Statutes, 1*, 340. This comes from a 1692 agreement between trustees of the Middlesex County Court and two builders.

11 QUARTERED FOR A TIME: Bacon first led his "army" of small freemen against the Indians whose land they coveted, and then, when curbed by British officials who did not think it politic to break treaties, attacked the redoubtable and enduring Governor Berkeley and the entrenched Assembly at Jamestown, breaking the tight control of a powerful few and opening the way for greater representation on the part of the freemen—and for less governmental control of the colonist's encroachment on Indian lands. See Morgan, . . . *Slavery* . . . *Freedom*, 250–270.

12 UNTIL A DECADE LATER: Letter of Nov. 14, 1980, from Cary Carson, Director of Research, Colonial Williamsburg Foundation.

13 MAKE THEMSELVES SECURE: Joseph W. Barnwell, "The Second Tuscarora Expedition," *South Carolina Historical and Genealogical Magazine, 10* (Jan. 1909), 33–48; Elias Johnson, *Legends, Traditions and Laws of the Iroquois or Six Nations and History of the Tuscarora Indians* (Lockport, N.Y., 1881), 61–69.

13 THE ESTABLISHED CHURCH: Harold Wickliffe Rose, *The Colonial Houses of Worship in America* (New York, 1963), 13–26. For South Carolina, Arthur Henry Hirsch, *The Huguenots of Colonial South Carolina* (Durham, 1928), 102–130, and Frederick P. Bowes, *The Culture of Early Charleston* (Chapel Hill, 1942), 13–33.

14 DEGREE SELF-GOVERNING: George Maclaren Brydon, *Virginia's Mother Church*, 2 vols. (Richmond, 1947), *1*, 90–94, 98.

14 GENERALLY KNOWN: In my discussion of colonial churches in the South I am grateful to Mrs. Sue Walker, Mrs. Carol Mann, Mrs. Sarah Bailey Luster, and Mrs. Regina Scotto Wedig, graduate students in art history at Tulane University, for information and insights contributed in seminars.

14 TOWERS OR STEEPLES: Rose, *Houses of Worship*, 451, 459–460.

14 THAN THE ALTAR: For discussions of colonial Virginia churches: Thomas Jefferson Wertenbaker, *The Old South: The Founding of American Civilization* (New York, 1942), 107; George Carrington Mason, *Colonial Churches in Tidewater Virginia* (Richmond, 1945); James Scott Rawlings, *Virginia's Colonial Churches: An Architectural Guide* (Richmond, 1963); Rose, *Houses of Worship*, 13–18, 446–526; and Marcus Binney, "Virginia Country Churches," *Country Life* (London), *162* (April 27, 1978), 1138–1140.

14 "NOT ALL BUILT ALIKE": William J. Hinks, ed. and trans., "Report of the Journey of Francis Louis Michel from Berne, Switzerland, to Virginia, October 2, 1701–December 1, 1702," *Virginia Magazine of History and Biography, 24* (Jan. 1916), 21–22.

14 BUILDING A NEW ONE: Rawlings, *Virginia's Colonial Churches*, 27–30; Rose, *Houses of Worship*, 462–463; Mason, *Colonial Churches*, 76–79.

15 EARLY SEVENTEENTH CENTURY: James F. White, *Protestant Worship and Church Architecture* (New York, 1964), 78–117; G.W.O. Addleshaw and Frederick Etchells, *The Architectural Setting of Anglican Worship* (London, 1948), 22–29, 52, and Appendix I, 245–246.

15 SEATED IN THEIR PEWS: Marian Card Donnelly, *The New England Meeting Houses of the Seventeenth Century* (Middletown, 1968).

15 TO OTHER ACTIVITIES: Perry Miller, *Errand into the Wilderness* (Cambridge, Mass., 1956), 99–140, esp. 106 and 138–140; William H. Seiler, "The Anglican Parish in Virginia," *Seventeenth-Century America*, ed. James Morton Smith (Chapel Hill, 1959), 120–142; Brydon, *Virginia's Mother Church*, *1*, X, 28–29, n. 22; Richard Beale Davis, *Intellectual Life in the Colonial South* (Knoxville, 1976), *2*, 631.

15 MORE THAN FOUR: Brydon, *Virginia's Mother Church*, *1*, 380–381.

15 BY ENGLISH STANDARDS: Ibid., *1*, 28–29, 86–88, 94, 506–515.

15 "CURRENT AMONG US": Hinks, "Report . . . of Michel," 21.

16 "UPON THEIR KNEES": Hugh Jones, *The Present State of Virginia* (London, 1724; reprint ed., New York, 1865), 69; or Brydon, *Virginia's Mother Church*, *1*, 399.

16 "FITTED FOR AUDITORIES": Stephen Wren, *Parentalia: or, Memoirs of the Family of the Wrens: viz. of Mathew Bishop of Ely, Christopher Dean of Windsor etc., But Chiefly of Sir Christopher Wren* (London, 1750), 320.

16 CENTER AISLE: Addleshaw and Etchells, *Architectural Setting*, 53–77; White, *Protestant Worship*, 94–98. Wren may well have known Solomon de Brosse's 1623 Protestant Temple at Charenton, France, with its open central space and high galleries. See Margaret Whinney, *Christopher Wren* (New York, 1971), 32, 48–49.

17 THREE FEET THICK: Rawlings, *Virginia's Colonial Churches*, 120–126; Rose, *Houses of Worship*, 501–502; Stephen P. Dorsey, *English Churches in America* (New York, 1952), 72–75. See also Alan Gowans, *King Carter's Church*, University of Victoria Maltwood Museum, Studies in Architectural History, no. 2 (1969); Marcus Whiffen's review, *Journal of the Society of Architectural Historians, 29* (May 1970), and reply, *29* (Dec. 1970), 363–364. Also, Marcus Whiffen, *The Public Buildings of Colonial Williamsburg* (Williamsburg, 1958), 77–85; and White, *Protestant Worship*, 93–94, 103–104. It may be relevant to mention that Christ Church and its sister church, St. Mary's White Chapel, had both been served for nearly thirty years by the Reverend Andrew Jackson, a Presbyterian minister, who died in 1710. For various references, see Brydon, *Virginia's Mother Church*, *1*, 29, 243, 255, 269, 480. He was dead by the time Christ Church was built, but may have in-

fluenced his congregation toward a taste for simplicity—this is conjecture only, but it is an interesting coincidence.

17 "PERFECT THE BUILDING": *Virginia Magazine of History and Biography, 6* (1898), 3.

17 FOUR CARPENTERS: Ibid., 367–370.

18 "HAND OF MY WIVES": Ibid., 3; Bishop William Meade, *Old Churches, Ministers and Families of Virginia,* 2 vols. (Philadelphia, 1857), *2,* 115–123; and Rawlings, *Virginia's Colonial Churches,* 120.

18 PRECEDENT OR MODEL: Gowans, *King Carter's Church,* 22–32, Plates VII and IX, cites two churches, Durisdeer in northern Dumfriesshire of c. 1695, and Farley in Wiltshire of 1689–1690 as possible models.

18 "I EVER PERFORMED": Meade, *Old Churches, 2,* 118.

18 NORTH CAROLINA, 1734: Rose, *Houses of Worship,* 191–192, 327–328. St. Thomas's once had a brick tower which was destroyed by a hurricane in 1905, but it appears to have been of a later date than the main fabric of the church.

18 ON BOTH SIDES: Frederick Dalcho, *An Historical Account of the Protestant Episcopal Church in South Carolina* (Charleston, 1820), 244–263; Rose, *Houses of Worship,* 425–426; Dorsey, *English Churches in America,* 96–97; White, *Protestant Worship,* 102.

19 ENGLISH COUNTRY CHURCHES: Addleshaw and Etchells, *Architectural Setting,* 179–180 and n. 2. Harold Kalman and John De Visser, *Pioneer Churches* (New York, 1976), 63, say the present pulpit was "inserted into the chancel" later in the eighteenth century. They do not indicate where it might have been earlier.

20 ITS KIND IN AMERICA: *Gentleman's Magazine* (June, 1753), 260. From the moment it was erected, St. Philip's was described as "a large, regular beautiful building exceeding any that are in his Majesty's dominions in America," as cited in a 1723 document by Rev. William Tredwell Bull, in Edward McCrady, *The History of South Carolina Under the Royal Government, 1719–1776* (New York, 1899), p. 43.

20 "STRUCTURE IN AMERICA": Quoted in Anna Wells Rutledge, "Charleston's first artistic couple," *Antiques, 52* (Aug. 1947), 101.

20 "WE HAVE IN AMERICA": Edmund Burke [and William Burke], *An Account of the European Settlements in America,* 2 vols. (London, 1761; 4th ed., 1765), *2,* 258. There is no evidence to show Burke visited America; his materials seem to have been gathered from others, including his nephew William.

20 "OTHER PUBLIC STRUCTURES": Edward McCrady, "An Historic Church, The Westminster Abbey of South Carolina," *Year Book, City of Charleston, 1896* (Charleston, 1896), 319–374; Edward G. Lilly, ed., and Clifford L. Legerton, *Historic Churches of Charleston* (Charleston, 1966), 19; John

Fitzhugh Millar, *The Architects of the American Colonies* (Barre, Mass., 1968), 24–25; Dalcho, *Episcopal Church in S.C.,* 120–126.

21 KEEP IT SO: Hirsch, *Huguenots,* esp. 102–130; Bowes, *Culture of Early Charleston,* 13–33.

21 BARREL-VAULTED INTERIORS: Lilly and Legerton, *Churches of Charleston,* 19. No source is given for the quotation.

21 "INDIANS TO BEGIN WITHALL": Quoted in Peter H. Wood, *Black Majority* (New York, 1974), 133–142.

21 CALLED "MEETING HOUSES": Charles Fraser, *My Reminiscences of Charleston* (Charleston, 1854; reprinted., 1969), 65.

22 NUMBER OF WHITES: Wood, *Black Majority,* 35–62.

22 INCREASED SUBSTANTIALLY: Morgan, . . . *Slavery . . . Freedom,* 296–308.

22 HOLLAND AND FRANCE: Hugh Morrison, *American Colonial Architecture* (New York, 1952), 174; John Summerson, *Architecture in Britain, 1530 to 1830,* 4th ed. (Baltimore, 1969), 32, fig. 6.

22 THE FIRST PLAN: Reps, *Tidewater Towns,* 117–193; John W. Reps, *The Making of Urban America: A History of City Planning in the United States* (Princeton, 1965), 103–114; Whiffen, *Public Buildings,* 1–33, 227–228.

23 "NAME OF THE CAPITOL": Beverley, *Present State of Virginia,* 105.

23 "OF ANY IN AMERICA": Ibid., 289.

23 "IN BRITISH AMERICA": Burke, *European Settlements, 2,* 213.

23 "POST AND RAILS": Reps, *Tidewater Towns,* 148, 174; Marcus Whiffen, *The Eighteenth-Century Houses of Williamsburg* (Williamsburg, 1960), 53–56.

24 IN A DRAWING: Whiffen, *Houses of Williamsburg,* 106–109.

25 SOME IN THE INTERIORS: Paul E. Buchanan, "The Eighteenth-Century Frame House of Tidewater Virginia," in Charles E. Peterson, ed., *Building Early America* (Radnor, Pa., 1976), 54–73; Dell Upton, "Vernacular Domestic Architecture in Eighteenth-Century Virginia," *Winterthur Portfolio, 17* (Summer/Autumn 1982), 95–119.

26 HEMP AND TOBACCO: Louis R. Caywood, "Green Spring Plantation," *Virginia Magazine of History and Biography, 65* (Jan. 1957), 67–83.

27 WITH ABSOLUTE CERTAINTY: Modern scholarship now makes use of microscopic analysis of woods, and this often helps to suggest the area in which a piece was made; in some cases documents exist, but most other evidence is circumstantial. In recent years the staff of the Museum of Early Southern Decorative Arts in Winston-Salem has been carefully gathering evidence about furniture

and other artifacts believed to have been made in the Southeast before 1820; pieces have been photographed, construction examined, and if any history is known, this is recorded. They have thus built a useful body of comparative material concerning forms, use of woods, and methods of construction. They are also compiling, from available legal and printed materials, detailed listings concerning the existence and practices of craftsmen and artists of this period.

27 "WILL YEELD PROFITE": Quinn, *Roanoke Voyages, 1,* 330.

28 SURRY COUNTY, VIRGINIA: I am grateful to Mrs. Mary Rose Boswell, Curator, Society for Preservation of Virginia Antiquities, for giving me a copy of this and other inventories.

29 "PAINTER, A GERMAN": J. Hall Pleasants, "Justus Engelhardt Kühn, An Early Eighteenth Century Maryland Portrait Painter," *Proceedings of the American Antiquarian Society, 46* (Oct. 1936), 243–280, is the most important reference on Kühn.

30 "ABLE TO LIVE": Frank J. Klingburg, *Carolina Chronicle: The Papers of Commissary Gideon Johnston, 1707–1716* (Berkeley and Los Angeles, 1946), 31.

31 JAQUELIN-AMBLER FAMILIES: Mary Black, "The Case of the Red and Green Birds," *Arts in Virginia, 3* (Winter 1963), 3–9; Mary Black, "The Case Reviewed," *Arts in Virginia, 10* (Fall 1969), 12–21; see also Mary Black, "Contributions Toward a History of Early Eighteenth-Century New York Portraiture: Identification of the Aetatis Suae and Wendell Limners," *American Art Journal, 12* (Autumn 1980), 4–31. Though Black suggests Nehemiah Partridge, who worked in New York and whose style is close to this artist, as the painter of this group, Partridge's name has not yet been found in Virginia records. I am grateful to Carolyn Weekley of Colonial Williamsburg Foundation for this latter information.

32 BEFORE 1700: Graham Hood, *Charles Bridges and William Dering, Two Virginia Painters 1735–1750* (Charlottesville, 1978), 29, n. 33.

32 AND IS NOTCHED: I am grateful to Professor Joseph Ewan, Tulane University, for this information.

32 "CONVENIENCE TO GO TO": Mark Catesby, *The Natural History of Carolina, Florida and the Bahama Islands* (London, 1754), *1,* i.

34 "PAINTER-LIKE WAY": Catesby, *Natural History, 1,* vi.

34 NATURAL HISTORY ILLUSTRATIONS: George Frederick Frick and Raymond Phineas Stearns, *Mark Catesby, the Colonial Audubon* (Urbana, 1961), 50.

34 "ESPECIALLY IN CATTLE": B. R. Carroll, ed., *Historical Collections of South Carolina,* 2 vols. (New York, 1836), *2,* 128.

35 FAILED TO DISCOVER: E. Milby Burton, *South*

Carolina Silversmiths, 1690–1860 (Rutland, 1968), 47–49, 105–110.

35 OF THE SAME PERIOD: Burton, Silversmiths, 178–179; Kathryn C. Buhler and Graham Hood, American Silver: Garvan and Other Collections in the Yale University Art Gallery, 2 vols. (New Haven and London, 1970), 2, 253–254.

36 "WATERED BY THEM": Isaac J. Cox, ed., The Journeys of René Robert Cavalier Sieur de La Salle, 2 vols. (New York, 1905–1906), 1, 145, 167.

36 SOLDIER-SAILOR: For a summary of this period, Marcel Giraud, A History of French Louisiana, the Reign of Louis XIV, 1698–1715 (Baton Rouge, 1974), 1.

37 TONE WITH SKILL: Samuel Wilson, Jr., "Architecture in Eighteenth-Century West Florida," in Eighteenth-Century Florida and Its Borderlands, ed. Samuel Proctor (Gainesville, 1975), 102–139.

38 BUILDINGS SURVIVE: Many of these drawings are reproduced in Samuel Wilson, Jr., Bienville's New Orleans: A French Colonial Capital, 1718–1768, Friends of the Cabildo, Louisiana State Museum (New Orleans, 1968).

39 EARLIER MEN'S WORK: David I. Bushnell, Drawings by A. De Batz, Smithsonian Miscellaneous Collections, 80, no. 5, 1928, and Samuel Wilson, Jr., "Louisiana Drawings by Alexandre De Batz," Journal of the Society of Architectural Historians, 22 (May 1963), 75–89.

39 "THEIR MOTHER COUNTRY": [James Oglethorpe], A New and Accurate Account of the Provinces of South-Carolina and Georgia (London, 1733), reproduced in Trevor R. Reese, ed., The Most Delightful Country of the Universe, Promotional Literature of the Colony of Georgia, 1717–1734 (Savannah, 1972), 130, 135.

39 "LAID OUT THE TOWN": Letter from James Oglethorpe to Trustees, in Reasons for Establishing the Colony of Georgia (London, 1733), reprinted in Collections of the Georgia Historical Society (Savannah, 1840), 1, 233–234.

39 WRITTEN AND CONJECTURED: For the best discussion of the Savannah and other early Georgian town plans, see Reps, Making of Urban America, 175–203.

41 WERE BEING BUILT: For development of London, see especially Sir John Summerson, Georgian London (New York, 1946), 22–35, 81–94.

41 PUBLIC BUILDINGS: Select Tracts Relating to the Colonies, printed for J. Roberts (London, 1732). Reprinted in Reese, Delightful Country, 76–112. Reference to the Irish experience is found in Oglethorpe's Accurate Account, 115–156, esp. 117–118.

41 "THE ROOF SHINGLED": Francis Moore, A Voyage to Georgia Begun in the Year 1735 (London, 1744), reprinted in Trevor R. Reese, intro., Our

First Visit in America, Early Reports from the Colony of Georgia, 1732–1740 (Savannah, 1974), 96.

41 "PLAINED AND PAINTED": Ibid., 97.

41 "AND AN ATTIC": Samuel Urlsperger, Detailed Reports on the Salzburger Emigrants Who Settled in America, 1733–1734, George Fenwick Jones, intro., Hermann J. Lacher, trans. (Athens, 1968), 1, 139.

41 "A RUINOUS HEAP": Colonial Records of the State of Georgia (Atlanta, 1915), 25, 174.

41 IN COPENHAGEN: Kristian Huidt, Von Reck's Voyage, Views of Georgia in 1736 (Savannah, 1980).

42 VINEYARDS, AND TRADE: George Fenwick Jones, trans. and ed., Henry Newman's Salzburger Letters (Athens, 1966), 392.

43 IN 1740: Urlsperger, Detailed Reports, 1, 135–148; Huidt, Von Reck's Voyage, 24.

43 (IN FLORIDA): Phinizy Spalding, Oglethorpe in America (Chicago, 1977), 101, n. 11.

PART TWO An Established Society, 1735-1788

47 "IN THE ENGLISH TASTE": Harriet Horry Ravenel, Eliza Pinckney (New York, 1896), 5.

47 1700 AND 1750: Edmund S. Morgan, American Slavery, American Freedom: The Ordeal of Colonial Virginia (New York, 1975), 296–299.

48 "UTTERLY DESTROYED": March 1, 1773, as quoted by Anna Wells Rutledge, Artists in the Life of Charleston, Transactions of the American Philosophical Society, N.S., 39, part 2 (Philadelphia, 1949), 117.

49 PUBLISHED DESIGNS: For a good short list of the more important architectural books and carpenters' handbooks published in the middle years of the eighteenth century, see Hugh Morrison, Early American Architecture (New York, 1952), 290–291.

51 NO SMALL COMPLIMENT: Henry A. M. Smith, "The Ashley River: Its Seats and Settlements," South Carolina Historical and Genealogical Magazine, 20 (Jan. 1919), 11.

52 PLATE XXXV: Frederick D. Nichols, "Drayton Hall, plantation house of the Drayton family," Antiques, 97 (April 1970), 576–578.

52 INDIGO WERE GROWN: For a history of the Drayton family, see Margaret Babcock Meriwether, ed., The Carolinian Florist of Governor John Drayton of South Carolina, 1766–1822 (Columbia, 1943), xxiii–xxxiv, esp. xxv.

52 WEALTHIER COUNTERPART: This hypothesis is put forth by the scholar Edmund S. Morgan, whose detailed analysis of "the ordeal of colonial Virginia" traces the roots of this complex paradox, . . . Slavery . . . Freedom, 380–381.

52 "EXCEEDING SIX FEET": Thomas Cooper and

David J. McCord, eds., The Statutes at Large of South Carolina, 10 vols. (Columbia, 1830–1841), 7, 17. As quoted in Beatrice St. Julien Ravenel, Architects of Charleston (Charleston, 1945), 2.

52 INDIAN ANTECEDENTS: Albert Simon, "Architectural trends in Charleston," Antiques, 97 (April 1970), 545–555.

52 "TOWARDS THE RIVER": Description of Nicolas de La Salle, 31 Aug. 1704, Mobile, from Archives Nationales, Section Outre-Mer, Paris, C-13A-II, 468, as quoted in Samuel Wilson, Jr., Gulf Coast Architecture, Historic Pensacola Preservation Board (Pensacola, 1977), 85.

52 TERRAIN AND CLIMATE: Peter J. Hamilton, Colonial Mobile (Boston, 1910), 87.

52 "GREAT HOUSE": George Whitefield, A Journal of a Voyage from London to Savannah in Georgia (London, 1739–1741), reproduced in Trevor R. Reese, ed., Our First Visit in America (Savannah, 1974), 298, 302.

53 "CONVENIENTLY DIVIDED": Gentleman's Magazine (April 1767), 168.

53 IN THE NEW WORLD: Samuel Wilson, Jr., "Architecture in Eighteenth-Century West Florida," in Eighteenth-Century Florida and its Borderlands, ed. Samuel Proctor (Gainesville, 1975), 102–139.

53 BY SEBASTIANO SERLIO: See especially the Scene of Pillage in the Large Miseries of War series, reproduced in Howard Daniel, Callot's Etchings (New York, 1974), no. 268. In an unpublished paper, "The Bolduc House, St. Genevieve," given at the January 1968 annual meeting of the Society of Architectural Historians held at St. Louis, Dr. Ernest Connally pointed out the close relationship between this upper Mississippi Valley house and the sixteenth-century drawings prepared by Sebastiano Serlio of designs for French farmhouses. See Sebastiano Serlio, On domestic architecture: Different dwellings from the meanest level to the most ornate palace . . . The sixteenth-century manuscript of Book VI in the Avery Library of Columbia University, foreword, Adolf K. Placzek; intro., James S. Ackermann; text, Myra Nan Rosenfeld (New York, 1978), 50–51, and Plate I, esp. B-2, "Farmhouse of the middle class citizen at two levels of poverty," and C-3, "Farmhouse of the rich citizen for two levels of wealth."

54 REAR OF THE BUILDING: Samuel Wilson, Jr., Bienville's New Orleans: A French Colonial Capital, 1718–1768, Friends of the Cabildo, Louisiana State Museum (New Orleans, 1968), 46.

54 "WEST-INDIA STYLE": Thomas Ashe, Travels in America performed in the year 1806 (London, 1809), 299–300.

55 ON FOUR SIDES: Diego Angulo Iñiguez, Planos de Monumentos Arquitectonicos de America y Filipinas existentes en el Archivo de Indios, Catalogo, 2 (Seville, 1934), Lám. 144, p. 38, Siglo XVIII, Estados Unidos.

56 A FEW YEARS LATER: George Howe, History of the

Presbyterian Church in South Carolina, 2 vols. (Columbia, 1870), *1*, 187; for another reference to the simple country meetinghouses of South Carolina, with illustration, see T. Addison Richards, "The Rice Lands of the South," *Harper's New Monthly Magazine, 19* (Nov. 1859), 721–738, esp. 728, 733.

56 WILLIAM'S PARISH: Alice R. Huger Smith, intro., *A Charleston Sketchbook, 1796–1806, by Charles Fraser* (Charleston, 1940; reprint ed., Charleston, 1971), 11, 9.

56 "INTO A ROOM": William Attmore, *Journal of a Tour to North Carolina*, in *James Sprunt Historical Publications, 17*, no. 2 (Chapel Hill, 1922), 45–46.

57 "SOLID AT FIRST": Samuel Wilson, Jr., "An Architectural History of the Royal Hospital and the Ursuline Convent of New Orleans," *Louisiana Historical Quarterly, 29* (July 1946), 3–103, quoted p. 47; Wilson, "Louisiana Drawings by Alexandre De Batz," *Journal of the Society of Architectural Historians, 22* (May 1963), 75–89.

59 FAIRLY COMMON: Albert Manucy, *The Houses of St. Augustine, 1565–1821*, St. Augustine Historical Society (St. Augustine, 1962), 93.

59 ENTRANCE WAY: Ibid., 131.

59 PORCH OR GALLERY: *Historic St. Augustine Preservation Board, Guide Book*, Department of State, State of Florida (1971), 70.

59 CATCH THE BREEZES: For various typical plans of St. Augustine's houses, see Manucy, *Houses*, 56–69.

60 "UP THE WINDOW": John Bartram, *Diary of a Journey Through the Carolinas, Georgia and Florida from July 1, 1765 to April 10, 1766*, Francis Harper, ed. (Philadelphia, 1942), 55. As quoted in Manucy, *Houses*, 31.

60 AMERICAN ERA: See, for example, William Cullen Bryant, *Letters of a Traveller, or Notes of Things Seen in Europe and America* (1850; reprint ed., New York, 1870), 101–102.

61 FOOD STORAGE: The July 1965 issue of *Antiques, 88*, was devoted to a series of articles on Old Salem. Most pertinent are Chester Davis, "The Moravians of Salem," 60–64, and William J. Murtagh, "The Architecture of Salem," 69–76.

61 BUILT 1769-1774: James Scott Rawlings, *Virginia's Colonial Churches: An Architectural Guide* (Richmond, 1963), 228–232; Harold Wickliffe Rose, *The Colonial Houses of Worship in America* (New York, 1963), 510–512; Pohick Church Vestry, *Minutes of the Vestry Truro Parish, 1732–1785* (Lorton, Va., 1974), 114–117, 121–136.

63 "CARVED WORK": For Sears at Pohick, see Luke Beckerdite, "William Buckland and William Bernard Sears: The Designer and the Carver," *Journal of Early Southern Decorative Arts, 8* (Nov. 1982), 6–40, esp. 28–29.

63 "FINISHING THE SAME": Pohick Church Vestry, *Minutes*, 129.

63 THE LONG SIDE: Marian Card Donnelly, *The New England Meeting Houses of the Seventeenth Century* (Middletown, 1968), 87–90; John Betjeman, "Nonconformist Architecture," *Architectural Review, 88* (Dec. 1940), 161–174.

63 RELIGIOUS FREEDOM: Rhys Isaac, "Religion and Authority: Problems of the Anglican Establishment in Virginia in the Era of the Great Awakening and the Parson's Cause," *William and Mary Quarterly*, 3rd ser., *30* (Jan. 1973), 1–36, esp. 23–29.

64 "LIKE WAINSCOT": *Legislative Journals of the Council of Colonial Virginia, 1*, 422–423. I am grateful to Roy Eugene Graham, Resident Architect of Colonial Williamsburg, for sending me a copy of this.

64 "SHILLINGS A YARD": As quoted in Alfred Coxe Prime, *The Arts and Crafts in Philadelphia, Maryland and South Carolina*, 2 vols. (1929; reprint ed., New York, 1969), *1*, 299.

64 IN IRELAND: Desmond Guinness, *Irish Houses and Castles* (New York, 1971), 79–82, 108, 156, 158, 203, 220–221.

64 AROUND 1750: W. J. Johnson Thomas, "Seven great Charleston houses," *Antiques, 97* (April 1970), 558.

67 BY ELIZA LUCAS: Ravenel, *Eliza Pinckney*, 54.

67 "GENTLEMEN'S SEATS": *South Carolina Historical and Genealogical Magazine, 15* (July 1914), 144–145.

68 "SINGULARLY BEAUTIFUL": "Journal of Josiah Quincy, Junior, 1773," *Massachusetts Historical Society Proceedings, 49* (June 1916), 444–446.

69 "ME OUT AGAIN": Josiah Quincy, *Memoire of the Life of Josiah Quincy, Jr. of Massachusetts Bay, 1744–1775*, 3rd ed. (Boston, 1875), 152.

69 ORIGINAL OWNERS: A. S. Salley, Jr., "Col. Miles Brewton and Some of His Descendants," *South Carolina Historical and Genealogical Magazine, 2* (1901), 142–143; Mrs. St. Julien Ravenel, *Charleston, the Place and the People* (New York, 1906), 230–231.

70 STRUCTURE AND DECORATION: For William Buckland's roles as craftsman and designer, see Beckerdite, "Buckland and Sears," ibid., and "William Buckland Reconsidered: Architectural Carving in Chesapeake Maryland, 1771–1774," also in *Journal of Early Southern Decorative Arts, 8* (Nov. 1982), 42–88.

71 "SHORTEST NOTICE": Cited in Prime, *Arts and Crafts, 1*, 290.

71 LATEST MODE: Rosamond Randall Breine, "The Chase House in Maryland," *Maryland Historical Magazine, 49* (Sept. 1954), 177–195; George B. Tatum, "Great houses from the golden age of Annapolis," *Antiques, 111* (Jan. 1977), 174–193; Professor Tatum also cites Sterling M. Boyd, "The Adams' style in America: 1770–1820," diss., Princeton University, 1966, 176.

71 FAMILY HOUSES: See C. A. Weslager, *The Log*

Cabin in America (New Brunswick, 1969), esp. 99–258, 316–342; Weslager, p. 205, n. 38, cites Fred Kniffen and Henry Glassie, "Building in Wood in the Eastern United States," *Geographical Review, 56* (Jan. 1966), 40–66, as "the most significant paper on log housing that has yet been written," but corrects some of their statements.

71 "THAT ARE NAILED": Louis B. Wright, ed., *The Prose Works of William Byrd of Westover* (Cambridge, Mass., 1966), 174, 206.

72 "SADDLE-BAG": Thomas Tileston Waterman, *The Early Architecture of North Carolina* (Chapel Hill, 1941), 3–8; James C. Thomas, "The log houses of Kentucky," *Antiques, 105* (April 1974), 791–798.

72 MARCH 1785: Howe, *Presbyterian Church in S.C.*, 288–289, 504–505.

72 ENGLISH NAMES: Carolyn Murray Wooley, "Kentucky's early stone houses," *Antiques, 105* (March 1974), 592–602.

73 THIS ARTIST: The basic reference is Graham Hood, *Charles Bridges and William Dering, Two Virginia Painters, 1735–1750* (Charlottesville, 1978), esp. 16–21; see also Henry Wilder Foote, "Charles Bridges: Sergeant-Painter of Virginia," *Virginia Magazine of History and Biography, 60* (Jan. 1952), 3–55; Thomas Thorne, "Charles Bridges, Limner," *Arts in Virginia, 9* (Winter 1969), 22–31. I have not seen the M.A. thesis by Susanne Neale, "Charles Bridges: Painter and Humanitarian," College of William and Mary, 1969.

75 "OF VIRGINIA": Quoted in Foote, "Charles Bridges," 11.

75 ST. PAUL'S PARISH: Bishop William Meade, *Old Churches, Ministers and Families of Virginia*, 2 vols. (Philadelphia, 1857), *1*, 419–420.

75 CAPTAIN BOLLING: Hood, *Bridges and Dering*, 9.

75 VARIABLE SKILL: Carolyn J. Weekley, "Further Notes on William Dering, Colonial Virginia Portrait Painter," *Journal of Early Southern Decorative Arts, 1* (May 1975), 21–28; Hood, *Bridges and Dering*, 99–122; J. Hall Pleasants, "William Dering, A Mid-Eighteenth Century Williamsburg Portrait Painter," *Virginia Magazine of History and Biography, 60* (Jan. 1952), 56–63.

76 UPHOLSTERED CHAIR: Walden Phoenix Belknap, Jr., *American Colonial Painting* (Cambridge, Mass., 1959), Fig. 39.

76 AT HIS HOUSE: Pleasants, "William Dering," 56–63; Hood, *Bridges and Dering*, 99.

76 INTEREST IN PAINTING: Hood, *Bridges and Dering*, 101.

76 1735 OR 1736: The major study on Theus is Margaret Simons Middleton, *Jeremiah Theus, Colonial Artist of Charles Town* (Columbia, 1953). See also Rutledge, *Artists in Charleston*, esp. 114, 220.

76 "PLANTATIONS": Middleton, *Theus*, 33.

77 FRANCIS COTES: Barbara B. Lassiter, "American paintings in the Reynolda House collection," *Antiques*, *98* (Nov. 1970), 758; Belknap, *Colonial Painting*, no. 55.

78 "CAME HOME": Mabel L. Webber, "Extracts from the Journal of Mrs. Ann Manigault," *South Carolina Historical and Genealogical Magazine*, *20* (April 1919), 128–129.

78 "HIS JUDGMENT": "Peter Manigault's Letters," *South Carolina Historical and Genealogical Magazine*, *31* (Oct. 1930), 277–278.

78 1750 OR 1751: Theodore Bolton and Harry Lorin Binsse, "Wollaston, An Early American Portrait Manufacturer," *Antiquarian*, *16* (June 1931), 30–33, 50–52; George C. Groce, "John Wollaston (FL. 1736–1767): A Cosmopolitan Painter in the British Colonies," *Art Quarterly*, *15* (Summer 1952), 133–149; Carolyn J. Weekley, "John Wollaston, Portrait Painter: His Career in Virginia 1754–1758," M.A. thesis, University of Delaware, June 1976.

78 ST. CHRISTOPHER'S ISLAND: I am grateful to Carolyn Weekley for this information.

78 "IN LONDON": As quoted in John Sartain, *The Reminiscences of a Very Old Man, 1808–1897* (New York, 1899), 147.

79 FROM HIS FATHER: Richard K. Doud, "John Hesselius, Maryland Limner," *Winterthur Portfolio*, *5* (1969), 129–153; also, "The Fitzhugh Portraits by John Hesselius," *Virginia Magazine of History and Biography*, *75* (April 1967), 159–173; and Doud's M.A. thesis, "John Hesselius: His Life and Work," University of Delaware, 1963.

79 IN 1764–1765: Charles Scarlett, Jr., "Governor Horatio Sharpe's Whitehall," *Maryland Historical Magazine*, *46* (March 1951), 10.

79 ENGLISH MEZZOTINTS: Belknap, *Colonial Painting*, 5E, 15B, 15A, and 15.

79 SOMEWHAT SIMILAR: Cf. Belknap, *Colonial Painting*, 15; the portrait of Elliott owned by the Carolina Art Association, reproduced in *Art in South Carolina 1670–1970*, no. 33, and Rutledge, *Artists in Charleston*, 172, Fig. 5.

80 BY KNELLER: Belknap, *Colonial Painting*, no. 47.

80 AN ENGLISH MEZZOTINT: Ibid., 57, 57A.

80 "GENERALLY POSSESS": William Dunlap, *History of the Rise and Progress of the Arts of Design in the United States* (New York, 1834); intro., William P. Campbell, ed. Alexander Wyckoff (New York, 1965), *3*, 169.

81 IN 1720: E. P. Richardson, "Gustavus Hesselius," *Art Quarterly*, *12* (Summer 1949), 220–226.

81 "TEN COMMANDMENTS": *William and Mary Quarterly*, *5* (Oct. 1896), 115.

81 "LAST JUDGMENT": Meade, *Old Churches*, 1, 323.

81 EASTERN SEABOARD: The most complete listing is in the files of the Museum of Early Southern Decorative Arts in Winston-Salem. For Charleston, see Rutledge, *Artists in Charleston*, 183–236; for Maryland and South Carolina, Prime, *Arts and Crafts*, *1*, 1–14. There are no references to artists or painters working before 1788 in James H. Craig, *The Arts and Crafts in North Carolina* (Winston-Salem, 1965), 1–11.

81 HAS SURVIVED: Anna Wells Rutledge, "Charleston's first artistic couple," *Antiques*, *52* (Aug. 1947), 100–102.

82 BY HER HAND: Frank L. Horton, "America's Earliest Woman Miniaturist," *Journal of Early Southern Decorative Arts*, *5* (Nov. 1979), 1–5.

82 NATURAL HISTORY: Joseph Ewan, intro. and ed., *William Bartram, Botanical and Zoological Drawings, 1756–1788* (Philadelphia, 1968).

83 LAFCADIO HEARN: N. Bayllion Fagin, *William Bartram, Interpreter of the American Landscape* (Baltimore, 1933).

83 DE LA NATURE: Ibid., 13.

83 IN THAT CITY: Robert G. Stewart, *Henry Benbridge (1743–1812), American Portrait Painter*, National Portrait Gallery (Washington, D. C., 1971).

83 REPAINTED IN 1775: Stewart, *Benbridge*, 20, 48, no. 44.

83 FEDERAL CONSTITUTION: Rutledge, *Artists in . . . Charleston*, 122–123.

83 IN NORFOLK: Carolyn J. Weekley, "Henry Benbridge: Portraits in Small from Norfolk," *Journal of Early Southern Decorative Arts*, *4* (Nov. 1978), 52–55.

84 UNDERSTOOD IT: Ellis Waterhouse, *Painting in Britain 1530 to 1790* (London, 1953), 197–206; Jules D. Prown, *John Singleton Copley*, *2*, *England* (Cambridge, 1966).

84 "CHARLES W. PEALE": Robert Gilmor, "Correspondence Book I (1844–48)," Maryland Historical Society, as quoted by Romaine Stec Somerville, "A Peale exhibition at the Maryland Historical Society," *Antiques*, *107* (March 1975), 502–515.

84 AS SOURCES: Charles Coleman Sellers, *Portraits and Miniatures by Charles Willson Peale*, Transactions of the American Philosophical Society, N.S. *42* (Philadelphia, 1952). Alphabetical listing.

85 "IN THE EVENING": Sellers, *Portraits and Miniatures*, 197–198; also *Charles Willson Peale with Patron and Populace*, Transactions of the American Philosophical Society, N.S. *59* (Philadelphia, 1969), 28.

86 CHARLESTON NEWSPAPERS: Beatrice St. Julian Ravenel, "Here lies buried, taste and trade in Charleston tombstones," *Antiques*, *41* (March 1942), 193–195.

86 IN 1766: Rutledge, *Artists in . . . Charleston*, 142; Wayne Craven, *Sculpture in America* (New York, 1968), 47–48.

86 CLASSICAL IMAGE: For a discussion of the theories behind this idea, and the controversy re modern or antique for historical subjects in eighteenth-century England, see Charles Mitchell, "Benjamin West's 'Death of General Wolfe' and the Popular History Piece," *Journal of the Warburg and Courtauld Institutes*, *7* (1944), 20–33.

86 APPROPRIATE STATUE: Craven, *Sculpture*, 49; Wallace B. Gusler, *Furniture of Williamsburg and Eastern Virginia, 1710–1790* (Richmond, 1979), 8–9.

86 BE COMMISSIONED: Cravens, *Sculpture*, 51–53; Gilbert Chinard, *Houdon in America* (Baltimore, 1930).

88 "MODERN COSTUME": Chinard, *Houdon*, 33.

89 WILLIAMSBURG AREA: The pioneer study is E. Milby Burton, *Charleston Furniture, 1700–1825* (Columbia, 1955). The recent research of the Museum of Early Southern Decorative Arts in the Charleston area had not been published at the time of writing.

89 HAS SURVIVED: Stephen P. Dorsey, *English Churches in America* (New York, 1952), 96.

89 PIECE OF FURNITURE: Gusler, *Furniture*, 13–23. A sketch of the chair is reproduced in Fred Sheeley, ed., "The Journal of Ebenezer Hazard in Virginia, 1777," *Virginia Magazine of History and Biography*, *62* (1954), 409.

90 WITH WILLIAMSBURG: Gusler, *Furniture*, 16–17, Fig. 8.

90 TECHNIQUES AND STYLES: Gusler, *Furniture*, 25–41 and n. 21, 56, Fig. 16; see also Ann W. Dibble, "Fredericksburg-Falmouth Chairs in the Chippendale Style," *Journal of Early Southern Decorative Arts*, *5* (May 1978), 1–24.

90 PETER SCOTT: Gusler, *Furniture*, 25–41 and n. 21, 56.

91 A SHOP THERE: Gusler, *Furniture*, 141, Fig. 95.

92 OF A PAIR: Frank L. Horton, "Carved Furniture of the Albemarle: A Tie with Architecture," *Journal of Early Southern Decorative Arts*, *1* (May 1975), 14–20; Horton, intro., *The Museum of Early Southern Decorative Arts*, Catalogue (Winston-Salem, 1979), 38. This pair, along with six related pieces by two different but closely associated cabinetmakers, is to be discussed in a forthcoming study, *The Furniture of Coastal North Carolina, 1700–1820*, by John Bivins, Jr., of the Museum of Early Southern Decorative Arts. I am grateful to him for this information. This supersedes Gusler's tentative speculation that these chairs may have originated in Norfolk, Virginia. Gusler, *Furniture*, 156–157.

92 AND MOTIF: Anthony Coleridge, *Chippendale Furniture* (London, 1968), Fig. 171.

92 VARIOUS CRAFTSMEN: Joseph Downs, *American Furniture, Queen Anne and Chippendale Periods* (New York, 1952), Figs. 151 and 159, for examples with Massachusetts and New York histories; for Charleston example, Burton, *Charleston Furniture*, Fig. 112; for a chair with a New Hampshire history, Myrna Kaye, "Marked Portsmouth furniture," *Antiques*, 113 (May 1978), 1099.

92 MASONIC CHAIRS: Bradford L. Rauschenberg, "Two Outstanding Virginia Chairs," *Journal of Early Southern Decorative Arts*, 2 (Nov. 1976), 1–23; Gusler, *Furniture*, nos. 46, 47, 49, 59, 60; pp. 70–73, 75–77, 92–96, 105–108, 110–113. One of the ceremonial chairs identified by Gusler is the Capitol, or Royal Governor's, chair, his Fig. 46. This has long been believed to be English. Gusler argues that it was probably made in Williamsburg and in the shop of Anthony Hay. Bradford Rauschenberg of MESDA has recently stated that he "feels as if there is not enough proof to establish the Williamsburg, Virginia, 'Capitol' or Royal Governor's chair as an American-made example. It probably represents the English prototype for the Williamsburg ceremonial type." Note 55, p. 31, in Rauschenberg, "The Royal Governor's Chair: Evidence of the Furnishing of South Carolina's First State House," *Journal of Early Southern Decorative Arts*, 6 (Nov. 1980).

93 AN EASY CHAIR: Gusler, *Furniture*, 59–113; Ivor Noël Hume, *Williamsburg Cabinetmakers: The Archaeological Evidence*, Colonial Williamsburg Foundation (Williamsburg, 1971).

93 "BY MR. HAY": Gusler, *Furniture*, 59.

93 PROBABLY INVOLVED: Gusler, *Furniture*, 79.

94 OF THIS WORK: Gusler, *Furniture*, 59.

94 MASONS THEMSELVES: Albert G. Mackey, *An Encyclopedia of Freemasonry*, 2 vols. (1873; Chicago, 1921). Alphabetical references. The quotations given below are from this. Alan Gowans, "Freemasonry and the neoclassic style in America," *Antiques*, 77 (Feb. 1960), 172–175. Gusler, *Furniture*, 110–113.

95 WESTMINSTER ABBEY: Rauschenberg, "Two . . . Chairs," 14–15.

95 OF WILLIAMSBURG: Frederick M. Hunter, *The Regius Manuscript* (Research Lodge of Oregon, 1952), 91–92.

95 MADE IN AMERICA: Gusler, *Furniture*, no. 51, 81–85.

96 OF WILLIAMSBURG: Gusler, *Furniture*, no. 82, 123–124.

96 "RICHEST IN AMERICA": *The London Magazine* (June 1762), 276.

96 THE EXPORTS: Ibid. (Aug. 1761), 448.

97 POWER, AND INFLUENCE: J. Hector St. John Crèvecoeur, *Letters from an American Farmer* (London, 1782; reprint ed., 1908), intro. Ludwig Lewisohn, 222–225.

97 HAS SURVIVED: "The Thomas Elfe Account Book, 1768–1775," *South Carolina Historical and Genealogical Magazine*. Portions are recorded in every issue from vol. 35 (Jan. 1934) through vol. 42 (Jan. 1941); Burton, *Charleston Furniture*, 84–90.

97 BY HIS SHOP: In Rauschenberg, "Royal Governor's Chair," 1–32, official accounts, while not specific, are cited as convincing evidence that a chair known as the Royal Governor's chair in the collection of the South Caroliniana Library in Columbia, South Carolina, was made by Elfe and Hutchinson c. 1756–1758.

97 EVEN CHEAPER: Burton, *Charleston Furniture*, 29.

98 MAHOGANY FURNITURE: Burton, *Charleston Furniture*, 29; Edgar G. Miller, Jr., *American Antique Furniture* (New York, 1937), Fig. 1043.

98 INVENTORIES: Burton, *Charleston Furniture*, 59.

98 BERKELEY COUNTY: Susan Stitt, *Museum of Early Southern Decorative Arts* (Winston-Salem, 1972), 24; Burton, *Charleston Furniture*, 69; Samuel Gaillard Stoney, *Plantations of the Carolina Low Country* (Charleston, 1938), 64–66, 177–183.

99 CONSTRUCTION DETAILS: Burton, *Charleston Furniture*, 42–45, Fig. 36.

101 "WEALTHY BRITON": William Eddis, *Letters from America*, Aubrey C. Land, ed. (Cambridge, Mass., 1969), 13, 57–58.

101 BEEN ESTABLISHED: William Voss Elder III, "Maryland furniture, 1760–1840," *Antiques*, 111 (Feb. 1977), 354–361.

101 JOHN SHAW: Lu Bartlett, "John Shaw, cabinetmaker of Annapolis," *Antiques*, 111 (Feb. 1977), 362–377.

102 SHIPPED FROM THERE: Eddis, *Letters*, 50.

102 "WAS INCREASING": Maurice A. Crouse, ed., "The Letterbook of Peter Manigault, 1763–1773," *South Carolina Historical Magazine*, 70 (July 1969), 191.

102 AND AUGUSTA: Carl Bridenbaugh, *Myths and Realities, Societies of the Colonial South* (Baton Rouge, 1952), 129.

103 IT WAS NEW: Family tradition from owner.

103 AROUND 1770–1780: Robert E. Winters, Jr., *North Carolina Furniture, 1700–1900* (Raleigh, 1977), 17.

104 SHORE OF VIRGINIA: Gusler, *Furniture*, 178–179.

104 ELFE'S ACCOUNT BOOK: 37, 155; 38, 59; 41, 128.

104 SOME OF MAHOGANY: Jessie J. Poesch, *Early Furniture of Louisiana*, Louisiana State Museum (New Orleans, 1972), no. 11, 3.

104 MATERIALS ARE LIMITED: Though there were

several collectors in the area in the 1930s there were no publications on the subject until 1968. Since then, there have been several: Jessie J. Poesch, "Early Louisiana *armoires*," *Antiques*, 94 (Aug. 1968), 196–205; H. Parrott Bacot, *Southern Furniture and Silver: The Federal Period, 1788–1830*, Anglo-American Art Museum (Baton Rouge, 1968); Poesch, *Early Furniture*; Jack Holden and Robert E. Smith, *Louisiana French Furnishings, 1700–1830*, Art Center for Southwestern Louisiana (Lafayette, La., 1974); Poesch, "Furniture of the River Road plantations in Louisiana," *Antiques*, 111 (June 1977), 1184–1193.

105 DIFFERENT PLANES: Henry P. Dart, "Inventory of the Estate of Sieur Jean Baptiste Prevost, Deceased Agent of the Company of the Indies, July 13, 1769," *Louisiana Historical Quarterly*, 9 (July 1926), 411–457, esp. 445–447, 449, 451.

105 GOODS AND CHATTEL: Henry P. Dart, "The Career of DuBréuil in French Louisiana," *Louisiana Historical Quarterly*, 18 (April 1935), 281–331.

105 BLACKSMITH SHOP: As quoted by Alcée Fortier, *A History of Louisiana*, 4 vols. (Paris, 1904), 2, 33.

106 WITH CANE SEATS: George C. H. Kernion, "Reminiscences of the Chevallier Bernard de Verges, an Early Colonial Engineer of Louisiana," *Louisiana Historical Quarterly*, 7 (Jan. 1924), 80.

106 "IN OUR PROVINCES": Wilson, "Drawings by De Batz," esp. 85–87.

107 RICE BARRELS: David Duncan Wallace, *South Carolina: A Short History* (Chapel Hill, 1951), 294; Burton, "Decorative Arts," in Francis W. Bilodeau, Mrs. Thomas J. Tobias, and E. Milby Burton *Art in South Carolina, 1670–1970*, The South Carolina Tricentennial Commission (Charleston, 1970), 217.

107 BY 1775: E. Milby Burton, *South Carolina Silversmiths, 1690–1860* (Rutland, 1968).

107 FROM THOMAS ELFE: Ibid., 40–41.

107 "WARRANTED STERLING": Prime, *Arts and Crafts*, 1, 67–68.

107 OR IN AMERICA: For the development of the classical or "Adam" taste in English silver, see Robert Rowe, *Adam Silver, 1765–1795* (London, 1965).

108 WITH SCROLL FEET: David B. Warren, *Southern Silver*, Museum of Fine Arts (Houston, 1968), 74.

108 "ON THE BUSINESS": Burton, *Silversmiths*, 203–206; Prime, *Arts and Crafts*, 1, 100–101.

108 "MANY YEARS": Burton, *Silversmiths*, 146–149, 208–209.

108 "THENCEFORTH EMPLOY": Burton, *Silversmiths*, 207–208.

108 IMPORTED MERCHANDISE: Ivor Noël Hume, "James Geddy and sons, colonial craftsmen: evidence from the earth," *Antiques*, 95 (Jan. 1969), 106–111.

109 IN 1771–1772: JOHN D. DAVIS, "The silver," *Antiques*, *95* (Jan. 1969), 137.

109 THIS TASTE: Kathryn C. Buhler and Graham Hood, *American Silver: Garvan and Other Collections in the Yale University Art Gallery*, 2 vols. (New Haven and London, 1970), *2*, 246–247.

110 CREEK MOUND: I am grateful to James Arthur Williams and the Telfair Academy of Arts and Sciences, Savannah, for this information.

110 OFFICIAL COMMISSIONS: George Barton Cutten, *The Silversmiths of Georgia* (Savannah, 1958), 83.

110 DIED AROUND 1756: Burton, *Silversmiths*, 185–186.

110 COMMUNAL SYSTEM: Frank P. Albright, "The crafts at Salem," *Antiques*, *88* (July 1965), 94–97.

111 IN THE 1750S: John Bivins, Jr., "An Introduction to the Decorative Arts of North Carolina 1776–1976," in *200 Years of the Visual Arts in North Carolina*, North Carolina Museum of Art (Raleigh, 1976), 124.

111 SILVER, AND FURNITURE: Letter written on April 2, 1771, in Crouse, "Letterbook of Peter Manigault," 188–189. See also Julia Cherry Spruill, *Women's Life and Work in the Southern Colonies* (Chapel Hill, 1938); Anne Firor Scott, *The Southern Lady* (Chicago, 1970); Catherine Clinton, *The Plantation Mistress* (New York, 1982).

111 AND EMBROIDERY: Susan Burrow Swain, *Plain & Fancy: American Women and Their Needlework, 1700–1850* (New York, 1977).

111 AGE THIRTY-FIVE: Elizabeth Donaghy Garrett, "The Theodore H. Kapnek collection of American samplers," *Antiques*, *114* (Sept. 1978), 542.

112 ARE INTRODUCED: I am grateful to Miss Mildred Lanier, Curator of Textiles, Colonial Williamsburg, for information about this coverlet.

112 "FOR MISS PRISSY": Phillip Vickers Fithian, *The Journal and Letters of Philip Vickers Fithian, 1773–1774: A Plantation Tutor of the Old Dominion*, ed. Hunter Dickinson Farish (Williamsburg, 1943), Dec. 28 and 29, 1773, entries, 57.

PART THREE *A New Nation, 1788–1824*

117 "SCIENCES IN AMERICA": Howard C. Rice, intro., *Travels in North America in the Years 1780, 1781, and 1782, by the Marquis de Chastellux*, 2 vols. (Chapel Hill, 1963), *2*, 529–548.

117 "OF LIBERTY": Rice, *Travels of Chastellux*, *2*, 545.

117 TO PUBLISH IT: Ibid., *2*, 531.

118 "ENCOURAGES ARTISTS": Ibid., *2*, 537.

118 "AND PUBLIC HAPPINESS": Ibid., *2*, 538.

118 "TEMPLES OF DEMOCRACY": Henry-Russell Hitchcock and William Seale, *Temples of Democracy: The State Capitols of the USA* (New York, 1976).

118 "FROM THE WEATHER": Rice, *Travels of Chastellux*, *2*, 391.

118 "ELEGANCE AND DIGNITY": Hitchcock and Seale, *Temples of Democracy*, 28–35; also, William H. Pierson, Jr., *American Buildings and Their Architects: The Colonial and Neo-classical Styles* (Garden City, N.Y., 1970), 286–333; S. Fiske Kimball, *Thomas Jefferson, Architect* (Cambridge, 1916); William Howard Adams, ed., *The Eye of Th. Jefferson*, National Gallery of Art (Washington, D.C., 1976), 221–229.

119 FOR THE NEW CITY: Kimball, *Thomas Jefferson, Architect*, 49–52. The sketch is in the Papers of Thomas Jefferson, Library of Congress, sec. 4, *1*, 121.

119 AT MONTICELLO: Thomas Jefferson to Governor William Miller, Monticello, Jan. 22, 1816. Papers of Thomas Jefferson, Library of Congress. As cited in Ulysses Desportes, "Giuseppe Ceracchi in America and His Busts of George Washington," *Art Quarterly*, *26* (Summer 1963), 169; Wayne Craven, *Sculpture in America* (New York, 1968), 61–64.

119 "PUNY EFFECT": Craven, *Sculpture in America*, 62. Jefferson letter dated Jan. 22, 1816.

119 OF THE MOUTH: Desportes, "Ceracchi," 171.

120 JOHN IZARD MIDDLETON: Carolina Art Association, *Selections from the Collections of the Carolina Art Association* (Charleston, 1977), 12–13.

120 MARCH 1821: Copy of manuscript receipt, North Carolina State Archives.

120 "POWERFUL INTEREST": *Raleigh Gazette*, Dec. 28, 1821.

121 THEIR STATEHOUSE: Hitchcock and Seale, *Temples of Democracy*, 65–67.

121 STILL SURVIVES: Ibid., 69–70, 90–92.

121 AFTER 1813: Ben F. Williams, *Jacob Marling, Early North Carolina Artists*, North Carolina Museum of Art (Raleigh, 1964), 5–11.

123 THOMAS SULLY: Resolution, 1816 (LP296), General Assembly. Information in letter of Sept. 19, 1978, from Paul P. Hoffman, Head, Archives Branch, Division of Archives and History, Raleigh, N.C.; Philipp B. Fehl, "Thomas Sully's *Washington's Passage of the Delaware*: The History of a Commission," *The Art Bulletin*, *55* (December 1973), 584–599. For a personal and romanticized view, see *Diary of William Dunlap*, New-York Historical Society, 62–64 (New York, 1929–1931), *2*, 473, 522–527; *3*, 698, 703; and William Dunlap, *History of the Arts of Design*, 3 vols. (New York, 1834; reprint 1965), *1*, 328; *2*, 272.

123 "DISTANCES SUBLIME": Dunlap, *Diary*, *3*, 524.

123 "FAULTY CONDEMNS": Dunlap, *Arts of Design*, *2*, 273.

123 FROM THE SETTING: *Raleigh Register*, March 11, 1825, as quoted in Edgar Ewing Brandon, ed., *A Pilgrimage of Liberty* (Athens, Ohio, 1944), 24–37.

124 "'I SO SORRY'": R. S. Tucker, comp., *Early Times in Raleigh* (Raleigh, 1867), 9.

124 IN THIS COUNTRY: Craven, *Sculpture in America*, 64.

124 STILL SURVIVES: Hitchcock and Seale, *Temples of Democracy*, 88–93.

124 "ALTOGETHER YOUTHFUL": Miss Conner, as quoted in James Bennett Nolan, *Lafayette in America Day to Day* (Baltimore, 1934), 278.

125 (PORTRAIT LATER): For the best known, by Samuel F. B. Morse, the general sat for a study; the artist completed the full-length painting later. A similar situation may have prevailed with Peticolas. See Edward Lind Morse, *Samuel F. B. Morse*, 2 vols. (Boston and New York, 1914), *1*, 259–264, 270. The Peticolas painting, as with Morse, seems to be an original conception.

125 "OF THAT CITY": Dunlap, *Art of Design*, *3*, 103.

125 OF THE CINCINNATI: Anna Wells Rutledge, *Artists in the Life of Charleston*, Transactions of the American Philosophical Society, N.S., *32* (Philadelphia, 1948), 133–135; Ruel P. Tolman, "The technique of Charles Fraser, miniaturist," *Antiques*, *27* (Jan. 1935), 19–22.

126 NINETEENTH CENTURY: For a good summary of neoclassicism in American architecture see Pierson, *American Buildings*, 205ff.

127 USED IN PATTERNS: For a study of Adam's decorative work and his sources, see Damie Stillman, *The Decorative Work of Robert Adam* (London, 1966).

127 THE SAME YEAR: George B. Tatum, *Penn's Great Town* (Philadelphia, 1961), Figs. 24 and 27.

127 AROUND 1799: Richard Hubbard Howland and Eleanor Patterson Spencer, *Architecture of Baltimore* (Baltimore, 1953), 13–14, Plates 7 and 8.

128 REVOLUTIONARY GENERATION: Wilbur H. Hunter, "Baltimore in the Revolutionary Generation," John B. Boles, ed., *Maryland Heritage: Five Baltimore Institutions Celebrate the American Bicentennial* (Baltimore, 1976), 183–233.

129 AS MANY AS TWENTY: Howland and Spencer, *Architecture* of Baltimore, 3–6, 4–18; Mary Ellen Hayward, "Urban Vernacular Architecture in Nineteenth-Century Baltimore," *Winterthur Portfolio*, *16* (Spring 1981), 33–63.

129 "AS ANY IN IRELAND": Alfred Coxe Prime, *The Arts and Crafts in Philadelphia, Maryland and South Carolina* (1929; reprint ed., New York, 1969), *2*, 320, quoting advertisements in the *Maryland Journal* (Baltimore) of May 14, 1790, and Oct. 6, 1789.

129 TO CHARLESTON: Gene Waddell, "The Charleston Single House: An Architectural Survey," *Preser-

vation Progress, Preservation Society of Charleston, 22 (March 1977), 4–7.

130 FROM EUROPE: Ibid., 5.

130 "A PORTE COCHERE": Samuel Wilson, Jr., ed., *Impressions Respecting New Orleans by Benjamin Henry Boneval Latrobe* (New York, 1951), 26.

132 BEFORE THAT TIME: Italo William Ricciuti, *New Orleans and Its Environs: The Domestic Architecture, 1727–1870* (New York, 1938), and Samuel Wilson, Jr., Roulhac Toledano, Sally Kittredge Evans, and Mary Louise Christovich, *New Orleans Architecture: The Creole Faubourgs* (Gretna, La., 1974), 4, esp. 41–56, 85, 95–96, 131, 159.

132 ENFILADE ARRANGEMENT: The two watercolors are among a group done by specialists in architectural renderings in the middle years of the nineteenth century. They were made when buildings were put up for sale and are filed in the Notarial Archives in New Orleans, providing a remarkable record of the city's architecture, unlike that available anywhere else.

132 "SPACE FOR PASSAGES": Wilson, *Impressions*, 105–106.

132 BUILT IN 1820: Wilson et al., *New Orleans Architecture*, 4, 95. Though these are now identified as "Creole cottages," they were not so identified in the nineteenth century.

132 ARCHITECTURAL TREATISE: Sebastiano Serlio, *On domestic architecture: Different dwellings from the meanest level to the most ornate palace . . . The sixteenth-century manuscript of Book VI in the Avery Library of Columbia University*, foreword, Adolf K. Placzek, intro., James S. Ackermann; text, Myra Nan Rosenfeld (New York, 1978).

132 OR LOT LINE: Serlio, *Domestic architecture*, Plate XLVIII. For dating, see p. 32.

132 PEOPLE OF COLOR: Evans, "Free Persons of Color," in Wilson et al., *New Orleans Architecture*, 4, 35–36.

132 HARASSMENT AND DISCRIMINATION: David C. Rankin, "The Forgotten People: Free People of Color in New Orleans, 1850–1870," diss., Johns Hopkins University, 1976, 40–135, 291–307; see also Herbert E. Sterkx, *The Free Negro in Antebellum Louisiana* (Rutherford, 1972).

132 WRITERS AND MUSICIANS: A volume of their collected poetry, *Les Cenelles*, was published in New Orleans in 1845. See Alfred J. Guillaume, Jr., "Love, Death, and Faith in the New Orleans Poets of Color," *Southern Quarterly*, 20 (Winter 1982), 126–144.

132 OVER ADVERSITY: Ira Berlin, *Slaves Without Masters* (New York, 1976), esp. 216–249.

133 ORIGINAL PLAN: For a detailed study see Samuel Wilson, Jr., and Leonard V. Huber, *The Cabildo on Jackson Square* (New Orleans, 1970), esp. 1–57.

135 "OR THE LEVEE": Wilson, *Impressions*, 40.

135 AND SOIREE: Pierre Clement de Laussat, *Memoirs of My Life*, trans. Sister Agnes-Josephine Postwa (Baton Rouge, 1978), 88–91.

135 "TE DEUM" WAS SUNG: *Niles' Weekly Register*, 8 (1815), 163, as quoted in Jane Lucas Degrummond, "The Fair Honoring the Brave," *Louisiana History*, 3 (Winter 1962), 54–58.

135 YOUNG REPUBLIC: Joe Gray Taylor, *Louisiana* (New York, 1976), 55.

136 PARADED BELOW: Henry Renshaw, "Lafayette's Visit to New Orleans," *Louisiana Historical Quarterly*, 1 (Sept. 1917), 5–8.

136 "ROOF IS ENORMOUS": Wilson, *Impressions*, 45.

136 "TWO ADDITIONAL ROOMS": C. C. Robin, *Voyage to Louisiana, 1803–1805*, Stuart O. Landry, Jr., ed. (New Orleans, 1966), 122.

137 "AT THEIR EASE": Thomas Ashe, *Travels in America performed in the year 1806* (London, 1808), 329–330.

137 NEAR HAHNVILLE: For a good recent description of these riverside plantations, see William Nathaniel Banks, "The River Road plantations of Louisiana," *Antiques*, 111 (June 1977), 1170–1183.

137 FRENCH PROTOTYPES: See pages 130–131.

137 LOUISIANA ARCHITECTURE: Samuel Wilson, Jr., "Destrehan Plantation, St. Charles Parish," *Louisiana Architect*, 8 (March 1969), 8–9.

138 OBLIGATIONS DISCHARGED: Ibid.

138 BY STAKES: Ibid.

139 SUGAR MILLS: Robin, *Voyage to Louisiana*, 109.

141 INCLEMENT WEATHER: T. T. Waterman and F. B. Johnston, *The Early Architecture of North Carolina* (Chapel Hill, 1941), 9.

141 MIDDLE TENNESSEE: Thomas B. Brumbaugh, *Architecture of Middle Tennessee: The Historic American Buildings Survey* (Nashville, 1974), 110–115; Ward Allen, "Cragfont, Grandeur on the Tennessee Frontier," *Tennessee Historical Quarterly*, 23 (June 1964), 103–120; James Patrick, *Architecture in Tennessee, 1768–1897* (Knoxville, 1981), 71, 75.

141 "FOR THE COUNTRY": F. A. Michaux, *Travels to the Westward of the Allegheny Mountains in the States of Ohio, Kentucky, and Tennessee in the Year 1802* (London, 1805), 254.

142 HOUSE WAS BUILT: Ibid., 254.

142 IN THE PARLOR: Albert W. Hutchinson, Jr., "Domestic architecture in Middle Tennessee," *Antiques*, 100 (Sept. 1971), 404.

142 "LOG HOUSES": Michaux, *Travels*, 256–257.

143 THE MOUNTAINS: Ibid., 150.

143 "EUROPEAN ELEGANCE": Ashe, *Travels in America*, 191.

145 "ATHENS OF THE WEST": Timothy Flint, *Recollections of the Last Ten Years, Passed in Occasional Residences and Journeyings in the Valley of the Mississippi* (Boston, 1826; reprint ed., New York, 1968), intro. James D. Norris, 67–68; George W. Ranck, *History of Lexington, Kentucky* (Cincinnati, 1872), esp. 42–49.

145 "LITERARY PLACE": Ranck, *History of Lexington*, 42–49.

145 MANUFACTURED HEMP: Clay Lancaster, *Ante-Bellum Houses of the Bluegrass* (Lexington, 1961), 47–49.

145 *AMERICAN BUILDER'S COMPANION*: 3rd ed. (Boston, 1816). At time of writing, this is only edition available. Plate 32, designed by D. Raynard, appears to have been in the first edition of 1811.

145 LEVI WEEKS: Milly McGehee, "Auburn in Natchez," *Antiques*, 111 (March 1977), 546–553. Miss McGehee is also the author of an M.A. thesis, "Levi Weeks, Early Nineteenth-Century Architect," University of Delaware, 1975.

145 "ORDERS OF ARCHITECTURE": As quoted in Wilson, *Impressions*, 176. The original letter is in the Weeks Collection, Mississippi State Department of Archives and History, Jackson, Mississippi.

146 "AND PIAZZAS": Fortescue Cuming, *Sketches of a Tour to the Western Country* (Pittsburgh, 1810), in Reuben Gold Thwaites, ed., *Early Western Travels, 1748–1846* (Cleveland, 1904), 4, 320.

146 VISITING INDIANS: Ibid., 321.

146 *IN ARCHITECTURE*: McGehee, "Auburn," 548.

147 RENAISSANCE SOURCES: Leslie Frank Crocker, "Domestic Architecture of the Middle South, 1795–1865," diss., University of Missouri, Columbia, 1971. University Microfilms, Ann Arbor, 97–100, summarizes the problem. He arrives at the term "Palladian Neo-Classicism" as best describing the style of buildings found in the area roughly enclosed by the triangle formed by the capitals of Tennessee, Mississippi, and Alabama.

147 IN A LECTURE: Published in the *Journal of the Franklin Institute*, 31 vols., 3rd ser., 1 (Jan. 1841), 11–12, as cited in Talbot Hamlin, *Greek Revival Architecture in America* (New York, 1944), 62

147 TIME OF HIS DEATH: McGehee, "Auburn," esp. 547–553.

148 ENTRANCE HALL: Ibid., 549.

148 "MAGNIFICENT MANNER": Appendix B, Letter of Julia Latrobe to her brother, Cadet H. J. B. Latrobe, written April 1, 1820, from St. Francisville, Louisiana, in Wilson, *Impressions*, 175–176.

148 "MISSISSIPPI VALLEY": Ronald W. Miller, "Historic preservation in Natchez, Mississippi," *Antiques*, 111 (March 1977), 543.

149 MAY BE UNIQUE: Frederick D. Nichols, *The Architecture of Georgia*, rev. ed. (Savannah, 1976), 45–48, 188–193; Edward V. Jones, "The Owens-Thomas

house," *Antiques*, *91* (March 1967), 341–346; "The Owens-Thomas House," reprint for *Architectural Digest*, no date given, 13 pp. There is a dissertation by James Vernon McDonough, "William Jay—Regency Architect in Georgia and Carolina," Princeton University, 1950, listed in *Dissertation Abstracts*, *15* (1955), 554.

150 TOWN IN 1810: G. L. M. Goodfellow, "William Jay and the Albion Chapel," *Journal of the Society of Architectural Historians*, 22 (Dec. 1963), 225–227.

151 IN SAVANNAH: Jones, "Owens-Thomas," 344.

151 "FALLEN A MONUMENT": Mills Lane, *Savannah Revisited: A Pictorial History* (Savannah, 1977), 56–73.

151 GRADUALLY NAMED: Harvey de Courcy and John Gilmary Shea, *History of the Catholic Church in the United States* (New York, 1904), 63, 537.

152 INSTITUTIONS OF LEARNING: For a good summary of the roots of the nineteenth-century taste for the Gothic in America, and the history of the style in this country, see William H. Pierson, Jr., *American Buildings and Their Architects: Technology and the Picturesque, the Corporate and the Early Gothic Styles* (Garden City, N.Y., 1978). For St. Mary's, see p. 118. See also Lois L. Olcott, "Public architecture of Kentucky before 1870," *Antiques*, *105* (April 1974), 835–836.

152 AND KENTUCKY: Charles W. Upton, "The Shaker utopia," *Antiques*, *98* (Oct. 1970), 582–587.

153 "CONCEIVABLE STYLE": Quoted by James G. Thomas, "Micajah Burnett and the buildings of Pleasant Hill," *Antiques*, *98* (Oct. 1970), 601–602.

153 1813 AND 1840: Ibid., 600–605.

154 BUILT AROUND 1820: Thomas J. Kirkland and Robert M. Kennedy, *Historic Camden, Part Two, Nineteenth Century* (Columbia, 1926), 294–296.

154 "HEARING AND SEEING": Robert Mills, *Statistics of South Carolina, Including a View of its Natural, Civil, and Military History, General and Particular* (Charleston, 1826), 591–592.

154 OF THE UNITED STATES: There is a large bibliography on Mills. Two of the most useful studies are H. M. Pierce Gallagher, *Robert Mills, Architect of the Washington Monument, 1781–1855* (New York, 1935), esp. 23–30, 42; and John Morrill Bryan, *Robert Mills, Architect, 1781–1855*, Catalogue for an exhibition, Columbia Museum of Art, Columbia, S.C., 1976. Professor Bryan has discovered many hitherto unknown documents relating to Mills and is at work on a new biography.

154 "AS A PROFESSION": Gallagher, *Mills*, 168.

155 "BUILDINGS FROM": Ibid., 170.

155 WHAT HE PREACHED: Ibid.

155 NATIVE STATE: Ibid., 42–43.

156 "EACH FRONT": Mills, *Statistics*, 410.

156 STATE AGENCIES: Gene Waddell, "Robert Mills's Fireproof Building," *South Carolina Historical Magazine*, 80 (April 1979), 105–135.

156 IRREPLACEABLE RECORDS: Ibid., 114.

157 "CONSTITUENT PARTS": Mills's "Autobiographical Notes," in Gallagher, 170.

157 COMPLETED IN 1825: Samuel Wilson, Jr., "The Pentagon Barracks, 1825," *Louisiana Architect*, 4 (Nov. 1964), 9–10.

158 OF OLD TREES: Dunlap, *Arts of Design*, 2, 296–297.

158 HIS OTHER PAINTINGS: Sona K. Johnston, "American Painting of the Revolutionary Period," *Maryland Heritage*, ed. Boles, 80–81; and Linda Crocker Simmons, *Charles Peale Polk, 1767–1822; A Limner and His Likenesses*, Corcoran Gallery of Art (Washington, D.C., 1981), 42.

158 "AND KIND": Alexander Graydon, *Memoirs of a Life Passed Chiefly in Pennsylvania within the Last Sixty Years* (Harrisburg, 1811), 95, as quoted in Aaron Baroway, "Solomon Etting, 1764–1847," *Maryland Historical Society*, 15 (March 1920), 2–3.

159 "AT THE TIME": Whaley Batson, "Charles Peale Polk: Gold Profiles on Glass," *Journal of Early Southern Decorative Arts*, 3 (Nov. 1977), 51–57.

159 COUNTY, VIRGINIA: Richard B. Woodward, *American Folk Painting, Selections from the Collection of Mr. and Mrs. William E. Wiltshire III*, Virginia Museum of Fine Arts (Richmond, 1977).

160 DIED IN 1817: Mimeographed data provided by the Maryland Historical Society. Gerald Levin, of the Society's staff, was responsible for locating the will.

160 VIRGINIA FAMILIES: J. Hall Pleasants, "Joshua Johnston, the First American Negro Portrait Painter," *Maryland Historical Magazine*, 37 (June 1942), 121–149. Carolyn Weekley is doing further research on this artist.

160 "NELSON ST.": *Baltimore City Directory for 1817–1818* (Baltimore, 1817), printed by James Kennedy, 217.

160 SOME CONFIDENCE: Quite recently a signed painting by this artist has been found: Linda Crocker Simmons, *Jacob Frymire, American Limner*, Corcoran Gallery of Art (Washington, D.C., 1975), 45–46.

160 "GIVE SATISFACTION": Quoted in Simmons, *Charles Peale Polk*, 84.

160 OR "PAINTER": Simmons, *Frymire*, 6–13.

161 NINETEENTH CENTURY: Robin Bolton-Smith, *Portrait Miniatures from Private Collections*, National Collection of Fine Arts, Smithsonian Institution (Washington, D.C., 1976), 4.

161 DIED IN 1860: Alice R. Huger Smith and D. E. Huger Smith, *Charles Fraser* (Charleston, 1924);

Martha R. Severens, "Charles Fraser of Charleston," *Antiques*, *123* (March, 1983), 606–611.

162 JUDGE'S TOMBSTONE: "Tombstones at Holy Cross Church, Stateburg, S.C.," *South Carolina Historical and Genealogical Magazine*, 50 (Jan. 1929), 59.

162 BEEN A PASTIME: Theodore Bolton, *Early American Portrait in Crayons* (New York, 1923), 62–70; Fillmore Norfleet, *Saint-Mémin in Virginia* (Richmond, 1942); Madeleine Herard, *Contribution à l'étude de l'émigration de Charles-Balthazar-Julien Fevret de Saint-Mémin aux États-Unis de 1793 à 1814* (Dijon, 1970).

163 AMATEUR ARCHITECT: Information from Maryland Historical Society catalogue sheet.

164 AND HIS DAUGHTER: I am grateful to Carmen Lord for summarizing research about the Salazars. Some of the material was compiled by the WPA researchers of the 1930s, some by the indefatigible Samuel Wilson, Jr., some by curators at the Louisiana State Museum, notably Nadine Russell and Vaughan Glasgow. Ms. Lord is the first to identify clearly Francisca Salazar and to locate a commission to her.

164 BAROQUE TRADITION: For a reproduction, see Mrs. Thomas N. C. Bruns, comp., *Louisiana Portraits*, National Society of the Colonial Dames of America (New Orleans, 1975), 18.

164 SEPTEMBER 22, 1801: I am grateful to the late Sidney Villere, genealogist, for this information.

164 HIS CORTEGE: Wesley Jackson, "Père Antoine Reappears for Round 2 in New Orleans," *Times-Picayune*, June 3, 1973, sec. 3, p. 2; Clarence Wyatt Bishpam, "Fray Antonio de Sedella, An Appreciation," *Louisiana Historical Quarterly*, 2 (Jan. 1919), 24–37 and (Oct. 1919), 369–392; and Albert A. Fossier, *New Orleans, the Glamour Period, 1800–1840* (New Orleans, 1957), 326–335.

164 EARN A LIVING: Data from Isaac Delgado Museum of Art Project, WPA, Typescript, Ms 42, Howard-Tilton Memorial Library, Tulane University.

165 "DON ANTONIO": Howard Corning, ed., *Journal of John James Audubon Made During his Trip to New Orleans in 1820–21* (Boston, 1929), 199–200. Among the many studies of Audubon, one of the most useful is Alice Ford, *John James Audubon* (Norman, 1964).

165 "ANTOINE COAT": Corning, *Journal*, 202.

165 "FATHER ANTOINE": Ibid., 203.

165 "PUPILS OF NOTE": Ibid., 204.

165 "SOON AS POSSIBLE": Ibid., 210.

165 SENT TO HAVANA: Francis Hobard Herrick, *Audubon the Naturalist*, 2 vols. (New York, 1917; reprint ed., 1968), *1*, 321. See also Ford, *Audubon*, 116.

166 DRAWING SKILL: Corning, *Journal*, 115–116,

143–146, 149, 153, 209–210, 217–218, 220, 222, 225.

166 SINGLE MORNING: Ibid., 125–126.

166 JEAN BAPTISTE WILTZ: John Burton Harter and Mary Louise Tucker, *The Louisiana Portrait Gallery, to 1870*, Louisiana State Museum (New Orleans, 1979), *1*, 26.

166 TRY CHARLESTON: Paul Staits, "Samuel F. B. Morse in Charleston, 1818–1821," *South Carolina Historical and Genealogical Magazine*, 79 (April 1978), 87–112, with bibliography.

167 BESIDE A FAWN: *Godey's Magazine*, 33 (1846), 213.

168 SOUTH CAROLINA HALL: Rutledge, *Artists in Charleston*, 137–140.

168 WITH STUART: John Hill Morgan, *Gilbert Stuart and His Pupils*, New-York Historical Society (New York, 1939), 81–93. See also William Barrow Floyd, *Matthew Harris Jouett, Portraitist of the Ante-Bellum South*, Transylvania University (Lexington, 1980).

168 "BEGINS TO PAINT": Morgan, *Stuart*, 85.

168 "(DEADNESS OR SADNESS)": Ibid., 83.

169 GENIUS SMILED: As quoted in S. W. Price, *The Old Masters of the Bluegrass* (Louisville, 1902), 44.

169 "FRIENDLY SPIRITS": "The Life of Olaudah Equiano or Gustavas Vassa, the African, Written by Himself," in Arna Bontemps, comp., *Great Slave Narratives* (Boston, 1969), 35. I am grateful to Peter Wood for calling this to my attention.

170 IN MASSACHUSETTS: Chester Harding, *My Egotistigraphy* (Cambridge, Mass., 1866).

170 "NOTHING ELSE": Ibid., 27.

170 "IN THEIR BOSOMS": Ibid., 32.

171 OF HIS DAUGHTER: Correspondence in private collection cited in Agnes M. Dods, "Nathan and Joseph Negus, itinerant painters," *Antiques*, 76 (Nov. 1959), 434–437.

172 BATTLE OF NEW ORLEANS: Jerome R. Mac-Beth, "Portraits by Ralph E. W. Earl," *Antiques*, 100 (Sept. 1971), 390–393; the portrait was described in detail in the *Nashville Whig* and *Tennessee Advertiser* of May 9, 1818, and is now owned by the Tennessee Historical Society.

172 AFTER THE REVOLUTION: Information from James Gergat, of the Valentine Museum, Richmond, as cited in Virginius Dabney, *Richmond: The Story of a City* (New York, 1976), 29.

172 "INTO HIS EMBRACE": Dabney, *Richmond*, 106.

172 UNKNOWN ARTIST: Information from Valentine Museum files.

173 AND ORANGEBURG: Beatrix Rumford, "Folk art in America: a living tradition," *Antiques*, 107 (Feb. 1975), 334.

174 OF YORUBA ORIGIN: Ibid. Information from Lorenzo Turner of Roosevelt University cited.

174 LOWER CREEKS: Museum of Early Southern Decorative Arts, Acq. no. 2312.

174 REAL POSSIBILITY: MESDA catalogue files.

174 TALENTED AMATEUR: J. Leitch Wright, Jr., *William Augustus Bowles, Director General of the Creek Nation* (Athens, Ga., 1967), 4.

174 EIGHTEEN EDITIONS: See British Library catalogue listing.

174 SCENE PAINTING: Wright, *Bowles*, 24, 38, 51; [Benjamin Baynton], *The Authentic Memoirs of William Augustus Bowles* (London, 1791; reprint ed., 1971), 46–47, 70, 75.

175 INDIAN CHIEF: Wright, *Bowles*, vii; Baynton, *Memoirs*, 70–73. Among his Indian progeny was Chief Bowles, the friend of General Sam Houston.

176 NATURAL TO HIM: Rutledge, *Artists in Charleston*, 123–124, 191–192; Whaley Batson, "Thomas Coram: Charleston Artist," *Journal of Early Southern Decorative Arts*, *1* (Nov. 1975), 35–47.

176 HENRY BENBRIDGE: Dunlap, *Arts of Design*, *1*, 165, 286–287.

176 RESIDENCE IN BALTIMORE: J. Hall Pleasants, "Four Late Eighteenth Century Anglo-American Landscape Painters," *Proceedings of the American Antiquarian Society*, *52* (1943), 186–324, esp. 239–300; Stiles Tuttle Colwill, *Francis Guy, 1760–1820*, Museum and Library of Maryland History (Baltimore, 1981).

177 "INVITING LOCALITY": From Rembrandt Peale, "Reminiscences—Desultory," in *The Crayon* (Jan. 1856), as quoted by Pleasants, "Landscape Painters," 263; Colwill, *Guy*, 20.

178 FORMAT ON OCCASION: For examples, see Carl Paul Barbier, *William Gilpin* (London, 1963), Plate 8.

178 "SQUARE YARD": Pleasants, "Landscape Painters," 165.

179 NORFOLK, VIRGINIA: Ibid., 195–214.

179 GOING TO AMERICA: Ibid., 197.

179 "LIGHT AND SHADE": William Gilpin, "Essay III, The Art of Sketching Landscape," *Three Essays* (London, 1794; reprint ed., 1972), 75.

180 "30 GUINEAS 52-10-1": As quoted in Pleasants, "Landscape Painters," 208.

180 ESTABLISH HIMSELF: Frank H. Goodyear, Jr., *Thomas Doughty, 1793–1856: An American Pioneer in Landscape Painting*, Pennsylvania Academy of the Fine Arts (Philadelphia, 1973), esp. 13–15, 21.

181 GILMOR'S COLLECTION: Ibid., 13–14.

181 ROSA, AND OTHERS: Dunlap, *Arts of Design*, 3,

272–275. See also Anna Wells Rutledge, "One Early American's Precocious Taste," *Art News*, 98 (March 1949), 28–29, 51.

182 OF THESE CITIES: Information from Mantle Fielding, *Dictionary of American Painters, Sculptors and Engravers* (Philadelphia, 1926); Fielding, *American Engravers upon Copper and Steel* (Philadelphia, 1917); biographical folder, Louisiana Collection, Howard-Tilton Memorial Library, Tulane University; City Museum of St. Louis, *Mississippi Panorama* (St. Louis, 1949), 67–68; and *Virginia Historical Society Occasional Bulletin*, 14 (April 1967), 7–8.

182 IN THIS COUNTRY: John Sartain, *The Reminiscences of a Very Old Man, 1808–1897* (New York, 1899), 176.

182 "IN Yᵉ U.S.": Dunlap, *Diary*, 3, vol. 63, 527.

182 "UNSUNG AND UNDESCRIBED": Joshua Shaw, *Picturesque Views of American Scenery* (Philadelphia, 1820), intro. As quoted in John Wilmerding, *American Art* (New York, 1976), 75.

182 RUGGED BEAUTY: Gilpin, "On Picturesque Beauty," *Three Essays*, 4–7.

183 STEPMOTHER IN FRANCE: Ford, *Audubon*, 10–38. Recently some publications have identified Audubon as a mulatto; Ford's careful research refutes this.

183 THEIR SURROUNDINGS: Marshall B. Davidson, *The Original Water-Color Paintings by John James Audubon for The Birds of America*, New-York Historical Society (New York, 1966), Plate 377. This is Havell, Plate 160, which Audubon identified as a Black-Capped Titmouse.

184 OF HIS SUBJECTS: Davidson, *Paintings by Audubon*, xvii–xviii, xxiii, xxxi.

184 MORE EXACT STUDY: For an excellent study of the role of natural history at this time, see William Martin Smallwood, *Natural History and the American Mind* (New York, 1941).

184 IN VIRGINIA REVEAL: As reproduced in *The Virginia Journals of Benjamin Henry Latrobe, 1795–1798*, 2 vols., Edward C. Carter, ed., Maryland Historical Society (New Haven, 1977), see esp. *1*, xxvii, and *2*, 457–531. There are 14 sketchbooks in all; it is to be hoped that they will all be published in time.

185 "SIMILAR CIRCUMSTANCES": *Virginia Journals of Latrobe*, *1*, 234–235.

185 IN 1797–1798: Ibid., *2*, 457–531.

185 "PRECEDING SEASONS!": Ibid., *2*, 518, 519.

186 "HAS BEEN FORMED": Robert Southey, *Letters from England*, 3 vols. (London, 1807), *2*, 42–43.

186 "IN AMERICA": Charles Eliot Norton, "The First American Archaeologist," *American Journal of Archaeology*, *1* (1895), 3–9.

186 ACCURATE PICTURES: As cited in Edwin L. Green, "John Izard Middleton," *Dictionary of Ameri-*

can Biography (New York, 1973). Middleton's rare volume was not available to me at time of writing, though I had seen it earlier.

186 "UNDER THE LENS": Norton, "American Archaeologist," 9.

188 1791 TO 1793: Peter Ward-Jackson, *English Furniture Designs of the Eighteenth Century*, Victoria and Albert Museum (London, 1958), 65–68, see Plates 315, 317, 320, and 327. Of the many publications on English furniture design, this is one of the most useful.

188 1789 AND 1794: In lieu of original editions of these: Ralph Fastnedge, *Shearer Furniture Designs from the Cabinet-Makers' London Book of Prices 1788* (London, 1962); and Ralph Edwards, *Hepplewhite Furniture Designs from the Cabinet-Maker and Upholsterer's Guide 1794* (London, 1965).

188 AND DILETTANTES: See especially Eileen Harris, *The Furniture of Robert Adam* (London, 1963); and Clifford Musgrave, *Adam and Hepplewhite and Other Neoclassical Furniture* (London, 1966). For cabinetmakers in London, Ambrose Heal, *The London Furniture Makers from the Restoration to the Victorian Era, 1660–1840* (London, 1953). For a list of design sources, price books, English and American, and bibliography on English background for Federal period furniture, Charles F. Montgomery, *American Furniture: The Federal Period* (New York, 1966), 487–489.

188 FROM 1802 TO 1819: *Baltimore Furnitures, The Work of Baltimore and Annapolis Cabinetmakers from 1760 to 1810*, Baltimore Museum of Art (Baltimore, 1947), 193; William Voss Elder III, "Maryland furniture, 1760–1840," *Antiques, 111* (Feb. 1977), 359–360. Gregory Weidman is preparing a catalogue of the furniture collection of the Maryland Historical Society in which the work of William Camp will be discussed. An exhibit of the work of Camp and another Baltimore cabinetmaker, John Needles, is also being planned.

188 DESK-DRESSING TABLE: I am grateful to Gregory Weidman for this information about Camp and for the identification of the original owners.

188 FOR THEIR HOME: Baroway, "Solomon Etting," 1–20; and William Vincent Byars, *B. and M. Gratz, Merchants in Philadelphia* (Jefferson City, 1916).

189 AT THIS PERIOD: William Voss Elder III, "American Decorative Arts of the Revolutionary Period," *Maryland Heritage* (Baltimore, 1976), 119.

189 IN THIS TECHNIQUE: Batson, "Polk," 53.

189 THE FINAL FORM: For two excellent brief discussions of the business of cabinetmaking and the interaction among specialized craftsmen, see Montgomery, *Federal Period*, 11–26, and Wallace B. Gusler, "The Arts of Shenandoah County, Virginia, 1770–1825," *Journal of Early Southern Decorative Arts, 5* (Nov. 1979), esp. 8–10.

189 ADAM-HEPPLEWHITE CONCEPTS: Lu Bartlett, "John Shaw, cabinetmaker of Annapolis," *Antiques, 111* (Feb. 1977), 362–377.

190 THESE TWO OVALS: Richard H. Hulan, "Tennessee textiles," *Antiques, 100* (Sept. 1971), 989.

190 CAROLINA CABINETMAKER: Frank L. Horton, "The work of an anonymous Carolina cabinetmaker," *Antiques, 101* (Jan. 1972), 169–176. The work of this craftsman was first identified as a group by Paul H. Burroughs, *Southern Antiques* (Richmond, 1935), Chapter XV, Plate V.

193 JOHNATHAN LONG: Frank L. Horton and Carolyn J. Weekley, *The Swisegood School of Cabinetmaking*, Museum of Early Southern Decorative Arts (Winston-Salem, 1973).

193 JOHN SWISEGOOD: Ibid., Cat. 5.

193 ALBEMARLE REGION: Betty Dahill, "The Sharrock Family: A Newly Discovered School of Cabinetmakers," *Journal of Early Southern Decorative Arts, 2* (Nov. 1976), 37–51.

193 URBAN EXAMPLES: Several other North Carolina cabinetmakers have been identified: John Bivins, Jr., "A piedmont North Carolina cabinetmaker: The development of a regional style," *Antiques, 103* (May 1973), 968–973, discusses Jesse Needham; Carolyn Weekley, "James Green, piedmont North Carolina cabinetmaker," ibid., 940–944.

195 MADE BY SPECIALISTS: Montgomery, *Federal Period*, 30–31, 33–40.

195 FURNITURE FORMS: Bradford L. Rauschenberg, "A Study of Baroque and Gothic-Style Gravestones in Davidson County, North Carolina," *Journal of Early Southern Decorative Arts, 3* (Nov. 1977), 24–47.

195 COUNTY IN VIRGINIA: Gusler, "Shenandoah," 14, Fig. 5; and Donald Walters, "Johannes Spiter, Shenandoah County, Virginia, furniture decorator," *Antiques, 108* (Oct. 1975), 733.

196 AFTER 1788: Klaus Wust, *Virginia Fraktur: Penmanship as Folk Art*, Shenandoah History (Edinburg, Va., 1972), 18.

196 "STONY CREEK ARTIST": Ibid., 17–19.

197 (FATHER AND MOTHER): John Bivins, Jr., "Fraktur in the South: An Itinerant Artist," *Journal of Early Southern Decorative Arts, 1* (Nov. 1975), 1–23.

197 OF HIS WORK: Christian Kolbe and Brent Holcomb, "Fraktur in the 'Dutch Fork' Area of South Carolina," *Journal of Early Southern Decorative Arts, 5* (Nov. 1979), 36–51.

197 REFORMED CONFESSION: Ibid., 39, n. 20.

198 IN THE REGION: Edna Talbott Whitley, *A Checklist of Kentucky Cabinetmakers from 1775 to 1859* (Paris, Ky., 1969), Addenda, 5.

198 "AND NEW YORK": *Kentucky Gazette and General Advertiser*, Dec. 12, 1805, Lexington, quoted Whitley, *Checklist*, 18.

198 "NEWEST FASHIONS": *American Republic*, Oct. 26, 1810, Frankfort, as quoted by Lois L. Olcott,

"Kentucky Federal furniture," *Antiques, 105* (April 1974), 875.

198 "IN CABINET-MAKING": F. André Michaux, *The North American Sylva* (Paris, 1819), 2, 90–91. This was first published in France between 1810 and 1813, and in English between 1817 and 1819. Much of the data were gathered by the author's father, André Michaux, when he visited America with his son between 1785 and 1796. François André came to America between 1801 and 1803.

198 "IMMENSE EXPENSE": Cuming, *Sketches in Early Western Travels*, 185–186.

199 IN GREEN COUNTY: Keith N. Morgan, "Josiah reconsidered: a Green County school of inlay cabinetmaking," *Antiques, 105* (April 1974), 883–893, see esp. Figs. 8, 15, and 16.

199 IN THE CAROLINAS: Mary Rolls Dockstader, "Sugar chests," *Antiques, 25* (April 1934), 140–143; Olcott, "Kentucky Federal," 875, 878–879; J. B. Speed Art Museum, *Kentucky Furniture* (Louisville, 1974), 65–71. These references mention only sugar chests. In Tennessee and Kentucky I have also heard pieces identified locally as meal chests, and these would apparently have held white cornmeal.

201 HIS WORK: Olcott, "Kentucky Federal," 877, Fig. 14.

201 NEW FRONTIERS: Whitley, *Checklist*, 109, and Addenda, 5.

201 "PLAIN AND INLAID": E. Milby Burton, *Charleston Furniture, 1700–1825* (Charleston, 1955), 55–57. See also Montgomery, *Federal Period*, 357–360.

201 SOUTHWESTERN FRONTIER: Virginia Van der Veer Hamilton, *Alabama* (New York, 1977), 3–12.

201 SOUTH ALABAMA: Albert B. Moore, *History of Alabama*, rev. ed. (University of Ala., 1934), 75, 105.

201 IN CHARLESTON: Burton, *Charleston Furniture*, 58 and Figs. 72–74.

201 SOUTHERN IN ORIGIN: For some other examples, see Montgomery, *Federal Period*, 431–432; Jan Garrett Hind, *The Museum of Early Southern Decorative Arts* (Winston-Salem, 1979), 46, 49, 91; Henry D. Green, *Furniture of the Georgia Piedmont*, High Museum of Art (Atlanta, 1976), 75–77; Helen Comstock, "Furniture of Virginia, North Carolina, Georgia and Kentucky," *Antiques, 61* (Jan. 1952), 62–64.

201 OF ITS CITIZENS: For some examples, see Figs. 18, 19, 20, 23, and 24, in Burton, *Charleston Furniture*. See also E. Milby Burton, "Charleston furniture," *Antiques, 97* (June 1970), 910–914.

201 FOR THAT CITY: Burton, *Charleston Furniture*, 6.

202 HOSPITAL IN BALTIMORE: Bryan, *Robert Mills*, Cat. 69.

202 BEDS THEMSELVES: See Montgomery, *Federal Period*, 56–57.

203 WAR OF 1812: Catalogue information, Textiles, Smithsonian Institution, P 63157, Cat. no. T.12815, Accession no. 242609.

203 FEW ARE KNOWN: Sandra Shaffer Tinkham, "A Southern bed rugg," *Antiques, 105* (June 1974), 1320–1321.

203 "INTO THE ARM HOLES": Thomas Webster, *An Encyclopedia of Domestic Economy* (New York, 1845), 304.

203 ONES ABOVE: Re usage of the terms clothespress and wardrobe, see Montgomery, *Federal Period*, 440–442.

203 HAS SURVIVED: Burton, "Charleston furniture," *Antiques, 97* (June 1970), 913.

203 VENEERS AND INLAYS: Burton, *Charleston Furniture*, 125.

203 BELOW THE CENTER: Jessie Poesch, "Early Louisiana *armoires*," *Antiques, 94* (Aug. 1968), 196–205.

205 WITH LION PAW FEET: Ward-Jackson, *English Furniture Designs*, 65–66, Plates 332 and 335.

205 EARLY AS 1812: *Le Courrier de la Louisiane*, April 10, 1812, p. 3, col. 4, reference to a shop fronting that of Mr. Seignouret, upholsterer.

206 IMPORTED WINES: See Maud O'Bryan Ronstrom, "Seignouret and Mallard, cabinetmakers," *Antiques, 46* (Aug. 1944), 79–81. Mr. William A. Feuillan is researching the history of this firm.

206 AT THE HERMITAGE: Benjamin H. Caldwell, Jr., "Tennessee silversmiths," *Antiques, 100* (Sept. 1971), 382–385.

206 TIME AS GRECIAN: See, for example, Plate 6 in Sheraton's *Encyclopedia of 1804–1808*, reproduced in John Harris, *Regency Furniture Designs* (London, 1961), no. 44. For William King, Jr., see Anne Castrodale Golovin, "Cabinetmakers and chairmakers of Washington, D.C., 1791–1840," *Antiques, 107* (May 1975), 898–922.

207 ANOTHER RENOVATION: Golovin, "Cabinetmakers," 901, 916; Museum of the Daughters of the American Revolution, Washington, D.C., Accession Sheet information, for chairs 61.133.1 and .2 (they own two of the chairs).

207 "DOMESTIC MANUFACTURE": Hans Huth, "The White House Furniture of the Time of Monroe," *Gazette des Beaux Arts*, Series 6, *29* (Jan. 1946), 23–46, esp. 29; Lucius Wilmerding, Jr., "James Monroe and the Furniture Fund," *New-York Historical Society Quarterly, 44* (April 1960), 133–149.

207 HOUSEHOLD FURNITURE: Huth, "White House Furniture," 30.

207 GREEK HAD BECOME: Reproduced in David B. Warren, *Southern Silver*, Museum of Fine Arts (Houston, 1968), Fig. C-1-D.

207 WORK ON THE CAPITOL: James A. Bear, Jr.,

"Thomas Jefferson's silver," *Antiques, 74* (Sept. 1958), 236.

208 SEVENTEENTH CENTURY: Louise Durbin, "Samuel Kirk, nineteenth-century silversmith," *Antiques, 94* (Dec. 1968), 868–873.

209 FASHIONED THESE: Bradford L. Rauschenberg, "A School of Charleston, South Carolina, Brass Andirons," *Journal of Early Southern Decorative Arts, 5* (May 1979), 26–74.

209 ON THE TABLE: Ibid., esp. 58–59, Figs. 13a, 14a, 14c, and 15c.

209 MARKET STEEPLE: Kirkland and Kennedy, *Historic Camden, Part One*, 20–22.

209 FROM 1815 TO 1834: Rutledge, *Artists in Charleston*, 209; and Kirkland and Kennedy, *Historic Camden*, 21.

210 BY A SHAWNEE: Kirkland and Kennedy, *Historic Camden*, 48–55, 66.

210 WAR HERO: E. Milby Burton, *South Carolina Silversmiths, 1690–1860* (Rutland, 1968), 9–11.

PART FOUR *The Sense of Separation,*
1825–1860

215 GREEK REVIVAL TASTE: William Barrow Floyd, "The restored Old Capitol, Frankfort, Kentucky," *Antiques, 114* (July 1978), 108–116; Henry-Russell Hitchcock and William Seale, *Temples of Democracy* (New York, 1976), 76–83; Clay Lancaster, "Gideon Shryock and John McMurty, Architect and Builder of Kentucky," *Art Quarterly, 6* (Autumn 1943), 257–275.

215 "PRIENE IN IONIA": *Atkinson's Casket: Gems of Literature, Wit, and Sentiment, 3* (1833), 553–554, cited in both Floyd and Hitchcock and Seale, but quoted in full, without full citation, in Elizabeth S. Field, "Gideon Shryock, His Life and Work," *Kentucky State Historical Society Register, 50* (April 1952), 117–118.

215 IONIC CAPITALS: See, for example, A. W. Lawrence, *Greek Architecture* (London, 1957), 192–195.

215 WILLIAM STRICKLAND: The above-mentioned authors do not cite Shryock's book source. It may have been the *Antiquities of Ionia*, published by the Society of Dilettante in London in four parts between 1769 and 1771. All twelve plates of Part II show details from the Temple of Minerva Polias at Priene in Ionia. I am grateful to Mr. Roger Mortimer, Head, Special Collections, University of South Carolina Library, Columbia, for checking the plates in these rare volumes.

216 DESIGNED BY SHRYOCK: For the Harrisburg Capitol, Hitchcock and Seale, *Temples of Democracy*, 59–63. To me the staircase seems close to Robert Adam's at Calzean Castle, Ayrshire, in Scotland, but I do not know if there is a direct connection.

216 "WESTERN WORLD": *Frankfort Commentator*, Dec. 8, 1829, as quoted in Bayless E. Hardin, "The

Capitols of Kentucky," *Kentucky State Historical Society Register, 43* (July 1845), 183.

217 CHOSEN PLAN: Hardin, "Capitols of Kentucky," 173–182.

217 FINISHED TO MEASURE: Ibid., 182–185.

217 "SUCH A SITUATION": Field, "Gideon Shryock," 117.

217 HENRY MORDECAI: Ibid., and Hitchcock and Seale, *Temples of Democracy*, 80.

217 NAMED IT ATHENS: E. Martin Coulter, *College Life in the Old South* (New York, 1928), 1–10.

217 "IN THE INTERIOR": As quoted in both Coulter, *College Life*, 178, and Frederick D. Nichols, *The Early Architecture of Georgia* (Chapel Hill, 1957), 240. They cite different page references in the manuscript of Minutes of the Trustees at the University of Georgia Library. See also John Linley, *The Georgia Catalog, Historic American Building Survey* (Athens, Ga., 1982), 264.

217 TO MEET THERE: Leola Selman Beeson, "The Old State Capitol at Milledgeville and Its Cost," *Georgia Historical Quarterly, 34* (Sept. 1950), 195–202.

217 1834 AND 1835: Leola Selman Beeson, *History Stories of Milledgeville and Baldwin County* (Macon, 1943), 34–36.

217 "GOTHIC ARCHITECTURE": Adiel Sherwood, *Gazetteer of the State of Georgia* (Philadelphia, 1829), 133, See also Linley, *Georgia Catalog*, 42, 120, 125, and 312.

217 MAN'S INSTITUTIONS: It has been suggested that the Gothic may have been chosen here because many of the legislators were Masons. The style was much revered by the society because it was associated with the Freemasons of the Middle Ages, whom they saw as their spiritual, if not actual, antecedents. There is no specific evidence to support this suggestion. See Hitchcock and Seale, *Temples of Democracy*, 74–76.

218 "BUT SUFFICIENT": Thomas Hamilton, *Men and Manners in America*, 2 vols. (London, 1833), 2, 272–273.

218 "OF MILLEDGEVILLE": J. S. Buckingham, *The Slave States of America*, 2 vols. (London, 1842), 2, 535, 538.

218 WAS COMPLETED: Hitchcock and Seale, *Temples of Democracy*, 76.

219 "PANTHEON AT ROME": Arthur Scully, Jr., *James Dakin, Architect, His Career in New York and the South* (Baton Rouge, 1973), 193, n. 14, gives three sources in which the comparison to St. Paul's was made.

219 "BUT OF STUCCO": Fredrika Bremer, *Homes of the New World*, 2 vols. (New York, 1853), 2, 194–195.

219 "AT NEW ORLEANS": Buckingham, *Slave States, 1,* 331–333. For a history of hotels, see Niko-

laus Pevsner, *A History of Building Types* (Princeton, 1976), 169–192.

219 PHILADELPHIA, AND BALTIMORE: Norman Walker, "Commercial and Mercantile Interests," in Henry Rightor, *Standard History of New Orleans* (Chicago, 1900), 538–577; U.S. Dept. of State, *Compendium of the Enumeration of the Inhabitants and Statistics of the United States* (Washington, D.C., 1841).

219 50,000 PEOPLE: T. P. Thompson, "Early Financing in New Orleans, 1831—Being the Story of the Canal Bank—1915," *Publications of the Louisiana Historical Society*, 7 (New Orleans, 1915), 37–38.

219 "IN NEW YORK": As cited in James Robert Bienvenu, "Two Greek Revival Hotels in New Orleans, the St. Charles by James Gallier, Sr., and the St. Louis by J. N. B. D. and J. I. De Pouilly," M.A. thesis, Tulane University, 1961, 8.

219 AMERICAN ARCHITECTURE: The interrelationships among these men have been best sorted out by Scully in *Dakin*. Information is threaded throughout, but see esp. 4–8, 39–42, 43–46.

219 NEW YORK CAREERS: Dakin's work in New York has been described in Scully, *Dakin*, 8–38.

219 TOWN, DAVIS, AND DAKIN: Ibid., 8

219 *MODERN ARCHITECTURE:* Ibid., 31.

219 THE CONSTRUCTION: Ibid., 26–32.

220 THE *LOUISIANA:* James Gallier, *Autobiography* (Paris, 1864; reprint ed., New York, 1973), 17.

220 "MUCH ENLARGED": Ibid., 16.

220 IN 1806–1811: Sir John Summerson, *Architecture in Britain, 1530–1830*, 5th ed. (London, 1969), 303.

220 "IN THAT DIRECTION": Gallier, *Autobiography*, 17.

220 "MY LABOURS": Ibid.

220 LECTURES ON ARCHITECTURE: James Gallier, manuscript notes, Special Collections Division, Howard-Tilton Memorial Library, Tulane University.

220 "HAS EVER SEEN": Ibid., Lecture Three, 23–24.

221 "BEAR THE CLIMATE": Gallier, *Autobiography*, 20–21.

221 THEY WERE REUNITED: Norman Walker, "Municipal Government," in Rightor, *History of New Orleans*, 96–98.

221 COLONNADED DOME: Scully, *Dakin*, 44, 50, 51.

222 SEAT 500, ETC.: Buckingham, *Slave States*, 322; and Lester B. Shippee, ed. and intro., *Bishop Whipple's Southern Diary, 1843–1844* (Minneapolis, 1937), 196–197.

222 "IS ALSO GREATER": Shippee, *Bishop Whipple*, 196.

222 COMMERCIAL EXCHANGE: T. L. Nichols, *Forty Years of American Life* (London, 1874), 134–135.

222 IN THE ROTUNDA: Martha Ann Peters, "The St. Charles Hotel: New Orleans Social Center, 1837–1860," *Louisiana History*, 1 (Summer 1960), 191–211.

222 "DID NOT SUIT ME": Bremer, *New World*, 2, 195.

222 "LIFE IN ENGLAND": Buckingham, *Slave States*, 1, 334.

222 "MAY BE ENJOYED": Ibid., 333.

222 ISAIAH ROGERS: Bienvenu, "Greek Revival Hotels," 32–38, Fig. B. See also Hamlin, *Greek Revival*, 118.

223 GENERAL PRECEDENT: For a picture, see Summerson, *Architecture in Britain*, 208 B.

223 HOUSE OF DETENTION: Hitchcock and Seale, *Temples of Democracy*, 86–89; Roger Hale Newton, *Town and Davis* (New York, 1942), 160, Fig. 26; Scully, *Dakin*, 8–10, 37.

223 (PRESUMABLY JAMES): *Norman's New Orleans* (1845). See also Scully, *Dakin*, 44, 50–51.

225 ACROSS THE STREET: Scully, *Dakin*, 51–55.

225 PART OF THE CITY: Bienvenu, "Greek Revival Hotels," 19–38, 42–51.

225 "OF ENCHANTMENT": Shippee, *Bishop Whipple*, 201.

226 IN THE REGION: For Gallier, see also Samuel Wilson, Jr., and Marion Dean Ross, *James Gallier, Architect: An Exhibition of His Work* (New Orleans, 1950). Ann M. Masson is working on a study of de Pouilly's architectural career.

226 OF ARCHITECTS: Scully, *Dakin*, 66–67.

227 1833 AND 1835: Pitts and Clark, *New Orleans Directory for 1842* (New Orleans, 1842), 56.

227 WINTER SEASON: See Robert C. Reinders, *End of an Era, New Orleans, 1850–1860* (New Orleans, 1964), 33–46.

227 NEW YORK ROUTE: James P. Baughman, *Charles Morgan and the Development of Southern Transportation* (Nashville, 1968).

227 SHEDLIKE BUILDINGS: For illustrations, see especially Gibson's *Guide and Directory of the State of Louisiana and the Cities of New Orleans and Lafayette* (New Orleans, 1838), 310–313.

227 "SCENE IN NEW ORLEANS": Shippee, *Bishop Whipple*, 103; see also Buckingham, *Slave States*, 337.

227 ON THE SCENE: Newton, *Town and Davis*, 119–200, Figs. 1, 2, 34; Scully, *Dakin*, 5, 16–17 and Plate 3; 68–72 and Plate 5.

227 "OF ORIGINALITY": *Journal of the Franklin Institute*, 31 vols., 3rd ser., 1 (Jan., 1841), 11–12, as cited in Talbot Hamlin, *Greek Revival Architecture in America* (New York, 1944), 62.

229 "EVER REMEMBER": Buckingham, *Slave States*, 1, 282–283.

229 DAKIN AND DAKIN: Scully, *Dakin*, 68–84.

229 IMPOSING SITE: Nell Savage Mahoney, "William Strickland and the Building of Tennessee's Capitol, 1845–1854," *Tennessee Historical Quarterly*, 4 (June 1945), 99–153; Clayton B. Dekle, "The Tennessee State Capitol," *Tennessee Historical Quarterly*, 25 (Fall 1966), 213–238; James Patrick, *Architecture in Tennessee* (Knoxville, 1981), 132.

229 "FROM TAXATION": *Acts of Tennessee*, 25th Assembly, 1st Sess., 1843–1844, Ch. CCXVII, 252–253, as cited in Dekle, "Tennessee Capitol," 218.

229 "IMPLICITLY RELIED ON": Robert H. White, *Messages of the Governors of Tennessee*, 6 vols. (Nashville, 1952–1953), 4, 62, as cited in Dekle, "Tennessee Capitol," 219. See also Mahoney, "William Strickland," 106–108.

229 OF THAT YEAR: Mahoney, ibid., 110–112.

231 "MORE BEAUTIFUL": Benjamin H. Latrobe, *The Journal of Latrobe* (New York, 1905), 140, as cited in Mahoney, "William Strickland," 114, n. 69.

231 ROBERT MILLS: H. M. Pierce Gallagher, *Robert Mills* (New York, 1935), 100–101, 114.

231 "OF DEMOSTHENES": A. R. Newsome, ed., *North Carolina Manual, 1927*, North Carolina Historical Commission (Raleigh, 1927), 300–301. *See also* George Dardis, *Description of The State Capitol of Tennessee* (Nashville, 1854), 71, where the term is used.

231 BASEMENT PORTICO: Mahoney, "William Strickland," 150; Hitchcock and Seale, *Temples of Democracy*, 120.

231 AT ABBOTSFORD: Mrs. John Trotwood Moore, "The Tennessee State Library in the Capitol," *Tennessee Historical Quarterly*, 12 (March 1953), 8–11.

231 "DESTINED TO CONTAIN": Moore, "State Library," 11.

231 "GOTHIC STYLE": Newsome, *North Carolina Manual*, 301.

232 JOHN C. CALHOUN: Moore, "State Library," 10–11.

232 HENRY WADSWORTH LONGFELLOW: Ibid., 9.

232 "IN THIS COUNTRY": Ibid., 10.

232 "AND THERMOPYLAE": Edgar Ewing Brandon, ed., *A Pilgrimage of Liberty* (Athens, Ohio, 1944), as for example at Raleigh, 28, Natchez, 209, and Nashville, 235.

232 "ATHENIAN DESTINIES": Andrew A. Lipscomb, ed., *The Writings of Thomas Jefferson*, 20 vols.,

(Washington, D. C., 1904), *13*, 179, in a letter of July 12, 1812.

232 OXFORD AND CAMBRIDGE: For the Gothic revival in general, Sir Kenneth M. Clark, *The Gothic Revival* (London, 1928). For the American genesis and development, William H. Pierson, Jr., *American Buildings and Their Architects, Technology and the Picturesque, the Corporate and Early Gothic Styles* (Garden City, N. Y., 1978).

232 AND INFLUENTIAL: For a study of his career, see Phoebe B. Stanton, *Pugin* (London, 1971).

232 BECOME DECADENT: Phoebe B. Stanton, *The Gothic Revival and American Church Architecture, An Episode in Taste, 1840–1856* (Baltimore, 1968), 18. This book is an excellent study of one phase of the Gothic revival.

232 DOCTRINE AND SPIRIT: Ibid., 17; *New York Ecclesiologist*, *1* (Oct. 1848), 8.

233 OF THE GOTHIC: Stanton, *Gothic Revival*, 21.

234 HIS COLLEGE YEARS: For information on the technique, the decisions, and the sources I am grateful to Captain Richard Anderson, who has been closely involved with the recent restoration. Letter to author, Nov. 6, 1978.

234 OF THE CENTURY: For a brief summary of his career, see Beatrice St. Julien Ravenel, *Architects of Charleston* (Charleston, 1945), 201–216.

235 ACHIEVE THEM: *New York Ecclesiologist*, *1* (Oct. 1848), 5–8.

235 HALE COUNTY: For information about the church, William M. Spencer, "St. Andrew's Church, Prairieville," reprint with additions from *The Alabama Review* (Jan. 1961); Winston Smith and Gwyn Collins Turner, "History in towns: Demopolis, Alabama," *Antiques*, *117* (Feb. 1980), 413; and brochure, with plan, from the church. I am grateful to the Reverend William B. Wright for answering inquiries, and to Mr. Robert Matthews for opening the church for me.

235 "BY THE FALL": Smith and Turner, "History," 6.

235 MUCH TO PUGIN: Everard M. Upjohn, *Richard Upjohn, Architect and Churchman* (New York, 1939); Stanton, *Gothic Revival*, 61–63; for a somewhat critical appraisal, see *New York Ecclesiologist*, *1* (Oct. 1848), 34–39.

235 THE ECCLESIOLOGISTS: Stanton, *Gothic Revival*, 68–83.

235 VERTICAL EMPHASIS: For a reproduction of this, see Upjohn, *Upjohn*, Fig. 68.

235 PARISH CHURCH: Pierson, *Technology and the Picturesque*, 432–455.

235 OWN MODIFICATIONS: Upjohn, *Upjohn*, 214, accepts the design as from Upjohn on the basis of internal evidence, though he mistakenly identifies it as St. Michael's.

235 HENRY A. TAYLOE: Spencer, "St. Andrew's," 6–7.

235 OF HONEST AIMS: See especially *New York Ecclesiologist*, *2* (July 1849), 135.

235 CLEARLY SEEN: For a more comprehensive survey, see James Patrick, "Ecclesiological Gothic in the Antebellum South," *Winterthur Portfolio*, *15* (Summer 1980), 117–138.

235 HARPER'S IN 1857: [William Gilmore Simms], "Charleston," *Harper's New Monthly Magazine*, *15* (June 1857), 1–22, esp. 9–10.

236 "BETTER PROPRIETY": Ibid., 13.

237 THROUGH 1857: Ravenel, *Architects of Charleston*, 219–228.

237 FAÇADES OF BUILDINGS: Turpin C. Bannister, "Bogardus Revisited, Part I: The Iron Firsts," *Journal of the Society of Architectural Historians*, *15* (Dec. 1956), 12–22. See also William H. Jordy, *American Buildings and Their Architects, Progressive and Academic Ideals at the Turn of the Twentieth Century* (New York, 1972), 9–11.

238 SOURCE OF PRIDE: "Improvements," New Orleans *Times-Picayune*, Sept. 25, 1859, unpaginated (p. 7); see also Mary Louise Christovich, Roulhac Toledano et al., *New Orleans Architecture*, *2*, *The American Sector* (Gretna, La., 1972), 102–103. In the latter an incorrect date is given for the newspaper article cited above.

238 BENNETT AND LURGES: For a brief history of the latter, see Ann M. Masson and Lydia J. Owen, *Cast Iron and the Crescent City*, Exhibition, Gallier House (New Orleans, 1975), 45.

238 TO THE MASONRY: Christovich, *New Orleans, American Sector*, 102. The original building contract is in New Orleans Notarial Archives, S. Wagner, 14 June 1859, vol. 7, no. 227, fol. 1073.

238 "RULES OF THE ART": "Improvements," *Times-Picayune*, Sept. 25, 1859, 7.

238 BUILT 1858–1860: Lois T. Olcott, "Public architecture of Kentucky before 1870," *Antiques*, *105* (April 1974), 830–831, 837.

239 AND WELL LIGHTED: S. F. A. Tarrant, ed., *Hon. Daniel Pratt: A Biography* (Richmond, 1904), 63.

239 TO A CARPENTER: For biographical information, Tarrant, *Pratt*, and Merrill E. Pratt, *Daniel Pratt, Alabama's First Industrialist* (Birmingham, 1949).

239 INDUSTRIAL TOWNS: Pierson, *Technology and the Picturesque*, 22–90.

240 "AND BACKGROUND": Pratt, *Daniel Pratt*, 9.

241 HOT CLIMATE: Hamlin, *Greek Revival*, 133, suggests a New York origin for these cast-iron verandas.

242 TO GEORGIA: Robert S. Raley, "Daniel Pratt, architect and builder," *Antiques*, *102* (Sept. 1972), 425–433; William Nathaniel Banks, "The Architec-

tural Legacy of Daniel Pratt," *Papers of Athens Historical Society*, *2* (Athens, Ga., 1979), 52–62; and Linley, *Georgia Catalog*, 57, 60–63, 316.

242 IT WAS COMPLETED: It has recently been restored and moved about a hundred miles from its original site.

242 FROM THEIR HOMES: Wilbur Zelinsky, "The Greek Revival House in Georgia," *Journal of the Society of Architectural Historians*, *13* (May 1954), 9–12.

242 IN SUCH HOUSES: Ibid.

244 CLASSICAL VERNACULAR: Hamlin, *Greek Revival*, Appendix A, 339–355, esp. 343; see also Pierson, *American Buildings, Colonial and Neoclassical*, 456–458.

244 WADE HAMPTON: See William Nathaniel Banks, "The River Road plantations of Louisiana," *Antiques*, *111* (June 1977), 1172–1174, with notes.

244 "BYE-GONE DAYS": Charles Fraser, *Reminiscences of Charleston* (Charleston, 1854), 58.

245 ON THE PROPERTY: Dwight S. Young, "Historic preservation in Mobile," *Antiques*, *112* (Sept. 1977), 461, and Margaret Rose Ingate, "History in towns: Mobile, Alabama," *Antiques*, *85* (March 1964), 304.

245 BUILT IN 1853: Ernest Allen Connally, "Architecture at the End of the South: Central Texas," *Journal of the Society of Architectural Historians*, *11* (Dec. 1952), 8–12; Drury Blakeley Alexander, *Texas Homes of the Nineteenth Century* (Austin, 1966), 85–90, 253–254, and Fig. 135.

246 WITH BOARDS: For some descriptions of other modest structures in Georgia, see Nichols, *Architecture of Georgia*, 36–37.

246 NORTH OR SOUTH: Jesse G. Whitfield, *Gaineswood and Other Memories* (Demopolis, n.d.); "The Story of Gaineswood," *House & Garden* (Nov. 1939), 41–44, 66–68; Ralph Hammond, *Ante-Bellum Mansions of Alabama* (New York, 1951), 114–120; and Smith and Turner, "History in towns," 402–413. I am grateful to W. H. Britton of Demopolis for sharing some of his notes with me, as well as parts of a typescript article by Walter S. Patton. Mr. Britton is responsible for the superb wood-graining and marbleizing to be seen in the present restoration.

248 BUILDER'S GUIDE: Scully, *Dakin*, 8, cites the frontispiece and Plate 75 in Lefever.

248 GRANDSON REMEMBERED: Whitefield, *Gaineswood*.

248 IN 1845: I am grateful to Mr. and Mrs. Amon Carter Evans and John W. Kiser for providing me with information on the thoroughgoing research done on the house during the recent restoration. See also Thomas B. Brumbaugh, Martha I. Strayhorn, and Gary C. Gore, eds., *Architecture of Middle Tennessee* (Nashville, 1974), 150–152; Hamlin, *Greek Revival*, 207; Albert W. Hutchinson, "Domestic architecture in Middle Tennessee," *Antiques*, *100* (Sept. 1971), 403–405; Patrick, *Architecture in Tennessee*, 179, 181.

250 SURVIVING EXAMPLE: Brumbaugh et al., *Middle Tennessee*, 134–137; Patrick, *Architecture in Tennessee*, 17.

251 OF SMALL FARMS: "Tullie Smith House, Progress Report," *The Atlanta Historical Society Newsletter* (April 1971); Nichols, *Architecture of Georgia*, 36–38, 136–137; Linley, *Georgia Catalog*, 22.

251 "COMPOSED THE WALLS": John Townsend Trowbridge, *The South, A Tour of its Battlefields and Ruined Cities* (Hartford, 1866), 484.

252 EGALITARIAN AMERICANS: For an analysis of this movement in America, see Pierson, *Technology and the Picturesque*, 270–431.

252 OF A COTTAGE: Alexander Jackson Downing, *The Architecture of Country Houses* (1850; reprint ed., New York, 1969), 42.

252 PLEASING COMBINATIONS: Patty T. Murfee, "History in towns: Columbus, Mississippi," *Antiques*, 100 (Dec. 1971), 914–918.

253 COLUMNS ARE USED: There is an even simpler one in Lexington, Georgia. See Nichols, *Architecture of Georgia*, 398, and Linley, *Georgia Catalog*, 149–150, 156, and 264–265.

253 APALACHICOLA, FLORIDA: Carol Matlock, "Eufaula," *American Preservation*, 2 (Oct.–Nov. 1978), 9–21; Joel P. Smith, "History in towns, Eufaula, Alabama," *Antiques*, 114 (Sept. 1978), 520–527.

254 AND MORTON: Nichols, *Architecture of Georgia*, 65, based on information prepared for National Register Nomination by Janice Biggers, March 23, 1971, and Linley, *Georgia Catalog*, 140–143, 145, and 288.

255 "WELL MANAGED": Calvert Vaux, *Villas and Cottages* (New York, 1857), 54.

255 OR COMPANILE: Samuel Sloan, *The Model Architect*, 2 vols. (Philadelphia, 1852), 1, 31–32.

256 "OF THE COUNTRY": Ibid.

256 BATON ROUGE: Henry W. Krotzer, Jr., "The restoration of San Francisco (St. Frusquin), Reserve, Louisiana," *Antiques*, 111 (June 1977), 1194–1203; Samuel J. Dornsife, "San Francisco Plantation House, An Exercise in Restoration," *Connoisseur*, 197 (April 1978), 275–282.

257 "HONORARY HOTEL": Sloan, *Model Architect*, 2, 55, 81.

257 HOME THERE: The surviving papers concerning the building of Longwood are printed in Ina May Ogletree McAdams, *The Building of Longwood* (Austin, 1972).

258 "NOT HANGED": McAdams, *Longwood*, 63–64.

258 OF THE CAUSE: The story of the strong Union sentiments of Natchezians is well documented in William Banks Taylor, *King Cotton and Old Glory* (Hattiesburg, 1977).

259 COMPLETED IN 1857: Charles L. Dufour, "Henry Howard: Forgotten Architect," *Journal of the Society of Architectural Historians*, 11 (Dec. 1952), 21–24; William R. Cullison III, *Historic Mississippi Delta Architecture*, Louisiana Landmarks Society (New Orleans, 1978), 46–47; Henry Howard, Manuscript Autobiography, Special Collections, Howard-Tilton Memorial Library, Tulane University, Ms 623, Box 1, folder 6. A number of descriptions of this mansion, particularly romanticized narrative versions, erroneously assign this to James Gallier.

259 THIRTY-SEVEN YEARS: Ms 372, Special Collections, Howard-Tilton Memorial Library, Tulane University. Belle Grove Plantation advertisement, no date. Some of the undocumented descriptions of the plantation say Andrews came in 1850.

259 "UNITED STATES": Quoted by Dufour, "Henry Howard," 21.

259 AUTOBIOGRAPHY: Ms 623, Box 1, folder 6, Special Collections, Howard-Tilton Memorial Library, Tulane University. Victor McGee, who is working on a study of Howard and his oeuvre, believes that this manuscript is not written in Howard's own hand, was possibly dictated by him, and contains some errors.

261 "IN OUR COUNTRY": John Neal, "American Painters—and Painting," *The Yankee*; and *Boston Literary Gazette* (N.S., no. 1, 1829), 48–51, as quoted in H. E. Dickson, ed., *Observations on American Art, Selections from the Writings of John Neal (1793–1876)* (State College, Pa., 1943), 42.

261 AND ASSESSED: Some idea of the number and variety can be gained by examining the Bicentennial Index of American Painting at the National Collection of Fine Arts in Washington, D.C. The recent publications of the National Society of the Colonial Dames, in which they are recording all portraits before 1870 which they can locate in individual states, such as those for Alabama, North Carolina, Georgia, Kentucky, and Louisiana, represent a useful first step for the study of portraiture in the South.

261 MAY 29, 1837: Edward Biddle and Mantle Fielding, *The Life and Works of Thomas Sully* (Philadelphia, 1921), 129.

262 "OR A LOVER": Dickson, *John Neal*, 81.

262 SKILL AND GRACE: Mrs. Orville Lay and Sidney A. Smith, *Alabama Portraits Prior to 1870*, National Society of the Colonial Dames of America (Mobile, 1969), 71.

263 SIR THOMAS LAWRENCE: Margaret M. Bridwell, "Oliver Frazer, early Kentucky portrait painter," *Antiques*, 12 (Nov. 1967), 718–721; see also William Barrow Floyd, "Portraits of ante-bellum Kentuckians," *Antiques*, 105 (April 1974), 813; George W. Ranck, *History of Lexington, Kentucky* (Cincinnati, 1872), 147–149.

263 AND INDIANA: Floyd, "Portraits of Kentuckians," 813.

264 APPLE ORCHARDS: Papers of Mr. and Mrs.

Leonard Mee, Archives of American Art, Washington, D.C., Microfilm roll 960, frames 80–498.

264 $75 OR $100: Ibid., June 28, 1846, entry, while in Nashville. Mee papers, frame 274.

264 UNIDENTIFIED ARTIST: John Burton Harter and Mary Louise Tucker, *The Louisiana Portrait Gallery, to 1870*, Louisiana State Museum (New Orleans, 1979), 1, 44.

264 ON SOUTHERN CASES: Richard Harrison Shryock, *Medicine in America, Historical Essays* (Baltimore, 1966), esp. 7–21, 49–70.

265 NEW ORLEANS IN 1822: Harter and Tucker, *Portrait Gallery*, 119, and Anna Wells Rutledge, *Artists in the Life of Charleston*, Transactions of the American Philosophical Society, N.S. 32 (Philadelphia, 1949), 130, 153, 190; Typescript, WPA New Orleans Artists' Roster, Ms 42, Special Collections, Howard-Tilton Memorial Library, Tulane University.

266 IN 1831: Typescript, WPA New Orleans Artists' Roster; Lynne W. Farwell, "Jean Joseph Vaudechamp and New Orleans," *Antiques*, 94 (Sept. 1968), 371–375; Lynne W. Farwell, *Jean Joseph Vaudechamp*, Louisiana State Museum (New Orleans, 1976). See also *Diary of William Dunlap*, 3, 785, in *New-York Historical Society Collection*, 64 (New York, 1931).

266 DEATH IN 1890: Harter and Tucker, *Portrait Gallery*, 42.

266 1831 TO 1837: Mary Louise Tucker, "Jacques Amans, Portrait Painter in Louisiana, 1836–1856," M.A. thesis, Tulane University, 1970.

267 AND DATED 1845: The larger version, for which this may be a study, is owned by a descendant, Madame Jackie Valabrègue-Landreaux of France.

267 MOST SYMPATHETIC: Tucker, "Amans," 40, 81, 167.

268 VERSIONS OF THIS: Tucker, "Amans," 68–69, 163–166. Susan Clover Symonds, "Portraits of Andrew Jackson, 1815–1845," M.A. thesis, University of Delaware, 1968, lists four paintings based on an original 16- by 24-inch version, two signed and dated in private collections, and two others, one at Brown University and another at the Chicago Historical Society. The one given as at Brown University is now owned by the Historic New Orleans Collection. Amans subsequently did a larger equestrian portrait of Jackson with Theodore Moise in 1844, owned by City Hall, New Orleans.

269 1840S OR '50S: Tucker, "Amans," 108.

269 CUVIER AND REDOUTÉ: John James Audubon, *Audubon and His Journals*, ed. Marie R. Audubon and notes by Elliott Coues, 2 vols. (New York: reprint ed., 1962), 231–234.

269 DESCRIBED EARLIER: Mrs. Thomas Nelson Carter Bruns and George Jordan, *Louisiana Portraits*, National Society of the Colonial Dames of America (New Orleans, 1975), 19.

269 MIDDLE TENNESSEE: Budd H. Bishop, "Art in Tennessee; the Early 19th Century," *Tennessee Historical Quarterly*, 29 (Winter 1970–1971), 379–389; Bishop, "Three Tennessee painters: Samuel M. Shaver, Washington B. Cooper, and James Cameron," *Antiques*, 100 (Sept. 1971), 432–437.

269 MISSISSIPPI: Elizabeth P. Reynolds, *To Live upon Canvas: The Portrait Art of Thomas Cantwell Healy*, Mississippi Museum of Art (Jackson, 1980).

269 HAVE BEEN TRACED: William B. O'Neal, *Primitive into Painter: Life and Letters of John Toole* (Charlottesville, 1960).

269 AND NORFOLK: Helen G. McCormack, *William James Hubard, 1807–1862*, Valentine Museum and Virginia Museum of Fine Arts (Richmond, 1948).

271 NEW CAPITAL: Rutledge, *Artists in Charleston*, 154, 168–169; Helen Hennig, *William Harrison Scarborough, Portraitist and Miniaturist* (Columbia, 1937).

272 "STRANGELY NEGLECTED": Rutledge, *Artists in Charleston*, 155, quoting *Courier* of Oct. 3, 1837.

272 "OAK TREE GROWS": Bremer, *New World*, 1, 283–285.

272 "INDIFFERENT TO ALL . . . ": Ibid.

272 "OF HIS FOREST": Ibid.

272 IN EUROPE: Bilodeau et al., *Art in South Carolina*, 127.

272 BY AN AMERICAN: Rutledge, *Artists in Charleston*, 155.

272 GEORGE CATLIN: Emma Lila Fundaburk, *Southeastern Indians, Life Portraits, A Catalogue of Pictures, 1564–1860* (Luverne, Ala., 1957), nos. 284–292.

273 IN THIS WAY: The best study of Catlin's work is William H. Truettner, *The Natural Man Observed: A Study of Catlin's Indian Gallery* (Washington, D. C., 1979). A good, short review of Catlin's career is John C. Ewers, *George Catlin: Painter of Indians of the West*, reprinted from the Annual Report of the Smithsonian Institution for 1955.

273 TO THE WEST: Fundaburk, *Southeastern Indians*, nos. 188–197.

273 AN AGED MAN: George Catlin, *North American Indians, Being Letters and Notes on Their Manners, Customs and Conditions*, 2 vols. (London, 1841; reprint ed., Edinburgh, 1926), 1, letter nos. 36, 36–40, and letter nos. 57, 247–251; Truettner, *Cat.*, no. 302.

273 BANDIT'S BRIDE: These two paintings are in the Vincent L. Bradford Collection at Washington and Lee University.

273 MAY 26, 1856: Smith, *Alabama Portraits*, 404, and information from Mr. Caldwell Delaney, Director of the Museum of the City of Mobile.

274 DEEP SOUTH: John Fulton, *Memories of Frederick A. P. Barnard* (New York, 1896), 89–90. For a general history of photography in America, see Robert Taft, *Photography and the American Scene* (New York, 1938; reprint ed., 1964), re Barnard, 38. For Barnard and Harrington, Margaret Denton Smith and Mary Louise Tucker, *Photography in New Orleans, The Early Years, 1840–1865* (Baton Rouge and London, 1982), 26–27, 159.

275 "THE MINIATURE": Smith and Tucker, *Photography in New Orleans*, 42.

275 IN NEW ORLEANS: Leo Stashin, "Portraits of notable nineteenth-century Americans in daguerreotype," *Antiques*, 103 (April 1973), 788.

275 DONE IN NEW ORLEANS: Smith and Tucker, *Photography in New Orleans*, 60–65, 160–161.

276 ONLY KNOWN WORKS: Rutledge, *Artists in Charleston*, 186; Bilodeau et al., *Art in South Carolina*, 148.

276 HENRY JACKSON: Martha R. Severens, *Selections from the Collection of the Carolina Art Association* (Charleston, 1977); Rutledge, *Artists in Charleston*, 158, 202.

277 1834 TO 1836: Information from files of Maryland Historical Society, Baltimore.

277 IN 1787: For a brief history of the panorama, see John Francis McDermott, *The Lost Panoramas of the Mississippi* (Chicago, 1958).

278 AS LUMINIST: John Wilmerding, *American Light: The Luminist Movement, 1850–1875*, National Gallery of Art (Washington, D. C., 1980). Among the essays in this volume, one of the most interesting is that by Theodore E. Stebbins, Jr., "Luminism in Context: A New View," 211–233; see also Barbara Novak, "Grand Opera and the Still Small Voice," *Art in America*, 59 (March–April 1971), 64–73.

278 AND CURIOSITIES: Museum of Fine Arts, Boston, *M. & M. Karolik Collection of American Water Colors & Drawings* (Boston, 1962), 92–93.

278 KNOWN ELSEWHERE: Marilou Alston Rudulph, "George Cooke and His Paintings," *Georgia Historical Quarterly*, 44 (June 1960), 117–153; William Nathaniel Banks, "George Cooke, painter of the American scene," *Antiques*, 102 (Sept. 1972), 449–454; Beth Abney, "George Cooke and the Chapel Painting," *Athens Historical Society Papers*, 2 (1979), 62–73.

279 GREAT SUCCESS: William Dunlap, *History of the Rise and Progress of the Arts of Design in the United States* (New York, 1834), intro. William P. Campbell, ed. Alexander Wyckoff (New York, 1965), 2, 274; E. Bénézit, ed., *Dictionnaire critique et documentaire des peintres, sculpteurs, dessinateurs et graveurs* (Paris, 1976), 5, "Granet, François Marius," 165–166; Biddle and Fielding, *Sully*, 339,

279 "SCULPTURE AND PAINTING": George Cooke, "The Fine Arts, No. III," *Southern Literary Messenger*, 1 (May 1835), 477–478.

279 CONSIDERATIONS: E. P. Richardson and Otto Wittman, Jr., *Travellers in Arcadia*, Detroit Institute of Arts and Toledo Museum of Art (Detroit, 1951); Barbara Novak, "Americans in Italy: Arcady Revisited," *Art in America*, 61 (Jan.–Feb. 1973), 56–59.

280 ATMOSPHERIC SKIES: *The Southern Literary Messenger*, 1 (1834–1835), 98–99; ibid., 6 (1840), 775–777.

280 COOKE'S WIFE: William P. Campbell, *John Gadsby Chapman*, National Gallery of Art (Washington, D.C., 1962); Georgia S. Chamberlain, "John Gadsby Chapman, Painter of Virginia," *Art Quarterly*, 24 (Winter 1961), 378–390.

280 REPRODUCE DRAWINGS: Sinclair Hamilton, *Early American Book Illustrations and Wood Engravers* (Princeton, 1958), foreword by Frank Weitenkampf, vii; re Chapman, 90–91.

281 COLORED ENGRAVINGS: Three of his paintings from the Linton-Surget collection are now in the Tulane University collection.

282 KNOWN TODAY: Alexander Moore, "A Charleston Artist and a National Art," *Art in the Lives of South Carolinians, Nineteenth Century Chapters*, 2, 4; Martha Severens, of the Gibbes Art Gallery of Charleston, is working on a study of Fraser's landscapes.

282 SUCH ARTISTS: P.H.S., "A Painting of Oakland," *J. B. Speed Art Museum Bulletin*, 18 (Louisville, 1957), unpaged.

282 TO BE DISCOVERED: Robert Brammer had a studio in New Orleans in June 1853 and a summer home in Biloxi. His landscapes were highly praised. *Daily Orleanian*, June 11, 1853, and June 16, 1853, as recorded in WPA New Orleans Artists' Roster, Ms 42, Special Collections, Howard-Tilton Memorial Library, Tulane University. At present I know of only one Louisiana or Mississippi landscape by him, a swamp scene. He died in Biloxi in the summer of 1853, *Daily Orleanian*, August 6, 1853. For the swamp scene, see the R. V. Norton Gallery, *Louisiana Landscape and Genre Painting of the 19th Century* (Shreveport, 1981), 7, Fig. 5.

282 AND LOUISIANA: John Hervey, *Racing in America, 1665–1865*, 3 vols., Jockey Club (New York, 1944), 2, 103, 121–128.

282 IN THE SOUTH: Ibid., 2, 378–379.

282 GREAT RIVER: McDermott, *Lost Panoramas*.

283 "'LOW COUNTRY'": William C. Richards, ed., *Georgia Illustrated* (Penfield, Ga., 1842), 1.

284 OIL PAINTINGS: Louis T. Griffith, "T. Addison Richards, Georgia Scenes by a Nineteenth Century Artist and Tourist," *Bulletin of Georgia Museum of Art*, University of Georgia, Athens, 1 (Fall 1974), 9–16. An exhibition of Richards's drawings was held at the Washburn Gallery in New York in May–June 1974, reviewed in the *New York Times*, June 1, 1974.

285 "FROM HIS EASEL": *Rambler* (Dec. 30, 1843), 2, as cited in Rutledge, *Artists in Charleston*, 166.

285 TO VISITORS: William Howard Adams, ed., *The*

Eye of Th. Jefferson, National Gallery of Art (Washington, D. C., 1976), no. 582, 337–38, 390; *The Natural Bridge of Virginia*, Natural Bridge of Virginia (n.d.), 14–45; and Pamela H. Simpson, *So Beautiful an Arch: Images of the Natural Bridge, 1787–1890*, Washington and Lee University (Lexington, 1982).

285 "INDESCRIBABLE": Thomas Jefferson, *Notes on the State of Virginia*, ed., intro. and notes by William Peden (Chapel Hill, 1955), 24–25, 263–264, n. 5.

285 BY JEFFERSON: Howard C. Rice, intro., *Travels in North America in the Years 1780, 1781, and 1782, by the Marquis de Chastellux*, 2 vols. (Chapel Hill, 1963), *1*, 16; *2*, viii., engraving bet. 446–447, 406–408, and 445–456.

285 "EVER REMEMBERED": Andrew Reed and James Matheson, *A Narrative of the Visit to the American Churches*, 2 vols. (New York, 1835), *1*, 167–169.

285 VISIT IN 1852: This is now at the University of Virginia Art Museum in Charlottesville; see Adams, *Eye of Th. Jefferson*, 337.

285 INFINITE VARIETY: Johnson's early work is in the process of "rediscovery." See Jo Miller, "Drawings of the Hudson River School: The Second Generation, Part 2," *Connoisseur, 175* (Sept. 1970), 53; William H. Gerdts, *Revealed Masters, 19th Century American Art*, American Federation of Arts, New York (New York, 1974), 88–89; Wilmerding, *American Light*, 99, 108, 138, 214, 216, 237; John I. H. Bauer, "'. . . the exact brushwork of Mr. David Johnson,' An American Landscape Painter, 1827–1908," *American Art Journal, 12* (Autumn 1980), 32–65.

286 DATED 1847: Museum of Fine Arts, Boston, *M. and M. Karolik Collection of American Painting* (Cambridge, Mass., 1949), 495–497.

286 NOT SHOWN: Page 237. The vessel is also different.

286 "OF THE WEST": Cited by Varian Feare, "Varian Feare Reaches Wetumpka," *Birmingham News-Age-Herald*, April 7, 1975, 3, in E. Walter and Varian F. Burkhardt, *Alabama Ante-Bellum Architecture*, Alabama Historical Commission (Montgomery, 1976), 29.

288 ACADEMIC TRADITION: E. Bénézit, *Dictionnaire, 9*, 492. H. Stewart Leonard, *Mississippi Panorama*, City Art Museum of St. Louis (St. Louis, 1949), 115. I am grateful to Joseph Newell for insights and information presented in a seminar paper on this painting in December 1979.

288 L. J. M. DAGUERRE: For the early career of Daguerre see Helmut and Alison Gernsheim, *L. J. M. Daguerre* (New York, 1968), 3–47.

288 "DOUBLE-EFFECT" DIORAMA: Gernsheim, *Daguerre*, 33–34.

289 AND SEBRON: Ibid., 33, 184.

289 WORE OFF: Ibid., 143.

290 OF THE SHOWING: New Orleans *Commercial Times*, p.3, col. 4, as recorded in WPA New Orleans

Artists' Roster, Ms 42, Special Collections, Howard-Tilton Memorial Library, Tulane University. This painting is not listed as among Daguerre's oil paintings, or among the diorama paintings in Gernsheim, *Daguerre*, 180, 182–184.

290 "MINIATURE PAINTERS": New Orleans *Commercial Bulletin*, Feb. 26, 1848, as recorded in WPA New Orleans Artists' Roster.

290 "IS THE CREATOR": *Daily Delta*, Feb. 23, 1849; *New Orleans Bee*, Feb. 27, 1849, as recorded in WPA New Orleans Artists' Roster. See also *Daily Picayune*, Feb. 20, 1849, and Feb. 27, 1849, and *Daily Crescent*, March 6, 1849.

290 IN NEW ORLEANS: *Courier*, May 12, 1852, and *New Orleans Bee*, May 11, 1852. WPA New Orleans Artists' Roster.

290 VIEWS OF CITIES: Gernsheim, *Daguerre*, Figs. 38, 39, 40, all by Daguerre in 1838–1839.

290 APRIL 30, 1852: New Orleans *Daily Picayune*, April 30, 1852; Pauline A. Pinckney, *Painting in Texas* (Austin, 1967), 68–73.

290 TO JAPAN: *New Orleans Bee*, June 5, 1857.

290 TO BE CHOCTAW: This painting has been reproduced in various publications, such as City Museum of St. Louis, *Mississippi Panorama* (St. Louis, 1949), 67; Jesse Burt and Robert B. Ferguson, *Indians of the Southeast: Then and Now* (Nashville and New York, 1973), 129. Russell Harper, *Early Painters and Engravers in Canada* (Toronto, 1970), 37; Hugh Honour, *The European Vision of America*, Cleveland Museum of Art (Cleveland, 1976), cat. no. 299.

291 TROPICAL BAYOUS: "The Northern Lands, Paintings of Canada, Alaska and the Arctic," *Kennedy Quarterly, 12* (Dec. 1973), 241.

291 AMONG HIS WORKS: Rutledge, *Artists in Charleston*, 163–164, 237, 240, 242–245; Patricia Hills, *The Painters' America, Rural and Urban Life, 1810–1910* (New York, 1947), 59.

293 "HUMAN TRAFFIC": Eyre Crowe, *With Thackeray in America* (London, 1893), 133–136.

293 ACADEMY IN LONDON: Algernon Graves, comp., *The Royal Academy of Arts, A Complete Dictionary of Contributors and Their Work from Its Foundation in 1769 to 1904* (London, 1905–1906; New York, reprint ed., 1972), *2*, 211.

293 AROUND 1858: The New Orleans *Daily Crescent*, Jan. 26, 1859. References to Antrobus were given to me by the Historic New Orleans Collection.

293 WORTHY OF PURSUIT: *Daily Times Delta*, New Orleans, April 29, 1860.

294 "CARROLL PARISH": *Daily Times Delta*, April 22, 1860. For a discussion of Afro-American graveyard decoration, see John Michael Vlach, *The Afro-American Tradition in Decorative Arts*, Cleveland Museum of Art (Cleveland, 1908), 139–147.

295 "VISIBLE MOURNERS": T. Addison Richards,

"Rice Lands," *Harper's* (Nov. 1859), 735.

295 TIME TO TIME: Mrs. Lyn Allison Yeager of Bowling Green, Kentucky, is working on a study of Antrobus's career.

295 AND BOSTON: Rutledge, *Artists in Charleston*, 136, 225–226; Paul R. Weidner, ed., "The Journal of John Blake White," *South Carolina Historical and Genealogical Magazine, 42* (1941), 55–71, 99–117, 169–185; *43* (1942), 35–46, 103–117, 161–174; see esp. 104, 107, 117, 164–165.

295 "PUBLIC MIND": Weidner, "Journal," *43* (April 1942), 162, 165.

295 BY SOUTH CAROLINA: For a reproduction of the engraving, see Bilodeau et al., *Art in South Carolina*, 92.

295 "FROM THE SERVICE": Brig. Gen. P. Horry and M. L. Weems, *The Life of Gen. Francis Marion, A Celebrated Partisan Officer in the Revolutionary War Against the British and Tories in South Carolina and Georgia* (1809; Philadelphia, 1845), 153–156.

295 HISTORY PAINTINGS: See Bilodeau et al., *Art in South Carolina*, 93.

295 AFTER IT: William Gilmore Simms, *The Life of Francis Marion*, 8th ed. (New York, 1846), 176–180.

295 IN 1859: Ethelbert Nelson Ott, "William D. Washington (1833–1870), Artist of the South," M.A. thesis, University of Delaware, June 1968, 44. Frequently listed as William de Hartburn Washington, Ms. Ott has convincingly indicated that his correct name was William Dickinson Washington.

295 ROBIN HOOD: The large finished painting is at the Reading Public Museum and Art Gallery in Reading, Pennsylvania.

296 WEST INDIES: The definitive study is Alexander Mackay-Smith, *The Race Horses of America, 1832–1872, Portraits and Other Paintings by Edward Troye*, National Museum of Racing (Saratoga Springs, 1981). See also J. Winston Coleman, Jr., *Edward Troye, Animal and Portrait Painter* (Lexington, 1958), and "Edward Troye, sporting artist," *Antiques, 105* (April 1974), 799–805.

296 NORTH AMERICA: Hervey, *Racing in America, 1*, 53, 62.

297 UNTIL 1845: Duncan MacLeod, "Racing to War, Antebellum Match Races Between the North and South," *Southern Exposure, 7* (Fall 1979), 7–10.

297 IN VIRGINIA: Mackay-Smith, *Troye*, 18–24, 40–42, and 413–414.

298 ALSO IN CANADA: Ibid., 187–202, 425–426. Replicas were given by Richards to Bethany College in West Virginia, where they remain. The originals were apparently burned in 1875.

298 IN EUROPE: Ibid., 202.

298 JACK PORTER: Jean Jepson Page, "Francis Blackwell Mayer," *Antiques, 109* (Feb. 1976), 316–323.

300 BEING ATTACKED: In the Baltimore Museum of Art, dated 1849.

300 INCLUDING ENGRAVING: Rutledge, *Artists in Charleston*, 27, 139, 181; Bilodeau et al., *Art in South Carolina*, 108, no. 115; David McNeely Stauffer, *American Engravings upon Copper and Steel*, 2 vols. (New York, 1907), *1*, 180.

301 BENJAMIN H. LATROBE: John E. Semmes, *John H. B. Latrobe and His Times, 1803–1891* (Baltimore, 1917).

301 POPULAR BOOKS: Ibid., 103–105.

301 "ART CRUSADE": Peter C. Marzio, *An Analysis of American Drawing Manuals, 1820–1860*, Smithsonian Studies in History and Technology, no. 34 (Washington, D.C., 1976).

301 "NATIONAL CHARACTER": *Lucas' Progressive Drawing Book* (Baltimore, 1827), vi.

301 AVAILABLE: Albert Ten Eyck Gardner, *History of Water Color Painting in America* (New York, 1966), 7–8.

302 OF THE VISITORS: Many of these are reproduced by Semmes. The Maryland Historical Society in Baltimore has an extensive collection of J. H. B. Latrobe's watercolors, dating from 1826 through 1889.

302 "GOOD MANNERS": Semmes, *Latrobe*, 255–256.

302 BALTIMORE COTTAGES: Ibid., 444, and reproduction of watercolor opp. 354.

302 ART COLLECTION: Ibid., 167–169, 417.

302 SAMUEL F. B. MORSE: Cecil D. Eby, Jr., *"Porte Crayon": The Life of David Hunter Strother* (Chapel Hill, 1960), 20–26.

303 TO HARPER'S: Ibid., 63.

303 WHITE WASHES: I am planning to do a comprehensive study of Strother's drawings.

304 "IN MYSTERY": D. H. Strother, "The Dismal Swamp," *Harper's New Monthly Magazine*, 13 (Sept. 1856), 449.

304 AND PHOTOGRAPHER: Eleanor H. Gustafson, "Museum accessions," *Antiques*, 111 (June 1977), 1128, and materials from H. Parrott Bacot, Curator, Anglo-American Museum, Louisiana State Museum, Baton Rouge.

304 SILHOUETTE ARTISTS: Anna Wells Rutledge, "William Henry Brown of Charleston," *Antiques, 60* (Dec. 1951), 532–533; Rutledge, *Artists in Charleston*, 150, 240–241.

304 "BLACK PAPER": William Henry Brown, *The History of the First Locomotives in America* (New York, 1874), 182–183.

304 "MARINE VIEWS": Ibid.

304 NATCHEZ FENCIBLES: Ibid., 198.

305 IDENTIFIABLE: Ibid., opp. 174.

305 TWENTY-TWO: Rutledge, *Artists in Charleston*, 144–145, 189–190; Wayne Craven, *Sculpture in America* (New York, 1968), 94–95; Anna Wells Rutledge, "Cogdell and Mills, Charleston sculptors," *Antiques*, 41 (March 1942), 192–193, 205–208.

305 ITS PRESIDENT: Rutledge, *Artists in Charleston*, 138–147.

305 THE MEMBERS: Dunlap, *Arts of Design*, 2, 371–373.

305 FOREIGN-BORN ARTISTS: Constance Vecchione Hershey, "Mortuary art in Charleston churches," *Antiques*, 98 (Nov. 1970), 800–807.

305 IN ITALY: Craven, *Sculpture*, 100–144; William H. Gerdts, *American Neo-Classic Sculpture* (New York, 1973).

306 OHIO RIVER: Craven, *Sculpture*, 111–123; Sylvia E. Crane, *White Silence* (Coral Gables, 1972), 167–269.

306 REFLECTED THIS: See various references in Crane, *White Silence*.

306 SMALL-SCALE REPLICA: Bilodeau et al., *Art in South Carolina*, 144.

306 STATE OF VIRGINIA: For a brief history of the equestrian statue in America, and for the Jackson monument, Craven, *Sculpture*, 168–172; for the Richmond *Washington*, 130–131; see also Rutledge, "Cogdell and Mills," *41*, 192–193, 205–208.

307 ITS PLACEMENT: New Orleans *Courier*, Jan. 6, 1856, and the *American Exponent*, Jan. 19, 1856, both as cited in Ms 42, New Orleans Artists' Roster, Special Collections, Howard-Tilton Memorial Library, Tulane University.

307 JACKSON SQUARE: *American Exponent*, Feb. 2, 1856, as cited in Ms 42, *op. cit.*

307 IN RICHMOND: Craven, *Sculpture*, 130–131, 143, Fig. 4.14.

308 "OF THE PAST": Frederick Law Olmsted, *A Journey in the Back Country* (New York, 1863), 280.

308 AND NEW ORLEANS: Craven, *Sculpture*, 155, 197–199.

308 BEEN REDISCOVERED: H. Parrott Bacot and Bethany B. Lambdin, "Edwin Lyon, an Anglo-American sculptor in the lower Mississippi River valley," *Antiques*, 111 (March 1977), 554–557.

308 FIRE IN 1863: Craven, *Sculpture*, 205–206.

308 THE TELFAIRS: Telfair Academy catalogue; Louis T. Cheney, "The Telfair and its paintings," *Antiques*, 91 (March 1967), 353–360; Craven, *Sculpture*, 192–196.

308 AROUND 1833: Lester Burbank Bridaham, "Pierre Joseph Landry," *Antiques*, 72 (Aug. 1957), 157–159.

309 MANUAL DEXTERITY: The Louisiana State Museum in New Orleans owns a hand-illustrated military drill book of about 1815 which is by a Landry, possibly by him or by his father.

309 DIED IN 1821: See, for example, Leonard V. Huber, *Louisiana: A Pictorial History* (New York, 1975), 128.

309 NAPOLEON'S DEATH: Olivia Blanchard, "The Death Mask of Napoleon," *Louisiana Historical Quarterly*, 8 (Jan. 1925), 71–83; Louisiana State Museum, *Death Mask of Napoleon* (New Orleans, 1936).

310 CONSTANTINOPLE: John C. Chase, *Frenchmen, Desire, Good Children, and Other Streets of New Orleans* (New Orleans, 1949), 145–147.

311 TOMBSTONES: This is especially true in New Orleans, but they can be seen elsewhere. For New Orleans tombstone imagery, see Leonard V. Huber, *Clasped Hands, Symbolism in New Orleans Cemeteries* (Lafayette, 1982).

311 CITIES OF AMERICA: Thomas O'Connor, *History of the Fire Department in New Orleans* (New Orleans, 1895). This also gives information on firefighting in the eighteenth century.

311 WERE PLACED: Ibid., 39–44, 54–57, 69–75.

311 FOLK SCULPTURE: See Tom Armstrong, "The Innocent Eye, American Folk Sculpture," in Whitney Museum of Art, *200 Years of American Sculpture* (New York, 1976), 75–111.

312 THEIR TASK: Christie Zimmerman Fant, *The State House of South Carolina* (Columbia, 1970), 108–109. For Werner, see Vlach, *Afro-American Tradition*, 110; J. Francis Brenner, Jr., "Master Ironworkers Came to Practice Art in City," Charleston *Courier*, Aug. 21, 1932 (10B); and South Carolina Archives, Columbia: General Assembly, 1831–1859, Public Improvements, Petition of Christopher Werner for aid to complete Palmetto Monument, Resolution re Palmetto Monument, and Senate resolution re Palmetto Monument 1856.

312 THE CONFEDERACY: Arthur Mazyek, *Charleston in 1885, being a sketch of the history of Charleston, S.C.* (Charleston, 1885), 35–36.

312 WAR THAT FOLLOWED: Col. L. M. Keitt, "Patriotic Services of the North and the South," *De Bow's Review, 21* (Nov. 1856), 491–508.

312 ANCIENT MODELS: Useful surveys are Serge Grandjean, *Empire Furniture 1800 to 1825* (London, 1966); Clifford Musgrave, *Regency Furniture* (London, 1961); and John Harris, *Regency Furniture Designs* (London, 1961).

312 NEW FASHIONS: A useful survey is Celia Jackson Otto, *American Furniture of the Nineteenth Century* (New York, 1965), esp. 44–121.

312 CAP THE FEET: Helen Scott Townsend Reed, "Decorative arts in the Valentine Museum," *Antiques*, 103 (Jan. 1973), 167–168.

313 BOOK FOR FURNITURE: Robert C. Smith, "John

Hall, a busy man in Baltimore," *Antiques*, *92* (Sept. 1967), 300–366; Otto, *American Furniture*, 114–117.

314 AND CHARLESTON: Re the Meeks, see John N. Pearce, "The Meeks family of cabinetmakers," *Antiques*, *85* (April 1964), 414–420; John Pearce, "More on the Meeks cabinetmakers," *Antiques*, *90* (July 1966), 68–73; and Edith Gaines, "Collectors' notes," *Antiques*, *98* (July 1970), 127.

314 "SUPERIOR ARTICLES": As quoted in James H. Craig, "The 1840 North Carolina capitol and its furniture," *Antiques*, *88* (Aug. 1965), 205–207.

314 ORNAMENT CHAIRS: Ibid. See also Craig, *The Arts and Crafts in North Carolina, 1699–1840* (Winston-Salem, 1965), 98, 213, and index refs.

315 SKILLED CRAFTSMAN: Not all legal documents list them as such, but, for example, at the time of his wife's death the elder is identified as a free man of color: Petition of Pierre Charles Dutreuil Barjon, f.m.c., in the Succession of his wife, Eulalie Lanna, filed in New Orleans Probate Court, after 19 Feb. 1836. His marriage contract, dated Feb. 1, 1821, identifies him as born in Santo Domingo: New Orleans Notarial Archives, Carlyle Pollock, vol. 2, fol. 575. I am grateful to Charles Mackie for this legal information.

315 POSSESSIONS: Meeting of Creditors of Pierre Dutreuil Barjon, July 25, 1843, New Orleans Notarial Archives, Louis T. Caire, Notary Public.

315 AND WAREHOUSES: A useful discussion of the furniture trade, craft and business, for one region, is found in Lonn Taylor and David B. Warren, *Texas Furniture: The Cabinetmakers and Their Work, 1840–1880* (Austin, 1975), 13–37; see also Elizabeth A. Ingerman, "Personal experiences of an old New York cabinetmaker," *Antiques*, *84* (Nov. 1963), 576–580.

315 COMPETITION: North Carolina Museum of History, *Thomas Day, Cabinetmaker* (Raleigh, 1975). For other craftsmen in Milton and in Caswell County, see the index entries in Craig, *Arts and Crafts in North Carolina*.

316 (1786–1852): E. Milby Burton, *South Carolina Silversmiths, 1690–1860* (Rutland, 1968), 54–57; David B. Warren, *Southern Silver*, Museum of Fine Arts (Houston, 1968), I-5-A.

316 IN THE 1850s: Benjamin H. Caldwell, Jr., "Tennessee silversmiths," *Antiques*, *100* (Sept. 1971), 382–385. See also William Barrow Floyd, "Kentucky coin-silver pitchers," *Antiques*, *105* (March 1974), 576–580.

319 FINE SPECIMEN: [Samuel Allen], "Sketches of the West," *American Agriculturist*, *2* (May, Dec. 1843), as cited in Eugene L. Schwaab, ed., with Jacqueline Bull, *Travels in the Old South, Selected from Periodicals of the Times* (Lexington, 1973), *2*, 300.

320 BAFFLE A STRANGER: Information from accession file of Historic Columbia Foundation, Columbia, S.C.

321 "MODERATE TERMS": *De Bow's Review*, *21* (Nov. 1856), no page given.

322 MALLARD AND CO.: *Acts Passed at the First Session of the First Session of the First Legislature of the State of Louisiana Begun and Held in the City of New Orleans on the 9th Day of February 1846* (New Orleans, 1846), Act Number 37; *Humphrey's Journal*, *6* (May 1, 1854), 31. I am grateful to Kurt Thomas for calling my attention to the first item and to Margaret Denton Smith for the second.

324 OWN PREMISES: Thomas Webster, *An Encyclopedia of Domestic Economy* (New York, 1845), 207.

325 ROSEWOOD BOOKCASES: Romaine S. Somerville, "Furniture of the Maryland Historical Society, *Antiques*, *109* (May 1976), 988–989; Katherine Susman Howe, "The Gothic revival style in America, 1830–1870," *Antiques*, *109* (May 1976), 1014–1023.

326 STRANDS OF WIRE: This example is very similar to the cake basket, no. 49, p. 48, shown in Cary T. Mackie, H. Parrot Bacot, and Robert L. Mackie, *Crescent City Silver*, Historic New Orleans Collection, and Anglo-American Museum (New Orleans, 1980); see also 4–5, 30, 41, 121, 126.

327 VALUED AT $8,500: Civil District Court Records, Parish of Orleans, La., Succession of Adolph Himmel, No. 39710, August 23, 1877, New Orleans Public Library. Charles L. Mackie kindly provided me with a copy.

327 LEX. KY.: Henry H. Harned, "Ante-bellum Kentucky silver," *Antiques*, *105* (April 1974), 818–824; Hervey, *Racing in America*, *2*, 350.

327 DECORATED WORK: Warren, *Southern Silver*, Catalogue E-5-B. The cover design is a detail taken from the sugar bowl exhibited there. See also Margaret M. Bridwell, "Asa Blanchard, early Kentucky silversmith," *Antiques*, *37* (March 1940), 135–136; Lockwood Barr, "Kentucky silver and its makers," *Antiques*, *48* (July 1945), 25–27; and Margaret M. Bridwell, "Kentucky Silversmiths Before 1850," *Filson Club History Quarterly*, *16* (1942), 111–125.

327 POST STAKE: The earliest representations of the Metairie course of which I know are post–Civil War; one in *Frank Leslie's Illustrated Weekly* of May 4, 1872, 17, and a painting of 1876 by Pierson and Moise. See Leonard V. Huber, *New Orleans, A Pictorial History* (New York, 1972), 248–249. There are not enough distinguishing features in the Warfield Cup scene to confirm a comparison.

327 SMITHSONIAN INSTITUTION: Hervey, *Racing in America*, *2*, 273–317; for the 1854 race, 286; on Lexington's death, 316.

327 KENTUCKY TURF: Hervey, *Racing in America*, *1*, 229–231.

328 "SAME KIND": Robert Mills, *Statistics of South Carolina, Including a View of Its Natural, Civil, and Military History, General and Particular* (Charleston, 1826), 523–524, 526.

328 QUALITIES DEFINED: John A. Burrison, "Alkaline-glazed stoneware: A Deep-South Pottery Tradition," *Southern Folklore Quarterly*, *39* (Dec. 1975), 377–403; Stephen T. Ferrell, *Early Decorated Stoneware of the Edgefield District, South Carolina*, Greenville County Museum of Art (Greenville, 1976); Georgeanna H. Greer, "Alkaline glazes and groundhog kilns: Southern pottery traditions," *Antiques*, *111* (April 1977), 768–773; and Vlach, *Afro-American Tradition*, 76–97. I am grateful to Dr. Greer, potter-researcher and collector, for the opportunity of seeing her extensive collection, and for information about these and other wares. Burrison and Greer are both at work on specialized studies of pottery.

329 MATTER OF CONJECTURE: Burrison, "Alkaline-glazed stoneware," 385–388. See notes 27 and 31.

329 AROUND 1835: Information from Dr. Georgeanna H. Greer.

329 COLUMBIA, SOUTH CAROLINA: Vlach, *Afro-American Tradition*, 77–81; Ferrell, *Edgefield*.

330 DURING FIRING: Greer, "Alkaline glazes," Plate. III, 770.

330 THAT LINE: Statement by Bradford L. Rauschenberg as quoted by Burrison, "Alkaline-glazed stoneware," 379.

330 POTTERY THERE: John Ramsay, *American Potters and Pottery* (New York, 1947), 87, 91, 235.

329 AROUND 1840-1850: Information from Dr. Georgeanna H. Greer.

330 BEING DISCOVERED: For a useful but now out-of-date summary of pottery in the South, see Ramsay, *American Potters*, 81–92, 235–243.

330 RECENT STUDY: Mint Museum of History, *Potters of the Catawba Valley* (Charlotte, 1980).

330 "FROM MICE": Catherine E. Beecher, *Domestic Receipt Book*, 3rd ed. (New York, 1857), 266–267.

331 TOO WARM: Eliza Leslie, *Miss Leslie's Lady's House-Book* (Philadelphia, 1852), 244.

331 "FOUR DOLLARS": Civil District Court Records, Parish of Orleans, La., Succession of Adolph Himmel, No. 39710, August 23, 1877, New Orleans Public Library.

331 HALF AN HOUR: Irma S. Rombauer, *The Joy of Cooking* (New York, 1946), 453; *American Heritage Cookbook and Illustrated History of American Eating and Drinking* (New York, 1964), 124, 144; Howard Weeden, *Bandana Ballads* (New York, 1899), 70. I am grateful to Mrs. Sidney A. Smith for providing me with several recipes for beaten biscuits.

331 TRADITIONAL CRAFT: Margaret R. Knight, "A Craft Revived," *Times-Picayune*, Dixie roto section, New Orleans, Nov. 19, 1978, 21–24.

332 OF THE SOUTH: "Charleston," *Harper's New Monthly Magazine*, *15* (June 1857), 9–10.

332 "SOUTHERN STATES": Downing, *Architecture of Country Houses*, 312–317.

332 ROOMS FOR SLEEPING: Sloan, *Model Architect, 2,*
55–57, 81–82, Designs 44 and 53.

334 ''ITS SUBLIMITY'': Written in 1835. Reprinted in
John W. McCoubrey, ed., *American Art, 1700–1960*
(New York, 1965), 98.

Notes on an After-Image

335 AND ITS PEOPLE: Francis Pendleton Gaines, *The
Southern Plantation* (New York, 1925), esp. 1–35; I.
A. Newby, *The South: A History* (New York, 1978),

174–179. See also William A. Taylor, *Cavalier and
Yankee* (London, 1963).

335 MARKS OF AGE: Herbert S. Fairall, *The World's Industrial and Cotton Centennial Exhibition, New Orleans
1884–1885* (Iowa City, 1885), 167.

336 COLUMNS AND COLONNETTES: Halsey C. Ives,
intro., *The Dream City. A Portfolio of Photographic
Views of The World's Columbian Exposition* (St. Louis,
1893). No page numbers.

336 COLONIAL PERIOD: Cuyler Reynolds, *New York at*

the Jamestown Exposition, Norfolk, Virginia, April 26 to
December 1, 1907* (Albany, 1909), 143.

336 CENTRAL PAVILION: Jamestown Exposition Com-
mission of the State of Louisiana, *Louisiana at the
Jamestown Tercentennial Exposition 1907* [Baton
Rouge?, 1908], 2.

336 AT THAT TIME: Fraser, *Reminiscences of Charleston*
(Charleston, 1854), 58.

Select Bibliography

ARCHITECTURE

Books and Exhibition Catalogues

Alexander, Drury Blakeley. *Texas Homes of the Nineteenth Century*. Austin, 1966.

Andrews, Wayne. *Pride of the South, A Social History of Southern Architecture*. New York, 1979.

Brumbaugh, Thomas B., Strayhorn, Martha I., and Gore, Gary C., eds. *Architecture of Middle Tennessee, The Historic American Buildings Survey*. Nashville, 1974.

Bryan, John Merrill. *Robert Mills, Architect, 1781–1855*. Catalogue from an exhibition, Columbia Museum of Art. Columbia, 1976.

Burkhardt, E. Walter, and Varian. *Alabama Antebellum Architecture*. Alabama Historical Commission. Montgomery, 1976.

Christovich, Mary Louise; Toledano, Roulhac; et al. *New Orleans Architecture. 2: The American Sector*. Gretna, La., 1972.

Crocker, Mary Wallace. *Historical Architecture in Mississippi*. Jackson, 1973.

Cullison, William R., III. *Historic Mississippi Delta Architecture*. Louisiana Landmarks Society. New Orleans, 1978.

Dardis, George. *Description of the State Capitol of Tennessee*. Nashville, 1854.

Dorsey, Stephen P. *English Churches in America*. New York, 1952.

Gallagher, H. M. Pierce. *Robert Mills, Architect of the Washington Monument, 1781–1855*. New York, 1935.

Gallier, James. *Autobiography*. Paris, 1864; reprint ed., New York, 1973.

Gowans, Alan. *King Carter's Church*. University of Victoria Maltwood Museum, Studies in Architectural History Number Two. Victoria, B.C., 1969.

Hammond, Ralph. *Ante-Bellum Mansions of Alabama*. New York, 1951.

Hitchcock, Henry-Russell, and Seale, William. *Temples of Democracy, The State Capitols of the USA*. New York, 1976.

Howland, Richard Hubbard, and Spencer, Eleanor Patterson. *Architecture of Baltimore*. Baltimore, 1953.

Kalman, Harold, and De Visser, John. *Pioneer Churches*. New York, 1976.

Lancaster, Clay. *Ante-Bellum Houses of the Bluegrass*. Lexington, 1961.

Lilly, Edward G., ed., and Legerton, Clifford L. *Historic Churches of Charleston*. Charleston, 1966.

Linley, John. *The Georgia Catalog, Historic American Building Survey*. Athens, 1982.

Manucy, Albert. *The Houses of St. Augustine, 1565–1821*. St. Augustine Historical Society. St. Augustine, 1962.

Mason, George Carrington. *Colonial Churches in Tidewater Virginia*. Richmond, 1945.

Masson, Ann M., and Owen, Lydia J. *Cast Iron and the Crescent City*. Gallier House. New Orleans, 1975.

McAdams, Ina May Ogletree. *The Building of Longwood*. Austin, 1972.

McClure, Harlan, and Hodges, Vernon. *South Carolina Architecture, 1670–1970*. Clemson Architectural Foundation and the Columbia Museum of Art. Columbia, 1970.

Mills, Robert. *Statistics of South Carolina, Including a View of Its Natural, Civil, and Military History, General and Particular*. Charleston, 1826.

Nichols, F. D. *The Early Architecture of Georgia*. Chapel Hill, 1957.

————. *The Architecture of Georgia*. Rev. ed. Savannah, 1976.

Patrick, James. *Architecture in Tennessee, 1768–1897*. Knoxville, 1981.

Ravenel, Beatrice St. Julian. *Architects of Charleston*. Charleston, 1945.

Rawlings, James Scott. *Virginia's Colonial Churches*. Richmond, 1963.

Ricciuti, Italo William. *New Orleans and Its Environs, The Domestic Architecture, 1727–1870*. New York, 1938.

Rose, Harold Wickliffe. *The Colonial Houses of Worship in America*. New York, 1963.

Scully, Arthur, Jr. *James Dakin, Architect, His Career in New York and the South*. Baton Rouge, 1973.

Severens, Kenneth. *Southern Architecture: 350 Years of Distinctive American Buildings*. New York, 1981.

Smith, J. Frazer. *White Pillars: Early Life and Architecture of the Lower Mississippi Valley Country*. New York, 1941.

Swaim, Doug, ed. *Carolina Dwelling. Towards Preservation of Place: In Celebration of the North Carolina Vernacular Landscape*. Student Publication of the School of Design, *26*, North Carolina State University. Raleigh, 1978.

Upjohn, Everard M. *Richard Upjohn, Architect and Churchman*. New York, 1939.

Waterman, Thomas Tileston, and Johnston, F. B. *The Early Architecture of North Carolina*. Chapel Hill, 1941.

Weslager, C. A. *The Log Cabin in America*. New Brunswick, N. J., 1969.

Whiffen, Marcus. *The Eighteenth-Century Houses of Williamsburg*. Williamsburg, 1960.

————. *The Public Buildings of Colonial Williamsburg*. Williamsburg, 1958.

Whitfield, Jesse G. *Gaineswood and Other Memories*. Demopolis, Ala., n.d.

Wilson, Samuel, Jr. *Bienville's New Orleans, A French Colonial Capital, 1718–1768*. Friends of the Cabildo. New Orleans, 1968.

————, ed. *Impressions Respecting New Orleans by Benjamin Henry Boneval Latrobe*. New York, 1951.

————, and Huber, Leonard V. *The Cabildo on Jackson Square*. New Orleans, 1970.
————, and Ross, Marion Dean. *James Gallier, Architect, An Exhibition of His Work*. New Orleans, 1950.
————; Toledano, Roulhac; Evans, Sally Kittredge; and Christovich, Mary Louise. *New Orleans Architecture. 4: The Creole Faubourgs*. Gretna, La., 1974.

Articles, Dissertations, and Theses

Allen, Ward. "Cragfont, Grandeur on the Tennessee Frontier." *Tennessee Historical Quarterly*, *23* (June 1964), 103–120.

Banks, William Nathaniel. "The Architectural Legacy of Daniel Pratt." *Papers of Athens Historical Society*, *2* (Athens, Ga.,1979), 52–62.
————. "The River Road plantations of Louisiana." *Antiques*, *111* (June 1977), 1170–1183.
Beeson, Leola Selman. "The Old State Capitol at Milledgeville and Its Cost." *Georgia Historical Quarterly*, *34* (Sept. 1950), 195–202.
Betjeman, John. "Nonconformist Architecture." *The Architectural Review*, *88* (Dec. 1940), 161–174.
Bienvenu, James Robert. "Two Greek Revival Hotels in New Orleans, the St. Charles by James Gallier, Sr., and the St. Louis by J. N. B. and J. I. De Pouilly." M. A. thesis, Tulane University, 1961.
Binney, Marcus. "Virginia Country Churches." *Country Life* (London), *162* (April 27, 1978), 1138–1140.
Bonner, James C. "Plantation Architecture of the Lower South on the Eve of the Civil War." *Journal of Southern History*, *11* (1945), 370–388.
Breine, Rosamond Randall. "The Chase House in Maryland." *Maryland Historical Magazine*, *49* (Sept. 1954), 177–195.
Buchanan, Paul E. "The Eighteenth-Century Frame House of Tidewater Virginia." In *Building Early America*, edited by Charles E. Peterson, 54–73. Radnor, Pa., 1976.

Carson, Cary. "The Virginia House in Maryland." *Maryland Historical Magazine*, *69* (Summer 1974), 185–196.
————; Barka, Norman F.; Kelso, William M.; Stone, Gary Wheeler; and Upton, Dell. "Impermanent Architecture in the Southern American Colonies." *Winterthur Portfolio*, *16* (Summer/Autumn 1981), 135–196.
Caywood, Louis R. "Green Spring Plantation." *Virginia Magazine of History and Biography*, *65* (Jan. 1957), 67–83.
Connally, Ernest Allen. "Architecture at the End of the South: Central Texas." *Journal of the Society of Architectural Historians*, *11* (Dec. 1952), 8–12.
Crocker, Leslie Frank. "Domestic Architecture of the Middle South, 1795–1865." Diss., University of Missouri, Columbia, 1971. University Microfilms, Ann Arbor.

Dekle, Clayton B. "The Tennessee State Capitol." *Tennessee Historical Quarterly*, *25* (Fall 1966), 213–238.
Dornsife, Samuel J. "San Francisco Plantation House, An Exercise in Restoration." *Connoisseur*, *197* (April 1978), 275–282.
Dufour, Charles L. "Henry Howard: Forgotten Architect." *Journal of the Society of Architectural Historians*, *11* (Dec. 1952), 21–24.

Field, Elizabeth S. "Gideon Shryock, His Life and Work." *Kentucky State Historical Society Register*, *50* (April 1952), 117–118.
Floyd, William Barrow. "The restored Old Capitol, Frankfort, Kentucky." *Antiques*, *114* (July 1978), 108–116.

Gowans, Alan. Reply to Marcus Whiffen's review of his *King Carter's Church*. *Journal of the Society of Architectural Historians*, *29* (Dec. 1970), 363–364.

Hardin, Bayless E. "The Capitols of Kentucky." *Kentucky State Historical Society Register*, *43* (July 1845), 183.
Hayward, Mary Ellen. "Urban Vernacular Architecture in Nineteenth-Century Baltimore." *Winterthur Portfolio*, *16* (Spring 1981), 33–63.
Hutchinson, Albert W. "Domestic architecture in Middle Tennessee." *Antiques*, *100* (Sept. 1971), 402–407.

Ingate, Margaret Rose. "History in towns: Mobile, Alabama." *Antiques*, *85* (March 1964), 294–309.

Jones, Edward V. "The Owens-Thomas House." *Antiques*, *91* (March 1967), 341–346.

Krotzer, Henry W., Jr. "The restoration of San Francisco (St. Frusquin), Reserve, Louisiana." *Antiques*, *111* (June 1977), 1194–1203.

Lancaster, Clay. "Gideon Shryock and John McMurty, Architect and Builder of Kentucky." *Art Quarterly*, *6* (Autumn 1943), 257–275.

Mahoney, Nell Savage. "William Strickland and the Building of Tennessee's Capitol, 1845–1854." *Tennessee Historical Quarterly*, *4* (June 1945), 99–153.
Matlock, Carol. "Eufaula." *American Preservation* (Oct.–Nov. 1978), 9–21.
McCrady, Edward. "An Historic Church, The Westminster Abbey of South Carolina." *Year Book, City of Charleston, 1896*. Charleston, 1896, 319–374.
McGehee, Milly. "Auburn in Natchez." *Antiques*, *111* (March 1977), 546–553.
————. "Levi Weeks, Early Nineteenth-Century Architect." M. A. thesis, University of Delaware, 1975.
Miller, Ronald W. "Historic preservation in Natchez, Mississippi." *Antiques*, *111* (March 1977), 538–545.
Moore, Mrs. John Trotwood. "The Tennessee State Library in the Capitol." *Tennessee Historical Quarterly*, *12* (March 1953), 8–11.
Murfee, Patty T. "History in towns: Columbus, Mississippi." *Antiques*, *100* (Dec. 1971), 914–918.
Murtagh, William J. "The architecture of Salem." *Antiques*, *88* (July 1963), 69–76.

Nichols, Frederic D. "Drayton Hall, plantation house of the Drayton family." *Antiques*, *97* (April 1970), 576–578.

Olcott, Lois T. "Public architecture of Kentucky before 1870." *Antiques*, *105* (April 1974), 830–839.

Patrick, James. "Ecclesiological Gothic in the Antebellum South." *Winterthur Portfolio*, *15* (Summer 1980), 117–138.
Peters, Martha Ann. "The St. Charles Hotel: New

Orleans Social Center, 1837–1860." *Louisiana History*, *1* (Summer 1960), 191–211.

Raley, Robert S. "Daniel Pratt, architect and builder." *Antiques*, *102* (Sept. 1972), 425–433.
————. "Early Maryland Plasterwork and Stuccowork." *Journal of the Society of Architectural Historians*, *20* (Oct. 1961), 131–135.
Roth, Rodris. "Interior Decoration of City Houses in Baltimore: The Federal Period." *Winterthur Portfolio*, *5* (1969), 59–86.

Simon, Albert. "Architectural trends in Charleston." *Antiques*, *97* (April 1979), 40–44.
Smith, Joel P. "History in towns: Eufaula, Alabama." *Antiques*, *114* (Sept. 1978), 520–527.
Smith, Winston, and Turner, Gwyn Collins. "History in towns: Demopolis, Alabama." *Antiques*, *117* (Feb. 1980), 402–413.
Spencer, William M. "St. Andrew's Church, Prairieville." Reprinted with additions from *The Alabama Review* (Jan. 1961).

Tatum, George B. "Great houses from the golden age of Annapolis." *Antiques*, *111* (Jan. 1977) 174–193.
"The Story of Gaineswood." *House and Garden* (Nov. 1939), 41–44.
Thomas, James C. "Micajah Burnett and the buildings of Pleasant Hill." *Antiques*, *98* (Oct. 1970), 600–605.
————. "The log houses of Kentucky." *Antiques*, *105* (April 1974), 791–798.
Thomas, W. J. Johnson. "Seven great Charleston houses." *Antiques*, *97* (April 1970), 556–570.
"Tullie Smith House, Progress Report." *The Atlanta Historical Society Newsletter* (April 1971).

Upton, Charles W. "The Shaker Utopia." *Antiques*, *98* (Oct. 1970), 582–587.
Upton, Dell. "Early Vernacular Architecture in Southeastern Virginia." Diss., Brown University, 1980.
————. "Vernacular Domestic Architecture in Eighteenth-Century Virginia." *Winterthur Portfolio*, *17* (Summer/Autumn 1982) 95–119.

Waddell, Gene. "Robert Mills' Fireproof Building." *South Carolina Historical Magazine*, *80* (April 1979) 105–135.
————. "The Charleston Single House, An Architectural Survey." *Preservation Progress*, Preservation Society of Charleston, *22* (March 1977), 4–7.
Whiffen, Marcus. Review of *King Carter's Church*, by Alan Gowans. *Journal of the Society of Architectural Historians*, *29* (May 1970).
Wilson, Samuel, Jr. "An Architectural History of the Royal Hospital and the Ursuline Convent of New Orleans." *Louisiana Historical Quarterly*, *29* (July 1946), 3–103.
————. "Architecture in Eighteenth-Century West Florida." In *Eighteenth-Century Florida and Its Borderlands*, edited by Sameul Proctor, 102–139. Gainesville, 1975.
————. "Destrehan Plantation, St. Charles Parish." *The Louisiana Architect*, *8* (March 1969), 8–9.
————. "The Pentagon Barracks, 1825." *The Louisiana Architect*, *4* (Nov. 1964), 9–10.
Wooley, Carolyn Murray. "Kentucky's early stone houses." *Antiques*, *105* (March. 1974), 592–602.

Young, Dwight S. "Historic preservation in Mobile." *Antiques*, *112* (Sept. 1977), 460–465.

Zelinsky, Wilbur. "The Greek Revival House in Georgia." *Journal of the Society of Architectural Historians, 13* (May 1954), 9–12.

PAINTING AND DRAWING

Books and Exhibition Catalogues

Adams, William Howard. *The Eye of Th. Jefferson.* National Gallery of Art. Washington, D.C., 1976.

Audubon, John James. *Audubon and His Journals.* Edited by Marie R. Audubon. Notes by Elliott Coues. 2 vols. New York, 1897; reprint ed., 1962.

Biddle, Edward, and Fielding, Mantle. *The Life and Works of Thomas Sully.* Philadelphia, 1921.

Bilodeau, Francis W., and Tobias, Mrs. Thomas J., comps. and eds., and Burton, E. Milby. *Art in South Carolina, 1670–1970.* Carolina Art Association. Charleston, 1970.

Boles, John B., ed. *Maryland Heritage: Five Baltimore Institutions Celebrate the American Bicentennial.* Maryland Historical Society. Baltimore, 1976.

Bolton-Smith, Robin. *Portrait Miniatures from Private Collections.* National Collection of Fine Arts, Smithsonian Institution. Washington, D.C., 1976.

Bright, Marion Converse, comp. *Early Georgia Portraits, 1715–1870.* National Society of the Colonial Dames of America in the State of Georgia. Athens, 1975.

Bruns, Mrs. Thomas Nelson, and Jordan, George, comps. *Louisiana Portraits.* National Society of the Colonial Dames of America. New Orleans, 1975.

Bushnell, David I. *Drawings by A. De Batz.* Smithsonian Miscellaneous Collections, *80,* no. 5., 1928.

Campbell, William P. *John Gadsby Chapman.* National Gallery of Art. Washington, D.C., 1962.

Carter, Edward C., ed. *The Virginia Journals of Benjamin Henry Latrobe, 1795–1798.* 2 vols. Maryland Historical Society. New Haven, 1977.

Catesby, Mark. *The Natural History of Carolina, Florida and the Bahama Islands.* 2 vols. London, 1754.

Catlin, George. *North American Indians, Being Letters and Notes on Their Manners, Customs and Conditions.* 2 vols. London, 1841; reprint ed., Edinburgh, 1926.

City Art Museum of St. Louis. *Mississippi Panorama.* Cat. H. Stewart Leonard. St. Louis, 1949.

Coleman, J. Winston, Jr. *Edward Troye, Animal and Portrait Painter.* Lexington, 1958.

Colwill, Stiles Tuttle. *Francis Guy, 1760–1820.* Museum and Library of Maryland History. Baltimore, 1981.

Corning, Howard, ed. *Journal of John James Audubon Made During His Trip to New Orleans in 1820–1821.* Boston, 1929.

Craig, James H. *The Arts and Crafts in North Carolina.* Winston-Salem, 1965.

Crowe, Eyre. *With Thackeray in America.* London, 1893.

Davidson, Marshall B. *The Original Water-Color Paintings by John James Audubon for The Birds of America.* New-York Historical Society. New York, 1966.

Driskell, David C. *Two Centuries of Black American Art.* Los Angeles County Museum of Art. New York, 1976.

Eby, Cecil D., Jr. *"Porte Crayon": The Life of David Hunter Strother.* Chapel Hill, 1960.

Ewan, Joseph, intro. and ed. *William Bartram, Botanical and Zoological Drawings, 1756–1788.* Philadelphia, 1968.

Ewers, John C. *George Catlin: Painter of Indians of the West.* Reprinted from the Annual Report of the Smithsonian Institution, 1955.

Fagin, N. Bayllion. *William Bartram, Interpreter of American Landscape.* Baltimore, 1933.

Farwell, Lynne W. *John Joseph Vaudechamp.* Louisiana State Museum. New Orleans, 1976.

Floyd, William Barrow. *Matthew Harris Jouett, Portraitist of the Ante-Bellum South.* Transylvania University. Lexington, 1980.

Ford, Alice. *John James Audubon.* Norman, Okla. 1964.

Fraser, Charles. *My Reminiscences of Charleston.* Charleston, 1854; reprint ed., 1969.

Frick, George Frederick, and Stearns, Raymond Phineas. *Mark Catesby, The Colonial Audubon.* Urbana, 1961.

Fundaburk, Emma Lila. *Southeastern Indians, Life Portraits, A Catalogue of Pictures, 1564–1860.* Luverne, Ala., 1957.

Harter, John Burton, and Tucker, Mary Louise. *The Louisiana Portrait Gallery. 1: to 1870.* Louisiana State Museum. New Orleans, 1979.

Hennig, Helen. *William Harrison Scarborough, Portraitist and Miniaturist.* Columbia, 1937.

Hérard, Madeleine. *Contribution à l'étude de l'émigration de Charles-Balthazar-Julien Fevret de Saint-Mémin aux États-Unis de 1793 à 1814.* Dijon, 1970.

Herrick, Francis Hobard. *Audubon the Naturalist.* New York, 1917; reprint ed., 1968, *1.*

Hood, Graham. *Charles Bridges and William Dering, Two Virginia Painters, 1735–1750.* Williamsburg and Charlottesville, 1978.

Huidt, Kristian. *Von Reck's Voyage, Views of Georgia in 1736.* Savannah, 1980.

Hulton, Paul, and Quinn, David Beers. *The American Drawings of John White, 1577–1590, with Drawings of European and Oriental Subjects.* London and Chapel Hill, 1964.

Jones, Arthur F., and Weber, Bruce. *The Kentucky Painter from the Frontier Era to the Great War.* University of Kentucky Art Museum. Lexington, 1981.

Lay, Mrs. Orville, comp. *Alabama Portraits Prior to 1870.* National Society of Colonial Dames of America. Mobile, 1969.

Lorant, Stefan, ed. *The New World, The First Pictures of America Made by John White and Jacques Le Moyne and Engraved by Theodore De Bry.* New York, 1946.

Mackay-Smith, Alexander. *The Race Horses of America, 1832–1872: Portraits and Other Paintings by Edward Troye.* National Museum of Racing. Saratoga Springs, 1981.

McCormack, Helen G. *William James Hubard, 1807–1862.* Valentine Museum and Virginia Museum of Fine Arts. Richmond, 1948.

McDermott, John Francis. *The Lost Panoramas of the Mississippi.* Chicago, 1958.

Middleton, Margaret Simons. *Jeremiah Theus, Colonial Artist of Charles Town.* Columbia, 1953.

Norfleet, Filmore. *Saint-Mémin in Virginia.* Richmond, 1942.

North Carolina Museum of Art. *Two Hundred Years of the Visual Arts in North Carolina.* Raleigh, 1976.

O'Neal, William B. *Primitive into Painter, Life and Letters of John Toole.* Charlottesville, 1960.

Pinckney, Pauline A. *Painting in Texas.* Austin, 1967.

Price, S. W. *The Old Masters of the Bluegrass.* Louisville, 1902.

R. V. Norton Gallery. *Louisiana Landscape and Genre Painting of the 19th Century.* Shreveport, 1981.

Reynolds, Elizabeth P. *To Live upon Canvas, The Portrait Art of Thomas Cantwell Healy.* Mississippi Museum of Art. Jackson, 1980.

Richards, William C., ed. *Georgia Illustrated.* Penfield, Ga., 1842.

Rutledge, Anna Wells. *Artists in the Life of Charleston.* Transactions of the American Philosophical Society, N.S., *39,* Part 2. Philadelphia, 1949.

Sellers, Charles Coleman. *Charles Willson Peale with Patron and Populace.* Transactions of the American Philosophical Society. N.S., *59.* Philadelphia, 1969.

———. *Portraits and Miniatures by Charles Willson Peale.* Transactions of the American Philosophical Society. N.S., *42.* Philadelphia, 1952.

Semmes, John E. *John H. B. Latrobe and His Times, 1803–1891.* Baltimore, 1917.

Severens, Martha R. *Selections from the Collection of the Carolina Art Association.* Charleston, 1977.

Simmons, Linda Crocker. *Charles Peale Polk, 1767–1822: A Limner and His Likenesses.* Corcoran Gallery of Art. Washington, D.C., 1981.

———. *Jacob Frymire, American Limner.* Corcoran Gallery of Art. Washington, D.C., 1975.

Smith, Alice R. Huger, intro. *A Charleston Sketchbook, 1767–1806, by Charles Fraser.* Charleston, 1971.

———, and Smith, D. E. Huger. *Charles Fraser.* Charleston, 1924.

Stewart, Robert G. *Henry Benbridge (1743–1812), American Portrait Painter.* National Portrait Gallery. Washington, D.C. 1971.

Truettner, William H. *The Natural Man Observed: A Study of Catlin's Indian Gallery.* Washington, D.C., 1979.

Williams, Ben F. *Jacob Marling, Early North Carolina Artist.* North Carolina Museum of Art. Raleigh, 1964.

Articles, Dissertations and Thesis

Abney, Beth. "George Cooke and the Chapel Painting." *Athens Historical Society Papers, 2* (1979), 62–73.

Banks, William Nathaniel. "George Cooke, painter of the American scene." *Antiques, 102* (Sept. 1972), 449–454.

Batson,, Whaley. "Thomas Coram: Charleston Artist." *Journal of Early Southern Decorative Arts, 1* (Nov. 1975), 35–47.

Bauer, John I. H. " '. . . the exact brushwork of Mr. David Johnson,' An American Landscape Painter, 1827–1908." *American Art Journal, 12* (Autumn 1980), 32–65.

Bishop, Budd H. "Art in Tennessee: The Early 19th Century." *Tennessee Historical Quarterly, 29* (Winter 1970–1971), 379–389.

———. "Three Tennessee painters: Samuel M. Shaver, Washington B. Cooper, and James Cameron." *Antiques*, 100 (Sept. 1971), 432–437.

Black, Mary. "Contributions Toward a History of Early Eighteenth-Century New York Portraiture: Identification of the Aetatis Suae and Wendell Limners." *American Art Journal*, 12 (Autumn 1980), 4–31.

———. "The Case of the Red and Green Birds." *Arts in Virginia*, 3 (Winter 1963), 3–9.

———. "The Case Reviewed." *Arts in Virginia*, 10 (Fall 1969), 12–21.

Bolton, Theodore, and Binsse, Harry Lorin. "Wollaston, An Early American Portrait Manufacturer." *The Antiquarian*, 16 (June 1931), 30–33, 50–52.

Bridwell, Margaret M. "Oliver Frazer, early Kentucky portrait painter." *Antiques*, 12 (Nov. 1967), 718–721.

Chamberlain, Georgia S. "John Gadsby Chapman, Painter of Virginia." *Art Quarterly*, 24 (Winter 1961), 378–390.

Coleman, J. Winston, Jr. "Edward Troye, sporting artist." *Antiques*, 105 (April 1974), 799–805.

Cooke, George. "The Fine Arts, No. III." *Southern Literary Magazine*, 1 (May 1835), 477–478.

Dods, Agnes M. "Nathan and Joseph Negus, itinerant painters." *Antiques*, 76 (Nov. 1959), 434–437.

Doud, Richard K. "John Hesselius: His Life and Work." M.A. thesis, University of Delaware, 1963.

———. "John Hesselius, Maryland Limner." *Winterthur Portfolio*, 5 (1969), 129–153.

———. "The Fitzhugh Portraits of John Hesselius." *Virginia Magazine of History and Biography*, 75 (April 1967), 159–175.

Ewers, Joseph C. "An Anthropologist Looks at Early Pictures of North American Indians." *New-York Historical Society Quarterly*, 32 (Oct. 1934), 223–225.

Farwell, Lynne W. "John Joseph Vaudechamp and New Orleans." *Antiques*, 94 (Sept. 1968), 371–375.

Fehl, Philipp B. "Thomas Sully's *Washington's Passage of the Delaware*: The History of a Commission." *Art Bulletin*, 55 (Dec. 1973), 584–599.

Floyd, Wiliam Barrow. "Portraits of ante-bellum Kentuckians." *Antiques*, 105 (April 1974), 808–817.

Foote, Henry Wilder. "Charles Bridges: Sergeant-Painter of Virginia." *Virginia Magazine of History and Biography*, 60 (Jan. 1952), 3–55.

Griffith, Louis T. "T. Addison Richards, Georgia Scenes by a Nineteenth Century Artist and Tourist." *Bulletin of Georgia Museum of Art* (University of Georgia, Athens), 1 (Fall 1974), 9–16.

Groce, George C. "John Wollaston (fl. 1736–1767): A Cosmopolitan Painter in the British Colonies." *Art Quarterly*, 15 (Summer 1952), 133–140.

Horton, Frank L. "America's Earliest Woman Miniaturist." *Journal of Early Southern Decorative Arts*, 5 (Nov. 1979), 1–5.

Johnston, Sona K. "American Painting of the Revolutionary Period." In *Maryland Heritage*, edited by John B. Boles, 55–95. Baltimore, 1976.

Mac Beth, Jerome R. "Portraits by Ralph E. W. Earl." *Antiques*, 100 (Sept. 1971), 390–393.

Ott, Ethelbert Nelson. "William D. Washington (1833–1870), Artist of the South." M.A. thesis, University of Delaware, 1968.

Page, Jean Jepson. "Francis Blackwell Mayer." *Antiques*, 109 (Feb. 1976), 316–323.

P. H. S. "A Painting of Oakland." *The J. B. Speed Art Museum Bulletin*, 18 (Louisville, 1957), n.p.

Pleasants, J. Hall. "Four Late Eighteenth Century Anglo-American Landscape Painters." *Proceedings of the American Antiquarian Society*, 52 (1943), 186–324.

———. "Joshua Johnston, The First American Negro Portrait Painter." *Maryland Historical Magazine*, 37 (June 1942), 121–149.

———. "Justus Engelhardt Kühn, An Early Eighteenth Century Maryland Portrait Painter." *Proceedings of the American Antiquarian Society*, 46 (Oct. 1936), 243–280.

———. "William Dering, A Mid-Eighteenth Century Williamsburg Portrait Painter." *Virginia Magazine of History and Biography*, 60 (Jan. 1960), 53–63.

Richardson, E. P. "Gustavius Hesselius." *Art Quarterly*, 12 (Summer 1949), 220–226.

Rudulph, Marilou Alston. "George Cooke and His Paintings." *Georgia Historical Quarterly*, 44 (June 1960), 117–153.

Rutledge, Anna Wells. "Charleston's first artistic couple." *Antiques*, 52 (Aug. 1947), 100–102.

———. "One Early American's Precocious Taste." *Art News*, 98 (March 1949), 28–29, 51.

———. "William Henry Brown of Charleston." *Antiques*, 60 (Dec. 1951), 532–533.

Severens, Martha R. "Charles Fraser of Charleston," *Antiques*, 123 (March 1983), 606–611.

Staits, Paul. "Samuel F. B. Morse in Charleston, 1818–1821." *South Carolina Historical Magazine*, 79 (April 1978), 87–112.

Symonds, Susan Clover. "Portraits of Andrew Jackson, 1815–1845." M.A. thesis, University of Delaware, 1968.

Thorne, Thomas. "Charles Bridges, Limner." *Arts in Virginia*, 9 (Winter 1969), 22–31.

Tolman, Ruel P. "The technique of Charles Fraser, miniaturist." *Antiques*, 27 (Jan. 1935), 19–22.

Tucker, Mary Louise. "Jacques Amans, Portrait Painter in Louisiana, 1836–1856." M.A. thesis, Tulane University, 1970.

Weekley, Carolyn J. "Further Notes on William Dering, Colonial Virginia Portrait Painter." *Journal of Early Southern Decorative Arts*, 1 (May 1975), 21–28.

———. "John Wollaston, Portrait Painter: His Career in Virginia, 1754–1758." M.A. thesis, University of Delaware, June 1976.

Weidner, Paul R., ed. "The Journal of John Blake White." *The South Carolina Historical and Genealogical Magazine*, 42 (1941), 55–71, 99–117, 169–185; 43 (1942), 35–46, 103–117, 161–174.

Wilson, Samuel, Jr. "Louisiana Drawings by Alexandre De Batz." *Journal of the Society of Architectural Historians*, 22 (May 1963), 75–89.

PHOTOGRAPHY

Books

Fulton, John. *Memories of Frederick A. P. Barnard*. New York, 1896.

Smith, Margaret Denton, and Tucker, Mary Louise. *Photography in New Orleans, The Early Years, 1840–1865*. Baton Rouge and London, 1982.

Taft, Robert. *Photography and the American Scene*. New York, 1938; reprint ed., 1964.

Articles and Theses

Smith, Margaret Denton. "Photography in New Orleans, 1840–1865." M.A. thesis, Tulane University, 1977.

Stashin, Leo. "Portraits of notable nineteenth-century Americans in daguerreotype." *Antiques*, 103 (April 1973), 784–800.

SCULPTURE

Books

Crane, Sylvia E. *White Silence*. Florida, 1972.

Craven, Wayne. *Sculpture in America*. New York, 1968.

Gerdts, William H. *American Neo-Classic Sculpture*. New York, 1973.

Huber, Leonard V. *Clasped Hands. Symbolism in New Orleans Cemeteries*. Lafayette, 1982.

Articles

Armstrong, Tom. "The Innocent Eye, American Folk Sculpture." In Whitney Museum of Art, *200 Years of American Sculpture* (New York, 1976), 75–111.

Bacot, H. Parrott, and Lambdin, Bethany B. "Edwin Lyon, an Anglo-American sculptor in the lower Mississippi River valley." *Antiques*. 111 (March 1977), 554–557.

Brenner, J. Francis, Jr. "Master Ironworkers Came to Practice Art in City." Charleston *Courier*, August 21, 1932 (10B).

Bridaham, Lester Burbank. "Pierre Joseph Landry." *Antiques*, 72 (Aug. 1957). 157–159.

Cheney, Louis T. "The Telfair and its paintings." *Antiques*, 91 (March 1967), 353–360.

Desportes, Ulysse. "Giuseppe Ceracchi in America and His Busts of George Washington." *Art Quarterly*, 26 (Summer 1963), 141–179.

Hallam, John S. "Houdon's *Washington* in Richmond: Some New Observations." *American Art Journal*, 10 (Nov. 1978), 72–80.

Hershey, Constance Vecchione. "Mortuary art in Charleston churches." *Antiques, 98* (Nov. 1970), 800–807.

Ravenel, Beatrice St. J. "Here lies buried, taste and trade in Charleston tombstones." *Antiques, 41* (March 1942), 193–195.
Rutledge, Anna Wells. "Cogdell and Mills, Charleston sculptors." *Antiques, 41* (March 1942), 192–193, 205–208.

PRODUCTS OF CRAFTSMEN

Books and Exhibition Catalogues

Bacot, H. Parrott. *Southern Furniture and Silver, The Federal Period, 1788–1830.* Anglo-American Art Museum. Baton Rouge, 1968.
Baltimore Furniture. The Work of Baltimore and Annapolis Cabinetmakers from 1760 to 1810. Baltimore Museum of Art. Baltimore, 1947.
Burroughs, Paul H. *Southern Antiques.* Richmond, 1935.
Burton, E. Milby. *Charleston Furniture, 1700–1825.* Columbia, 1955.
———. *South Carolina Silversmiths, 1690–1860.* Rutland, 1968.

Craig, James H. *The Arts and Crafts in North Carolina, 1699–1840.* Winston-Salem, 1965.
Cutten, George Barton. *The Silversmiths of Georgia.* Savannah, 1958.

Ferrell, Stephen T. *Early Decorated Stoneware of the Edgefield District, South Carolina.* Greenville County Museum of Art. Greenville, 1976.

Green, Henry D. *Furniture of the Georgia Piedmont Before 1830.* High Museum of Art. Atlanta, 1976.
Gusler, Wallace. *Furniture of Williamsburg and Eastern Virginia, 1710–1790.* Richmond, 1979.

Holden, Jack, and Smith, Robert E. *Louisiana French Furnishings, 1700–1830.* Art Center for Southwestern Louisiana. Lafayette, 1974.
Horton, Frank L., and Weekley, Carolyn J., *The Swisegood School of Cabinetmaking.* Museum of Early Southern Decorative Arts. Winston-Salem, 1973.
Hume, Ivor Noël. *Williamsburg Cabinetmakers: The Archaeological Evidence.* Colonial Williamsburg Foundation. Williamsburg, 1971.

J. B. Speed Art Museum. *Kentucky Furniture.* Louisville, 1974.

Mackie, Cary T.; Bacot, H. Parrot; and Mackie, Charles L. *Crescent City Silver.* Historic New Orleans Collection, and Anglo-American Museum. New Orleans, 1980.
Mint Museum of History. *Potters of the Catawba Valley.* Charlotte, 1980.

North Carolina Museum of History. *Thomas Day, Cabinetmaker.* Raleigh, 1975.

Otto, Celia Jackson. *American Furniture of the Nineteenth Century.* New York, 1965.

Poesch, Jessie J. *Early Furniture of Louisiana.* Louisiana State Museum. New Orleans, 1972.

Swain, Susan Burrow. *Plain & Fancy, American Women and Their Needlework, 1700–1850.* New York, 1977.

Taylor, Lonn, and Warren, David B. *Texas Furniture, The Cabinetmakers and Their Work, 1840–1880.* Austin, 1975.
Theus, Mrs. Charlton M. *Savannah Furniture, 1735–1825.* Savannah, 1967.

Vlach, Michael. *The Afro-American Tradition in Decorative Arts.* Cleveland Museum of Art. Cleveland, 1978.

Warren, David B. *Southern Silver.* Museum of Fine Arts. Houston, 1968.
Whitley, Edna Talbott. *A Checklist of Kentucky Cabinetmakers from 1775 to 1859.* Paris, Ky., 1969.
Winters, Robert E., Jr., *North Carolina Furniture, 1700–1900.* Raleigh, 1977.
Wust, Klaus. *Virginia Fraktur: Penmanship As Folk Art.* Shenandoah History. Edinburg, Va., 1972.

Articles, Dissertations, and Theses

Albright, Frank P. "The crafts at Salem." *Antiques, 88* (July 1965), 94–97.
Antiques, 61 (Jan. 1952), *30th Anniversary Edition Featuring Furniture of the Old South, 1640–1820* (entire issue).

Barr, Lockwood. "Kentucky silver and its makers." *Antiques, 48* (July 1945), 25–27.
Bartlett, Lu. "John Shaw, cabinetmaker of Annapolis." *Antiques, 111* (Feb. 1977), 362–377.
Batson, Whaley. "Charles Peale Polk: Gold Profiles on Glass." *Journal of Early Southern Decorative Arts, 3* (Nov. 1977), 51–57.
Bear, James A., Jr. "Thomas Jefferson's silver." *Antiques, 74* (Sept. 1958), 233–236.
Beckerdite, Luke. "William Buckland and William Bernard Sears: The Designer and the Carver." *Journal of Early Southern Decorative Arts, 8* (Nov. 1982), 6–40.
———. "William Buckland Reconsidered: Architectural Carving in Chesapeake Maryland, 1771–1774." *Journal of Early Southern Decorative Arts, 8* (Nov. 1982), 42–88.
Bivins, John, Jr. "A piedmont North Carolina cabinetmaker: The development of a regional style." *Antiques, 103* (May 1973), 968–973.
———. "An Introduction to the Decorative Arts of North Carolina, 1776–1976." In *200 Years of the Visual Arts in North Carolina.* North Carolina Museum of Art. Raleigh, 1976, 124.
———. "Fraktur in the South: An Itinerant Artist." *Journal of Early Southern Decorative Arts, 1* (Nov. 1975), 1–23.
Bridwell, Margaret M. "Asa Blanchard, early Kentucky silversmith." *Antiques, 37* (March 1940), 135–136.
———. "Kentucky Silversmiths Before 1850." *The Filson Club History Quarterly, 16* (1942), 111–125.
Burrison, John A. "Alkaline-Glazed Stoneware: A Deep-South Pottery Tradition." *Southern Folklore Quarterly, 39* (Dec. 1975), 377–403.

Burton, E. Milby. "Charleston furniture." *Antiques, 97* (June 1970), 910–914.

Caldwell, Benjamin H., Jr. "Tennessee silversmiths." *Antiques, 100* (Sept. 1971), 382–385.
Comstock, Helen. "Furniture of Virginia, North Carolina, Georgia and Kentucky." *Antiques, 61* (Jan. 1952), 62–64.
Craig, James. "The 1840 North Carolina capitol and its furniture." *Antiques, 88* (Aug. 1965), 205–207.

Dahill, Betty. "The Sharrock Family, A Newly Discovered School of Cabinetmakers." *Journal of Early Southern Decorative Arts, 2* (Nov. 1976). 37–51.
Dibble, Ann W. "Fredericksburg-Falmouth Chairs in the Chippendale Style." *Journal of the Early Southern Decorative Arts, 5* (May 1978) 1–24.
Dockstader, Mary Rolls. "Sugar chests." *Antiques, 25* (April 1934), 140–143.
Durbin, Louise. "Samuel Kirk, nineteenth-century silversmith." *Antiques, 94* (Dec. 1968), 868–873.

Elder, William Voss, III. "American Decorative Arts of the Revolutionary Period." *Maryland Heritage.* (Baltimore, 1976), 97–123.
———. "Maryland furniture, 1760–1840." *Antiques, 111* (Feb. 1977), 354–361.

Floyd, William Barrow. "Kentucky coin-silver pitchers." *Antiques. 105.* (March 1974), 55–580.

Golovin, Anne Castrodale. "Cabinetmakers and chairmakers of Washington, D.C., 1791–1840." *Antiques, 107* (May 1975), 898–922.
Greer, Georgeanna H. "Alkaline glazes and groundhog kilns: Southern pottery traditions." *Antiques, 111* (April 1977), 768–773.
Gusler, Wallace B. "The Arts of Shenandoah County, Virginia, 1770–1825." *Journal of Early Southern Decorative Arts, 5* (Nov. 1979), 8–10.

Harned, Henry H. "Ante-bellum Kentucky silver." *Antiques, 105* (April 1974), 818–824.
Horton, Frank L. "Carved Furniture of the Albemarle, A Tie with Architecture." *Journal of Early Southern Decorative Arts, 1* (May 1975), 14–20.
———. "The work of an anonymous Carolina cabinetmaker." *Antiques, 101* (Jan. 1972), 169–176.
Howe, Katherine Susman. "The Gothic revival style in America, 1830–1870." *Antiques, 109* (May 1976), 1014–1023.
Hudson, J. Paul. "Jamestown artisans and craftsmen." *Antiques, 71* (Jan. 1957), 47–50.
———, and Watkins, C. Malcolm. "The earliest known English pottery in America." *Antiques, 71* (Jan. 1957), 51–54.
Hulan, Richard H. "Tennessee textiles." *Antiques, 100* (Sept. 1971), 386–389.
Hume, Ivor Noël. "First Look at Lost Virginia Settlement." *National Geographic, 155* (June 1979), 735–767.
———. "James Geddy and sons, colonial craftsmen: Evidence from the earth." *Antiques, 95* (Jan. 1969), 106–111.
Huth, Hans. "The White House Furniture of the Time of Monroe." *Gazette des Beaux Arts.* Series 6, *29* (Jan. 1946), 23–46.

Kolbe, Christian, and Holcomb, Brent. "Fraktur in

the 'Dutch Fork' Area of South Carolina." *Journal of Early Southern Decorative Arts*, 5 (Nov. 1979), 36–51.

Morgan, Keith N. "Josiah reconsidered: A Green County school of inlay cabinet making." *Antiques*, 105 (April 1974), 883–893.

Olcott, Lois L. "Kentucky Federal furniture." *Antiques*, 105 (April 1974), 870–882.

Poesch, Jessie J. "Early Louisiana armoires." *Antiques*, 94 (Aug. 1968), 196–205.
——. "Furniture of the River Road plantations in Louisiana." *Antiques*, 111 (June 1977), 1184–1193.

Rauschenberg, Bradford L. "A School of Charleston, South Carolina, Brass Andirons." *Journal of Early Southern Decorative Arts*, 5 (May 1979), 26–74.
——. "A Study of Baroque and Gothic-Style Gravestones in Davidson County, North Carolina." *Journal of Early Southern Decorative Arts*, 3 (Nov. 1977), 24–50.
——. "The Royal Governor's Chair: Evidence of the Furnishing of South Carolina's First State House." *Journal of Early Southern Decorative Arts*, 6 (Nov. 1980), 1–32.
——. "Two Outstanding Virginia Chairs." *Journal of Early Southern Decorative Arts*, 2 (Nov. 1976), 1–23.

Reed, Helen Scott Townsend. "Decorative arts in the Valentine Museum." *Antiques*, 103 (Jan. 1973), 167–174.

"Report on the first Antiques and Decorations Forum held at Williamsburg, Virginia, January 24 through February 4, 1949." *Antiques*, 55 (April 1949), special supplement.

Ronstrom, Maud O'Bryan. "Seignouret and Mallard, cabinet-makers." *Antiques*, 46 (Aug. 1944), 79–81.

Smith, Robert C. "John Hall, a busy man in Baltimore." *Antiques*, 92 (Sept. 1967), 300–366.

Somerville, Romaine S. "Furniture of the Maryland Historical Society." *Antiques*, 109 (May 1976), 970–989.

Tinkham, Sandra Shaffer. "A Southern bed rugg." *Antiques*, 105 (June 1974), 1320–1321.

"The Thomas Elfe Account Book, 1768–1775." *The South Carolina Historical and Genealogical Magazine*, 35 (Jan. 1934) through 42 (Jan. 1941).

Wahlman, Maude Southwell. "The Art of the Afro-American Quilt: Origins, Development and Significance." Diss., Yale, 1980.

Walters, Donald. "Johannes Spitler, Shenandoah County, Virginia, furniture decorator." *Antiques*, 108 (Oct. 1975), 730–735.

Weekley, Carolyn. "James Gheen, Piedmont North Carolina cabinetmaker." *Antiques*, 103 (May 1973), 940–944.

Wilmerding, Lucius, Jr. "James Monroe and the Furniture Fund." *New-York Historical Society Quarterly*, 44 (April 1960), 133–149.

TOWN PLANNING

Books

Reps, John W. *Tidewater Towns: City Planning in Colonial Virginia and Maryland*. Williamsburg and Charlottesville, 1972.
——. *The Making of Urban America, A History of City Planning in the United States*. Princeton, 1965.

Index

Credits

MUSEUMS AND COLLECTIONS

Alabama Department of Archives and History, 170, 262

Anglo-American Art Museum, Louisiana State University, Baton Rouge, 197 (upper right), 303, 326

Courtesy of Antiques Magazine, 48, 51 (upper right and mid-left), 70, 72, 143, 144, 146, 147, 148, 150, 151, 211, 228 (above), 234, 236, 238, 244, 250 (below)

Courtesy of Antiques Magazine (photographs only), 102 (upper left), 108, 111 (lower left), 113 (left), 190, 191 (lower right), 198, 204, 205 (upper left), 207, 263, 264 (upper left), 305, 313 (below), 315, 317 (left), 325

Archives Nationales Section outre-mer, Paris, France, 37, 38, 54, 55

Archivo General de Indias, Seville, Spain, 56 (upper left)

Collection of The Art Institute of Chicago, 80 (lower right)

Association for the Preservation of Virginia Antiquities, 11, 204 (upper left)

Atlanta Historical Society, 331

The Baltimore Museum of Art, 80 (upper left), 127 (above), 158, 179 (Charlotte G. Paul Bequest Fund), 188, 270 (upper left; Gift of Dr. and Mrs. Michael A. Abrams), 278

Courtesy of William Nathaniel Banks, 138, 216, 240, 241, 243

Bocage Restoration (Mrs. Richard Genre), 315

The British Museum, Map Library, London, England, 59, 60

Courtesy of the Trustees of the British Museum, Department of Prints and Drawings, London, England 6, 7

Courtesy of the Trustees of the British Museum, Natural History, London, England, 82

The Carolina Art Association, Gibbes Art Gallery, 1, 21, 31 (upper right), 45, 57 (lower left), 58 (upper left), 77 (upper right), 120, 161, 163 (upper left), 176, 187 (above), 277, 300

Courtesy of Amon Carter Museum, Fort Worth, 245

Courtesy of The Charleston Museum, Charleston, South Carolina, 98 (lower right), 101 (lower right), 108 (lower right), 111 (lower left), 204, 272

Cheekwood Botanical Gardens and Fine Arts Center, 171, 264 (lower right)

Chicago Historical Society, 160, 180

The City of Charleston, South Carolina, 126

The College of William and Mary in Virginia, 73 (lower left and right), 74 (upper left), 87

P. & D. Colnaghi & Co., Ltd., London, 33 (lower right)

Colonial Williamsburg, 8, 9, 23, 24, 75, 81, 90, 91 (upper right and upper left), 92, 96 (lower right and upper left), 100 (lower right), 101 (upper left), 104 (upper left and lower left), 109 (lower right), 113 (upper right), 193

Columbia Museum of Art, 282

Columbia University, Butler Library, 20, 133 (below)

Commonwealth of Virginia, Virginia State Library, Richmond, 88, 90, 186

In the Collection of The Corcoran Gallery of Art, Gift of William Wilson Corcoran, 181, 299

Daughters of the American Revolution Museum, 78

Courtesy of Arthur Q. Davis, 133 (above)

Drayton Hall, A Property of the National Trust for Historic Preservation, 51 (lower left)

The Fine Arts Museum of the South at Mobile, 333

The Florence Museum, 270 (lower right)

The Gallier House, 323, 324 (upper left)

"The Galt Family Collection" of Williamsburg, 92 (upper left)

Courtesy of John Geiser III, 205 (lower right)

Georgia Department of Archives and History, 218

Georgia Museum of Art, 279

Courtesy of Dr. Judith Hardy-Stashin, 274 (lower right)

Historic Columbia Foundation, 321

The Historic New Orleans Collection, 220, 261, 294, 304, 309 (lower right)

Howard-Tilton Memorial Library, Tulane University, 135, 137, 223, 225, 240, 269 (below), 288, 322, 324 (lower right)

Collection of Leonard V. Huber, 310 (upper left)

Courtesy of Dr. and Mrs. Robert C. Judice, 105 (upper left), 139

Judson College, 274 (upper left)

Keeneland Association, 327

Kennedy Galleries, Inc., 293, 301

Kentucky Historical Society, 215, 264 (upper left), 320

The Kirk Stieff Company, 208

John W. Kiser, Antioch, Tennessee, 249, 250 (above)

Ladies' Hermitage Association, 206 (above), 208 (upper right)

The Liberty Corporation Textile Collection, Greenville, S.C., 113 (left)

Library of Congress, Washington, D.C., 14, 16, 17, 19, 50, 62, 93, 129, 141 (above), 142, 144 (above), 206 (below), 228 (below), 231, 247 (below), 248, 251, 253, 259, 260

Courtesy of Mr. and Mrs. Earle Long III, 200 (below)

From the Collections of the Louisiana State Museum, 56 (lower), 105 (lower right), 106, 107, 134, 165, 166, 221, 237, 265, 266, 267 (upper right), 309 (upper left)

Louisiana State University Library, Baton Rouge, 224

Maryland Hall of Records, Annapolis, Maryland, 22

Maryland Historical Society, 25, 30, 84, 127 (below), 138 (below), 159, 163 (lower right), 177, 178, 185, 189 (right), 313 (below), 325

Cyrus Hall McCormick Library, Washington and Lee University, 273 (lower left)

Courtesy of Mr. and Mrs. William McGehee, Ms. Milly McGehee, 205 (upper left)

The Metropolitan Museum of Art, New York, N.Y., 64

Middleton Place Foundation, 66, 187 (below)

Museum of Early Southern Decorative Arts, 26, 27, 28, 29, 74 (lower right), 89, 91 (lower right), 92 (lower right), 94, 95, 97, 98, 100 (upper left), 102 (lower right), 109 (above), 175, 191 (left), 192, 193, 194, 196, 199, 200 (above), 202, 209 (below)

Courtesy, Museum of Fine Arts, Boston, 124, 189 (upper left), 287

National Geographic Society, 8

National Museum of American Art (formerly National Collection of Fine Arts), Smithsonian Institution, 162, 273 (upper right; Gift of Mrs. Joseph Harrison, Jr.), 298 (Bequest of Harriet Lane Johnston), 306

National Portrait Gallery, Smithsonian Institution, Washington, D.C., 83, 275

The Nelson-Atkins Museum of Art (Charles T. Thompson Fund), 31 (lower left)

Courtesy of the Newberry Library, Chicago, the Edward E. Ayer Collection, 36

New Orleans Museum of Art, New Orle-

PHOTOGRAPHERS

PAPERS

Permission to use the J. W. Dodge papers residing in the Archives of American Art granted by Leonard S. Mee.

A NOTE ON THE TYPE

This book was set in a modern adaptation of a type designed by William Caslon (1692–1766). The first of a famous English family of type designers and founders, he was originally an apprentice to an engraver of gunlocks and gun barrels in London. In 1716 he opened his own shop for silver chasing and making bookbinders' stamps. The printers John Watts and William Bowyer, admirers of his skill in cutting ornaments and letters, advanced him money to equip himself for type founding, which he began in 1720.

In design Caslon was a reversion to earlier type styles. Its characteristics are remarkable regularity and symmetry, and beauty in the shape and proportion of the letters; its general effect is clear and open but not weak or delicate. For uniformity, clearness, and readability it has perhaps never been surpassed. After Caslon's death his eldest son, also named William (1720–1778), carried on the business successfully. Then followed a period of neglect of nearly fifty years. In 1843 Caslon type was revived by the firm of Caslon for William Pickering and has since been one of the most widely used of all type designs in English and American printing.

Production Manager: Dennis Dwyer; Production Editor: Nancy Clements; Designer: Maria Epes; Art Director: Betty Anderson.